2004 Edition

Archer's Bible®

The Ultimate Archery Reference Guide

Stoeger Publishing Company Accokeek, Maryland

Stoeger Publishing
Great Outdoor Books Since 1925

STOEGER PUBLISHING COMPANY
is a division of Benelli U.S.A.

Benelli U.S.A.
Vice President and General Manager:
  Stephen Otway
Director of Brand Marketing and Communications:
  Stephen McKelvain

Stoeger Publishing Company
President: Jeffrey Reh
Publisher: Jay Langston
Managing Editor: Harris J. Andrews
Design & Production Director: Cynthia T. Richardson
Photography Director: Alex Bowers
Imaging Specialist: William Graves
Copy Editor: Kate Baird
Publishing Assistant: Christine Lawton
Sales Manager Assistant: Julie Brownlee
Administrative Assistant: Shannon McWilliams

Published by:
Stoeger Publishing Company
17603 Indian Head HIghway, Suite 200
Accokeek, Maryland 20607

BK0303
ISBN:0-88317-246-1
Library of Congress Control Number: 2002110064

Manufactured in the United States of America
Distributed to the book trade and
to the sporting goods trade by:
Stoeger Industries
17603 Indian Head Highway, Suite 200
Accokeek, Maryland 20607
www.stoegerindustries.com

OTHER PUBLICATIONS:
Shooter's Bible 2004 - 95th Edition
  The World's Standard Firearms
  Reference Book
Gun Trader's Guide - 26th Edition
  Complete, Fully-Illustrated
  Guide to Modern Firearms with
  Current Market Values

Hunting & Shooting
Conserving Wild America
Hunting Whitetails East and West
Hounds of the World
The Turkey Hunter's Tool Kit:
  Shooting Savvy
Complete Book of Whitetail Hunting
Hunting and Shooting with
  the Modern Bow
The Ultimate in Rifle Accuracy
Advanced Black Powder Hunting
Labrador Retrievers
Hunting America's Wild Turkey
Taxidermy Guide
Cowboy Action Shooting
Great Shooters of the World

Collecting Books
The Truth About Spring Turkey
  Hunting According to "Cuz"
The Whole Truth About Spring Turkey
  Hunting According to "Cuz"
Hounds of the World
Sporting Collectibles
The Working Folding Knife
The Lore of Spices

Firearms
Antique Guns
P-38 Automatic Pistol
The Walther Handgun Story
Complete Guide to Compact Handguns
Complete Guide to Service Handguns
America's Great Gunmakers
Firearms Disassembly with
  Exploded Views

Rifle Guide
Gunsmithing at Home
The Book of the Twenty-Two
Complete Guide to Modern Rifles
Complete Guide to Classic Rifles
Legendary Sporting Rifles
FN Browning Armorer to the World
Modern Beretta Firearms
How to Buy & Sell Used Guns
Heckler & Koch: Armorers
  of the Free World
Spanish Handguns

Reloading
The Handloader's Manual of
  Cartridge Conversions
Modern Sporting Rifle Cartridges
Complete Reloading Guide

Fishing
Bassing Bible
Ultimate Bass Boats
The Flytier's Companion
Deceiving Trout
The Complete Book of Trout Fishing
The Complete Book of Flyfishing
Peter Dean's Guide to Fly-Tying
The Flytier's Manual
Flytier's Master Class
Handbook of Fly Tying
The Fly Fisherman's Entomological
  Pattern Book
Fiberglass Rod Making
To Rise a Trout

Motorcycles & Trucks
The Legend of Harley-Davidson
The Legend of the Indian
Best of Harley-Davidson
Classic Bikes
Great Trucks
4X4 Vehicles

Cooking Game
Fish & Shellfish Care & Cookery
Game Cookbook
Dress 'Em Out
Wild About Venison
Wild About Game Birds
Wild About Fresh Water Fish

CONTENTS

FOREWORD

Gear Up, Go Forth and Enjoy Archery

This is a great era to be an archer and a bowhunter. Compound bows have become much more high-tech and feature-packed engineering marvels in recent years. If you like traditional archery, recurve bows are now offered in more woods and material options than ever before, and longbows are as much fun as ever. There are also more models of crossbows available. With so many bows—but only two arms and hands—which should you shoot, buy or try next?

Well it all depends. I do, however, hope that this edition of the Archer's Bible will help you answer your gear-related questions. And when you see something that you like—or must have—I trust that you can find it at your local archery pro shop. Take this book along and point it out to the pro shop staff if they do not have it in stock and maybe they'll want to place an order to cover your needs and those of your archery friends. After you gear up, it's time to release some arrows in practice or on the hunt.

Another benefit for bowhunters and arrow shooters these days are the hunting options. Bowhunting has grown far beyond white-tailed deer hunting to become a year-round lifestyle. During the spring many bowhunters are taking gobblers with bow and arrow. Other archery enthusiasts spend summer months bagging varmints, stalking groundhogs, and shooting carp. The numbers of big game species that you can hunt with a bow in the fall—and the places to hunt them—now seem almost endless. Life is short, bowhunt often.

Bowhunting can be your ticket to travel and explore the Southeast swamps, tall mountains in the West, deserts in the Southwest and sprawling tundra in the far north. Is this the year for you to hunt a new area or try for a new species? Gear up, go forth and have a grand bowhunting adventure. Bowhunting camps are special places where you can relive the past, savor the present and dream about the future. Ask a friend, your wife or husband, or your kid(s) to join you on your next trip. Archery and bowhunting can be the thread that keeps families connected.

And when you're home, there's the practice side to keep you tuned, ready and motivated. Blocks, bags, and 3-D targets are popping up in backyards across America for good reasons. If you do not have a backyard range, take the family or your friends to a local archery range or 3-D course and have a great time. Releasing an arrow is a great way to release stress. We can all use more of that in our lives these days.

. . I hope that you find the 2004 Archer's Bible to be a great shopping guide and wish book. The various authors and their feature articles should also help you become a more successful bowhunter and skilled archer. Reread the articles before you start your rigorous fall hunting season and maybe a tidbit of information garnered from the pages of this Archer's Bible will help you bag the buck, bull or bruin of a lifetime.

I hope that this edition of the Archer's Bible will serve you well and will show many worn pages in future years. I'm proud to do my part to make you a better-educated archer and bowhunter. Good luck and shoot straight.

Michael D. Faw, Editor

FEATURE ARTICLES

Insure Your Bowhunt Instinctively
By Judd Cooney

"**W**e've got to turn around and go back to camp," shouted the white-faced bow-hunter, above the deep throated burble of the eighty-five horsepower Suzuki outboard, as we slid down the glass-smooth lake toward our evening rendezvous with several of Saskatchewan's humongous black bears. The lake was too smooth for seasickness, the hunter hadn't indicated a bad heart or ulcers on his contract, and I knew that he'd been the last one out of the outhouse before we left. I already had a suspicion about his need to return to camp when I asked what the problem was.

"My release won't work, and I can't hunt tonight without one," he complained. Unfortunately for him, we were 20 miles down the lake and I had two other hyped bowhunters in the boat and wasn't about to return to camp and delay or ruin their evening hunt. I dropped off the other hunters first and finally dropped the grumbling

Careful practice and training in instinctive shooting techniques allows a bowhunter to eliminate the need for complicated and fragile devices such as peep sights, sight pins and mechanical string releases.

and reluctant bowhunter off at his bait for the evening. "It's only 15 yards from the stand to the bait, just use your fingers and shoot instinctively," I coaxed the distraught hunter. The client was so disturbed about losing the use of his release that he wouldn't even take a practice shot or two using his God-given, never fail, fingers.

It was almost a forgone conclusion he'd see the colossal bear that had been hitting the bait. Sure enough, when I picked him up later that evening he was a basket case, having watched a monstrous Pope & Young-class bear feed from the bait can for half an hour at point-blank range. According to him, he'd never shot his bow with fingers and was convinced it wouldn't shoot without the use of sights, string peep and release. Hog-wash!

The following afternoon in camp I took his bow and after a dozen practice shots, I could keep all the arrows in a 3-inch circle at 20 yards using my fingers and ignoring his fancy sight setup. This happened even though the bow's draw length was an inch shorter than

my normal draw. I simply let instinct take over and concentrated on where I wanted the arrows to hit.

That evening the frustrated bowhunter killed a much smaller bear on the bait than the one he saw the previous evening. His equipment failure and uncompromising mindset had cost him a record book bear.

As an outfitter I've seen dozens of times when equipment failure or inadequacies has cost one of my clients a chance at a big game animal. If I hadn't already been a confirmed instinctive shooter, these avoidable occurrences sure would have prompted me to learn the basics of instinctive shooting as a failsafe backup for my hunting ventures.

True instinctive shooting depends on nothing more than your eye,

Bowhunter Mike Kraetsch holds a full draw with an arrow tipped with a Zwicky broadhead. Instinctive bow shooting depends on having the shooter's eye, bow arm and string fingers all work together to place the arrow accurately within a reasonable range.

Author Judd Cooney lights a scent-producing "smoke stick" to lure a bear into the ideal range for an instinctive shot. Constant practice trains the archer's "mental computer" to instantly judge the distance and best angle for an accurate shot.

bow arm and string fingers working together to put the arrow right where you want it at ANY distance within reasonable bow range. "That's too tough, I could never master that!" you say. How about throwing a rock, shooting a basketball, tossing a football, hitting a golf ball, baseball or tennis ball? All these are truly instinctive actions, no sight pins, peeps, cross-hairs or release aids needed in accomplishing these tasks. If you can accomplish any of the above, or walk while eating an ice cream cone, there's no reason you can't shoot your bow instinctively when you need to.

There are a number of definite advantages to shooting instinctively. It's the most natural way to shoot a bow, whether you're using a compound, recurve or long bow. Being the most natural way to shoot also makes it the most adaptable. You don't have to be in a perfect bow stance to take your shot. You can easily learn to shoot instinctively and accurately from just about any position you choose, including prone.

When shooting instinctively, the archer should ignore arrow and other aim points and concentrate on the intended point of impact. The shooter's left hand should be pointing the bow while the archer concentrates on the target.

When developing an instinctive shooting style, always avoid using the arrow tip or any part of the bow as an aiming or reference point.

Try that with sights and a peep!! You can also shoot much quicker instinctively. This can be a definite advantage under adverse hunting conditions, and in my experiences, all hunting conditions come under the heading of ADVERSE! Running game, flying birds, and fast swimming fish are only a few of the situations where quick, accurate, instinctive shooting can make the difference between success and getting "skunked."

An instinctive shooter's bowhunt doesn't depend on devices such as sight pins that fall out or get out of adjustment, string peeps that won't line up when the shooter gets a bit excited, or don't function effectively in the low light situations when game is most active, releases that won't release or that release, prematurely and unexpectedly. These are just a few problems that can crop up under hunting conditions and either ruin your hunt entirely or give you a lame excuse for not connecting. Why take a chance on a small mechanical device's failure ruining your hunting trip?

It always amazes and exasperates me when I have a client come toddling out of the woods when there is still another half hour of legal shooting time left, the best half hour of the whole damn bowhunt! Without fail the reason given for this early exodus is the fact they can't see well enough to make use of their peep sight and sight pins. The fact that bow sights and string peeps often cost a bowhunter a half hour to an hour of premium early morning and late evening hunting time, is just one of the reasons YOU should learn to shoot instinctively.

Instinctive shooting really shines under abysmal conditions such as rain, snow, fog, and early or late evening hunting. All that you need is to see your target well enough to pick a spot to focus all your concentration and leave the rest to your instincts. There are no pins to focus on and line up on your quarry while you're mentally worrying about guesstimating the range and picking the correct pin to keep from over- or undershooting your target. Just concentrate on where you want the arrow to hit, and release. Simple, fast and effective!

Like throwing a rock or tossing a baseball, once learned and mastered, instinctive shooting is not forgotten. Mastering this method of shooting also makes you much more adaptable with different bows. I have little trouble switching from one compound to another or from a compound to a recurve. A few practice shots and my arrows start going where they should, regardless of how long I've laid off my shooting or whether I have ever shot that particular bow before.

Few things in life are without some disadvantages and instinctive shooting is certainly not one of them. Probably the biggest disadvantage is the time it takes to feed your mental computer (your brain) enough data and information to make you an effective instinctive shooter. The reason you can throw a small rock reasonably accurately and then throw a much heavier rock further and just as accurately is that your arm has been working for and supplying your mental computer information all your life. Your arm and brain have performed the task of throwing objects of different sizes, shapes and weights, varying distances, thousands and thousands of times while providing your mental computer with a complete backlog of data to work with.

To become a competent instinctive shooter you must get your brain, arms and string fingers working together the same way. This takes time and effort and the results will not be as quick in coming as with your

Shooting from behind a brush pile of fallen birch, an archer prepares to release his arrow on a big Canadian black bear at close range. The ability to make a quick and accurate shot under a wide range of conditions can be the key to successful hunt.

mechanical aids. Most new bowhunters want instant results and aren't willing to take the time involved to become proficient without mechanical aids. However, learning to shoot your hunting bow instinctively with fingers at short range is darn good insurance and may make the difference in the success or failure of your hunts under the right circumstances.

It's difficult to find someone to show you how to shoot instinctively because there aren't many "true" instinctive shooters roaming the woods and ranges. With a little patience and perseverance, however, you can self learn the basics of instinctive shooting.

Your primary objective is to program your mental computer with as much data on your shooting as you can. Like all computers, your brain functions on a GIGO basis, which in computerese stands for Garbage In, Garbage, Out. Don't try to THINK when you're shooting instinctively 'cause all you'll do is screw up your mental instincts and ruin your shooting. Be natural and let your body and brain work together along with your bow to get the arrow where you want it.

Forget thinking in terms of distance when

shooting instinctively!!! You don't think of distance when you throw a baseball from center field to home plate or shoot a basketball from the corner of the court so, DON'T THINK DISTANCE when shooting instinctively.

Concentration is the real key to successful instinctive shooting and it's something you can work on and practice any time, any place. A bowhunting acquaintance of mine, who is an excellent instinctive shot, once told me a good instinctive shooter should be able to look at a blank white wall and concentrate hard enough to PICK A SPOT. Try it sometime and the results might surprise you! The sharper you can tune your ability to focus your concentration, the more successful your instinctive shooting will be and this mental practice will definitely help your sight shooting, too.

Start your instinctive, finger release shooting session with your bow and arrow set at a distance of 7-10 yards. Leave your string peep, sights or whatever accessories fastened to your bow in place. Use a large target with NO bull's-eye or scoring rings. Use any kind of small spot, blemish, hole, or shadow on the target as a beginning concentration point. When practicing I'll move my concentration point all over the target face. Vital areas on game animals are rarely if ever centered either horizontally or vertically, so why get used to this on your targets? Remember, this is the first step in programming your mental computer. The key to that is by repetition after repetition until your shooting at this range is truly instinctive.

With an arrow on the string push your bow arm out and point with it toward the target, as you concentrate on where you want the arrow to hit. Ignore the bow, arrow, sights, etc. as you concentrate on the intended point of impact. To get the feel of this technique, point your left index finger (for a right-handed shooter,) at your point of concentration as you extend your bow arm. You're actually pointing your bow with your left hand. Reach out and grasp the string, still concentrating on the spot. Draw and hold as long as it takes to center your full concentration on the spot and release smoothly. Simple, no?

From this close distance, shoot three to five arrows at the target. Don't worry if they aren't hitting anywhere near the spot at first but keep shooting and trying for tight grouping. If the groups are not hitting the spot, concentrate on mentally moving the arrows to the spot. Do not use the arrow tip or any part of the bow as an aiming point or reference point. It may take several days or only a few minutes to get your arrows grouping where you're looking. Remember, every shot you take is providing that mental computer with valuable data. Don't take these shooting sessions lightly! When your concentration begins to lag and you start scattering arrows all over the target—quit. Keep shooting at this distance until you can keep all your arrows in a cup-sized group or smaller.

When your groups are tight and centered around the spot, move back five more yards and go through the process again. Stay with it until the same goal is accomplished. This second session should take a lot less time, but DO NOT move further back until you are shooting small groups around the spot. When you're hitting the spot consistently at this distance, move up to the previous distance and repeat the drill to keep programming your mental computer with accurate, repetitious data. Impatience at this point can create real problems in your shooting so stick to the routine!

Keep repeating these steps and moving back in five yard increments until you get to the maximum range to meet your goal, by grouping your arrows consistently in a kill zone-sized area. Keep varying the distances until you can get good groupings around the spot from any distance you might shoot from under actual hunting conditions. Once you get the hang of instinctive finger shooting, you might just decide to extend your range with more practice and throw away those sights, peeps, and release aids.

If you're patient, develop your concentration, and mix a bit of finger release instinctive shooting into each of your pre-hunt shooting sessions, it won't be long before you'll amaze yourself with your ability to put an arrow on target with nothing but concentration, instinct, and your unfailing fingers. What could be better insurance for your bowhunting success?

A bear hunter finds his bow sights knocked out of adjustment after a bumpy boat ride on a rough Canadian lake. With sufficient experience and practice, the instinctive bow shooter can dispense with fragile sights.

The Camo Conundrum
By Bob Humphrey

Today's hunters are faced with myriad choices when it comes to selecting camouflage patterns, making it all the more difficult to solve the riddle of which pattern or patterns work best for various hunting applications.

What's the right camouflage pattern for you? Not so many years ago that was an easy question to answer, as the choices were limited. But with the vast number and variety of camouflage patterns available today, selecting the right one can seem a daunting task to bowhunters. Having so many more options available, however, is not necessarily a bad thing.

Modern technology and the competitive nature of the camouflage industry have resulted in some innovative designs in both the patterns themselves and the process by which they are applied to fabrics and other materials. Where bowhunters used to have to live with a "one-type-fits-all" approach to camouflage, they can now choose from a broad array of patterns and colors to find the most appropriate type for a specific application, habitat or hunting season. There are patterns available for just about any application imaginable.

Trebark Bigwoods camouflage is designed to help the tree stand hunter blend in against a woody background.

OBJECTIVE

The objective of camouflage clothing is to conceal its wearer by creating contrast and breaking up the outline of the human form. This is done largely with a mosaic of light- and dark-colored shapes. Deer and other ungulates see most colors as shades of gray. So, for big game hunters, color accuracy is not as important as the contrast and tonal range of colors. Color accuracy becomes more important when hunting other species like bears, turkeys or predators, which can distinguish colors quite well. All of these species can readily spot movement, but the proper camouflage pattern can help reduce the risk of detection.

Most modern camouflage patterns consist predominantly of various shades of gray, green and brown that offer both accurate colors for the turkey hunter and proper tonal ranges for the deer hunter. Some patterns are quite similar. Others differ radically in terms of colors, shapes, patterns, and the camouflaging principles used. Some patterns are designed for general use, while others are most effective at certain times of year or in certain habitats. Some camouflages go one step further by incorporating very accurate renditions of actual vegetation, while others rely on more basic principles of dark linear patterns against a light background.

Another key principle to effective camouflage is that it should hold its contrast at any distance. Some of the older, obsolete patterns were criticized because they tended to blob at a distance. They looked great from 20 yards away, but if you backed away to 50 or 100 yards, the contrast disappeared and the camouflage-and its wearer-appeared as a solid, dark blob. That no longer seems to be the case with newer patterns, and those that have stood the test of time.

In full sunlight or shadow, branch patterns effectively assist in breaking up the hunter's outline, adding an extra dimension of concealment.

CAMO TYPES
General Purpose

Many of the more popular camouflage patterns are designed for broad application, allowing the hunter to blend into a wide variety of habitats. Some accomplish this using accurate patterns of vegetation such as leaves, branches and bark to add realism. Examples include: Advantage Classic and Advantage Timber, Mossy Oak Break-Up and Mossy Oak Forest Floor, Predator Deception, Tru-Woods Autumn, Trebark Bigwoods, Skyline Excel, Superflauge and Image Country Reflection Brownleaf. Others patterns, like Predator, ASAT, and Skyline rely on the general principle of breaking up the human outline with contrasting shapes of dark and light color shades. Still others, like Natural Gear, Diamondback and Snake Skin Illusions, use natural prin-

Camo Selection Guide

GENERAL/ ALL-PURPOSE:
- Advantage Classic, Timber
- Mossy Oak New Break Up, Forest Floor
- NaturalGear Natural
- Predator Deception, Evolution
- Tru-Woods Autumn
- Trebark Superflauge, Bigwoods
- Skyline Excel, Xtreme
- Image Country Reflection Canada, Reflection Brownleaf

EARLY-SEASON TREESTAND:
- Realtree Hardwoods Green
- Mossy Oak
- Predator Fall Brown
- Image Country Image

LATE-SEASON TREESTAND:
- ASAT
- Realtree Hardwoods
- Mossy Oak Shadow Branch
- Predator Fall Gray
- Brush Country Tree Stand
- Skyline Horizon, Apparition Horizon
- Sticks N Limbs
- Field's Edge

SPRING/EARLY FALL/SOFTWOODS:
Advantage Timber
Realtree Hardwoods Green, Xtra Brown
Mossy Oak Shadow Leaf

By mimicking the regional foliage patterns, Rocky Mountain Camo's Aspen Pattern provides perfect concealment for the early-season elk hunter.

- Image Country Reflection Greenleaf
- Tru-Woods EF/S
- Predator Spring Green
- Skyline Apparition Green

LATE FALL/WINTER- NO SNOW:
- Reeltree Xtra Gray, Hardwoods
- Mossy Oak Break Up, Shadow Branch
- NaturalGear Natural
- Skyline Apparition
- Predator Fall Brown, Fall Gray
- Tru-Woods Autumn
- Trebark
- Image Country Reflection Brownleaf

SNOW:
- NaturalGear Snow
- Predator Winter White
- Image Country Snow Country
- Sticks N' Limbs Snow Camo Skyline Horizon

- Superflauge Snow
- Realtree Xtra Snow
- Prairie Ghost Snow

SPECIALTY:
- Blackbrush Pearflat, Cedarbreak
- NaturalGear Evergreen
- Brush Country Hill Country, South Texas, Coastal Plains, Post Oak
- DK Flatwoods
- Montana Camo Prairie Ghost, Ridge Ghost

CORNFIELD/GRASSLAND:
- Advantage: Wetlands
- Mossy Oak: Shadow Grass
- Skyline: Fall Flight
- Blackbrush: Canefield
- Image Country: Refuge

ciples of camouflaging colors to fool the eye.

Most general purpose patterns feature a range of colors that make them more versatile. The dark and light gray matrix of most, which is designed to simulate a tree trunk, disguises you well against the trunk of a tree, or the gray background of forest light. Conversely, the greens help you blend in against leafy foliage at ground level or against the forest canopy when you're up in a tree stand. Meanwhile, lighter browns simulate the effect of mottled sunlight filtering down through the overhead canopy onto the forest floor.

Special Purpose

A recent trend in camouflage is patterns with narrower, more specific applicability. Some are designed for a specific type of hunting, such as from a tree stand, for example. Others are more effective at a particular time of year, or in a specific habitat or region of the country.

Tree Stand

The vast majority of camo patterns are designed primarily with the bowhunter in mind, and while most have broader applications, some are designed specifically for the tree stand bowhunter. The most effective patterns for that purpose are those that provide the greatest contrast, and usually consist of a light, open background mottled with darker lines and shapes. Breaking up your outline becomes more important late in the season after the foliage has dropped, and several patterns are particularly well-suited to this application (see table).

Season-Specific

Other patterns may have broad application but are most effective during a particular season or time of year. The best patterns for spring turkey hunters, early fall deer, elk, or spring or fall bear hunters are those with more green in them, as they'll blend better with the lush, green foliage. Winter in the south, or early spring before leaf-out, might call for more open patterns with dull browns and grays. Any bowhunter with a stand in a late fall oak tree with its dull brown leaves intact knows how effective Advantage Classic can be in that situation. Meanwhile, late season in the north country often means snow, which calls for patterns with a white matrix and smaller, dark patterns. Again, the general purpose patterns may also work under a variety of habitats, but those designed for a specific season will usually work better.

Habitat/Locale

While most camouflage patterns are designed for broad geographical or environmental applications, a handful were created for very specific conditions. For example, Brush Country's four patterns-Hill Country, South Texas, Coastal Plains and Post Oak-are all designed to match various regions or habitats of Texas they're named after.

Mossy Oak's Forest Floor can be effective for tree stand hunters who place their stand in trees that tend to retain their leaves in the fall.

Many habitat-specific patterns also blend in well in non-target habitats. This is Rocky Mountain Camo's Aspen against a background of oak trees.

Realtree Hardwoods Grey

Realtree Hardwoods

Blackbrush's Pear Flat and Cedar Break are designed specifically for hunting in the arid southwest. Montana Camo's Prairie Ghost mimics the sagebrush habitat of the western plains, while their Ridge Ghost blends best in the evergreen "black" timber. Likewise, the palmetto-leaf pattern of DK Flatwoods is best suited to the Deep South.

There are even a few patterns that work remarkably well for situations other than their intended purpose. Though they are designed primarily for waterfowl hunters, the marsh grass and cornfield patterns also work well in any grassland habitat, like spot-and-stalk hunting for plains mulies or still-hunting whitetails in a Midwestern cornfield.

Camo Companies

**BLACKBRUSH
CAMOUFLAGE CO., INC.**
P.O. Box 830
Ingram, TX 78025
800-752-2970
Fax: 830-367-5076
www.camo@blackbrush.net

**BRUSH COUNTRY
CAMOUFLAGE
BIG RACK TRADING CO.**
P.O. Box 4314
Bryan, TX 77805
979-778-2404 or 877-599-7225
Fax: 979-778-2446
www.brushcountrycamo.com

DIAMONDBACK CAMOUFLAGE
Business Information:
P.O. Box 1419
Marble Falls, TX 78654
800-909-9972
Fax: 830-693-9688
www.diamondbackcamo.com

DK FLATWOODS, INC.
P.O. Box 922
Odessa, FL 33556
888-910-CAMO(2266)
www.dkflatwoods.com

**DOWNWIND
3D CAMOUFLAGE**
P.O. Box 861
Solana Beach, CA 92075-0861
858-792-7738
Fax: 858-792-7738
www.downwind3dcamo.com

**FIELD'S EDGE
CONCEALMENT
SOLUTIONS**
P.O. Box 1205
Stone Mountain, GA 30086
404-272-7291
www.fields-edge.com

**FOUR SEASONS
OUTDOORS, INC.**
1020 Front St.
Conway, AR 73032
501-327-2253
Fax: 501-327-2253
www.snakeskinillusions.com

HUNTER'S PINE
8107 Good Carter Rd.
Nicholls, GA 31554
912-285-9681
www.hunterspine.com

IMAGE COUNTRY CAMOUFLAGE
14 Mountain Dr.
Rutland, VT 05071
802-747-3009
www.imagecountry.com

MONTANA CAMO INC.
P.O. Box 1327
Victor, MT 59875
406-961-6829
Fax: 406-961-6819
www.montanacamo.com

Realtree Hardwoods Green

Mossy Oak Forest Floor

Added Dimension

Until fairly recently, the camouflage industry was largely two-dimensional. Designers of some more recent patterns have devised ways to use dark shadows to trick the eye into perceiving three-dimensional depth. Nothing, however, beats the real world. The military figured this out a long time ago when they developed ghillie suits. It took the sport camouflage industry a while to catch on, but now there's a whole array of three-dimensional leaf-cut fabrics and add-ons you can use to enhance your disappearing act. Companies like Shelter-Pro, DownWind and Ashford Springs Hunting Products all have garments

MOSSY OAK
Haas Outdoors, Inc.
P.O. Box 757 200 E. Maine St.
West Point, MS 39773
662-494-8859
www.mossyoak.com

NATURAL GEAR
5310 S. Shackleford, Ste. D
Little Rock, AR 72204
800-590-5590
Fax: 501-228-4838
www.naturalgear.com

PREDATOR, INC.
2605 Coulee Ave.
Lacrosse WI 54601
608-787-0500
www.predatorcamo.com

SKYLINE COVER, LLC
S-3950 McKinley Parkway
Blasdell, NY 14219
716-649-2312
Fax: 714-648-5700
www.skylinecamo.com

STICKS N' LIMBS CAMOUFLAGE
CLARKFIELD OUTDOORS
1032 10th Ave.
Clarkfield, MN 56223
320-669-7140
Fax: 320-669-4923
www.bowhunting.net/sticks

TEAM REALTREE
Address:
P.O. Box 9638
Columbus, GA 31908
800-992-9968
Fax: 706-569-9346
www.realtree.com

TREBARK CAMO ENTERPRISES, INC.
200 E Main St.
West Point, MS 39773
662-494-8859
Fax: 662-494-8742
www.trebark.com

TRU-WOODS CAMO
629 Upland St.
Pottstown, PA 19464
888-288-2177
Fax: 610-970-5491
www.truwoods.com

UNDERBRUSH BY SHELTER-PRO
P.O. Box 337
Stearns, KY 42647
606-376-2004
Fax: 606-376-4314
www.underbrushblinds.com

WACKER BACKER
Dept. PB
12261-D Cleveland
Nunica, MI 49448
877-922-5372
www.wackerbacker.com.

Mossy Oak Break-up

Mossy Oak Shadow Leaf

Mossy Oak Shadow Grass

Realtree Hardwoods Green

that use camouflage patterns and loose-cut fabric to create a perceptual and actual three-dimensional camouflage. Not only do they further break up the two-dimensional shape of the human form, but they also add natural movement when wind flutters the ragged fabric.

You can also go one step farther by adding faux foliage to your body, equipment and surroundings. Quality Archery Designs' SneakyLeaf system includes synthetic leaves that you can attach to your clothing or equipment. A.S.A.P.'s Micro-Flage system and Gameslayer Necessities' Real Stuff Brush Holding Camo System hold natural vegetation in telescoping, swivel arms, or rods that can be attached to trees or treestands. The Wacker Backer and PMI Cover System kits include artificial branches, ground stakes, and inserts for building ground blinds or breaking up treestand outlines. When using any and all products that attach to or that are located near a tree,stand, be certain that the products do not interfer with a safe entry into and exit out of the stand.

Conclusion

People are sometimes critical of the camouflage industry when they see the vast array of patterns available from various manufacturers. But that variety is as much an artifact of user demand as marketing, and those companies wouldn't be in business if the demand wasn't there. A quick flip through the pages of any hunting catalog will reveal the wide array of patterns and huge assortment of selections.

Today's bowhunters are more sophisticated. It also seems nowadays many bowhunters have more disposable income, but less surplus time for recreation. Thus, they want hunting equipment that will allow them to maximize their time and effort afield. Having more choices in camouflage patterns does that. If you want one design that will fit a variety of conditions, there are plenty of patterns with broad applicability to

The Wacker Backer system allows hunters to add 3-D camouflage components to their stands and ground blinds, adding an additional factor of concealment.

choose from. Conversely, if you want a pattern that will match the precise habitat and season you'll be hunting in, chances are good it exists.

Imagine you've invested several thousand dollars in a New Mexico elk bowhunt or a Texas deer hunt. When that trophy of a lifetime suddenly steps into view, it would be a shame if he spotted you because you failed to invest a few more dollars in the right camouflage clothing. On the other hand, selecting the right pattern could pay off in dividends that far exceed the original investment.

SneakyLeaf's pin-on synthetic leaves allow the hunter to add 3-D camo to any apparel.

Mossy Oak's **Forest Floor** pattern is designed to blend in with a leaf-covered forest floor. It is equally effective in seasons and habitats where dead leaves tend to remain on branches.

You can add another dimension to your concealment by selecting 3-D camouflage clothing. This suite by **Downwind-3D** is in Advantage Timber and features a layer of false leaves to add in breaking up the human silhouette.

BILL JORDAN'S
ADVANTAGE
TIMBER

Bowhunting for Whitetails

By Bill Winke

SWhitetail deer are North America's most popular big game animal. The fact that bucks are crafty enough to grow old right in our own backyards - despite fairly heavy hunting pressure - makes them both fascinating and borderline mystical. Hunting them with a bow is an adrenaline roller coaster that will make you cry and laugh, probably in the same day.

Here are several of the fundamental strategies that have proven most important when bowhunting whitetails. There are many more lessons to learn about deer and how to hunt them, but if you will stick with these basics while you gain experience, you will enjoy more than your share of success.

PREDICTING BUCK MOVEMENT

Question number one: where do I put my stand? There are a lot of trees out there. When most bowhunters place their stands they make the common mistake of immediately looking for scrapes and rubs – buck sign. Granted, these torn patches of ground and scuffed trees have stories to tell, but they are not the final word in bowhunting strategy. Buck sign simply serves to complement a broader strategy based on the terrain and cover. Actually, terrain and cover are better predictors of where a buck will travel than sign. This is especially true when you begin hunting the prime time of the rut when bucks abandon any semblance of a pattern and travel much more randomly in search of does. It pays to know what sign can reveal and what it can't.

Scrapes: Just prior to the time when bucks begin chasing does they will visit their scrapes more consistently. A line of scrapes is better than a single scrape because it denotes a travel route that at least one buck is using. A scrape line is a good place for your stand during the week leading up to the rut. In general, scrapes will be abandoned when the does actually start to come into estrus and bucks are actively chasing and breeding.

Rubs: Again, a line of rubs is a better find than a single rub because the line points out a buck's travel route. Once again, this sign is best hunted prior to the time when bucks start chasing. Some woodsmen would have you believe

Planning your bowhunting strategy and careful attention to the habits of your quarry can lead to success -- such as this truly impressive drop-tine White tail buck.

that big rubs are always made by big bucks. This isn't always true. I've seen enough small bucks rubbing big trees that I've given up attributing anything to rub size unless the tree is simply gigantic.

Rubs are somewhat directional, which means that they can be used to guess at the direction the buck was walking when he made it. That, in turn, helps to reveal time of day. For example, a rub on the side a tree facing a bedding area was likely made during the afternoon as the buck moved away from his bedding area. Of course, a rub facing away from a bedding area would likely indicate that the buck made the rub in the morning as he approached his bedding area.

Tracks: Big tracks are a good indicator of a buck's maturity. Bucks with big hooves are usually mature and that means they'll have nice racks. If you find an area with a concentration of big tracks, you need to start looking for good stand sites nearby. In the same way that rubs can offer some clues about when they were made, so, too, can tracks. Tracks pointing toward a bedding area were likely made during the morning and tracks pointing away from a bedding area were likely made in the evening.

Effects of terrain and cover: because of the limited range of a bow, bottlenecks should become your best friend. Terrain and cover can form bottlenecks that force traveling bucks toward a narrow corridor. Finding and hunting these spots can increase your odds because more bucks are likely to be within range. A classic terrain-related funnel is a ditch or creek crossing. Deer like to take the path of least resistance whenever possible. This means they will use gradual banks and shallow water crossings whenever possible. When such crossings are located 100 yards or more apart, they become funnels for traveling bucks and worthy places for your tree stand.

A typical cover-related funnel is a brush-choked fence line connecting two wood lots, or the middle of the hourglass shaped bottleneck that occurs when two large blocks of cover share a common corner. Other examples include the corner where a field juts abruptly into the timber and even an edge where bucks travel around a jungle of briars.

THE IMPORTANT ELEMENT OF SURPRISE

Once you've used the sign, terrain, and cover to pick out a general area for your stand, you need to consider how you will hunt it. The most important thing you can do to assure success is to keep the deer from knowing they're being hunted. Keep that in mind when evaluating your options. Many things can happen when you put pressure on a buck, and almost all of them are bad. One of the primary ways that

By carefully examining the characteristics of a rub and comparing them with other information, a bowhunter may be able to determine the movement patterns of a particular buck.

new bowhunters hurt their chances for success is by giving too little thought to the routes they take to get to and from their stands.

Deer are phenomenally adept at detecting human intrusion, and when they do, they begin to avoid that part of their range. If you are not careful, there's no telling how many deer may see you, hear you or smell your scent in the air or on the ground as a result of your approach to and from your tree stand each day. Spend lots of time planning this aspect of your hunt. In general, avoid the places where deer feed when approaching your morning stands and when leaving your evening stands, and avoid the places where they bed when leaving your morning stands and when approaching your afternoon stands.

HUNT THE HOTSPOTS LAST

Where you put your stand has a lot to do with how many deer you'll see and potentially how many you'll educate. Everybody likes to hunt the

A successful hunter approaches a downed buck. By carefully selecting a stand location that does not disrupt deer movement patterns, hunters can increase their chance of success.

hottest sign in the woods. When walking to a stand that's located right in the middle of the action, you get that feeling that "today is the day." But stands located in places where lots of deer pass are a double-edged sword. They are fun to hunt because you have the potential for seeing a lot of deer at close range. But if the set up is not perfect (and few are) you may end up educating a high percentage of the deer in your hunting area. If that happens, you are likely in for a slow season.

By saving the hotspots for last while hunting the fringes nearby, you keep your whole hunting area fresh and productive much longer. You won't get flooded with action on the first hunt and then have to endure a whole season of thumb-twiddling as you wonder why your hotspot suddenly "went cold." The action will be a little slower on the fringes but more consistent throughout the season. Besides, as your vacation time draws to a close you can always hunt the hotspot. By then you have nothing to lose.

With these basic fundamentals of successful whitetail hunting in mind, here are specific strategies for the two most commonly hunted portions of the season.

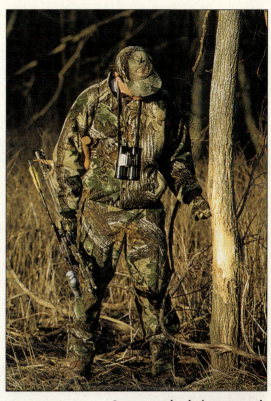

Scrapes are buck signposts and can be one useful factor among many in determining the movement patterns and habits of the deer in a hunting area.

EARLY SEASON

Bucks are much more patternable when the season first opens than they are during the rut that follows. They live their lives between their bedding areas and their feeding areas. To keep from over-pressuring them, it is best to focus only on their feeding areas and stay away from their bedding areas at this point in the season. We'll save them for later.

Spend at least two or three evenings before the season opens glassing feeding areas from a safe distance. Hunting a big buck during the early season is a lot easier once you've actually seen him. And ideally, you'll see him do something at least twice so you can establish some type of pattern. It's just as important to determine what the other deer using the feeding area are doing too. You'll need to avoid getting picked off by them, as well, or the buck will never materialize.

Rarely will the big buck be the first to come out in the evening. More than likely does, fawns and young bucks will come out first. If they catch your scent, they'll sound the alarm and you can forget about seeing your buck. If that happens more than once, the other deer using the feeding area will become wary. Then you can forget about seeing the buck again until possibly the rut. Study the situation and take all the factors into consideration before you pick a stand location. Here are two more details to consider.

Getting out clean: You may not get the buck the first time you hunt him, so you need a good plan for getting back to your vehicle without spooking any of the deer using the feeding area. This usually means a wide detour around the field. If it's impossible to come up with a good exit scenario, you will need to arrange to have someone drive up to the edge of the field and scatter the deer more naturally with a vehicle so you can climb down and get out unnoticed. The deer seem to forgive these intrusions much more readily than they will a man climbing down from a tree right on the edge of their feeding area.

Morning vs. evening: If you've got a buck on a feeding pattern, count yourself lucky. Don't push him by trying to find a way to hunt him in the morning. All the morning options (including hunting bedding areas) carry a higher probability of spooking him. Keep him feeling safe and traveling naturally as you stand in wait near his food source. Spend the mornings either finishing work around the house or office or glassing the food source from a safe distance. As long as the buck is still cooperative, hunt him only at the food source and only in the evening.

THE RUT

One of the prime advantages a whitetail bowhunter has is the ability to hunt during the early stages of the rut. This is the time when most experienced bowhunters schedule their annual hunting vacation. When bucks start chasing does, forget the sign and shift your strategy to the places where the does concentrate.

This buck with his massive, non-typical rack was the product of a carefully planned hunting strategy. By learning and developing field-craft and hunting skills, a bowhunter can reduce elements of chance and dramatically increase the potential for a successful hunt.

Bedding areas in the mornings: One morning, a couple of seasons back, I experienced the most excitement I've ever had on stand. Three different does - all of them obviously in heat - ran past, each followed by several bucks hot on their trails. The action took place well back in the timber on the edge of doe bedding area during the middle of the morning. As soon as I see bucks chasing does through areas, these are the spots I reserve for my morning hunts. Bucks will begin showing up shortly after sunrise and will mill in and out of the areas all morning as they hunt for a doe in heat.

The tricky part about hunting bedding areas is managing your impact. You can't afford to educate the does or they will stop using the area prematurely and the bucks will stop visiting. Keep your stand to the downwind fringe of the bedding area in a place where you can get in and out without being seen, heard or smelled. You'll find that this requirement eliminates a lot of potential stand sites.

Feeding areas in the evenings: Feeding areas are a lot like bedding areas. They start to produce excellent results when the bucks start chasing does. While bedding areas are great morning stand locations, feeding areas are best hunted in the afternoons. Does will use their customary feeding areas heavily until the bucks get to hounding them so badly that they start to avoid these areas. This typically doesn't happen until the middle of the breeding phase of the rut.

Set up along the main trails heading into the feeding area, but pay particular attention to the edge trail that runs the perimeter about 20 to 30 yards inside the cover. Bucks will often cruise along this edge trail to intersect trails leading in and out of the feeding area while sniffing for signs of a hot doe. It is also good, whenever possible, to cover the field edge from the same stand. Bucks sometimes cruise right along the edge of the timber where they can also cut trails and visually watch for does.

CONCLUSION

For whitetail enthusiasts, bowhunting offers a seasonal advantage in many states because you are able to chase big bucks during the best days of the rut. Bowhunting also offers a longer hunting season. You may come to the sport hoping for a way to increase the number of deer you can shoot in a season, but soon you'll realize that the close-range nature of every encounter is reward enough in itself. Welcome to the wonderful world of bowhunting whitetails.

A hunter examines a large whitetail track along a muddy road. Reading tracks is a valuable skill in close-up bowhunting.

Stand Placement Tips

WIND DIRECTION:
Normally the lesson is but a single statement: "Keep the wind in your face." But there's more to it than that. You also have to avoid placing stands in sheltered locations because when the wind blows it will swirl into these pockets of still air and carry your scent in every direction.

HEIGHT:
Strive to put your stands at least 15 feet up, and 18 to 20 feet is better. This gets you above low brush for improved visibility and high enough that deer aren't going to notice you easily. But, you won't be so high that the shot angle becomes tough with a bow or the sheer height produces anxiety.

SET UP ON THE BACK OF THE TREE:
You can stay better hidden in medium-sized trees by placing your stand on the backside of the tree – away from the direction you expect the deer to pass. You are basically hiding behind the tree.

SHOOTING LANES:
Make sure you can get a shot at a deer passing at every reasonable range and in any direction.

Before or after the season making the required brush cuts is a simple saw job. Heck, you can even use a small chainsaw. But during the season, keep your cutting to a minimum or deer will notice the change and shy from your scent. Keep your shooting lanes about four to six feet wide. That gives you plenty of room to stop a walking deer but doesn't open up the woods and attract attention to your stand.

TREE SIZE:
Whenever possible, choose trees that are just a bit larger than your waist. Trees of this size are easy and safe to climb and offer reasonable concealment while remaining fairly easy to shoot around.

DISTANCE FROM TRAILS:
Place your stands about 20 yards from the expected travel route as often as possible. This is close enough for an easy shot, but far enough that you won't be noticed easily.

SITTING VS. STANDING:
Standing is better in general because it puts you in position to respond quickly to shots in any direction. Sit for a few minutes to rest, but plan to stand most of the time.

Dress For Success

By Bob Robb

One key to bowhunting clothing is to make sure your upper body garments do not interfere with the bowstring during the shot. Wearing an armguard and tight-fitting binocular strap around the neck will help keep the string free and clear.

Why is it that bowhunters spend so many hours agonizing over their bows and equipment, but give their clothing little thought other than what camouflage pattern they think they need?

That's a huge mistake. Wearing the wrong type of clothing inhibits your comfort, making you a less efficient hunter. In wet, cold, and inclement weather the wrong clothing can also be dangerous. Yet it's easy to see why bowhunters make mistakes in selecting the best clothing available. The latest high-tech clothing, while a much better choice for most bowhunting applications, is expensive. Yet by taking a seasonal approach, you can remain comfortable, safe, and hunting at peak efficiency. Here's how to go about it.

The Purpose of Outerwear

Outerwear has two primary functions. First, it must keep the body's microclimate as close to normal as possible, regardless of external conditions. And second, it should protect the body, whether it be from the briars of a swamp thicket, sharp rocks of a Montana mountain, or any one of a hundred other "gotchas." But before we delve into outerwear, a word about clothing systems.

When choosing hunting clothing, do so with a layered approach in mind. Depending on the weather, choose a wicking underlayer followed by various additional layers topped with outerwear, all designed to function together as a team whose goal is to keep the body comfortable and protected all day long. Like any team, the success of your clothing system to do this is dependent on its weakest link. Choosing the wrong layering garments can defeat the ability of other high-tech layers to function at peak efficiency. For example, wearing all-cotton undershirts or longjohns – which will soak up perspiration like a sponge, and hold it near the body where it will make you cold and clammy – instead of a wicking material like CoolMax, Thermax, Capilene, or polypropylene, will defeat the ability of high-tech Gore-Tex and Windstopper garments to permit perspiration vapor to wick away from the skin and out through the outer layers of the system.

It's also important to remember that there is no "magic" garment that's perfect for every conceivable condition throughout the year. A light cotton shirt and pant ideal for hot September bowhunts is way too thin for late November treestand hunting in the frigid upper Midwest. Heavily-insulated jackets built for late-season warmth will torch you up if you wear them while hiking up a steep mountain in mild weather. Use common sense, and you'll be much happier, and more efficient in the field.

Early-season bowhunters are best served with lighter-weight outerwear worn over wicking undergarments.

Early-Season Outerwear

In much early-season bowhunting, the concern is staying cool, not staying warm. This is where cotton garments shine. As long as it isn't raining, nothing beats cotton for early-season comfort and quiet, making it ideal for everything from western elk and mule deer stalking to sitting a treestand over a food plot in whitetail country. When it gets a bit chilly, adding a light jacket or vest made from synthetic fabrics like polar fleece, microsuede, and similar materials are very quiet and warm, and don't add a lot of bulk.

There are a ton of cotton hunting garments available in stores as varied as Wal-Mart to local hunting shops and in the mail-order giants like Cabela's, Bass Pro Shops, and Gander Mountain.

If choosing garments for early-season is something of a no-brainer, when the weather turns nasty, selecting the right garments becomes more problematic.

In bitter weather, using a muff to keep the hands warm allows you to wear light gloves, which will not inhibit your ability to make the shot.

Late-Season Outerwear

Is there anything worse than being cold, wet and miserable on a late-season deer hunt? You've waited all year for the rut, and it's finally here. The bucks are moving like madmen, but the weather has turned worse than expected and you're not prepared. You're so cold you can't help but fidget enough to make the tree shake. After it's rained for an hour, you're wet and chilled to

the bone and can't concentrate. You end up heading back to camp, defeated by a lack of the right clothing system.

The key is the base layer of undergarments, which should be made from a synthetic material like CoolMax, Thermax, Polypropylene, or another space-age fabric designed to both insulate and wick moisture off the skin. Wet skin is cold skin. Wearing cotton undergarments or tee-shirts will seriously hamper the ability of the rest of your clothing system to do its job.

Late-season hunters should wear outer garments made from only two types of fabrics – wool, or a wool-synthetic blend; and hydrophobic man-made fibers designed to wick moisture. Cotton, while an outstanding material early in the year, becomes useless when wet, losing most of its insulating ability and turning into an ice box. Smart hunters know this, and choose only fabrics designed for optimum performance when Mother Nature turns cold and nasty.

There are literally more outerwear fabrics available on today's market than you can shake a stick at. As in everything in life, there are tradeoffs to be made.

Some, like Ambush Cloth, DuPont's Cordura nylon and Highland Industries' Ten Mile Cloth, among others, are extremely durable, resisting abrasion almost like steel. The tradeoff? They're very noisy, making them a poor choice for bowhunting. However, the latest generation of microsuede and micro-fleece fabrics are tough yet quiet enough for close-range bowhunting.

In recent years, progress has also been made in the polar fleece, knit acrylic, and nylon fields, primarily in the backpacker market but now spilling over into the hunting market. Space-age nylon materials like Supplex, Taslan, Packcloth and others offer light weight, great strength, and reasonable quiet. Fleece, which includes fabrics with manufacturer's brand names like Polarfleece, Polartec, Polartuff, and others, as

Late in the season, wearing a layered system featuring synthetic fibers or wool and/or wool blends is the smart choice.

Extreme Measures For Odor Elimination

It is imperative that all big game bowhunters—and especially those who hunt from static locations such as tree stands and ground blinds—take extreme measures to control their scent. Such measures should include:

• Wash all your clothing, both outerwear and underwear, in unscented laundry soap. Double rinse it. Store the clothing in a scent-free bag. Avoid exposing it to unnatural odors like cooking, gasoline, etc.

• Shower head-to-toe each morning using unscented soap/shampoo. Pay special attention to head, armpits, crotch, and feet.

• Brush your teeth and tongue with baking soda and lots of water.

• Use unscented body deodorants and/or gels. There are several available from various hunting product makers, but you can also buy them in the grocery store.

• Wear scent-absorbing outerwear and/or underwear. Products made from Gore-Tex and Gore Windstopper Supprescent fabric have the advantage of being able to be laundered regularly with no loss of effectiveness. Garments made by ALS Enterprises (Scent-Lok) and Robinson Laboratories (ScentBlocker) also use activated carbon, but should not be laundered.

• Wear scent-proof boots, either classic knee-high rubber boots or those featuring a waterproof, breathable Gore-Tex Supprescent membrane. These boots are both waterproof and breathable for increased comfort, and block 100 percent of human odor.

• Spray everything—equipment, daypack, clothing, etc.—with an odor-eliminating spray. This includes the inside of your boots, outerwear, under garments, caps, gloves and facemasks.

Activated carbon clothing will absorb human scent, keeping your smell away from the radar-like noses of big-game animals. Unlike other brands of carbon clothing, in which the carbon is held in place by glue, the activated carbon in Gore-Tex and Windstopper Supprescent fabric is held in place by the nodes and fibrils of the Gore Windstopper membrane itself. Imagine a bunch of horizontal layers of spider webs. The carbon particles, wedged in between the layers of the webs, are too large to get through the web; therefore, they're permanently held in place. They can't come out, even if the membrane is washed during normal home laundry cycles using unscented soap, or under the toughest field-use conditions.

well as knit acrylics, are ultra-quiet, retain their insulative value when wet, and dry extremely quick. The downside of fleece-like materials? They block virtually no wind, though that problem has been addressed by a few select manufacturers offering both acrylic and fleece garments laminated with breathable membranes like Gore-Tex, Windstopper, WindBloc, and Sympatex that block virtually 100 percent of the wind, yet add virtually no extra weight or bulk.

Finally, in a world of space-age fibers and materials, don't overlook the deer hunter's traditional favorite—wool. Wool still provides great comfort, tremendous insulative properties that it retains when wet, a reasonable amount of toughness, and is ultra quiet in the deer woods. Woolrich's CamWoolflage jackets and pants are superb garments, and available in both Realtree and Advantage patterns.

Rain Gear

I've had lots of experience hunting around the world in wet, rainy weather. The first item I pack for any hunting trip is a rain suit.

For stationary hunting in heavy rains—long sits in a tree stand or ground blind comes immediately to mind—old-style, non-breathable rainwear made from rubber—a thick coating of PVC over heavy cotton, nylon, or rayon— and waxed cotton garments are hard to beat. This stuff will shed 100 percent of the water. Period. Its downside? Water vapor in the form of sweat can't pass through it, meaning you'll end up clammy and cold if you sweat much when hiking.

Tree stand hunters are the big beneficiaries of high-tech activated carbon outerwear systems. If deer come downwind of you, the chances of them detecting your odor are greatly lessened when outfitted in these garments. J.D. McCay of Colorado wore Gore-Tex Supprescent garments when he shot his first-ever whitetail buck in western Kentucky in October, 2002.

For active hunting, where hiking makes up part or all of your day, a breathable rain suit that allows perspiration vapor to exit the fabric, yet keep out water molecules, is an excellent choice. Here there are several different choices available. It's hard to beat today's versions of waterproof, breathable membranes. These include Gore-Tex, Sympatex, Patagonia's Gridstop and Super Pluma, and Browning's Hydro-Tech. Kool-Dri Rainwear is a top-quality product and in a separate category, attacking this concept with microporous pores in the tough shell fabric itself. There are several variations of polyurethane coatings that have a different ratio of waterproofness to breathability, depending on the coating's thickness when applied to the garment's base fabric. These include Toray Industries' Entrant, Helly Hansen's Helly-Tech, Patagonia's H2No, Solstice's Microshed, Columbia's Omni-Tech, and Burlington Industries' Ultrex.

One key for the bowhunter is wearing outerwear made from a fabric that is quiet when scraped up against tree trunks, brush, or when swishing against itself when walking. The last thing you need to do is scare off an animal with noisy clothing.

Choosing the Right Boots & Socks

Bowhunters need comfortable footwear. However, not all boots are right for every situation – meaning you need a boot designed for the situation at hand.

"The human foot was really not designed to wear a shoe or boot," said Tom Casti, Hunting Footwear Product Specialist for W.L. Gore & Associates, makers of the Gore-Tex and Gore-Tex Supprescent membranes found in many high-quality hunting boots. "Wearing the wrong boot during hunting activities can be both uncomfortable and damaging to the foot and entire lower body."

The key is to get properly fitted before buying a new boot, Casti said. "It's best to visit a shoe store with a wide boot selection and have a trained sales person measure your feet with a Brannock device," Casti said. "This is the only way to get a precise measurement of your foot, including length, width, and arch height," he said.

"People should be aware that boot sizes will vary slightly by manufacturer, and even between different boot models from the same manufacturer. Also, as you age your foot size will change, so a boot that fit like a glove 10 years ago may not fit you today."

After being measured, Casti said, choosing a boot designed for the specific bowhunting application you will be engaged in is critical. "You don't want a heavily-insulated boot for early-season hunting," he said. "Boots with soft, flat soles may be great for flatland whitetail hunting, but awful for chasing elk in the Rockies."

Casti noted that managing moisture – sweat – is the key to comfort in a hunting boot. "One of the most important things in maintaining comfort is keeping the feet dry," Casti said. "That means keeping moisture like rain and dew out of the boot,

and wicking sweat away from the foot. While an all-rubber boot will certainly keep moisture out, it will also keep it in because it doesn't breathe. A waterproof, breathable membrane like Gore-Tex Supprescent, which also blocks 100 percent of human odor just like rubber boots do, will allow sweat to wick off the foot and pass through the membrane, keeping the feet as comfortable as they can be while not compromising scent control."

Casti also noted that using a synthetic sock, like those from SmartWool, Thorlo, and other high-tech manufacturers, is critical to moisture management. "Cotton socks absorb water, and will keep it on the foot, creating a cold, damp environment," he said. "Wicking socks are the only way to go for all hunting."

I'm a big fan of breathable rain gear, simply because venting moisture off the body is the key to staying dry and comfortable regardless of the conditions at hand. While this is not the place to debate the merits of each of the above individual products, suffice it to say that all are not created equal. In my experience — both in the field and observing laboratory testing — while all the above will work under light mist and very light rain, when the going gets really tough, the waterproof/breathable membranes are tops. One advantage a Gore-Tex membrane has over the polyurethane coatings is that it cannot be broken down by any chemical, acid, or other product on the planet. An example is DEET, the active ingredient in the best insect repellents. DEET will eat right through the polyurethane and PVC coatings, but will not affect Gore-Tex.

Scent-Control: The Next Generation

You stink. But then, so do all your friends. So do I. Always have, always will. Maybe not to your wives and girlfriends, but certainly to most big game animals. Here's a charming thought. Dr. Louis Leakey, the world-famous paleontologist, once said he believed that ancient man smelled so badly they probably repelled predators with their stench. Hear a deer snort or elk bark and run, and you have to think that's exactly how

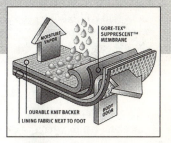

Here's how a Gore-Tex Supprescent membrane works in footwear. The Gore-Tex membrane is selectively permeable, meaning it permits moisture vapor – sweat – to vent out, yet blocks human odor molecules from leaving. At the same time, it is 100% waterproof. This provides unsurpassed comfort and performance, and means you don't have to wear uncomfortable rubber boots to remain scent-free when big game hunting.

Tree stand hunters gain the greatest benefit from high-tech activated carbon outerwear. The author shot this buck in western Kentucky while wearing Gore-Tex scent control garments and boots.

Never forget you must hide a shiny face and hands when bowhunting. That means using either face paint, as Chuck Jones prefers, or a face mask or head net.

we smell to game, no matter how hard we try not to.

Defeating the radar-like noses of big game animals has always been a bowhunter's toughest challenge. Enter activated carbon clothing. In a nutshell, the activated carbon in this clothing adsorbs human odor molecules, preventing them from reaching an animal's nose. Used properly, this clothing can tremendously up your odds at success.

It all began in 1992, when Scent-Lok stormed onto the scene with the introduction of their now-famous green liner system, featuring head covering, top, pants, and gloves made from a nylon fabric impregnated with millions of tiny nodules of activated charcoal that absorbed odors, including human smells. The suits were designed to be worn under the archer's outerwear. In 1997, the company introduced its first Scent-Lok Camo Clothing, an outerwear system made from a 50/50 poly/cotton brushed twill available in three camouflage patterns and designed to be worn as the outer final layer. In 1999 the company took the system one step further by making their material available to the manufacturers of accessory items like day packs.

In late 1998 W.L. Gore & Associates — best known for their Gore-Tex and Windstopper membranes — entered the market with the introduction of Gore Windstopper Supprescent fabric. It also contains activated carbon, yet also provides the benefits of the Gore-Tex and Windstopper membranes. Both membranes are highly breathable, which means that any moisture vapor produced by the wearer — sweat — can pass quickly through the membrane, drastically reducing the effects of convective heat loss, or wind chill. This makes this high-tech fabric ideal for wearing in a wide range of activities, from hard hiking to sitting for hours on stand, in a wide range of temperatures.

Just as importantly, the activated carbon in Supprescent fabric is held in place by the nodes and fibrils of the Gore Windstopper membrane itself. Imagine a bunch of horizontal layers of spider webs. The carbon particles, wedged in between the layers of the webs, are too large to get through the web; therefore, they're permanently held in place. They can't come out, even if the membrane is washed during normal home laundry cycles using unscented soap, or under the toughest field-use conditions.

Today Robinson Laboratories also markets activated carbon clothing under license from Scent-Lok, under the name ScentBlocker.

Great strides are being made in the activated carbon clothing business annually. The bottom line is this – if you are serious about your bowhunting, you will be wearing this type of clothing

Early-season elk hunters need garments that allow them to cover lots of ground quickly and quietly, yet keeps them protected from the elements. I shot this nice 6x6 bull in Colorado while wearing lightweight Gore-Tex Supprescent outerwear and boots – a big advantage in the swirling winds of early September.

When the weather is really bitter, you have to choose a clothing system specifically designed for the task at hand. When I shot this record book muskox bull in the Northwest Territories, it was -40 degrees, with a wind blowing about 20 mph. That's cold!

Being the Boss
By Michael D. Faw

Ben Pearson Archery's hunting camp and testing facility in the deep woods of Alabama has been in Tom McPherson's family since 1915.

E ver think about owning an archery shop or bow company? Do you think this would be a way to meet new hunting friends and could result in offers and hunting opportunities across America? Well, yes and no, and it depends, according to Tom McMillan, Jr., the owner of Alabama-based Ben Pearson Archery and McPherson Archery companies.

Tom bought the McPherson Archery Company in 1993 and jumped right into the bow manufacturing process. Tom's son, Tom III, had a strong interest in archery and bowhunting at that time and the two worked as a team to advance the company. In 1997, the McMillans obtained Ben Pearson Archery, a company that has been in business since 1927, when master archer Ben Pearson began making recurves and longbows.

In addition to moving the archery company's headquarters and manufacturing facilities to Brewton, Alabama, the McMillans began the tedious task of quickly learning about the archery industry on an advanced level.

Ben Pearson owner Tom McMillan, Jr. displays his favorite Pearson hunting compound bow.

Tom McMillan Jr. soon discovered that his loyal customers and dedicated sales staff were willing to help his companies grow.

"We have relied on our dealer representatives and customer word-of-mouth to help us grow," said Tom Jr. "I also find the archery industry exciting. I enjoy seeing the new products, learning about what's new and discovering the latest thing and break-through products."

One thing that Tom and his 16 employees strongly believe in is customer service. When you call the plant and headquarters, you get a quick response and instant help. McMillan also believes that dealer loyalty, along with the innovative designs and features found on the Pearson and McPherson bows, are what set him and his products apart from the large corporate mass-produced bow manufacturers. Innovation shines through from the company's 20-degree bio-slant bow grips to their 2003 Freedom Pro compound bow with its eye-catching red, white and blue All American camou-

Tom McMillan holds his company's new Freedom Pro compound bow. The Freedom Pro is finished in a patriotic red, white and blue camo design.

flage. All of the company's bows have a lifetime guarantee that also sets them apart from the pack.

"We are aggressive in our goals and growth," says Tom Jr. "We're also small and lean, and this offers advantages in many areas of our business." The companies can normally develop and incorporate a new idea into their product line in less than six months. Another aggressive move that has been well received by Pearson and McPherson customers is the lifetime warranty. The company's rigorous testing and triple layer inspection process ensures that each bow leaving the factory will perform flawlessly, so few bows ever return for repairs.

On my visit to the plant, I saw bow limbs being stressed 100,000 plus bends by what could best be described as a medieval torture machine. Another machine in a dark corner slowly and methodically drew a bow thousands of times each day for weeks at a time. I'm not sure that I'd ever want to hook any of my bows to these tests, but I'm glad Pearson and McPherson set such rigorous testing requirements! The standard Pearson and McPherson compound bows have 56 parts and each part is inspected before, during and after assembly. Will all these parts mean we'll see new futuristic bows in the years ahead?

"I believe that bows will basically be the same in future years," said Tom Jr. "You can tweak them to make 'em better, but they'll have the same basic design and mechanics. On the other side, there are a lot of things that you can do to a bow to add weight and make 'em more expensive. This is not always a good thing for the shooter." One detail that does find its way on most Pearson and McPherson bows is a factory-installed antler velvet finish on the arrow rest shelf. No need to add strips of moleskin.

Now, what about traveling and hunting the country? The Pearson company-sponsored shooting team travels around the U.S. each summer promoting the brands as they compete in numerous archery tournaments. During hunting season, however, they're back in Alabama and working to assist dealers and customers who are preparing for the pending archery seasons and hunting season shopping sprees.

When things do slow, you might find Tom Jr. and some employees sitting in a tree stand at their Dozier Camp testing and hunting ground. This rigorous research is one of the benefits of owning, and working for, a bow company.

Below Top:
Ben Pearson Marketing Manager Dave Coldwell take aim with the company's new Centurion Crossbow. The crossbow, introduced in 2003, has a 165-pound draw weight and produces 330 foot-pounds of energy with a 480-grain bolt.

Below Bottom:
Coldwell tries the Ben Pearson Freedom Pro Z-cam bow on a range at the company's Alabama hunting camp. The Freedom Pro has a newly-designed machined riser with 42° limb pockets and an improved noise and vibration reduction system.

Be a Better Bow Shot!
By Chuck Adams

Most bowhunters learn to shoot "by the seat of their pants". They teach themselves with little or no instruction from books, videotapes, or experienced archers. The result is seldom good and never great.

To become an excellent shot on live animals, you must do two important things. First, practice basic, time-tested shooting moves until these become habit. Second, refine your field-shooting talents by launching arrows from natural hunting positions at a variety of distances. If you simply shoot without discipline and forethought, you'll develop poor habits that preclude top hunting bow accuracy. Once ingrained, such habits can be difficult to break.

Stand Correctly

Stand close to the target to begin with, 15 or 20 yards at most. Your feet should be parallel and 12 to 18 inches apart, with your body weight equally distributed on both feet. Point your toes at about 45 degrees toward the target. Some beginning archers stand with feet pointing 90 degrees (at right angles) to the target. This is a big mistake.

An "open", face-the-target, stance is favored by almost every top archer, since this moves the bowstring farther from your chest and bow arm during the shot. If the string brushes clothing in these areas even slightly, the arrow will fly wildly to the right or left — usually left for a

An archer prepares to launch his arrow from a kneeling position. Constant target practice in a variety of fundamental hunting positions is vital to the development of disciplined and effective shooting.

right-hand shooter. Slightly facing the target will shorten your draw length by an inch or so. You might need to adjust your compound bow if you've already been shooting awhile.

Get a Grip
Hold the bow loosely with thumb and fingers closed to lightly touch in the front. Do not tightly squeeze the bow. In general, bows with the smallest grips shoot the best, because it's too easy to squeeze or grab a large bow grip too hard during the shot.

Grabbing too tightly tenses your hand and arm, throwing your shot off the mark. Also, a white-knuckle hold on the bow will cause it to twist or torque, causing the arrow to wobble from side to side. Wobbling arrows do not fly well with hunting broadheads attached and will dart and dive off the mark. The bow should rattle loosely in your closed hand after you release. With practice, you should be able to keep your bow hand relaxed throughout the shot.

A few archers mistakenly aim with an open bow hand, then grab the bow as they release. The result is a severe loss of accuracy. If you have this habit, or cannot keep your bow hand relaxed, try a commercial wrist sling that ties the bow to your hand. This allows a wide-open hand throughout the shot, without reduced accuracy. Wrist slings are most practical for shooting from a tree stand, where you usually have time to slip your hand inside. At ground level, a wrist sling can be slow and cumbersome if sudden shots present themselves.

After mastering the basics, you should practice field archery techniques, such as shooting from one knee.

Draw Smoothly
Whether you opt to draw with fingers or a release aid is strictly a matter of personal preference. A trigger-operated, mechanical release is potentially more accurate, but slower and noisier to use. A finger release requires more practice to perfect, but ensures fast, simple, and trouble-free shooting. I recommend release aids to all beginning bowhunters, and about 85% of modern archers use them because they are easier to shoot with. Take your pick.

If you do decide to draw and release with your fingers, here are three solid tips. First: use a tab to protect your fingers from the string. A glove might feel more natural at first, but tends to develop a groove over time and impede an accurate release. Second: shoot a compound bow at least 40 inches long from axle to axle. Shorter bows create radical string pinch around your fingers and hang up the string. Finally, draw with three fingers and release with two. Whether you drop your

A tight and accurate grouping of arrows indicates well-honed expertise. Practice with attention to detail is an important step in developing effective hunting skills.

top or bottom finger from the string is personal preference, but relax one or the other. Best accuracy results from a two-finger release.

When you want to shoot an arrow, grip the bowstring with your fingers or a mechanical release, lift the bow and point it at the target and draw the string straight back to your face. If you find yourself dipping the bow or hoisting it overhead to draw, the bow is too heavy for your muscles. Reduce the bow's weight if it feels too heavy. After practicing for several weeks, you can gradually increase the weight as you become fit.

Anchor Solidly

At full draw, the bowstring hand should be locked solidly against your face with the bowstring more or less in line with your aiming eye. Most modern archers use a peep sight on the bowstring to guarantee consistent through-the-string aiming. A large aperture (at least 3/16-inch) is necessary for ample light to reach your aiming eye at dawn and dusk.

Find a comfortable, solid anchor point along the jaw or side of your face, then adjust the bowstring peep for perfect alignment with your eye. Most finger shooters and release users drop the thumb below the jawline with the index finger or release aid pressed against the upper jaw. There should be solid hand pressure against your face as you aim and release.

Aim Consistently

The vast majority of archers aim using one or more sight pins set for ranges like 20, 30, and 40 yards. But even if you prefer to shoot by "feel" without sights, aiming should be a consistent and familiar operation.

Move slowly but steadily on target from the same direction every time. The majority of bowhunters come up on the target, some come down, and a few swing on the target from left or right. I prefer to smoothly lift my bow as I aim. I can see the target clearly above my sights and I can count the pins until the correct sight is on target.

If you own a laser rangefinder (every sight shooter should have one), you'll usually know the precise range to your target. But in quick hunting scenarios, you might need to estimate distance by eye. Practice judging distances as you practice with your bow. Either way, bring the correct sight pin on target, hesitate a second, then release the arrow. If you aim the same way every time, this move will become automatic and deadly.

Get A Good Release

With a release aid or fingers, a slick string release is crucial to accuracy. With a trigger device, be sure to squeeze gently until the string disengages. Never slap or punch the release. With fingers, simply relax and let the bowstring pull free.

Keep your string hand against your face as you release, letting it slide naturally backward along the jaw and neck. Flipping your hand away from your face will cause arrows to scatter to the left or right of center.

Follow Through The Shot

Correctly following through is critical to any projectile sport. In golf, you smoothly swing the club completely through the shot. In tennis, you smash the ball with your eye glued to the target.

In archery, follow-through is equally important. Try to keep your sight on the target until the arrow actually hits. Don't drop your bow or lift your head to "peek" at the arrow after you release. The target and the sight are all you should see until the arrow impacts.

Your bow will naturally recoil during the shot, but if you try to stay on target, the arrow will be accurately on its way before recoil occurs. Correctly follow through the shot, and you'll hit what you aim at most of the time.

Learn Your Distance Limitations

With practice, most bowhunters can increase their effective animal-bagging distance. You should never shoot at game beyond your own sure-kill capability, but you should work at extending and controlling that capability. Here are some rules on how to proceed.

First, know the size of your intended target's vital zone. For example, the average deer or black bear has a chest cavity about 8 inches in diameter. A

A dedicated archer practices shots at various ranges so that he knows at which range he can hit an animal's vital chest zone every time. Practicing on 3-D deer targets can help.

Perfecting realistic tree and ground shots can help you become a more deadly hunter.

caribou has a 12-inch chest, and an elk has a kill zone 16 inches deep.

Second, practice shooting at bull's-eye and 3-D animal targets at various ranges with kill zone sizes in mind. A very good bow shot can hit a 3-inch bull's-eye almost every time from 20-yards, a 6-inch target from 40-yards, and a 9-inch target from 60-yards.

Third, never shoot at an animal unless you know you can control your arrow at a particular distance. For example, a 40-yard shot at a relaxed, broadside deer is entirely acceptable if you can hit a 6-inch spot every time at that range. If you can only shoot 6-inch groups from 20 or 25 yards, you have no business shooting at game beyond these distances. If you push your limits on the target range, you will tighten your arrow groups and be in better control on closer as well as longer shots.

Practice Natural Positions

Upright, classic target practice is the foundation for all shooting at game -- master the fundamentals first. But very few chances at animals are perfect. In a tree, you'll always be shooting downward and sometimes from a sitting position. You'll may need to twist left or right, and you'll be trussed with a safety belt or harness that impedes free movement. On the ground, a bowhunter must sometimes kneel or crouch to shoot, or launch an arrow while standing on uneven ground. Such moves must be anticipated and practiced before hunting season begins.

Summer target-practice clothes and bulkier late autumn hunting duds can require different shooting moves and gear. You'll definitely need an armguard and possibly an archer's chest guard to compress a coat or vest along your upper body. You might need to face the target more directly when wearing heavy clothing to avoid an accuracy-ruining collision between the bowstring and fabric.

Practice under conditions that accurately imitate hunting situations. Erect an elevated platform and shoot practice arrows at targets on the ground. Wear the clothes you expect to bowhunt in. Learn to bend at the waist, using a tree stand safety belt, to ensure proper upper body shooting form. Learn to compensate for a slightly higher arrow impact from a tree stand. Learn to shoot from a tree stand stool, placing the lower bow limb between your legs as you slightly face the target. Learn to shoot while twisting left and right at the waist.

Fine-tune your shooting skills at ground level. Learn to shoot from one or both knees, and while sitting on your heels. Shoot practice arrows into dirt banks and rotten stumps from crouched, twisted positions over uneven terrain. Work at estimating distance by eye, and practice using your rangefinder quickly.

Final Thoughts

By mastering the basics of accurate archery and applying them to real field shooting situations, you'll learn to grip, draw, anchor, aim and release with deadly effect. There's no shortcut for practicing with a bow, and no substitute for practicing correctly. The extra effort is well worth it as you become a better bowshot and feel your confidence increase.

The author practices what he preaches. His giant 1400-pound Alaska brown bear is one of 116 official Pope and Young record animals to his credit—more than any archer in history.

By Rick Sapp

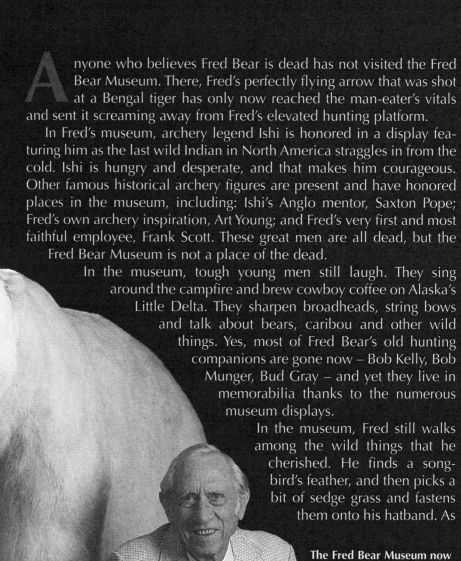

Anyone who believes Fred Bear is dead has not visited the Fred Bear Museum. There, Fred's perfectly flying arrow that was shot at a Bengal tiger has only now reached the man-eater's vitals and sent it screaming away from Fred's elevated hunting platform.

In Fred's museum, archery legend Ishi is honored in a display featuring him as the last wild Indian in North America straggles in from the cold. Ishi is hungry and desperate, and that makes him courageous. Other famous historical archery figures are present and have honored places in the museum, including: Ishi's Anglo mentor, Saxton Pope; Fred's own archery inspiration, Art Young; and Fred's very first and most faithful employee, Frank Scott. These great men are all dead, but the Fred Bear Museum is not a place of the dead.

In the museum, tough young men still laugh. They sing around the campfire and brew cowboy coffee on Alaska's Little Delta. They sharpen broadheads, string bows and talk about bears, caribou and other wild things. Yes, most of Fred Bear's old hunting companions are gone now – Bob Kelly, Bob Munger, Bud Gray – and yet they live in memorabilia thanks to the numerous museum displays.

In the museum, Fred still walks among the wild things that he cherished. He finds a songbird's feather, and then picks a bit of sedge grass and fastens them onto his hatband. As

The Fred Bear Museum now in Gainsville, Florida is the personal legacy of Fred Bear to the achers of the world. In this remarkable, but undated photo from the 1980s when the archery pioneer was in his 80s, Fred poses in a Museum "Picture Place" beside his polar bear.

long as he lives, the spirits of his hunting buddies have nothing to fear. Together, they still ride horseback through the deep valleys and across the barren, wind swept mountain passes of the Yukon. They chop wood to heat the stove for grilling flapjacks. They field dress moose and grizzly bears harvested by single arrows, and they laugh and pose for pictures. And today, as long as we, the inheritors of this incredible archery and hunting legacy, can stare up at the life-size pictures that cover the walls of Fred's Museum, we share his immortality, too. The museum is no longer just Fred Bear's Museum or Frank Scott's or even Ishi's, it is ours.

Fred Bear dreamed about having a museum that would highlight his hunting adventures, sell the products he made at Bear Archery in Grayling, Michigan, and promote the sport of archery. At the age of 65 and just one year before he sold his company to Victor Comptometer, his wish came true in 1967.

Arlyne Rhode, who now publishes The U.S. & International Archer magazine, remembers the original Fred Bear Museum in Grayling as a well-lighted and beautiful place. "Fred was so proud of it. People spent hours wandering around and staring at his trophies," she says. "If you visited the museum in Grayling or now in Gainesville, Florida, you know Fred was a collector. He never traveled but what he didn't come home with strange and wonderful archery artifacts, including: bows and poison-tipped arrows used by pygmy hunters in Africa, a bodkin-style broadhead thought to have been shot during the battle of Marathon in Greece 2,500 years ago, snowshoes, a "jackalope" rabbit, and a pair of mounted timber wolves he bought from a taxidermist in Alaska."

Frank Scott, Fred's first employee, called his boss a "scrounger" and he was. Everything that Fred Bear collected that was not lost or given away when his wife, Henrietta, died in 1997, is in the museum today and can be easily viewed, admired and savored. Thousands of trophies and artifacts are collected under one roof. The items range from the rare and precious to the sometimes bizarre, such as the mounted fish that swims in one direction, but runs on long legs in another, or the model rocket mounted in a slingshot that was given to Fred by astronaut and Air Force Major General Joe Engle.

Many of Fred's hunting trophies, like his 1957 world-record Stone's

Fred Bear hired Frank Scott in 1939 to blow up ballons at a shooting exhibition. Frank soon went to work for Fred full time and, practically speaking, was employed by Bear Archery for more than 50 years. When he died in 2000 at 79 years of age, Frank was the Director of the Fred Bear Museum. He went to his office every day. the African lion bringing down a water buffalo is just one of thousands of exhibits and archery items of interest in the Fred Bear Museum.

sheep, are on display in the museum. Some are mounted life-size, including brown bears, a moose, and Fred's polar bear with its curious blue tongue and massive paw holding a seal. There are special treasures here, too, such as a full-sized lion attacking a Cape buffalo, a grizzly emerging from its cave and, of course, the Bengal tiger. Fred called his 1963 trip to India as guest of the Maharaja of Bundi, his "greatest hunt ever." Today, the huge tiger is thoughtfully posed standing on two hind legs sharpening its claws on a tree. Visitors like to place their hand against its paw and have their picture taken, as if they were giving the bloodthirsty man-killer a "high five."

The Fred Bear Museum is not just a gallery of stuffed animals, though. A special showcase is devoted to Fred's personal hunting gear. The most prized is Fred's trademarked brown Borsalino hat, but other items include his fishing vest—Fred was an ardent fly fisherman—his size "huge" hunting boots, the tiny stub of a pencil and pocket-size notebook he used taking notes for his hunting classic Fred Bear's Field Notes, which was published in 1976. Fred's quiet humor and steadfast vision animates the trophies and fills the rooms and the long carpeted halls with his brilliant, quirky personality.

The effect the lanky Pennsylvania farm boy had on archery, hunting and conservation in America and around the world is on display, too.

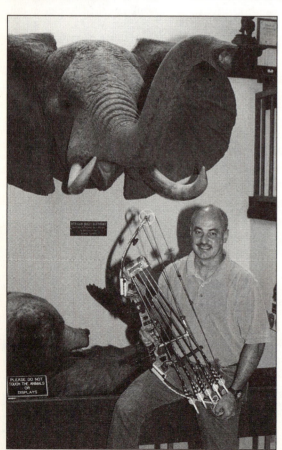

Evern today, archers such as bowhunter and NFAA Field Champion Dan Massimillo like to pose for pictures on the stairs of the Fred Bear Museum. Behind him is Fred Bear's African bull elephant, taken on safari in Mozambique in 1964. Below and beside one of Fred's life-size brown bears, but not visible in the photograph, is a life-size bull moose.

History comes to life with photos of Fred with governors, foreign dignitaries, movie stars and astronauts that cover the walls. Letters and testimonials from universities and from the people who worked with and loved him are here, too … along with the gifts.

Everyone who met Fred Bear—and many who did not—gave him presents: hand-tooled leather saddles, ancient archery artifacts, trophies that Fred perhaps never hunted (a red fox, a bobcat, a beaver!), a moose with monstrously deformed antlers, and hunting and archery club patches they would rip off their sleeves and hand him for the museum's growing collection. This giving was the individual archer's way of participating in and living through Fred's astonishing life. It was a way of returning something to a man who gave so much, to honor a man who would autograph anything, and to connect with a hunter who would patiently listen to a million hunting stories and who always had a kind and wondering word about his worshippers' small adventures.

When Fred Bear purchased the six acres for his original 8,500 square-foot manufacturing facility in 1946, after a historic horseback ride with Grayling banker John Brunn, he was already an accomplished field archery champion and bowhunter. Over the next ten years, Fred would become an internationally recognized video pro-

Longtime Museum Director Frank Scott poses in the Frank Scott Alcove of the Fred Bear Museum in Gainsville, Florida shortly before his death in 2000. Frank toured the country with his vaudeville family, *The Shooting Mansfields,* and became Fred's first employee in 1939.

ducer and manufacturer as well. Today's expansive archery manufacturing facility, which includes the Fred Bear Museum, is twenty times larger than the original shop.

In its current quarters, in the Bear Archery (now, with Jennings and Golden Eagle as part of The North American Archery Group, LLC) plant in Gainesville, Florida, large picture windows allow visitors to watch bows being built, tested and packaged. This is the very heart of the business of archery. Programmed CNC machines chisel raw billets of aluminum into bow risers and cams. A computerized conveyor moves drying racks loaded with freshly painted compression-molded carbon limbs through a temperature-controlled drying room. Bows by the thousands, including compounds, recurves, longbows, children's bows and the latest high-tech shooting gear, are packaged, sorted and stacked two stories high for sale and shipment around the world.

Fred's business has grown into a huge manufacturing enterprise, but the visitor who is not in a hurry can pause to watch people building equipment. A visitor might spot a man inspecting recurve limbs for any hint of a flaw, and then polishing and rubbing them to a high gloss. Another sight could be a woman packaging the 145-grain Super Razorhead broadhead that Fred designed in the mid '50s—a product that remains virtually unchanged. An interested visitor can watch teams assembling fast, camouflaged one-cam compound bows, the same bows that have become an international standard for hunting and competition.

The picture windows highlight the depth of Fred's intellectual curiosity and his persistence. Far more than just a sportsman or a business dilettante, Fred Bear was a tough-minded entrepreneur and a fair employer. He was an innovator with fiberglass and aluminum, with fresh designs and patents and a forward-looking approach to competition. When fire practically destroyed the factory in 1952, Fred found investors and rebuilt, larger and more modern than before. He was unlettered, a farm boy turned pattern maker and archer, but he drove

When and Where To Go

More than 20,000 people visit the Fred Bear Museum and Pro Shop each year. It is open to the public five days a week, Tuesday through Saturday, from 10:00 a.m. until 6:00 p.m. The museum closes on major holidays and visitors should call in advance to verify its operating schedule. For more details, contact: (352) 376-2327 x 278.

Admission to the museum is $3.50 per adult and $2.00 for children 6-12 years of age. A family admission (two adults and two children) is $8.50. The museum is located inside The North American Archery Group LLC manufacturing facility—home to Bear, Jennings and Golden Eagle. It may be reached easily by taking the frontage road—Fred Bear Drive, of course!—west of Interstate 75 in Gainesville, Florida between State Roads 24 (exit 75) and 121 (exit 74).

himself to accomplishment after accomplishment.

Fred Bear won every award that archery and the shooting sports could hand out. He was inducted into the Archery Hall of Fame and the Safari Club International's Hunting Hall of Fame. Fred was a winner of archery's Compton Medal, the National Archery Association's Maurice Thompson Medal of Honor and much more. In 1957, he was elected to the prestigious Explorer's Club. All of these honors are on display in Fred's museum.

In 1978, following a prolonged and bitter strike in Grayling, Michigan, Bear Archery moved south to Gainesville, Florida. Fred's museum remained open at the new "Bear Mountain" for two more years. When it again reopened in 1985, the museum was inside the Bear factory next to Interstate 75 in Gainesville, just two hours from Disney World.

Eventually, the Fred Bear Museum in Gainesville came to be all about many men, but two especially, rather than just one. Fred, of course, was the foundation. Without his genius and leadership there would never have been an archery and hunting museum.

But in 1939, Fred recruited Frank Scott to blow up balloons for him at a shooting exhibition. Fred was trading archery demonstrations for booth space wherever crowds gathered. Frank was traveling with his family, a vaudeville troupe called The Shooting Mansfields that specialized in trick .22 rifle shooting. Soon after, Frank went to work for Fred full-time and, practically speaking, for the rest of his life.

Forty-seven years after meeting Fred and just two years before Fred died, Bear Archery re-hired Frank Scott as the museum's director. Frank, who was working in sales at Bear at the time, had been the museum director in Grayling from 1974 until it relocated to Florida. The museum was a long way from the vaudeville and county fair circuit where Frank and Fred first met, but the return to promotion and curator responsibilities was pure genius. Frank thrived and the idle museum took on renewed life.

Frank Scott's pride and innate feeling for his opportunity kept the museum and pro shop from languishing through several corporate sales, numerous company presidents and frequent policy changes. He promoted Fred's museum, reorganized the exhibits, installed a button-activated electronic tour system and, along the way, found time to publicize his own exploits.

Frank Scott passed away in November 2000, outliving his mentor by a dozen years. He was still hunting bears every year in Nova Scotia, still shooting his Fred Bear Custom Kodiak Take-Down recurve, still employed as the museum curator and still going to work every day. He was 79 years old. To the very end, he inspected the Fred Bear Museum hourly, and could be spotted straightening, dusting, touching, caring for his precious charges, cheerfully greeting visitors, working with the staff and planning new exhibits. On his last day at the museum, he walked the halls with a screwdriver and aligned every brass screw head

In this post card from The Fred Bear Museum, Frank Scott poses beside Fred Bear's Bengal tiger. In his hand is a Japanese war arrow designed to cut the rigging lines of attacked ships and outfitted with a special whistling head to terrify the sailors on those ships.

vertically. Frank was a guardian, hovering protectively over many of the archery industry's most precious artifacts and historical collections.

Frank's commitment to promoting the sport of archery and conserving the Fred Bear Museum was rewarded in 1996 with a special exhibit of its own in the museum. Today, Frank's Alcove is a 250 square-foot room near the African elephant at the head of the stairs. The alcove is devoted to Frank, his historic vaudeville family and his long relationship with Fred Bear. It is a credit to Fred, who passed away in April 1988, that the umbrella of his name and accomplishments is expansive enough to cover a wider slice of history than solely his own. The visitor will notice that Frank has packed his alcove with his own bowhunting trophies, with wonderful pictures from the early days of Bear Archery and with hundreds of souvenirs symbolic of a life well-lived in archery … right alongside his mentor and friend, Fred Bear.

More than any other place in the world, the Fred Bear Museum tells the story of bowhunting and archery innovation in the 20th century. Its thousands of artifacts are a living testament to its founder's energy and vision. The Museum is the ultimate gift from Fred Bear to the world.

Wearing his familiar Borsalino hat, Fred Bear sits in the bow of a canoe during a hunt for white-tailed deer in southern swamp country while J. Wayne Fears serves as his oarsman. The legacy of this and a thousand other bowhunting adventures are preserved in the Fred Bear Museum.

Picking Your New Archery Partner
By C.J. Davis

Some people say that choosing a spouse is more challenging than picking a bow. I disagree. A good bow is, well, a good bow. And unlike dealing with people, there's rarely any guesswork when selecting a bow.

There's no better time to dive into bowhunting than right now. The gear is better than ever, pro shops are more knowledgeable and there is a bow and arrow combination that will work for anyone and their hunting style. Of course, all this gear and knowledge can seem overwhelming to the new archer. Don't worry. With a little thought and pre-planning you can make buying your bow and accessories enjoyable.

Equipped For Success

The biggest and most expensive part of the setup is the bow. Plus, there are many factors that go into the bow-buying equation: What brand? What poundage? One cam or two design? And how about brace height? But before you get overwhelmed, set a budget that includes a bow, arrows and the necessary accessories. It will help you make the right decision. Decide exactly how much you are willing to spend and stick to it. A good starting point is $350 to $500 for the bow and up to $150 for the accessories.

Next, do your research. If you have access to the Internet, spend time perusing chat rooms and checking out several bow manufacturers' Web sites. Then visit all the pro shops in your area and read catalogs.

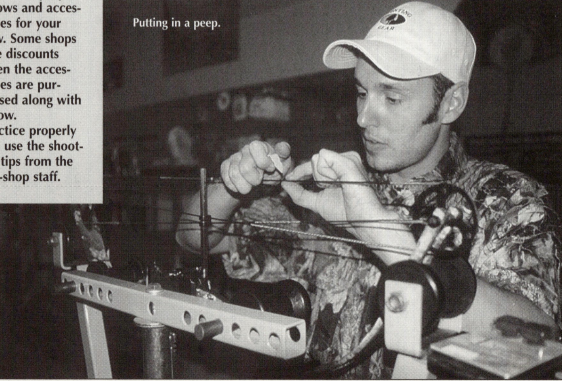

Putting in a peep.

All of the top companies make good bows, but there are some that will work better for you. Make a list of features you want in a bow. Single-cam bows are generally easier to tune and stay tuned longer. A shorter bow is easier to shoot from a treestand, but you may want a longer bow (measured from axle to axle length) if you plan on shooting with your fingers instead of a release. The longer length allows for less finger pinch at full draw and a cleaner release.

Expert Advice

If you've never shot a bow, or have only shot a little, head straight to your local archery pro shop. You'll find them by asking other hunters or by looking in the phone books. By telling the pro shop staff about the game animals that you plan to hunt, they can help fit a bow to your needs and save you a lot of frustration and wasted time. A good pro shop can take a novice shooter and a properly tuned bow and have them shooting respectable groups in a matter of minutes. A good friend who knows how to set up and shoot a bow can do a great job as well.

Buying your first bow from a pro shop is a good idea. Have the sales person recommend a few different models, then go with how the bow feels in your hand. The bow's grip is the key for proper feel, and it is the most critical contact point on the bow. A narrow throat on the grip is generally better, as it promotes a torque-free shot. A bow is a very personal choice, so make sure you like the bow you pick. As you gain experience, then take advantage of catalogs and Web sites to do your ordering.

The Right Measurements

Once you have narrowed down your decision, ask to shoot the bow(s). The next step is making certain the bow fits you. Your personal draw weight and draw length are the determining factors here. Start with a weight that you can comfortably draw back and hold for a few seconds. If you have to contort your body to get the bow back, lower the weight. Draw length will affect your accuracy if it's incorrect. So it is best to have a pro shop do it for you.

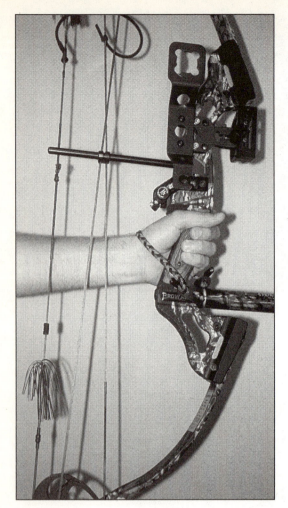

The grip of a bow is key to accuracy and comfort.

Staying In Tune

Once you have the draw length and poundage set, and have established a consistent anchor point, it's time to choose arrows and tune your bow.

Again, more choices: Carbon or aluminum arrow shafts or maybe even carbon/aluminum composites could be right for you. They are all good arrows and each has its benefits and downfalls. The main thing to remember is to select an arrow that is properly spined for your bow, meaning that the arrow fits the draw weight and draw length of your bow. An arrow that is too light can be difficult to tune and makes your bow louder than it should be. An arrow with the spine too stiff can cause tuning problems. But a stiffer arrow is better than a light one.

Carbon arrows are very durable and remain straight under normal use. Plus, carbon arrows are less expensive than ever, so giving them a shot won't drain your wallet. The only drawback with carbon arrows are their small diameter. You may have to pay a little more attention to fletching clearance through your rest. However, that is a small price to pay for the other benefits carbon offers. Aluminum shafts, a somewhat cheaper alternative, can bend or dent a lot easier than carbon ones. Pro shops can often straighten the shafts so that you can reuse them

Tuning is when the shooter sets the bow so that it and the arrow work together to achieve the best accuracy possible. If you follow a plan, tuning is usually a simple task. But it takes some patience. The objective is for the arrow to leave the bow flying straight to have the best accuracy. A tuned bow is simply more accurate and more forgiving. Your broadheads will fly better and the bow will be extra quiet. You will also have better penetration. Bows are like people; they have their own personality and each may tune a little differently. Some will shoot almost any arrow well, while others have a decided preference.

The most common way to tune a bow is through paper tuning. First set your nocking point and rest per the manufacturer's instructions. While this may not be the location you end with, it's a good starting point. Basically you are using the tear the arrow makes through a piece of paper set up in front of a safe backstop to determine how the arrow is flying. Many books, articles and videos have been produced on this subject and finding one should be a simple task. Your local pro shop also can help you with this and probably should if it is your first experience tuning a bow.

Another tuning method is bare shaft tuning. This method is used a lot by traditional shooters but can work equally well for compound shooters. It is a more complicated process and should be left until you

The grip on this Browning is a good example of a consistent grip.

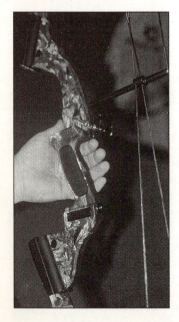

have gained some experience tuning a bow on your own.

Some archers have their bow tuned at the shop and then make small adjustments while shooting their broadheads. Consistent accuracy is the goal, and good tight broadhead groups are the reward. Don't worry if your broadheads and field points don't impact at exactly the same spot. As long as your broadheads are grouping well, adjust your sights so that they dead on for your broadheads.

Getting In Sync With Your Bow

Now that you have a well-tuned bow, it's time to tune the shooter. My friend summed it up best, "Generally, it ain't the arrow, it's the Indian that could use a little help." Practice is most important, as is putting what the pro shop taught you to use. Concentrate on each arrow. Shooting three arrows well is much better than shooting 20 poorly. Concentrate on your form and executing the shot properly. Aiming should be constant while you squeeze the release. The shot should come as a surprise.

As you work on the mechanics of shooting, your muscle memory takes over and your accuracy improves. Don't try to hold the pin completely still. Allow it to move slowly about the center while aiming and releasing. Continue aiming until the arrow hits the target. Correct follow-through after the release—and keeping your body and arms rock steady—is just as important as your actions are prior to the release when shooting a bow.

Until your muscles are built up, don' shoot more than 20 to 30 arrows per day. Most people do better shooting every other day instead to keep from getting tired.

Remember archery is supposed to be fun; don't get too upset over a few stray arrows. And if you start having trouble, head back to your pro shop for a tune-up—on your bow and you.

Silence is Golden

Many accessory companies are adding silencing materials to their gear.

Compared to models from a few years ago, today's bows are whisper-quiet right out of the box. As good as they are manufactured, they can still be better. Making your bow as quiet as possible is a definite plus in the woods. You need silence before, during, and after the shot. Loud bows make for missed game because weary game animals can be easily spooked by strange noises. Bows that have a lot of vibration can also have more problems with sights jarring loose, or arrows not staying in the quiver. New vibration reduction devices, such as those offered by Sims Laboratories, are a simple addition well worth the small cost. They reduce shock, keep everything tight on the bow and keep it quiet.

When drawing your bow, a little moleskin or heat-shrink tubing on the rest eliminates any noise the arrow makes while sliding across the rest. String silencers and other devices silence the bow during the shot and prevent vibrations after the shot.

The easiest things to add are string silencers, which can be tied directly to the string. Rubber "spider legs" or other devices work wonders. Small mushroom-shaped devices on the back of limbs quiet the bow even more. Sims also makes smaller models to mount on quivers and sights.

Moleskin strips or heat-shrink tubing or Teflon coating on the arrow rest is a must for silence. Remember, when it comes to bowhunting, silence is golden. And in today's market, it's cheaper than ever.—C.J.D.

Recruiting Tomorrow's Archers
By J.R. Absher

An improvised backstop and straw-filled targets convert a high school basketball court into a practice range for beginning archers. Encouragement of young bow enthusiasts is vital to the survival of archery sports.

A young woman practices her draw with a compound bow. Women's archery has been a well-established sport in American colleges for over a century.

Throughout the late 1980s and early '90s, archery, and particularly the sport of bowhunting, was on a roll. Compound bows were being produced and sold at record numbers, and the sales charts that donned the walls and boardroom easels of the major archery equipment manufacturers were anything but vertically challenged.

For nearly a decade, the growth in archery and the bowhunting boom was nothing short of phenomenal. As an example, the 11 percent excise tax (Pittman-Robertson Funds) paid on archery equipment totaled $7.3 million in 1984. It rose to $11.3 million in 1987, to $14 million in 1989, $15.2 million 1991, and hit $20.8 million in 1993.

At the same time, the ranks of bowhunters were also growing dramatically, with some popular hunting states experiencing license sales increases of 30 percent or greater. Figures from the Archery Manufacturers and Merchants Organization (AMO) indicate that more than 40 states reported substantial jumps in bowhunter numbers from the late '80s to mid-'90s.

As a point of reference, the total number of bowhunting licenses reported in the U.S. rose from around 1.9 million in 1987, to nearly 3 million in 1996-an increase of more than one million, representing a 65 percent growth rate in less than ten years.

As would be expected, during the same period other aspects of archery experienced an equally impressive upturn in popularity, including the competitive sport of shooting 3-D animal targets. In its infancy in the 1980s, 3-D archery rode the wave created by bowhunting's growth, and the two shooting disciplines fed from each other's success. The International Bowhunting Organization formed in 1987, standardizing 3-D competition rules, organizing tournaments and holding regional and national championship events.

But, that was then. Since 1993, the total sales revenues of archery equipment nationwide have remained about as flat as a Kansas highway. Any increases in revenues realized among the industry leaders in manufacturing a have been generally attributed to the sales of more expensive, higher-end bows, rather than by any substantial increase of participation. As a result, the hot topic of discussion among bow makers, industry leaders, retailers, distributors, bowhunting writers, archery coaches, state game agencies and lovers of archery in recent years has become the question of how to jumpstart interest and participation in the sport, or even maintain the current archer and bowhunter numbers for years down the road.

A Place to Start

An obvious area to cultivate for needed growth in archery and bowhunting ranks is in the often overlooked demographic of women and youth.

A look inside the sport as it exists today and a little number-crunching reveal the harsh realities of a pastime with a less-than-stellar growth curve in the past decade. The fact is, today's bowhunters are graying rapidly, as the age of the average hunting archer is 36. Further, more than three quarters of all bowhunters are between the ages of 25 and 54.

Demographic studies also reveal that more than 95 percent of bowhunters are male, though the participation of women has shown a marked, yet modest, increase. Through the '90s the number of women involved in archery and bowhunting increased more than 150 percent, a respectable trend, to be sure-but a hardly a blip on the big radar screen of the total number of bow shooters.

But, when the subject turns to the unsure future of archery, it's generally agreed among industry leaders and demographers alike that youth archers, both male and female, are key to the health and well-being of the sport, as well as other shooting sports.

"Archery is a great way to introduce kids to the shooting sports. Once they try it, every kid wants to shoot a bow and arrow, and they really love doing it," said Lloyd W. Brown Jr., who heads the National Archery Association (NAA) and served as an assistant coach for the U.S. Olympic Archery Team.

"I like to tell parents that the skills that I teach their kids in archery can be used to prepare for a math test or job interview," Brown said. "It also helps them increase upper body strength. It's a great lifetime sport for men, women and kids. Plus, it's something the whole family can do together."

The NAA level one instructor course includes emphasis on getting young shooters started early, at summer camps, schools, and through the 4-H Shooting Sports Program. Instructors are taught to use positive communications, never to say "no," or "don't." By design, the experience should be a positive one, Brown and his coaches believe, to make it interesting for the youngsters and to make them want to come back for more.

"Millions of kids shoot bows and arrows at summer camp," Brown said. "When they come home, a lot of times they have no place to continue shooting. We need to help them locate the nearest archery shop, archery club or a place to shoot."

Open Doors and Open Minds

Back in 1976, George Chapman used to assist Precision Shooting Equipment (PSE) founder and archery pioneer Pete Shepley build some of the first commercially-produced compound bows in a converted chicken coop just outside of Mahomet, Illinois.

Selected Youth Bow Manufacturers

Bow Tech
600 Dale Kuni Rd.,
Suite 220
Creswell, OR 97426
888-689-1289
www.bowtecharchery.com

Browning Archery
P.O. Box 5487
Tucson, AZ 85703
800-644-0283
www.browning-archery.com

Forge Bow Company
2860 S. 171st St.
New Berlin, WI 53151
414-732-7400

Genesis (by Mathews)
2035 Riley Rd.
Sparta, WI 54656
608-269-1779
www.genesisbow.com

Golden Eagle
4600 SW 41st Blvd.
Gainesville, FL 32608
352-376-2327

Parker Compound Bows
P.O. Box 105
Mint Spring, VA 24463
800-707-8149

Precision Shooting Equipment
P.O. Box 5487
Tucson, AZ 85703
520-594-5169
www.pse-archery.com

Stacey Archery Sales
6866 Jennifer Ln.
Idaho Falls, ID 83401
208-523-7278

XI/Indian Archery
817 Maxwell Ave.
Evansville, IN 47711
812-467-1200

Today, PSE is known worldwide as one of the industry leaders, and Chapman busies himself coaching archers and teaching archery dealers how to succeed in their business. PSE and Chapman began the first-ever training program for its retailer network in 1988. Since then the program has graduated thousands of dealers and has led other manufacturers to mirror its training instruction.

"Unfortunately, within most of the archery retail network, women and youth are still a fairly untouched market," Chapman said. "Sadly, we really haven't done a good job reaching them."

Chapman pointed to the fishing tackle industry, noting that youth and women contribute greatly to its growth in participation, thanks in part to national marketing efforts. Unlike with fishing gear, the nature of archery tends to be more hands-on, bows and accessories must be matched to shooters, and some expert advice and instruction is often necessary, especially for beginners, Chapman noted.

"That's why so much of the responsibility lies with the retailer," he said. "The beginner must be fitted correctly and must receive at least basic lessons on form and shooting. Anybody can buy a rod and reel and catch fish. It's not the same with archery." Chapman said he stresses the importance of making archery shops "more female friendly," in an environment that is more often than not dominated by men and "good ol' boy" attitudes.

"I tell retailers, you've got to clean up your act so women will feel comfortable coming into your shop. If you don't, you're missing a great opportunity to make money," said PSE's Chapman.

Besides the noted demographics and numbers relating to archery, another statistic that merits mention is the number of single parent households in the U.S., most of them headed by the mother. With clearly half of all marriages today ending in divorce, millions of men and fathers do not have the opportunity to influence their sons and daughters, particularly with their choices for hobbies and other interests.

"There's a limit to the things a single mom can do with her kids, especially as a mother and son. Archery shops need to open their doors to this great opportunity," Chapman said.

Clubs Reaching Out

The International Bowhunting Organization (IBO) is the largest, membership-based 3-D archery-shooting group in the country that sanctions qualifying matches at hundreds of clubs and affiliate ranges. At least a dozen of its shooting classifications are women-and youth-specific, with participation and competitive levels among these classes as intense as those among male archers.

Additionally, the IBO encourages family memberships and hosts special shooting venues for very young shooters (ages 8 and under) at its "Future Bowhunter," non-competition events in which every youngster receives a prize.

"The hundreds of local and regional archery clubs across the country can serve as a focal point for clean and healthy social interaction for entire families," said IBO president Ken Watkins. "The most simple way to double, triple and quadruple participation in archery is for a husband and father to take his wife and kids to the local range or club and get them involved. There's nothing as contagious as a youngster's enthusiasm-and soon they want to bring their friends and peers into the mix."

School Programs Can Succeed

While many middle-aged archers (and non-archers) have less than fond memories of their first experience shooting a bow in a school physical education class, an innovative and ambitious program now underway in Kentucky is on track to change the entire future of archery in public schools.

A physical education curriculum, "Archery: On Target for Life" is the result of an equal partnership of the state Departments of Education and Fish & Wildlife Resources. It was implemented as a pilot program in 22 Kentucky middle schools in the spring of 2002, hoping to reach a goal of 120 schools statewide by 2005. The program has proven so popular that nearly 100 schools were participating by fall, 2002, and the three-year goal may be reached in 12 months.

A well-equipped young bowman, fitted with a fully outfitted youth-sized compound bow, joins in an archery club target event. Many archery clubs welcome family membership and participation.

Designed to teach Olympic-style target archery to sixth, seventh and eighth-graders, class content covers archery history, safety, technique, equipment, mental concentration, and self-improvement. Before presenting the course, teachers undergo the NAA Level I archery-training program.

Roy Grimes, Deputy Commissioner of the Kentucky Department of Fish and Wildlife Resources-and a longtime archer and bowhunter-attributes the program's success to the cooperation between his department and the state department of education.

"It simply would not have succeeded without the support of two department commissioners who both believe in archery," Grimes said. He reports that word of the programs has spread across the state, and the country, due to its positive results, in the classroom and beyond.

"Teachers report enthusiastic students, improved student behavior on archery days, eager participation by students who are non-athletic and those who previously resisted PE class," Grimes said.

Upon witnessing a class demonstration, Gene Wilhoit, Kentucky Commissioner of Education, said, "As I watched the students and their teachers cheering for one another, it was evident this archery program has provided a common experience from which students and teachers can relate to one another. I'm convinced this will improve teacher/student relationships in other classes throughout the year."

Building on the success of the Kentucky program, state officials and members of the archery industry are hoping to take the successful blueprint from the Bluegrass State and utilize it in other state school programs within a few years.

B.O.W. Wows 'Em

It all started with a 1990 workshop, "Breaking Down Barriers to Participation of Women in Angling and Hunting," headed by Dr. Christine Thomas, a professor of natural resources at the University of Wisconsin, Stevens Point. The workshop attendees examined and identified 21 barriers to women's participation in outdoors activities and discussed reasons for the disparity between sexes.

As a result, the first "Becoming an Outdoors-Woman" program was started in 1991 as an experiment to determine whether providing a hands-on educational opportunity would be enough to welcome women to outdoor activities traditionally enjoyed mostly by their male counterparts. Since then, the workshop has enjoyed popular and critical acclaim worldwide. It has expanded to 44 states and eight Canadian provinces, with many states offering multiple opportunities.

What state agencies have learned through the BOW program is clear: Women are interested in learning outdoor skills. When the opportunity is offered, they line up for the chance to be involved.

Dr. Thomas' premise is a simple one: "I learned that you don't have to be superwoman to enjoy the outdoors. Take it at your own level. Enjoy what you enjoy and avoid what you don't like."

Thomas, who has since become something of an outdoor icon to those involved in the hunting and fishing industry, attributes much of the program's success to creating a relaxed type of atmosphere in which women learn best, one that is supportive and non-threatening.

B.O.W. course activities include orienteering, archery, basic camping skills, fly fishing, outdoor cooking, introduction to firearms and firearm safety, nature appreciation, canoeing, and more. Women who seek continuing instruction may learn advanced shotgun and intermediate bowhunting as well.

In their combined foresight and expertise, individuals like Dr. Thomas, Chapman, Grimes, Brown and Watkins have correctly identified the pathway to recruiting both women and youth to the rewards offered by the sport of archery-and to a lifelong enjoyment and respect of the outdoors-by removing the barriers and stigmas related to education, and offering a common experience in which individuals may achieve success at their own pace.

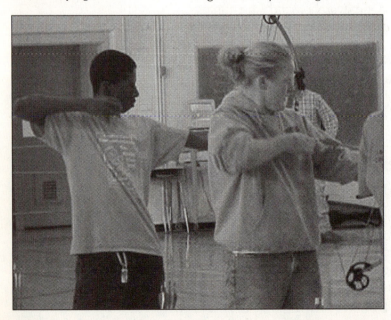

High school students learn the fundamentals in a classroom setting. Some states have added Olympic-style archery to their physical education programs.

NEW PRODUCTS

COMPOUND HUNTING BOWS

CROSSBOWS

ARCHERY PRODUCTS

NEW Products: **Compound Bows**

ALPINE ARCHERY

Fatal Impact

Alpine's Fatal Impact successfully combines speed with quiet, smooth and relatively shock and vibration free shooting. This bow is part of the VX line of high performance risers that feature a parallel limb design and Alpine's new Bi-Polar Riser dampening and Inter-Loc Limb Mounting System. This unique system is designed to stop the limbs from moving during the shot sequence, which will quiet the shot and reduce vibration. An innovative limb-pocket acts to dampen the shock and vibrations of each shot. The Fatal Impact delivers outstanding performance and control with a long reflexed riser for a longer field of view than most bows today. This bow has a mass weight of 4.2 pounds, is 34" axle-to-axle. It is available in Realtree Hardwoods Green HD camo with a two-piece wood grip.

BOW SPECIFICATIONS
AMO Draw Length: 27-, 28-, 29-, 30- and 31-inches
Draw Weights: 50, 60 and 70 pounds with 65 or 80% let-off
Bow Speed: NA
Axle-to Axle: 34 inches
SRP: **$415**

Ravage

Here is a short bow, made for maneuverability and speed with the stability and balance usually found only in longer compounds. The Ravage is part of Alpine's new VX series that feature a parallel limb design and Bi-Polar Riser with an Inter-Loc Limb Mounting System. In addition, the bow features Alpine's patented FastTrac one cam system with sealed ball bearings in both the idler and the lower cam. The limb system stops the limbs from moving during the shot sequence to silence the shot and reduce vibration. The design encases the limb in a nylon liner, preventing it from contacting the riser. This is then fitted into an innovative limb pocket where it dampens the shock and vibration of each shot. The Ravage has a mass weight of 4 pounds with a 7½-inch brace height and 80% let-off. It is available in Realtree Hardwoods Green HD camo with a two-piece wood grip.

BOW SPECIFICATIONS
AMO Draw Length: 25-, 26-, 27-, 28- and 29-inches.
Draw Weights: 50, 60 and 70 pounds
Bow Speed: NA
Axle-to Axle: 28 Inches
SRP: **$650**

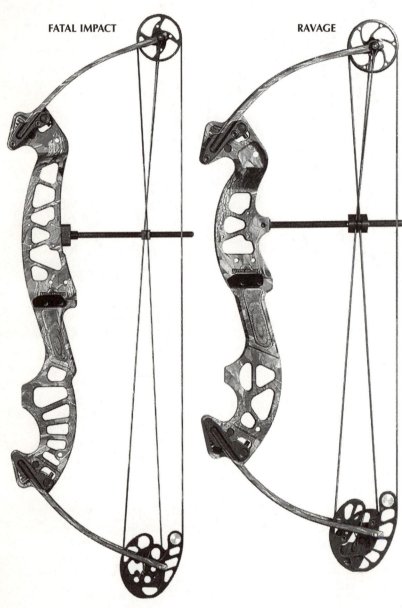

FATAL IMPACT   RAVAGE

CHEROKEE

COLT KIT

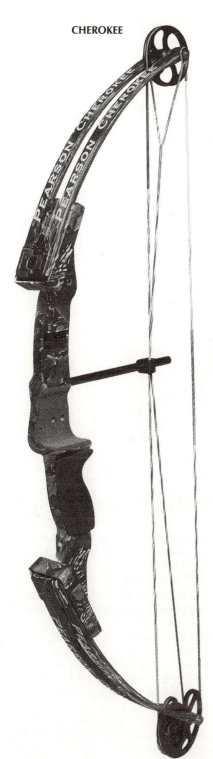

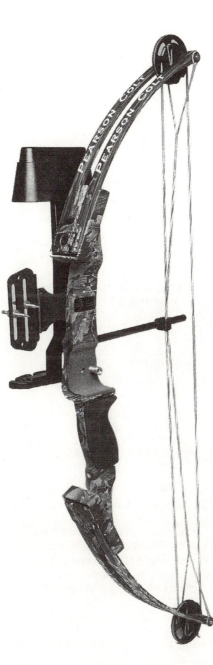

BEN PEARSON ARCHERY

Cherokee

This bow is similar to Pearson's Warrior model and is designed for young bowhunters. It features a 16-inch straight raiser design with velvet antler finished shelf, 12½-inch quad limbs, and a wide track idler wheel. Other features are a cable guard with slide and molded grip. The Cherokee is backed with a lifetime guarantee.

BOW SPECIFICATIONS
AMO Draw Length: 22 to 26 inches with modular adjustments
Draw Weights: 25, 35 or 45 pounds
Bow Speed: NA
Axle-to Axle: 29½ inches
SRP: **$299**

Colt Kit

A complete package that includes the bow, quiver, sights and arrow rest—all you need to add is a young archer or small-framed shooter. The Colt bow has a CNC machined riser, Two-Cam system and quad limbs. It comes equipped and camouflaged with Superflage camo.

BOW SPECIFICATIONS
AMO Draw Length: 19-21 or 22-24 inches
Draw Weights: 20, 30, 40, or 50 pounds
Bow Speed: NA
Axle-to Axle: 29 5/16 inches
SRP: **$299**

Know The Winds
Knowing the direction of small, fickle winds is important because it can carry the human odor—a sure game spooker—to approaching or nearby game animals. You can reduce this chance by wearing an odor absorbing suit such as those made by Scent-Lok or Browning clothing with Gore's Supprescent.—MDF

NEW Products: **Compound Bows**

DIAMONDBACK VX

DIVA VX

FREEDOM

BEN PEARSON ARCHERY

Diamondback VX
This hunting compound bow features the VIB-X noise and vibration reduction module in a pocket on the riser. Other features include the Laser cam and Accu-Trac idler wheel, both with ball bearings. The Diamondback has 14½-inch limbs and a lifetime guarantee. This bow has a 7⅞-inch brace height and is covered with Lynch Worldwide's Superflage.

BOW SPECIFICATIONS
AMO Draw Length: 24 to 31 inches, modular adjustments
Draw Weights: 50, 60 or 70 pounds, with 85% standard and 65% or 75% let-off optional
Bow Speed: 302 fps IBO
Axle-to Axle: 31⅜ inches
SRP: **$599**

Diva VX
The unique and flashy leopard—caged cat camo—skin finish on this compound bow will be the first thing that you notice. The Diva features an 85% pet-off Laser PhD cam and an Accu-Trac idler wheel. The machined riser has the VIB-X noise and vibration reduction module built in. This system works unlike any other and is a plus at reducing felt hand vibration upon arrow launch. This bow has a 6⁹⁄₁₆-inch high brace height,

BOW SPECIFICATIONS
AMO Draw Length: 24 to 31 inches adjustable with modulars
Draw Weights: 30, 40, 50, 60 or 70 pounds
Bow Speed: 303 fps IBO
Axle-to Axle: 35 ⅜ inches
SRP: **$619**

Freedom
The Freedom has 42-degree limb pockets, the Vib-X noise and vibration reduction system installed in the riser and a Z-Cam with PHd (perfect horizontal delivery). The cam and the Accu-Tracidler wheel are based on ball bearings and the quad limbs are 12½ inches long. This bow has a wooden grip and 6¹¹⁄₁₆-inch brace height. The shelf is covered with a factory installed velvet antler finish. This bow has a lifetime guarantee and is covered with Superflage Freedom camouflage.

BOW SPECIFICATIONS
AMO Draw Length: 23 to 30 inches, modular adjustments
Draw Weights: 50, 60 or 70 pounds
Bow Speed: 315 fps IBO
Axle-to Axle: 35³⁄₁₆ inches
SRP: **$699**

FREEDOM PRO

PREDATOR VX

BEN PEARSON ARCHERY

Freedom Pro

The Freedom Pro features a red, white and blue patriotic All-American color scheme. Beyond this, the Freedom Pro has 42-degree limb pockets, the Vib-X noise and vibration reduction system installed in the riser and a Z-Cam with PhD (perfect horizontal delivery). The cam and the idler wheel are based on ball bearings and the quad limbs are 14½-inches long. This bow has a wooden grip and 8⅝-inch brace height.

BOW SPECIFICATIONS

AMO Draw Length: 26 to 33 inches, modular adjustments
Draw Weights: 50, 60 or 70 pounds
Bow Speed: 303 fps IBO
Axle-to Axle: 37⅛ inches
SRP: **$739**

Predator VX

The quad limb compound bow has a wooden grip, cable guard with slide and the VIB-X noise and vibration reduction system. The shelf is covered with a factory installed velvet antler finish. Other features include a laser cam with PhD and cable guard with slide. This hunting bow is covered with Superflage camouflage.

BOW SPECIFICATIONS

AMO Draw Length: 225 to 32 inches with modular adjustments
Draw Weights: 50, 60 and 70 pounds with 85% let-off stock and 65% or 75% optional
Bow Speed: 304 fps IBO
Axle-to Axle: 34½ inches
SRP: **$599**

NEW Products: **Compound Bows**

ADRENALINE SX

ADRENALINE SX COMPETITION

ECLIPSE ZLX

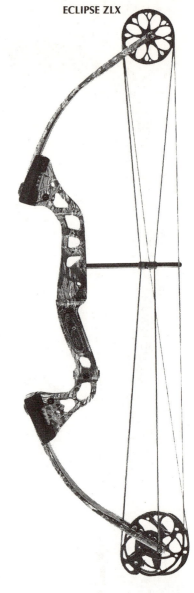

BROWNING

Adrenaline SX

This Browning compound bow uses the company's Lightning cam system along with solid Contour XP limbs. Other features include a two-piece wooden grip, machined aluminum riser and cable guard with slide. The Adrenaline is finished in Mossy Oak camouflage.

Bow Specifications
AMO Draw Length: 24-27, 27-29 and 29-31 inches
Draw Weights: 40-50, 50-60 and 60-70 with 70% let-off
Bow Speed: 305 fps

Axle-to Axle: 33 inches
SRP: **$745**

Adrenaline SX Competition

This is a competition version of the Adrenaline with the option of a blue or red riser. The components and design are similar and this bow has chromed cams and idler wheels.
SRP: **$799.95**

Eclipse ZLX

This new model compound bow by Browning features the Split harness system with its unique one cam and counter rotating twin idlers. The split harness supports the bottom limb tip

to provide adjustability to balance the limb fork load. Other features include a machined aluminum riser, Cyber ZX cam, adjustable let-off, Radial-Lok pivoting limb pockets and Impact-stop vibration dampening pocket inserts. This bow has custom two-piece grips and is camouflaged with Mossy Oak Break Up.

Bow Specifications
AMO Draw Length: 27 to 31 inches
Draw Weights: 50-60 and 60-70 pounds with 65% or 75% let-off
Bow Speed: 302 fps
Axle-to Axle: 36 inches
SRP: **$799**

**ECLIPSE ZLX
COMPETITION**

MIRAGE ZX

MIRAGE ZX COMPETITION

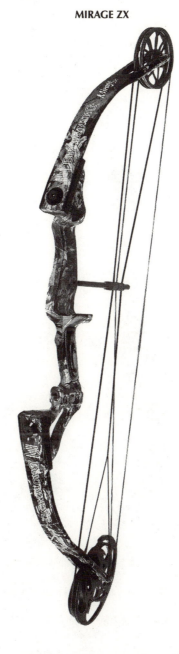

BROWNING

Eclipse ZLX Competition

A compound bow similar to the Eclipse ZLX but this bow has glossy black limbs, chromed cams and idler wheels and a dark blue riser. This bow is also available in red.
SRP: **$849**

Mirage ZX

A bow that utilizes Browning's new Split Limb harness One-Cam technolo-gy and twin idler. The Mirage provides 5 inches of draw length adjustment and has two-piece wooden grips. This bow has 15-inch Contour XP limbs, pivoting machined limb pockets and Impact stop limb pocket inserts to reduce vibration. The Mirage weighs 3.8 pounds and has a 7½-inch brace height.

BOW SPECIFICATIONS
AMO Draw Length: 26 to 30 inches
Draw Weights: 50-60 and 60-70 with 75% or 65% let-off

Bow Speed: 300 fps
Axle-to Axle: 33 inches
SRP: **$749**

Mirage ZX Competition

This bow is similar to the standard camouflaged Mirage but has chromed limb pockets, cam and idler, plus a choice of red or blue riser. The competition model also has a cable guard and wooden grip.
SRP: **$799**

RAGE

TORNADO

TORNADO COMPETITION

BROWNING

Rage

A bow designed for hunters on a budget, this compound has a machined aluminum riser and HyperMax cam system that permits 10 inches of adjustment. Other features include Contour XP limbs, a one-piece grip and cable guard with slide. The Rage weighs 3.9 pounds and is covered with Mossy Oak Break Up camouflage. This bow is offered as a package with a two-piece quiver, sight, three fiber optic pins and an arrow rest for $399

BOW SPECIFICATIONS
AMO Draw Length: 21-31 inches

Draw Weights: 45-55 and 55-65 with 70% let-off
Bow Speed: 292 fps
Axle-to Axle: 35 inches
SRP: **$319**

Tornado

An ergonomically designed bow with a moderately reflexed machine riser with a one-piece logo grip. The Tornado uses Contour XP limbs and the Cyber5 cam system. The tips of the 15½-inch limbs fit into pockets. This bow is camouflaged with Mossy Oak and uses a Dynaflite 97-inch string. This bow is also available in a package complete with quiver, sight, rest, stabilizer and sling for $539.

BOW SPECIFICATIONS
AMO Draw Length: 24-28 and 27-31 inches
Draw Weights: 50-60 and 60-70 with 80% let-off and 65% let-off optional
Bow Speed: 292 fps
Axle-to Axle: 37 inches
SRP: **$439**

Tornado Competition

A competition version of the Tornado compound bow by Browning. This bow is only available in blue and has black limbs. All other components are similar in design and color and the performance and specifications are the same.
SRP: **$479.95**

AVALANCHE EXTREME

EXCITER

MAGNUM EXTREME

DARTON ARCHERY

Avalanche Extreme

The Avalanche Extreme combines Darton's new C/P/S Extreme cam system and reflex machined riser for a high-energy producing power stroke. The 7½-inch brace height helps provide overall shootability while the highly efficient UltraFlexPower Limbs, with their unique mounting angle, and the new Integral Dampening System makes a fast shooting bow. This bow is available in both right- and left-hand models.

Bow Specifications

AMO Draw Length: 26½ inch to 30½ inch with 70 or 80% let-off
Draw Weights: 50, 60 and 70 pounds
Bow Speed: 308 IBO
Axle-to Axle: 34⅜ inch
SRP: **$630**

Exciter

Darton's new Exciter compound bow is designed for kids around a rugged

and dependable machined aluminum riser matched up with a pair of machined pultruded fiberglass limbs and versatile Short Draw P/F/C single-cam system. It is available in a draw weight range suitable for bowhunting and with the Short Draw P/F/C single cam and four interchangeable modules it can be made to fit the growing archer for years of shooting excitement. The bow comes in either SuperFlage camo or black as a single unit or as a package with camouflaged bow quiver, 3-pin fiber optic sight and arrow rest. The Exciter is available in both right and left hand models, has a 6⅝-inch brace height and weighs a light 2.8 pounds.

Bow Specifications

AMO Draw Length: 21½ to 25½ inches
Draw Weights: 20 to 45 pounds with 80% let-off
Bow Speed: NA
Axle-to Axle: 32⅝ inches
SRP: **$399**

Magnum Extreme

The Magnum Extreme begins with the new C/P/S Extreme cam system for power, performance and accuracy. It is then outfitted with a pair of matched UltraFlexPower energy efficient limbs utilizing high strength modulus materials. To complete this impressive package it all comes together on a redesigned version of the Maverick forged aluminum riser with new Integral Dampening System. The Magnum Extreme is available in both right and left hand models, has a 6½-inch brace height, is axle-to-axle, and weighs 3.4 lbs.

Bow Specifications

AMO Draw Length: 25½ to 30 inches
Draw Weights: 50 to 70 pounds with 70% or 80% let-off
Bow Speed: 312 IBO fps
Axle-to Axle: 32⅝ inches
SRP: **$469**

NEW Products: **Compound Bows**

FRED BEAR ARCHERY

Fred Bear TRX32

This Fred Bear TRX32 bow offers a Perimeter weighted One-cam. Other features include four Carbon Quad straight limbs, a 6061 T-6 machined aluminum riser and a vibration-suppressing grip. This bow is coated with Advantage camouflage and has a string shock stop system attached to the tip of the cable guard. The bow's riser has quiver-mounting holes and speed buttons are factory installed on the TechTwist bowstring. The limb pockets are a unique gold color.

BOW SPECIFICATIONS

AMO Draw Length: 28, 29 and 30 inches adjustable ranges from 24 to 31 inches

Draw Weights: 40-50, 50-60 and 60-70 pounds with 75% let-off, 65% optional

Bow Speed: 303 fps IBO and 234 fps AMO

Axle-to Axle: 32 inches

SRP: **$399.95**

Fred Bear Family Bow

A unique compound bow that's designed to be used by every archer at any level of experience. This bow has no specific draw length, has 48½-inch string and weighs approximately 2 pounds. It is offered in right hand models only and is a blue and granite color.

BOW SPECIFICATIONS

AMO Draw Length: 14 to 28 inches

Draw Weights: 20 pounds adjustable

Bow Speed: NA

Axle-to Axle: 33 inches

SRP: **$129.99**

FRED BEAR TRX32

FRED BEAR FAMILY BOW

MOSSY OAK 32

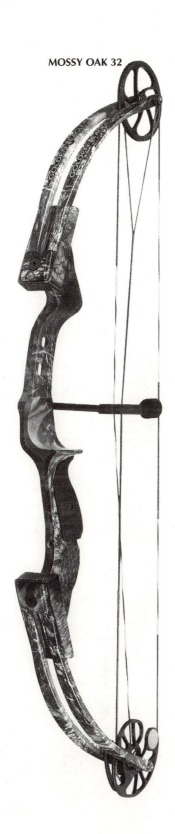

MOSSY OAK 36

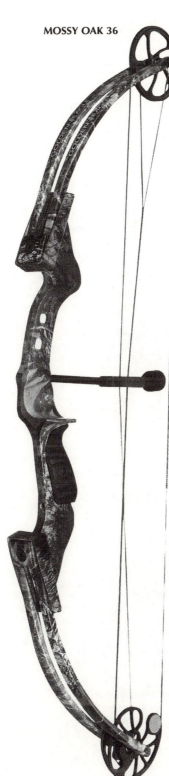

GOLDEN EAGLE

Mossy Oak 32

Golden Eagle's new Mossy Oak 32 offers a 75% let-off with a Gold Dot Perimeter weighted One-cam. Other features include four Carbon Quad straight limbs, a straight 6061 T-6 machined aluminum riser and an elasto-polymer grip. This bow is coated with Mossy oak camouflage and has a string shock stop system. The bow's riser has quiver-mounting holes pre-bored and you can install optional Adjustable Dampening System brass weight rings to reduce vibration. This bow is offered in right-hand models only.

BOW SPECIFICATIONS
AMO Draw Length: 28 and 29 inches adjustable with modules to range from 27 to 31 inches
Draw Weights: 50-60 and 60-70 pounds
Bow Speed: 284 fps IBO and 226 fps AMO
Axle-to Axle: 32 inches
SRP:. **$399**

Mossy Oak 36

This compound bow is similar in design to the Mossy Oak 32 but has a longer 36-inch axle-to-axle length thanks to longer limbs. This bow weighs 4 pounds, 2 ounces and is designed for finger shooters.

BOW SPECIFICATIONS
AMO Draw Length: 28 and 29 inches adjustable with modules to 28 to 32 inches
Draw Weights: 50-60 and 60-70 pounds with 75 or 65% let-off
Bow Speed: 284 fps IBO and 226 fps AMO
Axle-to Axle: 36 inches
SRP:. **$399**

NEW Products: **Compound Bows**

OBSESSION

RAPTOR

SPARROWHAWK II

GOLDEN EAGLE

Obsession

The Obsession features precision engineering and the unique ShockStop string suppressor. Other features include a machined reflex riser equipped with a two-piece checkered hardwood grip with an interior leather wrap. The straight carbon cable guard is located above the grip and it can be located below the grip if desired. The Obsession also has the Gold Dot Perimeter One Cam system and compression molded CarbonAir Qud limbs and a four-inch ball bearing mounted idler wheel. This bow is available in left- and right-hand models and is coated with new Mossy Oak Break Up camouflage.

BOW SPECIFICATIONS
AMO Draw Length: 27, 28 and 29 inches adjustable with modules
Draw Weights: 40-50, 50-60,and 60-70 pounds with 75% let-off and 65% let-off optional

Bow Speed: 284 fps IBO, 226 fps AMO
Axle-to Axle: 34 inches
SRP: **$499**

Raptor

The Raptor utilizes one-cam efficiency, a machined aluminum riser and CarbonAir quad limbs. The limbs are anchored in a Split-Loc limb box to eliminate noise and vibration. The raptor is coated with new Mossy Oak Break Up camouflage and is offered in right-hand only. This bow has a 6.8-inch brace height and weighs 3 pounds, 10 ounces.

BOW SPECIFICATIONS
AMO Draw Length: 29 inches plus/minus 1 inch
Draw Weights: 50-60 and 60-70 pounds with 65% let-off
Bow Speed: 292 fps IBO and 229 fps AMO
Axle-to Axle: 36 inches
SRP: **$249.65**

Sparrowhawk II

Golden Eagle created this bow with the short draw archer in mind. The riser is computer designed and machined from aluminum and has a large 7-inch brace height. Other features include straight CarbonAir quad limbs, Rapid Cam twin cams, molded grip and cable guard with slide. This bow is offered in right-hand models only and is camouflaged with Mossy Oak Break Up.

BOW SPECIFICATIONS
AMO Draw Length: 24, 25, 26, 27 and 28 inches
Draw Weights: 30-40 and 40-50 pounds with 75% let-off
Bow Speed: 278 fps IBO and 218 fps AMO
Axle-to Axle: 36½ inches
SRP: **$199**

MAX-XTREME

PERFX CAM

HIGH COUNTRY ARCHERY

Max-Xtreme

The new Max-Xtreme Carbon compound bow is light—just over 2 pounds and will handle any arrow from lightweight carbon to heavy aluminum. This bow has a weatherproof, military grade carbon riser that features a semi-reflex riser and the L.E.T. System, (Limb Equalization Timing) with Solid Vibra Damp S-D Tech bushing system that reduces noise and vibrations. The Quad Loc Pockets with Super S-D Tech Pad also aid in shock reduction. The Max-Xtreme is available in three cam configurations and with 14- or 16-inch Vibra Flex Armor V-Split limbs. It is coated with Mossy Oak camouflage. It is protected by a lifetime warranty.

BOW SPECIFICATIONS
AMO Draw Length: varies widely
Draw Weights: 60- to 70 pounds
Bow Speed: up to 375 fps
Axle-to Axle: 32 or 37 inches
SRP:. **$815**

PerFX Cam

HCA's new PerFX CAM can cover six draw lengths ranging from 24 to 32 inches and has three peak weight ranges from 25 to 80 pounds in two let-offs. The features include a new two-track system, lighter cam with more velocity and improved tracking to keep the string and harness completely in line while eliminating side pressure. This bow system delivers a full 35-pound weight range.

BOW SPECIFICATIONS
AMO Draw Length: ranges from 24 to 29 inches, 225 to 30, 26 to 31 and 27 to 32 inches
Draw Weights: 45, 50, 60, 70 and 80 pounds with 65 or 80% let-off
Bow Speed: NA
Axle-to Axle: dependant upon setting with cam module
SRP:. **$865**

NEW Products: **Compound Bows**

RAZORTEC   **CMX**

HOYT

RazorTec

A design that includes a new technology that permits both cams to work together without timing. Other features include a dual locking limb pocket design, cable guard with a Pro cable guard slide, and quiver attachment holes. This bow continues Hoyt's odd-looking TEC multi-cut riser design that reduces vibration. Sims Limb Savers are factory installed and the riser has a stainless steel stabilizer bushing installed. This camouflaged model has wooden panel grip inserts

BOW SPECIFICATIONS
AMO Draw Length: 25 to 31 inches
Draw Weights: 50, 60 and 70 pounds
Bow Speed: 302 fps
Axle-to Axle: 31½ inches
SRP:. **$665**

JENNINGS

CMX

The CMX (Carbon Master Extreme) has a vibration-suppressing grip and machined riser that will accept the optional Adjustable Dampening System with brass weights. Other features include the unique blue-and-black twist tech string, high mount carbon cable guard, and Perimeter Weighted OneCam. This bow is camouflaged has solid carbon limbs. It weighs 3 pounds, 8 ounces.

BOW SPECIFICATIONS
AMO Draw Length: 27, 28 and 29 inches adjustable up to 32 inches with modules
Draw Weights: 40-50, 50-60 and 60-70 pounds
Bow Speed: 300 fps IBO, 228 fps AMO
Axle-to Axle: 37½ inches
SRP:. **$299**

ONZA II

CONQUEST 3

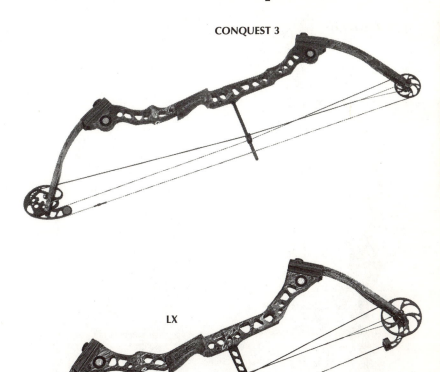

LX

MARTIN

Onza II

The Onza II has a unique riser with its long shelf and grip with a brace. It is available in three styles: Elite, Straight and SE. The cam options are Fury, Fury-X and Fusion. Color options include Advantage Timber or standard carbon, and the target series can be acquired in sunburst yellow, blue fade to red, platinum and Procat burgundy.

BOW SPECIFICATIONS

AMO Draw Length: 26 to 32 inches and varies by cam selection.
Draw Weights: 50, 60 and 70 pounds
Bow Speed: 305 fps
Axle-to Axle: 32 inches in the SE, 36⅜ inches for the Straight and 39⅞ inches for the Elite model
SRP:. . . . . . . $1,131.12 to $1,263.12

MATHEWS

Conquest 3

This compound bow features the new V-lock limb tips and pockets, plus harmonic damping system and a wooden competition grip. It is coated in camouflage and has a standard cable guard with slide. This bow weighs 4.4 pounds.

BOW SPECIFICATIONS

AMO Draw Length: 28 to 32 inches
Draw Weights: 40 to 70 pounds with 80, 65 or 60% let-off
Bow Speed: 310 fps IBO, 236 AMO
Axle-to Axle: 41 inches
SRP: $749

LX

This compound bow by Mathews has the company's new V-Lock zero tolerance limb system where the v-shaped limb tip fits into a specially designed V-shaped limb cup. Other features include the HP (high performance) single cam, string suppressors at the cams, a ball bearing roller guide instead of a cable guard, and parallel limb design. The cams incorporate perimeter-weighted technology and the bow has a Zebra Zs twist string. It features a wooden grip, harmonic damping system and camouflage coating. The LX weighs 4½ pounds.

BOW SPECIFICATIONS

AMO Draw Length: 25 to 30 inches
Draw Weights: 40 to 70 pounds with 80 or 65% let-off
Bow Speed: 315 fps IBO
Axle-to Axle: 35 inches
SRP: $719

NEW Products: **Compound Bows**

ESC BLACK EAGLE

HAWK

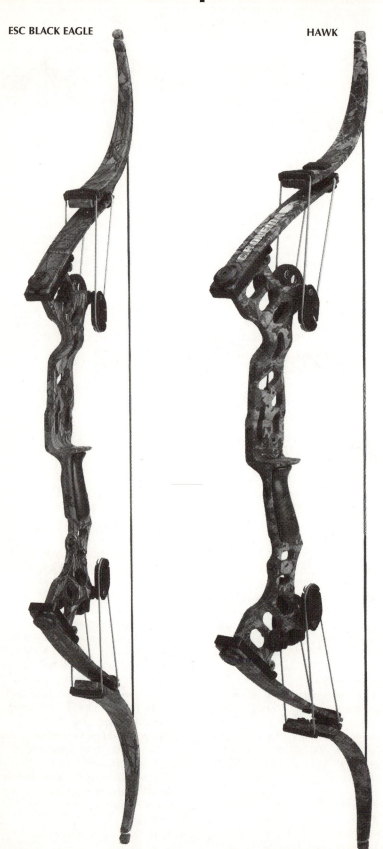

ONEIDA EAGLE

ESC Black Eagle

This Onedia bow continues the company's traditional look with limbs that break at a junction. The Engineered Structural Composite limbs can withstand temperatures up to 550 degrees Fahrenheit. This bow is camouflaged with Skyline Excel and has a wooden grip. This bow is up to 46 inches long and weighs 4½ pounds.

BOW SPECIFICATIONS
AMO Draw Length: 26 to 34 inches
Draw Weights: 35-55, 50-70, and 60-80 pounds
Bow Speed: NA
Axle-to Axle: NA, up to 46 inches long
SRP: **$649.99**

Hawk

An Oneida-style bow with a wooden grip and brace height up to 6⅛ inches. It is similar in design to all Oneida bows and has a sturdy aluminum riser and weighs 3.8 pounds. This bow is camouflaged with Mossy Oak Break Up.

BOW SPECIFICATIONS
AMO Draw Length: 22 to 26 inches
Draw Weights: 25 to 45 pounds
Bow Speed: NA
Axle-to Axle: NA, but its 40 inches tip-to-tip
SRP: $499.99

MOUNTAIN 30

MOUNTAIN SUPREME

MOUNTAIN 32

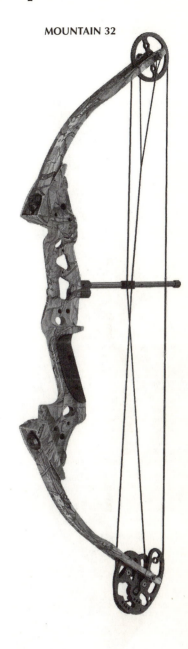

PROLINE

Mountain 30
This short axle-to-axle length bow incorporates a CNC machined aluminum riser with solid Dual Flex limbs. This bow uses Proline's PFC single cam system and has an 8-inch brace height. Other features include cable guard with slide, molded grip and camouflaged finish.

BOW SPECIFICATIONS
AMO Draw Length: 25½ to 30 inches
Draw Weights: 50, 60 and 70 pounds

with 75% let-off
Bow Speed: 294 fps IBO
Axle-to Axle: 30 inches
SRP: $615.31

Mountain Supreme
The Mountain Supreme by Proline is similar to the Mountain 30 but has QuadFlex limbs and a 7⅝-inch brace height.
BOW SPECIFICATIONS
AMO Draw Length: 25½ to 30½ inches
Draw Weights: 50, 60 and 70 pounds with 75% let-off

Bow Speed: 297 fps IBO
Axle-to Axle: 32 inches
SRP: $661.46

Mountain 32
This bow is similar to the Mountain 30 Proline bow but has longer limbs.
BOW SPECIFICATIONS
AMO Draw Length: 25½ to 30½ inches
Draw Weights: 50, 60 and 70 pounds
Bow Speed: 305 fps IBO
Axle-to Axle: 32 inches
SRP: $553.77

NEW Products: **Compound Bows**

FIRESTORM LITE

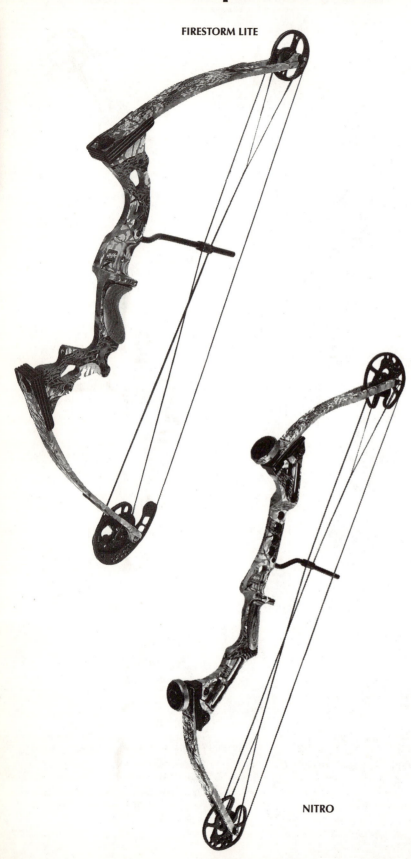

NITRO

PSE (PRECISION SHOOTING EQUIPMENT)

Firestorm Lite

A compound bow that uses PSE's Lightning-3 One-Cam with solid limbs to improve the draw cycle. This bow's ultra-lightweight machined aluminum riser has an 8-inch brace height and aggressive design. The metal components and limbs have a lifetime warranty. Other features include a TRM wooden grip, cable guard and a totally redesigned model that's different from previous versions of this bow. It weighs 3.2 pounds.

BOW SPECIFICATIONS
AMO Draw Length: 26 to 30 inches
Draw Weights: 50, 60 or 70 pounds with 80% let-off, 65% optional
Bow Speed: 300 fps
Axle-to Axle: 30 inches
SRP: $579.99

Nitro

This PSE compound bow is available with Maxi-Plus Twin cams or Centerfire One-Cams. Other features include Trimline pivoting limb pockets, the Phase III grip system, integrated cam-lock cable guard, and the NV vibration dampening system. The bow's brace height is approximately 6 inches and this model is coated with PSE brush camo. This bow is also available in three competition colors for additional costs.

BOW SPECIFICATIONS
AMO Draw Length: from 25 to 31 inches, varies by cam selection
Draw Weights: 60 or 70 pounds
Bow Speed: 315 fps One-Cam, 308 fps Twin cam
Axle-to Axle: 36 inches
SRP: $669.99

PSE (PRECISION SHOOTING EQUIPMENT)

Primos STL

A PSE bow designed with input by hunting pro Will Primos, the Primos STL is designed for hunting and is coated with PSE Brush camo. Features are Phase III grips, a 7³/₄-inch brace height, integrated cam-lock cable guard and Centerfire one-cam system. This bow is also available in blue and red tournament colors. This bow weighs 3.95 pounds and has the NV vibration dampening system.

BOW SPECIFICATIONS
AMO Draw Length: 26 to 31 inches
Draw Weights: 60 and 70 pounds with 85% or 65% let-off
Bow Speed: 305 fps
Axle-to Axle: 38 inches
SRP: **$629.99**

Supra

PSE's Supra is a competition bow with recurve Magnaglass limbs, machined limb pockets, chrome wheels, a cable guard and molded grip. The new lightweight machined riser significantly reduces felt vibration. This bow is offered in blue, red and good vibrations graphics. Two cam options are offered: Stinger or Synergy Pro-65 cams.

BOW SPECIFICATIONS
AMO Draw Length: 25 to 30 dependent upon cam selection
Draw Weights: 40, 50 or 60 pounds with 75% or 65% let-off based on cam selection
Bow Speed: 280 fps Stinger, 298 fps Pro-65 cam
Axle-to Axle: 39½ inches
SRP: . . . . **Starting at $529.99**

PRIMOS STL

SUPRA

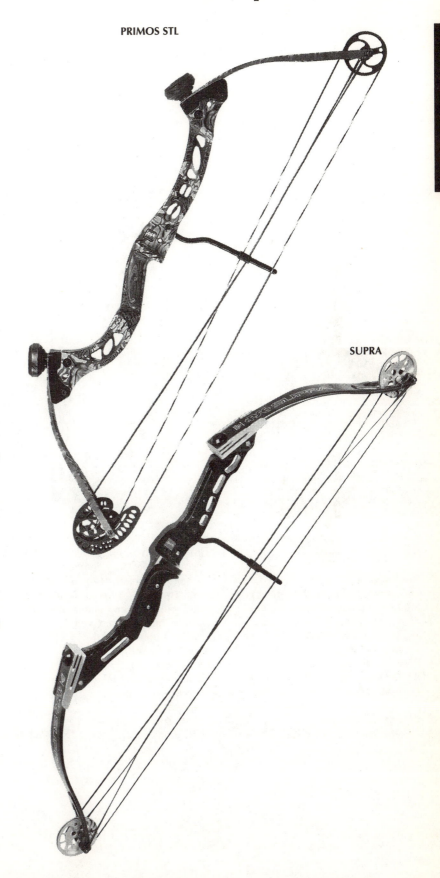

BUCKSKIN

TIMBER WOLF

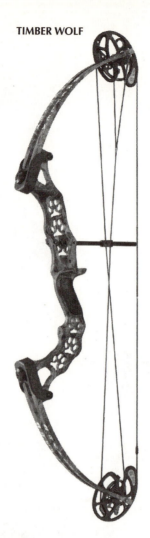

ALPHA-1

REFLEX

Buckskin

This bow is similar to the Timber Wolf but has a tamer riser with cut outs of deer tracks along the aluminum riser. This bow is camouflaged and has a 7½-inch brace height.

BOW SPECIFICATIONS
AMO Draw Length: 27 to 30 inches
Draw Weights: 50-60 and 60-70 pounds
Bow Speed: 306 fps IBO
Axle-to Axle: 34 inches
SRP:. **$369**

Timber Wolf

This new Renegade compound bow has split limbs and a 6-inch brace height, molded rubber grip, cable guard with slide and unique riser with cut outs that resemble wolf tracks. The bow is camouflaged.

BOW SPECIFICATIONS
AMO Draw Length: 27 to 30 inches
Draw Weights: 50-60 and 60-70 pounds
Bow Speed: 315 fps IBO
Axle-to Axle: 36 inches
SRP:. **$419**

RENEGADE

Alpha-1

Renegade's Alpha-1 expands this Wisconsin bowyer's line. This compound bow has a short axle-to-axle length and large 8-inch brace height. It uses the radical flamethrower cams—cams that resemble small saw blades. Two models are available and both have PTS limbs, Mossy Oak camouflage and weigh 3.6 pounds. A one or two-piece grips is optional. One model offers 75% let-off and the other model delivers 65 or 80% let-off.

BOW SPECIFICATIONS
AMO Draw Length: 25-31 or 26-29-inches
Draw Weights: 45-60, 55-70,65-80
Bow Speed: 302 fps
Axle-to Axle: 31½ inches
SRP:. **$549**

CENTURION
CROSSBOW

ELITE CROSSBOW

LEGEND II

DURANGO EXPRESS

BEN PEARSON ARCHERY

Centurion Crossbow

This high performance hunting bow has a Teflon impregnated aluminum barrel assembly and Superflage camouflaged stock with an open shoulder mount. Other features include a dry fire inhibitor, peep sight and pins, a Weaver-style scope mount base and built in fittings for a cocking device that is sold separately.

BOW SPECIFICATIONS
Draw Weight: 165 pounds
Bow Speed: 330 fps
SRP: $729

GREAT LAKES CROSSBOWS

Durango Express

The new Durango Express crossbow features a machined aluminum front riser and split limbs outfitted with alloy energy wheels. The performance also comes from the 17-inch power stroke, precision machined track and hard anodized Teflon impregnated barrel. The special pre-curved limb design

with 0-Deflex produces a longer, more efficient power stroke while the synthetic power yoke cables feature split anchor attachments on each limb to balance limb torque. The patented, machined trigger mechanism with controlled sensitivity and a smoother pull also incorporates a patented dry-fire prevention system and positive safety that can be comfortably used by either right or left handed shooters. This crossbow weighs 7½ pounds and is 28½ inches wide, tip to tip. It is available in both 150-pound and 165-pound peak draw weight. It comes standard with a universal Weaver style scope mount, adjustable arrow retention system and a built in fitting that will accept a wide choice of cocking devices. The Durango Express is available in Timber Top Brown or Advantage camouflage. Available accessories items include a Crossbow Winch, Nylon Sling, Five-Arrow Quiver and Cocking Rope.
SRP: $559

HORTON HUNTER

Elite Crossbow

This 2003 introduction by Horton has external axle limb tips to eliminate drilled axle holes and reducing noise while strengthening the limb tips. The Hunter Elite features wide-body limbs, high output speed wheels, a composite thumbhole stock and Am-Busch camouflage. The arrow travels on a machined micorflite barrel. This crossbow weighs 8 pounds and has a 175-pound pull weight.
SRP: $450

Legend II

This crossbow has Toughboy wide limbs, high output wheels a Dial-A-Range trajectory compensator and peep-pin sights. The stock length is adjustable and the arrow launcher is based on steel cables. This crossbow has a 175-pound pull and a stirrup to assist with cocking.
SRP: $400

NEW Products: **Broadheads and Points**

SCORPION

XP Broadhead

Nap has released the Scorpion, a new mechanical broadhead with a super-penetrating, cut-on-contact tip. The replaceable tip has a low profile. The broadhead's extra strong aluminum ferrules have PowerGrooves for quick penetration. Three tough and sharp .030-inch thick knife grade stainless steel blades open to provide a 1½-inch cutting diameter. The ScorpionXP is offered in 100 grains.

SRP:. . . . . **per three $22.99**

SATELITTE ARCHERY

Slik Tips

Target friendly field points that are 27.6% easier to remove describes these new tips. Tests found these tips could be removed with approximately 28.5 lbs. of force from foam targets. A self-lubricating Dupont Derine collar combined with an oversized nickel-plated point makes the easy extraction possible.

SRP:. . . . . **per dozen $ 5.25**

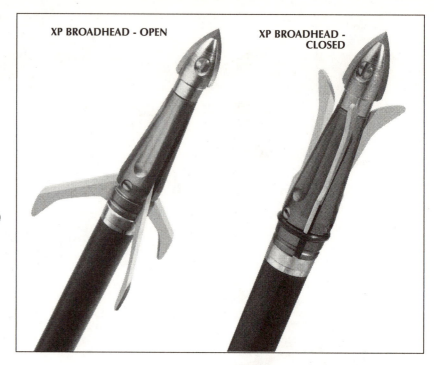

XP BROADHEAD - OPEN

XP BROADHEAD - CLOSED

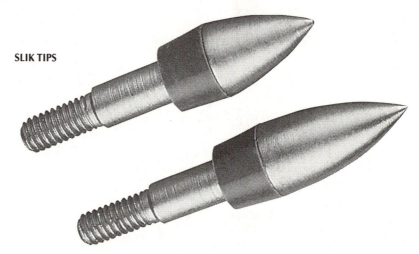

SLIK TIPS

Easy Out
When using foam 3-D targets for practice, you'll find that arrows are easier to remove if you spray them with Pam or a similar cooking spray prior to shooting. You can also try coating them with car wax. You should not use these on your designated hunting arrows since the odors could spook game animals.

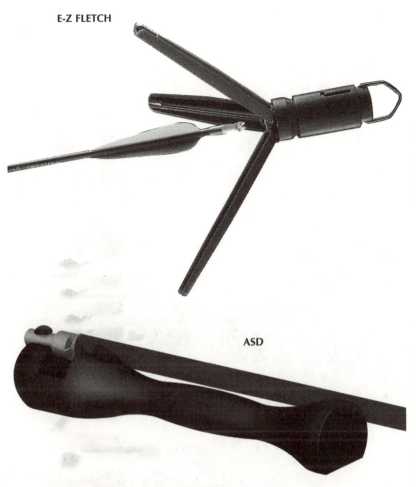

E-Z FLETCH

ASD

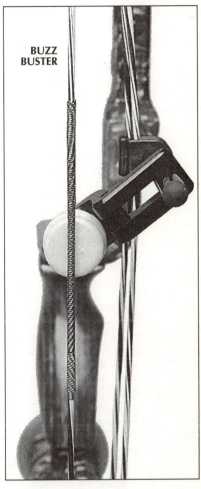

BUZZ BUSTER

ARIZONA RIM COUNTRY

E-Z Fletch

The E-Z Fletch is a compact, light-weight arrow-fletching unit that is easy to use, even in the field. The E-Z Fletch Pro automatically adjusts to any size arrow shaft from 2013 to 2613. It comes in straight, straight offset, right- or left-helical design and will also do any style of three or four fletch with nothing extra to buy. The E-Z Fletch's new Carbon Arrow model will fletch the smallest carbon shaft up to a 2018 aluminum shaft. This new, patented design ensures precision alignment and includes interchangeable arms.
SRP: $46.99

G5

ASD

The ASD is an Arrow Squaring Device used to machine, deburr and clean the face of an insert or to square and arrow shaft. Two models are available: the aluminum cutter and the carbon cutter. The carbon cutter has a dia-mond-cutting surface. Both models are easy to operate and help increase arrow accuracy.
SRP: aluminum $33.99
carbon $36.99

BEN PEARSON ARCHERY

Buzz Buster

This small arm mounts on any cable guard with the turn of a hex wrench. Align the pad with the string and its ready to go, it's that simple. How does it work? When your string moves for-ward at the release to propel the arrow, it reaches a point in line with bow's axles. The string continues beyond this point, pulled by the arrow, and works to slow the arrow down. When the arrow nock breaks free of the string, you'll frequently hear a slight buss or twang as the string oscil-lates back in line with the axles. The buzz buster stops the string in line with the axles and the arrow breaks free under maximum power.
SRP: $15.95

BLACK GOLD

Dusk Devil

This is Black Gold's newest sight and it is bright because the fibers don't bend—they are located in line along a fin in the middle of the sight—in a straight away design. Other features of the Dusk Devil include direct mount bracket machined from 6061, T6 aluminum, horizontal and vertical gang adjustment and a black or Multi-Match camouflage finish. The sight is secured into place with a precision-machined dovetail bracket and oversized bolts. Dusk Devil comes in three pin colors—red, green and yellow—and two pin sizes and the pins are easy to add or switch. Calibrations are clearly marked on the brackets. The pin guard has three quick-alignment dots to help you secure the target faster and align your sights.

SRP: black $79.25
   camouflage $87.10
Dusk Devil w/ smaller
   Micro Dot pins black $83.95
      camouflaged $94.25
   4-pin models . . . . add $6.25
Standard sight replacement pins
SRP: . . . . ea. $8.35
Micro Dot pins
SRP: . . . . ea. $9.25

BRUNTON

BattPack Battery Charger

An innovative battery charger that recharges AA and AAA batteries with an in-home AC connection or in your truck, car or RV with DC outlets. The Brunton Solarport cell will generate a charge when the units are connected in tandem. You can also use the Battpack as a direct power source. The charger weighs less than 10 pounds and all necessary cables are included.
SRP: $40

SOLO Portable Power Units

This portable solar power cell has three outputs—7.5-volt, 12-volt and 110-volt—and the unit can operate laptops, TVs, air pumps and cell phones when fully charged. The cords and cables are provided. The SOLO measures a small 11.5x12.5x3.7 inches when closed.

DUSK DEVIL

SOLO PORTABLE POWER UNITS

BATTPACK BATTERY CHARGER

SOLARPORT 2.2

SOLARIS 25

It's covered by a one-year warranty. The SOLO 2 is larger and has twice as much power.
SOLO1
SRP: $649
SOLO 2
SRP: . . . . $949.

Solaris 25

Here's a tri-fold solar cell system that's the size of a standard notebook when folded and weighs less than 8 ounces but will convert sunshine into 25 watts of 12V DC power. It has a rugged Cordura case and three high-perform-ance Moncrystalline Solor Cells. You can link these together for more

power. This system in voltage regulat-ed to protect devices.
SRP: $399

Solarport 2.2

A portable recharger that converts sun-light into energy. It delivers 2.2 watts of energy and can be linked in tandem with other units. The Solarport weighs 11 ounces and can be connected to a cell phone car adapter. The unit folds like a small notebook for easy storage and transporting. This will turn any remote camp into a powered base and can also be useful in emergencies.
SRP: $80

SAVEYUR GATORS

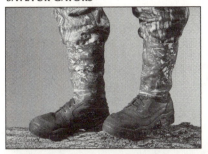

SAVEYUR 11 ARM GUARD

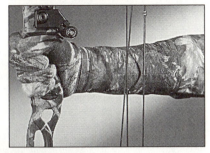

SUPER PORTA ROOF

TURKEY AND DEER HUNTER GROUND SEAT

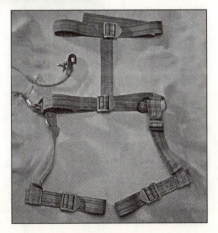

WAIST /LEG CLIMBING AND SAFETY HARNESS

BUCKWING

Saveyur Tick Chigger and Fire Ant Gators

These heavy-duty stretch gators cover your boots and laces while keeping crawling insects from reaching you. The gators cover your pants cuffs to prevent insects from entering. Now available in women and youth sizes and in camouflage patterns.
SRP: $12.95

Saveyur 11 Arm Guard

This stretch to fit arm guard keeps sleeves and bulky coats out of the way for a smooth release. It's now available in a larger men's size and in smaller sizes for women and youths.
SRP: $7.68

Super Porta Roof

The Super Porta Roof is big and provides extra protection from the elements. It's only 21 inches long when collapsed but expands to 67 inches when opened. The roof weighs less than a pound, is easy to carry, takes seconds to mount and is windproof. It can also double as a ground blind. This item is available in woodland, Break Up and hardwoods camouflage.
SRP: . . . . Starting at $32.95

Turkey and Deer Hunter Ground Seat

A seat that will keep you off the ground and warmer and drier. The legs are adjustable from 6- to 12-inches so you can fine-tune your seating level. The unit can be carried with a strap and quick release. It will support 250 pounds yet weighs mere ounces. It has camo webbing for concealment.
SRP:

Waist /Leg Climbing and Safety Harness

A unique harness that works without annoying shoulder straps. The webbing wraps around your legs and waist and keeps you attached to the tree with a rope while climbing and web belt when at your hunting height. The heavy-duty webbing is olive green and is now available for women and kids.
SRP: $33.99

CAROLINA NORTH MFG.

Hang 'Em High Hoist

The Hang 'Em High Hoist is designed for hoisting loads under 250 pounds and features the rope ratchet as the center point. Easy to use, the pulley S-Hook is secured while the object to be hoisted is secured to the ratchet hook. Once in place, the ratchet rope is pulled and raises the item. There is no need to tie off since the ratchet locks into place as the rope is pulled. The Hang 'Em High offers a 2:1 pulling ratio and comes with 20 feet of sturdy, ³/₈-inch solid braid camouflage rope. The unit weighs a light 1.5 pounds making it the perfect hoist for field dressing game and many other hoisting jobs at the workplace, shop or home. The Hoist features an easy-to-use ¹/₈-inch rope pull release that is activated to lower the item hoisted.
SRP: **$25.99**

HANG 'EM
HIGH HOIST

CAVALIER EQUIPMENT

Avalanche Extreme Fall Away Arrow Rest

The Avalanche Extreme cord activated fall-away arrow rest by Cavalier Equipment provides micro vertical and horizontal adjustments. The Avalanche Extreme's cord can be placed at variable activation positions to ensure trouble-free operation. The enhanced arrow launcher is wider and an arrow holder is optional. Several mounting brackets are offered to accommodate various risers from several major bow manufacturers.
SRP: .... **from $29.95**
with the regular mount and add $2 for any other mounts. Call 480-497-2977 for additional details.

COBRA

E-Z Adjust Pro Caliper Junior

The new E-Z Adjust Pro Caliper Junior has a reduced length, custom padded loop lock strap designed to fit women and youth, and a black anodized release head. The trigger is gun-style and curved. This release has distinctive gold COBRA letters on the black head.
SRP: **$21.99**

Sidewinder Sight

This all metal bowhunting sight by Cobra features fiber optic pins with more than 2-feet of light gathering fiber optic cord to ensure brighter sight pins with .030-inch diameter. The Posi-Stop module permits quick detachment with a turn of the knob. Comes with three sight pins and a unique cylinder with the fiber optic cord coiled inside. A mounting bracket and pin guard are included on this black sight.
SRP: black **$44.99**
    Mystik camouflage **$49.99**

AVALANCHE EXTREME FALL
AWAY ARROW REST

E-Z ADJUST PRO
CALIPER JUNIOR

SIDEWINDER
SIGHT

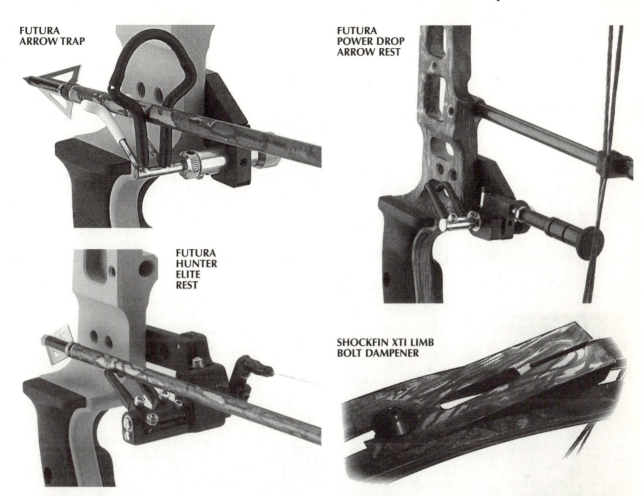

FUTURA
ARROW TRAP

FUTURA
POWER DROP
ARROW REST

FUTURA
HUNTER
ELITE
REST

SHOCKFIN XTI LIMB
BOLT DAMPENER

GOLDEN KEY

Futura Arrow Trap

The Arrow Trap is a top-quality, adjustable bowhunting rest that makes it almost impossible for your arrow to fall off the launcher. This rest's special design features both rear and side loading with a keeper frame that automatically centers and holds the arrow in the shooting channel. This keeper frame secures the arrow in the shooting channel and will not damage fletching, does not affect arrow speed and is whisper quiet during the draw and the shot. The Arrow Trap is unaffected by weather and the durable frame launcher is also spring loaded for easy tuning.

SRP: **$65.99**

Futura Power Drop Arrow Rest

The new Power Drop rest is a revolutionary bow-driven rest with total clearance in a drop-away design that's easy to install and tune. It is designed for clean, unimpeded arrow flight at the release without the need for connecting strings, cables or other bulky, cumbersome attachments. It never needs to be reset or cocked.

SRP: **$57.99**

Futura Hunter Elite Rest

The Hunter Elite features dual synthetic bearings for quiet stability, a selection of hunting launchers for a stable draw, fully adjustable vertical and horizontal movement for total tuning and the accuracy and forgiveness of a precise drop-away launcher system in one package. With this rest the shooter is able to choose the lifting linkage type—rubber tube, cord with spring or static line—that best suits their shooting situation. Users also have the choice of attaching the linkage to the buss cable or to the special cable slide provided.

SRP: **$49.99**

GLOBAL RESOURCES INC.

Shockfin XTI Limb Bolt Dampener

The ShockFinXTI Limb Bolt Dampener works equally well on solid-limb or split-limb bows and crossbows to defeat shock, vibration and torque. These forces, especially prevalent in the higher poundage bows and crossbows, not only degrade the equipment and accessories, but also make shooting noisy, uncomfortable and inaccurate. These Hi-Tech Dampeners affix solidly under the limb bolt without additional hardware or having to remove the limb bolt, or with lightweight washers at any location along the split limb.

SRP: **$29.99**

NEW Products: **Archery Products**

SCENTS

HOT TRAILS

Scents

Hot Trails are light, unbreakable and easy to use. Each scented candle will burn for up to 5 hours, releasing a constant flow of scent out to 500 yards and more. These scented hunting candles and mini lantern are small, lightweight, convenient, and simple to use. Just light and let the candle and wind do the rest. The Hot Trails Starter Kit comes with a mini lantern and four scent candles. Candles are now available in these enticing scents: Doe-n-Heat, Dominate Buck, Deer Corn, White Oak Acorn, Deer Corn, Deer Apple, Persimmon, Earth, Elk, Anise For Bear, Honey For Bear and new for 2003, Cinnamon Scented Candles For Bears, Bacon Scent Candles for Bear and Coyote and Fox Attractant Scent Candles.

SRP: $14.99

VITA-RACK 26

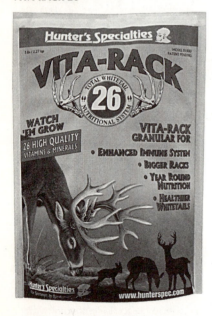

TROPHY ROCK

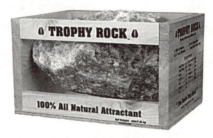

HUNTER SPECIALTIES

Vita-Rack 26

A mineral supplement for white-tailed deer, Vita-Rack 26 has 14 trace elements and 12 vitamins and nutrients to provide proper nutritional balance to deer on a year-round basis. The results include increased weight, antlers and reproduction. The mineral system is easy to maintain. Vita-Rack 26 contains calcium phosphorus, magnesium, copper, vitamin B-6 vitamin E and other ingredients. 25 and 50 pound bags are available.

SRP: . . . . 5 pounds $13.35

Trophy Rock

A natural lure and attractant that is mined from sea salt and has trace minerals in it. This product is 100% natural and available in a 16-pound rock.

SRP: $20

Avoid Metal Noise
You can avoid loose rattling broadheads—and field points—by using plumber's Teflon tape when screwing the point into the arrow shaft insert. An inexpensive roll will last for years.—MDF

JIM DANDY RELEASES

TOM TURKEY

HIP BOW HOLDER

SQUARE DEER STAND BOW HOLDER

JIM FLETCHER ARCHERY AIDS

Jim Dandy Releases
This wrist strap secured release has a forward trigger near the tip of the jaws to help reduce draw length loss found in many releases. The Jim Dandy Release clips easily to a bowstring or loop and has an infinitely adjustable trigger pull and a small, compact release. It's available with a camouflaged anodized finish and has a smooth, double-roller trigger action.
SRP: $49.95

MONTANA DECOY

Tom Turkey
This strutting tom decoy is a one-plane cutout that's compact and portable. It's printed on durable polyester fabric with a realistic photograph finish image on both sides. A spring steel band and fiberglass support rods keep the decoy in place. Other decoys are also available including: elk, whitetails and pronghorns.
SRP: $35.95

MOUNTTEK

Hip Bow Holder
An innovative hanger that permits you to hang your bow at your waist. The kit includes a bow mount, hip holder and the hardware.
SRP: $29.95

Round Stand Bow Holder
This holder permits you to secure your bow on the front or side of your tree stand so it's ready for action and nearby. The unique holder securely holds the bow until you lift it out of the bracket.
SRP: $26.95

Square Deer Stand Bow Holder
Similar to the Round Stand bow holder, but the attachment is made to fit square-edged stands.
SRP: $24.95

NEW PRODUCTS

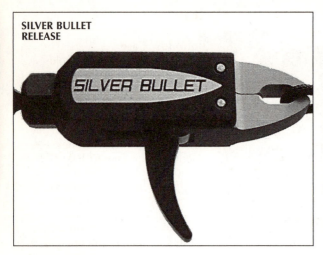

SILVER BULLET RELEASE

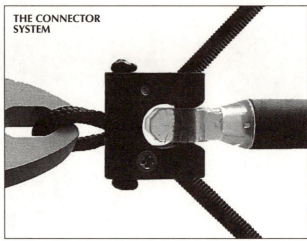

THE CONNECTOR SYSTEM

VIDEO HUNTER

LIP BLOCKER

SCENT SHIELD SHOWER KIT

Introducing the
Video Hunter

PRO RELEASE

Silver Bullet Release

This release aid has been CNC machined for close tolerances from aircraft aluminum and steel. The precision calipers provide incredible performance and a perfect arrow release every time. The jaws open extra wide and the trigger is adjustable. This release will fit either right or left hands and is available with a pistol grip, concho style or Wrist strap.

SRP: wrist $68.95
    Concho. $62.95
    Pistol grip $74.49

The Connector System

A loop and base unit that attaches to a bowstring to make a consistent and convenient connection between the archer, release aid and bowstring. The connector works with either fixed-head or rotating head release aids. The Connector 1 model allows up to 180-degrees of rotation and the Connector 2 rotates 360-degrees. This item eliminates string and serving wear and maintains a perfect loop position behind the arrow every time.

SRP: Connector 1 . . . . $19.95
    Connector 2 . . . . $21.95

ROBINSON OUTDOORS

Lip Blocker

Prevent the sun's rays and wind's chill from affecting your lips with this scent-free lip balm. No game spooking odors from this .15-ounce tube that's made by

SRP: $1.99

Scent Shield Shower Kit

Here's a great idea for traveling hunters. This shower kit has liquid body soap, underarm deodorant, shampoo and a liquid hair and body deodorant. The kit also includes a razor, towel and mirror. All items are securely stored in a camouflage carrying case.

SRP: $29.99

SHED HUNTER COMPANY

Video Hunter

A unique bracket that lets you mount a camcorder on the front of your bow to film you hunt as the action takes place. The bracket is lightweight, quiet, stable and easy to use.
The bracket can also be used off the bow.

SRP: $29.99

ROTO BOW CASE

INTERIOR

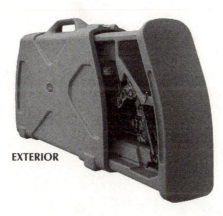

EXTERIOR

SKB

Roto Bow Case

A hard-shell case that will hold a compound bow with the quiver attached. Most stabilizers and hunting sights can also remain on the bow. This case opens from the end and an interior panel slides out to accept and hold the bow and accessories. The exterior shell is constructed of sturdy, rotational molded HDPE and strong structural ridges give support and protection to the bow inside. Additional features include: several interior cargo straps, two zippered interior storage pockets, and storage for up to 6 arrows, plus those in the quiver. The handle is molded in and the case is lockable and airline approved.
SRP: **$189.99**

STRAWBERRY WILDERNESS ARCHERY PRODUCTS

Machined Vibr-Tech 3-D Stabilizer

An odd looking bow stabilizer that uses a series of four Sims Limb Savers to stop noise and vibration. The body of this unit is machined from 6061 T-6 aluminum and three cut outs reduce the weight. Available colors include red, purple, blue and black. The stabilizer is 12 inches long and weighs 9.9 ounces.
SRP: **$89.95**

Machined Vibr-Tech Stabilizer

Similar to the 3-D stabilizer (above) but the base is solid and five Sims Limb Savers are mounted on the camouflaged base. This unit is 7 inches long and weighs 9.5 ounces.
SRP:. **$63**

MACHINED VIBR-TECH 3-D STABILIZER

PRODIGY SIGHT

ARCHERY
STAND-BY

STEALTH FIRETACKS

SURE-LOC

Prodigy Sight

This new target sight by Sure-Loc provides the novice target archer with a dependable starter sight. The features include elevation and windage adjustments, positive elevation locking knob and it's totally reversible from right- to left-handed. This sight is made for all bows—compound and recurves—up to 44 pounds pull. Includes a 550-size frame, 6-inch extension, mounting block and sight aperture. Available in black only.

SRP: **$89.99**

WILDTECH

Stealth Firetacks

The new Stealth Firetacks trail markers are three times brighter than the original FireTacks and twice as bright as the common white flat tacks. They are also a lighter tan color making them easier to see in daylight. These markers maintain their brightness when wet, unlike other flat tacks or push pins. These are also available in new Diamond Firetacks that are an amazing 500 times brighter than push pins when wet with dew, fog or rain. WildTech also has a full line of retro-reflective tape and marker products marking trails, tree stands, steps, gates, mailboxes, trail posts or any other application that

would require high nighttime and daytime visibility. These are available in new ice, stealth and blaze colors and are shipped 25 per pack.

SRP: . . . ranges from $9.99 to $12.99

WILDWOOD INNOVATIONS

Archery Stand-By

A unique bow and arrow stand that can be used in the backyard or at the range. A wide 10x14-inch base that's filled with sand securely supports the load and a tube holds the arrows. A bracket holds the bow and will not damage limbs or cams.

SRP: **$39.95**

MCKENZIE CARBON BLOCKS

CARBON BUCK

HANDIBLOCK

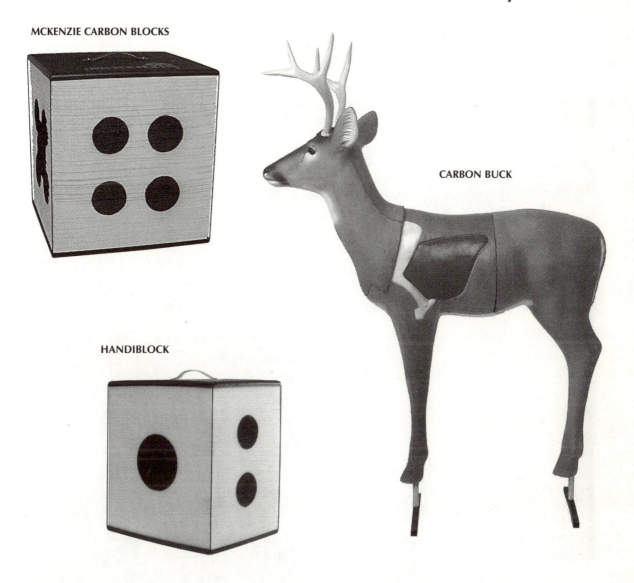

MCKENZIE

McKenzie Carbon Blocks
These McKenzie targets are designed for carbon arrows and have non-bonded layered foam with a unique four-corner cable system to keep the target together. Two sizes are available: 18x18x16-inch and 18x24x16-inches.
SRP: small **$89.95**
     Large **$99.95**

Carbon Buck
This life-like 3-D target has a super flex foam midsection for easy arrow removal and has painted 3-D vitals to help archers learn about deadly arrow placement. The target can be shot with broadheads, field points and expandables. This target will easily release carbon arrows and will last for thousands of shots.
SRP: **$149.95**

HandiBlock
This compact 16x18x12-inch block can be shot on four sides and is constructed with layered foam. The Handiblock by McKenzie works well for compound bows and carbon arrows. It provides easy arrow retrieval and is designed to last for years of use.
SRP: **$69.95**

NEW Products: **Archery Products**

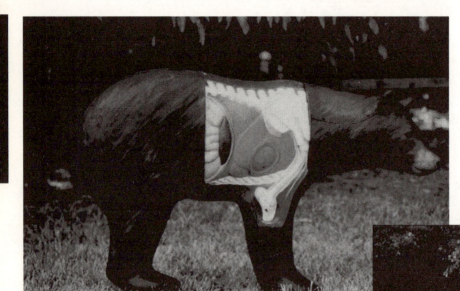

VITAL ZONE DEER

VITAL ZONE BLACK BEAR

Vital Zone Black Bear
This target accurately resembles a black bear on all fours and shows the organs on one side in vivid color and details. This target was created in cooperation with the National Bowhunter Education Foundation and is scaled to represent a 140-pound animal. It can be easily and steadily secured in the ground with two metal stakes that are provided. This target is a great training aid for beginning archers or anyone planning to go on a black bear hunt in the future.
SRP: $129.95

Vital Zone Deer
This three-dimensional foam target depicts a white-tailed deer buck while revealing the vital organs. It was designed in cooperation with the National Bowhunter Education Foundation as a training aid but can help all archers discover whether their arrows are accurately entering the kill zone.
SRP: $129.95

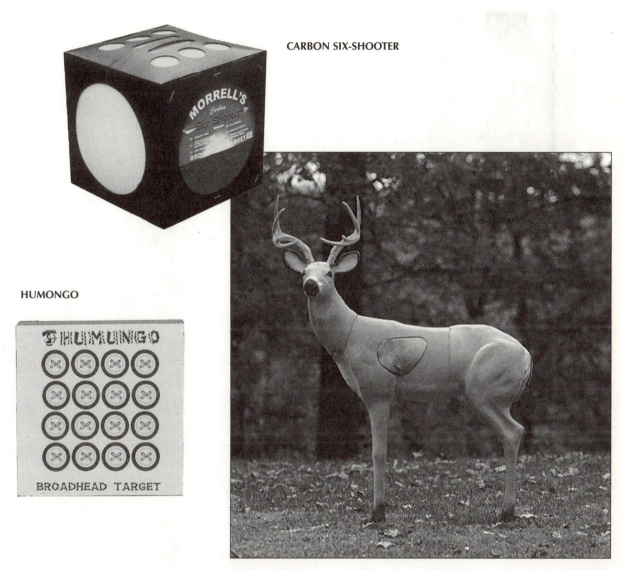

CARBON SIX-SHOOTER

HUMONGO

SON OF A BUCK

BLUERIDGE

Son Of A Buck

This realistic 3-D target includes two replaceable vitals—one for field points and one designed to work well with broadheads. The rear of the buck target has a pocket to secure the vital that is not in use. This target disassembles into three sections and has removable antlers. Stakes are included. Call 417-451-4438 for more details or visit www.outlandsports.com.
SRP: $129.99

MORRELL

Carbon Six-Shooter

The Carbon Six-Shooter foam box target by Morrell is now sporting an easy-carry handle. This long lasting 6-sided target is a rugged, free standing foam target that's made to handle today's high performance equipment, broadheads and field points and all arrow shafts, including carbon. Special high density, layered foam allows for easy arrow removal, even broadheads. It is 100% waterproof.
SRP: $49.99

Humongo

The Humongo is made from a special multi-layered foam and is designed so it will easily stop carbon, wood and aluminum arrows regardless of the broadhead or the speed, yet arrow removal is easy. It is a large 30x30x10-inch target and now features a 100% waterproof cover. It's designed for long life and fairly impervious to the weather.
SRP: $34.99

NEW Products: **Archery Products**

MOOSE TARGET

BIGBUTT TARGET

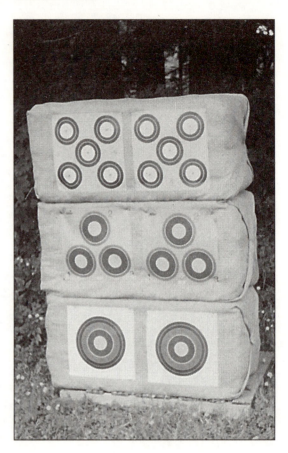

RINEHART

Moose Target

When you want a big target or to prepare for a moose-oriented bowhunt, this target will serve the purpose. It is constructed of dense foam and stands nearly 5-foot tall at the shoulder.

SRP: **$1,393.25**

PACIFIC BOW BUTTS

BigButt Target

Designed for pro shops and clubs, this target backstop by Pacific Bow Butts is 44 inches wide, 21 inches high and 20 inches thick. These targets can easily be stacked three high and rotated to provide years of dependable and carefree use. The targets are constructed with compressed, biodegradable straw and wrapped with burlap. The package is secured with 1/2-inch galvanized bands. Arrows are easily removed after a shot and the backstop can easily withstand more than 75,000 penetrations.

SRP: **$69.96**

COMPOUND HUNTING BOWS

Alpine Archery Compound Hunting Bows

COMPOUND HUNTING

1 CAM

INFERNO CAM

XTREME FOREST FLOOR

XTREME HARDWOODS

FAST TRAC XL WIDE BODY CAM

ALPINE ARCHERY prides itself with offering cutting edge hunting bows at a fair price. The company's engineers are always seeking ways to push the envelope on bow design, construction and technology. Their new Ravage compound shows the direction this effort is taking. Alpine Archery is located in Lewiston, Idaho and makes a complete line of hunting oriented compound bows. The company began operation in 1988.

CHALLENGER

The Challenger bow offers the same features as Alpine's Stealth Force but is also outfitted with a standard 1-Cam or Inferno cam system. The Challenger's features include: split limbs, two-piece wood checkered grip panels and a machined Inverse twin limb mounting system. This bow weighs 3.5 pounds and is coated with Mossy Oak Forest Floor camouflage.

BOW SPECIFICATIONS: CHALLENGER
AMO Draw Length: 26- to 31-inch in 1-inch increments with Inferno Cam; begins at 27- inch with the One-Cam system
Draw Weights: 50#, 60# and 70#, 80% let-off standard and 65% let-off optional with standard cam; Note that only 65% let-off is offered with Inferno cams
Bow Speed: NA
Axle-to Axle: 39 inches
SRP: with Inferno cams. $459
    with the 1-Cam system. $489

FAST TRAC

The Fast Trac X-Treme utilizes a compact riser and is designed for comfortable tree stand hunting. The X-Treme features a two panel checkered wood grip for torque-free shooting and a straight, carbon cable guard with a Teflon impregnated slide. The bow also utilizes the Fast Trac Four Point Bearing Control System and Wide Body Cam Technology. It's available in two camouflage patterns and with split limbs, arrow shelf and silicone bedded limbs. The bow weighs 3.4 pounds, uses a weighted one-cam and has a 7-inch brace height. This bow is being discontinued in 2003.

BOW SPECIFICATIONS: FAST TRAC X-TREME
AMO Draw Length: 28- to 32-inch in 1-inch increments
Draw Weights: 50#, 60# and 70# with 80% let off standard (65% optional)
Bow Speed: NA
Axle-to Axle: 33 inches
SRP:. $499

IMPACT X-TREME

MICRO

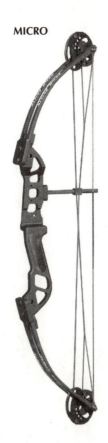

RAVAGE

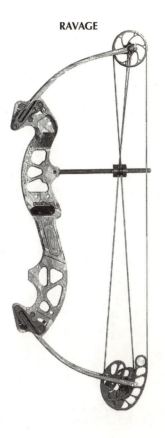

IMPACT X-TREME

The Impact X-Treme was designed to be a lightweight machined riser bow equipped with factory-selected accessories. The Impact features a very slim, two piece grip that allows a glove to be worn in cold weather without making the bow torque when shot. It is fitted with a Soft Loc 5-arrow Mossy Oak camo quiver, fiber optic sight, Whisper Flite rest and Pro Flex stabilizer with bow sling. The bow weighs 2.4 pounds, uses Inverse Twin limb mounting and is available with Stalker II cams or Alpine's 1-Cam system.

BOW SPECIFICATIONS: IMPACT X-TREME
AMO Draw Length: 23- to 30-inch with Stalker cams; 26- to 30-inch in 1-inch increments in the 1-Cam version
Draw Weights: 50#, 60# and 70# with 80% let off standard (65% let-off optional). Note that 65% let-off is the only option with Stalker cam models
Bow Speed: NA
Axle-to Axle: 34 inches
**SRP: for Stalker models. $309
     for 1-Cam models. $369**

MICRO

The Micro is the choice for starting serious young shooters. All of the hardware and riser are completely CNC machined aluminum. The Micro sports adult bow features such as Alpine's split limb technology, two panel ABS grips, and carbon cable guard rod. Another feature is the easy-adjust Stalker II Cam with 8-inch draw adjustment. The bow's draw length is adjusted by removing one screw and rotating the take-up side of the cam. Each hole is one inch of draw and about two pounds of peak weight gained or lost depending on whether you lengthen or shorten the draw. No bow press is required and the adjustment only takes minutes. This cam is perfect for growing children and weighs only 2¼ pounds. The Micro is available in black finish only.

BOW SPECIFICATIONS: MICRO
AMO Draw Length: 21- to 28-inch
Draw Weights: 30#, 40# and 50#; 65% let off
Bow Speed: NA
Axle-to Axle: 32 inches
SRP:. $189

RAVAGE

The Alpine bow's design is a top example of today's technology with its aggressive VX riser and Bi-Polar dampners. Another new feature is Inter-loc limbs with a nylon dampening system. The Ravage model also advances parallel limb technology to a new higher level to deliver a very short and compact bow. This bow's design was the result of an application of state-of-the-art computer modeling software.
Other features of this bow include: Fast Trac cam system with wide body technology, Bi-Flex composite limbs, a cable guard and a two-piece wooden grip. This bow weighs 4 pounds, has a 7½-inch brace height and is offered in Realtree's Hardwoods Green High-Definition camouflage finish.

BOW SPECIFICATIONS: RAVAGE
AMO Draw Length: 25- to 29-inch in 1-inch increments
Draw Weights: 50#, 60# and 70# with 80% let-off standard (65% let-off optional)
Bow Speed: NA
Axle-to Axle: 28 inches
SRP:. $675

SIDEWINDER FOREST

SIDEWINDER HARDWOODS

STEALTH FORCE FOREST

STEALTH FORCE HARDWOODS

COMPOUND HUNTING

SIDEWINDER

The Sidewinder is the fastest bow in Alpine's Fast Trac Series. It is designed for the shooter who demands a quality fit and finish in a technically advanced arrow shooting machine. Speed, accuracy and reliability are maintained without sacrificing smooth, quiet shooting characteristics. This bow utilizes the ultra reflex riser with a two panel, checkered wood grip. The Sidewinder is for the more seasoned shooter that is comfortable with reflexed risers. Other features include a four- point Bearing Control System (patent pending) and Wide Body Cam Technology to make this Fast Trac Series bow the most technically advanced reflexed bow on the market. This bow is available in Realtree Hardwoods and Mossy Oak Forest

Floor camouflage dipped finish. This bow weighs 3.5 pounds, has split limbs and a 6-inch brace height.

BOW SPECIFICATIONS: SIDEWINDER
AMO Draw Length: 26 to 30 inches in 1-inch increments
Draw Weights: 50#, 60# and 70# with 80% let off standard (65% optional)
Bow Speed: NA
Axle-to Axle: 36 inches
SRP:. $589

STEALTH FORCE

The Stealth Force combines Alpine's Fast Trac technology with a higher brace height than many of the bows. The Stealth Force comes in two axle-to-axle lengths, with the shorter version producing the greater arrow velocity. The bow's riser is designed for balance and has a two piece,

checkered wood panel grip and a full-view sight window cutout. The straight, carbon cable guard and Teflon slide provide a smooth draw and whisper-quiet operation. The bow uses perimeter weighted cams and Bi-Flex composite limbs set in machined pockets. Other features include: Alpine's Fast Trac Four Point Bearing Control System, Wide Body Cam Technology and split limbs.

BOW SPECIFICATIONS: STEALTH FORCE
AMO Draw Length: 27- to 31-inch (down to 26 for the shorty models) in 1-inch increments
Draw Weights: 50#, 60# and 70# with 80% let-off standard (65% let-off optional)
Bow Speed: NA
Axle-to Axle: 39 or 36 inches
SRP:. $549

Alpine Archery Compound Hunting Bows

TETON LITE

TETON LITE

Alpine's Teton Lite compound bow has all of the features of the company's Sidewinder model, but is offered with either the standard perimeter weighted 1-Cam or Inferno cam systems. The Teton Lite is covered in Mossy Oak Forest Floor camo. This bow uses silicone imbedded Bi-Flex composite limbs and an Inverse twin limb mounting system.

BOW SPECIFICATIONS: TETON LITE
AMO Draw Length: 25- to 30-inch in 1-inch increments with Inferno Cam
Draw Weights: 50#, 60# and 70#, 80% let-off standard and 65% let-off optional with standard cams. Note that 65% let-off is the only option with Inferno cams
Bow Speed: NA
Axle-to Axle: 36 inches
**SRP: for Inferno cam models. . . $489
       for 1-Cam models. $519**

Steady and Ready

While practicing and shooting can help improve archery shots, some archers fall into the habit of pulling, anchoring and releasing. When hunting and faced with suddenly moving game animals, some archers have a difficult time holding steady because of the pause.

You can prepare for this situation by spending practice time drawing your bow, aligning the sights, and holding without releasing. A good way to reinforce this practice is to go to the range, prepare to shoot draw and HOLD. Do this repeatedly and increase your duration of steadiness. If you do this for 15 to 30 minutes, then leave the range without ever releasing an arrow, you'll find the practice pays big rewards.

This is a way to mentally prepare for bowhunting and all archery disciplines. Much of your archery skills involve mental preparation and this practice skills set helps teach steadiness without a follow-through release. Try it. –MDF

WHEN JOHNNY MORRIS set up his first fishing lure display in a liquor store, no one thought it would go this far. The first clue should have been when the lures were outselling the liquor. Today Bass Pro Shops continues to cater to more than just anglers. The company outfits bowhunters with a thriving catalog ordering service and the company's 20 super stores across the eastern half of the US. The company recently opened a wildlife museum near their Springfield, Missouri, headquarters. Johnny and the Redhead pro staff roam North America each fall in search of hunting opportunities.

Bass Pro also contacts archery manufacturers to create special exclusive purchasing opportunities for bowhunters and archery enthusiasts. Many of these bow and accessory packages can be obtained at great savings when compared to purchasing the components individually. These exclusive bows and accessories can only be obtained through Bass Pro Shops. In addition to visiting a store, buyers can order on line at www.basspro.com or by calling (800) BASS-PRO (227-7776).

NOVA HUNTER PACKAGE

This bow and matching components begins with PSE's Nova compound bow as a base. The bow's features include a solid machined aluminum riser, solid Magnaglass limbs, and Vector-4 machined aluminum cams. The add-ons include: fiber optic sight, arrow rest and Mongoose six-arrow quiver in PSE's Brush camouflage finish to match the bow.

BOW SPECIFICATIONS:
NOVA HUNTER PACKAGE
AMO Draw Length: 25-27, 27-29, 28-30 and 29-31 inches
Draw Weights: 40# to 50#, 50# to 60# and 60# to70# with 75% let-off
Bow Speed: NA
Axle-to Axle: 39 inches
SRP: **$199.99**

WHITETAIL EXTREME PACKAGE

This hunting bow assembly starts with PSE's short Whitetail compound bow which features solid limbs, a machined aluminum reflex riser and the Arson OneCam system. The bow has a black molded grip and cable

guard. The accessories include: FX Hunter 3-pin sight with pin guard, 5-inch stabilizer, camo wrist sling, peep sight and quiver that holds six arrows. The package is ready for hunting with PSE's Brush camouflage coating.

BOW SPECIFICATIONS:
WHITETAIL EXTREME PACKAGE
AMO Draw Length: 28, 29 and 30 inches
Draw Weights: 50# to 60# and 60# to70# with 70% let-off
Bow Speed: NA
Axle-to Axle: 34 inches
SRP: **$299.99**

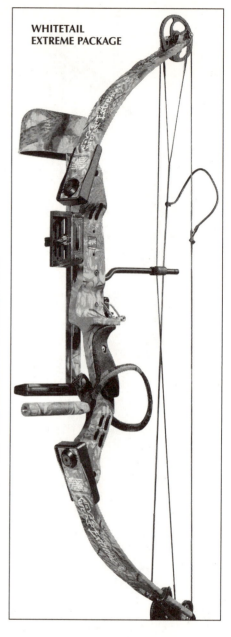

WHITETAIL EXTREME PACKAGE

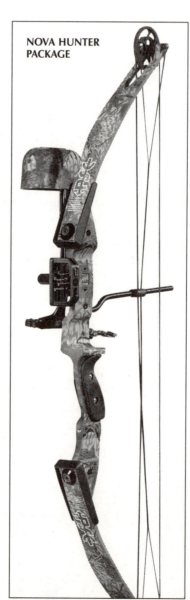

NOVA HUNTER PACKAGE

Bass Pro Shops Compound Hunting Bows

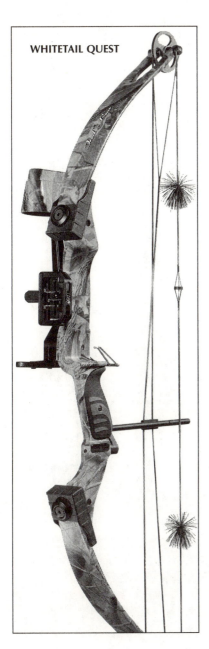

WHITETAIL QUEST

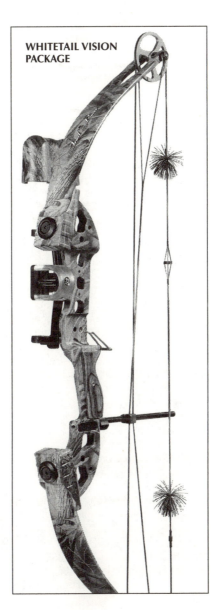

WHITETAIL VISION PACKAGE

WHITETAIL QUEST

This bow is similar to the Whitetail Vision model and uses an aluminum Super Cam. It has a solid riser, stylish molded grip and matching black limb pockets. The bow is available in six right-hand models and three left-hand versions. The accessories include a 3-pin fiber optic sight with a level attached and a quiver for arrows. The bow is camouflaged by Realtree Hardwoods.

BOW SPECIFICATIONS: WHITETAIL QUEST
AMO Draw Length: 28, 29 and 30 inches
Draw Weights: 50# to 60#, 60# to70# with 75% let-off
Bow Speed: NA
Axle-to Axle: 34 1/2 inches
SRP: $249.99

WHITETAIL VISION PACKAGE

This Bass Pro exclusive compound bow is manufactured by Bear Archery and begins with a machined aluminum reflexed riser and then adds on solid compression molded carbon/glass limbs. The bow moves arrows with a Perimeter OneCam system. Other features include a wood two-piece grip, cable guard and interchangeable modules to adjust the draw length. Accessories include: quick detach 4-arrow quiver, 3-pin fiber optic sight, arrow rest, peep sight and string silencers. Left- and right-hand models are available and all bows are coated with Realtree's Hardwoods High- Definition camo pattern.

BOW SPECIFICATIONS:
WHITETAIL VISION PACKAGE
AMO Draw Length: 28 to 30 inches
Draw Weights: 60# to 70# with 75% let-off
Bow Speed: NA
Axle-to Axle: 34 inches
SRP: $399.99

A Bow's Back
The back of a bow is the side facing away from you as you draw an arrow. The bow's front is what you're looking at as you draw the bow. –MDF

Bear Archery Compound Hunting Bows

BADGE

THE NAME FRED BEAR is synonymous with the modern archery movement in America. From his crude early workshop in Grayling, Michigan, Fred began to handcraft recurve bows and eventually sell bows and archery hunting accessories. Fred helped establish one of the nation's first archery-only hunting seasons and his films were watched by millions as he trotted around the globe with bow in hand. Fred Bear can be credited with promoting archery to the masses as he traveled across America and displayed bows. He routinely showed how simple and effective bows were for hunting and recreation. After the creation of compound bows, Bear Archery fueled America's renewed interest in archery with innovations like the Whitetail 4-wheel bow and the mass production and distribution of the Bear Razorhead with its changeable bleeder insert blade. Bear Archery's compound bows have continued to show cutting-edge designs and ground-breaking innovations such as the angled riser and adjustable cams that permit the user to make changes without using a vice or going to a pro shop. The culmination of this technology, which began when Fred Bear was in control, resulted in the Custom Borsalino takedown compound bow. This could be one of the archery industry's most innovative bows ever produced. Other unique bow features that are incorporated into many Bear models include the swing arm cable guard and weighted OneCams.

The company continues to produce innovative designs and helps archers everywhere enjoy the sport of archery.

Bear bows are produced and distributed by the North American Archery Group in Gainesville, Florida. This company is the parent firm for Bear Archery and Fred Bear Traditional Bowhunting Company with its full line of recurve bows. All of the company's compound bows are camouflaged and designed for hunting but could be used successfully on the 3-D tournament trails.

The manufacturing and assembly facility in Florida is also the headquarters of the famed Fred Bear museum and houses many of the bows and momentos from Fred's round-the-world bowhunting adventures. The museum and plant are open for tours and are a must-see if you are in that region of Florida.

BADGE

This Bear Archery bow is designed for young and small framed archers. Its features include a rugged, lightweight riser with integral grip and limb pockets. Other features include solid carbon recurve limbs and 20 pound adjustable draw weight range. This bow is only available as a right-hand model and in Hardwoods High Definition camouflage.

BOW SPECIFICATIONS: BADGE

AMO Draw Length: 21 or 25 inches
- adjustable range for 21-inch is 20 to 23 inches
- adjustable range for 25-inch is 24 to 27 inches

Draw Weights: 15-25# or 35-45# with 65% let-off
Axle-to Axle: 34.875 inches
Weight in hand: 2 lbs., 15 oz.
SRP: . . . . **Starting at $159.**

CUSTOM BORSALINO TAKE-DOWN

CUSTOM WHITETAIL PINNACLE

EPIC XTREME

CUSTOM BORSALINO TAKE-DOWN

This technologically advanced compound bow folds in half and sets up again in less than a minute. It can be easily transported in an optional soft-sided carrying case. Other features include bronzed hardware, draw length adjustable OneCam system and a Realtree Hardwoods camouflage finish. This compound bow incorporates the Shock Stop noise and vibration elimination system and is available as a right-hand only model. A tip of the famous Fred Bear Borsalino hat is offered to the company on the creation of this bow.

BOW SPECIFICATIONS:
CUSTOM BORSALINO TAKE-DOWN
AMO Draw Length: 25- to 33-inch
Draw Weight: 60-70#
Bow Speed: IBO fps = 321;
AMO fps = 237
Axle-to Axle: 38¼ inches
Weight in hand: varies by selection of cams and other options
SRP: $749

CUSTOM WHITETAIL PINNACLE

This advanced design bow is custom built to owner specifications at the North American Archery Group's Gainesville, Florida, facility. Its features include the innovative ZenCam that produces virtually no hand shock and a superbly energy efficient design that reduces limb travel. This bow is available in Realtree Harwoods High Definition camouflage and left- and right-hand models. This is one of the few offerings in the archery industry where you can have a custom hunting compound bow built to your specifications.

BOW SPECIFICATIONS:
CUSTOM WHITETAIL PINNACLE
AMO Draw Length: 28- to 31-inch
Draw Weights: 50-60# and 60-70# with let-off dependant upon cam selection
Bow Speed: IBO fps = 298;
AMO fps = 233
Axle-to Axle: 38 inches
Weight in hand: varies
SRP: $499

EPIC XTREME

This hunting compound bow utilizes a modular weighted OneCam that permits eight inches of draw length adjustment and one inch of micro adjustment. The stylish bronze anodized and brass weighted dampening system contrasts against the bow's Realtree Hardwoods High Definition camouflage finish. The machined aluminum riser offers a 7½-inch brace height and is available in left- or right-hand models with a checkered laminated wood grip complete with an inlaid compass. This model has a swing-arm cable guard and a distinct Fred Bear signature inset on the riser.

BOW SPECIFICATIONS: EPIC XTREME
AMO Draw Length: 28-, 29- and 30-inch; adjustable range from 24 to 31 inches.
Draw Weights: 50-60# and 60-70# with 75% let-off (65% let-off optional)
Bow Speed: IBO fps = 303;
AMO fps = 234
Axle-to Axle: 32 inches
Weight in hand: 3 lbs., 15 ozs.
SRP: $399

COMPOUND HUNTING

Bear Archery Compound Hunting Bows

LITTLE DELTA

TRX

VAPOR 300

LITTLE DELTA

The Little Delta was designed to help kids step into the archery arena in adult-like style. Features include a Mossy Oak Break-Up camouflage finish, magnesium riser, carbon solid straight limbs and the use of solid composite modular cam. This model includes a cable guard and all weather composite grip. Left- and right-hand versions are available and the bow will accommodate accessories.

BOW SPECIFICATIONS: LITTLE DELTA
AMO Draw Length: 25 inches, adjustable 24 to 27 inches
Draw Weight: 25-35# or 40-50#
Axle-to Axle: 34.625 inches
Weight in hand: 3 lbs., 10 oz.
SRP:. **$129**

TRX

This special-edition Fred Bear 100th Birthday Anniversary commemorative Team Realtree bow wears a Realtree Hardwoods High Definition finish on the machined 6061-T-6 aluminum riser and four carbon recurve limbs. Other features include a Shock Stop tipped cable guard and checkered laminated wood grip with inlaid compass. The TRX is available in left- and right-hand versions with a 94¾-inch long Tech Twist string and gold colored accents on the limb pockets, idler wheel and cam.

BOW SPECIFICATIONS: TRX
AMO Draw Length: 28-, 29- or 30-inch: adjustable range from 24 to 31 inches
Draw Weights: 40-50#, 50-60#, or 60-70#; 70% let-off (65% let-off optional)
Bow Speed: IBO fps = 305; AMO fps 230
Axle-to Axle: 35.875 inches
Weight in hand: 3 lbs., 15 oz.
SRP: . . . . **Starting at $399**

VAPOR 300

This high-tech 4-limb compound bow was designed to assist bowhunters on the hunt. Features of the Vapor 300 include a machined aluminum riser, powerful V-Tech OneCam and a vibration dampening Elasto-Polymer grip. Other features include an adjustable cable guard and tan/olive Tech Twist string. This bow is coated in Realtree Hardwoods High Definition camo and the left-hand model has a checkered laminated wood grip.

BOW SPECIFICATIONS: VAPOR 300
AMO Draw Length: 28-, 29- and 30-inch; adjustable range from 24 to 31 inches.
Draw Weights: 40-50#, 50-60#, 60-70#; 75% let-off (65% let-off optional)
Bow Speed: IBO fps = 302; AMO fps = 223
Axle-to Axle: 34.25 inches
Weight in hand: 4 lbs., 6 oz.
SRP:. **$279**

Ben Pearson Archery Compound Hunting Bows

440 QUAD KIT

ANACONDA

BEN PEARSON ARCHERY was established in 1938 and has remained active in the archery industry since the beginning. As archery has changed through the years and decades, so have the company and its products. The company has been aggressive in its research, development and manufacturing of bows.

In 2002 McPherson bows were merged into Ben Pearson to become the Pro Shop series. These bows are only available through select archery shops.

Many popular bows in the Pearson line returned in 2002-or similar models took their place—and the company's line has expanded. Of special interest in some of these bows is the vibration dampening shock built into the riser and the 20-degree bio grip that is offered on some models. Some bows are offered as competition models. Contact the company to determine the models and the colors currently being produced. Ben Pearson Archery is located in Brewton, Alab

440 Quad Kit

The 440 has been the work horse bow in the Pearson line for five years. In 2002, Pearson offered the 440 Quad Kit which includes the bow and all the accessories. The 440 Quad features: 15½-inch quadra-flex split limbs, wide track idler wheel, Z3 catapult PhD Cam, soft-feel thermo grip, velvet antler finish in rest area, and Superflauge camo.

The accessories include: bow with fiber optic sight, stabilizer, string silencer, peep, arrow rest, quiver and four arrows.

BOW SPECIFICATIONS: 440 QUAD KIT
AMO Draw Length: 25- to 32-inch
Draw Weights: 50#, 60# and 70# with 75% let-off
Bow Speed: IBO fps= 303
Axle-to Axle: 36¾-inches
Weight in hand: 3.6 lbs.
SRP: $469

ANACONDA

The machined aluminum riser on the Anaconda has withstood the torture of over 100 dry fires. This bow has a 20-degree bio grip slant handle—a "must have" requirement by a growing number of experienced hunters--and an IBO speed of 310 fps. Other features include: a wood grip; 15½-inch quadra-flex split limbs, Z3 weighted catapult PhD cam, and Superflauge camo.

BOW SPECIFICATIONS: ANACONDA
AMO Draw Length: 25- to 32-inch
Draw Weights: 50#, 60# and 70# with 75% let-off
Bow Speed: IBO fps= 310
Axle-to Axle: 36¼-inches
Weight in hand: 3.6 lbs.
SRP: $489

COMPOUND HUNTING

Ben Pearson Archery Compound Hunting Bows

DIAMONDBACK VX AND DIAMONDBACK

HORNET VX

MARK XII

DIAMONDBACK VX AND DIAMONDBACK

This bow is Pearson's number one seller. The Diamondback VX's features include: a 20-degree bio grip handle to reduce shooting fatigue and arm slap, a low torque wood grip and the VIB~X noise and vibration reduction system built into the riser below the hand position. This bow also has a velvet antler finish in the rest area, machined aluminum limb pockets and retainers, 14½-inch quadra-flex split limbs and the Whisper Cam with PhD (perfect horizontal delivery) single cam system. The Diamondback VX has 85% let-off and Superflauge camo.

The Diamondback model is similar to the Diamondback VX without the VIB-X shock reduction under the grip. This bow has a reflex riser, the 20° bio grip and 85% let-off. This bow has a 30¹⁵⁄₁₆-inch axle-to-axle length.

BOW SPECIFICATIONS: DIAMONDBACK VX
AMO Draw Length: 24- to 31-inch
Draw Weights: 50#, 60# and 70# with 85% let-off

Bow Speed: IBO fps= 302
Axle-to Axle: 31⁷⁄₁₆-inches
Weight in hand: 3.8 lbs.
SRP: Diamondback VX $609
standard Diamondback. $529

HORNET VX

With a 31-inch axle-to-axle length, this "shortie" is powerful, maneuverable, lightweight and a top contender for treestand hunters. This bow has the VIB-X vibration dampening shock below the grip. Other features include: a machined aluminum reflex riser with a full sight window, below center grip that puts the arrow in the exact center of the bow, wide track idler wheel, velvet antler finish in the rest area and four 14½-inch quadra-flex split limbs. The Hornet VX also has a cable guard with slide and uses the single cam design with a Whisper PhD cam. This bow is finished in Superflauge camo. The new Hornet VX was reintroduced in 2002.

BOW SPECIFICATIONS: HORNET VX
AMO Draw Length: 24- to 31-inch
Draw Weights: 50#, 60# and 70# with 85% let-off (and 65% and 75%

let-offs are possible when modules are purchased and installed)
Bow Speed: IBO fps= 302
Axle-to Axle: 31½-inches
Weight in hand: 3.7 lbs.
SRP:. $589

MARK XII

This compound bow has an 87% let-off—one of the highest in the archery industry. It has similar design features and components to the other McPherson bows. It uses the Thruster PhD cam and Widetrack idler wheel system. The bow is camouflaged, has a wooden grip and a cable guard with slide. The Mark XII has an aluminum riser and split limbs. For any archer with shoulder pains, this could be the bow for you with its high let-off rating.

BOW SPECIFICATIONS: MARK XII
AMO Draw Length: 26- to 33-inch
Draw Weights: 50#, 60# and 70# with 87% let-off
Bow Speed: IBO fps= 301
Axle-to Axle: 35 7/16 inches
Weight in hand: 3.5 lbs.
SRP:. $399

Ben Pearson Archery Compound Hunting Bows

MCPHERSON 38 SPECIAL

PENTRATOR VX

PIRANHA

MCPHERSON 38 SPECIAL

The lower part of the riser on this compound hunting bow features the new VIB~X noise and vibration reduction system. The chamber on this under-the-grip section incorporates a specially engineered polymer-Vibasorb that virtually eliminates vibration, noise and hand shock. Other features include: a machined aluminum riser and limb pockets; low torque wood grip; Pearson's exclusive velvet antler finish in the arrow rest area; all aluminum retainers; four 14½-inch quadra-flex split limbs tested to 300,000 cycles; catapult weighted Thruster cam with PhD—perfect horizontal delivery—single cam technology; wide track idler wheel and a new yellow and black string and harness assembly. The bow is coated with Lynch World Wide's Superflauge camo pattern.

BOW SPECIFICATIONS:
MCPHERSON 38 SPECIAL
AMO Draw Length: 25- to 32-inch

Draw Weights: 50#, 60# and 70# with 75% let-off (and 65% and 85% let-offs are possible when modules are purchased and installed)
Bow Speed: IBO fps= 310
Axle-to Axle: 38 inches
Weight in hand: 3.9 lbs.
SRP:.....................$759

PENTRATOR VX

The Penetrator, new in 2002, comes straight from the Pro Shop at Pearson Archery with enough accuracy for the 3-D archer and enough stored energy for the largest of big game species. The Penetrator features a 36½-inch axle-to-axle length, 6½-inch brace height, the VIB~X noise and vibration reduction system. This bow has a straight aluminum riser, four-limb design and a Thruster PhD single cam. It also has a cable guard and wood grip.

BOW SPECIFICATIONS: PENTRATOR VX
AMO Draw Length: 24- to 31-inch
Draw Weights: 50#, 60# and 70# with 85% let-off

Bow Speed: IBO fps= 310
Axle-to Axle: 36⁹/₁₆-inches
Weight in hand: 3.7 lbs.
SRP:.....................$579

PIRANHA

The Piranha will fit adult archers or those much smaller in size. This bow can provide growing youngsters a bow that will give them many years of shooting pleasure thanks to the Var-max PhD single cam, the most adjustable cam in the archery industry. Other features include: a machined aluminum riser; soft-feel thermo grip, velvet antler finish in the rest area, 14¼-inch quadra-flex split limbs, wide track idler wheel and Superflauge camo.

BOW SPECIFICATIONS: PIRANHA
AMO Draw Length: 24- to 32-inch
Draw Weights: 40#, 50#, 60# and 70# with 75% let-off
Bow Speed: IBO fps= 287
Axle-to Axle: 30½-inches
Weight in hand: 3.2 lbs.
SRP:.....................$399

Ben Pearson Archery Compound Hunting Bows

SCREAMER

SPOILER LITE

STINGER

SCREAMER

This McPherson compound bow uses a 2½-inch wide track idler wheel and Thruster PhD cam to propel arrows. Other features include: a machined aluminum riser, low torque wood grip, velvet antler finish at the arrow rest area; all aluminum retainers, 14½-inch quadra-flex split limbs, and Superflauge camo. Special features include 65% let-off modules for the Pope and Young minded archer or 85% let-off modules for the archer wanting a higher let-off capability. The modules are sold separately. This bow has a cable guard with slide.

BOW SPECIFICATIONS: SCREAMER
AMO Draw Length: 23- to 30-inch
Draw Weights: 50#, 60# and 70# with 75% let-off (65% and 85% let-offs optional)
Bow Speed: IBO fps= 318
Axle-to Axle: 33¼-inches
Weight in hand: 3.6 lbs.
SRP:. $519

SPOILER LITE

In 2002, the Spoiler returned to Pearsons line as the Spoiler Lite. While its legacy as a shorter more compact bow lives on, its previous cam has been replaced with a hybrid - the new and advanced Whisper PhD cam. This cam provides more speed, ease of draw, and better shooting performance. Other features include: a wood grip; Pearson's exclusive velvet antler finish at the arrow rest, a wide track idler wheel for straight string travel and Superflauge camo.

BOW SPECIFICATIONS: SPOILER LITE
AMO Draw Length: 24- to 31-inch
Draw Weights: 50#, 60# and 70# with 85% let-off
Bow Speed: IBO fps= 307
Axle-to Axle: 33½-inches
Weight in hand: 3.6 lbs.
SRP:. $519

STINGER

This bow was designed for small frame archers, ladies and youth. The Stinger features: a machined aluminum riser, soft-feel thermo grip, velvet antler finish in rest area, all aluminum retainers, 12½-inch split limbs and a Superflauge camo finish. This bow has the same design and features of many of their adult versions, including a cable guard with slide and single-cam system.

BOW SPECIFICATIONS: STINGER
AMO Draw Length: 20- to 26-inch
Draw Weights: 20#, 30#, and 40# with 75% let-off
Bow Speed: IBO fps= NA
Axle-to Axle: 28⅞-inches
Weight in hand: 2.8 lbs.
SRP:. $309

Browning Compound Hunting Bows

ADRENALINE 33

MIRAGE 33

THIS OGDEN, UTAH, based company has been in the firearms and hunting equipment business since John Browning first opened his gun shop. Browning entered the archery market in the 1970s with lightweight wood laminated bows such as the two-wheel Compound Cobra. Innovations progressed rapidly and the company has produced bows like the Micro Midas youth bow and other full-scale adult options like the Bridger in recent years. A full line of shooting and hunting accessories kept pace with the expanded bow model line up. The company has applied much of the same technology and marketing programs developed on its firearms side to its archery division and products to help it earn a solid reputation with archery enthusiasts. In recent years famed archer Ted Nugent traveled the archery circuits and represented Browning as a spokesperson.

In 2001, Browning Archery was licensed to PSE and is now located in Tucson, Arizona. There are still many bow models produced and many dealers who stock them. All Browning bows are camouflaged coated—most in Mossy Oak Break-Up—and ready for the hunt. You'll find them where the distinct Buckmark logo is displayed.

33 CLASS BOWS
This trio of bows—Mirage 33, Adrenaline 33 and Impulse LS—offer value for hunters seeking top-of-the-line components in an affordable one-cam compound bow. All bows feature forged/machined aluminum 33 risers (machined aluminum riser in the Impulse), Dynaflite strings and strong 450 Plus cables. The Mirage and Adrenaline models have 15-inch Contour XP limbs, integral cable guard, contoured two-piece foam grip and locking limb bolts and aluminum fixed position limb pockets. The lighter Impulse weighs 2.6 lbs. and has a 31½-inch axle-to-axle length and IBO speed of 277 fps. The Mirage uses the Cyber-Cam SX system to propel arrows and the Adrenaline and Impulse use Lightning cams and have 70% let-off. All of the bows are available in Mossy Oak Break-Up camouflage.

BOW SPECIFICATIONS:
MIRAGE AND ADRENALINE 33
AMO Draw Length: varies.
Draw Weights: varies; 75% let-off and 65% optional
Bow Speed: IBO fps = 300 (Mirage), 305 (Adrenaline)
Axle-to Axle: 33 inches (Mirage) and 33¼-inches (Adrenaline)
Weight in hand: 3.9 lbs.
SRP: **$499**
Impulse **$299**

The Long Pull
Wondering about the best way to remove an arrow? If it is buried in the target with the vane or fletching hidden, pull the arrow on through and consider buying another target with more solid arrow gripping power.

If your target is holding arrows correctly, try using one of the rubber arrow pulls that fit in the palm of your hand. These inexpensive devices give you more control and help you pull the arrow straight back. Do not pull and rotate an arrow or you can weaken the shaft wall and cause it to fly erratically when it is released the next time. –MDF

COMPOUND HUNTING

Browning Compound Hunting Bows

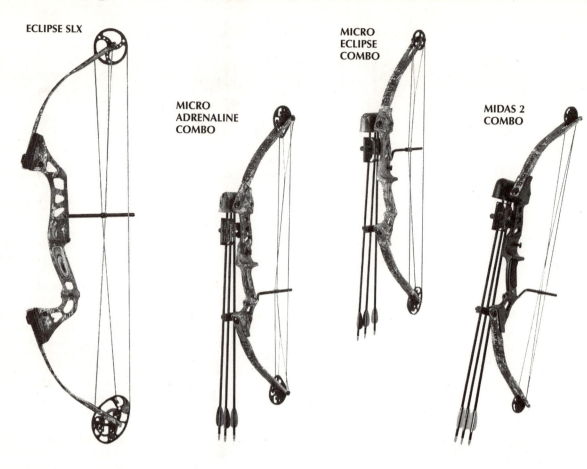

ECLIPSE SLX

MICRO ADRENALINE COMBO

MICRO ECLIPSE COMBO

MIDAS 2 COMBO

ECLIPSE SLX

This leader of the Browning pack of bows features a machined aluminum reflex riser that incorporates a machined self-grip with laminated wood insert panels. The riser makes the bow more comfortable to shoot. Other features include Radial-Lok pivoting limb pockets that are dampened with ImpacStop vibration dampening inserts. The limbs also assures positive limb to pocket alignment.

The Eclipse can be adjusted over a 3-inch draw length span and from 65% to 75% let-off. It has 15½-inch Contour XP limbs, an integral aluminum/carbon cable guard, two-piece wood grip, 8125 string and 450 plus cables and raised dome limb graphics. The idler wheel has a sealed ball bearing system. This compound bow is available in Mossy Oak Break-Up camouflage.

The Browning Eclipse SL 36 has a similar riser, limb and design as Eclipse SLX, including the use of Cyber-Cam SX system, and has a 36-in axle-to-axle length. This bow's limb pockets do not have the Radial Lok vibration system and the SL 36 has molded foam grip inserts.

BOW SPECIFICATIONS: ECLIPSE SLX
AMO Draw Length: varies.
Draw Weights: varies; 75% let-off and 65% optional
Bow Speed: IBO fps = 310
Axle-to Axle: 36 inches
Weight in hand: 4.3 lbs.
SRP:....................$745
    (add $16 for LH models)
SL 36....................$545

MICRO CLASS COMBOS

These youth-oriented bows—Micro Adrenaline, Micro Eclipse and Midas 2—are available in a complete combo that will have any young shooter increasing their skills and accuracy in record time. All bows have a 6¼-inch brace height, approximately 32-inch axle-to-axle length and Taperflex limbs. Other items offered in the combo package include: quivers, sights with pins, three matching carbon arrows, and a two-piece wood grip (foam only on the Midas 2). Each bow weighs slightly more than 2½-pounds and propels arrows at approximately 270-plus fps IBO. The Adrenaline and Midas 2 have under-the-grip cable guards and the Eclipse has an upper cable guard. All bows have dual cams (the Eclipse is single cam with idler wheel) and are camouflaged for hunting. The Midas has a black riser. All of these bows are available without the combo package for $70 less.

BOW SPECIFICATIONS: MICRO ADRENALINE, MICRO ECLIPSE AND MIDAS 2 COMBOS
AMO Draw Length: varies and can be adjusted approximately 6 inches.
Draw Weights: varies; 65% let-off (60% for the Adrenaline model)
Bow Speed: IBO fps = 270-plus
Axle-to Axle: approximately 32 inches
Weight in hand: 2.7 lbs.
SRP: Adrenaline and Eclipse . . . $335
Midas 2 .... $265

Browning Compound Hunting Bows

MIRAGE SX   ADRENALINE SX

SX CLASS BOWS

The two offerings in Browning's SX Class bows are the Mirage and Adrenaline. The Mirage has a forged/machined aluminum SX riser, Cyber-Cam SX system, adjustable let-off module with 65% or 75%, 15-inch Contour XP limbs and intergral aluminum/carbon cable guard. This bow's Radial-Lok pivoting machined aluminum limb pockets have ImpacStop vibration dampening pocket inserts. Other features include locking limb bolts, raised, domed limb graphics and 8125 string with 450 Plus cables. SX Class bows have two-piece wood grips and are camouflaged for hunting by a hand-dipped application of Mossy Oak Break-Up.

The Adrenaline SX compound bow features Lightning cams, a 6½-inch brace height, 70% let-off and the same axle-to-axle length and mass weight. Both SX bows have a Browning logo embedded in the riser under the grip.

BOW SPECIFICATIONS: MIRAGE SX
AMO Draw Length: varies.
Draw Weights: varies; 75% let-off and 65% optional
Bow Speed: IBO fps = 302
Axle-to Axle: 33 inches
Weight in hand: 3.9 lbs.
SRP:.....................**$675**
Adrenaline................**$675**

CYBER-CAM SX

Browning Compound Hunting Bows

SINGLE-CAM COMBOS

Browning takes the guess work and search out of finding the right accessories to perfectly match your hunting bow with the Tornado and Ambush combos.

The Tornado's accessories include: a seven-arrow one-piece Twist-Lok quiver in Mossy Oak Break-Up, TM Hunter arrow rest, 4½-inch solid tapered stabilizer, fiber optic sight with three metal sight pins and Whisper string silencers. This package also has an adjustable braided nylon sling, sight peep and nock. The Tornado bow has a machined aluminum riser, Contour XP limbs, molded grip with wood inserts and Dynaflite string. This bow's Cyber-Cam 5 provides 5 inches of draw length adjustability in half-inch increments and let-off that's adjustable from 65% up to 80%.

The Ambush combo includes: a two-piece quiver that will hold up to six arrows, a fiber optic sight, Toughman arrow rest, stabilizer, Whisper string silencers and a sling. A nock point and sight peep are included in the package to assist with accuracy when shooting. The Ambush has a unique black powder-coated machined aluminum riser and soft rubber grip with wood inserts. Other features include: a cable guard, Ignitor 3 cam and Dynaflite string. This bow also has solid Contour XP limbs coated with Ambush camouflage.

The Tornado and Ambush bows have a bold Browning logo on the limbs in black letters.

BOW SPECIFICATIONS:
AMBUSH AND TORNADO COMBOS
AMO Draw Length: varies.
Draw Weights: varies; 80% let-off adjustable to 65% (Tornado) and 75% let-off Ambush
Bow Speed: IBO fps = 292 (Tornado) and 280 (Ambush)
Axle-to Axle: 36 inches
Weight in hand: 3.9 lbs.
SRP: Tornado combo. $445
Ambush XB combo $299.99
Ambush separately $229

TORNADO COMBO

AMBUSH COMBO

CYBER-CAM 5

Buckmasters Compound Hunting Bows

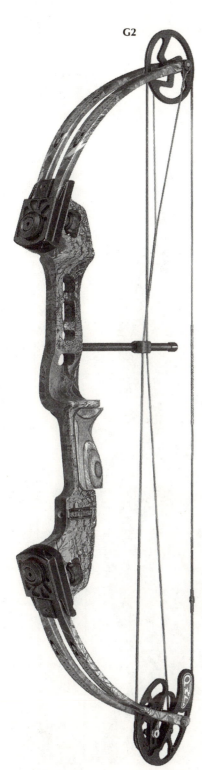

G2

THE BOWS that wear the Buckmasters name are produced and distributed by the North American Archery Group in Gainesville, Florida. This company is the parent of Buckmasters, Jennings, Fred Bear, Bear Archery and Golden Eagle bows. The company has worked with noted archery industry shooters and the staff and members of Buckmasters national organization to design and refine many of the products offered in this line. Many models incorporate the latest in archery design technology. All Buckmaster bows come with a limited lifetime warranty and most models feature Realtree camouflage patterns.

The bow manufacturing and assembly facility where these bows are produced in Florida is open for tours. If you want to earn money with your bow, consider joining Buckmasters and entering their archery competition that is held each summer during the group's annual member get together. Some events include shooting arrows at pop-up 3-D targets. A good time is had by everyone and even spectators enjoy the event.

2000

This performance oriented bow features a machined 6061-T-6 aluminum riser that provides a 7.375-inch brace height for its left- or right-hand versions. Other features include compression molded CarbonAir limbs, a synthetic string and the use of a SuperCam. Left-hand models feature a checkered laminated wood handle and the right-hand model has an elasto-polymer non-skid grip. It's available in Realtree Harwoods camouflage finish and with a solid cable guard equipped with a slide.

BOW SPECIFICATIONS: 2000
AMO Draw Length: 28-, 29- and 30-inch; adjustable range 26 to 32 inches
Draw Weights: 50-60# and 60-70# with 75% let-off (65% available)
Bow Speed: IBO fps = 292; AMO fps = 220
Axle-to Axle: 39½-inches
Weight in hand: 4 lbs., 10 oz.
SRP:. **$279**

G2

Representing the next generation of bows, the lightweight G2 incorporates Sims LimbSaver technology to cancel recoil, vibration and noise. Other features include a ball bearing mounted idler wheel, TechTwist string, lightweight carbon cable guard and a custom checkered hardwood grip. Special polymer wedges around the base ends of the Carbon Quad limbs help absorb shock and reduce noise. The G2 is available in right- and left-hand models with a Realtree Hardwoods camo finish. This hunting bow has a machined aluminum riser and a perimeter weighted cam.

BOW SPECIFICATIONS: G2
AMO Draw Length: 28-, 29- and 30-inch; adjustable range 28 to 30 inches
Draw Weights: 40-50#, 50-60# and 60-70# with 70% let-off (65% available)
Bow Speed: IBO fps = 309; AMO fps = 232
Axle-to Axle: 31 inches
Weight in hand: 3 lbs., 9 oz.
SRP:. **$499**

COMPOUND HUNTING

Buckmasters Compound Hunting Bows

HyperTech

The 34-inch axle-to-axle HyperTech features a perimeter weighted cam, Carbon Quad straight limbs and a Realtree Hardwoods camouflage finish. The right-hand model has an Elasto-Polymer grip and the left-hand version has a checkered laminated wood grip. Other features include a machined 6061-T-6 aluminum riser, solid cable guard and red-and-black TechTwist string.

Bow Specifications: HyperTech
AMO Draw Length: 27-, 28-, 29-, 30 and 31-inch; adjustable range 24 to 31 inches
Draw Weights: 50-60# and 60-70# with 70% let-off (65% optional with available modules)
Bow Speed: IBO fps = 298; AMO fps = 221
Axle-to Axle: 34 inches
Weight in hand: 4 lbs., 7 oz.
SRP: **$299**

Ultra Mag Set

This Buckmasters compound hunting bow arrives complete with sights, arrow rest and two-piece quiver. It's available in left- and right-hand versions with a black all-weather composite grip nestled against a magnesium riser. Other features include a Realtree Hardwoods camouflage finish, carbon quad limbs and a solid cable guard. Technology and matching accessories meet here to create a bow package that's ready for the hunt after you add arrows.

Bow Specifications: Ultra Mag Set
AMO Draw Length: 28-, 29- and 30-inch; adjustable range 24 to 30 inches
Draw Weights: 50-60# and 60-70# with 75% let-off (65% available)
Bow Speed: IBO fps = 291; AMO fps = 223
Axle-to Axle: 35.5 inches
Weight in hand: 4 lbs.
SRP: **$249**

Young Bucks

This feature packed bow is designed to introduce novice shooters to archery and bowhunting in an affordable package. The bow weighs less than 2 pounds, has adjustable draw weights and numerous high let-off options to make the bow compatible with growing arms and muscles. Other features include

Realtree Hardwoods camouflage finish, sight, two piece quiver and arrow rest. The Young Bucks bow is available in right-hand version only.

Bow Specifications: Young Bucks
AMO Draw Length: 20-, 21- and 22-inch
Draw Weights: 17 to 22# with 65% let-off
Axle-to Axle: 30 inches
Weight in hand: 1 lb., 9 oz.
SRP: bow only **$99**
    package costs additional

HYPERTECH

YOUNG BUCKS

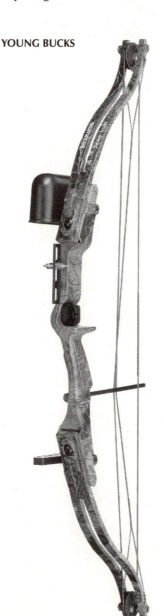

BROWNING
BUCKMARK PACKAGE

BROWNING GOLD
33 PACKAGE

ANY HUNTER AND ARCHERY addict knows about Cabelas', the world's foremost outfitter and catalog-based equipment source with an unlimited supply of gear. In recent years the company has opened destination oriented retail stores across the Midwest and Northeast. You should visit one of these if you've haven't yet, and take your family and neighbors along to see the conservation mountain display. The store in Owatonna, Minnesota, has become one the state's top tourist attractions! And all stores seem to be well stocked with archery gear and their knowledgeable sales staff can help you make selections.

Cabela's has also flexed its purchasing power muscles and hammered out exclusive bow deals with many manufacturers. While the bow might not arrive with a flashy Cabela's logo, the only way to obtain these compound hunting bow models is by ordering them through Cabela's at (800) 237-4444 or at www.cabelas.com. In some cases you can save serious money by ordering the bow and accessory kit. All products have a satisfaction guaranteed policy. The company also produces an archery-only catalog that most bowhunters will have a hard time putting down!

BROWNING BUCKMARK PACKAGE

This bow and accessory kit starts with Browning's popular Buckmark bow with the solid Contour XP limbs and Cyber Cam SX one-cam system. Other features of the bow include a molded riser and ergonomic grip. The Buckmark is coated with Ambush camouflage.

The package components include: a camouflaged two-piece quiver that hold six arrows, Lightning sight with three fiber optic pins, Huntsman Toughman rest and four carbon arrows along with the bow. All items are selected and designed to compliment the bow's in-the-field performance. The bow can be obtained in right- and left-hand models.

BOW SPECIFICATIONS: BROWNING BUCKMARK PACKAGE
AMO Draw Length: 28- to 30- inch
Draw Weights: 50/60# and 60/70# with 65% to 75% adjustable let-off
Bow Speed: IBO fps= 290, AMO fps= 224
Axle-to Axle: 36 inches
SRP: $299.99

BROWNING GOLD 33 PACKAGE

This kit is similar to the Browning Buckmark package and uses the Cyber Cam 5 system which delivers five full inches of draw length adjustment without taking the bow to a pro shop. This bow has limb pockets for the solid limbs, single cam, carbon cable guard with slide and a molded grip. The bow is coated with Ambush camouflage. The kit that accompanies the bow includes: a TL seven arrow quiver, adjustable arrow rest, Lightning sight and four Browning arrows. This bow is offered in RH models only.

BOW SPECIFICATIONS: BROWNING GOLD 33 PACKAGE
AMO Draw Length: 26- to 30-inch
Draw Weights: 50/60# and 60/70# with 65% or 80% adjustable let-off
Bow Speed: IBO fps= 300, AMO fps= 234
Axle-to Axle: 33³/₈-inches
SRP: $399.99

Safety First
When practicing and hunting, always be certain of your target and what is beyond it. Look before you shoot and shot only at the target. Be sure the range is clear and that no one else is shooting before you go to retrieve your arrows.—MDF

Cabela's Compound Hunting Bows

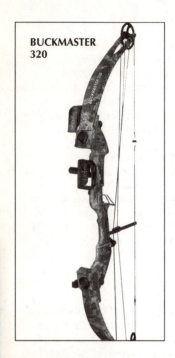

BUCKMASTER 320

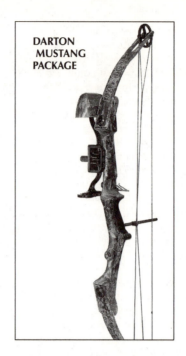

DARTON MUSTANG PACKAGE

PSE BABY-G PACKAGE

BUCKMASTER 320

This exclusive Cabela's bow has a short axle-to-axle length and a Perimeter OneCam system. Its compression molded carbon straight limbs are anchored in Quiet Tech limb cups to reduce game spooking noise and annoying vibrations. Other features include a radically reflexed machined aluminum riser, two-piece checkered wood grip and Posi-lock cable guard. This hunting bow is coated with Advantage Timber camouflage and has a 6-inch brace height. This bow is available as a left- or right-hand model.

A kit is offered for this bow that includes: a matching three-pin fiber optic sight with level, two-piece arrow quiver in matching camo, a Golden-Key Huntsman arrow rest, peep sight, and Whiskers string silencer.

BOW SPECIFICATIONS: BUCKMASTER 320
AMO Draw Length: 28-, 29- and 30-inch
Draw Weights: 60# to 70# with 65% let-off
Bow Speed: IBO fps =320, AMO fps= 236
Axle-to Axle: 35¼-inches
SRP: $299.99
   bow with kit $349.99

DARTON MUSTANG PACKAGE

This package is recommended for beginning or economically inclined archers and is big on features and low on price. The bow's features include: Darton's Post Feed Cam (PFC) single-cam technology, a solid die-cast riser, cable guard and molded grip. The package includes the bow, arrow rest, quiver and fiber optic sight with four pins. The entire assembly is covered in Superflage camo.

BOW SPECIFICATIONS:
DARTON MUSTANG PACKAGE
AMO Draw Length: 27- to 30-inch
Draw Weights: 50/60# and 60/70# with 75% let-off
Bow Speed: IBO fps= 277, AMO fps= 220
Axle-to Axle: 38¾-inches
SRP: $199.99

DARTON STRIKER PACKAGE

This Cabela's Exclusive package starts with a Striker compound bow by Darton and adds on an arrow rest, quiver and fiber-optic sight with pins. The bow features a solid riser with built-in overdraw, PFC single-cam system, molded grip and Superflage camo finish. There is a considerable savings by purchasing this package when compared to purchasing the parts separately.

BOW SPECIFICATIONS:
DARTON STRIKER PACKAGE
AMO Draw Length: 27- to 30-inch
Draw Weights: 50/60# and 60/70#

with 75% let-off
Bow Speed: IBO fps 277, AMO fps= 220
Axle-to Axle: 38¾-inches
SRP: $229.99

PSE BABY-G PACKAGE

One of PSE's top selling models is now available with a top-notch accessory package to make the trip from home to treestand much quicker and less stressful. Features of this bow include a split-harness string system to prevent the wheel from leaning, a Lightning One-Cam with positive draw stop, and a machined 6061 aluminum riser. The PSE Baby-G also has a wooden grip, solid Magnaglass limbs and Brush camouflage finish. The package components incorporate an FX sight, Mongoose arrow rest, stabilizer and peep, plus a one-piece quiver stocked with 4 carbon arrows.

BOW SPECIFICATIONS:
PSE BABY-G PACKAGE
AMO Draw Length: 28-, 29- and 30-inch
Draw Weights: 50/60# and 60/70# with 80% let-off
Bow Speed: IBO fps= 315, AMO fps= 246
Axle-to Axle: 36 inches
SRP: $399.99

Custom Shooting Systems Compound Hunting Bows

SWAMPMASTER

CUSTOM SHOOTING SYSTEMS (CSS) is based in Saltrock, West Virginia and offers it compound bows in more than 2,000 combinations. The buyer can select components, colors and options to create a true custom-built one-of-a-kind bow for hunting or target shooting. Imagination might be the only limiting factor. CSS also lets buyers register their bows on-line.

CHALLENGER

This CSS bow has a machined aluminum riser and soft touch molded grip or optional walnut grip. Other features for this bow include: Gordon thermal composite limbs, pro shop adjustable let-off and Mossy Oak Break-Up camo. This bow weighs 4 pounds and has a single-cam design.

BOW SPECIFICATIONS: CHALLENGER
AMO Draw Length: 25- to 33-inch
Draw Weights: 40#, 50#, 60#, 70#+ Max and Big game 80#+. Offers an adjustable let-off from 60% to 75%
Bow Speed: 310 fps IBO
Axle-to-Axle: 38, 40, 42 and 44 inches
SRP: **$625**

CONTENDER

The Contender has similar features and parts of the Challenger model, including cable guard and soft grip with walnut wood grip optional. This bow has a deflex style riser and is offered in the same colors as the Challenger and with a single-cam design.

BOW SPECIFICATIONS: CONTENDER
AMO Draw Length: 26- to 35-inch
Draw Weights: 40#, 50#, 60#, 70#+. The pro shop adjustable let-off ranges from 60% to 75%
Bow Speed: 290 fps IBO
Axle-to-Axle: 38, 40, 42 and 44 inches
SRP: **$625**

ECLIPSE

This bow is oriented around the same design as the CSS Swampmaster. This bow's features include: a T-6061 machined aluminum reflex riser, soft-touch one-piece grip, Gordon thermal composite limbs and Perimeter 1 cams. The Eclipse weighs 4 pounds and has a 7½-inch brace height. It is available in Mossy Oak Break-Up camouflage. A walnut wood grip is optional for an additional $10.

BOW SPECIFICATIONS: ECLIPSE
AMO Draw Length: 25- to 33-inch
Draw Weights: 40#, 50#, 60# and 70#+ Max. The let-off can be adjusted at the pro shop and ranges from 60% to 75%
Bow Speed: 305 fps IBO
Axle-to-Axle: 38 inches (optional 40 inches)
SRP: Starting at **$625**

SYSTEM

This CSS model uses T-6061 machined aluminum to create the riser that has soft-touch grips. Other features include perimeter 1 cam, adjustable let off, a 7¼-inch brace height and composite solid limbs. This bow is offered in Mossy Oak Break-Up.

BOW SPECIFICATIONS: SYSTEM
AMO Draw Length: 24- to 34-inch
Draw Weights: 40#, 50#, 60#, 70#+ Max and Big Game 80#. The pro shop adjustable let- off ranges from 60% to 75%
Bow Speed: 300 fps IBO
Axle-to-Axle: 38, 40, 42 and 44 inches
SRP: **$595**

SWAMPMASTER

This CSS compound hunting bow is offered only in Mossy Oak camo and is the company's flagship hunting bow. It has a T-6061 machined aluminum reflex riser, soft-touch grip, Gordon Thermal composite solid limbs and uses the perimeter 1-cam system to propel arrows. The Swampmaster weighs 3.7 pounds, has a cable guard and has a 6⅞-inch brace height.

BOW SPECIFICATIONS: SWAMPMASTER
AMO Draw Length: 24- to 30-inch
Draw Weights: 40#, 50#, 60#, 70#+; pro shop adjustable let off from 60% to 75%
Bow Speed: 300 fps IBO
Axle-to-Axle: 32 and 34 inches
SRP: **$565**

TALON

This hunting bow has the standard CSS riser, grip, cable guard and solid composite limbs with reinforced tips. It uses the perimeter 1 cam system and is offered only in Mossy Oak camo. The bow wears a distinct CSS logo on the limbs. The Talon has a 7½-inch brace height and a longer axle-to-axle length. The company markets this bow for hunters that desire a bow that will take big game without breaking the bank

BOW SPECIFICATIONS: TALON
AMO Draw Length: 24- to 31-inch
Draw Weights: 40#, 50#, 60#, 70#+. The pro shop adjustable let-off ranges from 60% to 75%
Bow Speed: 285 fps IBO
Axle-to-Axle: 36 inches
SRP: **$395**

Darton Archery Compound Hunting Bows

DARTON ARCHERY had humble beginnings more than 50 years ago under the watch of founder Ralph Darlington. The company opened its Flint, Michigan, factory doors in 1950 and designed and first manufactured arm guards, quivers, shooting gloves and finger tabs for the expanding archery industry.

Ralph's son, Rex, joined the company in 1961 and set about developing the designs and processes for manufacturing bows as the company wanted more control of the archery industry. Today Darton Archery is still under Rex's guidance.

Most Darton compounds produced today feature the patented C/P/S (Controlled Power System) single-cam design, a dual track upper control wheel with an eccentric bowstring groove and shorter bowstrings and cables to locate the nocking point near the center. All wheels are marked with easy-to-see tuning marks. Each bow is shipped with four interchangeable modules that can be changed without the use of a bow press. Darton risers are CNC machined from 6061-T6 and forged 7075-T6 aluminum. Each limb is computer designed and made with a pultruded process.

Darton offers its bows in groups such as: Premier Pro, Premier Assault, Trophy and the Action series. The premier bows are also available as tournament bows with competition colored risers and limbs and these models with elaborate paint schemes tend to cost about $100 more than the standard models. The Trophy series hunting bows are available as a ready-to-shoot package including arrows and a camouflaged coating. The Action series is an economical line and includes several starter models of youth bows.

Darton also produces and distributes the ProLine brand of bows.

DARTON'S PREMIER PRO SERIES

CYCLONE EXPRESS '3D'

Darton's Cyclone Express '3D' is designed for the highly competitive world of 3-D tournaments and the real world of bowhunting. This model incorporates a Deflexed machined riser and short limbs along with the C/P/S Express single-cam system. Its long axle-to-axle length makes it a good choice for finger shooters. Other features include limb pockets, cable guard and molded black grip. This bow is available in Superflauge camo and weighs 4.2 pounds.

BOW SPECIFICATIONS:
CYCLONE EXPRESS '3D'
AMO Draw Length: 27- to 31½-inch
Draw Weights: 50#, 60# and 70# with 80% let-off
Bow Speed: IBO fps= 304, AMO fps= 234
Axle-to Axle: 38 inches
SRP: $619.99

CYCLONE EXPRESS 'LD'

The Express 'LD' –Long Draw—shares many of the same quality features as Darton's Maverick Recurve, only with a longer deflexed machined riser. Other features include an 8-inch brace height, efficient cam/limb design, cable guard and molded grip. This bow is available in Superflauge camouflage.

BOW SPECIFICATIONS:
CYCLONE EXPRESS 'LD'
AMO Draw Length: 28- to 34¼-inch
Draw Weights: 50#, 60# and 70# with 80% let-off
Bow Speed: IBO fps= 300, AMO fps= 232
Axle-to Axle: 41¼-inches
SRP: $659.99

CYCLONE EXPRESS

Darton Archery Compound Hunting Bows

RAMPAGE EXPRESS

MAGNUM EXTREME

EXECUTIVE VEGAS

This bow features a long axle-to-axle measurement and the proven C/P/S 'SD' Single Cam System. Other specifications for this bow (model No. 9627) include a 9 ½-inch brace height—one of the archery industry's tallest— and weight of 4.3 pounds.

BOW SPECIFICATIONS: EXECUTIVE VEGAS
AMO Draw Length: 27- to 31-inch
Draw Weights: 50# and 60# with 75% let-off
Bow Speed: IBO fps= 275, AMO fps= 211
SRP: uperflage camo $659.99

EXECUTIVE VEGAS SD

The Vegas SD bow by Darton has shorter limbs and a shorter axle-to-axle length than the standard model and is available in a Superflage camo finish for hunting. Another feature of this bow is the proven C/P/S 'SD' single cam system. This model has an 8½-inch brace height, cable guard, molded black grip and weighs 4.3 pounds.

BOW SPECIFICATIONS:
EXECUTIVE VEGAS SD
AMO Draw Length: 27- to 31-inch
Draw Weights: 40#, 50#, 60# and 70# with 75% let-off
Bow Speed: IBO fps= 275, AMO fps= 211
Axle-to Axle: 41¼-inches
SRP: $749.22

RAMPAGE EXPRESS

The Rampage has a reflex machined riser with a brace height of slightly less than 7 inches. Other features include short FlexPower Limbs and the C/P/S 'Express' single-cam system. This bow is available in Darton's exclusive Superflauge camo.

BOW SPECIFICATIONS: RAMPAGE EXPRESS
AMO Draw Length: 25½- to 31¾-inch
Draw Weights: 50#, 60# and 70# with 80% let-off
Bow Speed: IBO fps= 310, AMO fps= 240
Axle-to Axle: 37¼-inches
SRP: $629.99

DARTON'S PREMIER ASSAULT SERIES

MAGNUM 33

The Magnum 33 spits out arrows at over 300 fps. Construction of the Magnum 33 starts with the C/P/S Express cam system matched with a pair of short, energy-efficient limbs utilizing high strength modulus materials. Other features include a forged aluminum riser, 7⅞-inch brace height, limb pockets and black molded grip. This hunting bow is available in Darton's Superflauge pattern and weighs 3.4 pounds.

Introduced in 2003, Darton's new Magnum Extreme is similar to the Magnum 33 in features and design and has an axle-to-axle length of 32.2 inches. The Magnum Extreme uses the CPS extreme cam system. An Avalanche model of this bow features C/P/S extreme cams.

BOW SPECIFICATIONS: MAGNUM 33
AMO Draw Length: 26¼- to 31⅜-inch
Draw Weights: 50#, 60# and 70# with 80% let-off
Bow Speed: IBO fps= 302, AMO fps= 237
Axle-to Axle: 33 inches
SRP: $549.99
Magnum Extreme
   (camouflage only) $569.99

On The Spot Records
A good way to make certain that the arrows you have match your bow is to place a small mailing label on the bow's limb with written details about it's set draw weight, length, and details about matching arrows that you own. This is very helpful if you have more than one bow and use numerous sizes of arrows. –MDF

Darton Archery Compound Hunting Bows

MAVERICK EXPRESS 'QL'

This Darton bow features the high-tech Quad Limb design along with a forged machined riser and the C/P/S 'Express' single-cam system. The Maverick Express QL also features a cable guard, 6-inch brace height and black molded grip. This bow is available in Superflauge camo and competition colors. This model weighs 3.8 pounds and was discontinued in 2003.

BOW SPECIFICATIONS:
MAVERICK EXPRESS 'QL'
AMO Draw Length: 24½- to 31-inch
Draw Weights: 50#, 60# and 70# with 80% let-off
Bow Speed: IBO fps= 314, AMO fps= 244
Axle-to Axle: 36 inches
SRP: $569.99

MAVERICK EXPRESS RECURVE

The Maverick Express 'Recurve' is actually a compound bow that features Darton's C/P/S Express single-cam system. This bow has been Darton's flagship bow. The lightweight bow–under 3.6 lbs.–has magnesium limb pockets attached to a 7075-T6 forged riser. Other features include a lightweight set of narrow, composite Recurve limbs, cable guard, and molded grip. This bow is available in Superflauge camo and Darton's competition colors.

BOW SPECIFICATIONS:
MAVERICK EXPRESS RECURVE
AMO Draw Length: 25½ to 33 inches
Draw Weights: 50#, 60# and 70# with 80% let-off
Bow Speed: IBO fps= 314, AMO fps= 244
Axle-to Axle: 38 inches
SRP: $579.99

MAVERICK RECURVE REW

This Maverick model features REW (Round Energy Wheels) technology and includes a machined forged riser and FlexPower recurve limbs. Other features include a 7-inch brace height, cable guard, and molded grip. The Maverick Recurve REW weighs 3.7 pounds and is available in Darton's Superflauge pattern.

BOW SPECIFICATIONS:
MAVERICK RECURVE REW
AMO Draw Length: 25¾- to 32⅝-inch
Draw Weights: 50#, 60# and 70# with 80% let-off
Bow Speed: IBO fps= 279, AMO fps= 219
Axle-to Axle: 44 to 44½-inches
SRP: $569.99

DARTON'S TROPHY SERIES

CHEROKEE EXPRESS

Here is an entry-level bow for short draw archers. The performance oriented Cherokee Express comes standard with the C/P/S SD single cam system for the beginner or intermediate archer looking for quality, reliability and increased performance. An added bonus is the ample draw length adjustment range. This model is built on the reliable 20K Magnesium Riser and uses power storing pultruded fiberglass limbs. Other features include: a solid one-piece riser with arrow shelf and grip, plus a cable guard, limb pockets and a camo finish. The Cherokee Express weighs 3 pounds and has a 5¾-inch brace height. The Cherokee Express was dropped from production in 2003.

BOW SPECIFICATIONS: CHEROKEE EXPRESS
AMO Draw Length: 20⅝ to 25½-inches
Draw Weights: 35# and 45# with 75% let-off
Bow Speed: IBO fps= 277, AMO fps= 220
Axle-to Axle: 32¾-inches
SRP: $219.99

MAVERICK EXPRESS 'QL'

MAVERICK EXPRESS RECURVE

EXCITER

EXCITER BLACK

EXPLORER

EXCITER

Darton is also introducing a new youth bow in 2003. This compound has many of the features found on their adult bows and can be adjusted to accommodate the needs of most short draw length archers. This bow is offered in three models. This is a serious bow for youngsters who want to pursue archery. Draw weights and lengths vary widely.

SRP: camouflaged **$279.99**
black. **$249.99**

EXPLORER

Built with a solid lightweight, tough 20K magnesium riser, the Explorer features reliable, high quality Gordon fiberglass camouflaged limbs and easy-to-draw molded eccentric wheels. Buyers have a choice of two different peak weights and adjustable Tri-Draw molded wheels.

The Explorer II has a 35# draw weight and slightly longer draw length along with 65% let-off. Both models

weigh 2.4 pounds.

BOW SPECIFICATIONS: EXPLORER
AMO Draw Length: 18- to 20-inch
Draw Weights: 25# with 65% let-off
Bow Speed: NA
Axle-to Axle: 32⅛ inches
SRP: Explorer. **$129.99**
Explorer II. **$139.99**

FURY EXPRESS

This single-cam compound uses a lightweight, machined riser along with Darton's C/P/S Express single-cam system. Other features include: interchangeable and adjustable draw length modules, cable guard and a molded grip. The Fury Express is also offered as a complete package with fiber-optic sight, bow quiver, launcher arrow rest and arrows. This model is available in TimberTop camouflage, weighs 3.8 pounds and has a 6⅛-inch brace height.

BOW SPECIFICATIONS: FURY EXPRESS
AMO Draw Length: 25 3/8- to 31 5/8-inch

Draw Weights: 50#, 60# and 70# with 80% let-off
Bow Speed: IBO fps= 301, AMO fps= 235
Axle-to Axle: 35⅛ inches
SRP: **$429.99**

FURY SD

The Fury SD is another unique design that makes Darton's C/P/S technology available to shorter draw archers. This lightweight model weighs 3.6 pounds and has a 6⅜-inch brace height. This shorter axle-to-axle length bow is available by itself or as a complete package with fiber optic sight, bow quiver, launcher rest and arrows.

BOW SPECIFICATIONS: FURY SD
AMO Draw Length: 21⅝- to 26½-inch
Draw Weights: 50#, 60# and 70# with 75% let-off
Bow Speed: NA
Axle-to Axle: 34¾-inches
SRP: **$429.99**

FURY EXPRESS

STORM

PIONEER

Manufacturing of the Pioneer starts with a solid, lightweight 20K Magnesium riser, pultruded fiberglass limbs and versatile short-draw PFC single-cam technology. The Pioneer arrives with 4 interchangeable modules and it can be made to fit the growing archer for years of shooting fun. Other features include: solid limbs, a cable guard and camouflage finish. To make things complete, a package with bow quiver, 3-pin sight and arrow rest can be added.

The Pioneer II has similar components and is available in 45# draw weight, 80% let-off and slightly longer draw length. It's designed for slightly larger built young archers. This bow weighs 2.8 pounds and has a 6-inch brace height.

BOW SPECIFICATIONS: PIONEER
AMO Draw Length: 21- to 24½-inch
Draw Weights: 35# with 75% let-off
Bow Speed: NA
Axle-to Axle: 33 inches
SRP: Pioneer $169.99
Pioneer II $199.99

STORM

Darton's Storm compound bow is a design achievement that utilizes short pultruded fiberglass limbs and a PFC single-cam system. This bow comes complete with four interchangeable draw length modules and has a cable guard and molded grip. A unique feature is camouflaged limb pockets. The Storm bow is available by itself or as a complete package with fiber-optic sight, bow quiver, launcher rest and arrows. This bow is available in TimberTop camo.

BOW SPECIFICATIONS: STORM
AMO Draw Length: 27- to 30-inch
Draw Weights: 50#, 60# and 70# with 75% let-off
Bow Speed: IBO fps= 290, AMO fps= 225
Axle-to Axle: 33½-inches
SRP: $349.99

STRIKER

This affordable bow starts with Darton's PFC single-cam technology. Features include a solid die-cast riser with a built-in overdraw and a molded grip for all weather comfort. A set of four modules are included with each bow. The bow's cable guard is positioned beneath the grip. The Striker is easy to set up and keep tuned for accurate, trouble free archery. This bow (No. 7951) is also available with a complete package that includes: fiber-optic sight, bow quiver and arrow rest. The Striker weighs 3.9 pounds, has a 7½-inch brace height and is available in TimberTop camo. This bow was discontinued in 2003.

BOW SPECIFICATIONS: STRIKER
AMO Draw Length: 27- to 30-inch
Draw Weights: 50#, 60# and 70# with 75% let-off
Bow Speed: IBO fps= 277, AMO fps= 220
Axle-to Axle: 36½-inches
SRP: $199.99

Firebrand Technologies Compound Hunting Bows

INTENSITY

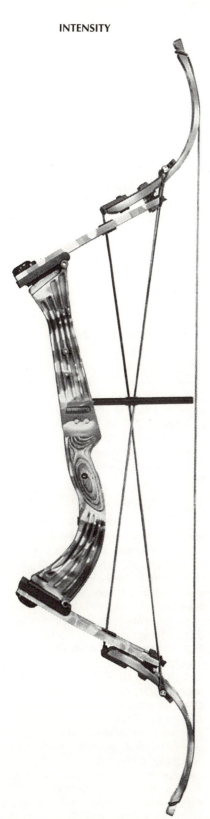

THESE BOWS HAVE NO CAMS and no eccentrics but use a riser with hinged limbs and a cable slide. Firebrand Technologies is headquartered in Fulton, New York, and offers two compound bow models to archers.

DISCOVERY BOW

The first thing you'll notice about this bow is no cams or wheels and the two-piece limbs. The bow has an aluminum riser and wooden two-piece grip. The let-off is adjustable over a wide range by moving a single set screw. Other features include: a cable guard and finish options that include Illusion and Fall Special camouflage and flat black.

BOW SPECIFICATIONS: DISCOVERY BOW
AMO Draw Length: 25 to 27, 28 to 30, and 30 to 32 inches, adjustable by 3 inches
Draw Weights: 25# to 45# or 50# to 70# with let-off from 0% to 90%
Bow Speed: up to 260 fps IBO
Tip-to-Tip: 39 inches (does not have axles and cams)
SRP:. $375

INTENSITY

The most noticeable feature about this compound bow is the ribbed riser —featuring Shadow Cast technology— that's crafted from aircraft grade aluminum and heat treated to a T-6 hardness. The riser ribs help add strength and increase the camouflage effectiveness of the bow. Other bow features include: carbon limb pockets, carbon composite limbs, machined walnut grip, weight forward riser, Saunders roller cable slide and 20-strand Dyneema cables. The Intensity by Forge has an extra wide sight window and up to 7-inch brace height. The bow is covered under an unconditional five-year warranty.

BOW SPECIFICATIONS: INTENSITY
AMO Draw Length: 25 to 27, 28 to 30, and 30 to 32 inches
Draw Weights: 25# to 45# or 50# to 70#
Bow Speed: up to 300 fps IBO
Tip-to-Tip: 43 inches (does not have axles and cams)
SRP:. $429

A Hat Trick
Wearing a hat with a brim will help you hide shiny eyeglasses and your face by casting a shadow over them. This could help keep you more concealed from wary game animals and help you see your target better.

If you will wear it while hunting or shooting, be sure to wear it while practicing to be certain the headwear does not interfere with your release.

Be certain to remember to remove the hat when it's time to get a photograph of you with your bowhunting trophy. The same shadow cast by the hat's brim can hide your face from the camera. You can also try tilting the hat back until the sun shines on your face for a picture perfect pose. –MDF

Forge Bow Company Compound Hunting Bows

DUSTER HP

F2 AND F2XL

FIRESTORM

COMPOUND BOWS BY FORGE

Bow Company offer some true industry innovations and some of the industry's longest axle-to-axle lengths. Most models are available in Autumn Leaves camouflage for hunting and various solid colors for target shooters. The company uses many limb styles throughout its lineup and a vibration dampening grip—the Anti-Vibe—with most bow models. The company uses cams with wide grooves to avoid string wear and the cams are easier to lull and can be adjusted in draw weight by changing modules. The company is based in New Berlin, Wisconsin and was founded in 1999. Their motto is: "Great Hunting Bows That Never Let You Down."

DUSTER HP AND DUSTER HB

Forge's Duster compound has a anti-vibe one-piece comfort grip, integrated cable guard and modular draw length adjustment. It has a machined aluminum riser and is available in LH and RH versions with an Autumn Leaf camo finish. The HP model has fiberglass limbs and the HB model has compression molded limbs.

BOW SPECIFICATIONS:
DUSTER HP AND DUSTER HB
AMO Draw Length: 25- to 30-inch with HP; 27- to 31½-inch with HB system
Draw Weights: 50#-60#, 60#-70# w/HP (note HB model is offered in 60#-70# only). Both styles offer 65% or 80% let-off versions.
Bow Speed: 305 fps IBO with HP; 290 fps IBO with HB
Axle-to-Axle: 32 inches with HP; 32½-inches with HB
SRP: **$459**

F2 AND F2XL

This F2 has a hybrid aluminum riser with billets, cable guard and anti-vibe one-piece grip. Other features include perimeter mass cam technology and vertical energy transfer technology incorporated into the design. This bow offers one of the archery industry's largest draw weight adjustment ranges and longest draw lengths—a popular point with finger shooters. This bow is available in left- and right-hand models and with a camouflaged coating.
BOW SPECIFICATIONS: F2 AND F2XL
AMO Draw Length: 26- to 31-inch with F2; 27- to 32-inch with F2XL system

Draw Weights: 50#-70# with F2 (Note: F2XL is offered in 55#-70# only). Both styles offer 65% or 80% let-off.
Bow Speed: 309 fps IBO with F2; 300 fps IBO with F2XL
Axle-to-Axle: 38 inches with F2; 40 inches with F2XL
SRP: **$569**

FIRESTORM

This model is similar to the Lightning Strike and has a longer axle-to-axle length. Other features include compression molded carbon and glass limbs, modular draw system, cable guard and molded grip. This bow is available in LH and RH options, in a camo finish and with a single cam or dual cam design.
BOW SPECIFICATIONS: FIRESTORM
AMO Draw Length: 25- to 28½-inch with single cam; 26- to 30-inch with double cams
Draw Weights: 40#-50#, 50#-60# with one-cam system (Note: the double cam model offers an additional 60#-70# option). Both styles offer 65% or 80% let-off options.
Bow Speed: 280 fps IBO w/ one cam; 305 fps IBO w/dual cam design
Axle-to-Axle: 35 inches one-cam; 36 inches w/dual cam
SRP: single cam **$329**
      double cam system **$299**

Forge Bow Company Compound Hunting Bows

LIGHTNING STRIKE

F34 AND PF36

X/STAR

LIGHTNING STRIKE

Forge's Lightning Strike comes with a $50 plus S&H limb exchange offer so that the bow can grow with the shooter or be upgraded without having to purchase an entire new bow. This bow features a machined aluminum riser, choice of one-cam or dual-cam layout, hardened stainless steel axles and a two-piece grip. The Lightning Strike weighs less than 3 pounds, is available in left- and right-hand models and has a camouflaged finish.

BOW SPECIFICATIONS: LIGHTNING STRIKE
AMO Draw Length: 23½- to 27½-inch with single cam; 22- to 28-inch with double cam
Draw Weights: 20#-30#, 30#-40#, 40#-50# (note double cam offers additional 50#-60#)
Bow Speed: NA
Axle-to-Axle: 33 inches one-cam, 33½-inches w/dual cam
SRP: $299

PF34 AND PF36

This Forge compound bow is offered in two axle-to-axle lengths—34 and 36 inches—and is based on an aluminum machined riser that provides a taller sight window—up to 8-inches on the PF36—and a larger grip area with the comfort grip system installed. Other features include a Forge cam and idler wheel, perimeter mass technology and cable guard. This bow offers a wider poundage adjustment range than other models. The main differences in the models are the PG fiberglass limbs on the PF34 and compression molded limbs on the PF36. According to the company, this was Forge's top seller in 2001 and is offered in LH or RH and with a camo finish.

BOW SPECIFICATIONS: PF34 AND PF36
AMO Draw Length: 25½- to 30-inch with PF34; 27- to 31¼-inch with PF36 system
Draw Weights: 45#-60#, 55#-70# with PF34 (note the PF36 model is available in 55#-70# range only). Both bows offer 65% or 80% let-off.
Bow Speed: NA
Axle-to-Axle: 34 inches with PF34; 36 inches with PF36
SRP: $539

X/STAR

Forge's X-Star series permits changing of a cable or bow string in the field without a press by alternately loosening the limb bolts. Warning: do not try this with other Forge bows or other compound bows from other manufacturers to avoid serious injury, per the company information. Forge set out to serve the tall archer with a longer draw length through the X/Star and it's mission accomplished. This bow has a 43-inch axle-to-axle length. Other features include anti-vibe grip, integrated cable guard, one-cam system and PG fiberglass limbs. This model has an 8¼-inch brace height and is offered in LH or RH models with the company's Autumn Leaves camo finish.

BOW SPECIFICATIONS: X/STAR
AMO Draw Length: 27½- to 33½-inch
Draw Weights: 50#-65#, with 58%, 65% or 80% let-off
Bow Speed: 284 fps IBO
Axle-to-Axle: 43 inches
SRP: $529

Golden Eagle Compound Hunting Bows

BRAVE SCOUT

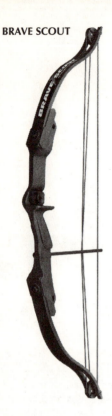

BRAVE SPORT

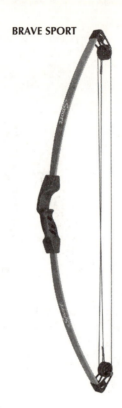

BRAVE WARRIOR

THE GOLDEN EAGLE compound bows are produced and distributed by the North American Archery Group in Gainesville, Florida. This company also produces the Jennings and Fred Bear bows. In the Golden Eagle product line, the compound bows have shown cutting-edge designs and ground-breaking innovations such as the angled riser and adjustable cams that permit the owner to make changes without using a vice or going to a pro shop. Other unique bow features that are incorporated into many models include the swing arm cable guard and weighted OneCams. The bows are known for being solidly built, easy to tune and based on innovative riser designs. Some models have evolved from the company's popular Evolution line that was released in the late 1990s. The company has worked with noted archery industry shooters Chuck Adams, Byron Ferguson and Rob Foulkrod to design and refine many of the products and nearly dozen models it offers this year.

North American Archery Group's manufacturing and assembly facility is located in Florida and open to the public for tours.

BRAVE SCOUT

This lightweight composite bow from Golden Eagle accommodates matching accessories to provide adult-scale satisfaction. It's available as a right-hand only model with Mossy Oak's Break-Up camouflage or black finish. This bow has an eye-catching yellow logo on its limb along with a cable guard and profiled grip. Buyers can sometimes spot this bow in mass merchandise retail stores but it is not a toy and should be used under adult supervision.

BOW SPECIFICATIONS: BRAVE SCOUT
AMO Draw Length: 20- and 22-inch
Draw Weight: 17-22# with 65% let-off
Axle-to Axle: 30 inches
Weight in hand: 1 lbs., 12 oz.
SRP:...................... $39

BRAVE SPORT

The Brave Scout is an entry-level basic compound bow with two lightweight composite wheels attached to the ends of limbs with brackets. Other features include a composite riser and fiberglass limbs. This bow is offered in a right-hand only model, and it arrives with two matched aluminum arrows and a paper target. The bow's color is appropriately Robin Hood Hunter Green. This and all youth bows should be used under adult supervision and guidance.

BOW SPECIFICATIONS: BRAVE SPORT
AMO Draw Length: 19-, 20- and 21-inch
Draw Weight: 15# with 50% let-off
Axle-to Axle: 30 inches
Weight in hand: 15 oz.
SRP:...................... $35

BRAVE WARRIOR

This threshold bow's 80% let-off means youngsters can use it to successfully learn about archery without a struggle. The bow's features include a Mossy Oak Break-Up finish, solid cams, cable guard and solid composite limbs and riser. It's available in a right-hand only model and as a solid black version for those opting to forgo camouflage.

BOW SPECIFICATIONS: BRAVE WARRIOR
AMO Draw Length: 23-, 24- and 25-inch, adjustable 23- to 28-inch
Draw Weight: 30-40# with 80% let-off
Axle-to Axle: 33 inches
Weight in hand: 2 lbs., 3 oz.
SRP:...................... $99

COMPOUND HUNTING

Golden Eagle Compound Hunting Bows

TITAN 38

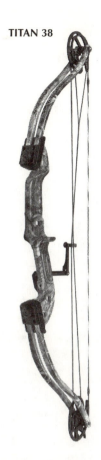

TITAN EXPRESS

CUSTOM Z-FIRE

CUSTOM TITAN EXPRESS/ TITAN 38

The Titan Express is one of the industry's longest bows with a 42.5-inch axle-to-axle length. This could be great news for finger shooters and tall archers with longer arms. This bow's features include a SwingArm II cable guard and solid 5% TurboTech cam. The Titan 38—a shorter model—utilizes a Controlled Power System that features level nock travel, Shock Stop vibration dampening technology and an all-synthetic string and harness system. Both bows feature laminated wood grips, a Realtree Hardwoods High Definition camouflage finish and are only available in right-hand models.

BOW SPECIFICATIONS: CUSTOM TITAN EXPRESS/TITAN 38

AMO Draw Length: 29 to 33-inch
Draw Weights: 65-75# (Titan 38 has 60-70#) and let-off varies
BOW SPEED: IBO FPS= 293;
AMO FPS= 231
Axle-to Axle: 42.5 inches
Weight in hand: varies
SRP: $429

CUSTOM Z-FIRE

This futuristic compound bow is designed to the purchaser's specifications at the Golden Eagle plant. Features of the Custom Z-Fire include the use of a 65% let-off ZenCam, angled natural reflex riser and four limbs. This model is available in left- and right-hand versions with Mossy Oak Break-Up camouflage. Many of the features are based upon customer selection. Price and weight may vary. This is one of the few places in the archery industry where you can have a custom hunting compound bow built to your specifications and with the components that you like.

BOW SPECIFICATIONS: CUSTOM Z-FIRE
AMO Draw Length: 28- to 30-inch;
Draw Weights: 50-60# and 60-70# with let-off dependant upon selections
Bow Speed: IBO fps = 288;
AMO fps = 230
Axle-to Axle: 34.5 inches
Weight in hand: varies
SRP: $449

EVOLUTION GOLD SET

This unique hunting bow package includes the company's carbon quad recurve limbs, magnesium riser, Gold Dot Perimeter Weighted cam system, plus sights, arrow rest, cable guard and a two-piece quiver. It's available in a right-hand only model and with the Mossy Oak Break-Up camouflage finish.

BOW SPECIFICATIONS:
EVOLUTION GOLD SET
AMO Draw Length: 30-inch; adjustable range 28 to 31 inches
Draw Weights: 50-60# and 60-70# with 75% let-off (65% optional with modules)
Bow Speed: IBO fps = 291; AMO fps = 227
Axle-to Axle: 38.5 inches
Weight in hand: 4 lbs., 5 oz.
SRP: $349

Golden Eagle Compound Hunting Bows

EVOLUTION XTR

SPLITFIRE 32 XTR

SPLITFIRE 36

EVOLUTION XTR

The Evolution by Golden Eagle incorporates a powerful MachOne OneCam with a unique tunnel design built into a magnesium riser. Other features include: carbon quad straight limbs, all-weather composite grip and a Mossy Oak Break-Up finish. This bow is offered in a right-hand model only. The Evolution series has included many models over the years and has a strong following among bowhunters.

BOW SPECIFICATIONS: EVOLUTION XTR
AMO Draw Length: 28-, 29- and 30-inch
Draw Weights: 50-60# and 60-70# with 65% let-off
Bow Speed: IBO fps= 290; AMO fp = 218
Axle-to Axle: 35.125 inches
Weight in hand: 4 lbs., 2 oz.
SRP:................... **$199**

SPARROWHAWK

This compact bow was developed for short-draw archers and young shooters. This model is legal for hunting in most states and is a great choice for small-framed beginning hunters. The Sparrowhawk's design features include power-packed carbon quad limbs, 75% let-off and the solid RapidCam system. It's available in right- and left-hand models with numerous draw lengths. This bow has a solid cable guard, magnesium riser and Mossy Oak Break-Up finish and uses a 52-inch Tech Twist string.

BOW SPECIFICATIONS: SPARROWHAWK
AMO Draw Length: 25-, 26-, 27-, 28-, 29- and 30-inch
Draw Weights: 30-40# and 40-50# with 75% let-off
Bow Speed: IBO fps= 281; AMO fps= 220
Axle-to Axle: 36.5 inches
Weight in hand: 4 lbs., 6 oz.
SRP:................... **$159**

SPLITFIRE 32 XTR

This 4-limb compound bow has an adjustable dampening system and unique 15-degree angled natural aluminum riser and modular Gold Dot cam. Ergonomic grip utilizes all-weather composite cover and is available in a right-hand model only. Other features include carbon quad straight limbs and Mossy Oak Break-Up camouflage finish.

BOW SPECIFICATIONS: SPLITFIRE 32 XTR
AMO Draw Length: 28-, 29- and 30-inch; adjustable range 27 to 31 inches

Draw Weights: 50-60# and 60-70# with 75% let-off
Bow Speed: IBO fps= 284; AMO fps= 226
Axle-to Axle: 32.75 inches
Weight in hand: 4 lbs., 4 oz.
SRP:................... **$379**

SPLITFIRE 36

This bow combines a lightweight aluminum riser with high-tech carbon limbs. Other features include a high-mount cable guard for maximum fletch clearance and a 15-degree angled Natural Series riser complete with an all-weather composite grip. The Splitfire 36 utilizes a Modular Perimeter OneCam and is covered under Golden Eagle's Solid Gold Assurance Plan. It's available as a right-hand model only in Mossy Oak Break-Up camouflage.

BOW SPECIFICATIONS: SPLITFIRE 36
AMO Draw Length: 28-, 29- and 30-inch; adjustable range 28 to 31 inches
Draw Weights: 50-60# and 60-70# with 70% let-off
Bow Speed: IBO fps = 284; AMO fps = 226
Axle-to Axle: 36 inches
Weight in hand: 4 lbs., 5 oz.
SRP:................... **$249**

High Country Archery Compound Hunting Bows

BRUTE ELITE

HIGH COUNTRY ARCHERY has been in business for 19 years and is the leader in using carbon materials—its Carbon Stealth Technology—in the construction of compound bows. Carbon is reportedly stronger than aluminum and less affected by cold and hot temperatures. The Dunlap, Tennessee, company employees more than 100 folks and runs its CNC machine 24/7 to make bow risers and parts. The company's Vibra Damp limb pockets use tech pads and limb porting to reduce noise and vibration. Limb Equalization Timing (LET) helps to further reduce any bow noise and vibration. The company holds nearly a dozen patents for archery innovations.

The Pro Series of bows are only available at authorized HCA pro shops. The HiLine and Short Draw series are available at numerous outlets.

BRUTE ELITE

This High Country compound model has 16-inch VFA limbs and standard limb pockets attached to the semi-reflexed forged and machined MR9 riser. Other features include an 8-inch brace height, one-piece grip and cable guard. These bows weigh approximately 4 pounds and are available with three cam options: Perimeter Weighted MX1 cam, Perimeter XD and D/S Hatchet cam systems. All models are available in Mossy Oak or High Country's Advanced 3-D camouflage.

BOW SPECIFICATIONS: BRUTE ELITE
AMO Draw Length: 26- to 30-inch
Draw Weights: 60# to 70#
Bow Speed: NA
Axle-to Axle: 36 inches
SRP: $455.99

CARBON 4-RUNNER AND 4-RUNNER EXTREME

These high-tech bows feature High Country's XCR1 stealth carbon riser, Vibra Damp limb pockets and the Vibra Flex V-Split limbs with LET limb stabilization technology. All models have a two-piece gray wooden grip. The shorter Extreme has 14-inch limbs and the standard 4-Runner models have 16-inch limbs. Numerous cam styles can be included with both groups of bows. All models are available in Mossy Oak or Advanced 3-D camouflage.

4-RUNNER, 4-RUNNER EXTREME AND 4-RUNNER MONSTER

These bows have the same style and cam options as the Carbon 4-Runners but are based on a forged and machined X-Rad1 riser. Of special interest is the 4-Runner Monster that can produce 80#, 90# and 100# draw weights with the round wheel-like Pro Cam and 16-inch V-Split limbs. Draw lengths range from 24 to 30 inches. SRPs for these bows start at $500.

BOW SPECIFICATIONS: CARBON 4-RUNNER
AMO Draw Length: 26- to 30-inch, and 25- to-29-inch length on the Extreme style
Draw Weights: 60# to 70#, and 50#, 60# and 70# with D/S hatchet cams
Bow Speed: NA
Axle-to Axle: 36 inches and 31 inches on the Extreme models
SRP: Both models starting at . . . $635

CARBON FORCE EXTREME

This bow has a CR2 carbon riser with a semi-reflex riser geometry and 14-inch Vibra Flex Armor V-Split limbs set in Vibra Damp limb pockets. Multiple cam options are available and the grip is a two-piece hardwood low-wrist style. HCA's Carbon Force Extreme weighs less than 3 pounds and has a 7-inch brace height. This model is available with Perimeter Weighted MX1 cams and Perimeter XD cams. All models are available in Mossy Oak or Advanced 3-D camouflage.

The Carbon Force bow is similar design and components with 29- to 33-inch draw length, 16-inch split limbs and the CR2 riser. This model weighs approximately 3 pounds and is available with the Perimeter Weighted MX1 cam, Perimeter XD and D/S hatchet cam systems. These systems provide a 39-inch axle-to-axle length.

BOW SPECIFICATIONS:
CARBON FORCE EXTREME
AMO Draw Length: 27- to 31-inch
Draw Weights: 60# to 70#
Bow Speed: NA
Axle-to Axle: 35 inches
SRP: $645.99

High Country Archery Compound Hunting Bows

LITE FORCE

The Lite Force was introduced in 2000 and is geared for ladies and young shooters. Features include the MR9 forged and machined riser with a split hardwood grip attached. The bow has 14-inch split limbs with a lifetime warranty and uses Mini Xtra-Draw one cams with XD or XL style cams. The Lite Force weighs 2.7 pounds and is coated in Mossy Oak Break-Up or Advanced 3-D camouflage.

BOW SPECIFICATIONS: LITE FORCE
AMO Draw Length: 22- to 26-inch
Draw Weights: 40# and 50#
Bow Speed: NA
Axle-to Axle: 31 inches
SRP:................... $357

MICRO QUAD

This youth and lady's bow is centered around the cast aluminum reflex designed AT2 riser by High Country. Other features include 14-inch Power Glass quad limbs, and the option of three cam systems: Perimeter Xtra-Draw, Mini XL or Pro Cam. This bow weighs less than 3 pounds and is coated with HCA standard camo colors.

BOW SPECIFICATIONS: MICRO QUAD
AMO Draw Length: 22- to 26-inch with Perimeter cams; 22- to 29-inch with the Pro Cam system
Draw Weights: 30#, 40# and 50#
Bow Speed: NA
Axle-to Axle: 31 inches
SRP: Perimeter cams......... $238
Pro Cam model $152

POWER FORCE X1

This bow utilizes a FR1 solid forged and machined riser and 16-inch solid power glass limbs to propel arrows. The power Force X1 is offered with three cam series: Perimeter Xl, D/S Hatchet and Pro cams. An optional accessory package that custom fits the bow includes sight, quiver and peep.

All models are available in Mossy Oak or Advanced 3-D camouflage.

BOW SPECIFICATIONS: POWER FORCE X1
AMO Draw Length: 23- to 33-inch
Draw Weights: 60# to 70#, and 50#, 60# and 70# with the Pro cams; 80% and 65% let-off based on cam selection
Bow Speed: NA
Axle-to Axle: 38 inches
SRP:.................... $238

QUAD RUNNER

This bow is similar to the Lite Force and has an MR10 style riser and 14-inch quad limbs and the same cam options.

BOW SPECIFICATIONS: QUAD RUNNER
AMO Draw Length: 22- to 26-inch
Draw Weights: 30#, 40# and 50#
Bow Speed: NA
Axle-to Axle: 31 inches
SRP: Starting at $346

SUPREME EXTREME

This HCA compound bow utilizes a patented, forged and machined MR11 riser along with 14-inch Vibra Flex Armor V-Split limbs set in Vibra Damp limb pockets and equipped with the L.E.T. limb stabilizing system. Multiple cam options are available and the bow has the center line idler wheel layout and a 7-inch brace height. Available cam systems include Perimeter Weighted MX1, Perimeter XD (Xtra Draw) and Perimeter XL (Xtra Lite). This bow includes a cable guard and wooden grip. All models are available in Mossy Oak or Advanced 3-D camouflage, weigh approximately 3.4 pounds and the limbs have a lifetime warranty.

BOW SPECIFICATIONS: SUPREME EXTREME
AMO Draw Length: 25- to 29-inch
Draw Weights: 60# to 70#
Bow Speed: NA
Axle-to Axle: 31 inches
SRP: $569.99

MICRO QUAD

POWER FORCE X1

ULTRA EXTREME

4-RUNNER PRO

BRUTE ELITE PRO

ULTRA EXTREME

This HCA bow series is based on a forged and machined FRM1 semi-reflexed riser and 14-inch VFA split limbs. The bows weigh approximately 3.7 pounds and are offered in two cam choices: the single-cam Perimeter XD Xtra Draw and dual cam D/S Hatchet. Both models are available in Mossy Oak or Advanced 3-D camouflage.

BOW SPECIFICATIONS: ULTRA EXTREME
AMO Draw Length: 24- to 30-inch
Draw Weights: 60# to 70#
Bow Speed: NA
Axle-to Axle: 36 inches
SRP:. $390

THE PRO SERIES

4-RUNNER EXTREME PRO AND 4-RUNNER PRO

These bows are similar to Carbon 4-Runner series except this group uses the forged and machined X-Rad1 riser instead of the carbon. Other features include: center line idler wheel, split limbs with the Lib Equalization Timing system, cable guards and wood grips. The Extreme Pro uses 16-inch limbs and yields a 7-inch brace height and the standard Pro has 14-inch limbs with a 6½-inch brace height. Cam options include HCA's Perimeter Xtra-Draw one cam and Perimeter Xtra-Lite one cam series.

The 4-Runner Pro models have 60# and 70# draw weight and a draw length ranging from 25 to 29 inches.

BOW SPECIFICATIONS:
4-RUNNER EXTREME PRO
AMO Draw Length: 25- to 29-inch

Draw Weights: 60# and 70#
Bow Speed: more than 300 fps IBO
Axle-to Axle: 31 inches on the Extreme models
SRP:. $635.99

BRUTE ELITE PRO

This bow's Vibra Damp Limb pockets are fastened to an MR9 forged and machined riser. Features of the Brute Elite Pro include LET system, Perimeter Xtra-Lite one cam, 8-inch brace height and 16-inch split limbs. This bow was introduced as a new model in 2001 and is available in Mossy Oak or Advanced 3-D camouflage.

BOW SPECIFICATIONS: BRUTE ELITE PRO
AMO Draw Length: 28- to 38-inch
Draw Weights: 60# and 70# with 65% or 80% let-off
Bow Speed: nearly 300 fps IBO
Axle-to Axle: 36 inches
SRP:. $460

CARBON 4-RUNNER PRO AND 4-RUNNER EXTREME PRO

These high-tech bows feature High Country's XCR1 stealth carbon riser, Vibra Damp limb pockets and the Vibra Flex V-Split limbs with LET limb stabilization technology. These bows use HCA's ball and socket limb mount bolts. All models have a two-piece gray wooden grip. The shorter Extreme Pro has 14-inch limbs and the standard 4-Runner Pro models have 16-inch limbs. All models use Perimeter XL cams, weigh approximately 2.6 pounds and are available in Mossy Oak or Advanced 3D camouflage.

The Carbon 4-Runner Pro has a 36-inch axle-to-axle length as a result of 16-inch limbs. It yields a 26- to 30-inch draw length and has similar components and design features of the upscale 4-Runner Extreme Pro.

BOW SPECIFICATIONS:
CARBON 4-RUNNER EXTREME PRO
AMO Draw Length: 25- to 29-inch
Draw Weights: 60# and 70#
Bow Speed: more than 300 fps IBO
Axle-to Axle: 31 inches on the Extreme models
SRP: Starting at $613.99

CARBON FORCE PRO AND CARBON FORCE EXTREME PRO

These bows have a CR2 carbon riser with a semi-reflex riser geometery and V-Split limbs set in Vibra Damp limb pockets. The bows weigh less than 3 pounds. Both models use Perimeter XL cams and are available in Mossy Oak or Advanced 3-D camouflage.

The Carbon Force Pro bow is similar design and components with 16-inch split limbs and the CR2 riser. This system provides a longer 39-inch axle-to-axle length and yields a draw length ranging from 29 to 33 inches.

BOW SPECIFICATIONS:
CARBON FORCE EXTREME PRO
AMO Draw Length: 27- to 31-inch

Draw Weights: 60# to 70#
Bow Speed: more than 300 IBO
Axle-to Axle: 35 inches
SRP:. $642

PREMIER EXTREME PRO AND PREMIER PRO

These bows are based on the forged and machined MR5 riser and feature wood grips and cable guards. Other features include Vibra Damp Pockets, center line sealed bearing idler wheels and split limbs.

The Premier Pro uses 16-inch limbs and offers a longer 38-inch axle-to-axle length. It also has 60# and 70# draw weights and a 29 to 33 inch draw length and is offered in three cam styles.

BOW SPECIFICATIONS:
PREMIER EXTREME PRO
AMO Draw Length: 22- to 31-inch
Draw Weights: 50#, 60# and 70# with Perimeter XD and XL cams
Bow Speed: more than 300 fps IBO
Axle-to Axle: 36 inches
SRP: $535.99

ULTRA EXTREME PRO

This High Country Archery compound bow was introduced in 2001 and works from an FRM1 riser with split limbs attached via the standard limb pockets. The LET limb vibration dampening system is installed and other features include a cable guard and molded one-piece grip. This bow uses the Perimeter Xtra-Lite one-cam, provides a 6½-inch brace height, and it's offered in the company's standard camouflage choices.

BOW SPECIFICATIONS: ULTRA EXTREME PRO
AMO Draw Length: 26- to 30-inch
Draw Weights: 60# and 70# with 65% or 80% let-off
Bow Speed: NA
Axle-to Axle: 36 inches
SRP: $356.99

CARBON FORCE PRO

Not A Toy
Remember that a bow and arrow are not a toy. Many bows deliver enough down range energy with an arrow to penetrate through a five gallon bucket filled with sand. That's more energy than a bullet fired from a .30-06 rifle! –MDF

BANSHEE

CYBERTEC
XT2000

HAVOCTEC
XT2000

HAVOCTEC
ZR200

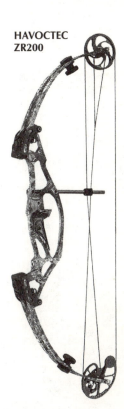

COMPOUND HUNTING

PUSHING THE LIMITS of bow-hunting technology is a continual pursuit for the engineers at Hoyt. The radically looking open riser with cross members that has become a Hoyt trademark continues to expand across the Utah based company's product line. Most of the company's bows are available with a split-limb design and with Accuwheels (two wheels), Excel (medium) or VersaCam (hard) options. Available styles on these compound bows include XT2000 limbs, XT 3000 limbs and ZR200. The company's standard camouflage color for its hunting bows is Mossy Oak Break-Up.

The company suggested that you visit a local dealer to determine their product prices since prices can vary from dealer to dealer, state to state and coast to coast.

BANSHEE

This bow is built specifically for young archers. The Banshee wheel is designed to be extremely easy to shoot and is adjustable to keep pace with growing young shooters. This bow is available in camouflage with a two-wheel configuration and cable guard. The Banshee has a 6¾-inch brace height.

BOW SPECIFICATIONS: BANSHEE
AMO Draw Length: adjustable
Draw Weights: 20# to 50#
Bow Speed: NA
Axle-to Axle: 32 inches
SRP: . . . . varies

CYBERTEC

The CyberTec compound bow uses shorter XT2000 limbs to provide greater vertical stability, and the bow's 36-inch axle-to-axle length makes it very accurate. The CyberTec also incorporates Hoyt's patented TEC design in the riser, which works like a bridge's truss to completely dampen shot vibration throughout the bow. The result is a vibration free and whisper quiet shot. Other bow features include a choice of standard, Excel cam (medium) or VersaCam (hard) to suit the shooter's preference. The CyberTec is available in Mossy Oak camouflage.

BOW SPECIFICATIONS: CYBERTEC
AMO Draw Length: From 21- to 31-inch dependant upon cam selected
Draw Weights: 40# to 80#
Bow Speed: Up to 309 fps dependant upon cam selection
Axle-to Axle: 36 inches
SRP:. . . . . varies by selection

HAVOCTEC

This lightweight (3.25 pounds), short axle-to-axle bow shoots like a dream and is patterned after the ever-popular Havoc while incorporating the patented Hoyt TEC riser design. This innovative design dampens vibration in the bow by channeling it through the truss and away from the hand. The result is an extremely quiet, smooth and accurate shot. This bow has a 7½-inch brace height and split-limb design with chrome or standard limb pockets.

BOW SPECIFICATIONS: HAVOCTEC
AMO Draw Length: 21- to 31-inch dependant upon cam and limb selection
Draw Weights: 40# to 80#
Bow Speed: From 270 to 300 fps IBO dependant upon cam and limb selection
Axle-to Axle: 31½-inches
SRP: . . . . varies by selection.

Hoyt Compound Hunting Bows

**HYPERTEC
XT2000**

**MAGNATEC
XT2000**

**MAGNATEC
ZR200**

**MT SPORT
ZR200**

HYPERTEC

The HyperTec features a shorter brace height to provide the long power stroke required for fast arrow speeds. The riser is stiff and lightweight with virtually no recoil or vibration at release. The HyperTec has a 6-inch brace height. This is a bow designed for advanced archers, so consult your local dealer to see if it's right for you.

BOW SPECIFICATIONS: HYPERTEC
AMO Draw Length: 24- to 30-inch dependant upon cam selection
Draw Weights: 40# to 80#
Bow Speed: 320 fps IBO
Axle-to Axle: 33 inches
SRP: . . . . varies

MAGNATEC

The lightweight MagnaTec was built with the bowhunter in mind and incorporates Hoyt's patented TEC design. The MagnaTec delivers a quiet and recoil-free shot. This bow is only available as a hunting bow in Mossy Oak Break Up and has a 7-inch brace height. Models available in Hoyt's XT2000 and ZR200 configurations.

BOW SPECIFICATIONS: MAGNATEC
AMO Draw Length: 21- to 32-inch based upon cam and limb selection
Draw Weights: 40# to 80#
Bow Speed: Up to 305 fps IBO.
Axle-to Axle: 35½-inches
SRP: . . . . varies

MT SPORT

The lightweight and affordable MT Sport also incorporates Hoyt's patented TEC engineering. This bow's shorter axle-to-axle length also makes it a more maneuverable bow in all hunting conditions. This bow is only available in Mossy Oak camo. The MT Sport utilizes Accuwheels and the company's ZR200 layout.

BOW SPECIFICATIONS: MT SPORT
AMO Draw Length: Available from 22 to 34 inches
Draw Weights: 40# to 80#
Bow Speed: Up to 286 fps IBO
Axle-to Axle: 34½-inches
SRP: . . . . varies

Hoyt Compound Hunting Bows

**PROTEC
XL2000**

**PROTEC
XL PRO**

**PROTEC
XL3000**

**SAPPHIRE
ZR200**

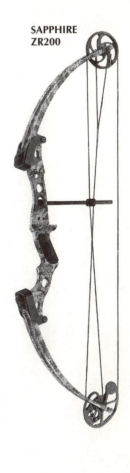

PROTEC

Hoyt's ProTec combines proven deflex geometry with a longer and stiffer riser along with the company's TEC design. This bow is available with Accuwheels, Excel cams and Versacams and with LXPRO, XT3000 and XT2000 limbs and styles. The bow's finish choices include Mossy Oak camouflage.

BOW SPECIFICATIONS: PROTEC
AMO Draw Length: 25- to 34-inch
Draw Weights: 40# to 80#
Bow Speed: Up to 290 fps IBO
Axle-to Axle: 38 to 46 inches dependant upon cam selection
SRP: . . . . varies

SAPPHIRE

This bow is designed for women and short-draw shooters. The Sapphire fully utilizes its moderately reflexed riser to provide superior speed. The specially-designed grip accommodates smaller hands and virtually eliminates hand-torque to improve shot accuracy. Available systems to move arrows include: Accuwheels, Excel and VersaCams. This bow has a standard riser (solid) and molded grip, plus a split-limb design. The Sapphire is available in Mossy Oak.

BOW SPECIFICATIONS: SAPPHIRE
AMO Draw Length: 21- to 28-inch
Draw Weights: 40# to 60#
Bow Speed: Up to 277 fps IBO
Axle-to Axle: 34¾-inches
SRP: . . . . $varies

Hoyt Compound Hunting Bows

ULTRATEC XL2000

ULTRATEC XL3000

VORTEC ZR200

UltraTec

The UltraTec's longer axle-to-axle length and shorter XT2000 limbs make this bow a solid performer. This bow is available in camouflage and has a 7-inch brace height. Models are available with Accuwheels, Excel cams, VersaCams and Hoyt's exclusive Redline cams and with XT3000 and XT2000 limb layouts.

BOW SPECIFICATIONS: ULTRATEC
AMO Draw Length: 22- to 33-inch dependant upon cam selection
Draw Weights: 40# to 80#
Bow Speed: Up to 305 fps IBO dependant upon limb and cam selection
Axle-to Axle: 38 inches
SRP: . . . . **varies**

VorTec

The VorTec features Hoyt's patented TEC riser design, which dampens shot vibration. Other features include wood grip, vibration dampening system and multiple cam options. This bow is available in Mossy Oak camouflage finish only with black limb pockets and ZR200 limb configuration. The VorTec opened the door for Hoyt's innovative risers and much of today's high-tech looks in bow design. Other cam system choices for the VorTec include Excel and VersaCam options.

BOW SPECIFICATIONS: VORTEC
AMO Draw Length: 22- to 33-inch dependant upon cam selection
Draw Weights: 40# to 80#
Bow Speed: Up to 300 fps IBO dependant upon cam selection
Axle-to Axle: 36 inches
SRP: . . . . **$varies**

CARBONMASTER XTREME

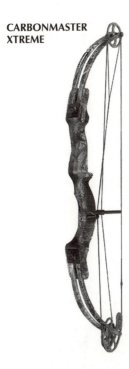

CUSTOM T-MASTER XTREME

GRANDMASTER

JENNINGS bows are produced and distributed by the Gainesville, Florida, based North American Archery Group LLC. The company and product line still wears the name of founder and archery industry leader Tom Jennings who designed numerous innovative bows during several decades of production. The Jennings line has been known through the years for top-notch mechanical performance. The high standards for these bows were assured under the watchful eye of industry pioneer Jennings. All bows are protected by a limited lifetime warranty.

CARBONMASTER XTREME

This 4-limb hunting bow has a solid cable guard and micro-adjustable brass spool in the cam for fine tuning precision. Other features include: a 93.75-inch Tech Twist string, Carbon Quad Straight limbs and a Perimeter Weighted Cam II system to propel the arrows. The Carbonmaster Xtreme uses the Shock Stop noise and vibration elimination system. This bow is available with a Realtree Hardwoods finish and in left- or right-hand versions with an all-weather composite grip.

BOW SPECIFICATIONS:
CARBONMASTER XTREME
AMO Draw Length: 27-, 28-, or 29-inch: adjustable range from

24 to 31 inches
Draw Weights: 40-50#, 50-60#, or 60-70# with 70% let-off (65% let-off optional)
Bow Speed: IBO fps= 298; AMO fps= 224
Axle-to Axle: 35.375 inches
Weight in hand: 4 lbs.
SRP: Starting at **$229**

CUSTOM T-MASTER XTREME

Here's a rare chance to have a 4-limb compound bow made to your specifications by the North American Archery Group plant in Gainesville, Florida. This custom bow's features include: a No-Torque pivoting wood grip, idler wheel mounted on ball bearings and the modular OneCam system that permits multiple draw length adjustments. Other construction features include left- or right-hand versions with the total-silence, vibration dampening limb pockets and a Mossy Oak Break-Up finish.

BOW SPECIFICATIONS:
CUSTOM T-MASTER XTREME
AMO Draw Length: 24- to 31-inch
Draw Weights: 60-70# with let-off dependant upon design selected features
Bow Speed: IBO fps= 311; AMO fps= 239
Axle-to Axle: 33½-inches

Weight in hand: varies
SRP: **$599**

GRANDMASTER

This high-tech bow was designed as a 3-D shooter and dons a camo skin in the hunting version. It has a 23-inch precision machined aluminum/titanium riser, modular cam that provides up to 8 inches of draw length adjustment and a 1-inch micro adjustment for a precision draw. The GrandMaster has Carbon Twill limbs and an adjustable dampening system that can use either a brass or titanium anodized weights to tame torque, dampen vibration and eliminate noise. This bow utilizes a SwingArm cable guard.

The GrandMaster is available in Realtree Hardwoods and left- and right-hand versions.

BOW SPECIFICATIONS: GRANDMASTER
AMO Draw Length: 27-, 28-, or 29-inch: adjustable range from 26 to 33 inches
Draw Weights: 40-50#, 50-60#, or 60-70# with 70% let-off (65% let-off optional)
Bow Speed: IBO fps = 300; AMO fps= 223
Axle-to Axle: 40½-inches
Weight in hand: 4 lbs., 5 ozs.
SRP: Starting at **$599**

Jennings Compound Hunting Bows

RACKMASTER

RACKMASTER LITE

TROPHYMASTER

RACKMASTER

This lightweight compound bow has a micro-adjustable SwingArm cable guard. Other features include the modular weighted OneCam system, ball bearing mounted idler wheel and a custom checkered hardwood grip. The riser design provides a 7½-inch brace height. The RackMaster is available in Realtree Hardwoods camouflage finish only.

BOW SPECIFICATIONS: RACKMASTER
AMO Draw Length: 27-, 28- and 29-inch; adjustable range from 24 to 31 inches.
Draw Weights: 40-50#, 50-60#, 60-70# with 70% let-off (65% let-off optional)
Bow Speed: IBO fps= 302; AMO fps= 230
Axle-to Axle: 34.375 inches
Weight in hand: 3 lbs., 10 oz.
SRP:. **$399**

RACKMASTER LITE

This hunting bow is designed for hunters with short draw lengths. Its features include: solid carbon-matrix limbs, titanium-styled Jennings hardware and a Perimeter OneCam. This bow uses a distinct blue/black Tech Twist string, has an all-weather comfort foam grip and has a solid cable guard. The Rackmaster Lite provides a 6¼-inch brace height on a machined 6061-T-6 aluminum riser. It's available in right- and left-hand versions and in Realtree Hardwoods camouflage finish.

BOW SPECIFICATIONS: RACKMASTER LITE
AMO Draw Length: 24-, 25- and 26-inch; adjustable from 22 to 26 inches.
Draw Weights: 20-30#, 30-40#, and 40-50# with 75% let-off
Bow Speed: IBO fps= 255
Axle-to Axle: 31½-inches
Weight in hand: 2 lbs., 12 oz.
SRP:. **$229**

STARMASTER

This four-limb bow utilizes a perimeter weighted cam, carbon quad limbs and machined aluminum riser to provide premium hunting performance. Other bow features include: a Mossy Oak Break-Up camouflage finish, checkered wood laminated grip and swinging cable guard. The StarMaster is available in right- and left-hand versions. This bow could be considered a top value that offers lots of technology at a bargain price.

BOW SPECIFICATIONS: STARMASTER
AMO Draw Length: 27-, 28- and 29-inch; adjustable from 25 to 32 inches.

Draw Weights: 40-50#, 50-60#, and 60-70# with 75% let-off (65% optional)
Bow Speed: IBO fps= 313; AMO fps= 234
Axle-to Axle: 38 inches
Weight in hand: 4 lbs., 10 oz.
SRP:. **$449**

TROPHYMASTER

This compact hunting bow uses Carbon Twill limbs and a modular cam to provide results oriented performance. The bow's features include: an adjustable dampening system, SwingArm cable guard, machined aluminum riser and titanium-anodized hardware. It has a checkered laminated wood grip and is available in left- and right-hand models and in Realtree Hardwoods camouflage.

BOW SPECIFICATIONS: TROPHYMASTER
AMO Draw Length: 27-, 28-, and 29-inch; adjustable range from 24 to 31 inches.
Draw Weights: 40-50#; 50-60#; and 60-70# with 70% let-off
Bow Speed: IBO fps = 308; AMO fps = 232
Axle-to Axle: 35.375 inches
Weight in hand: 4 lbs., 1 oz.
SRP: Starting at **$499**
marble finish **$549**

Martin Archery Compound Hunting Bows

ALTITUDE

MARTIN ARCHERY was founded by archery enthusiast Gail Martin and his wife, Eva. By the 1960s the business was growing and their sons, Terry and Dan, were hanging around the Walla Walla, Washington, shop so much that they soon become employees. Terry and Dan have been driving forces behind Martin's continued grow during recent years and already are being followed up by the third generation of Martin's to compete for market share in the archery industry. Through the years the company has acquired more than 2 dozen archery related patents and has produced ground breaking bow designs such as the Kam-Act bow. Today Martin's hunting bows are available in many patterns to include Mossy Oak Break-Up, Advantage Timber and the company's own Phantom camouflage.

Amazingly, the Martin factory has stood its ground at the same site for more than 50 years. Today, Martin Archery offers bows in its Pro and Gold Series.

JAGUAR

MARTIN'S PRO SERIES

ALTITUDE

Martin's Altitude compound bow is designed with the rigors of treestand hunting in mind. The short axle length is easily maneuvered through the woods and makes treestand hunting easier and more comfortable. The Altitude riser's compact design—machined from a solid aluminum block—also uses center line riser technology that allows you to hold steady and make better shots. This technology also makes the Altitude extremely smooth. Other features include solid limbs nestled in limb pockets and a black molded rubber grip. This bow weighs 3 pounds, 10 ounces and is available in Mossy Oak Break-Up and in right- or left-hand models.

BOW SPECIFICATIONS: ALTITUDE
AMO Draw Length: 24- to 29-inch
Draw Weights: 50#, 60# and 70# with 75% let-off (65% optional)
Bow Speed: 301 fps IBO
Axle-to Axle: 30 3/8-inches
SRP: Starting at **$626.64**

JAGUAR

The affordable Jaguar has a die cast riser and a short axle length. Other features include straight glass composite limbs set in limb pockets and a molded grip on this dual-cam bow. Martin's Jaguar is available in Advantage Timber, Cherry Red, or Deep Blue. This bow is offered in right-hand only.

The Jaguar Magnum is similar in design and uses the Fuzion single-cam system. This bow has wood panel grips. It's available in Mossy Oak Break-Up. The Jaguar Magnum is offered in right-hand only.

BOW SPECIFICATIONS: JAGUAR
AMO Draw Length: 25- to 31-inch
Draw Weights: 40# to 70# with 75% let-off (65% let-off optional)
Bow Speed: 291 fps IBO
Axle-to Axle: 36 3/8-inches
SRP: Starting at **$419.42**

BOW SPECIFICATIONS: JAGUAR MAGNUM
AMO Draw Length: 25- to 30-inches
Draw Weights: 50#, 60# and 70# with 75% let-off (65% optional)
Bow Speed: 310 fps IBO
Axle-to Axle: 33 1/4-inches
SRP: Starting at **$457.42**

MV2 ELITE

MV2 MAGNUM

PHANTOM MAGNUM

MV2 ELITE

The recently introduced MV2 Elite has proven itself. At the 2001 National Indoor Championships, in the hands of Martin Shooters Troy Knoll and George Ryals, it won 2 National Titles and gained one National Indoor Record. The feature packed MV2 uses Quick-Loc accessories and the VEM (Vibration Escape Module) system with dampners attached on the riser. The MV2's unique accessory attachment system makes it easier than ever to mount all your favorite hunting gear. The Quick Pin quiver system gives you a super-solid, rattle-free attachment to your bow with any Martin Direct Mount Quiver. The Lever-Loc Sight System allows the use of most any sight and permits a secure lock to The MV2 riser. Sights can be removed and replaced without affecting settings thanks to a double-pin alignment system. The lever action pulls the sight firmly against the bow and it is then locked into place against the sight bar. The quiver pin plugs into a receptacle on the riser and a knob on the opposite side is tightened to lock it into

place. The quiver easily separates from the bow. This permits users to quickly and quietly detach the quiver in a treestand without alerting game. This dual-wheel bow is available in Advantage Timber. The MV2 Elite is available in right- or left-hand models.

The MV2 Magnum bow is similar in design and uses a single cam system. It has a slightly shorter axle-to-axle length and slightly faster IBO rating and is available in Mossy Oak camouflage. This bow has an SRP less than the MV2 Elite.

BOW SPECIFICATIONS: MV2 ELITE
AMO Draw Length: 25- to 33-inch
Draw Weights: 40# to 70# with 75% let-off (65% let-off optional)
Bow Speed: 296 fps IBO
Axle-to Axle: 39⅞-inches
SRP: Starting with the Fury cams
. . . . **$1036.42**

PHANTOM

Martin's economical Phantom has a riser that is machined from a solid block of aluminum. Great attention to detail is evident in every curve and component of this bow. It's available

with Z-cams and Fuzion cams. Other features include solid limbs and wood panel grips. This bow weighs 3 pounds, 15 ounces and has a 6¾-inch brace height. The Phantom is coated with Martin Archery's own Phantom camouflage and is available in right- or left-hand models.

The Phantom bow is available in three styles. The Phantom Elite model uses Fury cams and has a long 38-inch axle-to-axle length. The Phantom Fusion uses a single cam design and has a rubber molded grip. The Phantom Magnum uses the Fusion single-cam system and has a 33-inch axle-to-axle length.

BOW SPECIFICATIONS: PHANTOM
AMO Draw Length: 25- to 32-inch
Draw Weights: 50#, 60# and 70# with 75% let-off (65% optional)
Bow Speed: 285 fps IBO
Axle-to Axle: 37¼-inches
SRP: Phantom Fuzion and Magnum,
    starting at **$506.64**
Phantom Elite with Fury cams,
    starting at **$785.06**

SCEPTER II ELITE

COUGAR

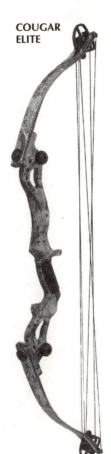

COUGAR ELITE

COUGAR MAGNUM

COMPOUND HUNTING

SCEPTER II ELITE

The Scepter II Elite is available with standard Fury cams or the popular Fury-X cams. The Scepter II Elite benefits from no limb tip torque, cam lean or cable friction. This solid limb bow is available in red, blue, or a selection of custom colors. This Martin bow is available in right- or left-hand models.

BOW SPECIFICATIONS: SCEPTER II ELITE
AMO Draw Length: 26- to 34-inch
Draw Weights: 40# to 80# with 75% let-off (65% let-off optional)
Bow Speed: 290 fps IBO
Axle-to Axle: 42 7/8-inches
SRP: Approximately **$1244.78**

SPEED FIRE MAGNUM

Martin's Speed Fire Magnum incorporates technological advancements such as the V.E.M. (Vibration Escape Module) and the Elevated Stabilizer Wing to improve the bow's feel and accuracy. Other features include: a single-cam Fuzion system,

solid limbs and a molded grip. This bow is available in Mossy Oak Break-Up and in right- or left-hand models.

BOW SPECIFICATIONS:
SPEED FIRE MAGNUM
AMO Draw Length: 25-to 30-inch
Draw Weights: 50#, 60# and 70# with 75% let-off (65% let-off optional)
Bow Speed: 301 fps IBO
Axle-to Axle: 32 inches
SRP: Starting at **$702.20**

MARTIN'S GOLD SERIES

COUGAR

Martin's Cougar has a long, sleek reflexed riser that's made from 6061-T6 aluminum. Other features include the V.E.M. (Vibration Escape Module), solid limbs set in pockets and a molded grip. The Cougar is available in two camouflage patterns, Advantage Timber and the new anodized Phantom camouflage. Fury Cams are available in high let-off and

65% let-off. This bow is also offered in right or left hand models.

The Cougar is also available in Elite, Fury-X, Fuzion and Magnum models. The Fury model uses the soft Fury Dual cam system and solid limbs and has a 42-inch axle-to-axle length. The Cougar Fuzion uses the Fuzion hard-cam system and has a 40-inch axle-to-axle length. The Magnum uses 14-inch limbs with tip reinforcements and a one-cam system. This model is available in Mossy Oak Break-Up camouflage.

BOW SPECIFICATIONS: COUGAR
AMO Draw Length: 24- to 32-inch and variable by cam selection
Draw Weights: 40# to 70# with 75% let-off (65% let-off optional)
Bow Speed: up to 310 fps IBO
Axle-to Axle: 40 1/8-inches and varies by limbs and model selection
SRP: **$710.86**

Martin Archery Compound Hunting Bows

COMPOUND HUNTING

PANTHER MAGNUM

Martin's Panther Magnum is built around a solid, machined aluminum riser that is super tough and light weight. Combine the riser with solid 14-inch limbs and the result is a very compact 33-inch axle-to-axle length. This bow has a black molded grip, weighs 3.7 pounds and has a 7¼-inch brace height. The Martin Fuzion single-cam system powers the bow that is available in Mossy Oak Break-Up. Specify right- or left-hand when selecting your bow.

BOW SPECIFICATIONS: PANTHER MAGNUM
AMO Draw Length: 26- to 31-inch and variable by cam selection
Draw Weights: 50#, 60# and 70# with 75% let-off (65% optional)
Bow Speed: 300 fps IBO
Axle-to Axle: 33⅙
SRP: Approximately $524.48

TIGER

Do you have a son, daughter, nephew, niece or grandchild that enjoys archery as much as you do?

Don't you think that child deserves equipment that is as enjoyable to shoot as your own? Check out the Martin Tiger with a solid machined riser and Mini Z-Cams that propel arrows to the target at more than 200 feet per second. Each Tiger compound bow comes complete with a full set of draw length modules that allow adjustment of draw over a 17- to 23-inch range so the bow can grow with the child. Other features include a solid cams and limbs plus a black molded grip. This bow is available in either anodized Reality camouflage and in right- or left-hand versions. The Tiger weighs approximately 2.3 pounds.

BOW SPECIFICATIONS: TIGER
AMO Draw Length: 17- to 24-inch adjustable
Draw Weights: 20#, 30# and 40# with 65% let-off
Bow Speed: 300 fps IBO
Axle-to Axle: 31½-inches
SRP: $270.70

TIGER

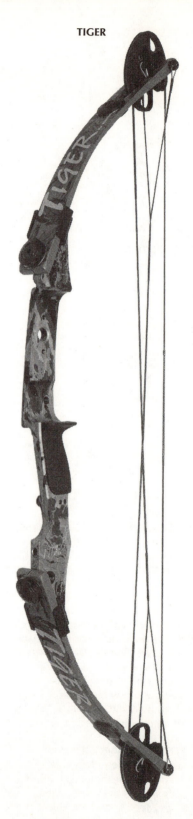

Cover Up

Suppose you've acquired the best camouflaged bow to match your bowhunting terrain, but deer look up, spot you and flee. Why does this happen?

Maybe they see your hands or face. Oils on your face can appear shiny under some lighting conditions. Wearing a facemask is one solution, but you'll need to wear the mask while practicing to make sure that it does not interfere with your release or become caught in your bowstring. The same applies to gloves—wear them while practicing if you'll wear them while hunting.

Soft leather gloves work best for getting a sure-grip on your bow and release. During warm weather you can wear fingerless gloves such as those used by weight lifters. Just be sure to wear them while practicing and be familiar with how they change you grip. –MDF

Mathews Compound Hunting Bows

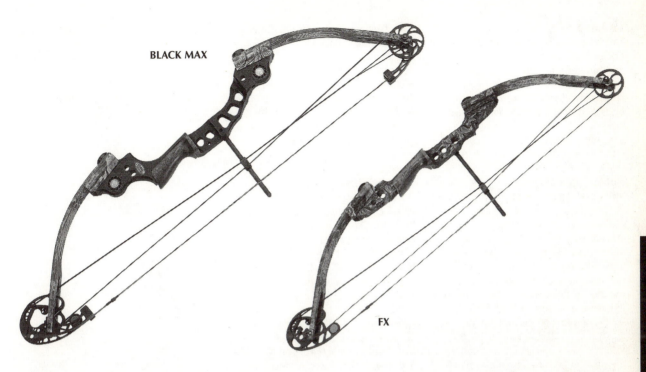

BLACK MAX

FX

MATHEWS needs no lengthy introduction to archery enthusiasts. The company's record of innovation speaks for itself with products ranging from the single cam technology to the Zebra Twist bow string. The company holds numerous patents and the rights to some of the same technology used by other archery equipment builders. In recent years the bow manufacturer released the perimeter weighted cam technology, harmonic dampening system and string suppressors. This brand of bow is also known for being lightweight and with a more open construction pattern on their innovative riser designs. Most of the Mathews bows have the company's name on the limbs in bold gold print. In recent years the company has produced and promoted the innovative Genesis bow that accommodates any beginning archer's draw length and weight. Many of the company's bows are also available in flavorable competition colors, such as blueberry, Kiwi and root beer.

An interesting fact is that this manufacturer also makes guitars, fly rods and an expedition sleeping bag under its subdivision companies! Mathews is based in Sparta, Wisconsin.

BLACK MAX

This lightweight compound, single-cam bow boasts possibly the fastest speed of any bow—a whopping 330 fps IBO. It utilizes the MaxCam system and has a flat black riser, solid limbs, cable guard and wooden grip. The bow's limbs are camouflaged with Trebark to offer a refreshing appearance in the market or they are offered as solid black limbs to match the riser.

BOW SPECIFICATIONS: BLACK MAX
AMO Draw Length: 25- to 30-inch
Draw Weights: 40# to 70# with 65% let-off
Bow Speed: 330 fps IBO; 252 fps AMO
Axle-to-Axle: 36 inches
SRP: **$699**

CONQUEST 2

This bow has a noticeably long riser for a Mathews model and even with parallel limbs it pushes a 41-inch axle-to-axle length. Other specs include: a competition one-piece grip, original MaxCam, Harmonic dampening, cable guard, a ball bearing idler wheel and Zebra Twist string. The Conquest 2 is available in Realtree Xtra camouflage. Archers with long draw lengths and finger shooters will find this bow appealing.

BOW SPECIFICATIONS: CONQUEST 2
AMO Draw Length: 28- to 32-inch; 24- to 29-inch with MiniMax cams and 28- to 32- inch with the SuperSoft cams
Draw Weights: 40# to 70# with 80%, 65% or 60% let-off
Bow Speed: 310 fps IBO; 236 fps AMO
Axle-to-Axle: 41 inches
SRP: **$429**

FX

Lightweight and short overall length best describe the FX. This Mathews creation weighs a scant 3.3 pounds and features a cable guard, solid limbs, competition one-piece grip and the original MaxCam system with weighted single cam. The riser is more standard in appearance than other Mathews' risers. The FX is offered in Realtree camo and with patented Zebra Twist strings.

BOW SPECIFICATIONS: FX
AMO Draw Length: 27- to 31-inch; 23- to 28-inch with MiniMax cams
Draw Weights: 40# to 70# with 80% or 65% let-off
Bow Speed: 308 fps IBO; 235 fps AMO
Axle-to-Axle: 34 inches
SRP: **$749**

Mathews Compound Hunting Bows

GENESIS

This Mathews bow was geared to help beginning archers learn the basics without working through complex measurements. The bow has zero let off and is adjustable from 10 to 20 pounds draw weight. Kids can't out-grow it! It features split limbs, single cam with idler wheel, limb pockets, molded grip, arrow rest and cable guard. This bow has a Realtree Xtra camouflage finish.

SRP: starting at . . . . $160.

ICON

This bow uses the concentric SoloCam—a round cam—for arrow energy. Other features include a ball-bearing idler wheel, Mathews' competition grip, Harmonic dampeners in plastic bushings, string suppressors, solid one-piece limbs and the innovative roller guard. The Icon is coated in Realtree Xtra camouflage and utilizes the parallel limb design. It also has threaded brass bushings to accept accessories such as a stabilizer below the grip. This bow has a $7^5/_8$-inch brace height and weighs 4.45 pounds.

BOW SPECIFICATIONS: ICON
AMO Draw Length: 24- to 30-inch, $27^1/_2$- to $29^1/_2$-inch half sizes
Draw Weights: 40# to 70# with 70% let-off
Bow Speed: 300 fps IBO; 225 fps AMO
Axle-to-Axle: 37 inches
SRP:. $749

LEGACY

The Mathews Legacy compound bow incorporates the latest company technology including string suppressors to reduce string vibration and noise, the roller guard that replaces the traditional cable guard and parallel limb design which was started in 1996. This bow has a wooden grip and is coated in Realtree camouflage. This flagship bow for Mathews uses the Harmonic dampening system—brass or aluminum discs inserted into the ends of the riser. The Legacy has a $7^1/_2$-inch brace height and weighs approximately 4.35 pounds.

BOW SPECIFICATIONS: LEGACY
AMO Draw Length: 24- to 30-inch, $27^1/_2$- to $29^1/_2$-inch half sizes
Draw Weights: 40# to 70# with 70% let-off

Bow Speed: 308 fps IBO; 235 fps AMO
Axle-to-Axle: 34 inches
SRP:. $699

MQ1

The MQ1 has the parallel limb design, straightline cam, a ballbearing mounted idler wheel, solid limbs and a cable guard. Other features include a wooden grip and camouflage finish. This bow weighs 3.75 pounds and has a $7^1/_2$-inch brace height.

BOW SPECIFICATIONS: MQ1
AMO Draw Length: 24- to 30-inch; $27^1/_2$- to $29^1/_2$-inch half sizes
Draw Weights: 40# to 70# with 80% or 70% let-off
Bow Speed: 308 fps IBO; 235 fps AMO
Axle-to-Axle: 37 inches
SRP:. $659

MQ-32

This bow grabbed Field & Stream's Best-of-the-Best award. The MQ-32 features a short riser and resulting short 32-inch axle-to-axle length. Other features include: straightline MaxCam, wooden grip, cable guard, Zebra twist string and solid limbs. This bow weighs only $3^1/_4$-pounds and is coated with a Mathews' camo finish.

BOW SPECIFICATIONS: MQ-32
AMO Draw Length: 24- to 30-inch; $27^1/_2$- to $29^1/_2$-inch half sizes
Draw Weights: 40# to 70# with 80% or 70% let-off
Bow Speed: 303 fps IBO; 228 fps AMO
Axle-to-Axle: 32 inches
SRP:. $599

RIVAL PRO

The Mathews Rival Pro uses a smaller MaxCam and mini idler wheel to control the string and launch arrows. Other features of this parallel limb designed bow include: long 27-inch plus riser, wooden grip, cable guard and Zebra twist string. It is camouflaged for hunting and has an 8-inch brace height.

BOW SPECIFICATIONS: RIVAL PRO
AMO Draw Length: 25- to 30-inch
Draw Weights: 40# to 70# with 65% let-off
Bow Speed: 308 fps IBO; 232 fps AMO
Axle-to-Axle: 40 inches
SRP:. $699

ICON

LEGACY

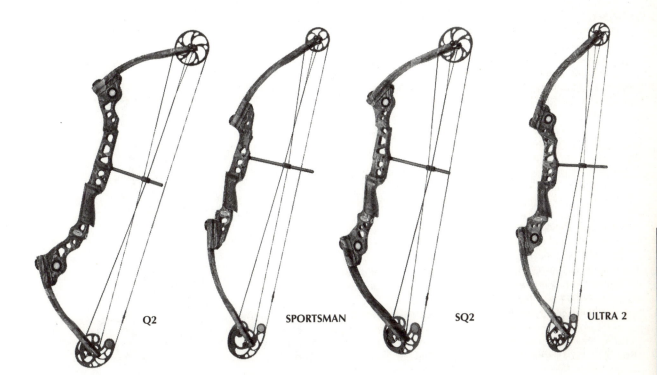

Q2   SPORTSMAN   SQ2   ULTRA 2

Q2

Mathews rates the Q2 as one of their best selling bows of all time. Features of the Q2 include: parallel limb design, Straighline MaxCam 2, Harmonic dampening system, cable guard, competition grip, and threaded brass bushings to accept accessories. It's available in Realtree Xtra camo.

BOW SPECIFICATIONS: Q2
AMO Draw Length: 23- to 30-inch; 26½- to 29½-inch half sizes
Draw Weights: 40# to 70# with 70% let-off
Bow Speed: 308 fps IBO; 235 fps AMO
Axle-to-Axle: 34 inches
SRP:. **$689**

Q2XL

Similar to the Q2 but is based on a longer 27-inch riser—compared to Q2's 23-inch riser—and made for finger shooters or those with longer draw lengths.

BOW SPECIFICATIONS: Q2XL
AMO Draw Length: 24- to 31-inch; 27½- to 30½-inch half sizes
Draw Weights: 40# to 70# with 70% let-off
Bow Speed: 308 fps IBO; 235 fps AMO

Axle-to-Axle: 38 inches
SRP:. **$699**

SPORTSMAN

This bow was developed with bow-fishermen and upland hunters in mind. It uses the fin or feather cam with perimeter weighting to create a low let off. The bow can be smoothly released at full draw or half draw without feeling a discernable let off "bump." There is no specific draw length for this bow and the same bow can be used by a wide group of shooters. Other features include Mathews' competition zebra twist string and solid limbs. The bow is coated in Realtree camo only and weighs 3.3 pounds.

BOW SPECIFICATIONS: SPORTSMAN
AMO Draw Length: 20- to 32-inch
Draw Weights: 40# to 70# with 70% let-off
Bow Speed: NA
Axle-to-Axle: 34 inches
SRP:. **$429**

SQ2

This Mathews compound bow has a short 31-inch axle-to-axle length and uses the Harmonic dampening system. Other features include: a competition

grip, cable guard, Straightline MaxCam 2, and a ball bearing idler wheel. The bow is offered in Realtree camo, has an 8½-inch brace height and weighs 3.3 pounds.

BOW SPECIFICATIONS: SQ2
AMO Draw Length: 23- to 30-inch, 26½- to 29½-inches half sizes
Draw Weights: 40# to 70# with 70% let-off
Bow Speed: 305 fps IBO; 230 fps AMO
Axle-to-Axle: 31 inches
SRP:. **$659**

ULTRA 2

This Mathews bow has features similar to the SQ2 but uses the Original MaxCam along with solid limbs and a cable guard. It's offered in Realtree camo and has a 6 ⅛-inch brace height and tips the scale at 3.7 pounds.

BOW SPECIFICATIONS: ULTRA 2
AMO Draw Length: 23- to 30-inch; 22- to 27-inch with MiniMax cams
Draw Weights: 40# to 70# with 80% or 65% let-off
Bow Speed: 320+ fps IBO (one of the industry's highest!); 245 fps AMO
Axle-to-Axle: 36 inches
SRP:. **$629**

Parker Compound Bows Compound Hunting Bows

PARKER COMPOUND BOWS is located in Spring Hill, Virginia, and was recently recognized as among the Top 500 Group for small companies and as one of the fastest growing privately-held companies in America by *Inc. Magazine*. That's big honors for any industry! The company manufactures nearly a dozen compound hunting bows and five 3-D competition models. Parker bows carry a lifetime warranty.

Parker dealers can also provide quivers, strings, fiber-optic sights, wood and Kraton grips, and carbon stabilizers for Parker bows. Other accessories include: peep sights, braided bow slings, Parker soft-side bow cases with the Parker logo, Sims limb savers, over-draws, rests and Whisker Biscuit shoot-thru arrow rests. Some bow accessories are sold together as a coordinated kit to fit on and enhance the performance of specific Parker bow models.

Parker shooting enthusiasts can also obtain Parker specialty hats, shirts, jackets and stickers. Call 540-337-5426 to order these items.

CHALLENGER

This smaller version of the popular Parker Ultra-Lite bows is designed for the shorter draw lengths of ladies and young archers. The Challenger has the same features as the Ultra-Lite series including an aluminum riser, walnut grip, and Power-Tuff composite limbs. This bow has a machined aluminum mini one-cam, cable guard and Superflauge finish.

BOW SPECIFICATIONS: CHALLENGER
AMO Draw Length: 23-, 24-, 25-, 26- and 27-inch with extra draw modules available.
Draw Weights: 30#, 40# and 50# with 10# adjustment down from set weight. 80 % let-off standard with 65% let-off optional.
Bow Speed: NA
Axle-to Axle: 32½-inches
SRP: **$319.95**

FEATHER-MAG II

The Feather-Mag uses a traditional deflex riser to provide a dependable and carefree compound bow. Most other features are same as the Ultra-Lite Pro. The Parker logo appears under the handle.
BOW SPECIFICATIONS: FEATHER-MAG II

AMO Draw Length: 26-, 27, 28-, 29-, 30-, 31-, 32- and 33-inch with extra draw modules available.
Draw Weights: 50#, 60# and 70# with 10# adjustment down from set weight. 80 % let-off standard with 65% let-off optional.
Bow Speed: 232 fps AMO; 298 fps IBO
Axle-to Axle: 37 inches
SRP: **$469.95**

FORCE-MULTIPLIER II

This radically appearing bow has a unique third idler wheel located below the grip and attached to the bottom of the machined aluminum riser. Here's a good example of archery technology expanding in new directions and this bow has helped draw attention to Parker's innovative bow line. The wheel absorbs torque to promote smooth arrow shots. This bow is available in left- and right-hand versions. The Force-Multiplier has Power Tuff composite limbs, a Force One-Cam, cable guard and a walnut wood grip. This bow has a 6-inch brace height, weighs 3.6 pounds and is covered in Superflauge.

BOW SPECIFICATIONS: FORCE-MULTIPLIER II
AMO Draw Length: 25-, 26-, 27, 28-, 29- and 30-inch with extra draw modules available.
Draw Weights: 50#, 60# and 70# with 10# adjustment down from set weight. 80 % let-off standard with 65% let-off optional.
Bow Speed: 250 fps AMO; 325 fps IBO
Axle-to Axle: 35 inches
SRP: **$599.95**

HUNTER-MAG

This one-cam compound bow is similar to the Stealth-Hunter but has a solid machined aluminum riser and black, shock-free Kraton handle. Parker's Hunter-Mag weighs 3.6 pounds and has a 7-inch brace height.

The Hunter-Mag bow is also available in a factory set-up combo with a shipping box that is suitable for use as a permanent bow case. Combo features include: a Parker quiver, four Beman carbon arrows, a fiber-optic sight, a caliper release, Quik-Tune 800 rest, pep sight, string silencers and a braided sling. The combo bows are only available in 28-, 29- and 30-inch draw lengths and as 50-60# and

HUNTER-MAG OUTFITTER COMBO

60-70# draw weights. These items have been specifically chosen to enhance the performance of and customer satisfaction with this bow.
BOW SPECIFICATIONS: HUNTER-MAG
AMO Draw Length: 25-, 26-, 27-, 28-, 29-, 30-, 31- and 32-inch with extra draw modules available.
Draw Weights: 50#, 60# and 70# with 10# adjustment down from set weight. 80 % let-off standard with 65% let-off optional.
Bow Speed: 239 fps AMO; 305 fps IBO
Axle-to Axle: 37 inches
SRP: **$319.95**
Hunter–Mag Outfitter Combo
. . . . **$429.95**

Parker Compound Bows Compound Hunting Bows

JUNIOR-MAG

**STEALTH-HUNTER
OUTFITTER**

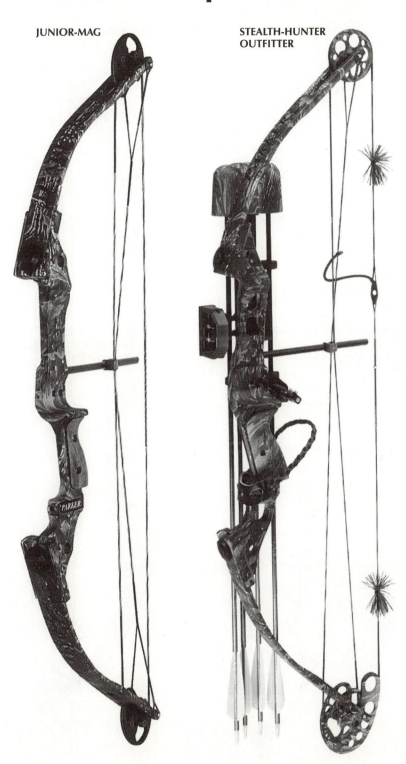

JUNIOR-MAG

The Junior-Mag is a scaled-down version of Parker's larger bows with a solid aluminum riser and with a 6-inch brace height, curved composite limbs and mini-cams. This model also has a walnut grip and Superflauge camo finish. This is a great consideration for a youth bow or a lady's first hunting bow when set at 40#.

BOW SPECIFICATIONS: JUNIOR-MAG
AMO Draw Length: 19-, 20-, 21-, 22-, 23- and 24-inch with extra draw modules available.
Draw Weights: 20#, 30# and 40# with 10# adjustment down from set weight. 80 % let-off standard with 65% let-off optional.
Bow Speed: NA
Axle-to Axle: 31½-inches
SRP: **$229.95**

STEALTH-HUNTER

This Parker compound bow was introduced in 2002 and has a sleek machined 6061 aluminum riser and unique camouflaged, shock-absorbing Kraton grip. This bow is available for left- and right-hand shooters. The Stealth-Hunter features the Super One-Cam, hand built Power-Tuff composite limbs and a Superflauge finish.

he Stealth-Hunter is also available in a factory set-up combination that includes: a Parker quiver, four Beman arrows, fiber optic sight, caliper release, Quik-Tune 1000 arrow rest, peep sight, string silencer and braided string. The unique shipping box can serve as a permanent carrying case. This factory prepared bow kit is only available in 28-, 29- and 30-inch draw lengths and as 50-60# and 60-70# draw weights.

BOW SPECIFICATIONS: STEALTH-HUNTER
AMO Draw Length: 25-, 26-, 27, 28-, 29-, 30-, 31- and 32-inch with extra draw modules available.
Draw Weights: 50#, 60# and 70# with 10# adjustment down from set weight. 80 % let-off standard with 65% let-off optional.
Bow Speed: 239 fps AMO; 305 fps IBO
Axle-to Axle: 37 inches
SRP: **$439.95**
**Stealth-Hunter Outfitter
    and case** **$549.95**

COMPOUND HUNTING

Parker Compound Bows Compound Hunting Bows

ULTRA-LITE 31

This Parker bow is available in left- and right-hand configurations with a machined 6061 aluminum riser that offers a 7-inch brace height. Other features include: power-tuff composite limbs, a super-One cam, carbon composite cable guard, crafted walnut grip and a Superflauge camouflage finish. This lightweight bow weighs only 2.9 pounds and is available in a competition model.

BOW SPECIFICATIONS: ULTRA-LITE 31
AMO Draw Length: 23-, 24-, 25-, 26-, 27, 28-, 29- and 30-inch with extra draw modules available.
Draw Weights: 50#, 60# and 70# with 10# adjustment down from set weight. 80 % let-off is standard with 65% letoff optional.
Bow Speed: 240 fps AMO; 310 fps IBO
Axle-to Axle: 31 inches
SRP: $569.95

ULTRA-LITE 35

This compound bow is similar to the Ultra-Lite 31 in design with a longer axle-to-axle length and weight of 3.1 pounds. The bow is designed to accommodate archers with a longer draw length and is available in Superflauge camouflage.

BOW SPECIFICATIONS: ULTRA-LITE 35
AMO Draw Length: 25-, 26-, 27, 28-, 29-, 30-, 31- and 32-inch with extra draw modules available.
Draw Weights: 50#, 60# and 70# with 10# adjustment down from set weight. 80 % let-off is standard with 65% let-off optional.
Bow Speed: 243 fps AMO; 300 fps IBO
Axle-to Axle: 35 inches
SRP: $569.95

ULTRA-LITE PRO

This Parker compound bow is a continuation of the Ultra-Lite series with similar features as the 31 and 35 model. The Pro model is designed for longer draw lengths, tall archers, finger shooters and for anyone who likes a longer bow. The bow weighs 3.6 pounds and is available in Superflauge camouflage. Parker's Ultra-Lite Pro is available in left- and right-hand versions and has a larger 7½-inch brace height.

BOW SPECIFICATIONS: ULTRA-LITE PRO
AMO Draw Length: 25-, 26-, 27, 28-, 29-, 30-, 31- and 32-inch with extra draw modules available.
Draw Weights: 50#, 60# and 70# with 10# adjustment down from set weight. 80 % let-off standard with 65% let-off optional.
Bow Speed: 240 fps AMO; 306 fps IBO
Axle-to Axle: 38 inches
SRP: $579.95

ULTRA-LITE 35

ULTRA-LITE 31

CORSAIR

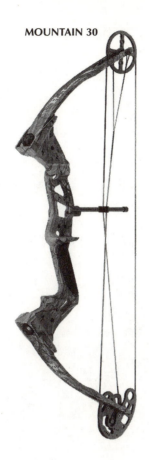

MOUNTAIN 30

RECRUIT

PROLINE'S patented cam design creates the unique Bowstring PFC (Post Feed Cam) System which not only controls nock travel, but also allows a single cam size to utilize six different draw length modules. By eliminating the third string groove on the Power Cam and using multiple post locations to control the bowstring feed out for the upper limb, ProLine is able to design greater flexibility and control into the cam system. Couple this with the company's patented tuning system and you will find one of the most cutting edge bow lines on the market.

These bows have been produced and distributed by Darton from their Michigan facility. All models are camouflaged and designed primarily for hunting applications. ProLine bows are being discontinued in 2003.

CORSAIR

The Corsair features ProLine's PFC single-cam system plus a tough, die cast magnesium riser with a built-in overdraw system. The slim throated,

snap-on grip is comfortable to shoot and hard to torque. Corsair's DualFlex limbs are high strength fiberglass with long, thick tips and deep slots. The bow has a cable guard, weighs four pounds and has a Skyline camouflage finish.

BOW SPECIFICATIONS: CORSAIR
AMO Draw Length: 26- to 31-inch
Draw Weights: 50#, 60# and 70# with 80% let-off
Bow Speed: IBO fps= 298, AMO fps= 228
Axle-to Axle: 37 3/16 inches
SRP: **$229.99**

MOUNTAIN 30

Short bows work better for some hunting situations. They are lighter, more maneuverable and make more efficient use of stored energy for a flatter shooting bow. The Mountain 30 covers this by starting with a short, CNC machined aluminum riser and adding a pair of solid, short DualFlex limbs. Next ProLine's PFC single-cam system is added along with a comfortable 8-inch brace height. Other

features include a molded handle and cable guard. This bow is available in Skyline's Excel camouflage finish.

The ProLine Mountain 32 is similar in design, construction and components and has a 32-inch axle-to-axle length. It's made for archers who want a longer bow to accommodate their longer draw length.

BOW SPECIFICATIONS: MOUNTAIN 30
AMO Draw Length: 25½- to 30-inch
Draw Weights: 50#, 60# and 70# with 80% let-off
Bow Speed: IBO fps= 290, AMO fps= 225
Axle-to Axle: 30 inches
SRP: **$499.99**
Mountain 32 . . . . **$439.99**

RECRUIT

The Recruit has single-cam technology and is designed to help young bowhunters and new archers start out with full confidence and excitement. The Recruit's features include a rugged, down-sized die-cast riser and DualForce limbs. Its single-cam

COMPOUND HUNTING

ProLine Compound Hunting Bows

SHORT STOP

SNIPER

STALKER

COMPOUND HUNTING

design includes a set of four draw length modules so you can easily custom fit this bow to the growing archer for years of enjoyable shooting. The Recruit is available alone or with an optional package that includes quiver, sight and arrow rest. This bow weighs 2.7 pounds, has a 6-inch brace height and is available in ProLine's TimberTop camo.

The Recruit II has similar features and design, plus the limbs are longer and the bow offers more pounds pull—up to 45#--with an 80% let off. To help young archers feel comfortable, and practice without tiring, the bow weighs 2.7 pounds.

BOW SPECIFICATIONS: RECRUIT
AMO Draw Length: 21- to 24½-inch
Draw Weights: 35# with 75% let-off
Bow Speed: NA
Axle-to Axle: 32 inches
SRP: $189.99

SHORT STOP
ProLine's Short Stop compound bow shares many of the Recruit's features

and this bow uses Tri-Draw Wheels along with solid limbs and a solid riser. This bow is available in black (the black limbs have ProLine's white logo emblazoned on them) and the Short Stop has a cable guard and weighs only 2.7 pounds. This bow could be one of the lightest models offered to archers today.

BOW SPECIFICATIONS: SHORT STOP
AMO Draw Length: 20- to 22-inch
Draw Weights: 30# with 65% let-off
Bow Speed: NA
Axle-to Axle: 34⅝-inches
SRP: $119.99

SNIPER
The new Sniper compound bow has a tight 33½-inch axle-to-axle length, weighs only 3½-pounds and can shoot up to 302 fps IBO. This bow has a machined aluminum riser, high mount cable guard, a 3-inch idler wheel with sealed ball bearings and a pair of solid DualFlex limbs. This bow weighs 3½-pounds and is available in Skyline's Excel camouflage.

BOW SPECIFICATIONS: SNIPER
AMO Draw Length: 25½- to 30½-inch
Draw Weights: 50#, 60# and 70# with 80% let-off
Bow Speed: IBO fps= 298, AMO fps= 228
Axle-to Axle: 33½-inches
SRP: $349.99

STALKER
The Stalker is a step up from ProLine's Sniper model. This bow has longer, high-tech two-piece QuadFlex limbs nestled into limb pockets, a 7¼-inch brace height and a longer axle-to-axle length. The Stalker weighs 3½ pounds and has a cable guard and black molded grip. The bow is finished in Skyline's Excel camouflage pattern.

BOW SPECIFICATIONS: STALKER
AMO Draw Length: 26- to 31-inch
Draw Weights: 50#, 60# and 70# with 80% let-off
Bow Speed: IBO fps= 298, AMO fps= 228
Axle-to Axle: 35¾-inches
SRP: $379.99

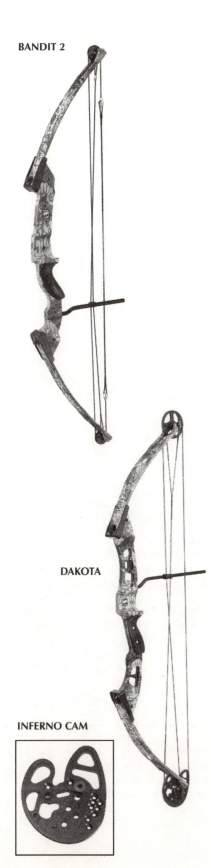

BANDIT 2

DAKOTA

INFERNO CAM

PSE (PRECISION SHOOTING EQUIPMENT) is based in Tucson, Arizona, and delivers one of the archery industry's largest lines of bows, accessories and services. The company has a popular tractor-trailer rig—complete with a fully-equipped workshop, bow parts, and all the shooting and hunting accessories—that tours the US each summer and fall to help archers tune bows, learn more about archery and hunting, and improve their skills. PSE also has a custom shop where you can get a bow built to your desired color and length. PSE's bow model line up and offered options makes it one of the most comprehensive and aggressive product lines that archers can consider today. The company offers schools for technicians, instructors and shooters.

Pete Shepley founded the company in 1971. Shepley is an avid hunter and has been featured in numerous videos and articles as he has hunted across North America and bagged numerous beasts, including a bison, with his bows.

In 2001 PSE acquired the rights to Browning archery products and continues to produce and distribute that brand of archery products.

Many PSE bow models are available in left-hand configuration for an additional $15. Some of the bow styles are available in vivid colors for competition shooting and the prices on those bows tend to run $40 to approximately $80 more. The prices listed can change if additional options are requested. Visit their web site–www.pse-archery.com–for the most up-to-date details or contact the company.

BANDIT 2

Here's another PSE youth bow that's big on features and made to successfully introduce small framed hunters and arrow enthusiasts to the thrills of archery. This bow is designed primarily for young bowhunters, and the Bandit is only available with a camouflage finish. Other construction features include: a molded wrap-around one-piece grip, solid riser and limbs and a reliable two-wheel cable system. This bow wears the PSE name, has PSE quality and is covered under the PSE warranty.

BOW SPECIFICATIONS: BANDIT 2
AMO Draw Length: 18-, 21-, 23- and 24-inch
Draw Weights: 20# in 18-inch draw, 30# and 40# in other draw lengths with 60% let-off
Bow Speed: IBO fps = 215
Axle-to Axle: 33 inches
Weight in hand: 2 lbs., 6 oz.
SRP:. $249

DAKOTA

The Dakota compound bow is designed for finger shooters who need longer axle-to-axle length bows to permit smooth finger releases and avoid string pinch. Dakota offers a slightly deflexed riser, PSE's Magnaglass limbs and three wheel options. Hunting versions are available in Brush camouflage and competition models are also available. A molded wrap-around grip ensures better control and shooter hand comfort.

BOW SPECIFICATIONS: DAKOTA INFERNO
AMO Draw Length: 27- to 31-inch in 1-inch increments.
Draw Weights: 60# and 70# with 75% let-off
Bow Speed: IBO fps = 300
Axle-to Axle: 39 inches
Weight in hand: 4 lbs., 3oz.
SRP:. $369

BOW SPECIFICATIONS: DAKOTA SYNERGY
AMO Draw Length: 28- to 30-inch in 1-inch increments.
Draw Weights: 60# and 70# with 65% let-off
Bow Speed: IBO fps = 300
Axle-to Axle: 41 inches
Weight in hand: 4 lbs., 3ozs.
SRP:. $339
   (add $15 for LH model)

BOW SPECIFICATIONS: DAKOTA SYNERGY
AMO Draw Length: 28- to 31-inch in 1-inch increments.
Draw Weights: 60# and 70# with 75% let-off
Bow Speed: IBO fps = 297
Axle-to Axle: 41 inches
Weight in hand: 4 lbs., 3 oz.
SRP:. $339
   (add $15 for LH models)

COMPOUND HUNTING

COMPOUND HUNTING

FIRESTORM

LIGHTNING CAM

MACH II

VECTOR 5 CAM

FIRESTORM LC

PSE's Firestorm was first introduced in 2001 and features an extremely short axle-to-axle length that works well for maneuvering and shooting in blinds and treestands. The bow has an 8-inch brace height and uses the company's Lightning Cam system to move arrows. The unique riser has a wrap-around solid wood grip and cable guard. This bow is available only in PSE's exclusive Brush camo finish.

BOW SPECIFICATIONS: FIRESTORM LIGHTNING CAM

AMO Draw Length: 27- to 30-inch in 1-inch increments.
Draw Weights: 50#, 60# and 70# with 80% let-off but the bow adjusts to a 65% let-off
Bow Speed: IBO fps = 300
Axle-to Axle: 30 inches
Weight in hand: 3 lbs., 10 oz.
SRP: **$669.99**

MACH II

The Mach II is sleek and very shootable. It's available in two models: the Vector 5 and the Stinger Cam version. The Mach II with the Vector 5 cam system is the tournament archery version of this model.

PSE's Mach II Stinger is available in Brush camo. This bow uses the modular Stinger Cam and has the NC Vibration Dampening System.

BOW SPECIFICATIONS: MACH II STINGER CAM

AMO Draw Length: 25- to 29-inch in 1-inch increments.
Draw Weights: 50#, 60# and 70# with 75% let-off
Bow Speed: IBO fps = 292
Axle-to Axle: 39 inches
Weight in hand: 4 lbs., 3 oz.
SRP: **$1089.99**

MONARCH

The Monarch, with PSE's Ultimate One Cam system, is a hunting model that's coated with a Brush Camo finish. This bow has a distinct solid black riser with a shoot-through center brace. Other bow features include: carbon solid limbs, arrow rest and cable guard with slide. This is a solid bow that's built to deliver years of sterling performance.

BOW SPECIFICATIONS: MONARCH ULTIMATE ONE CAM

AMO Draw Length: 26- to 31-inch in 1-inch increments.
Draw Weights: 60# and 70# with 80% let-off (65% let-off optional)
Bow Speed: IBO fps = 310
Axle-to Axle: 39 inches
Weight in hand: 4 lbs., 5 oz.
SRP: **$1169.99**

NITRO

ULTIMATE ONE
CAM

NOVA

ARSON CAM

Nitro Ultimate One Cam

This is an all-new high performance bow that provides smooth shoot-ablility. The bow's stout design incorporates a longer reflex handle and shorter limbs are mounted solidly in compact pivoting pockets. Other construction features include: NV System vibration control discs mounted on the front of the limb pockets, machined aluminum riser, a solid cable guard, Teflon coated cam and solid limbs. The Nitro is available in PSE's Autumn Brush camouflage or three vivid Color-Tech colors.

The Nitro Ultimate One Cam bow uses the Phase-3 grip system. You can use panels installed on each side of the riser, a full grip that wraps around the riser, or only the riser that has been radiused to permit hand-only shooting. This is one of the archery industry's top options for creating a true custom bow grip that suits the shooter's hand and personal preferences for feel.

Bow Specifications:
Nitro Ultimate One Cam
AMO Draw Length: 25- to 30-inch in 1-inch increments.
Draw Weights: 60# and 70# with 80% let-off (65% let-off optional)
Bow Speed: IBO fps= 314
Axle-to Axle: 36 inches
Weight in hand: 3 lbs., 10 oz.
SRP: $799.99

Nova

This compound bow by PSE has established a solid reputation as an affordable value that delivers quality in a simple, dependable package. The Nova is available with three cams: Arson, Vector Pro and Vector 5. Other features include integrated cam-lock cable guard, molded wrap around grips and solid carbon limbs. Note that the lower draw weights are available only in the shorter draw lengths in the Vector Pro model and that draw lengths are 24, 26, 28, 29 and 30 inches.

Bow Specifications: Nova Arson Cam
AMO Draw Length: 27- to 31-inch in 1-inch increments.
Draw Weights: 60# and 70# with 70% let-off
Bow Speed: IBO fps = 295
Axle-to Axle: 36½ inches

Weight in hand: 3 lbs., 12 oz.
SRP: $269
   (add $15 for LH models)

Bow Specifications: Nova Vector Pro
AMO Draw Length: 24- to 30-inch in 1-inch increments.
Draw Weights: 30#, 40#, 50#, 60# and 70# with 75% let-off
Bow Speed: IBO fps = 280
Axle-to Axle: 38 inches
Weight in hand: 3 lbs., 9 oz.
SRP: $249
   (add $15 for LH models)

Bow Specifications: Nova Vector 5
AMO Draw Length: 26- to 30-inch in 1-inch increments.
Draw Weights: 50# (26-inch draw length only), 60# and 70# with 65% let-off
Bow Speed: IBO fps = 275
Axle-to Axle: 39 inches
Weight in hand: 3 lbs., 9 oz.
SRP: $249
   (add $15 for LH models)

PSE Compound Hunting Bows

QUANTAM

SPYDER

STINGER CAM

**TEAM FITZGERALD
NOVA STAGE 3**

QUANTAM ULTIMATE ONE CAM

PSE's Quantum delivers a revolutionary design with a unique riser design that offers unequalled stability for the archer. This high-tech bow incorporates sleek lines and a trimline design to improve performance. This compound bow has a distinct multi-port vent system on the riser's upper and lower sections, plus solid limbs and cam. The Quantum Ultimate One Cam can use the Phase-3 grip system and is available in Brush camo. The Quantam's riser provides a 7½-inch brace height and the NV vibration dampening system can be installed.

BOW SPECIFICATIONS:
QUANTAM ULTIMATE ONE CAM
AMO Draw Length: 27- to 32-inch in 1-inch increments.
Draw Weights: 60# and 70# with 80% let-off (65% let-off optional)
Bow Speed: IBO fps = 305
Axle-to Axle: 39 inches
Weight in hand: 3 lbs., 10 oz.
SRP: **$799.99**

SPYDER

PSE's Spyder is designed for short-draw archers and can be adjusted across more than 5 inches of draw length. Other features for this compound bow include: a lightweight machined aluminum riser, integrated cam-lock cable guard, molded TRM grip and the

Stinger cam system. This bow has a 6¾-inch brace height and wears a distinctive PSE logo. The Spyder's shorter draw lengths and lighter draw weight combinations make this a great youth and lady's bow. The bow is available in Brush camo and blue colors.

The IBO speed for this bow was determined by shooting a 27-inch draw length.

BOW SPECIFICATIONS: SPYDER STINGER CAM
AMO Draw Length: 23- to 27-inch in 1-inch increments.
Draw Weights: 40#, 50# and 60# with 75% let-off
Bow Speed: IBO fps = 275
Axle-to Axle: 35 inches
Weight in hand: 3 lbs., 5 oz.
SRP: **$339**
  (add $15 for LH models)

SPYDER S4

A youth bow that's full of adult features best describes this compound bow. The Spyder S4 has a deflexed riser, molded composite wrap-around grip and cable guard. It utilizes solid limbs and is available in camouflage.

BOW SPECIFICATIONS: SPYDER S4
AMO Draw Length: 19- or 23-inch only.
Draw Weights: 20# in 19-inch draw, 30# and 40# in 23-inch draw with 65% let-off

Bow Speed: IBO fps = 240
Axle-to Axle: 32 inches
Weight in hand: 2 lbs., 6 oz.
SRP: **$179.99**

TEAM FITZGERALD NOVA STAGE 3

This package bow is endorsed by famed bowhunting advocates Dan Fitzgerald and Guy Fitzgerald and built by PSE. The bow package includes a two-prong arrow rest, fiber optic sight with clear pin guard, and one-piece arrow quiver. Other features include: a solid riser, wrap-around grip, cable guard and solid limbs. This bow is available only in PSE brush camouflage and with two-wheel technology. Other hunting related Fitzgerald products are available if you desire to increase the shooter's thrill and enthusiasm level. Just add arrows and start hunting!

BOW SPECIFICATIONS: TEAM FITZGERALD NOVA STAGE 3
AMO Draw Length: 24-, 27- and 29-inch.
Draw Weights: 40# (24-inch), 55# (27-inch) and 65# (29-inch) with 65% let-off
Bow Speed: IBO fps = 265
Axle-to Axle: 38 inches
Weight in hand: 3 lbs., 9 oz.
SRP: **$239.99**
  (add $15 for LH models)

COMPOUND HUNTING

THUNDERBOLT

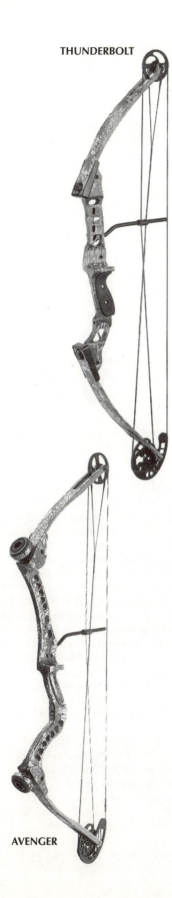

AVENGER

THUNDERBOLT

This lightweight and super fast bow is available with three powerful wheel options: Maxis HL, Lightning Cam and Stinger Cam systems. The Maxis cam provides traditional twin-cam technology with high let-off. The highly-adjustable Stinger cam features a pivoting module for easy draw length adjustment. The legendary Lightning cam delivers fast arrow speeds and flat trajectory. This bow uses MagnaGlass limbs and has a molded one-piece wrap around grip and cable guard. The Maxis model is available in Brush camo finish only and the Lightning cam and Stinger cam models are available in blue.

BOW SPECIFICATIONS: THUNDERBOLT LIGHTNING CAM

AMO Draw Length: 27- to 31-inch in 1-inch increments.
Draw Weights: 50#, 60# and 70# with 80% let-off but the bow adjusts to 65% let-off
Bow Speed: IBO fps = 300
Axle-to Axle: 36 inches
Weight in hand: 3 lbs., 9 oz.
SRP: $419.99

BOW SPECIFICATIONS: THUNDERBOLT MAXIS HIGH LET-OFF

AMO Draw Length: 26- to 30-inch in 1-inch increments.
Draw Weights: 50# (available in 26-inch draw length only), 60# and 70# with 75% let-off
Bow Speed: IBO fps = 300
Axle-to Axle: 38 inches
Weight in hand: 3 lbs., 9 oz.
SRP: $419
   (Add $15 for LH version)

BOW SPECIFICATIONS: THUNDERBOLT STINGER CAM

AMO Draw Length: 23- to 27-inch in 1-inch increments.
Draw Weights: 40#, 50# and 60# with 75% let-off

Bow Speed: IBO fps = 278
Axle-to Axle: 37½-inches
Weight in hand: 3 lbs., 9 oz.
SRP: $419

PSE PRO SERIES

The following PSE bows are part of the company's Pro Series and feature up-graded grips, upgraded strings and performance enhancing components in most models. These bows are developed with the advanced archer in mind.

AVENGER

With a unibody construction providing a machined one-piece riser and limb pockets combination, the Avenger provides un-compromised limb alignment. Other construction features include: PSE's NV System for vibration reduction, Phase-3 grip system and a Color-Tech Autumn Brush camouflage finish. PSE takes great pride and care in the finish of their bows and the new Color-Tech system seems to show this attention to detail. The Avenger's Phase -3 grip system permits the changing of panels or to a full grip or to no grip with the use of the bare radiused grip if desired—a true custom feel and hand fit. The bow's Ultimate One-Cam can be converted to a 65% let-off, has easily changed modular draw stop adjustments, a built in draw stop and is Teflon coated. This bow is available in RH only.

BOW SPECIFICATIONS: AVENGER ULTIMATE ONE-CAM

AMO Draw Length: 26- to 31-inch in 1-inch increments.
Draw Weights: 60# and 70# with 80% let-off (65% let-off optional)
Bow Speed: IBO fps = 305
Axle-to Axle: 37 inches
Weight in hand: 3 lbs., 15 oz.
SRP: $799.99

PSE Compound Hunting Bows

SYNERGY PRO 65 CAM

BEAST

DIAMONDBACK II

ENFORCER

BEAST

The Beast was unleashed with a new machined aluminum riser in 2002 and offers three cam options: Inferno, Synergy Pro 65 and Synergy Pro 75. This bow is geared toward perform-ance minded archers or hunters who also seek value. Other features include: an upper cable guard, 7–inch brace height, limb pockets securing solid limbs and a molded grip. The 40# and 50# draw weights are only available in the 26-inch draw length model. The Beast is also available only in PSE's Brush camouflage. LH models are available for an additional $15.

BOW SPECIFICATIONS: BEAST INFERNO CAM
AMO Draw Length: 27- to 31-inch in 1-inch increments.
Draw Weights: 60# and 70# with 75% let-off
Bow Speed: IBO fps = 290
Axle-to Axle: 36½-inches.
Weight in hand: 3 lbs., 10 oz.
SRP: $369.99

BOW SPECIFICATIONS: BEAST SYNERGY PRO 65
AMO Draw Length: 26- to 30-inch in 1-inch increments.
Draw Weights: 40#, 50#, 60# and 70# with 65% let-off

Bow Speed: IBO fps = 295
Axle-to Axle: 39 inches
Weight in hand: 3 lbs., 8 oz.
SRP: $249.99

BOW SPECIFICATIONS: BEAST SYNERGY PRO 75
AMO Draw Length: 26- to 30-inch in 1-inch increments.
Draw Weights: 40#, 50#, 60# and 70# with 75% let-off
Bow Speed: IBO fps = 290
Axle-to Axle: 39 inches
Weight in hand: 3 lbs., 8 oz.
SRP: $249.99

DIAMONDBACK II

This camouflaged compound hunting bow is the result of unequalled quality meeting incredible value. Features of the Diamondback II include: solid limbs, PSE's Lightning cam, a solid molded grip and an upper cable guard.
BOW SPECIFICATIONS: DIAMONDBACK II
AMO Draw Length: 27- to 31-inch in 1-inch increments.
Draw Weights: 60# and 70#; 80% let-off, adjusts to 65% let-off
Bow Speed: IBO fps = 305
Axle-to Axle: 36½-inches
Weight in hand: 3 lbs., 9 oz.
SRP: $419.99

(additional $15 for LH models)

ENFORCER

The unique unibody machined riser and partially reflexed riser with angled grip give this bow a space age appearance and advanced per-formance capabilities. The Enforcer offers sleek lines, lightweight construction and vibration-free performance. Other features include: PSE's Ultimate One-Cam system with 6 changeable modules, NV vibration reduction, Autumn Brush camouflage finish, and Phase-3 grip system. This hunting oriented compound bow also has a one-piece upper cable guard and solid limbs.
BOW SPECIFICATIONS: ENFORCER ULTIMATE ONE-CAM
AMO Draw Length: 26- to 31-inch in 1-inch increments.
Draw Weights: 60# and 70# with 80% let-off (65% let-off optional)
Bow Speed: IBO fps = 300
Axle-to Axle: 34 inches
Weight in hand: 4 lbs., 2 oz.
SRP: $799.99
   (add $15 for LH models)

MACH 10

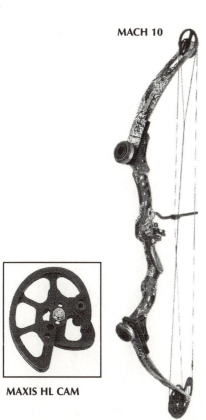

OUTLAW

STINGRAY

MAXIS HL CAM

MACH 10

This Pro Series compound bow uses PSE's Ultimate One-Cam system and NV vibration dampening system to deliver tack-driving accuracy and increased shooter comfort. Other features include: a Micro-Adjust two-prong rest, upper cable guard, Phase 3 grip system and PSE's Pivoting Limb Pockets. It's also available in PSE's Autumn brush only in the Maxis HL model. This bow is available in right-hand models only.

BOW SPECIFICATIONS: MACH 10 ULTIMATE ONE-CAM

AMO Draw Length: 26- to 31-inch in 1-inch increments.
Draw Weights: 60# and 70# with 80% let-off (65% let-off optional).
Bow Speed: IBO fps = 311
Axle-to Axle: 38 inches
Weight in hand: 4 lbs., 8 oz.
SRP: $999.99

BOW SPECIFICATIONS: MACH 10 MAXIS HL

AMO Draw Length: 27- to 30-inch in 1-inch increments.
Draw Weights: 60# and 70# with

75% let-off
Bow Speed: IBO fps = 307
Axle-to Axle: 39 inches
Weight in hand: 4 lbs., 8 oz.
SRP: $999.99

OUTLAW

The Outlaw was designed with one purpose: Getting youth interested and involved in archery. To meet this goal the bow is big on features and performance and low on price. Outlaw's features include: a mildly deflexed riser, PSE's 535 Magnaglass limbs, and the adjustable Synergy 4-cam system. Other features include: a lower cable guard, molded one-piece composite grip and an Autumn Brush camouflage finish. This bow is lightweight and offered at a low draw weight so that almost any youngster could pick it up and immediately have fun for a long period of time without tiring.

BOW SPECIFICATIONS: OUTLAW

AMO Draw Length: 20-inch
Draw Weights: 25# with 70% let-off
Bow Speed: IBO fps = 210
Axle-to Axle: 32½-inches

Weight in hand: 2 lbs., 4 oz.
SRP: $199.99

STINGRAY

The Stingray is a compact, lightweight bow—approximately 3 pounds!—that's highly maneuverable and easy to carry while in the field and hunting. This bow features a PSE Lightning cam system, narrow profile TRM grip and laid-back limb angle. Other features include: an upper cable guard, solid one-piece wooden grip and solid limbs securely anchored in sturdy limb pockets. This bow is available with the Autumn Brush finish.

BOW SPECIFICATIONS: STINGRAY LIGHTNING CAM

AMO Draw Length: 26- to 30-inches in 1-inch increments.
Draw Weights: 60# and 70# with 80% let-off and it adjusts to 65% let-off
Bow Speed: IBO fps = 305
Axle-to Axle: 32 inches
Weight in hand: 3 lbs., 2 oz.
SRP: $619.99
    (additional $15 for LH models)

COMPOUND HUNTING

PSE Compound Hunting Bows

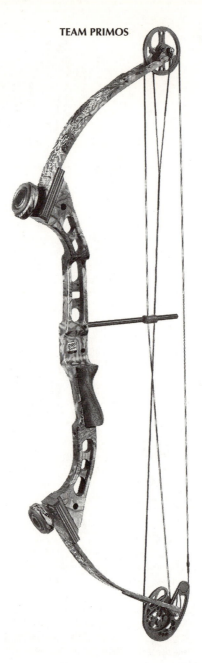

TEAM PRIMOS

XCELLERATOR

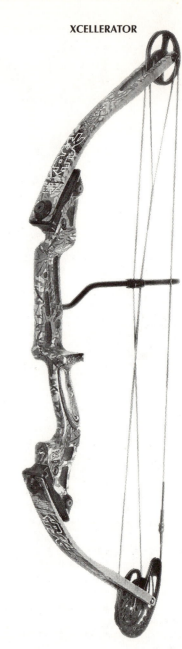

TEAM PRIMOS

This hunting oriented compound bow is endorsed by professional critter caller and call manufacturer Will Primos of Mississippi. Construction features include: a longer length, more than 40-inches overall, and a high brace height —7½-inches—that combine to create a fast bow that shoots with unbelievable forgiveness. Other features include: the NC vibration suppression system, Ultimate One-Cam with changeable parts, solid wood one-piece grip, solid limbs and an upper cable guard. The team Primos compound bow is available in PSE Autumn Brush camouflaged finish only. This is a good choice for any hunter with a long draw length and who wants a combination of speed and performance in a lightweight bow.

BOW SPECIFICATIONS: TEAM PRIMOS ULTIMATE ONE-CAM

AMO Draw Length: 27- to 32-inch in 1-inch increments.
Draw Weights: 60# and 70# with 80% let-off (65% let-off optional)
Bow Speed: IBO fps = 308
Axle-to Axle: 38 inches
Weight in hand: 3 lbs., 12 oz.
SRP: **$699.99**
(additional $15 for LH models)

XCELLERATOR

Exhaustive hours of attention to detail and painstaking design considerations have been invested into the Xcellerator. This bow has an all new pivoting limb pocket for unequalled adjustability and excellent limb alignment. Other design features include: a moderately reflexed short riser, Ultimate One-Cam eccentric, Phase-3 grip system and an upper cable guard. The Xcellerator has a large 7¾-inch brace height and solid limbs. This is a hunting bow that proudly wears the Autumn Brush finish with PSE's Color-Tech contrast enhancement and increased durability.

BOW SPECIFICATIONS: XCELLERATOR ULTIMATE ONE-CAM

AMO Draw Length: 25- to 30-inch in 1-inch increments.
Draw Weights: 60# and 70# with 80% let-off (65% let-off optional)
Bow Speed: IBO fps = 302
Axle-to Axle: 32½-inches
Weight in hand: 4 lbs., 3 oz.
SRP: **$749**
(add $15 for LH models)

The Proper Stance
To correctly shoot a bow, stand with your body at a right angle to the target and draw the arrow across your chest. Your feet should be shoulder width apart and your pulling arm should be parallel to the ground.—MDF

BIGHORN

CARIBOU

DENALI

REFLEX is a Hoyt bow company subsidiary that offers more mainstream designs when compared to Hoyt's radically appearing bridged risers and aggressive cam systems. Reflex compound bows are marketed as rugged and affordable bows for hunters who hunt hard and travel the extra mile to earn success. Reflex bows are sold at numerous outlets and all models are camouflaged and designed for hunting applications. Most models were designed with assistance from Chuck Adams. Reflex is based in Salt Lake City, Utah.

When pricing Reflex bows, the company reports that prices vary from dealer to dealer and coast to coast. The dealer has the final nod in determining the price so the company does not normally provide a suggested retail price. Call your local Hoyt/Reflex Dealer for more details.

BIGHORN

This hunting-oriented compound bow is coated with a durable camouflage finish that will help it blend in at many hunting sites. The Bighorn features a dual-cam system with solid limbs. Other specifications include: a 7⅝-inch brace height, cable guard with roller and black molded grip.

BOW SPECIFICATIONS: BIGHORN
AMO Draw Length: 25- to 28½-inch or 28½- to 32-inch
Draw Weights: 40# to 50#, 50# to 60#, or 60# to 70#, with 75% let-off
Bow Speed: NA
Axle-to Axle: 40 inches
SRP: Starting at **$220**

CARIBOU

This Reflex compound bow has a 9-inch brace height—one of the industry's biggest—and features an aluminum riser, split limbs and round wheel cams. This bow also has a molded grip, cable guard and unique limb pockets with a lip.

BOW SPECIFICATIONS: CARIBOU

AMO Draw Length: 28- to 31-inch adjustable
Draw Weights: 50# to 60#, or 60# to 70# with 65% let-off
Bow Speed: NA
Axle-to Axle: 45⅝-inches
SRP: . . . . . **varies by dealer and state**

DENALI

This compound bow continues Reflex's hunting line. It's very similar in components and design to the Tundra and Falcon models with split limbs, an aluminum riser and single-cam system. The Denali's shorter length increases its maneuverability in hunting situations. This bow has an 8½-inch brace height and is camouflaged.

BOW SPECIFICATIONS: DENALI
AMO Draw Length: 27½- to 30½-inch adjustable
Draw Weights: 50# to 60#, or 60# to 70# with 60% to 75% adjustable let-off
Bow Speed: NA
Axle-to Axle: 34 inches
SRP: Starting at **$450**

Reflex Compound Hunting Bows

FALCON   PROWLER   TETON   TUNDRA

 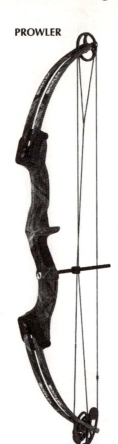  

FALCON

This Reflex model has a similar design and components of the Tundra. The cable guard has a roller bearing and the limb pockets are black and contrast against the bow's camo coating.

BOW SPECIFICATIONS: FALCON
AMO Draw Length: 27½- to 30½-inch adjustable
Draw Weights: 50# to 60#, or 60# to 70# with 60% to 75% adjustable let-off
Bow Speed: NA
Axle-to Axle: 36 inches
SRP: Starting at **$437**

PROWLER

The Prowler is an affordable compound bow that offers single-cam technology to archery enthusiasts. Its features include: split limbs, a weighted single cam and idler wheel system to propel arrows, and an under-the-grip cable guard. This bow's magnesium riser—

with a 7¼-inch brace height—is thicker than most Reflex models and has a unique camo finish.

BOW SPECIFICATIONS: PROWLER
AMO Draw Length: 27½- to 30½-inch adjustable
Draw Weights: 50# to 60#, or 60# to 70# with 60% to 75% adjustable let-off
Bow Speed: NA
Axle-to Axle: 38 inches
SRP: Starting at **$270**

TETON

This model is similar in design and components to Reflex's Prowler—including magnesium riser— but with dual cam technology. It's available with a camouflage finish and has a 6⅜-inch brace height.

BOW SPECIFICATIONS: TETON
AMO Draw Length: 27- to 30-inch adjustable
Draw Weights: 50# to 60#, or 60#

to 70#, with 75% let-off
Bow Speed: NA
Axle-to Axle: 38 inches
SRP: Staring at **$210**

TUNDRA

The Tundra comes with a camouflage finish and long aluminum riser. This bow also has split limbs nestled into limb pockets, a single-cam design that includes a weighted cam and idler wheel, plus a molded grip and cable guard. The Tundra has a 7⅜-inch brace height.

BOW SPECIFICATIONS: TUNDRA
AMO Draw Length: 27½- to 30½-inch adjustable
Draw Weights: 50# to 60#, or 60# to 70# with 60% to 75% adjustable let-off
Bow Speed: NA
Axle-to Axle: 38 inches
SRP: Starting at **$437**

FISHMASTER

KOMBOW

LS II 1 CAM

THIS WISCONSIN-BASED archery manufacturer has been coming on strong in the industry by gaining a growing legion of followers. Renegade currently offers seven compound and three recurve models to meet the needs of any archer. All bows are designed for hunting applications and the staff tests these products in the field and on the archery range. Almost all Renegade compound bows have an enlarged limb tip section to increase the limb's sturdiness and dependability.

Renegade also offers hats, shirts, soft-sided bow cases and a collectors hunting knife. Visit your local dealer for available items and prices. The company's logo is "Bows for Tomorrow and Today."

FISHMASTER EZ-1 SOLO WHEEL

Don't let the name of this bowfishing oriented bow fool you, this bow is designed for hunting also. Features include a machined aluminum deflex riser, one-piece wood grip, PTS limbs anchored in a limb pocket, upper cable guard, and accommodating large 7⅞ brace height. Renegades'

Fishmaster bow is coated in Mossy Oak Break-Up and utilizes the company's EZ-1 solo wheel system.

BOW SPECIFICATIONS:
FISHMASTER EZ-1 SOLO WHEEL
AMO Draw Length: 27- to 30-inch
Draw Weights: 50# with 75% let-off
Bow Speed: IBO fps = NA
Axle-to Axle: 33½-inches
Weight in hand: 3.4 lbs.
SRP:. $439

KOMBOW

The Kombow is designed by Renegade to serve the needs of finger and release shooters. It has a machined aluminum deflex riser that provides more than 8 inches of brace height. Other features include a comfortable wood grip, cable guard, PTS solid limbs and mossy Oak Break-Up finish.

The EZ-1 Solo Wheel Kombow model has a 37-inch axle-to-axle length, 28- to 31-inch draw length and 75% let-off.

BOW SPECIFICATIONS: KOMBOW 1 CAM
AMO Draw Length: 27- to 33-inch
Draw Weights: 60# or 70# with 80% or 65% let-off

Bow Speed: IBO fps = NA
Axle-to Axle: 36 inches
Weight in hand: 3.2 lbs.
SRP:. $439

LS-II 1 CAM

Renegade's LS-II is designed to help introduce youth, ladies and small-framed archers to bowhunting and to the sport of archery in an affordable manner. While this lightweight bow is smaller scaled, it incorporates many features found on full-sized bows like a wooden grip, cable guard, 1 Cam system and machined aluminum reflex riser. The bow also has PTS solid limbs and is coated with Realtree Hardwoods camouflage.

BOW SPECIFICATIONS: LS II 1 CAM
AMO Draw Length: 23- to 27-inch
Draw Weights: 30#, 40# and 50# with 65% let-off
Bow Speed: IBO fps = NA
Axle-to Axle: 32 inches
Weight in hand: 3 lbs.
SRP:. $329

Renegade Compound Hunting Bows

NON TYPICAL XL

SBD

TOMINATOR II

TROPHY RAC PLUS

NON TYPICAL XL

The Non Typical is one of the longest compound bows on the market today —41-inch axle-to-axle length— and is sure to attract the attention of finger shooters. The bow is available in the 1 Cam or EZ-1 Solo wheel systems and has a machined aluminum deflexed riser, wooden one-piece grip and solid limbs. Both models have large 9-inch plus brace heights. Renegade's Non Typical bow is coated in Mossy Oak Break-Up camouflage and uses a 104-inch string.

The EZ-1 Solo Wheel model offers 30- to 33-inch draw lengths and 75% let-off.

BOW SPECIFICATIONS:
NON TYPICAL XL 1 CAM
AMO Draw Length: 29- to 36-inch
Draw Weights: 60 or 70 pounds; 80% or 65% let-off
Bow Speed: IBO fps = NA
Axle-to Axle: 41 inches
Weight in hand: 4 lbs.
SRP:. **$459**

SBD

This new Renegade bow was introduced in 2002 and weighs in at 3 pounds. It has a short axle-to-axle length, one-piece wood grip, PTS solid limbs, upper cable guard, machined aluminum reflex riser and is coated in Realtree Hardwoods camouflage. This bow is only available with Renegade's 1 Cam system.

BOW SPECIFICATIONS: SBD 1 CAM
AMO Draw Length: 24- to 30-inch
Draw Weights: 60# or 70# with 80% or 65% let-off
Bow Speed: IBO fps = NA
Axle-to Axle: 31 inches
Weight in hand: 3 lbs.
SRP:. **$439**

TOMINATOR II

The Tominator is Renegade's newest compound bow model and was redesigned for its re-release in 2002. This lightweight hunting bow—only 3.2 pounds—is dipped in Realtree Hardwoods and designed for treestand hunting. It is available in a 1-Cam and EZ-1 solo wheel version. Both models offer a one-piece wood grip, PTS solid limbs, machined aluminum reflex riser and approximately 7-inch brace height. All models are available in 60# or 70# draw weights and have an upper cable guard with slide.

The Tominator II EZ-1 Solo Wheel model has a 90½-inch string, 33½-inch axel-to-axle length and 27- to 30-inch draw length.

BOW SPECIFICATIONS:
TOMINATOR II 1-CAM
AMO Draw Length: 24- to 31-inch

Draw Weights: 60# or 70# with 80% or 65% let-off
Bow Speed: IBO fps = NA
Axle-to Axle: 34 inches
Weight in hand: 3.2 lbs.
SRP:. **$439**

TROPHY RAC PLUS

This dependable, smooth shooting bow features a machined aluminum reflex riser dipped in Mossy Oak Break-Up camouflage. The Trophy Rac Plus is available with a 1-cam and EZ –1 Solo wheel system. Both models have one-piece wood grips and PTS solid limbs. Other features include a solid one-piece wood grip and upper cable guard with slide.

The EZ-1 Solo wheel model is similar to the 1 Cam version and has a 97 ⅝-inch cable, 6¾-inch brace height and 27- to 30-inch draw length with 75% let-off.

BOW SPECIFICATIONS:
TROPHY RAC PLUS 1-CAM
AMO Draw Length: 25- to 31-inch.
Draw Weights: 60# or 70# with 80% or 65% let-off
Bow Speed: IBO fps = NA
Axle-to Axle: 35¾-inches
Weight in hand: 3.8 lbs.
SRP:. **$439**

SUPER SWIFT

REVOLUTION ARCHERY PRODUCTS

This Canton, Kansas, company began manufacturing cams in 1995 and soon began manufacturing the entire bows. A solid understanding of cam design and the engineering features of compound bows are the hallmark of their products. The company's Swift model has been the basis for the rest of their product line.

SUPER SWIFT

This bow continues the Swift series traditions and features custom set draw weights and draw lengths, plus various axle lengths and numerous colors for the finish. Custom finishes for this bow include Mossy Oak camouflage. The bow has similar components to Revolution's Triumph bow model.

BOW SPECIFICATIONS: SUPER SWIFT
AMO Draw Length: From 25- to 30½-inch per customer request.
Draw Weights: From 30# to 65# with 65% let-off
Bow Speed: 319 fps IBO
Axle-to Axle: 36 and 37 inches
SRP:. **$675**

TRIUMPH

This bow is designed for archers wanting a longer axle-to-axle length. Design features of the Triumph include CNC machined limbs with three layers of fiberglass laminations and a machined aluminum riser. Other features can be selected by the buyer to include brace heights ranging from 6½- to 6⅞-inches and a custom draw length from 28 to 32 inches. The cams are machined and rotate on needle bearings. This bow arrives with a Mossy Oak finish.

BOW SPECIFICATIONS: TRIUMPH
AMO Draw Length: From 28- to 32-inch per customer request.
Draw Weights: From 38# to 65# with 65% let-off
Bow Speed: 312 fps IBO
Axle-to Axle: 39 and 40 inches
SRP:. **$695**

ULTRA SWIFT

This compound bow is designed for the shorter draw archer who desires speed and accuracy at lower pounds draw weight. The compact design makes this a good choice for women and kids. Features include fiberglass laminated limbs, machined riser and cams and finish colors like previous models. Brace heights for this bow range from 5¾- to 6⅜-inches.

BOW SPECIFICATIONS: ULTRA SWIFT
AMO Draw Length: From 23- to 28½-inch per customer request.
Draw Weights: From 28# to 65# with 65% let-off
Bow Speed: 312 fps IBO
Axle-to Axle: 32 and 34 inches
SRP:. **$650**

COMPOUND HUNTING

Practice That's Perfect

If you will be hunting with a quiver attached to your bow, and with arrows secured in it, then you should practice the same way. This will help you shoot a bow as it is normally balanced plus it lets you discover noises and other potential problems. —MDF

Stacey Archery Sales Compound Hunting Bows

MITEY MITE YOUTH

MITEY MITE ADULT

STACEY ARCHERY SALES This Idaho Falls, Idaho, bowyer produces eight compound adult models and two youth models, plus the innovative Tom Thumb series of compounds designed to help smaller kids gain the thrills and benefits of shooting an adult-like compound bow. Many of these bows can also be obtained in five tournament trail colors when you want to hunt on the 3-D circuit.

Stacey Archery Sales also offers archers a package deal that incorporates selected accessories to match a specific bow model. In addition to a cash savings, buyers can be certain the quivers, overdraw, release aid and other components will work with and fit the bow selected. The company also makes several models of release aids.

MITEY MITE

Stacey Archery Sales actively pursues the youth and small framed archer market with its Mitey Mite bows.

Both models feature CNC machined aluminum risers, a Mossy Oak Break-Up camouflage finish, a split two piece grip and steel insert bushings for installation of a cable guard and stabilizer. Other features include a lockdown cable guard, Power Glass split limbs and a choice of speed cams or five-step wheels. Steel pivoting centers for the limb pockets ensure 3-point limb alignment and a removable shelf guard is added for safety. Gold or black hardward and limb pockets are available to help add flash and a true custom appearance to the bow to suit any shooter's artistic tastes. These bows weight approximately 2.8 pounds.

The adult Mitey Mites are available as a package that includes the bow, a quiver, a dozen Easton arrows and a release aid. The youth model includes a stabilizer instead of a quiver.

BOW SPECIFICATIONS: MITEY MITE ADULT
AMO Draw Length: From 24- to 30-inch adjustable with modules.
Draw Weights: 20-30#, 30-40#, 40-50# and 50-60# with 65% let-off for speed cams, 65- to 70% let-off possible with wheels and draw length adjustments.
Bow Speed: NA
Axle-to Axle: 34 inches
SRP: $299.95
    package. $419.95

BOW SPECIFICATIONS: MITEY MITE YOUTH
AMO Draw Length: From 22- to 27-inch
Draw Weights: From 20-30#, 30-40# and 40-50# with 65% let-off for baby speed cams, 65% to 70% let-off possible with wheels and draw length adjustments
Bow Speed: NA
Axle-to Axle: 32½-inches
SRP: $259.95
    package. $369.95

SAWTOOTH

TARGHEE

TOM THUMB

SAWTOOTH

This compound has a machined aluminum riser and limb pockets sculpted from 6061-T6 aluminum. The pivoting limb pockets utilize steel pivoting centers to ensure three-point alignment. The bow's add-on accessories—cable guard, plunger button and stabilizer—can be mounted in the installed steel insert bushings. Other features include a 5½-inch center shot window, choice of two wood grips, graphite glass limbs and your choice of high speed cams or a weighted single cam. The Sawtooth is available in Mossy Oak Break-Up. This bow model is available in a manufacturer's package that includes a quiver, one dozen Easton arrows and a Stacey release aid.

BOW SPECIFICATIONS: SAWTOOTH
AMO Draw Length: From 23- to 31-inch
Draw Weights: From 40# to 80# with 65% let-off for speed cams and optional 80% with the single cam system.
Bow Speed: NA
Axle-to Axle: 35 and 37 inches
SRP: **$529.95**
 package. **$679.95**

TARGHEE

This compound bow is built with models for hunting and the 3-D tournament trail. Customers can custom build a bow with a choice of three limb lengths (15, 16 and 17 inches), three types of wheels and cams, five riser colors and two styles of wooden grips. With this many options you can have the company build your dream bow. The Targhee has the same design features as the Sawtooth plus 60% let-off wheels. Limb choices include 17-inch laminated carbon graphite recurve limbs or Power Tuff Griplite glass limbs. The Targhee weighs 4.2 pounds. This bow is also sold in a package that includes a quiver, overdraw, and release.

BOW SPECIFICATIONS: TARGHEE
AMO Draw Length: From 24- to 34-inch
Draw Weights: From 40# to 80# with 65% let-off for speed cams, 60% with wheels and 65% with single cam.
Bow Speed: NA
Axle-to Axle: 37, 39, 41 and 42 inches
SRP: **$449.95**
 package. **$529.95**

TOM THUMB II

With draw lengths as short as 16 inches and draw weights as low as 10 pounds, this creative feature packed bow will help young archers of any skill level and frame size find something to get excited about. Stacey Archery uses machined aluminum risers and wheels, machined limb pockets and power glass limbs to build the Tom Thumb compound bow. Other features include a split wood grip, five-inch adjustable wheels, removable shelf guard, lockdown cable guard and Fast Flite string and cables. Risers are available in Mossy Oak camouflage.

The company offers an up-grade policy with each bow. For a small fee the bow can be outfitted with the next larger wheel size and string to increase the draw length and weight. This bow is sold as a package with bow, rest, glove and half-dozen Easton arrows with points installed. There is a lightly higher cost for one dozen arrows with package.

BOW SPECIFICATIONS:
YOUTH TOM THUMB II
AMO Draw Length: From 16- to 25-inch, adjustable to many lengths with wheels, baby cams and modules.
Draw Weights: From 10- to 40# in 10# increments with 65% to 70% let-off possible
Bow Speed: NA
Axle-to Axle: 30 inches
SRP: **$179.95**
 package. **$199.95**
 (slightly higher cost with
 one-dozen arrows option)

Wing Archery Compound Hunting Bows

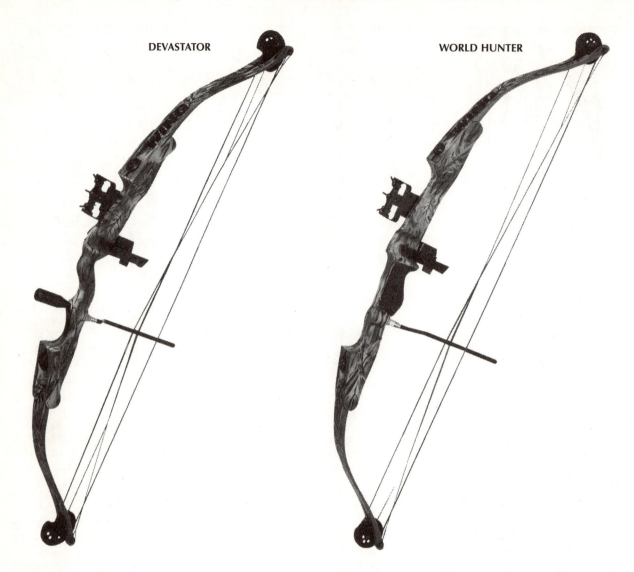

DEVASTATOR

WORLD HUNTER

WING ARCHERY These compound hunting bows are distributed by Wing Archery Products, a division of Dr. Bob's Archery Company in Randolph, New Jersey. Both models feature solid risers and solid limbs in a distinct gray and leaf pattern camouflage that will help hunters blend into their surroundings. All bow models have a unique limb pocket molded into the end of the riser as a one-piece unit.

DEVASTATOR EXPRESS

An excellent bow for hunting or 3-D shooting, the Devastator Express features a magnesium riser with a thin-waisted grip. The cut-away arrow rest accepts most overdraws easily. Limbs are constructed of multi-layered glass laminate in a recurve design.

All eccentrics are single-grooved, in-line design. This bow is available with a Super Flight Energy wheel or Kidney Kam. The Devastator Express is camouflaged in the company's unique Trailcover design. All bows are backed by a 3-year limited warranty and are available in right-hand models only.

BOW SPECIFICATIONS: DEVASTATOR EXPRESS
AMO Draw Length: 26- to 32-inch in 1-inch increments
Draw Weights: up to 80 pounds with 65% let-off
Bow Speed: NA
Axle-to Axle: 41 inches
Weight in hand: 4.4 lbs.
SRP: $339.95

WORLD HUNTER EXPRESS

This model is similar to the company's Devastator Express bow with a thicker riser and molded comfort grip. This bow is also camouflaged in Wing's Trailcover camouflage pattern and has a cable guard. The World Hunter Express uses either the Pass-Thru Power Kidney Kams or Super Flight Energy Wheels to propel arrows and control the string movement. The cables are fast flight split yoke design.

BOW SPECIFICATIONS:
WORLD HUNTER EXPRESS
AMO Draw Length: 26- to 32-inch in 1-inch increments
Draw Weights: up to 80 pounds with 65% let-off
Bow Speed: NA
Axle-to Axle: 42 inches
Weight in hand: 4.4 lbs.
SRP: $359.95

COMPOUND TOURNAMENT BOWS

CUSTOM SHOOTING SYSTEMS (CSS) is based in Saltrock, West Virginia and offers it compound bows in more than 2,000 combinations. Buyers can select from multiple components, colors and options to create a true custom-built one-of-a-kind bow for target shooting. Imagination might be the only limiting factor. Tournament models tend to be more expensive than the camouflaged versions in this line. CSS also lets buyers register their bows on-line.

CHALLENGER

This CSS bow has a machined aluminum riser and soft touch molded grip or optional walnut grip. Other features for this bow include: Gordon thermal composite limbs, pro shop adjustable let-off and in black, blue and burgundy target bow colors. This bow weighs 4 pounds and has a single-cam design.

BOW SPECIFICATIONS: CHALLENGER
AMO Draw Length: 25- to 33-inch
Draw Weights: 40#, 50#, 60#, 70#+ Max and Big game 80#+. Offers an adjustable let-off from 60% to 75%
Bow Speed: 310 fps IBO
Axle-to-Axle: 38, 40, 42 and 44 inches
SRP: Starting at $700

CONTENDER

The Contender has similar features and parts of the Challenger model, including cable guard and soft grip with walnut wood grip optional. This bow has a deflex style riser and is offered in the same colors as the Challenger and with a single-cam design.

BOW SPECIFICATIONS: CONTENDER
AMO Draw Length: 26- to 35-inch
Draw Weights: 40#, 50#, 60#, 70#+.
The pro shop adjustable let-off ranges from 60% to 75%

Bow Speed: 290 fps IBO
Axle-to-Axle: 38, 40, 42 and 44 inches
SRP: Starting at $700

ECLIPSE

This bow is oriented around the same design as the CSS Swampmaster. This bow 's features include: a T-6061 machined aluminum reflex riser, soft-touch one-piece grip, Gordon thermal composite limbs and Perimeter 1 cams. The Eclipse weighs 4 pounds and has a 7½-inch brace height. It is available in black, blue or burgundy. A walnut wood grip is optional for an additional $10.

BOW SPECIFICATIONS: ECLIPSE
AMO Draw Length: 25- to 33-inch
Draw Weights: 40#, 50#, 60# and 70#+ Max. The let-off can be adjusted at the pro shop and ranges from 60% to 75%
Bow Speed: 305 fps IBO
Axle-to-Axle: 38 inches (optional 40 inches)
SRP: Starting at $700

SYSTEM

This CSS model uses T-6061 machined aluminum to create the riser that has soft-touch grips. Other features include perimeter 1 cam, adjustable let off, a 7¼-inch brace height and composite solid limbs. This bow is offered in Mossy Oak Break Up and black, blue and burgundy competition colors.

BOW SPECIFICATIONS: SYSTEM
AMO Draw Length: 24- to 34-inch
Draw Weights: 40#, 50#, 60#, 70#+ Max and Big Game 80#.
The pro shop adjustable let- off ranges from 60% to 75%
Bow Speed: 300 fps IBO
Axle-to-Axle: 38, 40, 42 and 44 inches
SRP: Starting at $670

ECLIPSE

COMPOUND TOURNAMENT

Never Dry Fire
Never dry fire a bow—period. Without an arrow nocked and absorbing the energy, a bow's energy is transferred to its limbs, cables and cams. This can cause the bow to explode and seriously injure the shooter and anyone nearby. –MDF

Darton Archery Compound Tournament Bows

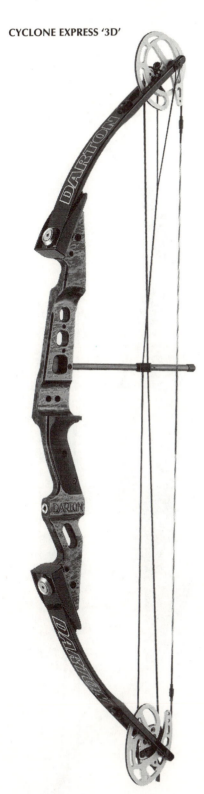

CYCLONE EXPRESS '3D'

DARTON ARCHERY began producing archery gear more than 50 years ago under the watch of founder Ralph Darlington. Darton first opened its Flint Michigan doors in 1950 and designed and manufactured arm guards, quivers, shooting gloves and finger tabs.

Ralph's son Rex joined the company in 1961 and spearheaded the development of designs and the industrial processes to manufacture bows. Today Darton Archery is still under his guidance.

Most Darton compounds feature the patented C/P/S (Controlled Power System) single cam design, a dual track upper control wheel with an eccentric bowstring groove and shorter bowstrings and cables to locate the nocking point near the center. All wheels are marked with easy-to-see tuning marks. Each bow is shipped with four interchangeable modules that can be changed without the use of a bow press. Darton risers are CNC machined from 6061-T6 and forged 7075-T6 aluminum. Each limb is computer designed and made with a pultruded process.

Darton offers its bows in groups such as: Premier Pro, Premier Assault and the Action series. The premier bows are also available as tournament bows with competition colored—red, yellow, green, etc.—risers and limbs. The Action series is an economical line and includes several starter models of youth bows.

Darton also produces and distributes the ProLine brand of bows.

DARTON'S PREMIER PRO SERIES

CYCLONE EXPRESS '3D'

Darton's Cyclone Express '3D' is designed for the highly competitive world of 3-D tournaments. This model incorporates a Deflexed machined riser and short limbs along with the C/P/S Express single-cam system. Its long axle-to-axle length makes it a good choice for finger shooters. Other features include limb pockets, cable guard and molded black grip. This bow is available in assorted competition colors and weighs 4.2 pounds.

BOW SPECIFICATIONS:
CYCLONE EXPRESS '3D'
AMO Draw Length: 27- to 31½-inch
Draw Weights: 50#, 60# and 70# with 80% let-off
Bow Speed: IBO fps= 304, AMO fps= 234
Axle-to Axle: 38 inches
SRP: **$729.99**
   in many competition colors

CYCLONE EXPRESS 'LD'

The Express 'LD' –Long Draw—shares many of the same quality features as Darton's Maverick Recurve, only with a longer Deflexed Machined Riser. Other features include an 8-inch brace height, efficient cam/limb design, cable guard and molded grip. This bow (item No. 9684) is available in several competition colors.

BOW SPECIFICATIONS:
CYCLONE EXPRESS 'LD'
AMO Draw Length: 28- to 34¼-inch
Draw Weights: 50#, 60# and 70# with 80% let-off
Bow Speed: IBO fps= 300, AMO fps= 232
Axle-to Axle: 41¼-inches
SRP: competition colors **$769.99**

EXECUTIVE VEGAS

This bow features a long axle-to-axle measurement and the proven C/P/S 'SD' Single Cam System. Other specifications for bow model No. 9627 include a 9½- inch brace height and weight of 4.3 pounds. It's available in competition colors which vary each year.

BOW SPECIFICATIONS: EXECUTIVE VEGAS
AMO Draw Length: 27- to 31-inch
Draw Weights: 50# and 60# with 75% let-off
Bow Speed: IBO fps= 275, AMO fps= 211
Axle-to Axle: 43⅛-inches
SRP: **$769.22**
   in various competition colors

Darton Archery Compound Tournament Bows

EXECUTIVE VEGAS SD

The Vegas SD bow by Darton has shorter limbs and a shorter axle-to-axle length than the standard model. Another feature of this bow is the proven C/P/S 'SD' single cam system. This model has an 8½-inch brace height, cable guard, molded black grip and weighs 4.3 pounds.

BOW SPECIFICATIONS:
EXECUTIVE VEGAS SD
AMO Draw Length: 27- to 31-inch
Draw Weights: 40#, 50#, 60# and 70# with 75% let-off
Bow Speed: IBO fps= 275, AMO fps= 211
Axle-to Axle: 41¼-inches
SRP: $749.22

RAMPAGE EXPRESS

The Rampage has a Reflex machined riser with a brace height of slightly less than 7 inches. Other features include short FlexPower Limbs and the C/P/S 'Express' single-cam system. This bow is available in many competition colors.

BOW SPECIFICATIONS: RAMPAGE EXPRESS
AMO Draw Length: 25½- to 31¾-inch
Draw Weights: 50#, 60# and 70# with 80% let-off
Bow Speed: IBO fps= 310, AMO fps= 240
Axle-to Axle: 37¼-inches
SRP: competition colors. . . . $739.99

PREMIER ASSAULT SERIES

MAVERICK EXPRESS 'QL'

This Darton bow features the high-tech Quad Limb design along with a forged machined riser and the C/P/S 'Express' single-cam system. The Maverick Express QL also features a cable guard, 6-inch brace height and black molded grip. This bow is available in the standard competition colors being used at the time. This model weighs 3.8 pounds and was discontinued in 2003.

BOW SPECIFICATIONS:
MAVERICK EXPRESS 'QL'
AMO Draw Length: 24½- to 31-inch
Draw Weights: 50#, 60# and 70# with 80% let-off
Bow Speed: IBO fps= 314, AMO fps= 244
Axle-to Axle: 36 inches
SRP: in competition colors. . $649.99

MAVERICK EXPRESS RECURVE

The Maverick Express 'Recurve' is actually a compound bow that features Darton's C/P/S Express single-cam system. This bow has been Darton's flagship bow. The lightweight bow–under 3.6 lbs.—has magnesium limb pockets attached to a 7075-T6 forged riser. Other features include a lightweight set of narrow, composite recurve limbs, cable guard, and molded grip. This bow is available Darton's assorted competition colors.

BOW SPECIFICATIONS:
MAVERICK EXPRESS RECURVE
AMO Draw Length: 25½- to 33-inch
Draw Weights: 50#, 60# and 70# with 80% let-off
Bow Speed: IBO fps= 314, AMO fps= 244
Axle-to Axle: 38 inches
SRP: $689.99

MAVERICK RECURVE REW

This Maverick model features REW (Round Energy Wheels) technology and includes a machined forged riser and FlexPower recurve limbs. Other features include a 7-inch brace height, cable guard, and molded grip. The Maverick Recurve REW weighs 3.7 pounds and is available in many competition colors.

BOW SPECIFICATIONS:
MAVERICK RECURVE REW
AMO Draw Length: 25¾- to 32⅝-inch
Draw Weights: 50#, 60# and 70# with 80% let-off
Bow Speed: IBO fps= 279, AMO fps= 219
Axle-to Axle: 44 to 44¼ inches
SRP: $649.99

EXECUTIVE VEGAS SD

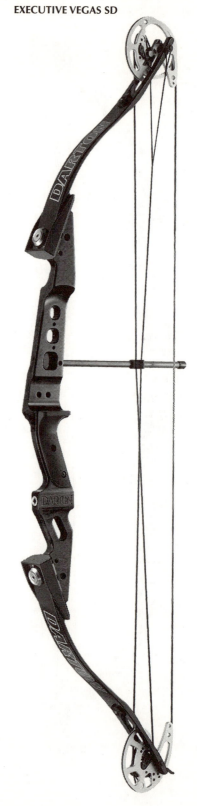

COMPOUND TOURNAMENT

Forge Bow Company Compound Tournament Bows

COMPOUND BOWS by the Forge Bow Company offer some true industry innovations and some of the industry's longest axle-to-axle lengths. This could be great news for tournament trail enthusiasts wanting a smooth finger release option. Most Forge bow models are available in multiple solid colors for target shooters. The company uses various limb styles and a vibration dampening grip—the Anti-Vibe grip—with most bow models. Other company manufacturing points of pride are wider cam grooves to reduce string wear, Eze-pull idler and cam wheel that permits the shooter to draw and hold up to 5 extra pounds and modules to change the draw weight.

For tournament bows the company offers eye-catching iridescent red, iridescent blue and Leopard. Yes, just like the real leopard with spots!

Forge also manufactures stabilizers.

The company motto: "A Great Bow That Will Never Let You Down."

Duster HP and Duster HB

Forge's Duster compound has an anti-vibe one-piece comfort grip, integrated cable guard and modular draw length adjustment. It has a machined aluminum riser and is available in left- and right-hand versions and arrives in various target colors. The HP model has fiberglass limbs and the HB model has compression molded limbs.

Bow Specifications:
Duster HP and Duster HB
AMO Draw Length: 25- to 30- inch with HP; 27- to 31½-inch with HB system
Draw Weights: 50#-60#, 60#-70# with HP (note HB model is offered in 60#-70# only). Both styles offer 65% or 80% let-off versions.
Bow Speed: 305 fps IBO w/ HP; 290 fps IBO w/HB
Axle-to-Axle: 32 inches w/HP; 32½-inches w/HB

F2 and F2XL

Forge's F2 series has a hybrid aluminum riser with billets, cable guard and anti-vibe one-piece grip. Other features include perimeter mass cam technology and vertical energy transfer technology incorporated into the design. This bow offers one of the archery industry's largest draw weight adjustment ranges and longest draw lengths—a popular point with finger shooters. This bow is available in LH and RH models and with a solid target color finish.

Bow Specifications: F2 and F2XL
AMO Draw Length: 26- to 31-inch with F2; 27- to 32-inch with F2XL system
Draw Weights: 50#-70# with F2 (note: F2XL is offered in 55#-70# only). Both styles offer 65% or 80% let-off.
Bow Speed: 309 fps IBO with F2; 300 fps IBO with the F2XL
Axle-to-Axle: 38 inches with F2; 40 inches with F2XL
SRP: $649
SRP: $539

PF34 and PF36

This Forge compound bow is offered in two axle-to-axle lengths—34 and 36 inches—and is based on an aluminum machined riser that provides a taller sight window—up to 8-inches on the PF36—and a larger grip area with the comfort grip system installed. Other features include a Forge cam and idler wheel, perimeter mass technology and cable guard. This bow offers a wider poundage adjustment range than other models. The main differences in the models are the PG fiberglass limbs on the PF34 and compression molded limbs on the PF36. According to the company, this was Forge's top seller in 2001 and is offered in LH or RH and target colors.

Bow Specifications: PF34 and PF36
AMO Draw Length: 25½- to 30 inches w/34; 27 to 31¼- inches w/36 system
Draw Weights: 45#-60#, 55#-70# w/PF34 (note the PF36 model is available in 55#-70# range only). Both bows offer 65% or 80% let-off.
Bow Speed: NA
Axle-to-Axle: 34 inches w/PF34; 36 inches w/PF36
SRP: $619

*See page 126-127 of Compound Hunting Bows for visual samples.

Which Way Are The Winds?
There are several simple ways to test wind direction.
The first is to tie a 6-inch section of sewing thread or floss to the end of your bowstring near the cam or wheel at the end of the limb. Place the fine string where it will not interfere with the cam's operation but where it is exposed to the elements.
When the wind blows, you'll see the string point the direction.
However, the string does not normally reveal up- and downdrafts. To discover these you'll need to use either floaters—small tufts of polyester material—or a spray of fine dust. Both of these inexpensive items are sold in archery stores nationwide.--MDF

Hoyt Compound Tournament Bows

CYBERTEC BLUE 2000

HAVOCTEC RED 2000

HAVOCTEC FLAME 2000

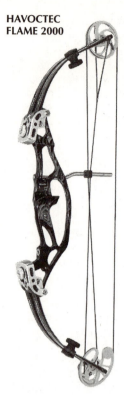

PUSHING THE LIMITS of archery technology is a continual pursuit for the engineers at Hoyt. The radically looking open riser design with cross members that has become a Hoyt trademark that continues to expand across the Utah based company's product line. Most of the company's bows are available with a split-limb design and with Accuwheels (two wheels), Excel (medium) or VersaCam (hard) options. Available styles on these compound bows include XT2000 limbs, XT3000 limbs and ZR200. The company offers numerous color options for 3-D archers who want to grip an eye-catching arrow slinger. The company's wild flame color might be one of the more interesting art options to enter archery shops.

Hoyt's pricing schedule is based on dealer preference. Prices can vary from dealer to dealer, state to state and coast to coast. Call your local dealer to inquire about prices.

BANSHEE

This bow is built specifically for young archers. The Banshee wheel is designed to be extremely easy to shoot and is adjustable to keep pace with growing young shooters. This bow is available with a two-wheel configuration and cable guard. The Banshee has a 6½ inch brace height.

BOW SPECIFICATIONS: BANSHEE
AMO Draw Length: adjustable
Draw Weights: 20# to 50#
Bow Speed: NA
Axle-to Axle: 32 inches
SRP: . . . . varies

CYBERTEC

The CyberTec compound bow uses shorter XT2000 limbs to provide greater vertical stability, and the bow's 36-inch axle-to-axle length makes it very accurate. The CyberTec also incorporates Hoyt's patented TEC design in the riser, which works like a bridge's truss to completely dampen shot vibration throughout the bow. The result is a vibration free and whisper quiet shot. Other bow features include a choice of standard, Excel cam (medium) or VersaCam (hard) to suit shooter preference. Color choices include: black, fade in blue, green and red and a wild flame pattern.

BOW SPECIFICATIONS: CYBERTEC
AMO Draw Length: From 21- to 31-inch dependant upon cam selected
Draw Weights: 40# to 80#
Bow Speed: Up to 309 fps dependant

upon cam selection
Axle-to Axle: 36 inches
SRP: . . varies by selection and dealer

HAVOCTEC

This lightweight (3.25 pounds), short axle-to-axle bow shoots like a dream and is patterned after the ever-popular Havoc while incorporating the patented Hoyt TEC riser design. This innovative design dampens vibration in the bow by channeling it through the truss and away from the hand. The result is an extremely quiet, smooth and accurate shot. This bow has a 7½-inch brace height and split-limb design with chrome or standard limb pockets. Combining the chrome parts and tournament colors—black, blue, green and red—creates an aesthetic compound bow.

BOW SPECIFICATIONS: HAVOCTEC
AMO Draw Length: 21- to 31-inch dependant upon cam and limb s election
Draw Weights: 40# to 80#
Bow Speed: From 270 to 300 fps IBO dependant upon cam and limb selection
Axle-to Axle: 31½-inches
SRP: . . . . varies by selection.

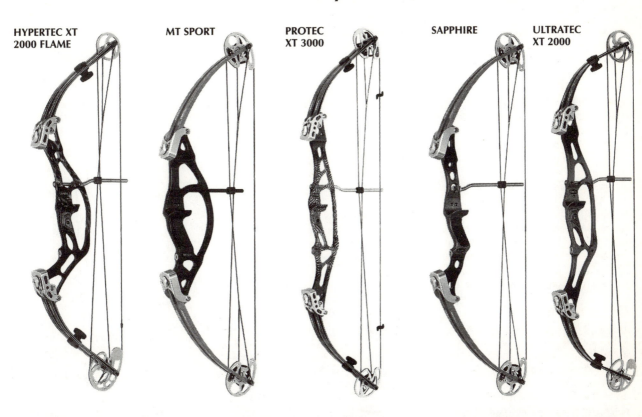

HYPERTEC XT 2000 FLAME   **MT SPORT**   **PROTEC XT 3000**   **SAPPHIRE**   **ULTRATEC XT 2000**

HYPERTEC

The HyperTec features a shorter brace height to provide the long power stroke required for fast arrow speeds. The riser is stiff and lightweight with virtually no recoil or vibration at release. The HyperTec has a 6-inch brace height. This is a bow designed for advanced archers, so consult your local dealer to see if it's right for you.

BOW SPECIFICATIONS: HYPERTEC
AMO Draw Length: 24- to 30-inch dependant upon cam selection
Draw Weights: 40# to 80#
Bow Speed: 320 fps IBO
Axle-to Axle: 33 inches
SRP: . . . . **varies**

MT SPORT

The lightweight and affordable MT Sport also incorporates Hoyt's patented TEC engineering. This bow's shorter axle-to-axle length makes it a more maneuverable bow in all hunting conditions. This bow is only available in standard red, black and blue colors. The MT Sport utilizes Accuwheels and the ZR200 layout.

BOW SPECIFICATIONS: MT SPORT
AMO Draw Length: Available from 22 to 34 inches

Draw Weights: 40# to 80#
Bow Speed: Up to 286 fps IBO
Axle-to Axle: 34 ½-inches
SRP: . . . . **varies**

PROTEC

Hoyt's ProTec combines proven deflex geometry with a longer and stiffer riser along with the company's TEC design. This bow is available with Accu-wheels, Excel cams and Versacams and with LXPRO, XT3000 and XT2000 limbs and styles. The bow's finish choices include: black, flame and the company's standard fade colors.

BOW SPECIFICATIONS: PROTEC
AMO Draw Length: 25- to 34-inch
Draw Weights: 40# to 80#
Bow Speed: Up to 290 fps IBO
Axle-to Axle: 38 to 46 inches dependant upon cam selection
SRP: . . . . **varies**

SAPPHIRE

This bow is designed for women and short-draw shooters. The Sapphire fully utilizes its moderately reflexed riser to provide superior speed. The specially-designed grip accommodates smaller hands and virtually eliminates hand-torque to improve shot accuracy. Available systems to move arrows include: Accuwheels, Excel and

VersaCams. This bow has a standard riser (solid) and molded grip, plus a split-limb design. The Sapphire is available in all standard Hoyt colors and the wild flame pattern.

BOW SPECIFICATIONS: SAPPHIRE
AMO Draw Length: 21- to 28-inch
Draw Weights: 40# to 60#
Bow Speed: Up to 277 fps IBO
Axle-to Axle: 34 ½-inches
SRP: . . . . **varies**

ULTRATEC

The UltraTec's longer axle-to-axle length and shorter XT2000 limbs make this bow a solid performer. This bow is available in Hoyt's color spectrum and has a 7-inch brace height. Models are available with Accuwheels, Excel cams, VersaCams and Hoyt's Redline cams and with XT3000 and XT2000 limb layouts.

BOW SPECIFICATIONS: ULTRATEC
AMO Draw Length: 22- to 33-inch dependant upon cam selection
Draw Weights: 40# to 80#
Bow Speed: Up to 305 fps IBO dependant upon limb and cam selection
Axle-to Axle: 38 inches
SRP: . . . . **varies**

COMPOUND TOURNAMENT

Jennings Compound Tournament Bows

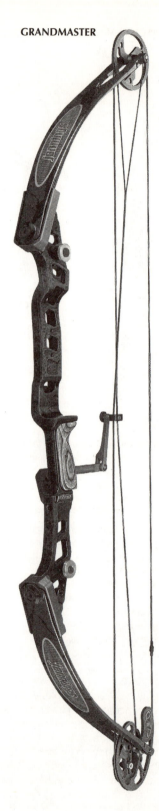

JENNINGS BOWS are produced and distributed by the Gainesville, Florida, based North American Archery Group LLC. These bows still bear the name of founder and archery industry leader Tom Jennings who designed numerous bow patterns during several decades of production. The Jennings line has been known through the years for innovation and top-notch mechanical performance. Many of their high standards were incorporated under the watchful eye of industry pioneer Jennings. All bows are protected by a limited lifetime warranty. These bows have garnered a strong following on the 3-D tournament trails across North America and feature an impressive marble color pattern on many models.

GRANDMASTER

This high-tech bow was designed as a 3-D shooter and dons a camo skin in the hunting version. It has a 23-inch precision machined aluminum titanium riser, modular cam that provides up to 8 inches of draw length adjustment and a 1-inch micro adjustment for a precision draw. The GrandMaster has Carbon Twill limbs and an adjustable dampening system that can use either a brass or titanium anodized weights to tame torque, dampen vibration and eliminate noise. This bow utilizes a SwingArm cable guard.

The GrandMaster is available in a blue/black marble finish and left- and right-hand versions.

BOW SPECIFICATIONS: GRANDMASTER
AMO Draw Length: 27-, 28-, or 29-inch: adjustable range from 26 to 33 inches
Draw Weights: 40-50#, 50-60#, or 60-70# with 70% let-off (65% let-off optional)
Bow Speed: IBO fps= 300; AMO fps= 223
Axle-to Axle: 40½-inches
Weight in hand: 4 lbs., 5 oz.
SRP: marble finish $699

TROPHYMASTER

This compact bow uses Carbon Twill limbs and a modular cam to provide results oriented performance. The bow's features include: an adjustable dampening system, SwingArm cable guard, machined aluminum riser and titanium-anodized hardware. It has a checkered laminated wood grip and is available in left- and right-hand models and with a blue/black marble finish.

BOW SPECIFICATIONS: TROPHYMASTER
AMO Draw Length: 27-, 28-, and 29-inch; adjustable range from 24 to 31 inches.
Draw Weights: 40-50#; 50-60#; and 60-70# with 70% let-off
Bow Speed: IBO fps= 308; AMO fps= 232
Axle-to Axle: 35.375 inches
Weight in hand: 4 lbs., 1 oz.
SRP:. $549

A Ground Level Indicator

A good way to determine ground level winds—which can be different that those at treestand level—is to tie a 12-inch piece of lightweight orange safety ribbon to a limb near a local deer trail. The ribbon will move at the slightest wind change and points out the wind direction. --MDF

COMPOUND TOURNAMENT

Martin Archery Compound Tournament Bows

JAGUAR MAGNUM

MARTIN ARCHERY was founded by archery enthusiast Gail Martin and his wife, Eva in the late 1950s. By the 1960s the family business was growing and sons Terry and Dan soon become employees. Terry and Dan have been driving forces behind Martin's continued grow during recent years and already are being followed up by the third generation of Martins to compete for market share in the archery industry. Here's a great combination of pursuing the American dream and combining it with a passion. Through the years the company has acquired more than 24 archery related patents and has produced numerous ground breaking bow designs, including the Kam-Act bow.

Amazingly, the Martin factory has stood its ground at the same Walla Walla, Washington, site for more than 50 years. Today, Martin Archery offers bows in its Pro and Gold Series. The company changes the colors offered on its tournament bows regularly. The 2003 colors are: Sunburst, Red-to-Blue Fade, Platinum and ProCat—adark green with red swirls throughout. The prices of tournament bow models can vary up to $60 because of the colors and components used. The prices listed are for guidelines only.

MARTIN'S PRO SERIES

ALTITUDE

Martin's Altitude compound bow is designed with the rigors of tournament contests in mind. The short axle-to-axle length makes maneuvering easier and more comfortable. The Altitude compact riser design—machined from a solid aluminum block—also uses center line riser technology that allows you to hold steady and make better shots. This technology also makes the Altitude extremely smooth. Other features include solid limbs nestled in limb pockets and a black molded rubber grip. This bow weighs 3 pounds, 10 ounces and is available in red, blue or a selection of custom colors and in right- or left-hand models.
BOW SPECIFICATIONS: ALTITUDE
AMO Draw Length: 24- to 29-inch
Draw Weights: 50#, 60# and 70# with 75% let-off (65% optional)
Bow Speed: 301 fps IBO

Axle-to Axle: 30⅞-inches
SRP: approximately $686.64

JAGUAR

The affordable Jaguar has a die cast riser and a short axle-to-axle length. Other features include straight glass composite limbs set in limb pockets and a molded grip on this dual-cam bow. Martin's Jaguar is available in Cherry Red or Deep Blue. This bow is offered in right-hand only.

The Jaguar Magnum is similar in design and uses the Fuzion single-cam system. This bow has wood panel grips. It's available in Cherry Red or Deep Blue. The Jaguar Magnum is offered in right-hand only.
BOW SPECIFICATIONS: JAGUAR
AMO Draw Length: 25- to 31-inch
Draw Weights: 40# to 70# with 75% let off (65% optional)
Bow Speed: 291 fps IBO
Axle-to-Axle: 36⅜ inches
SRP: approximately $479.42

BOW SPECIFICATIONS: JAGUAR MAGNUM
AMO Draw Length: 25- to 30-inch
Draw Weights: 50#, 60# and 70# with 75% let-off (65% optional)
Bow Speed: 310 fps IBO
Axle-to Axle: 33¼-inches
SRP: approximately $517.42

MV2 ELITE

The recently introduced MV2 Elite has proven itself. At the 2001 National Indoor Championships, in the hands of Martin Shooters Troy Knoll and George Ryals, it won 2 National Titles and gained one National Indoor Record. The feature packed MV2 uses Quick-Loc accessories and the VEM (Vibration Escape Module) system with dampners attached on the riser. The MV2's unique accessory attachment system makes it easier than ever to mount all your favorite hunting gear. The Quick Pin quiver system gives you a super-solid, rattle-free attachment to your bow with any Martin Direct Mount Quiver. The Lever-Loc Sight System allows the use of most any sight and permits a secure lock to The MV2 riser. Sights can be removed and replaced without affecting settings thanks to a double-pin alignment system. The lever action pulls the sight firmly against the bow and it is then locked into place against the sight

Martin Archery Compound Tournament Bows

bar. The quiver pin plugs into a receptacle on the riser and a knob on the opposite side is tightened to lock it into place. The quiver easily separates from the bow. This dual-wheel bow is available in red, blue or a selection of custom colors. The MV2 Elite is available in right- or left-hand models.

BOW SPECIFICATIONS: MV2 ELITE
AMO Draw Length: 25- to 33-inch
Draw Weights: 40# to 70# with 75% let-off (65% optional)
Bow Speed: 296 fps IBO
Axle-to Axle: 39⅞-inches
SRP: approximately $1096.42

PHANTOM

Martin's economical Phantom has a riser that is machined from a solid block of aluminum. Great attention to detail is evident in every curve and component of this bow. It's available with Z-cams and Fuzion cams. Other features include solid limbs and wood panel grips. This bow weighs 3 pounds, 15 ounces and has a 6¾-inch brace height. The Phantom is coated with your choice of target colors (red, blue, or purple) and is available in right- or left-hand models.

The Phantom bow is available in three styles. The Phantom Elite model uses Fury cams and has a long 38-inch axle-to-axle length. The Phantom Fuzion uses a single cam design and has a rubber molded grip. The Phantom Magnum uses the Fuzion single-cam system and has a 33-inch axle-to-axle length.

BOW SPECIFICATIONS: PHANTOM
AMO Draw Length: 25- to 32-inch
Draw Weights: 50#, 60# and 70# with 75% let off (65% optional)
Bow Speed: 285 fps IBO
Axle-to Axle: 37¼ inches
SRP: Fusion and Magnum
    approximately **$566.64**
Elite approximately $845.06

SCEPTER II ELITE

The Scepter II Elite is available with standard Fury cams or the popular Fury-X cams. The Scepter II Elite benefits from no limb tip torque, cam lean or cable friction. This solid limb bow is available in red, blue, or a selection of custom colors. This Martin bow is available in right- or left-hand models.
BOW SPECIFICATIONS: SCEPTER II ELITE

AMO Draw Length: 26- to 34-inch
Draw Weights: 40# to 80# with 75% let-off (65% let-off optional)
Bow Speed: 290 fps IBO
Axle-to Axle: 42⅞-inches
SRP: Approximately $1304.78

MARTIN'S GOLD SERIES.

PANTHER MAGNUM

Martin's Panther Magnum is built around a solid, machined aluminum riser that is super tough and light weight. Combine the riser with solid 14-inch limbs and the result is a very compact 33-inch axle length. This bow has a black molded grip, weighs 3.7 pounds and has a 7¼-inch brace height. The Martin Fuzion single-cam system powers the bow that is available in red, blue, or purple. Specify right- or left-hand when selecting your bow.
BOW SPECIFICATIONS: PANTHER MAGNUM
AMO Draw Length: 26- to 31-inch and variable by cam selection
Draw Weights: 50#, 60# and 70# with 75% let-off (65% let-off optional)
Bow Speed: 300 fps IBO
Axle-to Axle: 33 1/16
SRP: Approximately $762.20

TIGER

Do you have a son, daughter, nephew, niece or grandchild that enjoys archery as much as you do? Don't you think that child deserves equipment that is as enjoyable to shoot as your own? Check out the Martin Tiger with a solid machined riser and Mini Z-Cams that propel arrows to the target at more than 200 feet per second. Each Tiger compound bow comes complete with a full set of draw length modules that allow adjustment of draw over a 17- to 23-inch range so the bow can grow with the child. Other features include: solid cams and limbs plus a black molded grip. This bow is available in cherry red and in right- or left-hand versions. The lightweight Tiger weighs approximately 2.3 pounds.
Bow Specifications: Tiger
AMO Draw Length: 17- to 24-inch adjustable
Draw Weights: 20#, 30# and 40# with 65% let-off
Bow Speed: 300 fps IBO
Axle-to Axle: 31½-inches
SRP: Approximately $337.70

SCEPTER II ELITE

TIGER

Mathews Compound Tournament Bows

MATHEWS NEEDS NO LENGTHY introduction to archery enthusiasts. The company's record of innovation speaks for itself with products ranging from the single cam technology the Zebra Twist bow string. The company holds numerous patents and the rights to the technology used by other archery equipment builders. In recent years the bow manufacturer released the perimeter weighted cam technology, harmonic dampening system and string suppressors. This brand of bow is also known for being lightweight and normally has an open construction in its innovative riser designs. Most of the Mathews bows have the company's name emblazoned on the limbs in stylish gold print. In recent years the company has produced and promoted the innovative Genesis bow that accommodates any beginning archer's draw length and weight. Many of the company's bows are also available in flavorable—kiwi, blueberry, root beer and others—competition colors. This is a creative and light-hearted twist from a bow manufacturer that takes their products seriously.

An interesting fact is that this manufacturer also makes guitars, fly rods and an expedition sleeping bag under its subdivision companies! Mathews is based in Sparta, Wisconsin.

BLACK MAX
This lightweight compound, single cam bow boasts possibly the fastest speed of any bow—a whopping 330 fps IBO. It utilizes the MaxCam system and has a flat black riser, solid limbs, cable guard and wooden grip. The bow's limbs are offered in solid black to match the riser.

BOW SPECIFICATIONS: BLACK MAX
AMO Draw Length: 25- to 30-inch
Draw Weights: 40# to 70# with 65% let-off
Bow Speed: 330 fps IBO; 252 fps AMO
Axle-to-Axle: 36 inches
SRP: **$699**

CONQUEST 2
This bow has a noticeably long riser for a Mathews model and even with parallel limbs it pushes a 41-inch axle-to-axle length. Other specs include: a competition one-piece grip, original MaxCam, Harmonic dampening, cable guard, a ball bearing idler wheel and Zebra Twist string. Archers with long draw lengths and finger shooters will find this bow appealing. This bow is also offered in Mathew's competition colors.

BOW SPECIFICATIONS: CONQUEST 2
AMO Draw Length: 28- to 32-inch; 24- to 29-inch with MiniMax cams and 28- to 32-inch with the SuperSoft cams
Draw Weights: 40# to 70# with 80%, 65% or 60% let-off
Bow Speed: 310 fps IBO; 236 fps AMO
Axle-to-Axle: 41 inches
SRP: **$749**

GENESIS
This Mathews bow was geared to help beginning archers learn the basics without working through complex measurements. The bow has zero let off and is adjustable from 10 to 20 pounds draw weight. Kids can't outgrow it! It features split limbs, single cam with idler wheel, limb pockets, molded grip, arrow rest and cable guard. Available colors include: red cherry, key lime, lemon yellow, blue raspberry and wild berry.

SRP: Starting **$160**

ICON
This bow uses the concentric SoloCam—a round cam—for arrow energy. Other features include a ball-bearing idler wheel, Mathews' competition grip, Harmonic dampeners in plastic bushings, string suppressors, solid one-piece limbs and the innovative roller guard. The Icon utilizes the parallel limb design. It also has threaded brass bushings to accept accessories such as a stabilizer below the grip. This bow has a 7 5/8-inch brace height and weighs 4.45 pounds. Available colors include: black cherry, kiwi, root beer and blueberry.

BOW SPECIFICATIONS: ICON
AMO Draw Length: 24- to 30-inch, 27 1/2- to 29 1/2-inch half sizes
Draw Weights: 40# to 70# with 70% let-off
Bow Speed: 300 fps IBO; 225 fps AMO
Axle-to-Axle: 37 inches
SRP: **$749**

LEGACY
The Mathews Legacy compound bow incorporates the latest company technology including string suppressors to reduce string vibration and noise, the roller guard that replaces the traditional cable guard and parallel limb design which was started in 1996. This bow has a finely crafted wooden grip. This flagship bow for Mathews uses the Harmonic dampening system—brass or aluminum discs inserted into the ends of the riser. The Legacy a 7 1/2-inch brace height and weighs approximately 4.35 pounds. This bow is available in: black cherry, kiwi, root beer and blueberry for tournament trail shooters.

BOW SPECIFICATIONS: LEGACY
AMO Draw Length: 24- to 30-inch, 27 1/2- to 29 1/2-inch half sizes
Draw Weights: 40# to 70# with 70% let-off
Bow Speed: 308 fps IBO; 235 fps AMO
Axle-to-Axle: 34 inches
SRP: **$699**

ULTRA 2
This Mathews bow has features similar to the SQ2 but uses the Original MaxCam along with solid limbs and a cable guard. It has a 6 1/8 inch brace height and tips the scale at 3.7 pounds. This bow is also offered in Mathew's competition colors.

BOW SPECIFICATIONS: ULTRA 2
AMO Draw Length: 23- to 30-inch; 22- to 27-inch with MiniMax cams
Draw Weights: 40# to 70# with 80% or 65% let-off
Bow Speed: 320+ fps IBO (one of the industry's highest!); 245 fps AMO
Axle-to-Axle: 36 inches
SRP: **$629**

*See page 145-147 of Compound Hunting Bows for visual samples.

Parker Compound Bows Compound Tournament Bows

PARKER COMPOUND BOWS is located in Spring Hill, Virginia, and was recently recognized as among the Top 500 Group in America's small businesses and as one of the fastest growing privately-held companies in America by *Inc. Magazine*. The company manufactures numerous 3-D competition models that are known for marbled color schemes and the popular Force cam. Parker bows carry a life time warranty.

Parker shooting enthusiasts can also obtain Parker specialty hats, shirts, jackets and stickers. Some Parker bows can also be equipped with specially selected and designed gear from the company. These accessory packages can also translate into a cash savings when purchased together. Call 540-337-5426 to order these items.

CHALLENGER

This smaller version of the popular Parker Ultra-Lite bows is designed for the shorter draw length needs of ladies and young archers who want a true competition bow. This is a serious bow for serious tournament tests! The Challenger has the same features as the Ultra-Lite series including an aluminum riser, walnut grip and Power-Tuff composite limbs with a colorful marble finish. This bow has a machined aluminum mini one-cam, a solid cable guard and is offered in purple, red and blue finishes for tournament enthusiasts wanting to flash some splash on the 3-D trail.

BOW SPECIFICATIONS: CHALLENGER
AMO Draw Length: 23-, 24-, 25-, 26- and 27-inch with extra draw modules available.
Draw Weights: 30#, 40# and 50# with 10# adjustment down from set weight. Offers an 80 % let-off with 65% let-off optional.
Bow Speed: NA
Axle-to Axle: 33 inches
SRP: $319.95

Pick An Anchor Point
To be consistent with your release and aim, pick a spot on your face where you will always anchor your hand or part of a finger. Some shooters choose their nose, others use the corner of their mouth and others touch their ear. The best choice for you is the one that feels comfortable and that helps you stay consistent. –MDF

FORCE-MULTIPLIER II

ULTRA-LITE PRO

FORCE-MULTIPLIER II

This radical appearing bow has a unique third idler wheel located below the grip and attached to the bottom of the machined aluminum riser. The wheel absorbs torque to promote smooth arrow shots. Available in left- and right-hand versions, the Force-Multiplier has Power Tuff composite limbs, a Force One-Cam, cable guard and walnut wood grip. This bow has a 6-inch brace height and weighs 3.6 pounds. The bow's eye-catching finish is TQ Mist (Blue) on the riser and white Italian marble on the limbs and grip. This bow can be credited with making archers everywhere take note of Parker's bow model line up.

BOW SPECIFICATIONS: FORCE-MULTIPLIER II
AMO Draw Length: 25-, 26-, 27, 28-, 29- and 30-inch with extra draw modules available.
Draw Weights: 50#, 60# and 70# with 10# adjustment down from set weight. This bow arrives with an 80 % let-off (65% let-off optional).
Bow Speed: 250 fps AMO; 325 fps IBO
Axle-to Axle: 35 inches
SRP: $669.95

ULTRA-LITE 31

This Parker bow is available in left- and right-hand configuration with a machined 6061 aluminum lightweight riser with machined limb pockets. Other features include 1½-inch power-tuff composite limbs, a super-One cam and cable guard. This lightweight bow weighs only 2.9 pounds and is available in a flashy TQ mist finish and marble appearance.

BOW SPECIFICATIONS: ULTRA-LITE 31
AMO Draw Length: 23-, 24-, 25-, 26-, 27, 28-, 29- and 30-inch with extra draw modules available.
Draw Weights: 50#, 60# and 70# with 10# adjustment down from the set weight. Bows have an 80 % let-off (65% let-off optional).
Bow Speed: 240 fps AMO; 310 fps IBO
Axle-to Axle: 31 inches
SRP: $639.95

ULTRA-LITE 35

This Parker bow is similar to the company's Ultra-Lite 31 model with a longer axle-to-axle length and resulting weight of 3.1 pounds. The bow is designed to accommodate archers with a longer draw length and is available with the TQ mist finish and blue riser.

BOW SPECIFICATIONS: ULTRA-LITE 35
AMO Draw Length: 25-, 26-, 27, 28-, 29-, 30-, 31- and 32-inch with

extra draw modules available.
Draw Weights: 50#, 60# and 70# with 10# adjustment down from set weight. This bow has an 80 % let-off with 65% let-off optional.
Bow Speed: 243 fps AMO; 300 fps IBO
Axle-to Axle: 35 inches
SRP: $539.95

ULTRA-LITE PRO

This Parker compound bow is a continuation of the Ultra-Lite series with similar features as the 31 and 35 models. The Pro is designed for longer draws, tall and finger shooters and for anyone who likes a longer bow. The bow weighs 3.6 pounds and is available in left- and right-hand versions and has a larger 7½-inch brace height.

BOW SPECIFICATIONS: ULTRA-LITE PRO
AMO Draw Length: 25-, 26-, 27, 28-, 29-, 30-, 31- and 32-inch with extra draw modules available.
Draw Weights: 50#, 60# and 70# with 10# adjustment down from set weight. This model has an 80 % let-off with 65% let-off optional.
Bow Speed: 240 fps AMO; 306 fps IBO
Axle-to Axle: 38 inches
SRP: $649.95

COMPOUND TOURNAMENT

PSE Compound Tournament Bows

PSE (PRECISION SHOOTING EQUIPMENT) is based in Tucson, Arizona and delivers one of the archery industry's largest lines of bows, accessories and services for tournament and 3-D shooters. The company has a popular tractor-trailer outfit—complete with a workshop and bow parts and accessories—that tours the US each summer and fall to help archers tune bows and learn more about archery techniques while improving their shooting skills. PSE also has a custom shop where you can get a bow built to your desired color and length. This feature makes their bows some of the most prominent on the 3-D tournaments and at other competitions today. The company offers schools for technicians, instructors and shooters.

Pete Shepley founded the company in 1971. Visitors are welcome to stop in at the Tucson facility and discover the many options available for archers through the PSE product line.

Many PSE bow models are available in left-hand configuration for an additional $15. Some of the bow styles are available in vivid colors—black, black cherry, blue, copper, copper haze, forest green, ice blue, purple haze, red and violet— for competition shooting and the prices on those bows tend to run $40 to approximately $80 more. Prices for the PSE models are given but variations in colors, cams and left-hand models can increase the cost. Visit their web site—www.pse-archery.com—for the most up-to-date details or contact the company.

BANDIT 2

Here's another PSE youth bow that's big on features and made to successfully introduce small framed hunters and arrow enthusiasts to the thrills of archery. This bow is designed primarily for young bowhunters, and the Bandit is only available with a camouflage finish. Other construction features include: a molded wrap-around one-piece grip, solid riser and limbs and a reliable two-wheel cable system. This bow wears the PSE name, has PSE quality and is covered under the PSE warranty.

BOW SPECIFICATIONS:
BANDIT 2
AMO Draw Length: 18-, 21-, 23- and 24-inch.
Draw Weights: 20# in 18-inch draw, 30# and 40# in other draw lengths with 60% let-off
Bow Speed: IBO fps = 215
Axle-to Axle: 33 inches
Weight in hand: 2 lbs., 6 oz.
SRP: tournament package $269

DAKOTA

The Dakota compound bow is designed for finger shooters who need longer axle-to-axle length bows to permit smooth finger releases and avoid string pinch. Dakota offers a slightly deflexed riser, PSE's Magnaglass limbs and three wheel options. Tournament trail competition models are available in blue with chrome wheels. This could be one of the most popular bows on the tournament circuits as far as color scheme ranking. A molded wrap-around grip ensures better control and shooter hand comfort.

BOW SPECIFICATIONS:
DAKOTA INFERNO CAM
AMO Draw Length: 27- to 31-inch in 1-inch increments.
Draw Weights: 60# and 70# with 75% let-off
Bow Speed: IBO fps = 300
Axle-to Axle: 39 inches
Weight in hand: 4 lbs., 3ozs.
SRP:. $369

BOW SPECIFICATIONS:
DAKOTA SYNERGY PRO 65
AMO Draw Length: 28- to 30-inch in 1-inch increments.
Draw Weights: 60# and 70# with 65% let-off
Bow Speed: IBO fps = 300
Axle-to Axle: 41 inches
Weight in hand: 4 lbs., 3ozs.
SRP:. $369
    add $15 for LH model

BOW SPECIFICATIONS:
DAKOTA SYNERGY PRO 75
AMO Draw Length: 28- to 31-inch in 1-inch increments.
Draw Weights: 60# and 70# with 75% let-off
Bow Speed: IBO fps = 297
Axle-to Axle: 41 inches
Weight in hand: 4 lbs., 3 ozs.
SRP:. $369
    (add $15 for LH models)

DAKOTA

MACH II

MONARCH

MACH II

The Mach II is sleek and very shootable. It's available in two models: the Vector 5 and the Stinger Cam version. The Vector 5 is the 3-D t ournament archery version PSE's Mach II Stinger is available in Good Vibrations, Python Red and Marble Blue finishes. The Color-Tech versions of this design also retail for approximately $1100. This bow uses the modular Stinger Cam and has the NC Vibration Dampening System.

BOW SPECIFICATIONS:
MACH II STINGER CAM
AMO Draw Length: 25- to 29-inch in 1-inch increments.
Draw Weights: 50#, 60# and 70# with 75% let-off
Bow Speed: IBO fps = 292
Axle-to Axle: 39 inches
Weight in hand: 4 lbs., 3 oz.
SRP: $1169.99

MONARCH

The Monarch is available in a colorful 3-D tournament version so that shooters can stand out in the crowd. The Monarch features PSE's Ultimate One Cam and a riser with a shoot-through center brace. Other bow features include: carbon solid limbs, arrow rest and cable guard with slide. This is a serious bow for serious archers.

The tournament oriented Monarch Pro Vector 5 is available in red and blue.

BOW SPECIFICATIONS: MONARCH ULTIMATE ONE CAM
AMO Draw Length: 26- to 31-inch in 1-inch increments.
Draw Weights: 60# and 70# with 80% let-off (65% let-off optional)
Bow Speed: IBO fps = 310
Axle-to Axle: 39 inches
Weight in hand: 4 lbs., 5 oz.
SRP: $1269.99

NITRO ULTIMATE ONE CAM

This is an all-new high performance bow that provides smooth shootablility. The bow's stout design incorporates a longer reflex handle and shorter limbs are mounted solidly in compact pivoting pockets. Other construction features include: NV System vibration control discs mounted on the front of the limb pockets, machined aluminum riser, a solid cable guard, Teflon coated cam and solid limbs. The Nitro is available in three vivid Color-Tech colors. The Nitro Ultimate One Cam bow uses the Phase-3 grip system. You can use panels installed on each side of the riser, a full grip that wraps around riser, or grip only the riser that has been radiused to permit hand-only shooting. This is one of the archery industry's top options for creating a true custom bow grip that suits the shooter's hand and personal preferences for feel.

BOW SPECIFICATIONS:
NITRO ULTIMATE ONE CAM
AMO Draw Length: 25- to 30-inch in 1-inch increments.
Draw Weights: 60# and 70# with 80% let-off (65% let-off optional)
Bow Speed: IBO fps = 314
Axle-to Axle: 36 inches
Weight in hand: 3 lbs., 10 oz.
SRP: $889.99

PSE Compound Tournament Bows

NOVA

This compound bow by PSE has established a solid reputation as an affordable value that delivers quality in a simple, dependable package. The Nova is available with three cams: Arson, Vector Pro and Vector 5. Other features include integrated cam-lock cable guard, molded wrap around grips and solid carbon limbs. The tournament version has a riser with blue finish, black solid recurve limbs and chrome wheels. Note that the lower draw weights are available only in the shorter draw lengths in the Vector Pro model and that draw lengths are 24, 26, 28, 29 and 30 inches.

BOW SPECIFICATIONS:
NOVA ARSON CAM
AMO Draw Length: 27- to 31-inch in 1-inch increments.
Draw Weights: 60# and 70# with 70% let-off
Bow Speed: IBO fps = 295
Axle-to Axle: 36½-inches
Weight in hand: 3 lbs., 12 oz.
SRP: **$299**
(add $15 for LH models)

BOW SPECIFICATIONS:
NOVA VECTOR PRO
AMO Draw Length: 24- to 30-inch in 1-inch increments.
Draw Weights: 30#, 40#, 50#, 60# and 70# with 75% let-off
Bow Speed: IBO fps = 280
Axle-to Axle: 38 inches
Weight in hand: 3 lbs., 9 oz.
SRP: **$289**
(add $15 for LH models)

BOW SPECIFICATIONS:
NOVA VECTOR 5
AMO Draw Length: 26- to 30-inch in 1-inch increments.
Draw Weights: 50# (26-inch draw length only), 60# and 70# with 65% let-off
Bow Speed: IBO fps = 275
Axle-to Axle: 39 inches
Weight in hand: 3 lbs., 9 oz.
SRP: **$289**
(add $15 for LH models)

QUANTAM ULTIMATE ONE CAM

PSE's Quantum delivers a revolutionary design with a unique riser design that offers unequalled stability for the archer. This high-tech bow incorporates sleek lines and a trimline design to improve performance. This compound bow has a distinct multi-port vent system on the riser's upper and lower sections, plus solid limbs and cam. The Quantum Ultimate One Cam can use the Phase-3 grip system and is available in Good Vibrations, Python Red and Blue Marble finishes. This bow in PSE's Good Vibration paint scheme might be one of the most radically appearing bows on today's competition trail. It's a must see for every competition enthusiast's wish list. The Quantam's riser provides a 7½-inch brace height and the NV vibration dampening system can be installed.

BOW SPECIFICATIONS:
QUANTAM ULTIMATE ONE CAM
AMO Draw Length: 27- to 32-inch in 1-inch increments.
Draw Weights: 60# and 70# with 80% let-off (65% let-off optional)
Bow Speed: IBO fps = 305
Axle-to Axle: 39 inches
Weight in hand: 3 lbs., 10 oz.
SRP: **$899.99**

SPYDER

PSE's Spyder is designed for short-draw archers and can be adjusted across more than 5 inches of draw length. This is possibly one of the most adjustable bows in the industry. Other features for this compound bow include: a lightweight machined aluminum riser, integrated cam-lock cable guard, molded TRM grip and the Stinger cam system. This bow has a 6¾-inch brace height and wears a distinctive PSE logo. The Spyder's shorter draw lengths and lighter draw weight combinations make this a great youth and lady's bow. The bow is available in several blue colors.

The IBO speed for this bow was determined by shooting a 27-inch draw length.

BOW SPECIFICATIONS:
SPYDER STINGER CAM
AMO Draw Length: 23- to 27-inch in 1-inch increments.
Draw Weights: 40#, 50# and 60# with 75% let-off
Bow Speed: IBO fps = 275
Axle-to Axle: 35 inches
Weight in hand: 3 lbs., 5 oz.
SRP: **$369**
(add $15 for LH models)

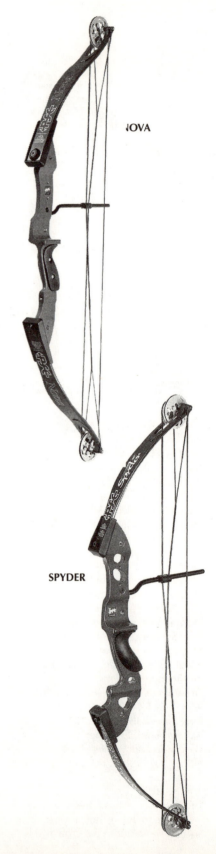

NOVA

SPYDER

SPYDER S4

A youth bow that's full of adult features best describes this compound bow. The Spyder S4 has a deflexed riser, molded composite wrap-around grip and cable guard. It utilizes solid limbs and is available in blue.

BOW SPECIFICATIONS:
SPYDER S4
AMO Draw Length: 19- or 23-inch only.
Draw Weights: 20# in 19-inch draw, 30# and 40# in 23-inch draw with 65% let-off
Bow Speed: IBO fps = 240
Axle-to Axle: 32 inches
Weight in hand: 2 lbs., 6 oz.
SRP: $179.99

THUNDERBOLT

This lightweight and super fast bow is available with three powerful wheel options: Maxis HL, Lightning cam and Stinger cam systems. The Maxis cam provides traditional twin-cam technology with high let-off. The highly-adjustable Stinger cam features a pivoting module for easy draw length adjustment. The legendary Lightning cam delivers fast arrow speeds and flat trajectory. This bow uses MagnaGlass limbs and has a molded one-piece wrap around grip and cable guard. The Lightning cam and Stinger cam models are available in blue.

BOW SPECIFICATIONS: THUNDERBOLT LIGHTNING CAM
AMO Draw Length: 27- to 31-inch in 1-inch increments.
Draw Weights: 50#, 60# and 70# with 80% let-off but the bow adjusts to 65% let-off
Bow Speed: IBO fps = 300
Axle-to Axle: 36 inches
Weight in hand: 3 lbs., 9 oz.
SRP: $449

BOW SPECIFICATIONS: THUNDERBOLT MAXIS HIGH LET-OFF
AMO Draw Length: 26- to 30-inch in 1-inch increments.
Draw Weights: 50# (available in 26-inch draw length only), 60# and 70# with 75% let-off
Bow Speed: IBO fps = 300
Axle-to Axle: 38 inches
Weight in hand: 3 lbs., 9 oz.
SRP: $419
  (add $15 for LH version)

BOW SPECIFICATIONS: THUNDERBOLT STINGER CAM
AMO Draw Length: 23- to 27-inch in 1-inch increments.
Draw Weights: 40#, 50# and 60# with 75% let-off
Bow Speed: IBO fps = 278
Axle-to Axle: 37½-inches
Weight in hand: 3 lbs., 9 oz.
SRP: $449

PSE PRO SERIES

The following PSE bows are part of the company's Pro Series and feature upgraded grips, upgraded strings and performance enhancing components in most models. These bows are developed with the advanced archer in mind.

BEAST

The Beast by PSE was unleashed with a new machined aluminum riser in 2002 and offers three cam options: Inferno, Synergy Pro 65 and Synergy Pro 75. This bow is geared toward performance minded archers or hunters who also seek value. Other features include: an upper cable guard, 7–inch brace height, limb pockets securing solid limbs and a molded grip. The 40- and 50# draw weights are only available in the 26-inch draw length model. LH models available for an additional $15.

BOW SPECIFICATIONS: BEAST INFERNO CAM
AMO Draw Length: 27- to 31-inch in 1-inch increments.
Draw Weights: 60# and 70# with 75% let-off
Bow Speed: IBO fps = 290
Axle-to Axle: 36½-inches
Weight in hand: 3 lbs., 10 oz.
SRP: $369.99

BOW SPECIFICATIONS: BEAST SYNERGY PRO 65
AMO Draw Length: 26- to 30-inch in 1-inch increments.
Draw Weights: 40#, 50#, 60# and 70# with 65% let-off
Bow Speed: IBO fps = 295
Axle-to Axle: 39 inches
Weight in hand: 3 lbs., 8 oz.
SRP: $249.99

BOW SPECIFICATIONS:
BEAST SYNERGY PRO 75

MACH 10

AMO Draw Length: 26- to 30-inch in 1-inch increments.
Draw Weights: 40#, 50#, 60# and 70# with 75% let-off
Bow Speed: IBO fps = 290
Axle-to Axle: 39 inches
Weight in hand: 3 lbs., 8 oz.
SRP: $249.99

MACH 10

This Pro Series compound bow uses PSE's Ultimate One-Cam system and NV vibration dampening system to deliver tack-driving accuracy and increased shooter comfort. Other features include: a Micro-Adjust two-prong rest, upper cable guard, Phase 3 grip system and PSE's Pivoting Limb Pockets. The Mach 10 is available in red, blue and graphic colors at an additional cost for the One cam model. This bow is available in right-hand models only.

BOW SPECIFICATIONS: MACH 10 ULTIMATE ONE-CAM
AMO Draw Length: 26- to 31-inch in 1-inch increments.
Draw Weights: 60# and 70# with 80% let-off (65% let-off optional)
Bow Speed: IBO fps = 311
Axle-to Axle: 38 inches
Weight in hand: 4 lbs., 8 oz.
SRP: $1059.99

Revolution Archery Compound Tournament Bows

THIS CANTON, KANSAS, company began manufacturing cams for bows in 1995, but wanted to be more involved in the archery industry and soon began manufacturing complete bows. A solid understanding of cam design and the engineering features of compound bows are the hallmark of their products. The company's Swift model has been the basis for the rest of their product line. Many of Revolution Archery Product's 3-D and tournament trail bows are offered in a wide assortment of colors.

SUPER SWIFT

This bow continues the Swift series traditions and features custom set draw weights and draw lengths, plus various axle lengths and numerous colors for the finish. Custom finishes include: red, blue, green, gold, black, silver, gray, maroon, teal and purple. The bow has similar components to the Triumph.

BOW SPECIFICATIONS: SUPER SWIFT
AMO Draw Length: From 25- to 30¼-inch per customer request.
Draw Weights: From 30# to 65# with 65% let-off
Bow Speed: 319 fps IBO
Axle-to Axle: 36 and 37 inches
SRP:..................... **$675**

TRIUMPH

This bow is designed for archers wanting a longer axle-to-axle length. Design features of the Triumph include CNC machined limbs with three layers of fiberglass laminations and a machined aluminum riser. Other features can be selected by the buyer to include brace heights ranging from 6½ to 6⅞- inches and a custom draw length from 28 to 32 inches. The cams are machined and rotate on needle bearings. Custom finishes include: red, blue, green, gold, black, silver, gray, maroon, teal, and purple. Pick your color to separate your bow from the crowds on tournament day.

BOW SPECIFICATIONS: TRIUMPH
AMO Draw Length: From 28- to 32-inch per customer request.
Draw Weights: From 38# to 65 # with 65% let-off
Bow Speed: 312 fps IBO
Axle-to Axle: 39 and 40 inches
SRP:..................... **$695**

ULTRA SWIFT

This compound bow is designed for the shorter draw archer who desires speed and accuracy at lower pounds draw weight. The compact design makes this a good choice for women and kids. Features include fiberglass laminated limbs, machined riser and cams and finish colors like the previous models. Brace heights for this bow range from 5¾ to 6⅜ inches.
Bow Specifications: Ultra Swift
AMO Draw Length: From 23- to 28½-inch per customer request.
Draw Weights: From 28# to 65# with 65% let-off
Bow Speed: 312 fps IBO
Axle-to Axle: 32 and 34 inches
SRP:..................... **$650**

Fletching Size
A faster arrow can use a smaller fletch and remain stable. A slower arrow requires a larger fletch(which will make it even slower). Choose an optimum size that stabilizes the arrow over the longest distance you will have to shoot. Use the fletch size that maintains arrow speed long enough to reach the target but is as large as you can get away with for the most forgiving shot. –MDF

Stacey Archery Sales Compound Tournament Bows

MITEY MITE

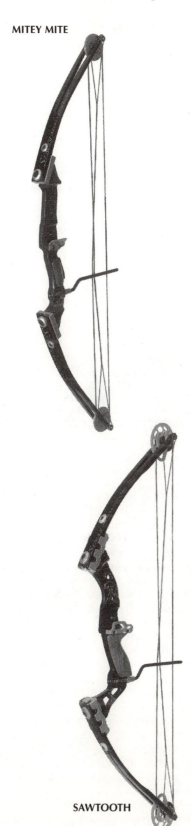

SAWTOOTH

THIS IDAHO FALLS, IDAHO, bowyer produces eight compound adult models and two youth models, plus the innovative Tom Thumb series of compounds designed to help smaller kids gain the thrills and benefits of shooting an adult-like compound bow. Many of the company's tournament models are available in five standard colors: red, blue, black, green and purple. The company also makes several models of release aids. The owners and employees take their products and sport seriously and are always aggressively looking for ways to improve their products. Stacey Archery also takes great pride in its products that are oriented toward getting young archers enthused about the sport.

MITEY MITE

Stacey Archery Sales actively pursues the youth and small framed archer market with its Mitey Mite bows. Both models feature CNC machined aluminum risers, anodized finishes available in five colors, a split two piece grip and steel insert bushings for installation of a cable guard and stabilizer. Other features include a lockdown cable guard, Power Glass split limbs and a choice of speed cams or five-step wheels. Steel pivoting centers for the limb pockets ensure 3-point limb alignment and a removable shelf guard is added for safety. Gold or black hardware and limb pockets are available to help add flash and a true custom eye-catching appearance to the bow to suit the shooter's artistic tastes. These bows weight approximately 2.8 pounds.

The adult Mitey Mites are available as a package that includes the bow, a quiver, a dozen Easton arrows and a release aid. The youth model includes a stabilizer instead of a quiver.

BOW SPECIFICATIONS: ADULT MITEY MITE
AMO Draw Length: From 24- to 30-inch adjustable with modules.
Draw Weights: 20-30#, 30-40#, 40-50# and 50-60# with 65% let-off for speed cams, 65- to 70% let-off is possible with wheels and draw length adjustments.
Bow Speed: NA
Axle-to Axle: 34 inches
SRP: $299.95
    package. $419.95

BOW SPECIFICATIONS: YOUTH MITEY MITE
AMO Draw Length: From 22- to 27-inch
Draw Weights: From 20-30#, 30-40# and 40-50# with 65% let-off for baby speed cams, and 65% to 70% let-off is possible with wheels and draw length adjustments
Bow Speed: NA
Axle-to Axle: 32½-inches
SRP: $259.95
    package. $369.95

SAWTOOTH

This compound has a machined aluminum riser and limb pockets sculpted from 6061-T6 aluminum. The pivoting limb pockets utilize steel pivoting centers to ensure three-point alignment. The bow's add-on accessories—cable guard, plunger butting and stabilizer—can be mounted in the installed steel insert bushings. Other features include a 5½-inch center shot window, choice of two wood grips, graphite glass limbs and your choice of high speed cams or a weighted single cam. Sawtooth competition models are available in five colors. This bow model is available in a manufacturer's package that includes a quiver, one dozen Easton arrows and a Stacey release aid. This package has almost everything any archer needs to start down the tournament trail.

BOW SPECIFICATIONS: SAWTOOTH
AMO Draw Length: From 23- to 31-inch
Draw Weights: From 40# to 80# with 65% let-off for speed cams and optional 80% let-off with single cam.
Bow Speed: NA
Axle-to Axle: 35 and 37 inches
SRP: $529.95
    package. $679.95

TARGHEE

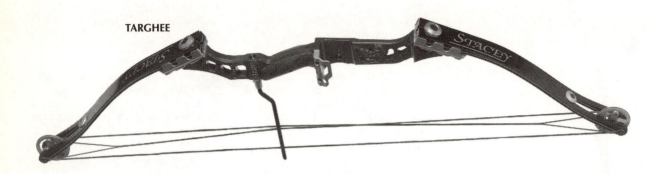

TOM THUMB II

TARGHEE

This bow is built for life on the 3-D tournament trail and the shooter can play a pivotal role in the bow's creation. Customers can custom build a bow with a choice of three limb lengths (15, 16 and 17 inches), three types of wheels and cams, five riser colors and two styles of wooden grips. With this many options you can have the company build your dream bow. The Targhee has the same design features as the Sawtooth plus 60% let-off wheels. Limb choices include 17-inch laminated carbon graphite recurve limbs or Power Tuff Griplite glass limbs. The Targhee weighs 4.2 pounds. This bow is also sold in a package that includes a quiver, overdraw, and release.

BOW SPECIFICATIONS: TARGHEE
AMO Draw Length: From 24- to 34-inch
Draw Weights: From 40# to 80# with 65% let-off for speed cams, 60% with wheels and 65% let-off with the single cam.
Bow Speed: NA
Axle-to Axle: 37, 39, 41 and 42 inches
SRP: **$449.95**
  package. **$529.95**

TOM THUMB II

With draw lengths as short as 16 inches and draw weights as low as 10 pounds, this creative feature packed bow will help young archers of any skill level and frame size find something to get excited about. Stacey Archery uses machined aluminum risers and wheels, machined limb pockets and power glass limbs to build the Tom Thumb compound bow. Other features include a split wood grip, five-inch adjustable wheels, removable shelf guard, lockdown cable guard and Fast Flite string and cables. Risers are available in: red, blue, black, green and purple.

The company offers an up-grade policy with each bow. For a small fee the bow can be outfitted with the next larger wheel size and string to increase the draw length and weight. This bow is sold as a package with bow, rest, glove and half-dozen Easton arrows with points installed. Slightly higher cost for one dozen arrows with package.

BOW SPECIFICATIONS:
YOUTH TOM THUMB II
AMO Draw Length: From 16- to 25-inch, adjustable to many lengths with wheels, baby cams and modules.
Draw Weights: From 10- to 40# in 10# increments with 65% to 70% let-off possible
Bow Speed: NA
Axle-to Axle: 30 inches
SRP: **$179.95**
  package. **$199.95**
  (slightly higher cost with one-dozen arrows option)

RECURVE BOWS

Black Widow Custom Bows Recurve Bows

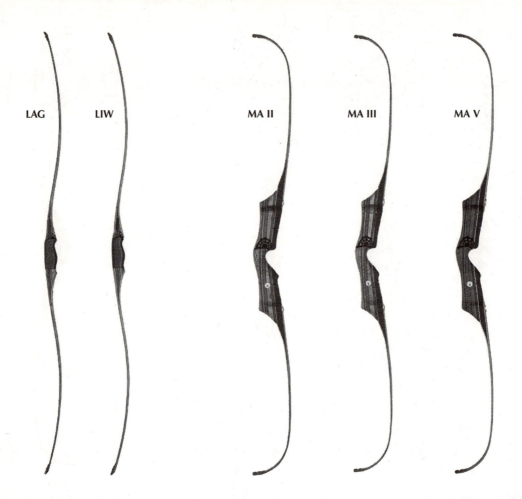

LAG   LIW   MA II   MA III   MA V

BUILDING A LAMINATE layered bow requires much work, including the up to 26 glue lines required to construct many Black Widow models. The company offers five series of models with each series in four different limb lengths and in two or three colors. Components include Dyna Flex limbs and Flemish twist DynaFLIGHT 97 strings. Each bow also comes with a bowstringer, bow tip protector, Spyder string silencers, Spider Webb shelf rest, one dozen nocking points and a detailed owner's manual. Some Black Widow models have a hard case or soft case and a free archery video included.

The company has a fleet of DEMO bows that you can check out for a week by paying for the shipping and insurance fees only when the bow is returned. This might be the only test-drive offer in the industry for bows! Contact Black Widow for details and tell them you discovered this option through this Archery Buyer's Guide!

LAG AND LIW

These longbows are available in one-piece and take-down models. Black Widow's LAGs and LIWs utilize DynaFlex limbs, DynaFlight 97 strings, deflex designed risers and Shur-Grip rubber handles that can be removed. Features of these bows include: 7-inch brace height, clear marine finish, radiused shelf, and reinforced limb core and tip overlay. A Navajo bow sleeve is included, plus a hardcase for the one-piece models. Draw lengths range from 24 to 34 inches.

The LAG (Long Autumn Gray) model has an Autumn Oak brown outer laminate over Graybark gray wood at the grip. The LIW features Ironwood in the riser.

SRP: LAG one-piece **$740**
    take-down **$860**
LIW one-piece **$830**
    take-down **$950**

MA II, MA III AND MA V

Black Widow's MA limbs have been redesigned and dynamically balanced in recent manufacturing runs. A longer deflex handle with long sight window permits use of sights. This take-down bow has a radiused shelf, marine epoxy finish and solid brass bushings. Dual-Pin take-down ensures perfect limb alignment. The limbs fit into reinforced areas on the face of the riser toward the shooter. Draw length options range from 58 to 64 inches. Black Widow's MA II bows are Graybark color, MA III bows are Autumn Oak and the MA V is dark brown Ironwood.

SRP: II/III series begins **$830**
    V series **$940**
Handle (riser) II/III series **$373**
    V series **$423**
Limbs II/III series **$457**
    V series **$517**

RECURVE BOWS

Black Widow Custom Bows Recurve Bows

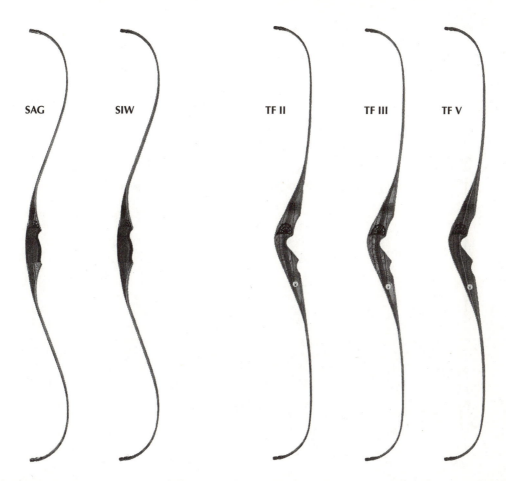

SAG   SIW   TF II   TF III   TF V

SA II, SA III AND SA V

SA model bows are similar in construction and components to Black Widow's MA series but with a 2-inch shorter handle to create a more maneuverable bow. This option is handy when hunting from treestands or ground blinds.

SRP: II/III series begins **$830**
    V series **$940**
Handle (riser) II/III series **$373**
    V series **$423**
Limbs II/III series **$457**
    V series **$517**

SAG AND SIW

These Black Widow short bows are based on a 1940s look—combining nostalgia and tradition—and are very maneuverable. This bow is available in a standard one-piece recurve design and as a take-down model with a unique locking device concealed under the leather grip. Features for the SAG and SIW series include: DynaFlex limbs, deflex riser, clear marine epoxy

finish and Flemish-twist DynaFLIGHT 97 string. These bows come with all of the previously mentioned accessories. SAG models are available in Autumn Gray and Autumn Oak, SIG models are offered in the darker brown Ironwood. A custom grip can be designed for an additional $70.

SRP: SAG one-piece **$740**
    take-down **$860**
SIW one-piece **$830**
    take-down **$950**

SENECA CONVERTIBLE TAKE-DOWN RECURVE

This youth bow is distributed by Black Widow and features black 46-inch solid fiberglass limbs. A unique feature is that this recurve can be easily converted from a left- to right-hand model by removing either of the two modules in the Ultra-Fiber black handle. The bow features: a Dacron bowstring, string silencers, knocking point, tip protector, and lock-on arrow rest. The complete kit includes

an arm guard, finger tab, two fiberglass arrows and a comprehensive instruction book. The draw weight is 20# at 24 inches draw length.

SRP: **$51.00**

TF II, TF III AND TF V

This Black Widow series of one-piece recurves uses TF limbs that are faced with transparent Bo-Tuff fiberglass. The deflex riser is pre-stressed and reinforced with multiple layers of Bo-Tuff fiberglass. This bow's sight window is cut ⅛-inch past center and the inserted brass bushings will accept side-mount quivers, sights or stabilizer. These bows arrive with a bow stringer, Spyder string silencers, tip protector, Spider Webb shelf protector, nocking points, video and owner's manual. They are available in the same colors as the previously listed bows.

SRP: II/III series begins **$830**
    V series **$940**

Bowhunting Traditions Recurve Bows

TAKE-DOWN LONGBOW

THESE BOWS ARE designed by expert bowyer Neil Jacobson and offered in longbow and recurve models. A unique color stripe runs through the risers and custom wood choices are available. Bowhunting Traditions is based in Sioux City, Iowa, and can be reached at (712) 276-0574.

BOWHUNTING TRADITIONS TAKE-DOWN LONGBOW

This unique longbow can be easily taken down for storage or transportation. It is similar in design and options to Bowhunting Tradition's Take-Down Recurve model and in 62-inches long. A Fast Flight Flemish string is included and custom woods, different lengths and other special features can be included in the construction of this longbow. Both right- and left-hand models are offered. Each bow is custom built one at a time.

BOW SPECIFICATIONS: BOWHUNTING TRADITIONS TAKE-DOWN LONGBOW
Draw Weight: varies
Length: 62-inch or other lengths are available
SRP: . . . . **varies by selections**

BOWHUNTING TRADITIONS TAKE-DOWN RECURVE

This 60-inch recurve bow by Bowhunting Traditions is offered in a right- or left-hand model and the grips can be low, medium or high. Handle risers are available in golden brown, rosewood or black laminated wood. Limbs are constructed of red elm with clear fiberglass laminates. All recurves have a special wedge built into the limb tip and the tips can be covered with antler tip, horn or mycarta. Buyer has the choice of wrench type bolts or hand-turned take-down knobs for the limb anchoring system.

BOW SPECIFICATIONS: BOWHUNTING TRADITIONS TAKE-DOWN RECURVE
Draw Weight: varies
Length: 60-inch and other lengths are available
SRP: . . . . **varies by selections**

TAKE-DOWN RECURVE

The Percentage Game
Most bows originally offered 50% let-off. Then 65%, 75% and higher percentage let-off bows appeared on the market. Any bow providing more than 65% does not qualify for the Pope and Young Club record books. Your record could, however, possibly qualify for the Safari Club International record books. Visit www.sci.org for more details.—MDF

RECURVE BOWS

Bruin Custom Recurves Recurve Bows

CLASSIC LONGBOW

DEFLEX EXPRESS

HUNTMASTER FAMILY

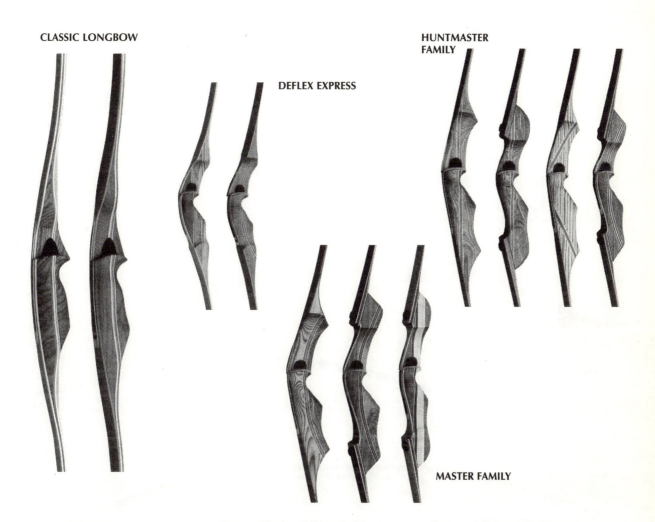

MASTER FAMILY

BRUIN CUSTOM BOWS are hand built to match the needs of the shooter after an in-depth interview which can be conducted over the phone or in person. Bruin bows are available in eight models, including the newer Classic Long-bows and Deflex Express. Bruin has been crafting bows since 1984 and is located in Antigo, Wisconsin. All bows are backed by a two year warranty. Call (715) 623-6537 for ordering information.

BRUIN CLASSIC LONGBOW

The buyer chooses the riser woods and limb cores to start the construction process for this bow and the overlays and tips will match those selections. This longbow is offered in 58- and 60-inch lengths. Bruin is one of a few companies that continues to make longbows.
SRP: Starting at $575

BRUIN DEFLEX EXPRESS

This traditional one-piece bow by Bruin provides a choice of riser woods, limb cores and the accent stripe through the riser. Other choices include overlays, limb wedges and tips that match or accent the color of the wood selections. This recurve is available in 58-, 60- and 62-inch lengths.
SRP: Starting at $795

BRUIN HUNTMASTER FAMILY

This series of recurves includes the Woodsmaster, Woodsmaster SE, and Huntmaster. These bows can be ordered as a traditional one-piece or in a take-down design. Length options include: 56-, 58- and 60-inch models.
SRP: from . . . . $465 to $695
set of extra limbs for the
T/D models up to. $350

BRUIN MASTER FAMILY

This family of bows includes the Master, Master SE, and Master Express. These recurves have stylish laminated wood risers. Master and Master SE bows have slightly larger hand grips. Bruin's take-down models are offered in 56-, 58-, 60- and 62-inch lengths. Traditional one-piece bows are offered in 60- and 62-inch lengths.
SRP: Master SE, starting at $550
Master, starting at $750
Master Express, starting at $825
The use of optional items and premium woods increases costs.

Custom Shooting Systems Recurve Bows

THIS WEST VIRGINIA company currently produces only one recurve bow model. Both hunting camouflage and target shooting color options are available. Contact CSS for more details.

RT RECURVE

This recurve uses a T-6061 machined aluminum riser—in the System or Contender style—to propel arrows. Other features include the soft-touch grip (walnut wood is optional), Gordon thermal composite limbs and a built-in arrow shelf. The RT Recurve is offered in Mossy Oak Break-Up for hunting and black, blue and burgundy for competition.

BOW SPECIFICATIONS: RT RECURVE
Draw Weight: 40#, 50#, and 60#.
Length: 60 or 66 inches
SRP:. . . . . varies by selection

Fred Bear Recurve Bows

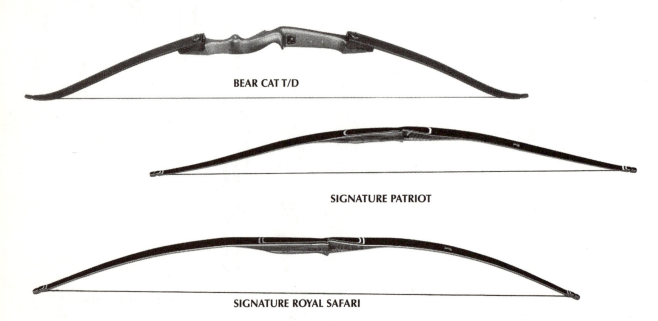

BEAR CAT T/D

SIGNATURE PATRIOT

SIGNATURE ROYAL SAFARI

MANY OF THE BOWS offered by the Fred Bear Archery Company continue to incorporate the designs and craftsmanship details provided by the master bowyer—Fred Bear—himself. You can see archery history—and many of the company's early proto-type bows—at the Fred Bear Museum in Gainesville, Florida.

BEAR CAT T/D

Technology and value take front stage on the Bear Cat T/D bow. The magnesium riser accepts the easy to bolt on fiberglass reinforced epoxy limbs. The Bear Cat uses a Dacron string and is drilled and tapped to accept any AMO standard accessories.

BOW SPECIFICATIONS: BEAR CAT T/D (MODEL 2293)
Draw Weight: RH only at 25#, 35# or 45#
Length: 60-inch
SRP:. $149

BYRON FERGUSON SIGNATURE PATRIOT

The Patriot blends longbow speed with a reflex/deflex design in a package that weighs less than 1.5 pounds. Each bow has Byron Ferguson's signature, a leather grip and FastFlight string. The rest shelf is crowned and radiused for smooth arrow take-off.

BOW SPECIFICATIONS: BYRON FERGUSON SIGNATURE PATRIOT (MODEL 2036)
Draw Weight: RH or LH models in 45#, 50#, 55#, 60# or 65#.
Length: 64-inch
SRP:. . . . . varies

BYRON FERGUSON SIGNATURE ROYAL SAFARI

This longbow is designed to famed archer Byron Ferguson's specifications and built on a core of laminated hard rock maple. The bow's face and back are laminated with black fiberglass. The riser is constructed of brown and black hard rock maple with a decorative face. Other features include a leather grip and Fast-Flight string. This would be a top contender as a longbow that's designed for hunting.

BOW SPECIFICATIONS: BYRON FERGUSON SIGNATURE ROYAL SAFARI (MODEL 2038)
Draw Weight: RH or LH models in 45#, 50#, 55#, 60#, 65# or 70#.
Length: 66-inch
SRP:. . . . . varies

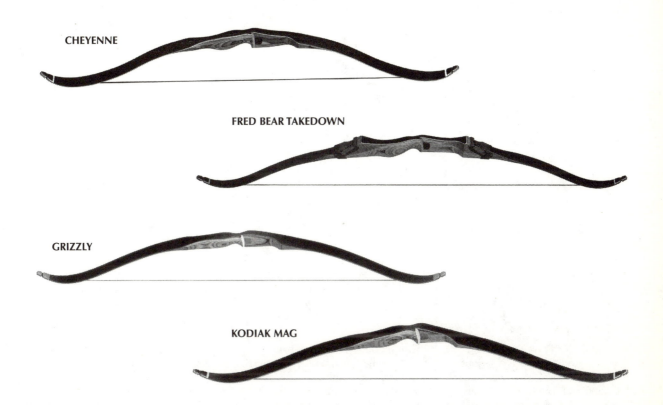

CHEYENNE

FRED BEAR TAKEDOWN

GRIZZLY

KODIAK MAG

CHEYENNE

This 55-inch recurve is constructed of select maple laminates and fiberglass laminate limbs. It incorporates a Radiused grip and FastFlight string. It weighs less than 1.5 pounds and is recommended for hunting whitetails and elk. Left- and right-hand versions are available in this flagship product for the Fred Bear Elite Series.

BOW SPECIFICATIONS: CHEYENNE (MODEL 2032)
Draw Weight: 45#, 50#, 55# or 60# models available.
Length: 55 inches
SRP:. $449

FRED BEAR TAKEDOWN

This bow is Fred Bear's masterpiece and is an excellent choice for the traveling hunter who visits remote regions. The TakeDown features a patented limb attachment system, crowned shelf with bear hair arrow rest and fiberglass reinforced tips. Two handle lengths—56-inch A-handle and 60-inch B-handle versions—are available.

BOW SPECIFICATIONS: FRED BEAR TAKEDOWN (MODELS 2075 (A) AND 2074 (B))
Draw Weight: 45#, 50#, 55#, 60# and 65# with left- and right-hand models available.
Length: 56-inch (A) or 60-inch (B)
SRP:. $999

GRIZZLY

This recurve bow is considered the working man's bow. Fred Bear designed this bow to be tough, yet economical. Construction components include black fiberglass surfacing over laminated hardwoods and a final coat of non-reflective satin gloss. This bow comes with a Dacron string. The bow can be shot off the bear hair rest or from a rest attached to the maple sight window.

BOW SPECIFICATIONS: GRIZZLY (MODEL 2086)
Draw Weight: RH or LH models in 45#, 50# or 55#. Additional RH model at 60#.
Length: 58-inch
SRP:. $299

KODIAK CUB

This Bear bow was designed to help the next generation enter into archery with a smooth transition. Handcrafted from North Country Hardwoods, the short-draw Kodiak Cub is hand sanded and hand surfaced and finished in satin. Other features include a Dacron string and stylish inlaid brass Fred Bear medallion.

BOW SPECIFICATIONS: KODIAK CUB (MODEL 2088)
Draw Weight: RH or LH models in 10#, 20# or 30# (at 24-inch AMO).
Length: 48-inch
SRP:. $179

KODIAK MAG

This Bear recurve bow is 52 inches long and features black fiberglass over select hardwood laminates. Other features include an inlaid Fred Bear brass medallion and rich satin finish. The medallion adds a true touch of prestige to this bow!

BOW SPECIFICATIONS: KODIAK MAG (MODEL 2030)
Draw Weight: 45#, 50#, 55#, 60# and 65# right-hand models available. 55# and 65# left-hand models are available.
Length: 52 inches
SRP:. $399

RECURVE BOWS

Fred Bear Recurve Bows

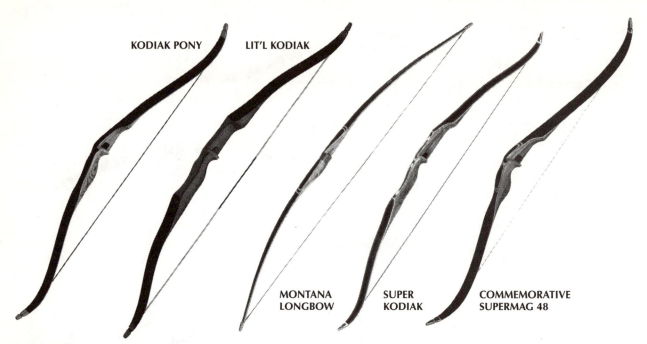

KODIAK PONY LIT'L KODIAK

MONTANA LONGBOW SUPER KODIAK COMMEMORATIVE SUPERMAG 48

KODIAK PONY

The Bear Kodiak Pony is a serious intermediate-level bow with a classic look and feel. The features of this bow include brown maple riser and matching wood tips that contrast against black glass. Other features include a crowned shelf, bear hair arrow rest and Dacron string.

BOW SPECIFICATIONS: KODIAK PONY (MODEL 2042)
Draw Weight: RH only models in 25#, 35# or 45# (at 25-inch AMO draw).
Length: 52-inch
SRP:. $299

LIT'L KODIAK

This is a scaled down recurve bow version that's designed to introduce small kids to archery. Features of the Lil' Kodiak include black glass limbs, lightweight maple laminate riser and an arrow shelf with bear hair rest and leather side plate. A distinctive brass Fred Bear medallion is inlaid in the handle.

BOW SPECIFICATIONS: LIT'L KODIAK (MODEL 2094)
Draw Weight: RH only at 5# to 8# and 14-inch draw length.
Length: 30-inch
SRP:. $100

MONTANA LONGBOW

This bow is a fine example of ancient bowyer's craftsmanship combined with modern materials. Features include maple laminates and black glass overlays with an arrow shelf that's crowned and cut to center. Other features include a standard leather grip, reinforced tips and FastFlight string.

BOW SPECIFICATIONS: MONTANA LONGBOW (MODEL 2040)
Draw Weight: 45#, 50#, 55#, 60# right-hand models. LH at 50# or 55#
Length: 64-inch
SRP:. $299

SUPER KODIAK

Fred Bear successfully hunted with this bow model on four continents. It is constructed with matched gray and brown laminates, black glass limbs and reinforced tips. The Super Kodiak includes a FastFlight string when purchased. The arrow shelf is crowned, cut past center and lined with bear hair.

The Commemorative Super Kodiak has a maple and rosewood riser, black and white glass laminates and scrimshawed medallion and compass inlays. Other features include an arrow shelf with leather side plate and Bear Hair rest and padded Fred Bear bow case. This bow looks like a true piece of art, but you could hunt with it in the fields and forests! It's a 1999 limited edition with limited supply. Available in RH or LH models at 50# or 55#. The Model

2010's SRP is $675.

BOW SPECIFICATIONS: SUPER KODIAK (MODEL 2020)
Draw Weight: 45#, 50#, 55#, 60# and 65# right-hand models available. 50#, 55# and 65# left-hand models are available.
Length: 60 inches
SRP:. $449

SUPERMAG 48

This 48-inch recurve bow is built by Bear Archery and has eye-catching black and white tips that accept the FastFlight string. Other construction components include a black hard rock maple riser with black fiberglass limbs. The crowned arrow shelf has a leather side plate and bear hair rest.

Commemorative SuperMag 48 has rosewood and black-over-white fiberglass laminates. Other features include an inlaid scrimshawed medallion and compass in the riser, FastFlight string and padded Fred Bear bow case. 2001 limited edition with limited supply. RH or LH at 50# or 55#. Model 2014/ SRP: $675.

BOW SPECIFICATIONS: SUPERMAG 48 (MODEL 2034)
Draw Weight: RH or LH models at 45#, 50#, 55#, or 65#.
Length: 48-inch
SRP:. $329

RECURVE BOWS

Fedora's Archery Shop Recurve Bows

THESE BOWS ARE DESIGNED by Olympic coach and archery consultant Mike Fedora Sr. at his Richland, Pennsylvania, shop. Call (717) 933-8862 for ordering details.

HUNTER 60-INCH ONE-PIECE

This bow has been in production for more than 40 years and has a strong following of users. It is designed for draw lengths up to 30 inches without stack, and is a fast, quiet and smooth shooter. Features of the Hunter 60-Inch One-Piece include a custom grip and selection of the finish by the buyer.

BOW SPECIFICATIONS:
HUNTER 60-INCH ONE-PIECE
Draw Weight: varies

Length: 60-inch
SRP: Starting at **$425**

STALKER 52-INCH

This bow is designed to shoot where you're looking without any stack to compensate for adjustments. It is a great model to select for hunting. Features of Fedora's Stalker 52-Inch include a custom grip fitted to the shooter and a Fedora thumb rest. This bow works well for short draw archers. The buyer can select the finish.

BOW SPECIFICATIONS: STALKER 52-INCH
Draw Weight: varies and ranges up to 75#
Length: 52-inch
SRP: Starting at **$425**

XCELLERATOR-HYBRID DEFLEX-REFLEX BOW

This longbow will change your mind about using longbows for hunting and shooting! The Xcellerator-Hybrid Deflex-Reflex bow is offered in 58-, 60-, 62-, 64-, and 66-inch lengths and as a right- or left-hand model. The AMO speed exceeds 200 fps. The draw length for this bow ranges from 25- to 32 inches. You can select a dull, satin or hand-rubbed finish to add to the personal touch of your bow.

BOW SPECIFICATIONS: XCELLERATOR-HYBRID DEFLEX-REFLEX BOW
Draw Weight: varies
Length: 58-, 60-, 62-, 64, and 66-inch
SRP: Starting at **$425**

Golden Eagle Recurve Bows

LIT'L BRAVE

THIS FLORIDA-BASED bow maker creates numerous youth recurves in addition to a full line of compound bows that have a strong world-wide following. Golden Eagle is owned by the North American Archery Group in Gainesville, Florida. These bow models are designed for educational and recreational purposes only and will not be legal for hunting in most states.

BRAVE RANGER

This discovery level recurve features a composite molded grip/riser with Robin Hood Green limbs. It has a distinctive Ranger logo that will be popular with any young shooter!
SRP: **$29**

LIT'L BRAVE

This starter level recurve bow helps teach youngsters the basics of archery in an exciting format. Features include composite limbs and riser, black finish and integral grip. This bow is available in right-hand models only.

BOW SPECIFICATIONS: LIT'L BRAVE
AMO Draw Length/Weight: 13# at 16-inch draw; 28# at 24-inch draw
Length: 45 inches
Weight in hand: 1 lbs., 9 oz.
SRP: **$39**

Great Plains Traditional Bow Co. Recurve Bows

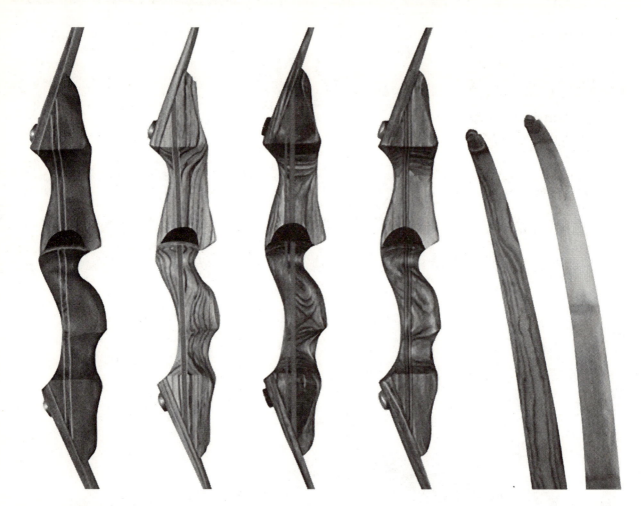

THIS BOW MANUFACTURER is based in Pampa, Texas, and creates longbows, recurves and target recurve bows. Each bow is handcrafted and finished with heavy duty epoxy. Other features include: reinforced limb tips, riser inserts, and the owner's name installed on the bow at no charge. B-models have an arched beam in the handle and are available in 58-, 60-, 62- and 64-inch lengths.

These bows have tips inlayed with Phonolic and antler tips are optional for some models. Prices can fluctuate based on options chosen.

GREAT PLAINSMAN LONGBOWS
SRP:
Cedar and Elm $480
  add $90 for T/D with elm cores
Gray Limb $505
  add $65 for T/D with elm cores
Osagian $505
  add $65 for T/D model

Rio Bravo $505
  add $65 for T/D model
Cazador-Yew Wood $535
  add $50 for T/D model
Tulip and Osage $550
  add $60 for T/D model
Bamboo $550
  add $60 for T/D model

YOUTH RECURVE BOW BY GREAT PLAINS
SRP: $185

TAKE-DOWN TARGET BOW BY GREAT PLAINS
SRP: $710

ONE-PIECE RECURVES
SRP:
Red River (gray or brown) $510
  add $40 for B-model
Wolf Creek $510
  add $40 for B-model
Palo Duro $510
  add $40 for B-model

Rio Bravo $510
  add $40 for B-model
Cazador $525
  add $40 for B-model
Bamboo $540
  add $50 for B-model
Kiowa $390
  available in standard model only

TAKE-DOWN RECURVES
SRP:
Red River (gray or brown) $560
  add $50 for B-model
Wolf Creek $560
  add $50 for B-model
Rio Bravo $560
  add $50 for B-model
Palo Duro $560
  add $50 for B-model
Estacado (B-model only) $610
Cazador $575
  add $50 for B-model
Bamboo $600
  add $50 for B-model

RECURVE BOWS

BRUSH BOW

COMBO HUNTER

IN YESTERYEAR, ARCHERS built their own bow. Horne's gives you that opportunity again with their truly custom recurves and longbows. You pick the materials and they do the work. This Texas based company permits you to custom design five models with your choice of wood(s) for the riser and limb, left- or right-hand models, lengths and color of glass laminates. You can also select: leather grip, quiver bushings, bamboo cored, decorative swoop and a two-wood swoop to suit your taste and please your eye. Wood choices include: Bamboo, osage orange, zebrawood, birdseye and curly maple, cocobolo, hickory, red elm, cherry, black locust and red cedar plus many others. Call (940) 433-3044 for the full details.

BRUSH BOW

This Horne's 28-ounce one-piece long-bow has limbs with a built-in reflex-deflex design for maximizing stored energy and reducing hand shock. The Brush Bow's riser has a 3-inch radiused sight window and radiused shelf covered with synthetic hair. The grip can be customized as medium or low. The Brush Bows are finished with matte or gloss finish, leather strike plate and hand-made Fast-Flight string. This custom bow is available in 60-, 62- or 64-inch lengths.

SRP: . . . . **varies by wood and option selections**

COMBO HUNTER

This is Horne's newest bow and combines superior craftsmanship with unmatched performance. This longbow riser has a 3-inch radiused sight window designed to be used with a take-down longbow or recurve limbs. With multiple limbs you can develop a personal bow for a wide assortment of hunting conditions and target shooting events.

The Combo Hunter is available in 60- and 62-inch recurve lengths and 62-, 64- and 66-inch lengths with the longbow limbs. This bow can be easily packed for travel.

SRP: Riser, starting at **$225**
Limbs in basic woods **$275**
There is an additional cost for premium woods.

Warm Up Often
It's a great idea to draw your bow periodically during a hunt to keep your muscles warm and flexible. Cold weather can make drawing difficult as it affects your joints and extremities.--MDF

Horne's Archery Recurve Bows

MOUNTAIN BOW

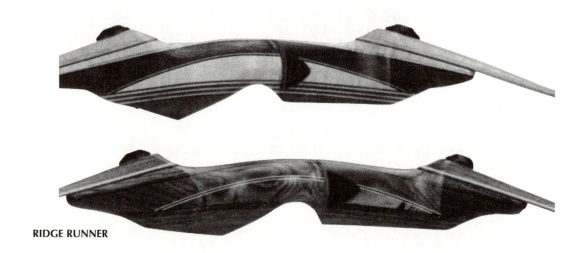

RIDGE RUNNER

MOUNTAIN BOW

Developed in the 1950s, this bow style has a medium or low grip that's wrapped in goat skin or sinew. You can have a take down model built with 56-, 58-, 60- or 62-inch length with a 3½-inch radiused sight window. A one-piece Mountain bow is available in 60-inch length. Mountain bows have hardwood overlays and fadeout limb tips that can be matched to the bow's handle colors.

SRP: Risers in basic wood, begins at $150
Limbs in basic wood. $275
   Premium woods cost more and take-down bows cost more.
   Call for pricing based on multiple options.

RIDGE RUNNER

This classic take-down recurve is available with a 15- or 17-inch hardwood riser. The handle is built with multiple glass and hardwood overlays. The Ridge Runner is offered in 56-, 58-, 60- and 62-inch lengths. The handle can be contoured as a low, medium or high wrist grip. This bow can be crafted from your choice of woods and with fade-out limb tips.

SRP: Ridge Runner risers, start at. $325
Solid-one-piece model riser, starts at $200
Limbs in basic woods $275

TRADITIONALIST

Available in 62-, 64-, 66- or 68-inch lengths, this Horne's longbow has a reflex-deflex design that forms a D-ring when strung. The contoured grip has a leather wrap to provide comfort.

SRP: Riser start at $150
Limbs in basic woods $275

RECURVE BOWS

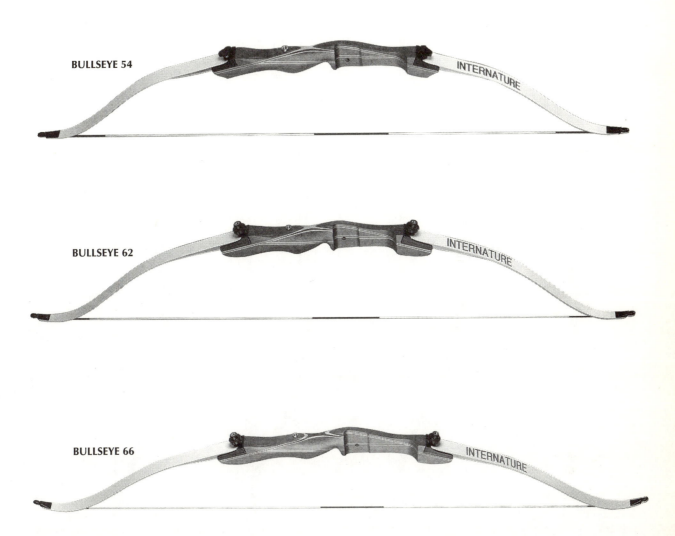

BULLSEYE 54

BULLSEYE 62

BULLSEYE 66

THIS PRODUCT LINE specializes in youth and recreation products in the archery arena. If you've ever shot a bow at a scout or 4-H camp, there's a good chance that you used one of these bows. One of the company's newest products is the economically priced TD Hunter recurve. These recurves are distributed by AIM (Archery International Marketing). This Connecticut based distributor provides recurves and other archery gear and accessories to archery enthusiasts around the world. AIM provides more than 18 recurve models to shooters under the Samick and interNature brands.

BULLSEYE

The Bullseye series of recurve bows are available in youth and recreation models. The youth bows are available in 48- (the Warrior) and 54-inch lengths with weights ranging from 15 to 38 pounds. Right- and left-hand models are also available. These bows feature laminated wood risers, limb pockets and threaded brass accessory receivers. All bows feature fiberglass limbs and stylish black reinforced tips. These bows are commonly used in youth camps, schools and scouting programs.

Adult Bullseye series bows are 62- and 66-inches long and are designed and built the same as the youth models. The longer length models achieve the upper 30, 33 and 38 pound draw weight ranges. All bows have components (limbs and risers) that can be purchased separately for upgrades and repairs. SRPs for the risers range from $42 to $66 and from $48 to $66 for the limbs.

BOW SPECIFICATIONS: BULLSEYE
Draw Weight: 15# to 38#.
Length: From 48 to 66 inches
SRPs: 48-inch Warrior:. $79.95
54-inch Bullseye:. $99.95
62-inch Bullseye:. $99.95
66-inch Bullseye:. $118.00

RECURVE BOWS

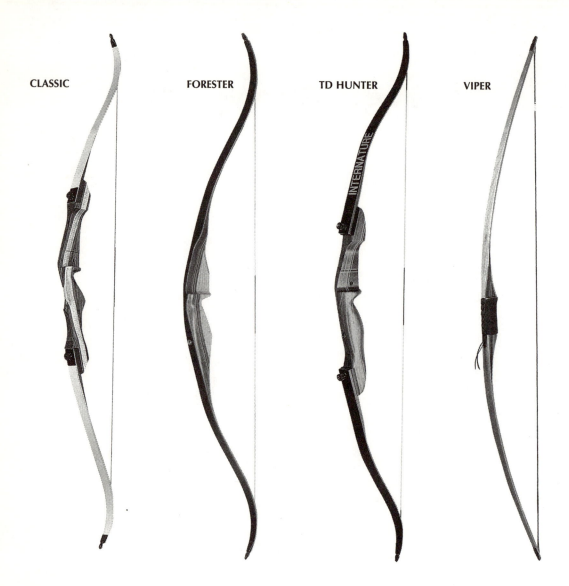

CLASSIC FORESTER TD HUNTER VIPER

CLASSIC

This 66-inch recurve has a two-color laminated wood riser with carved grip surface and white fiberglass limbs. It is recommended for recreational shooting or targets plinking. The Classic is available in left- and right-hand models.

BOW SPECIFICATIONS: CLASSIC
Draw Weight: 20#, 25#, 30# and 35#.
Length: 66 inches
SRP:. $155

FORESTER

This more traditional one-piece multi-laminate bow has dark and contrasting light wood layers. A threaded brass bushing will accept a stabilizer or other accessories. This recurve would be a good choice by hunters.

BOW SPECIFICATIONS: FORESTER
Draw Weight: 30#, 40#, 45#, 50#, 55# and 60#.
Length: 58 inches
SRP:. $195

TD HUNTER

This take down recurve by interNature is made for the traveling hunter and those seeking a compact bow for storage. Features include multi-laminated wood riser with a red laminate layer running through the middle of the riser. Each limb is black and constructed of laminates.

The TD Hunter is offered in right- and left-hand models.

BOW SPECIFICATIONS: TD HUNTER
Draw Weight: 40#, 45#, 50#, 55# and 60#.
Length: 58 inches
SRP:. $150

VIPER

This classically styled long bow has a leather grip wrapped around multiple wood laminated layers and reinforced limb tips. A unique construction process ensures that no two bows look alike. The Viper can be obtained in left- and right-hand models.

BOW SPECIFICATIONS: VIPER
Draw Weight: 30#, 40#, 45#, 50#, 55# and 60#.
Length: 68 inches
SRP:. $195

RECURVE BOWS

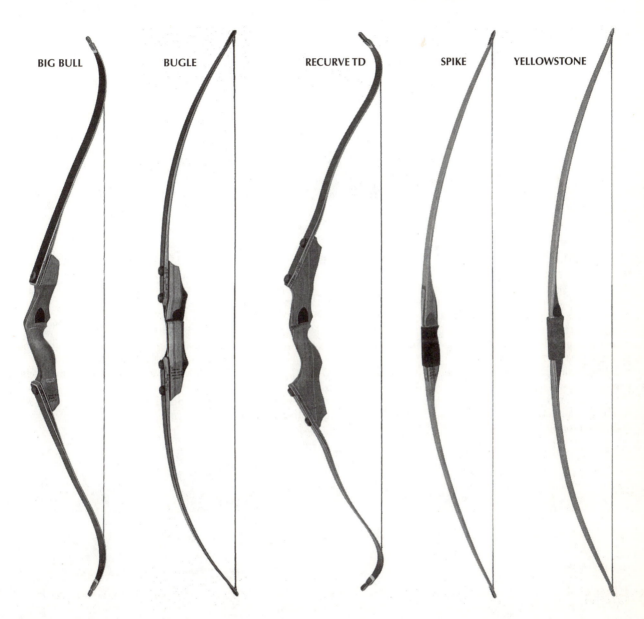

BIG BULL   BUGLE   RECURVE TD   SPIKE   YELLOWSTONE

THIS BOWYER IS based in Lakewood, Colorado, and has been hand-building custom bows since 1960. The recurves are cut to the riser center line only. Take-down bows are created in five basic designs: Quick-action snap lock, single bolt and pin, single bolt and pivot, slide-lock and two bolts per limbs. This company creates Wapiti recurves and longbows and the bows can be inscribed with the customer's name. Other features include crowned arrow shelf, hair rest and fiberglass reinforced limb mounting surfaces.

WAPITI BIG BULL SERIES RECURVES
SRP:.....................$495

WAPITI IMPERIAL SERIES RECURVES
SRP:.....................$695

WAPITI ROYAL SERIES RECURVES
SRP:.....................$595
   take-down series is the same price

**WAPITI LONGBOWS
WAPITI BUGLE**
SRP:.....................$525
   extra limbs.............$350

WAPITI QUIVERS
7- and 4-arrow capacity.....$49.95
   with a bow purchase.....$34.50

WAPITI SPIKE
SRP: one piece.............$495
   take-down.............$555

WAPITI YELLOWSTONE
SRP: one-piece.............$450
   take-down.............$510

RECURVE BOWS

Mahaska Custom Bows Recurve Bows

THIS BOWYER CRAFTS longbows and recurves one at a time to the specific demands of the customer and future owner. The customer selects the grip size and shape, draw length, and draw weight. More than two dozen handle woods and five different limb cores are available. Wood choices include: red gum, walnut, honey locust, flamewood, catclaw, lacewood, and coyote. These bows are backed by a three-year warranty. Call (641) 763-5501 for ordering information.

MAHASKA FLATBOW
This flatbow has shorter and wider limbs for smoothness and speed. The Flatbow can be built in any wood and handle shape desired and is available in 62-inch length.
SRP: Starting at **$360**

MAHASKA LONGBOW
Available in 62-, 64-, 66- and 68-inch lengths, these longbows have a deflex-reflex design with a straight traditional style. Other features include a semi-pistol grip and a slightly dished locator.
SRP: Starting at **$360**

MAHASKA TRADITIONAL RECURVE
This one-piece recurve is designed to shoot off the shelf, a desire of many instinctive archers. Bow lengths range from 58 to 60 inches.
SRP: Starting at **$380**

Check Your Clothing
One thing that can cause an arrow to miss its mark is your clothing. A puffy shirt front or sleeve that makes contact with the bowstring steals valuable arrow energy and can cause your arrow to fly erratically. You can use a chest protector and arm guard to prevent this problem. Remember that if you bowhunt, you wear thicker clothes and more clothing layers as the season progresses and the temperatures drop. Check your clothing to make sure that it does not interfere with your release and arrow flight.--MDF

RECURVE BOWS

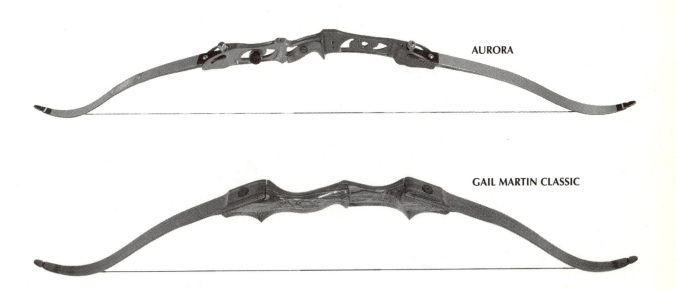

AURORA

GAIL MARTIN CLASSIC

THIS ARCHERY manufacturer makes recurves as well as a full line of popular compound bows. Martin Archery has been family owned and operated for more than 50 years and are still located at the facility where they began operation near Walla Walla, Washingotn. Now that's tradition! Martin Archery works to combine that tradition with archery design experience to create many quality bows.

AURORA
The technologically advanced Aurora target recurve bow by Martin Archery has an ergonomically designed riser that incorporates V.E.C. technology to eliminate riser vibration after arrow release. The riser uses a standard limb mounting system to use most any after-market target limb. The riser has a unique open design with appealing sculpted openings. The Aurora is available in Pro Red, Pro Blue, or Purple and in right- or left-hand models.

The Martin Design Team draws upon over 50 years of traditional bow making experience. This experience has been instrumental in the development of the Aurora Limb system. These limbs use the standard detent system and may be used on most any Olympic-style recurve handle with the detent system. The new Aurora limbs use proprietary core materials and

lamination designed to maximize stability and torsion resistance. This limb system, designed by Aurora R&D team member Mike Gerard, allows the shooter to independently adjust limb weight and limb center. The bolt has an independent cam action that permits shifting the center of the limb and adjusting the bow for individual needs. Once that adjustment is made, the weight can be changed without affecting the limb's center. The riser and limbs are sold separately for this target bow.
BOW SPECIFICATIONS: AURORA
AMO Draw Length/Weight: 30# to 50# at 28-inch draw
Length: Varies
Weight in hand: 3 lbs., 7 ozs.
SRP: **$1,100**

DREAM CATCHER
This one-piece 60-inch recurve by Martin has red elm laminations on the face that are backed with clear fiberglass. The bow's two-tone hardwood riser is sculpted from African hardwood and has accent strips. Other features include a Dacron string, bowstringer and traditional shelf rest. Sight and stabilizer bushings can be installed upon request. This bow is available in right- and left-hand versions and was introduced in 1997.

SPECIFICATIONS: DREAM CATCHER
Draw Weight: from 30# to 70# at 28-inch draw length in 5# increments.
Length: 60 inches
SRP: **$450.00**

GAIL MARTIN CLASSIC
The 60-inch Gail Martin Classic Take-Down, a bow displaying beauty and craftsmanship that reflects fifty years of pure archery enjoyment, graciously echoes the gratification and fulfillment that pioneer Gail Martin—the founder of Martin Archery—understands through traditional archery. The bow's smooth flowing lines are carefully sculpted by experienced hands and are showcased in a hand-applied glossy finish. Contrasting shades of color—gray and light brown—created by laminations of Bubinga and Maple create an eye-catching riser. Hand-laid laminations of Red Elm form limbs that gently accept the contours of the riser, tapering away to tips reinforced with layers of fiberglass and Bubinga wood. Hand-carved string-grooves gently cradle a hand-spliced Flemish bowstring. Everything about the Gail Martin Classic reflects a chance to own a piece of archery history.
SPECIFICATIONS: GAIL MARTIN CLASSIC
Draw Weights from 30# to 70#
Length: 60 inches
SRP: **$632.99**

Martin Archery Recurve Bows

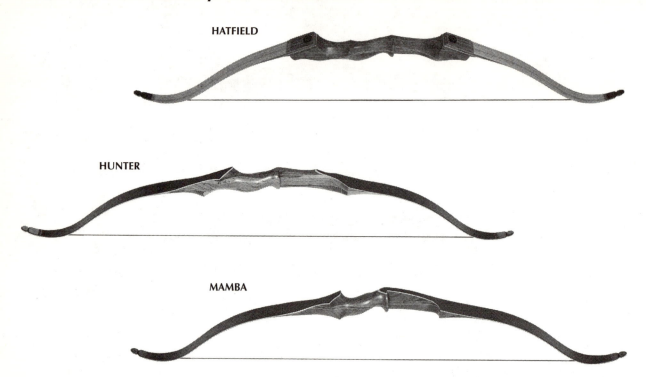

HATFIELD

HUNTER

MAMBA

HATFIELD

The 62-inch Hatfield take-down recurve bow by Martin Archery uses beautiful African hardwood laminations in the riser. Limbs are fashioned by hand from laminations of red elm and include reinforced tips that allow the choice of any bowstring material. This bow has an attractive brown riser with contrasting lighter limbs tipped with dark tips. Each Hatfield bow includes a traditional arrow rest, a bowstringer and a bowstring. The installation of sight and stabilizer bushings can be completed upon special request.

SPECIFICATIONS: HATFIELD
Draw Weight: from 30# to 70#
Length: 62 inches
SRP: **$479**

HAWK

Starting with its unfinished form, the 66-inch Hawk longbow lets the buyer decide the shaping of the grip, the decoration and the finish. The Hawk is also a very economical way to get started in traditional archery. Made of yellow birch and hickory, the bow's durability is enhanced with the addition of a fiberglass laminate. Other features include a 6½- to 7¼-inch brace height and a mass weight of 1

pound, one ounce. A bowstring is included.

SPECIFICATIONS: HAWK
Draw Weight: from 30# to 60#
Length: 66 inches
SRP: **$168.42**

HI-SPEED

This 58-inch take-down recurve by Martin Archery weighs 2 pounds 7 ounces and is for the archer who wants a short, quick bow that's great for traveling. The gently contoured Hi-Speed riser is sculpted from laminated maple for both beauty and strength and has an approximately 8-inch brace height. Limbs are hand laid laminations of red elm and clear glass and feature reinforced tips. The whole bow is immersed in a deep glossy finish. (Available in Semi-Gloss finish by special request.) The Hi-Speed comes complete with a traditional arrow rest, a bowstringer and a bowstring. The installation of sight and quiver bushings are available upon special request.

SPECIFICATIONS: HI-SPEED
Draw Weight: from 30# to 70#
Length: 58 inches
SRP: **$437.99**

HUNTER

This Martin manufactured one-piece recurve has 62-inch limbs with maple laminations and black fiberglass backing. The hardwood riser has distinct accent stripes running up through it. Other features include a string, and traditional shelf rest. The bow comes with a bowstringer and standard stabilizer insert. This bow is available in LH and RH models.

SPECIFICATIONS: HUNTER
Draw Weight: numerous available at 28-inch draw length
Length: 62 inches
SRP: **$350.00**

MAMBA

This one-piece recurve bow is crafted by Martin with 58-inch limbs with maple laminations and backed by black fiberglass. Other features of the Mamba include a hardwood riser, standard stabilizer insert, Dacron bowstring and traditional shelf rest. Bow is shipped with a bowstringer. The Mamba is available in left- and right-hand models.

SPECIFICATIONS: MAMBA
Draw Weight: from 35# to 70# at 28-inch draw length and 5# increments
Length: 58 inches
SRP: **$350.00**

RECURVE BOWS

Martin Archery Recurve Bows

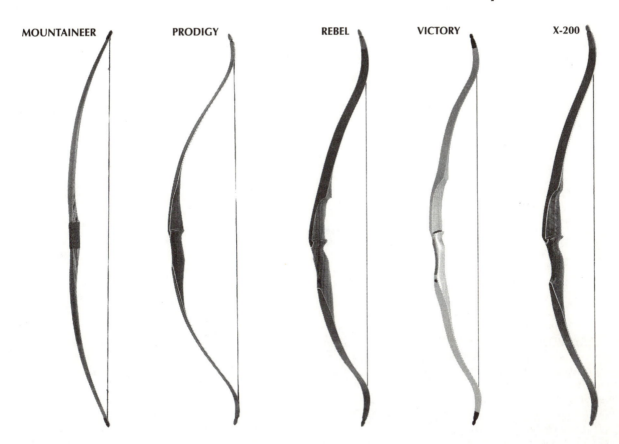

MOUNTAINEER   PRODIGY   REBEL   VICTORY   X-200

MOUNTAINEER

The 68-inch Mountaineer uses Zebra wood laminations and limbs with a reflex design to eliminate hand shock and stack. The grip section is enhanced with an attractive leather wrap. This bow weighs 1 pound, 5 ounces.

SPECIFICATIONS: MOUNTAINEER
Draw Weight: from 30# to 70#
Length: 68 inches
SRP: $350.00

PRODIGY

This Martin bow is for young archers who are serious about archery. The Prodigy is a scaled-down version of the company's adult bows and features a riser hand-crafted from African hardwoods and limbs of laminated maple. The bow has a contrsting red riser against dark limbs. The same hand-craftsmanship that goes into every Martin bow is used in the making of this 48-inch model. At only 10 oz., the Prodigy allows the young archer hours of enjoyable shooting without fatigue. Each Prodigy comes with a traditional rest and Dacron bowstring.

SPECIFICATIONS: PRODIGY
Draw Weight: from 10# to 25# at 24-inch draw
Length: 48 inches
SRP: $119.95

REBEL

While its design makes it look like a beginner or youth bow, or treestand hunting bow, the 52-inch Rebel recurve also excels at bowfishing. Durability and compact size are key elements required when the bowfishing action heats up. The Rebel by Martin is built to satisfy the most demanding bow fisherman, in the most demanding situations. Construction includes Shedua wood and fiberglass backings. A stabilizer or bowfishing reel adapter and sight mount bushing are each installed as standard equipment.

SPECIFICATIONS: REBEL
Draw Weight: from 20# to 50#
Length: 52 inches
SRP: $254.39

VICTORY

The 66-inch Victory's natural white color is derived from the use of hand-crafted hard maple. Its limbs have outer laminates of white glass and include reinforced tips that allow the use of any string material. A traditional arrow rest and a bowstringer are included with each Victory. Sight and stabilizer bushings are also installed as standard equipment.

SPECIFICATIONS: VICTORY
Draw Weight: from 20# to 50#
Length: 66 inches
SRP: $249.39

X-200

The X-200 packs value into a solid starter's recurve. Features include 60-inch maple laminated limbs and a brown Shedua hardwood riser. This bow is shipped with a Dacron bowstring and plastic Dura-Flip elevated arrow rest. The X-200 is available in LH and RH models.

SPECIFICATIONS: X-200
Draw Weight: from 35# to 45# in 5# increments at 28-inch draw length.
Length: 60 inches
SRP:. $225

RECURVE BOWS

Monarch Bows LLC Recurve Bows

LONGBOW

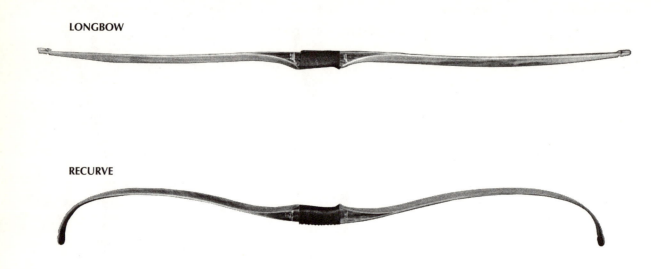

RECURVE

THIS DARBY, MONTANA, company has been producing bows since 1986. Buyer can create a custom bow by choosing: riser wood, limb wood, length, weight at draw length, size of riser to match hand, color of elk leather grip and personalized lettering. Features include elk horn tip, laced leather handle, tapered wood laminations, fiberglass reinforcement and satin finish. Most bows are available i

n 58-, 60-, and 62-inch lengths. The Spike Recurve is available in 56- and 58-inch length. Available wood choices include: tulipwood, red elm, Pacific yew, bocote, and featherwood. The Royal Flatbow and Royal Recurve bows joined the product line in 1996. The unique Royal Recurve has 1950's styling with a longbow like handle, wide limbs, riser wood tip overlays and sweeping limb curves. Most

models are shipped with a string and polar fleece bow sock. Call (800) 793-3224 for ordering details.
SRP:

Imperial Longbow	$590
Raghorn Longbow	$398
Royal Flatbow	$425
Royal Longbow	$510
Royal Recurve	$525
Spike Recurve	$495

Predator Custom Recurves Recurve Bows

THIS TAWAS, MICHIGAN, company takes great pride in producing bows the old fashioned way and with a quality product that's guaranteed to serve the shooter for years. Predator recurves are available in three models, including one the industry's few youth recurve models. Call (989) 362-7123 for details and to order.

CLASSIC CUSTOM TAKE-DOWN

This recurve is offered in a 60-inch length only and has a riser carved from sturdy bubinga wood and impregnated maple. The limbs are black glass or clear glass crafted over red elm wood. Other features include

a Flemish weave string and contoured pistol grip. Draw weights vary.
SPECIFICATIONS:
CLASSIC CUSTOM TAKE-DOWN
Length: 60 inches
SRP: $579.99

HUNTER RECURVE

This model features black glass limbs connected to a solid one-piece maple riser that's colored gray to blend in with the forest. The bow is 60 inches long and has a Flemish string. Draw weights vary per bow.
SPECIFICATIONS: HUNTER RECURVE
Length: 60 inches
SRP: $429.99

YOUTH 3-PIECE TAKE-DOWN

This youth oriented recurve displays the same colors as Predator's Hunter model with black glass limbs and a maple riser that's shaded gray. The Youth 3-Piece Take-Down is available in 48- and 52-inch lengths. The bow takes down via a bolt and beasel washer with stem system for packing, traveling and easy storage when not in use.
SPECIFICATIONS:
YOUTH 3-PIECE TAKE-DOWN
Length: 48 or 52 inches
SRP: $179.99

LONGBOW

MASTER BOWYER Gary Sentman pours more than 15 years of bow building experience into each handmade Moosejaw longbow. Each bow has a bamboo limb core, hand laminated African Bubinga wood and liner riser and Fast-Flite string. Available lengths include: 62, 64, 66 and 68 inches; 62, 64 and 66 inches

for the standard model with one-piece hardwood riser. Limb tips are laminated. A protective 72-inch bow sock is available for and additional $12 with purchase of a bow. This bow is backed by a 100% satisfaction guarantee for one year from date of purchase. Call (541) 592-6954 for full details.
SRP: Starting at $565

RAZORBACK BOW
The Razorback is similar to the Moosejaw longbow in 66- and 68-inch lengths with right- and left-hand pulls and with Ash or Bubinga wood risers.
SRP: Starting at $342

Palmer Bow Company Recurve Bows

LEGEND

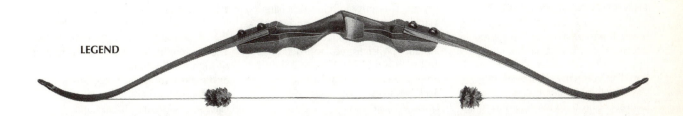

THIS SANIBAL, TEXAS, based bowyer produces bows one at a time with keen attention to balance, beauty, performance, fit and finish. Palmer bows are offered in any draw length from 24 to 34 inches and in draw weights ranging form 20 to 70 pounds. Available bow lengths range from 58 to 64 inches.

Riser styles offered range from the two-toned Legend to the Gray Bark gray and Classic which has a blend of light and dark woods. The Dead Leaf is a rich brown. Standard risers are constructed of laminated hardrock maple and legends are produced from Texas Ebony hardwood. Palmer bow limbs are available in standard 4-layer,

custom carbon 5-layer, and double carbon 7-layer laminates. All bows can be ordered with a choice of laminated limbs, with or without carbon fiber and finished in Dead Leaf, Gray Bark and Texas Ebony finishes. Limbs are attached to the risers with two bolts at each limb base.

Palmer also offers a bow quiver and a soft case. Call (830) 988-2568 for bow manufacturing details and pricing info.
SRP:
Dead Leaf Brown and
   Tree Bark Gray $495
Bows with single carbon
   limb layer $595

Bows with double carbon
   limb layers . . . . $695.
Classic designed double carbon
   . . . . $725
Legend designed double carbon . . . .
   . . . . $795

SRP: Limbs with carbon,
   from . . . . $270 to $470
   Palmer's Classic and Legend limbs
   are the most expensive.

SRP: Recurve quivers that hold
   4 or 7 arrows $39.95

RECURVE BOWS

INTREPID

SIERRA

THIS ARIZONA BOW CRAFTER is well known for innovative compound bows. It passes some of that same advanced technology and thinking into its comprehensive recurve bow line. The company recommends always using a recurve bow stringer to prevent limb tip twisting during the stringing process.

These bows are produced at the 4½-acre Tucson facility where PSE also makes compound bows and crossbows. While some models are tournament oriented, PSE (Precision Shooting Equipment) also makes hunting recurve models. Sometimes there is an additional charge for left-hand models or custom colors.

PSE HERITAGE LINE:

INTREPID

Integrated adjustable limb pockets on the Intrepid help the user achieve optimal bow riser and limb alignment. This bow features a strong, lightweight design and innovative limb mounting system. The Intrepid has a precision machined one-piece riser and stainless steel limb bolts. Available riser colors include: polished red, polished blue and polished black. Note that the limbs are sold separately.

BOW SPECIFICATIONS: INTREPID
Draw Weight: NA
Length: 25 inches, and can vary based on a total length determined by limbs selected.
SRP: **$479.99**
   (LH models are available)

SIERRA

An economically priced machined aluminum riser in a one-piece design makes PSE's Sierra a popular riser. The riser is 23 inches long, has a comfortable wood grip installed and is available in satin blue or red. The limbs for this bow are sold separately.

BOW SPECIFICATIONS: SIERRA
Draw Weight: NA
Length: 23 inches, total length determined by limbs selected.
SRP: **$274.99**
   (LH models are available)

PSE LIMBS

For the risers sold above, PSE offers their Competition and Pro Elite limbs. The Competition limbs are constructed of high quality hard rock maple wood and glass laminates. These limbs are shaped and crafted to precise tolerances for straightness and consistency. They are economically priced and available in 68-inch, 30-40# and above in additional 2lb. increments.

The Pro Elite limbs are carbon laminated layers and designed by Kyung Rae Park. They utilize the International Limb Fitting System and are available in 66-inch lengths with 30-42# draw weight. Also available as 68-inch with 30-42# draw and 70-inch limbs for a 32-40# draw in 2lb. increments.

SRP: The prices of the limbs vary widely based on models, length and poundage selected. Visit your local pro shop—or visit www.pse-archery.com– to determine availability and price.

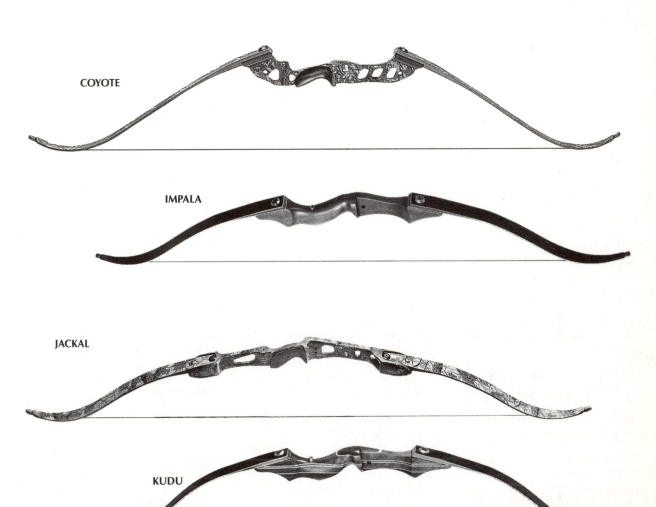

COYOTE

IMPALA

JACKAL

KUDU

COYOTE

The PSE Coyote represents value in a high-tech recurve. Features of this bow include a precision machined aluminum riser with a black wrap-around molded grip. This 60-inch bow is available in PSE's Brush camouflage finish and accepts PSE two-piece quivers.

BOW SPECIFICATIONS: COYOTE
Draw Weight: 35#, 40#, 45#, 50# and 55#.
Length: 60 inches
SRP: **$269.99**
   (LH models are available)

IMPALA

This PSE bow is perfect for the starting archer and features a new stylish handle. Other construction details include: a hardwood riser with detailed finish, bolt on laminated limbs and threaded receptors for accessories.

BOW SPECIFICATIONS: IMPALA
Draw Weight: 35#, 40#, 45# and 50#.
Length: 60 inches
SRP: **$189.99**
   (LH models are available)

JACKAL

The Jackal is a blend of high-tech Olympic style bows and traditional hunting recurves. It features a machined aluminum riser with wooden grip installed plus top-notch wood laminate limbs. The riser will accept a stabilizer and arrow rest. The Jackal is available in PSE's Brush camo.

BOW SPECIFICATIONS: JACKAL
Draw Weight: 40#, 45#, 50#, 55# and 60#

Length: 64 inches
SRP: **$439.99**
   (LH models are available)

KUDU

This takedown recurve is the latest in PSE's line up. It features eye-catching multi-layered laminates and solid brass accessory inserts which are the very best in quality, style and strength. The wide weight ranges offered with this model will accommodate bowfishermen and hunters.

BOW SPECIFICATIONS: KUDU
Draw Weight: 35#, 40#, 45#, 50#, 55# and 60#.
Length: 58 inches
SRP: **$299.99**
   (LH models are available)

RECURVE BOWS

Renegade Archery Company Recurve Bows

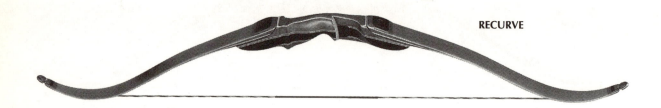

RECURVE

THIS WISCONSIN-BASED bow manufacturer offers numerous bows that are gaining a growing legion of followers each year. The company's sole recurve model is a unique traditional style bow that combines modern technology and yesteryear craftsmanship.

AGULLA AND AGULLA ULTRA

This competition bow offers a choice of machined Ultra riser or cast/forged Agulla riser. The Ultra riser features adjustable limb pockets and a riser with open design and points to accommodate accessories. Both bows feature weight and tiller adjustments. Available Agulla riser colors include: Sky blue, two tone blue, red, silver, and black. This recurve is sold as a separate riser and limbs and the riser will accept limbs from numerous manufacturers to suit the shooter's preference.

BOW SPECIFICATIONS: AGULLA AND AGULLA ULTRA
Draw Weight: 26#, 28#, 30#, 32#, 34#, 36#, 38#, 40#, 42# and 44#.
Length: 66 and 68 inches
SRP: Agulla riser. **$250**
Agulla Ultra riser. **$499.95**
Agulla Ultra Carbon limbs . . **$399.95**

HAWKEYE

This recurve has an unusual one-of-a-kind shaped laminated riser with unique rear limb mounting system that increases bow speed and accuracy. Black limbs with brown reinforced tips contrast against light wood riser. The Hawkeye is offered in LH and RH models by Samick.
BOW SPECIFICATIONS: HAWKEYE
Draw Weight: 40#, 45#, 50#, 55# and 60#.

Length: 62 inches
SRP: **$399.95**
    (riser and limbs also sold separately)

JAZZ

This youth bow has innovative high-tech carbon glass limbs with a scaled outer finish. Other features include a blue painted metal Cupid riser and a slotted sight with one pin. Left- and right-hand models are available.
BOW SPECIFICATIONS: JAZZ
Draw Weight: 15# and 20#
Length: 46 inches
SRP: **$89.95**

LAVITA

This Samick bow was created to inspire young Olympic oriented archers. Its features include a precision forged and machined riser, positive limb mounting pin, long window, clicker mount hole, and a contoured grip with rubber side inlays. The Lavita uses multi-laminated wood limbs and an inside the riser shock-dump system to provide a smooth and consistent arrow release. A threaded brass bushing accepts accessories and the white limbs have distinct black tips. Available riser colors include: blue, red, and black.
BOW SPECIFICATIONS: LAVITA
Draw Weight: 18#, 20#, 22#, 24#, 26#, 28#, 30#, 32#, 34#, 36# and 38#.
Length: 64 and 66 inches
SRP: riser. **$90**
limbs **$105**
    (sold separately)

LEGEND

A Samick one-piece longbow that has a traditional look and feel. The Legend offers a sleek design of laminate woods and one-of-a-kind true custom built. This bow is available in LH and RH versions.
BOW SPECIFICATIONS: LEGEND
Draw Weight: 40#, 45#, 50#, 55# and 60#
Length: 69 inches
SRP:. **$215**

PREDATOR

This lightweight Samick hunting recurve is sculpted from hard rock maple. Black laminate limbs fit into limb pockets that are a great contrast with light brown riser. The riser has a threaded bushing to accept accessories. The Predator is available in LH and RH models.
BOW SPECIFICATIONS: PREDATOR
Draw Weight: 40#, 45#, 50#, 55# and 60#.
Length: 58 inches
SRP:. **$195**
    (Note: the riser and limbs are also sold separately)

PROGRESS I

This competition oriented recurve features rear lock-down limb screws to ensure perfect alignment of the multi-laminated ultra glass wood limbs with the magnesium painted risers. The available bow colors include two-tone blue, red/silver and black/silver. Other features include white limbs with the distinct Samick logo and black reinforced limb tips.
BOW SPECIFICATIONS: PROGRESS I
Draw Weight: 20# to 40# in two pound increments.
Length: 66 inches
SRP:. **$195**

RECURVE BOWS

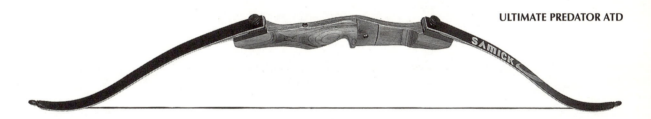

ULTIMATE PREDATOR ATD

THIS COMPANY and product line is one of the oldest and largest traditional custom bow manufacturers in the world. Samick produces an extensive line of traditional hunting and target bows. Its target bows have won top honors in many competitions.

All Samick bows are distributed by AIM (Archery International Marketing). This Connecticut based distributor provides recurves and other archery gear and accessories to archery enthusiasts around the world. AIM provides more than 18 recurve models to shooters under the Samick and interNature brands.

SPIRIT II

This hunting recurve has a new style rounded and shaped riser that is hand-crafted from rosewood and walnut.

No limb pockets are used since the limbs are aligned with a hidden dual pin system. Black laminate limbs with a white Samick logo in contrast with rich colored wood riser. LH and RH versions are available.

BOW SPECIFICATIONS: SPIRIT II
Draw Weight: 40#, 45#, 50#, 55# and 60#.
Length: 60 inches
SRP:.....................$225
   (riser and limbs also sold separately)

ULTIMATE PREDATOR ATD

This recurve has a 6061 machined aluminum riser, wooden one-piece grip, and laminate limbs with a hard maple core inside Bow Tuff laminates. A phenolic tip overlay ensures years of durable service. This unique bow has Mossy Oak Break-Up camouflage and

offers a three-year warranty.
BOW SPECIFICATIONS:
ULTIMATE PREDATOR ATD
Draw Weight: 45# - 70#
Length: 62-inch
SRP:.....................**$449**

WOODSMAN

Each Woodsman model is hand made and has a laminated riser with brown wood grain limbs. Look closely and you'll see a black stripe passing through the wood riser! These bows are prepared in LH and RH layouts by Samick.

BOW SPECIFICATIONS: WOODSMAN
Draw Weight: 45#, 50#, 55# and 60#
Length: 62 inches
SRP:.....................**$450**
   (riser and limbs also sold separately)

How Much Wind?
A fact of archery-shooting life: strong winds can affect arrow flight.
But how strong are the winds?
Brunton's Sherpa and Kestrel's wind meter have precision wind gauges that can help you determine how strong the winds are blowing. Both wind meters are small, lightweight and easy to use. Some units reveal temperature and altitude.
If the winds are gusting at more than 30 mph, then you should probably find something else to do since arrow flight could be erratic and game will normally bed since they cannot use their strong sense of smell to find hidden dangers in the fields and forests.--MDF

RECURVE BOWS

Wing Archery Products Recurve Bows

PRESENTATION I

PRESENTATION II

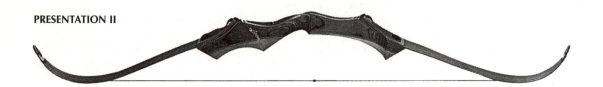

WING ARCHERY bows are a division of Dr. Bob's Archery Company and is based in Randolph, New Jersey. The company also produces compound bows.

PRESENTATION I

This Wing take-down hunter has been designed with an emphasis on strength and durability as well as grace and performance. Riser is constructed of Wingwood laminates and limbs feature laminates and maple with dark glass. The bow also has a brass stabilizer receiver and quiver bushings. The Presentation I features a crown and radius rest for sweet shooting. These bows have been manufactured since 1951 and are backed by a 2-year limited warranty.

BOW SPECIFICATIONS: PRESENTATION I
Draw Weight: 40# to 70#.
Length: 62 and 64 inches
SRP: **$369**

PRESENTATION II

Similar to the Presentation I, the Presentation II incorporates a myrtle-wood face and decorative padauk caps. The wood laminate riser provides up to 9 ½- inches of brace height. Red elm wood is used in the construction of the limbs. This bow is available in right-hand models only.

BOW SPECIFICATIONS: PRESENTATION II
Draw Weight: 40# to 70#.
Length: 62 inches
SRP: **$695**

Beginning Season Check Up
Before hunting season begins, and after your bow has been stored for extended periods of time, it is a good idea to slowly inspect limbs, bolts, attachments, risers and all parts for hairline cracks and loose or twisted parts. Pay close attention to the tips of limbs and where the axle passes through the limbs. Also inspect the string and serving for frayed areas. If something looks suspicious, try looking at it under a magnifying glass. If you have questions, take the bow to a pro shop for further inspections. –MDF

Barnett Crossbows

QUAD 300

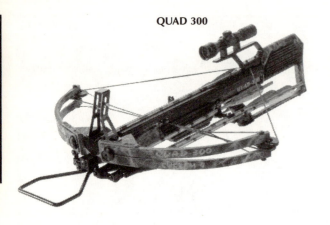

COMMANDO II

RC-150

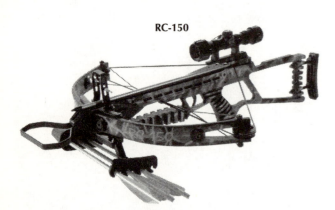

COMMANDO II
RECURVE

THIS CROSSBOW MANUFACTURER
uses state of the art machinery to create unique products with innovate stocks and take-down capabilities. Barnett makes compound and recurve crossbows, and also makes sling shots. The company is based in Odessa, Florida.

BARNETT QUAD 300

The crossbow uses quad limb technology teamed with cam technology to achieve high arrow speeds and peak performance. It has a synthetic harness system and 15¼-inch power stroke. This crossbow has a dark camouflaged stock, multiple rubber grip pads and a foot stirrup. The Quad 300 will accommodate a scope.

This bow is also offered in a kit that includes: bow, arrows, quiver, and 4X32 scope.

SPECIFICATIONS: BARNETT QUAD 300
Draw Weight: 150 lbs.
Max Speed: 335 fps
SRP: Starting at **$245**
Kit **$300**

COMMANDO II

This crossbow combines a rear pivoting stock, sturdy locking arms and precision extruded cocking hooks with self-aligning roller guides to increase accuracy. The installed Rhino trigger mechanism features a short, smooth, ultra-light trigger pull. This crossbow has a 10½-inch power stroke with solid limbs and e-wheels. It is recommended for hunting at up to 60 yards. One prominent feature of the Commando II is the protruding under-the-arm hook on the lower rear of the open-style stock.

The Commando II Recurve has similar stock and design as the standard Commando II but it has solid recurve limbs. This bow has a 10-inch power stroke, 150-pound draw weight and is recommended at up to 40 yards.

SPECIFICATIONS: COMMANDO II
Draw Weight: 150 lbs.
Max Speed: 260 fps
SRP: Compound mode starting . . **400**
Recurve model **$278**

RC-150

This Barnett crossbow is light—5½ pounds!—and compact. The bow has graphite composite limbs, aluminum flight track and machined alloy cams. It has a unique multi-ribbed forearm and rear bracket and open designed stock. The RC-150 is camouflaged in green and tan and has a 9½-inch power stroke. A metal foot stirrup helps control the bow while cocking. It will accommodate a scope and other accessories.

A recurve model by Barnett—the RX-150—has a similar stock and uses recurve limbs. It is a full-sized crossbow with an SRP of $105.

SPECIFICATIONS: RC-150
Draw Weight: 150 lbs.
Max Speed: 260 fps
SRP: Starting at **$165**
   bow, quiver and four arrows . **$178**

REVOLUTION

RHINO QUAD

REVOLUTION

The Revolution uses Veloci-Speed cams and 4-limb technology to move arrows. Users can adjust the stock's cheek piece and rear stock plate to ensure proper eye alignment with the sights or a scope when installed. The front of the bow can be easily removed for transportation and storage. This bow has a nonskid black rubber pistol grip. It will accommodate a scope.

This bow is offered in a kit that includes: bow, quiver, arrows and a 4X32 scope.

SPECIFICATIONS: REVOLUTION
Draw Weight: 133 lbs.
Max Speed: 340 fps
SRP: Starting at **$289**
   with a quiver and arrows . . . **$314**
Bow kit **$359**

RHINO QUAD

The Rhino Quad has an ultra-light trigger pull, scope adjustment dial and an analog range gauge to help increase shooter accuracy. Other features include: a Monte Carlo stock, patented lever-action breakdown mechanism, locking sight pins, ambidextrous safety, adjustable fore grip and a Veloci-Speed Synthetic String. This crossbow has a 13-inch power stroke and will accommodate numerous accessories.

SPECIFICATIONS: RHINO QUAD
Draw Weight: 150 lbs.
Max Speed: 310 fps
SRP: Starting at **$247**
   with a quiver and four arrows
      . . . . **$275**

Barnett Crossbows

WILDCAT III

RHINO SPORT MAGNUM

RHINO SPORT MAGNUM
This bow has a solid stock and uses 4-limb technology with Veloci-Speed cams to launch arrows. This unit has a lever-action take-down lever to make transportation and storage a breeze. The Rhino Sport Magnum has an adjustable foregrip, metal foot stirrup and is camouflaged.
SPECIFICATIONS: RHINO SPORT MAGNUM
Draw Weight: 150 lbs.
Max Speed: 260 fps
SRP: bow and a quiver stocked w/four arrows, starting at . . . $285

WILDCAT III
This crossbow has recurve limbs attached to a solid Monte Carlo ambidextrous stock. The entire unit is black and will accommodate multiple accessories. A stirrup assists with control while cocking. This bow is recommended at hunting ranges up to 40 yards.
SPECIFICATIONS: WILDCAT III
Draw Weight: 150 lbs.
Max Speed: 235 fps
SRP: Starting at $123

MAXPOINT 305

THESE CROSSBOWS are designed
for target shooting and hunting. Both Buckmaster models are also available with optional accessory kits. They are manufactured by the North American Archery Group in Gainesville, Florida.

MAXPOINT

This Buckmaster crossbow utilizes the exclusive MaxWing cam to deliver no let-off. The result—more stored energy. The Maxpoint features a four-limb design, machined aluminum riser and cocking stirrup. This crossbow is available with Realtree Hardwoods camo finish. The optional set model includes: sights, quiver and four bolts.
BOW SPECIFICATIONS: MAXPOINT
Draw Weight: 175 lbs.
Bow Speed: 340 fps
SRP:................... **$399**
   set.................. **$549**

MAXPOINT 305

This powerful crossbow delivers performance at an economical level. Features of this Buckmaster crossbow include: four Realtree Hardwoods camouflaged limbs, black aluminum riser and stock, and a grip that permits easy use by left- or right-hand shooters. The optional set includes: 1X30 Red Dot crossbow scope with cover and mount, plus four-arrow quiver, four bolts and field points.
BOW SPECIFICATIONS: MAXPOINT 305
Draw Weight: 150 lbs.
Bow Speed: 306 fps
SRP:................... **$349**
   set.................. **$499**

A Case Law
A bow case is a great piece of gear to use when traveling across town or across the country. Cases help protect your bow's string, sights and limb tips. You should also check the laws where you hunt. Some states require that a bow be in a case while being transported, and other states require that it be locked and inoperable during transporting. Some states, however, have no restrictions. —MDF

Excaliber Crossbows

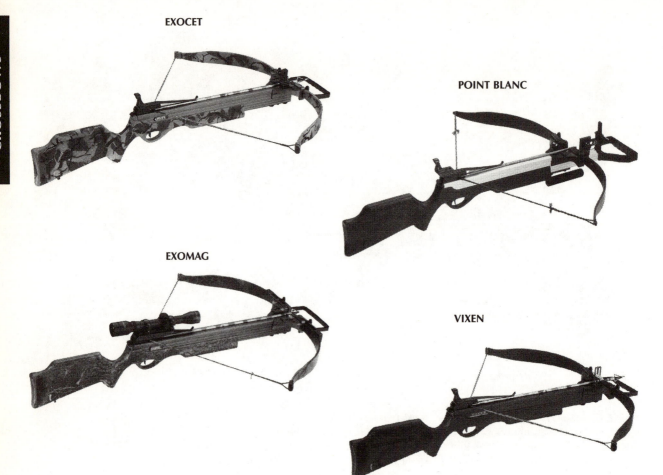

EXOCET

POINT BLANC

EXOMAG

VIXEN

THIS CANADIAN MANUFACTURER indicates that they are crossbow hunters who build crossbows. Their products follow their philosophy of sticking to the basics in design and manufacturing. All of their products are recurve based. The company was founded in 1983 and is located in Kitchner, Ontario.

EXOCET
This Excaliber crossbow has a solid, one-piece stock and forearm that's offered with a Realtree Hardwoods or four-color camouflage finish. This crossbow has an ambidextrous manual safety, Magtip limbs and quick detach sling studs. The Exocet has a fiber optic sight and is drilled and tapped to receive a scope base.
SPECIFICATIONS: EXOCET
Draw Weight: 175 lbs.

Max Speed: 300 fps
SRP: four-color camo **$465**
Realtree Hardwoods camo **$515**

EXOMAG
This recurve crossbow has a Realtree Hardwoods finish to help you blend in with your surroundings. Other features include: Magtip limbs and a Dissipator bar to reduce sound and recoil. The Exomag also has detachable sling swivels and a fiber optic sight.
SPECIFICATIONS: EXOMAG
Draw Weight: 200 lbs.
Max Speed: 330 fps
SRP: **$560**

POINT BLANC
This recurve crossbow is noticeable with its black stock and gold rail. The Point Blanc has a forward mounted stirrup, tuned trigger, and is drilled

and tapped for a scope mount. The Deluxe version includes a stabilizer, sight level, forward mounted target sight and elevated rear aperture.
SPECIFICATIONS: POINT BLANC
Draw Weight: 90 lbs.
Max Speed: NA
SRP: standard **$360**
  deluxe model **$450**

VIXEN
This no-frills crossbow has solid recurve limbs and a solid-one-piece stock—and all covered in basic black. The Vixen weighs 6 pounds, has an ambidextrous manual safety and peep sights. It is drilled and tapped to accommodate a scope mount base.
SPECIFICATIONS: VIXEN
Draw Weight: NA
Max Speed: 275 fps
SRP: **$390**

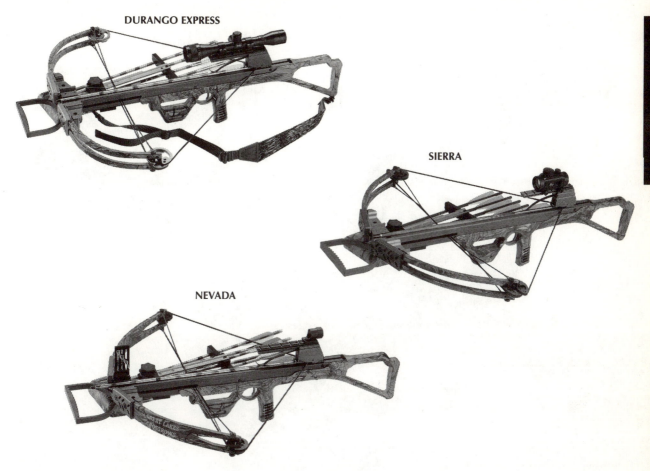

DURANGO EXPRESS

SIERRA

NEVADA

GREAT LAKES CROSSBOWS has successfully combined graceful aesthetics, incredible balance and rugged dependability with today's highest quality materials and workmanship to produce a true high performance sporting arm. The parent company—Darton Archery-has been in business for more than 50 years and is located in Hale, Michigan. It manufactures three models.

DURANGO EXPRESS

The Durango has a powerful 17-inch power stroke and round energy wheels attached to pre-curved limbs with "0" deflex for a longer, more efficient power stroke. It is similar in design and features to the other Great Lakes models and also has a Weaver-style scope mount base. The stock and limbs are coated in Skyline's Excel camouflage.
SPECIFICATIONS: DURANGO EXPRESS
Draw Weight: 165 lbs.
Max Speed: Up to 305 fps
SRP: **$649.99**

NEVADA AND NEVADA II

This crossbow features a one-piece solid limb design that helps produce pin point accuracy. It has a 13½-inch power stroke, precision machined arrow track, hard anodized Teflon coated barrel and a machined aluminum front riser. Its synthetic "Power Yoke" cables feature split anchor attachments on each limb to balance the limb torque. The Nevada has a patented dry-fire prevention mechanism and a center-balanced rifle-style safety for right- or left-handed shooters. Other features include: a universal Weaver-style scope mount and adjustable arrow hold down tension. The limbs are camouflaged.

The Nevada II is similar in design and features to the Nevada, and has stronger limbs and a fully camouflaged stock that's covered with Skyline's Excel camo.
SPECIFICATIONS: NEVADA AND NEVADA II
Draw Weight: 150 lbs. for Nevada, 165 for Nevada II

Max Speed: 265 fps for Nevada, 277 for Nevada II
SRP: Nevada **$549.99**
Nevada II **669.99**

SIERRA

This Great Lakes crossbow has composite laminated quad limbs with alloy energy wheels along with a 15-inch power stroke. Other features for this crossbow include: machined arrow track, an anodized and Teflon impregnated barrel and a machined aluminum front riser. The Sierra has a patented trigger and dry fire prevention device. The safety operates similar to that found on most rifles.
SPECIFICATIONS: SIERRA
Draw Weight: 150 lbs. and 165 lbs.
Max Speed: 275 fps for the 150# model, 294 for the 165# model
SRP: Starting at **$599.99**

Horton Manufacturing Crossbows

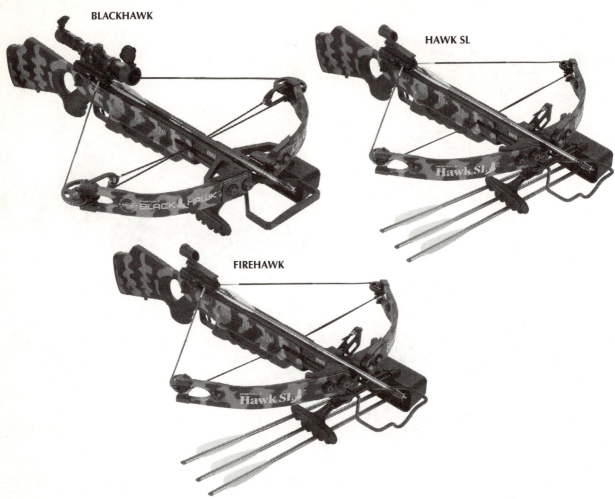

BLACKHAWK

HAWK SL

FIREHAWK

HORTON CROSSBOWS are designed for serious hunters. The products are regularly tested at the company's hunting grounds--Camp Opportunity. This company actively works with state game departments to open more opportunities for the use of crossbows. Their motto: "One Shot, One Choice." Horton is based in Tallmadge, Ohio.

Most Horton crossbows can be purchased at the company's Web site—www.crossbows.com. The crossbows can be purchased separately or as a package that includes the crossbow, scope and padded sling. Many accessories are available for these models.

BLACKHAWK

This crossbow has similar features as the Firehawk and is camouflaged in Horton's Hawk camo—a unique dark and light contrast that helps you blend in under any hunting condi-

tion. The choice to forgo a franchised camouflage pattern makes this crossbow a more economical selection consideration. The Blackhawk also has an adjustable stock length and laminated limbs.

SPECIFICATIONS: BLACKHAWK
Draw Weight: 200 lbs.
Max Speed: 310 fps
SRP:. $500
    package $650

FIREHAWK

This crossbow uses Horton's Toughboy wide-body DP2 solid laminated limbs to move arrows at up to 320 fps. The limbs are attached to a solid stock that can be adjusted to the desired length. Other features include: machined aluminum reflex riser, SpeedMax power wheels, peep/pin sight, steel trigger and trajectory compensator. The limbs are tipped with Horton's Dura-Tip integrated yoke system. The

stock is coated in Mossy Oak camouflage and has a scope base installed.

SPECIFICATIONS: FIREHAWK
Draw Weight: 200 lbs.
Max Speed: 320 fps
SRP:. $600
    package $750

HAWK SL

This Horton crossbow has a rugged and durable solid stock with a thumbhole and the Hawk camouflage pattern as a finish. The stock can be adjusted with ¾-inch stock plates that are sold separately. Other features for this bow include: diecast riser, wide-body solid limbs, machined aluminum round wheels, a peep/pin sight and a dial-adjustable trajectory compensator.

SPECIFICATIONS: HAWK SL
Draw Weight: 150 lbs.
Max Speed: 270 fps
SRP:. $320
    package $350

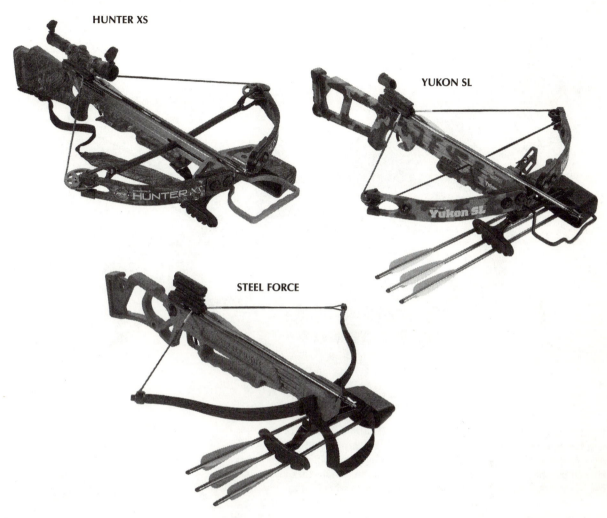

HUNTER XS

YUKON SL

STEEL FORCE

HUNTER XS

This Horton crossbow features a solid composite stock with a thumbhole cut in and Mossy Oak Break-Up camo finish. Other features include: cable mufflers, machined aluminum reflex riser, SpeedMax power wheels, peep and pin sight and a steel trigger. The cable mufflers are a unique feature that is easily noticed. This crossbow also has: a stirrup, machined barrel, dial-a-range trajectory compensator and Weaver-Style scope base installed. The Hunter XS has one of the biggest draw weights in the industry—200 pounds—and moves bolts at 320 fps. This crossbow is offered in a package that includes a scope.
SPECIFICATIONS: HUNTER XS
Draw Weight: 200 lbs.
Max Speed: 320 fps
SRP: **$600**
   pacakge **$750**

LEGEND SL

This unit has ICAD steel cables, solid Toughboy wide-body limbs with steel external axle limb tips and a stirrup. The Legend SL's composite stock has a thumbhole cut into the stock behind the grip and is coated with Am-Busch 3-D camouflage. Accessories for this crossbow must be purchased separately.
SPECIFICATIONS: LEGEND SL
Draw Weight: 175 lbs.
Max Speed: 300 fps
SRP: **$400**

STEEL FORCE

This recurve crossbow has limbs made of tempered steel. It also has a composite barrel in the stock with a thumbhole also cut in behind the grip. Other features include a red dot sight and quiver with four target arrows and points. It is available in two weight ranges.

SPECIFICATIONS: STEEL FORCE
Draw Weight: 150 or 80 lbs.
Max Speed: 240 fps for 150 lbs., and 175 fps for the 80 lbs.
SRP: bows and accessory package
  . . . . **$200**

YUKON SL

This crossbow features solid glass limbs, an ICAD cable system, round wheels and magnesium riser. The composite stock has a thumbhole and open-designed butt section. The Yukon SL is coated in Horton's brown camouflage finish.
SPECIFICATIONS: YUKON SL
Draw Weight: 150 lbs.
Max Speed: 260 fps
SRP: **$300**
   package **$340**

PSE Crossbows

DEERSLAYER

THIS TUCSON, ARIZONA, bow manufacturer has more than 300 employees and a factory sprawling across more than 4½ acres! PSE (Precision Shooting Equipment) makes one of the largest lines of compound and recurve bows and brings more than 30 years of experience into the crossbow arena.

DEERSLAYER

The Deerslayer has a power-touch trigger with an anti dry-fire mechanism. Other features for this crossbow include: a solid thumbhole stock with sling swivel studs installed, quad limb system with adjustable limb pockets and wheels, Acra-Angle barrel with patented Vibra-Crush and an aluminum barrel with PSE's Hard-Coat finish. The stirrup is custom coated and a scope mount base is included.

SPECIFICATIONS: DEERSLAYER
Draw Weight: 175 lbs.
Max Speed: NA
SRP: . . . . varies

PEREGRINE

This PSE crossbow is coated with the company's Brush camo finish and has an aluminum riser and machined aluminum wheels at the end of its solid limbs. It also has integrated cables and a Dacron string system. The solid stock is fitted with a Microflight aluminum barrel. A scope can be mounted on this crossbow.

SPECIFICATIONS: PEREGRINE
Draw Weight: 175 lbs.
Max Speed: NA
SRP: . . . . **contact a local dealer**

XB-270 PRO

This crossbow has a unique Oak Leaf camo finish on its stock and solid limbs. It is similar in design to PSE's Peregrine and has a rear peep sight and front pin sight system. It also has Dial-A-Range trajectory compensator and a machined trigger.

SPECIFICATIONS: XB-270 PRO
Draw Weight: 150 lbs.
Max Speed: 270
SRP: . . . . **contact a local deale**

Inspect Everything
Before releasing an arrow and starting a practice session, check your bow, it's limbs and cables and arrow rest for cracks or loose parts. Next, inspect your arrows for cracks, broken pr cracked nocks and missing parts. If you see a problem, have it repaired or replaced before using a damaged bow or arrow. —MDF

BOW ACCESSORIES

Bow Accessories Sights and Peep Systems

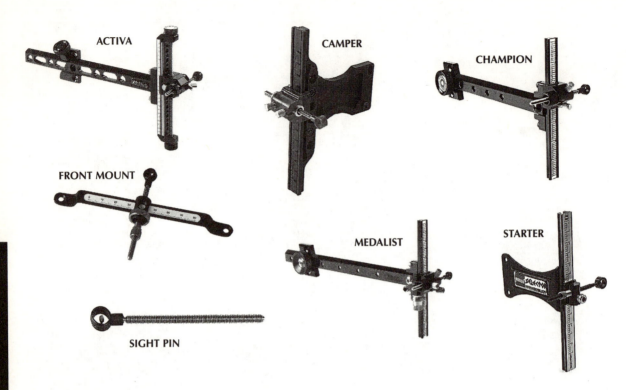

ACTIVA

CAMPER

CHAMPION

FRONT MOUNT

MEDALIST

STARTER

SIGHT PIN

A PIN-POINT PICTURE

Bow sights have evolved during recent years. From the small brass pins that fit into a few slots on a flat sheet of metal, the sights are now fiber optic pins that gather light and nearly glow in complete darkness. There are as many styles as there are bows, and that's a lot. Among the following sights you should be able to find some that help you place your arrows on the target with pin point accuracy. Shoot straight. –MDF

AIM

This company produces field archery recurves and the sights to place on them. Some styles are compatible for compound bows.

Activa Sight

This sight has ultra fine click adjustability with .002 increments. Parts are machined aluminum and level adjustments and 4-way sight pin. Other features include quick detach mounting bar, 9-inch extension bar and calibrated sight tape. Designed with 10/32 threads.
SRP: $199.95

Camper Sight

This sight's polymer and nylon construction means lightweight and durable construction. The Camper features a micro smooth windage adjustment, major elevation adjustment, embossed yardage bar and ring pin sight with a dot. Item 06102.
SRP: $17.00

Champion Sight

AIM's Champion sight was created for mid-level archers and has a streamline design and strong machined aluminum parts. Features include micro windage adjustment, quick detach 9-inch extension bar, calibrated sight tape and a free ring-pin sight.
SRP: $42.95

Front Mount Sight

This sight is designed by AIM for use on bows without any side-mount sight bushings. It can be attached with glue or a small wood screw. Item 06100.
SRP: $7.95

Medalist Sight

This competition sight is available in $^8/_{32}$ threads for recurves and $^{10}/_{32}$ for compound bows. It features a strong

aluminum 9-inch extension bar, quick detach mounting bar and fine-elevation adjustment with a worm gear. The compound model has a level adjustment and the unit includes a free ring pin sight.
SRP: (compound model) $110
SRP: (recurve model) $59.95

Starter Sight

AIM's Starter Sight is designed for the beginning archer and offers durability and affordability. Features a deluxe ring sight and calibrated yardage tape.
SRP: $10.95

Super Sight

A perfect sight for an intermediate archer. The Super Sight by AIM has the looks and features of a professional sight but is constructed of polymer and nylon to help control costs. Features include: smooth micro windage adjustments, a quick detach mounting base, major elevation adjustment, embossed yardage bar and a free ring sight.
SRP: $17.95

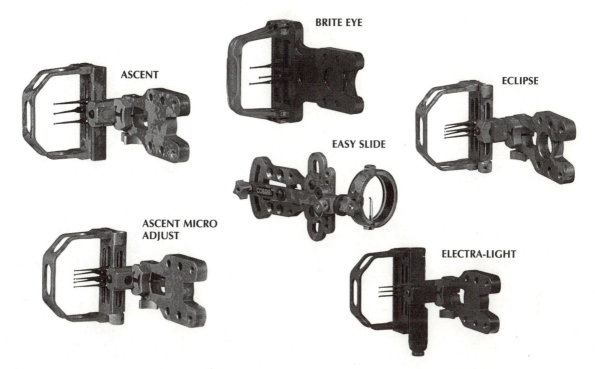

BRITE EYE

ASCENT

ECLIPSE

EASY SLIDE

ASCENT MICRO ADJUST

ELECTRA-LIGHT

COBRA

Cobra has been in the archery manufacturing business for nearly 30 years and has a 30,000 square-feet manufacturing facility in Oklahoma. The company's extensive product line includes more than 17 sights, 13 releases, 8 stabilizers and several arrow rests along with a wide assortment of sight pins. The company's products have won numerous awards from archery publications and organizations. Cobra is headquartered in Bixby, Oklahoma and enjoys worldwide distribution of its products.

Ascent Sight

The Ascent by Cobra incorporates dual angle pin tracks for zero pin gap spacing. The metal and fiber-optic pins are protected by a metal guard that's vented with slots. The design of this sight includes the Posi-Stop adjustment system, dovetail slide, and sturdy metal base for attachment and positioning on the bow. Available in black and Mystik camouflage. Replacement pins and fibers are available.

SRP: black **$33.99**
    camouflage **$38.99**

Ascent Micro Adjust

A bowhunting sight by Cobra with dual angled tracks to keep the pins in a single vertical sight plane. Features all metal constructions, five Micro TKO pins, easy adjustment, Posi-Stop module and a metal base with pre-drilled and tapped holes. The Ascent Micro has a vented square-edged metal sight guard and is available in black and Mystik camouflage.

SRP: black **$43.99**
    camouflage **$48.99**

Mini Ascent Sight

SRP: black **$36.53**
    camouflage **$41.60**

Brite Eye Sight

This Cobra sight uses three Brite Eye fiber optic and metal pins with double-lock hardware for separate windage and elevation adjustments. It has a solid non-glare smoked sight guard and a black one-piece base.

SRP: **$10.66**

Easy Slide Sight

A sight similar in design and construction to the Electra-Slide sight without the illumination system. This Cobra sight is easy to quickly adjust when mounted.

SRP: black **$40.99**
    camouflage **$45.99**

Eclipse Sight

Similar in design and construction to the Mini Eclipse Sight but with a more squared and slightly larger sight pin guard when compared to the rounder Mini Eclipse sight guard. This sight is also all metal construction. Incorporates dovetailed slides and quick turn knobs.

SRP: black **$54.56**
    camouflage **$59.63**

Mini Eclipse Sight

SRP: black **$56.59**
    Mystik camo **$61.66**

Electra-Light Sight

This Cobra sight is new in 2003 and has a white LED light module built into the sight pin bracket and positioned to shine on the three ELT pins that are included. No stray light shines on the bracket; all light is focused on the pins. Other features include machined dovetail elevation and windage adjustments, Posi-Stop module and sturdy base for attachment to the bow with pre-drilled and tapped holes.

SRP: black **$45.99**
    camouflage **$50.99**

Bow Accessories Sights and Peep Systems

ELECTRA-SLIDE

VENOM

FIBER OPTIC
TREE STAND
HUNTER LIGHT

VIEW MASTER
ELITE

FIBER OPTIC
LIGHT SIGHT PIN

VIEW MASTER
DELUXE

SIDEWINDER

LIGHT ALL

Electra-Slide Sight

This camouflaged bowhunting sight has a slide apparatus so that the shooter can adjust elevation quickly after turning a knob. A large round sight window contains a single metal fiber-optic pin. A red light—housed in the windage adjustment—illuminates the pin at dawn and dusk. The pin can only be illuminated from the side position. Accessories include: E Star replacement pins, Micro E Star replacement pins, replacement fibers and a spare battery for the light.

SRP: black............... $50.99
   Mystik camouflage....... $55.99

Sidewinder Sight

This all-metal sight features fiber optic pins with more than 2-feet of light gathering fiber optic cord to ensure brighter sight pins with .030-inch diameter. The Posi-Stop module permits quick detachment with a turn of the knob. It comes with three sight pins and a unique cylinder with the fiber optic cord coiled inside. A mounting bracket and pin guard are included on this black sight.

SRP: black............... $44.99
   Mystik camouflage $49.99

Venom Sight

Similar in design and all-metal construction to the Mini Venom but with a larger, rectangular sight pin guard and longer elevation bracket. Three TKO or Micro TKO pins are included.

SRP: black............... $19.99
   camouflage............ $23.99

Mini Venom Sight

SRP: black............... $21.30
   camouflage............ $25.36

View Master Elite Sight

A camouflaged bowhunting sight with a teardrop shaped pendulum suspended on ball bearings. A single all-metal STK fiber-optic pin is in the bottom of the teardrop. This sight is micro adjustable and has dovetailed bases and quick detach system. Vibration elimination buttons are mounted on the top and bottom of the sight guard.

SRP: black............... $49.99
   Mystik camouflage....... $54.99

View Master Deluxe Sight

SRP: black............... $39.99
   Mystik camouflage....... $44.99

COBRA ACCESSORIES FOR SIGHTS

These accessories are available for Cobra sights:

Light: All red............. $7.36
Fiber Optic light sight pin
   (red)................. $8.11

Starlight Pin:
(green or red)........... $2.75

Bright Eye Double locking pins:
(red, green and yellow) $3.99

Up/Down position Micro STK pins:
(green and yellow)........ $2.99

Lighted sight battery
per 2 pack:............. $2.99

Micro E-Star pins:
(green, red and yellow) $2.99

E-Star pins, standard:
(green, red and yellow) $2.99

Ultra TKO replacement fibers:
(assorted 3/pack)......... $3.99

ELT pins:
(red, green and yellow) $4.57

Fiber Optic Light Sight Pin

This Cobra pin has a positive locking system and a battery operated illuminated .040-inch diameter red fiber optic tip that illuminates brightly at dawn and dusk when turned on. Battery can be easily replaced.

SRP:.................... $8.11

Fiber Optic Tree Stand Hunter Light

SRP:.................... $14.20

Light All

SRP: with stem $7.36
SRP: without stem $6.45

ANTS TARGET

DEAD NUTS HUNTER 3-PIN

DUSK DEVIL

GRAND SLAM HUNTER

Q22 CAMO

DEAD NUTS PRO

DEAD NUTS HUNTER 5-PIN

GRAND SLAM HUNTER DELUXE

WORKHORSE CAMO

COPPER JOHN
Copper John ANTS Target Sight
This top-grade target sight has a quick adjust mounting bracket with a large finger-operated knob, a solid extension arm and double-sided quick adjust pin bracket. The pin bracket exterior frame features Sprung Relief Technology. A Third Axis knob assists with precision tuning options.
SRP: $249.95

Dead Nuts Hunter Sights
These sighs were introduced in 1999 and feature all metal construction, a round pin guard with an orange highlight ring surrounding it, and an open-style mounting bracket to reduce weight. Sights are offered with three or five pins and have a level installed inside the lower sight window circle. Available in Mossy Oak camouflage for approximately $20 more per unit.
SRP: three pin $59.95
five pin $69.95

Dead Nuts Pro Series
These pins are designed for competition archery and have smaller precision sight pin tips—down to 29- and 19 thousandths. The vertical gang adjustment and level setting feature are part of the same mechanism on this sight. The Pro II and Pro III models have a solid extension arm form the mounting bracket to the sight bracket.

SRP: Pro standard $79.95
Pro II $89.95
Pro III. 99.95

MONTANA BLACK GOLD
Montana Black Gold sights has been in business since 1992 and created the first bowsight machined entirely out of 6061-T6 aluminum. Black Gold sights are known for pin protection, durability, brass inserts in their sight pins, straight-away pins, calibrated horizontal and vertical adjustments and machined dovetails for a precise fit. The company uses 1-24 bolts to prevent stripping and they provide a lifetime warranty on all parts and sights. All sights are made in the USA. The company also makes the Trap Door arrow rests.

Dusk Devil
The fibers are located in line along a fin in the middle of the sight in a straight-away design. Other features include direct mount bracket machined from 6061 T6 aluminum, horizontal and vertical gang adjustment and a black or Multi-Match camouflage finish. The sight is secured by a precision-machined dovetail bracket. Dusk Devil comes in three pin colors—red, green and yellow—and two pin sizes. Calibrations are clearly marked on the brackets. The

pin guard has three quick-alignment dots to help you secure the target faster and align your sights.
SRP: black. $79.25
camouflage $87.10

Grand Slam Hunter
The economical version with calibrations marked and guard surrounding the pins.
SRP: standard $62.50
camouflage $71.25

Grand Slam Hunter Deluxe
SRP: standard $83.65
with Micro pins. $89.20

Q22
This Black Gold bow sight is specifically designed to fit a Mathews bow. It is a direct mount and has 4 standard or 4 Micro dot pins, plus calibrated brackets.
SRP: standard $39.00
black. $42.00
camouflaged $69.10
black sight with
Micro dots $74.15

Workhorse
This new economical bow sight has three pins and a direct base mount.
SRP: black. $39.95
camouflaged $44.25

Bow Accessories Sights and Peep Systems

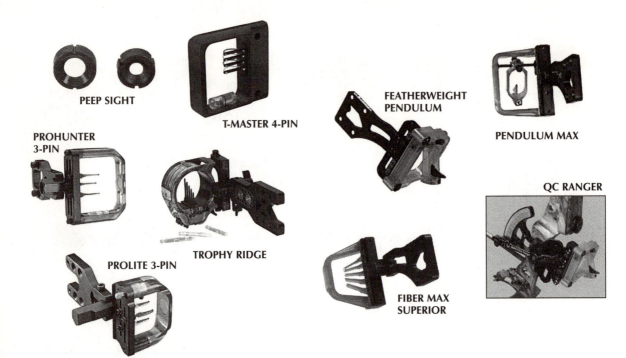

PEEP SIGHT

T-MASTER 4-PIN

FEATHERWEIGHT PENDULUM

PENDULUM MAX

PROHUNTER 3-PIN

QC RANGER

TROPHY RIDGE

PROLITE 3-PIN

FIBER MAX SUPERIOR

NORTH AMERICAN ARCHERY GROUP

Peep Sight
Round disc sight with beveled center. These peeps are available in medium, large and X-large sizes.
SRP: $2.49

ProHunter 3-Pin Fiber Optic
This 3-pin fiber optic sight has a machined aluminum body, smoke pin guard and level. The metal fiber optic pins can be adjusted vertical individually and vertical and horizontal as a gang.
SRP: $39.49

ProLite 3-Pin Fiber Optic Lighted Sight
A machined aluminum sight with a light built into the pin guard. Color: Black.
SRP: $45.99

T-Master 4-Pin Fiber Optic
A machined aluminum sight system with four pins and a level in the base of the pin guard. Color: Black.
SRP: $64.99

Trophy Ridge 5-Pin Fiber Optic
This sight incorporates a SIMS vibration dampener, Microtech and Camlock pin levers and Nitor light system. Available in Hardwoods High-Definition and Mossy Oak Break-Up camouflage. (Item 6085-065 is Custom Hardwoods model at same SRP)
SRP: $99.99

SAVAGE SYSTEMS

Featherweight Pendulum
This sight has twin riser mount holes so you can choose the best position. The Pendulum pin is house din a clear bracket. This sight is available in black or camouflaged.
SRP: with NightHawk Tritium pin,
. . . . $49.95 to $79.95
   Add $10 to $15 more for
   camouflaged sights

Fiber Max Superior
These fixed position standard designed bow sights by Savage Systems have sturdy mounting brackets and a calibrated sight window bracket. This sight has keyless adjustment thanks to awing nut on top. Your choice of three or five pin set ups with the sight. The sight is easily converted from left to right hand use.
SRP: three pin $36.95
   five pin $47.95
Nighthawk Tritium pin $62.95

Pendulum Max
This sight has a solid mounting bracket, and the swinging pins are housed inside a polycarbonate window. Numerous pin choices are available. The Smoke Featherweight sight is similar and has a smoke clear housing around the swinging pendulum sight.
SRP: . . . . $64.95 to $89.95

Pendulum Super Max
The single pin sight swings on a pendulum inside the sight window and is on line to nearly 30 yards distance from your tree stand. The Nighthawk pin uses a tritium light source to enhance the fiber optics.
SRP: Nighthawk pin $94.95
FiberGlo pin $69.95

QC Ranger
This Savage System sight is fully adjustable and adjusts to the bows speed out to 70 yards. It has laser engraved yardage markings, accepts pendulum sights and comes with fiber optic or Nighthawk sight pins. The lever swings across an arch at the back of the sight to rapidly adjust to the determined yardage. The pin moves freely inside a pendulum.
SRP: $134.95

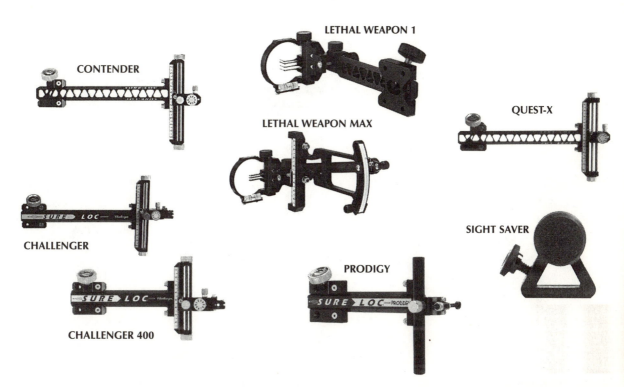

CONTENDER

LETHAL WEAPON 1

LETHAL WEAPON MAX

QUEST-X

CHALLENGER

SIGHT SAVER

CHALLENGER 400

PRODIGY

BOW ACCESSORIES

SURE-LOC

Sure-Loc sights are known for innovation and steadfast accuracy. The company uses the highest quality materials to create sights that stay where you want them to, and to move when you want them to. Steve Gibbs has been making these sights and outfitting archers ranging from bowhunters to Olympians since 1992. Sure-Loc is based in Versailles, Indiana.

Challenger

This package include either a 400 or 550 frame in black only, choice of 6-, 9- or 12-inch extension, mounting block and hardware, offset bracket, armored 3d axis, scope rod holder, durable carrying case. Available in left and right models (must specify.)
SRP: $177.99

Contender

Contender is similar to the Quest-X and is offered in black only. The Contender and the Quest-X are for recurve bow use only and not to be used with a scope.
SRP: $181.99

EZ-Adjust Eagle Eye

This sight has a bracket like the Fiber

Max and uses a smaller sight window and less pins.
SRP: $31.95

Lethal Weapon 1

A hunting bow sight with .0015-inch windage and elevation adjustments. A bubble can be placed on either side to check level. The windage block gives a full 1½-inch mass adjustment. Four steel pins with fiber optic in .019 and .029 sizes. Quiver mount is an accessory.
SRP: $178.95

Lethal Weapon 2M
SRP: $155.95

Lethal Weapon Max

This Sure-Loc hunting bow sight has 2 and 3 axes leveling capabilities and solid 2½-vertical slide action. Uses a lock to secure sight into position and the sight has three pins and numerous micro adjustment options.
SRP: $229.99

Prodigy Sight

Features include elevation and windage adjustments, positive elevation locking knob and it's totally reversible from right- to left-handed.

This sight is made for all bows—compound and recurves—up to 44 pounds pull. Includes a 550 size frame, 6-inch extension, mounting block and sight aperture. Available in black only.
SRP: $89.99

Quest-X

A target sight with no-lock vertical and horizontal tracking. Features a lightweight 5½-inch frame with 9-inch extension anodized in bright silver, black or the new Glory pattern. This sight package includes a 5.5-inch sight, a 9-inch extension and a recurve style ⁸/₃₂ aperture holder with Beiter washer package. This sight also has a carrying case. Specify right or left model when ordering.
SRP: $304.99

Sight Saver

Designed to use the popular Simms Vibration Knobs, this mini triangle can be mounted on a sight bar to reduce damaging vibration. Does not interfere with the sight's operation or use when mounted properly.
SRP: $24.99

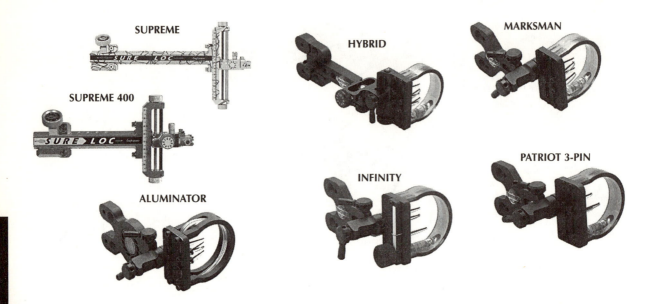

SUPREME

SUPREME 400

ALUMINATOR

HYBRID

INFINITY

MARKSMAN

PATRIOT 3-PIN

BOW ACCESSORIES

Supreme

Designed for compound bows with no-lock design and accurate tracking system. It is micro adjustable in repeatable increments up to .002-inch. Package includes either a 400 or 550 frame in silver, black or the new Glory pattern, choice of 6-, 9- or 12-inch extension, offset bracket, armored 3rd axis, scope holder, and carrying case. Must order as a right or left model.
SRP: $294.99

Supreme 400

This hunting sight has black knobs, a 6-inch extension, quiver mount and fixed pin attachment. The sights have black anodized sturdy metal surfaces. Buyer can choose from 5 brass pins or 3 fiber optic pins in this size or razor size. Package includes a 4-inch frame, 3- or 6-inch extension, mounting block, black offset bracket, quiver mount, choice of sight pins and a durable carrying case.
SRP: $294.99

Sure-Loc Challenger 400

SRP: $177.99

TOXONICS

Toxonics could be one of the first companies in the archery industry that permits you to build your own sights. The company sells modular components, then you select what you want and assemble your own custom designed sight.

Aluminator

Sight features all machined construction from 6061-T6 aircraft aluminum and superior light gathering capabilities with three feet of fiber optics strand housed in a durable Teflon coating. Two rows of sight pins are angled to meet perfectly in the middle of the sight. All models—three are available—feature the Aluminator sight system and quick knobs that permit finger operation.
SRP: $89.98
Model M-CT3 . . . . $104.98
Model M-CT2 . . . . $99.98

Hybrid Sight Series

This bow sight series by Toxonics have a phosphorous insert in the tinted pin guard to make pin detection easier at dawn and dusk. Add $10 extra and you purchase the camouflaged models for your hunting bow.
Hybrid III
   SRP: $39.99
Hybrid IV
   SRP: $59.99

Hybrid V
   SRP: $109.99

Infinity Sights

This sight has two fixed pins and a third adjustable pin that can be moved up and down with a quick turn of the dial. The third pin will adjust to infinite yardage settings and a yardage indicator shows distance marks around the dial. Other features include an easy adjust knobs, smoke clear sight guard and a level in the base of the sight window platform.
SRP: M-FT1 . . . . $79.98
Model M-FT3 . . . . $89.98
M-FT2 . . . . $89.98

Marksman 4-Pin

The Marksman is equipped with four long necked steel fiber optic sight pins backed by .040 fibers. The twin rows are angled to create a perfect pin alignment within the GLO-RING pin housing. Three Toxonics Marksman sight models are available, and an optional Photon light retails for $24.95.
Model M-DT1 . . . . $49.98.
Model M-DT2 . . . . $59.98

Patriot 3-Pin

SRP: $28.88

5000 NAILDRIVER

ALPHA CROSS

ALPHA

5300-RWB NAILDRIVER

MICRO MATRIX

SNIPER

5309-S09 NAILDRIVER

Sniper Sights

Toxonics' Sniper sights operate with a pendulum and three-pin fiber optic system. The top pin swings and is great for tree stand bowhunting situations. This sight is equipped with a level, tinted pin guard, GLO-RINGS, laser engraved yardage and windage scales. Sight must be adjusted with a hex wrench.

SRP: M-ET1 . . . . **$79.89**
M-ET2 . . . . **$89.98**

Naildriver Series

Sights for the tournament archers. The Naildriver series has a 10-click knob for compute generated sight tape compatibility. These sights are hand machined with a patented locking mechanism. Depress the knob for rapid movements, and twist the knob to lock the sight block and lead screw securely into position.

5000 Original Heavy Duty Naildriver
  SRP: **249.99**

5309-S09 Silver Naildriver
  SRP: **$299.99**
5300-RWB Naildriver
  SRP: **$359.99**

TROPHY RIDGE

The sights made by this Belgrade, Montana, manufacturer, along with its Drop Zone rest, have one thing in common—Dual Harmonic Dampers. The technology comes from Mathews but Trophy Ridge representative Mark Garcia said that the shock and vibration absorption system works and will reduce felt hand recoil and vibration. Trophy Ridge has pioneered vertical inline pin (VIPIN) technology. These sights use TRUGLO fiber optics.

Alpha

Base is for mounting on a bow's riser. This sight has vertical pins, a more open tubular sight window and is available with three or five pin design.
SRP: . . . . **$74.99 to $79.99**

Alpha Cross (crossbow)
SRP: . . . . **$49.99 to $57.99**

Micro Matrix

The prominent features of this sight include: a great field of view through the round sight window that rimmed by a reflective sight ring; clearly marked calibration markings on the sight bar and extension for adjustments; finger operated quick release on the mounting bracket and a level in the sight window. The pins are steel with fiber optic points. This sight is available in three and five-pin designs, with .029 and .019 size pin heads, and in right- or left-hand models. You can add Power plus lens to create magnification of the view and pins. You can install Nitro lights for low light situations. These sights are available in Mossy Oak and Realtree camouflage.
SRP: . . . . **$117 to $125**

Matrix (Steel pins and round sight ring)
SRP: . . . . **$109 to $119**

Bow Accessories Sights and Peep Systems

NITRO XTREME

GLO BRITE SITE

TRU SITE 3000

FLATLINER

RANGE ROVER

TRU SITE 5000

GLO BRITE SINGLE PIN

RITE SITE

Nitro Xtreme

Covered in Realtree X-tra Grey, this sight is offered with three or five pins and a bubble in the bottom of the round sight window. A five-pack of Nitro lights are included and these miniature light sticks last up to 12 hours. The vertical pins in the sight have fiber optic tips and the fiber optic coils wrap around the round sight window.

SRP: . . . . $79 to $89

Flat Liner (w/out camo or level)
SRP: . . . . $44.99 to $49.99

TRUGLO
Glo Brite Site

The sight pins have coils of fiber optic cable wrapped around their base and are protected by a smoke colored polycarbonate pin guard. The mounting bracket holds the sight bracket with a dove-tailed grip. Two slots permit pre-cision pin adjustments. A newer model of this sight is available with a battery-operated light installed in the pin guard for approximately $25 more.

SRP: three-pin $32.99
Five-pin camouflaged. $47.99

Glo Brite Single Pin

This sight has a single pin protruding up for the bottom of a light-gathering ring. The tritium coating in the pin keeps the tip glowing when light conditions drop below those collected but the 24 inches of fiber optic cable. This sight is easily adjusted and black in color.

SRP: $89.99

Range Rovers

This series of sights by TRUGLO has a finger-touch adjustment option and you can adjust the pins and sight for precise distances. The large aperture ring is 1½-inches diameter and the sight is also offered with a single pin within a rectangular pin guard.

SRP: $85.99
single pin $64.99

Rite Site

A basic and solid bow sight by TRUGLO with three brass-based blade pins that have a rib of fiber optics along the spine. Available in black and camouflage.

SRP: black. $32.99
camouflaged $37.99

Tru Site 5000

Constructed of machined metal, this sight offers precise micro-adjustable windage and elevation adjustments. Four pins are included and can be adjusted inside two slots on the pin bracket.

SRP: $72.99
with tritium sight pins $92.99

Tru Site 3000 (Without micro-adjust)
SRP: $62.99
with a tritium pin $82.99

BOW ACCESSORIES

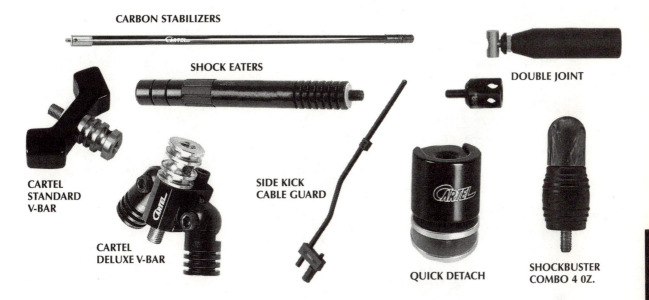

CARBON STABILIZERS

SHOCK EATERS

DOUBLE JOINT

CARTEL STANDARD V-BAR

CARTEL DELUXE V-BAR

SIDE KICK CABLE GUARD

QUICK DETACH

SHOCKBUSTER COMBO 4 0Z.

STABILIZERS

When you release an arrow and put your bow's string, cables, limbs and cams into motion, there's vibration and oscillation that begins—whether you see it or not. Stabilizers are designed to eliminate or dampen the effect and make the process go smoother. In recent year archers have seen incredible developments in this product arena. Whether you use a liquid filled, piston operated, or solid stabilizer, most bow manufacturers recommend that you use one—period.

These descriptions and models should help you in your search for the right stabilizer as you seek the right gear to help you shoot smoother and straighter. –MDF

CARTEL
Aluminum/Carbon Stabilizers
SRP: 1-inch diameter, 26-, 28-
and 30-inch length $79.95
same as 06213 in 10- and
12-inch length. $45.00

Carbon and Carbon Aluminum Stabilizers
SRP: $49.95
½-inch diameter model . . . $64.95
10- and 12-inch. $29.95
½-inch diameter model . . . $49.95

Hydraulic Carbon/Aluminum Stabilizers

SRP: 1-inch diameter, 26-, 28-
and 30-inch length
black. $89.95
camo $99.95
7-, 10- and 12-inch length
black. $49.95
camo . . . . $ 55.00

Deluxe V-Bar
This unit attaches to your bow's threaded bushing and permits the installation of two stabilizers at once. Can be set at any angle.
SRP:. $65
standard V-Bar. $24.95

Shock Eaters
This series of stabilizers has a flexible rubber ring near the tip to reduce bow recoil and shock. These stabilizers have vibration dispersal rings, three stackable end weights and hardened $5/16$-inch threads for connection with bow's threaded bushing. Available sizes include: 2-, 4-, 7-, 10-, and 12-inch.
SRP: . . . . $12.95 to $34.95

Stabilizer Quick Detach
A new item for Cartel in 2001. This unit permits archer to remove stabilizers and extenders from bow or V-bars with quick and easy quarter turn. Unique design keeps stabilizer tight through shooting sessions.
SRP. $17.95

COBRA
Double Joint
Use this item to disconnect and remove a stabilizer for storage or transportation. Simply turn the disconnect and remove the brass connector, or turn the brass connector to swing the stabilizer out of the way like a knuckle. Stabilizers can be moved up to 90 degrees.
SRP: $6.60
camouflage double joint . . . $8.11

Shockbuster
Designed to be placed between accessories and bow, this mini shock threads into AMO-ATA standard threaded holes and then accepts threaded studs.
SRP: $8.11

Shockbuster Stabilizer Combo
(4-, 6- and 8-ounce sizes placed on the front or back of the bow)
SRP: 4 ounce. $17.99
6 ounce. $18.99
8 ounce. $19.99

Side Kick Cable Guard and Threaded Cable Guard
Two cable guards are available from Cobra. One attaches to the bow's front or rear stabilizer hole and is adjustable from 10 to 13 inches long. The other model screws directly into the bow's handle and has a non-glare finish.
SRP: adjustable $9.39
standard threaded $6.19

Bow Accessories Stabilizers

COBRA STANDARD

COBRA DELUXE

COBRA LITTLE "C"

SHOCK FINS

SHOCKFIN PIRANHA

DOINKER D-2

WRAP AROUND
CABLE SAVER

MUZZY SPEED-LOC

SHOCKFIN STABILIZERS

Standard Stabilizer

This 12-ounce stabilizer has a durable non-glare matte finish over steel alloy construction.
SRP: $3.81

Deluxe Stabilizer (12-ounce, drilled and tapped receiver hole in the front for standard AMO/ ATA threaded stud.)
SRP: $4.99

Little "C" Stabilizer (8-ounce steel alloy, matte black finish.)
SRP: $3.70

Wrap Around Cable Saver

This cable guard slide wraps securely around the cable guard and reduces cable wear while it quiets the bow during release and draw.
SRP: $1.19

DOINKER
Doinker D-2

A lightweight mini stabilizer that weighs 2.3 ounces and has shock absorbing ribs. It can be used solo or attached on the tip or as a base for other stabilizers. Made of rubber.
SRP: $15.99

5-Inch Doinker
SRP: $36.95
Original Doinkers (4- or 7-inch, black or camouflage)
SRP: $41.95
Standard Doinkers (Fit between bow and other stabilizers)
SRP: $16

GLOBAL RESOURCES

Shock fins were designed and tested with the assistance of the Massachusetts Institue of Technology. The parent company is located in Stoughton, Massachusetts.

Shock Fins

These vibration and noise reduction fins are mounted on the tip of the bow limbs. They can be installed inside or outside on a bow limb with adhesive strips that are included.

SRP: 4 fins $18

Shockfin Piranha

These vibration reduction fins are joined by a flexible base that can be inserted in between split limbs on a quad limb bow.
SRP: per pair $26.96

Shockfin Stabilizers

These lightweight stabilizes are made of carbon and use inverted piston weight technology.
SRP: $34.99

MUZZY
Muzzy Speed-Loc

This adapter makes changing a stabilizer a snap. It can also be used to add a string tracker or to quickly break down your bow for easy storage and transportation. Made by the Muzzy broadhead company. (Item 400 and 400-Black)
SRP: $19.92

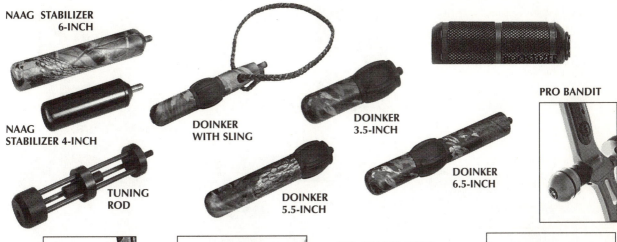

NAAG STABILIZER 6-INCH

NAAG STABILIZER 4-INCH

DOINKER WITH SLING

DOINKER 3.5-INCH

PRO BANDIT

TUNING ROD

DOINKER 5.5-INCH

DOINKER 6.5-INCH

BEAR OMNICOUPLER

DEADLY QUIET

PRO-DEADLY QUIET

BANDIT

NORTH AMERICAN ARCHERY GROUP

Bear OmniCoupler
Used to quickly attach and remove any standard threaded stabilizer from any bow for transportation and storage
SRP: $29.99

Doinker 3.5-Inch
This 3.5-inch stabilizers fits into a bow's standard threaded receptacle. Available in Mossy Oak Break-Up, Custom Hardwoods, and Realtree Hardwoods and Hardwoods High Definition camouflage patterns. Features a rubberized spacer/ bushing at the rear.
Weight: 3.6 ounces
SRP: $29.99

Doinker 5.5-Inch
Weight: 6 ounces
SRP: $34.99
Doinker 6.5-Inch
Weight: 7.2 ounces
SRP: $38.99
Doinker with Sling
Weight: 8.4 ounces
SRP: $39.99

Stabilizer 6-Inch
This camouflaged tube-type stabilizer is one solid piece and is distributed by the North American Archery Group. It's available in Mossy Oak Break-Up and Realtree Hardwoods High Definition camo. Also available in black.
Weight: 5.3 ounces
SRP: black $9.49
     camouflaged $13.99

Stabilizer 4-Inch
SRP: $7.49

Tuning Rod
An innovative design with end caps connected by three rods with a balance weight suspended between caps.
Weight: 6.4 ounces
SRP: $34.99

SAUNDERS ARCHERY EQUIPMENT COMPANY
Saunders archery has been in business many years and is based in Columbus, Nebraska. The company makes numerous innovative archery products ranging from stabilizers to targets and arrow components.

Bandit
A mini cap stabilizer and shock absorber that can be used solo or added to a stabilizer. With a dovetail bracket you can add this unit to a sight extension bar. This is an innovative unit you must see and try to believe.
SRP: $24.95
    bracket attachment $9.95

Pro Bandit (Two micro caps encased in visco-elastic polymer)
SRP: $38.95

Boostizer
A micro stabilizer than can enhance the performance of other units or used alone. It has three patented internal absorbers. This unit is available in black only.
SRP: $28.95

Deadly Quiet and Pro-Deadly Quiet
This system from Saunders Archery quiets the bow's string when the string reaches it. The units mount on a cable guard and the string stops when it reaches the rear of the Deadly quiet. This unit mounts on a standard $3/8$-inch cable guard rod.
SRP: Deadly Quiet $19.95
    pro model $34.95

Bow Accessories Stabilizers

SHOCK TAMER

SAUNDERS STRAIGHT ROD

XCHANGER

XCHANGER HUNTER

PRO-TAMER

TAMER V4

TAMER SS

WHISPER WHISKERS

NB101 RECOILLESS CAMOUFLAGED

Shock Tamer
This stabilizer has an internal chamber that's a death trap for shock and vibration. An adjustment plate neutralizes stabilizer sag and energy is converted to heat via a patented visco elastic polymer. Available in black, titanium gray and chameleon camouflage. A stand off unit can be installed on the bow to act as a base.

SRP: **$98.95**
stand off base **$10.95**

Pro-Tamer (Two cylinders on
floating delivery rod)
SRP: **54.95**
Tamer SS (Mini version of the
Pro-Tamer, 6.4 ounces)
SRP: **$42.95**

Straight Rod
A short aluminum rod that's ideal for mounting a deadly quiet unit from the rear port when front mounting interferes with sights.
SRP: **$8.95**

Torque Tamer and Tamer V4
These dynamic stabilizers use three internal shock chambers to kill shock and vibration. The tamer is not sensitive to cold, cannot leak and has no metal-to-metal moving parts. The torque tamer is 6.5 inches long and weighs 9 ounces. The Tamer V4 can be made into: a 5-inch unit weighing 9.5 ounces; a 6.25 inch unit weighing 10.4 ounces; a 9.25 inch unit weighing 12.2 ounces or a 10.5 inch system weighing 13.1 ounces.
SRP: Torque Tamer **$28.95**
SRP: Tamer V4 . . . . **$45.95**

Whisper Whiskers
The durable and waterproof rubber whiskers can be tied to the bow's string to provide quietness. Available in assorted colors or black.
SRP: **$2.45**

Toxonics
While the Missouri based Toxonics company is known for its sights and innovative target archery gear, it also produces this line of Recoilless stabilizers.

Recoilless Stabilizers
These Toxonics stabilizers work to offset the recoil of the release as well as dampen the vibration of the bow throughout the shot cycle. The stabilizers do not use hydraulics or oil, but do use an open cell foam piston and center shaft. Silicon rubber boots help with the dampening process. Several models are available:
**NB-100 Recoiless
black.** **$29.99**
**NB101 Recoilless
camouflaged** **$36.99**
**NB-105 Extender
SRP:** **$14.99**

TROPHY RIDGE
Xchanger
This new stabilizer uses Sorbodome and can be changed in length to fine tune your bow. The unit is lightweight, effective, 100% fluid free and can be telescoped from $6\frac{1}{2}$- to $10\frac{1}{2}$-inches long. It has a camouflaged exterior.
SRP: black. **$64.99**
camouflaged **$69.99**

Xchanger Hunter
Similar to the Xchanger but it does not lengthen. This stabilizer weighs 3 ounces and has open celled Sorbodome foam.
SRP: black. **$44.99**
camouflaged **$49.99**

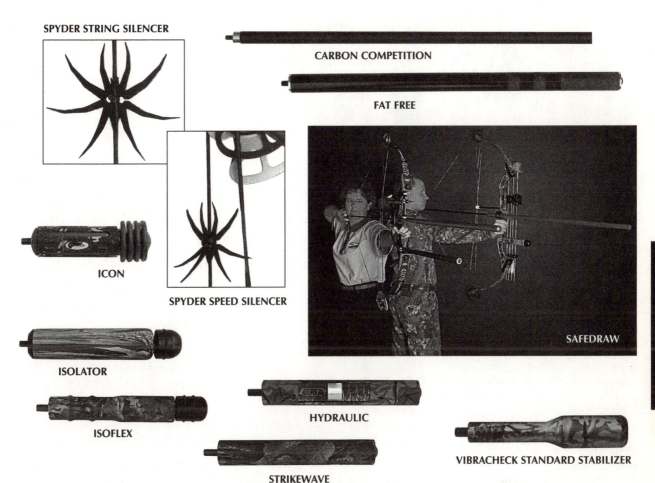

SPYDER STRING SILENCER

CARBON COMPETITION

FAT FREE

ICON

SPYDER SPEED SILENCER

SAFEDRAW

ISOLATOR

ISOFLEX

HYDRAULIC

STRIKEWAVE

VIBRACHECK STANDARD STABILIZER

BOW ACCESSORIES

T.R.U. BALL STABILIZERS
T.R.U. Ball Spyder Silencers
Made from durable Hypalon, these spider shaped silencers help gain bow speed and silence string twangs. The speed silencer attaches with a ball system and the string silencer attaches with serving thread.
SRP: String silencer per four . . $7.99
Speed silencer per four . . . $14.99

VIBRACHECK
Carbon Competition Stabilizers
These are designed for serious competitors. Available lengths include: 8, 20, 24, 28 and 34 inches long. Weights range from 2 to 6 ounces.
SRP: $124.95

Fat Free Stabilizers (3-D tournament, 18, 26 and 38 inches. 7, 8 and 9 ounces)
SRP: $125

Hydraulic and Strikewave.
The Hydraulic is 6.5 inches long, weighs 8 ounces and has an inner spring and weight. The Strikewave is the same length, weighs 6 ounces and has gel inside.
SRP: $29.95

Icon
A small unit that's 7 inches long and weighs 7 ounces. It has a nippled tip and uses VibraSORB gel inside an aluminum sleeve.
SRP: $39.95

Isolator
This unit is rubber coated and has a machined aluminum body. The inside is filled with VibaSORB gel and a 2-ounce activating weight.
SRP: $54.95
Isoflex. $44.95

Safedraw
This training aid by Virbacheck permits you to draw and fire your bow without an arrow. It is excellent for target panic therapy and can be used in a bow shop when customers are trying a bow. It mounts on a bow's rest and attaches to the bowstring. The shooter can use a bow exactly like it was being released at the target range.
SRP: $130

Standard Stabilizer
This unit is 5 inches long, weighs 5 ounces and is machined from solid aluminum stock.
SRP: $18.95

3-D Pro
These 10-inch long stabilizers by Vibracheck are either spring loaded or have Vibrasorb gel.
SRP: $69

Bow Accessories Strings

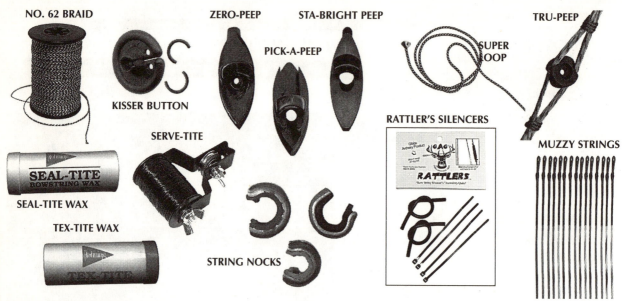

NO. 62 BRAID

KISSER BUTTON

SERVE-TITE

SEAL-TITE WAX

TEX-TITE WAX

ZERO-PEEP   STA-BRIGHT PEEP

PICK-A-PEEP

STRING NOCKS

RATTLER'S SILENCERS

SUPER LOOP

TRU-PEEP

MUZZY STRINGS

IT'S A STRING THING

Bows use a string to transfer energy from the limbs and cams onto the arrow. As you can tell, bowstrings are important. Here are the products and manufacturers of bowstrings for all types of bows. –MDF

BOHNING
No. 62 Braid

This material is durable Spectra and Polyester blended together. The polyester grips the bowstring and the Spectra rides on the outside for durability. Great for finishing bow strings. Available in .018-, .021- and .025-inch diameters.
SRP: $22.34

Kisser Button

This lightweight kisser button is easy to install and use.
SRP: $1.97

Seal-Tite Wax

Designed for high tensile bowstrings, this wax and silicone lubricates and holds strands together. 1 ounce tube.
SRP: $2.39

Serve-Tite String Server

You can adjust the tension and create smooth thread flow with this device. Mono and nylon serving models are available. Thread is also offered to fit each unit

SRP: $18.66
  mono thread, per spool $4.99
  nylon thread, per spool $5.25

String Nocks

Available in target (blue), cam (red) and Hunter (black) models to fit string sizes and needs.
SRP: per 6 . . . . $2.87

Tex-Tite Wax

A natural base wax for all bow strings. It is not sticky when cool. 1 oz. tube.
SRP: $2.22

Zero Peep

This standard peep is oval in shape, fits in the string and aligns with a tube and clip that are provided.
SRP: $6.99

Pick-A-Peep (Multiple adjustments)
SRP: $7.99

Sta-Bright Peep (Extra-large hole for low light conditions)
SRP: $6.99

GIBBS ARCHERY GEAR
Rattler's Bow String Silencers

These rubber tubes are woven and tied onto a bow string to reduce vibration and humming. Makes a unique rattlesnake rattler pattern when applied per directions.
SRP: $4.99

Super Loop

These loops can be affixed to a bowstring and used with a release aid to prevent string and serving wear. Multiple colors are available.
SRP: per pair $4.99

JIM FLETCHER ARCHERY AIDS
Tru-Peep Sights

These peeps fit into the string and are used to sight pins. The aluminum peeps are lightweight and provide a shaded hole at the draw. Available sizes include: hunter $1/8$-inch, Large $1/16$-inch, small $3/16$-inch and micro $1/32$-inch hole. A new Super Hunter model has a $3/16$-inch hole.
SRP: $3.50

MUZZY

The same Georgia based company that makes the Bad to the Bone broadheads also makes strings including custom strings.

Muzzy Strings

Numerous styles and colors are available. Additional charges are incurred for 450-plus braided centers, one color and two-color strings.
SRP: standard Dacron compound
  bowstrings $9.95
  traditional recurve and
    longbows strings 9.95
Fast-Flite standard strings. . . . $51.95
Yoke System cables $27.95

ERICKSON'S
CHRONOGRAPH
STAND

ERICKSON'S
OUTDOOR
CHRONOGRAPH
STAND

ERICKSON'S PAPER
TUNING RACK

QUIET ENHANCING KIT

EQUALIZER BOW PRESS

WORKBENCH
BOW VISE

BOW ACCESSORIES

TAKE THE TIME TO TUNE
When a bow is properly tuned, life is great. Some bow tuning tasks are so simple that you can do them at home with a few tools. These items should help lead you down the path of properly flying arrows and into the land of many bulls-eyes. Steady on the release and no jerking. –MDF

C.W. ERICKSON'S MFG.
This Buffalo, Minnesota company produces bow vises, multiple brackets for assorted uses and other archery accessories.

Chronograph Stand
This adjustable stand and base are lightweight and will securely and steadily hold a chronograph. Height adjustment is from 32- to 60-inches tall.
SRP: **$54.99**

Equalizer Double-Action Pull Lever Bow Press
This press is fully adjustable to hold any bow. It's quick, simple to operate and safe. Two rubber rollers protect the bow's limbs. Weighs 23 pounds.
SRP: **$144.89**

Outdoor Chronograph Stand
This stand spikes into the ground to hold a chronograph securely in place. Height adjustment is from 32- to 60-inches tall.
SRP: **$42.99**

Paper Tuning Rack
This rack hold paper steady while the shooter releases arrows and checks flight alignment. Provides a 20x18-inch shooting face and uses 18-inch freezer paper. Instructions and one roll of paper are included.
SRP: **$99.96**

Workbench Fully-Adjustable Bow Vise
Vise is secured to the edge of a workbench and grasps the limbs of any style bow. Can rotate the bow up to 360-degrees and will hold all bows, including crossbows. Holding prongs are vinyl coated to protect the bow.
SRP: **$46.99**

GOLDEN KEY-FUTURA
The folks at Golden Key-Futura make archery items ranging from release aids to rest to tuning tools.

Bow Quiet Enhancing Kit
This complete kit include all the items you need to silence a bow's rest, accessories and shelf. Includes adhesive felt, shrink tubes, eliminator buttons and string silencers.
SRP: **$20**

Bow Accessories Tuning Aids and Tools

COMPLETE TUNING KIT

BASIC TUNING KIT

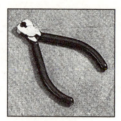

NOK SET PLIERS

QUICK NOK SHOOTING LOOP

DIGITAL GRAIN SCALE

HANSON BOW SCALE

SIMS LIMB SAVERS

METAL BOW SQUARE

Complete Tuning Kit

This bow kit includes a pocket tuning guide and instructional video to tell you how it's done, then a Tru-Center gauge, metal bow square and Nok-Set pliers will help you do it. Noks are included.

SRP:. $60

Basic Tuning Kit (Lacking the Tru-Center gauge)

SRP:. $18

DGS Digital Grain Scale

Precision weigh tips, broadheads and arrows to assist with proper selection and tuning. This electronic scale is a must for creating precision arrows. It will handle laods up to 750 grains. Has an Led digital displayand includes two precion weights for checking and calibrating. Can operate on a 9-Volt battery or AC adapter.

SRP:. $285

Hanson Bow Scale

These quality scales are used to determine a bow's draw weight and other needs. One scale ranges to 100 pounds and the other model will accommodate and record up to 300 pounds accurately.

SRP: 100-pound $78
　　　300-pound $85

MatchPoint Tuning Kit

Chuck Adams designed this bow and arrow tuning kit. It's features include a step-by-step tuning guide, three matchpoints, tackle box arrow rollers, tuning matchstrips, tuning marker and storage box. Matchpoint weights can be configured to dupli-cate and broadhead blade design and weight.

SRP: $24.99

Metal Bow Square

A one-piece solid square used for correctly setting nocks. Blue.

SRP:. $8

Nok Set Pliers

These are must have pliers for setting and removing nocks on a bowstring. The pliers are constructed of quality steel and have comfort grip handle wraps.

SRP:. $8

Quick Nok Shooting Loop

Eliminate string torque and serving wear with this easy to install nylon cord. It's strong and works well with all models of release aids. It's available in two diameters: 1 1/6- and 1/8-inch.

SRP:. $9

Sims Limb Savers

These mushroom shaped rubber buttons attach to a bows limbs and reduce shock, vibration and noise. Can be installed on split or solid limbs (must select proper model). These units are lightweight and will not interfere with strings or cables.

SRP: solid. $15
　　　split limb design. $20

TRU-CENTER GAUGE

BOW STRING WAX

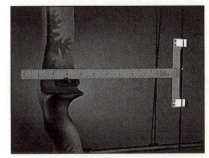

NAAG BOW SQUARE

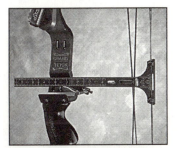

TAKE-DOWN BOW SQUARE

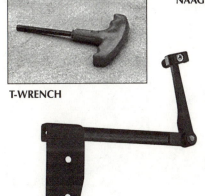

T-WRENCH

SWINGARM CABLE GUARD

NOCKING POINT PLIERS

Take-Down Bow Square
This square folds for easy and compact storage, plus it has levels to help determine proper string and sight alignment.
SRP:. $14

Tru-Center Gauge
Use this thin wire gauge to determine your bow's center shot. This model is improved and straddles the rest's mounting bolt.
SRP:. $15

T-Wrench
This is the same wrench used by the pro shops. It's a 3/16-inch hex wrench solidly attached to a large molded handle. It is easy to use to adjust a bow's draw weight.
SRP:. $7

NORTH AMERICAN ARCHERY GROUP
Bow String Wax
String wax helps increase life of your bow's string and reduce fraying and water absorption that can affect accuracy and arrow flight. (Item 7057)
SRP: $3.49

Bow Square
Check and adjust your nock's alignment against the arrow rest placement as you tune your bow. Color: blue.
SRP: $6.49

Nocking Point Pliers
The green rubber-coated grips on these pliers help assure a firm grip and precision nock alignment.
SRP: $5.49

Recurve Bow Stringer
Protect your recurve's tips and safely install the string with this system.
SRP: $11.99

Upper Mount SwingArm Cable Guard
This cable guard has a micro-adjust system and will mount on most bows.
SRP: $39.99

PROCHRONO
ProChrono Digital Chronograph
Features an expanded shooting area that's nearly two times the size of comparably priced models. Measures velocities from 56 to 9,999 feet per second and runs on a single .9-volt battery. Shoot in all weather since this chronograph operates in temperatures as low as 32° and as high as 100° Fahrenheit. Allows you to review 50 shots with power-down memory (review at home), high and low velocity settings, standard deviation, number of shots, average velocity, deletes current velocity and even has a printer interface so you can hook it to a printer to get a hard copy of the data. Shows metric or fps scales and features durable plastic diffusers. Measures just 16 x 3¼ inches. Mounting hole thread measures ¼ x 20 inches
SRP: $99.99

Bow Accessories Tuning Aids and Tools

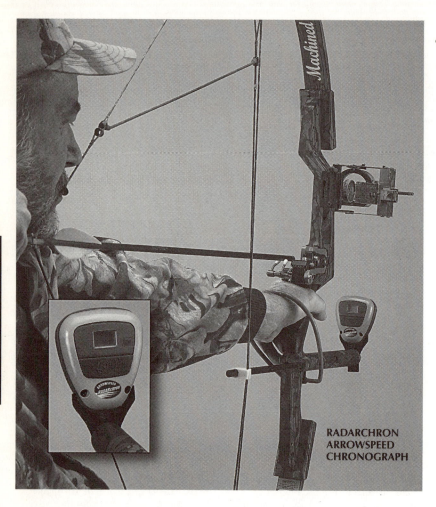

RADARCHRON
ARROWSPEED
CHRONOGRAPH

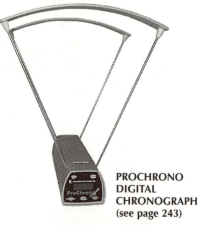

PROCHRONO
DIGITAL
CHRONOGRAPH
(see page 243)

ARCHERY SHOOTING CHRONY F-1
& BETA-CHRONY

R.S. ARCHERY
ArrowSpeed Chronograph
This chronograph is used by many pro shops when archers want to fine tune or enhance the performance of their bows. It's a small Doppler radar that measures the speed of the arrow as it is shot from the bow. The unit can be attached to the end of a stabilizer or to an extension rod that is provided.
SRP: $142.55

Bow Leveling Tuning System
This vise is used by the pros to hold bows in an upright position while offering the flexibility to hold the bow horizontally or vertically. A level tuning kit snaps to the string to check for horizontal and vertical positioning. Multiple accessories are offered. Call 800-444-9619 for details.
SRP: $89.95

SHOOTING CHRONY INC.
Archery Shooting Chrony F-1 & Beta-Chrony
Check velocities ranging from 30 fps to 7,000 fps with any Chrony Model and within 0.5 percent accuracy with any projectile: arrow, bullet, pellet, etc. LCD read-outs stay on the screen until next shot is fired. The Beta Chrony features a 60-shot memory (divided into six strings of 10 shots each); each string gives you Hi, Lo and Average velocity, ES and SD; it has a permanent memory for at-home data retrieval. All Chronys have steel housing for strength and less expansion/contraction deviation than plastic housings. Weight 2.5 lbs
Shooting F-1 Chronograph
SRP: $79.99

Shooting Beta Chronograph
SRP: $109.99

Shooting Chrony Beta Master
SRP: $139.99

SPORTS SENSORS, INC.
Radarchron Arrowspeed Chronograph
Using microwave Doppler radar, the RADARchron is accurate within +/- 2percent from 150 to 450 feet-per-second. LCD display toggles between hundredths and tenths of fps units. A threaded adapter attaches to the end of most stabilizers. The included extension rod can be used in place of stabilizer and connected directly to bow, and it can be carried anywhere, thanks to an ultra-compact size. Compatible with both aluminum and graphite/carbon arrows. Operates on a 3-volt lithium battery (included).
SRP: $99.95

Bow Accessories Cases and Slings

DELUXE
BOW CASE

MEGA BOW
SLING

BOONIE BOWSLING

FIELD
LOCKER

AIM
ARROW CASE

LOOP LOCK
BOW SLING

PACK IT AND SLING IT

Whether you're traveling across town or across country, you need to case your bow to protect it, the arrows and the bowstring from potential damage. And in some states it's the law. There are many hard and soft options. If you're traveling by plane or in a truck with a lot of gear, a sturdy hard side case is the best protection. Newer cases have room for an accessory box and lots of arrows.

And when you arrive in the field, there are new ways to carry or retain a good grip on your bow. A good bow sling can improve your shooting and use a more relaxed grip when you draw and release. You'll find something on these pages to help you travel and retain control. -MDF

AIM

AIM is headquartered in Willimantic, Connecticut, and make bows and accessories.

Arrow Case

AIM's heavy-duty clear plastic arrow case holds up to a dozen arrows and protects your arrows from damage while in storage or transit.
SRP: **$15.95**

BOONIE PACKER

While Boonie Packer is known for its gun slings, the Salem, Oregon, manufacturer also makes a simple and sturdy sling to carry a bow.

Boonie Bowsling

An over-the-shoulder sling that keeps your bow up front and ready when the sling is worn properly. The bow can also be carried over the shoulder and behind the back. The Boonie sling is 2-inch nylon webbing with a loop in each end. The sling is fully adjustable and available in Realtree Hardwoods, Woodland and Mossy Oak Break-Up.
SRP: **$21.99**

COBRA

Cobra is located in Oklahoma and also manufacturers sights, releases and rests.

Loop Lock Bow Sling

This sling has a metal bracket that fits over the bow's stabilizer hole and riser edge. It's drilled and tapped to accept a stabilizer. A ½-inch wide strap wraps over your hand and wrist. Available in black and camouflage.
SRP: **$4.25**

Mega Bow Sling

The cord loop fits over your hand and wrist and it has a dual lock. The metal bracket fits over the bow's

stabilizer hole and the extension is drilled and tapped to receive a standard stabilizer stud.
SRP: **$2.75**

DOSKOSPORT (formerly Doskocil)

For more than 40 years, this company has been making cases—period. Some of their original cases were made of hand stained wood. Today's cases are made of injection molded plastics in some cases. The Doskospor company is based in Arlington, Texas and their line of hard side bow cases continues to expand.

Deluxe Bow Case

Similar to the deluxe double bow (Bowguard) case, but it is designed to hold one bow and many arrows. Thick foam egg crate padding protects the bow.
SRP: . . . . **$79 to $89**

Field Locker Arrow Case

A hardside case by Doskosport that's designed to securely hold nearly two dozen arrows. The case latches closed and can be locked with three pad locks. Arrows are held in place by foam blocks. A must have for serious archers who travel with expensive carbon arrows.
SRP: . . . . **$14 to $19**

Bow Accessories Cases and Slings

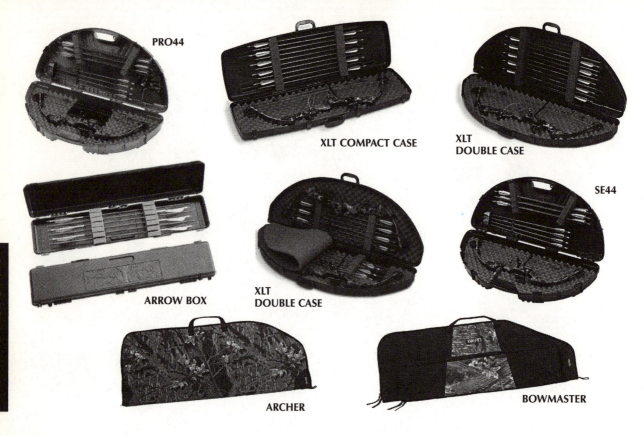

PRO44

XLT COMPACT CASE

XLT DOUBLE CASE

SE44

ARROW BOX

XLT DOUBLE CASE

ARCHER

BOWMASTER

Pro44

Hardside bow case – features include durable steel hinge pins, large and wide angled feet for stability, two inches of extra thickness permits safe storage of the bow. A post inside permits you to attach a quiver with arrows in a secure position away for the bow. An accessory box holds broadheads and other items securely. Tie-down straps hold the bow in place, and extra straps can hold arm guards, release aids, etc. Extra arrows can be securely stored in two rigid foam slotted blocks. The extra wide handle and four wide snap-over latches are recessed for easy carrying and loading. ATV tabs help tie this case to a four-wheeler's rack and it has two points for padlocks. This case is 44 inches long, 20 inches high and 9 inches thick outside dimensions when closed.
SRP: . . . . $49-99 to $59.99

SE44
SRP: (without the accessory box)
. . . . $29.99 to $39.99

XLT Compact Bow Case
Designed for smaller bows, such as those used by women and young archers. The case has 4 inches of inner locking foam to protect bows and hold them into place. Foam blocks hold up to 10 arrows. Latches are key lockable. This case's exterior is 47½-inches long by 15-inches tall.
SRP: . . . . $49 to $59

XLT Double Bow Case
The XLT Double Bow Case by Doskosport holds two full sized bows, arrows, and accessories. It features key lockable latches, slotted foam arrow retainer blocks and protective convoluted (egg crate) foam padding. The black case is 50 inches long and 18½ inches tall.
SRP: . . . . $79 to $89

XLT Single Bow Case
SRP: . . . . $59 to $69

KOLPIN
Kolpin manufactures archery cases and in recent years has begun manufacturing the popular Final Approach

hunting blinds. The company also produces firearm cases, accessory bags and a wide assortment of ATV gear and bags.

Archer
A basic no-thrills compound bow case made from heavy weave polyester and with a Rhino Hide tip. This Kolpin case is camouflaged with Mossy Oak Break Up and has a strap handle and full length zipper. Available styles include long and short and with or without an exterior pocket.
SRP: . . . . $27.99 to $32.99

Arrow Box
This box is specially designed to fit in all Kolpin bow cases arrow pockets. It will safely and securely hold up to a dozen arrows with broadheads attached. Other features are a Hinged top and flip lock front and an embossed wildlife scene. Color: Green.
SRP: $11.99

Bowmaster
Reinforced with weatherproof shell
SRP:starting at $44.99

Bow Accessories Cases and Slings

BOWTECTOR DELUXE

DOUBLE EDGE BOW GEAR BAG

YOUTH BOW CASE

BOWMASTER CROSSBOW

RECURVE BOW CASE

SEALTECTOR

LONGBOW CASE

COMPOUND BOW CASE

Bowtector
Exterior Rhino reinforced rib section, weatherproof. Models include a deluxe with exterior arrow case pocket, standard case and double bow case
SRP: starting at $64.99

Bowmaster Crossbow
The exterior of this case is reinforced with Rhino Hide in high wear areas. Closed cell foam liner and camouflaged Mossy Oak exterior. Padded wrap around handles make transportation easy on the hands. A sturdy zipper holds the contents inside and a metal ring helps hang the bag for storage.
SRP:. $74.99

Double Edge Bow Gear Bag
A soft-side case designed to hold two compound bows and lots of gear. The case is water repellent, has a center divide padded close cell foam partition and provide five exterior pockets for gear storage. A shoulder strap helps with transportation. Color: Brown.
SRP: $126.99

Sealtector Bow Case
Designed to strap onto the rack of any ATV. The case is waterproof with elec-

trically welded seams and has a rugged 600 Denier exterior shell. Additional features include: padded wrap around grip handle, inside pockets for arrows and accessories, web-reinforced attachment straps, and a stretchable cargo net to hold down gear. Available in Mossy Oak camouflage.
SRP: $179.99

NORTH AMERICAN ARCHERY GROUP
This bow case is distributed by the North American Archery Group of Gainesville, Florida. These cases will fit all bows but can be found anywhere where Bear, Golden Eagle and Jennings bows are stocked.

Compound Bow Case
A soft-side canvas shelled bow case with brown trim, loop handles and arrow box storage pocket on the side. Zippered closure and soft padding.
SRP: 44 inch $44.99
SRP: 39-inch $39.99

Recurve Bow Case
A stylish canvas case with zippered closure and brown nylon trim and

loop handles. Includes ID tag holder.
SRP: $45.99
Long Bow Case
SRP: $45.99

T/D Compound Bow Case
A compact canvas shelled case with two exterior pockets that's designed to hold the Bear Take-Down compound bow.
SRP: $59.99

Youth Bow Case
An adult-like version designed to hold the Brave youth bow. Features include a canvas shell with zippered closure and two loop handles. Length: 37 inches. Color: Green.
SRP: $19.99

PLANO MOLDING COMPANY
Plano Molding is well known for its series of gun cases and ammunition storage boxes. The company also makes bow cases and recently released the innovative Bow Max hip roof case. This company gets a nod of approval for making sturdy products at an affordable price. Plano is based in Plano, Illinois.

Bow Accessories Cases and Slings

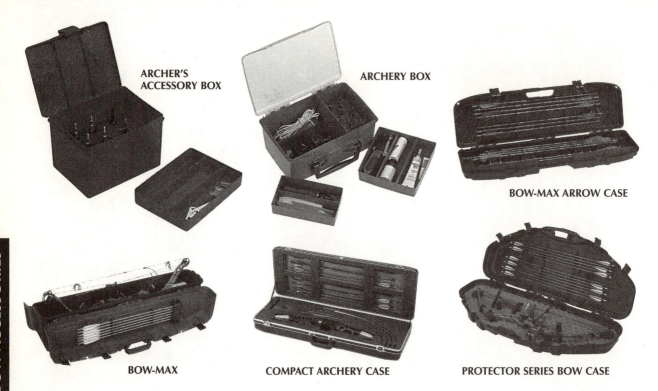

ARCHER'S ACCESSORY BOX

ARCHERY BOX

BOW-MAX ARROW CASE

BOW-MAX

COMPACT ARCHERY CASE

PROTECTOR SERIES BOW CASE

Archer's Accessory Box
A storage box designed to hold broadheads and touchy expandable broadheads also. A lift out tray is a good place to store nocks, field points and small items.
SRP: $6.99

Archery Box
A small multi-compartment storage box by Plano with a clear plastic lid and carrying handle to help you organize your must-have archery gear. Great for field or bench use. Has two lift out trays and foam area to securely hold broadheads.
SRP: $9.99

Bow-Max
A case with a two-part hip roof designed to cradle bows. A pivoting rubber bow retainer secures the bow in place and leaves room for the accessory box. A Sur-Lok arrow storage system retains arrows and covers the broadheads and points. It is lockable and airline approved. The case is 46 inches long and 19½-inches tall.
SRP: $99.99

Bow-Max Arrow Case
A strong case designed to securely cradle expensive arrows. Holds up to 18 arrows and has a Pillarlock locking system. Sur-Lok system grips and retains arrows in place. This black case has a molded in comfort handle and is 36 inches long.
SRP: $19.99

Protector Series Bow Case
A case with a compact design and thick wall patented PillarLock construction. Velcro straps hold bow in place and Sur-Lok grips arrows and secures them in place. The 49-inch long case is lockable and airline approved. It's available in black and camouflaged colors.
SRP: black $27.99
　　　 camouflage $34.99

SIMMONS SYSTEM ARCHERY
Simmons System Archery of Jasper, Alabama makes this unique tube quiver.

The BushMaster Quiver
A unique round tubular quiver that is carried over the shoulder by a strap. The case exterior is camouflaged by Mossy Oak and the precision cut foam inserts inside the tube hold arrows in place to ensure stealth quietness while hunting. Tree sizes are available and can hold arrows ranging from 30½ to 34½ inches long.
SRP: $55

SKB
These super-strong cases have been used by the military and by professional film crews for years. They are proven tough by the airlines and moving companies. The good news for bowhunters and archers is that the company offers nearly a dozen models in a wide assortment of styles to fit everything from crossbows to compounds to recurves. SKB is headquartered in Orange, California.

Compact Archery Case
A case that's designed to hold a breakdown recurve bow and two sets of limbs. This case has a sturdy HDPE shell, weather resistant O-ring seal and solid die cast zinc locks. Foam pre-cut strips will securely hold up to 18 arrows. A plastic toolbox is included and this also fits inside the case. The case is 36-inches long. Color: Black.
SRP: (Item 2SKB-3712RC) $169

BOW ACCESSORIES

Bow Accessories Cases and Slings

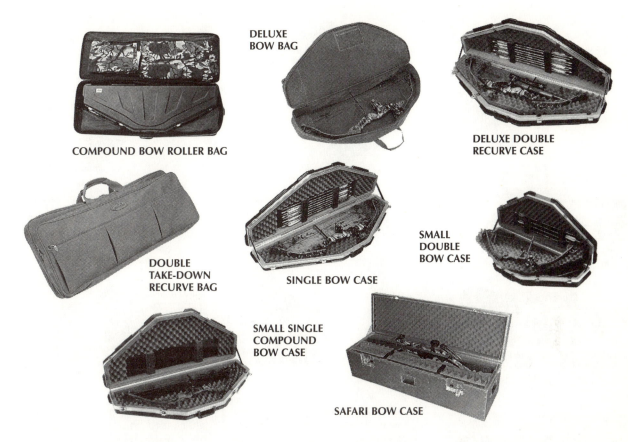

COMPOUND BOW ROLLER BAG

DELUXE BOW BAG

DELUXE DOUBLE RECURVE CASE

DOUBLE TAKE-DOWN RECURVE BAG

SINGLE BOW CASE

SMALL DOUBLE BOW CASE

SMALL SINGLE COMPOUND BOW CASE

SAFARI BOW CASE

Compound Bow Roller Bag

This roomy soft side bag will hold any SKB bow case plus an arrow box. It has oversized zippers, a strong 600 Denier exterior shell and wheels to keep the bag off the ground and provide easy airport movement. Color: Brown.
SRP: **$149.99**

Deluxe Bow Bag

A soft-side SKB case that holds one compound bow. D-rings inside can be used with bungee cords to hold smaller bows securely. Other features include a see-through mesh pocket to hold accessories, top quality leather trim and handles, arrow box storage section, full length pockets, and full padding to protect the bow and all contents. This case is large enough to hold a bow with a quiver and arrows attached. Color: Brown or green.
SRP: **$99.99**

Deluxe Double Recurve Case

Holds two takedown recurve risers, two sets of limbs, arrows, sights and a storage box. Color: Black.
SRP: **$189**

Double Take-Down Recurve Bag

This soft-side SKB bow case has leather reinforced pockets to hold risers and limbs safe and secure. Large exterior pockets can hold accessories and an arrow storage box. Other features include full padding to protect the contents, sturdy leather grip handles, oversized self-repairing nylon zippers and a 600 Denier exterior shell. Colors: Green or Brown.
SRP: **99.99**

Single Bow Case

A hard-side case that will hold one compound bow and up to 18 arrows. The interior is fully padded and the metal edge has a weather resistant O-ring seals to keep out dirt and moisture. Bumpers protect the case's hardware and it's lockable with solid die cast zinc locks. Color: Black
SRP: **$169**
Double Bow Case
    SRP: (Item 2SKB-6002) **$199**

Small Double Bow Case

Similar in design and style to the SKB small compound bow case but is designed to hold two smaller compound bows plus arrows. Thick egg-crate style foam separates the bows. A hard, swinging handle helps with transportation and two locks keep the contents secure. Color: Black.
SRP: **$189**

Small Single Compound Bow Case
SRP: **$179**

STRONG CASE

This Hayward, California, company builds a case unlike any other.

Strong Safari Bow Case

His heavy-duty metal case has sturdy one-piece construction of 14 gauge steel. A full-length piano hinge secures the top and recessed hardware makes moving easy. The foam interior liner is adjustable. Removable wheels help with airport moving. This case has a limited lifetime warranty and custom-built sizes are available.
SRP: Starting at **$225**

Bow Accessories Arm Guards

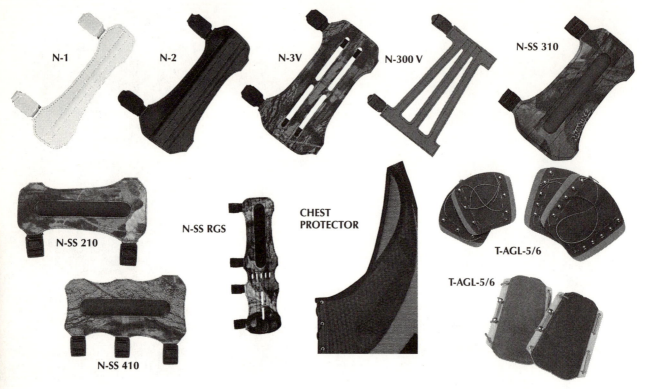

N-1 N-2 N-3V N-300 V N-SS 310 N-SS 210 N-SS RGS CHEST PROTECTOR T-AGL-5/6 T-AGL-5/6 N-SS 410

NEET

Based in Missouri, Neet makes one of the largest selections of arm guards, gloves, quivers, and archery accessories available today.

Armguard N-1

An armguard made for target shooters, this guard uses two adjustable straps and is made of vinyl. It's available in black and white.
SRP: $3.75

Armguard N-2
SRP: $4.00

Armguard N-3V
SRP: $7.00

Armguard N-300-V

A most unusual arm guard that's very open and it attaches to your arm with two straps. This guard is available in black, white, red, blue and camouflage.
SRP: starting at $6.90
more for camouflaged

Armguard N-SS-310

A camouflaged arm guard made with hunters in mind. This adult sized guard in 6¾-inch long and nearly 4 inches wide. It is fastened in place with two straps and has an exposed stave in a window. Made of Saddle Cloth or Cordura.
SRP: $6.75

Armguard N-SS-210
SRP: $5.95

Armguard N-SS-410
Three adjustable elastic straps.
SRP: $6.85

Armguard N-SS-RGS

A full-length arm guard that will cover your upper and lower arm. It has staves in the lower section and rods in the upper. It's available in Advantage and Break Up camouflage and with a Cordura or Saddle Cloth finish.
SRP: Starting at $9.95

Armguard N-SS-RGL
SRP: $10.00

Armguard N-RGL
SRP: $9.00

Chest Protector

An adjustable and comfortable nylon mesh over-the-shoulder guard from Neet that's designed to hold cloths away form the bowstring or release. A self-adjusting back strap with hook and loop front fastener keeps it securely in place. Interchangeable as left- or right-handed. This protector is available in black and white and sizes XS, S, M, L and XL.
SRP: $11.50

Hunter Guard N-3H

An armguard that's designed for hunters, this guard is wide and 7 inches long and is held securely in place with three adjustable straps.
SRP: $6.85

Mini Guard NY-MG

An arm guard for young archers. The stave is exposed in a window on the cover of this guard and two straps hold the unit in place on the arm.
SRP: $4.65

Traditional Armguards T-AGL-5/6

This Neet armguard is available in two sizes: 7½-x 8½-inch or 6⅜x 7-inch for the 6 model. One size fits all and the elastic cord lacing fits into boot lace hooks along the edge. It's available in burgundy and brown.
SRP: Starting at $12.65

Traditional Armguards T-AGS/T-AGL
SRP: Starting at $10.50

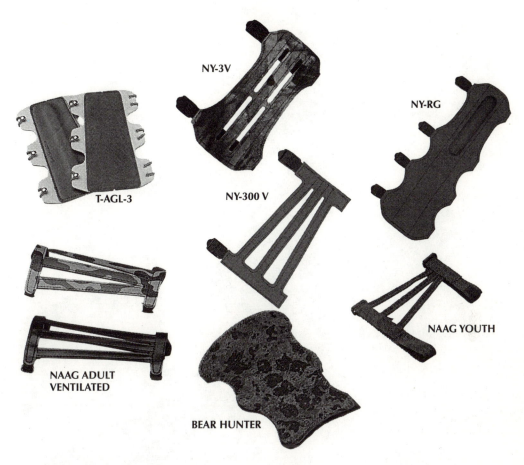

NY-3V

NY-RG

T-AGL-3

NY-300 V

NAAG YOUTH

NAAG ADULT
VENTILATED

BEAR HUNTER

Traditional Hunter Guard T-AGL-3
A leather armguard with 3-point hook up. It can be pre-laced to permit easy on/off with elastic cords.
SRP: $14.25

Ventilated Youth Guard NY-300V
This small arm guard is designed by Neet for you archers and has three staves, a Cordura outer layer and pull adjustable elastic straps. It's available in black, red, blue and camouflage.
SRP: $5.45

Ventilated Youth Guard NY-3V
SRP: $5.15

Youth Range Guard NY-RG
This full-length quiver gives protection to the full arm. The lower section has staves. It's held in place with adjustable pull elastic straps. Available in the same colors as the Ventilated Youth Guard.
SRP:. $7

NORTH AMERICAN ARCHERY GROUP
Adult Ventilated
This three-strap arm guard uses Velcro straps to securely hold it in place on you forearm. Available in camouflage and black.
SRP: camo. $7.49
     black. $6.49

Bear Hunter
This solid arm guard has a camo-printed leather surface and attached with three adjustable elastic bands.
SRP: $8.49

Youth
This three-strap guard is designed to fit young and small-framed archers. Color: black.
SRP: $5.99

BOW ACCESSORIES

N-CST

N-MT TAB

FG-2

FG-25C

NEET
Comfort Spacer Tab N-CST
A finger tab with a molded finger spacer, suede leather backing and leather front overlay. RH or LH available.
SRP: Starting at **$5.25**

Glove FG-2
A high quality tan suede glover with hook and loop fastners and an elstic back for a comfortable fit. This glove has three fingers with smooth leather or hair calf tips.
SRP: hair **$10.30**
    Leather **$6.75**

Glove FG-2SC
Advantage Timber or Mossy Oak Break Up camouflage.
SRP: hair **$10.00**
    Leather **$8.75**

Monster Tab N-MT
A tab designed for shooting three fingers under first, this tab has no finger cut out. Its' offered in LH and RH models and sizes S, M and L. Your choice of leather or hair calf finish.
SRP: **$5.15**

Whisper Quiet
While some hunters go to extremes to dampen any possible bow noise, they overlook noisy clothing. Cotton and fleece are quiet, but nylon and many waterproof outerwear garments can produce a subtle hiss when rubbed fabric-to-fabric. Hold your garment to your ear and rub them together to determine if you're missing a noise that game can possibly hear.—MDF

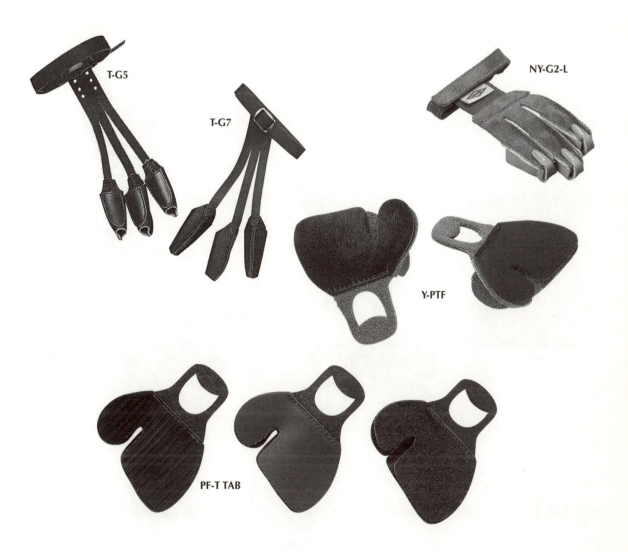

T-G5

T-G7

NY-G2-L

Y-PTF

PF-T TAB

Pinch Free Tab PF-T
A finger tab with a soft felt finger spacer and suede leather backing. Sizes offered include XS, S, M, L and XL. You choice of hair calf, super leather or Rib Tab facings. RH or LH models are available.
SRP: **$5.25**

Traditional Glove T-G5
A traditional glove with Cordovan leather tip overlays on the three fingers. This glove has a snap buckle wrist strap. Sizes S, M, L and XL and it's available in burgundy and honey brown.
SRP: **$12.55**

Traditional Glove T-G7
SRP: **$10.25**

Youth Glove NY-G2-L
This leather glove is made to fit small archer's hands and has a hook and loop fastener. It has smooth leather finger tips and is made of suede leather.
SRP: **$5.45**

Youth Tab Y-PTF
A small finger tab made by Neet with small young archers in mind. Left- and right-hand models are available.
SRP: . . . . **Starting at $4.85**

Bow Accessories Archer's Gloves and Tabs

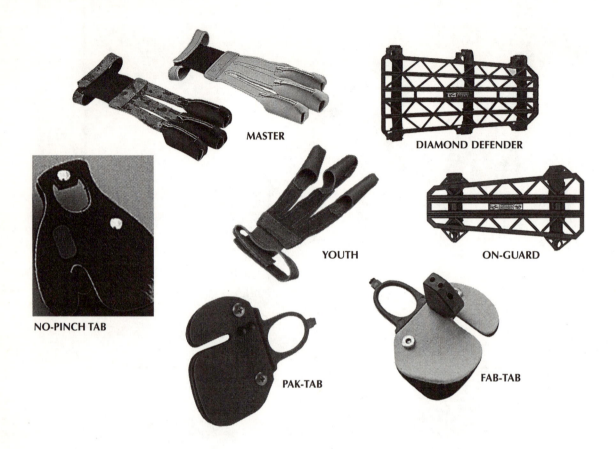

MASTER

DIAMOND DEFENDER

NO-PINCH TAB

YOUTH

ON-GUARD

PAK-TAB

FAB-TAB

NORTH AMERICAN ARCHERY GROUP

Master
A three-finger leather glove with elastic adjustment section and leather/Velcro wrist strap. The Master is available in sizes medium and large.
SRP: $9.49

No-Pinch Tab
This tab is available in medium and large, features durable leather layers and sturdy rivets.
SRP: $6.49

Youth
Smaller version of Master glove designed for smaller fingers and hands.
SRP: $8.99

SAUNDERS ARCHERY
Diamond Defender
This arm guard is 4x7.5-inches and is vented to be cool. Hooks latch easily and quietly. Adjustable elastic straps.
SRP: black $10.95
    camouflaged $12.95

On Guard
These arm guards are cool, comfortable and an eye-catcher at the range! They are available in black, camo and purple, yellow, blue, green and white.
SRP: black and assorted colors
   . . . . $8.95
   camoflaged $10.95

Pak Tab and Fab Tab
Finger tabs with felt string pads and leather backing. Offered in sizes small medium and large and the tabs can be changed to several options.
SRP: $10.95
   Fab Tab II $9.95

Pick A Spot
Most hunting misses with a bow are caused because the hunter shoots at an animal. Pick a spot on the animal and imagine a quarter placed against the animal at that spot. That's where you'll want to aim, and hit.--MDF

ARROWS

ARROWS

AIM Arrows

AIM is headquartered in Willimantic, Connecticut, and make bows and accessories.

AIM ARROWS
These fiberglass target arrows are distributed by AIM and are perfect for kids, camps and schools. Fletched with vanes and available in 26-, 28- and 30-inch lengths.
SRP: per _ gross box **$175**

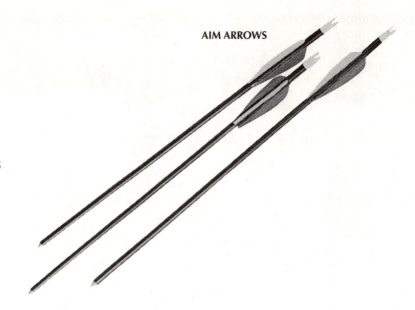

AIM ARROWS

Beman Arrows

FLASH

HUNTER

CAMO HUNTER PLUS

ICS ENERGY

ICS HAWK

BEMAN has years of experience in carbon arrow construction. The company is based in Salt Lake City, Utah.

CARBON FLASH
Similar to Carbon Hunter with outside diameters of $^{13}/_{64}$ and $^{14}/_{64}$.
SRP: **$40.32**

CARBON HUNTER
Made of pultruded carbon fibers and designed for hunters and target shooters. Outside diameter sizes are $^{15}/_{64}$ and $^{16}/_{64}$.

SRP: **$65.35**

CARBON METAL MATRIX
These carbon shafts are available in 460, 400, 340 and 300 sizes and have plus/minus .003-inch straightness. The shafts have an aluminum core and carbon fiber outer layers.
SRP: **$137.25**

ICS CAMO HUNTER PLUS
Similar to the ICS Trebark shafts but coated in Mossy Oak Break Up.
SRP: per dozen **$89.71**

ICS ENERGY
Super priced arrow for recreational use. Sizes include: 1000, 900, 780, 690, 600, 520, 460, 410 and 360.
SRP: **$70.25**

ICS HAWK
Affordable priced and excellent for 3-D shooting describes the Hawk. Super nocks are installed along with RPS point inserts.
SRP: **$66.85**

ARROWS

Beman Arrows

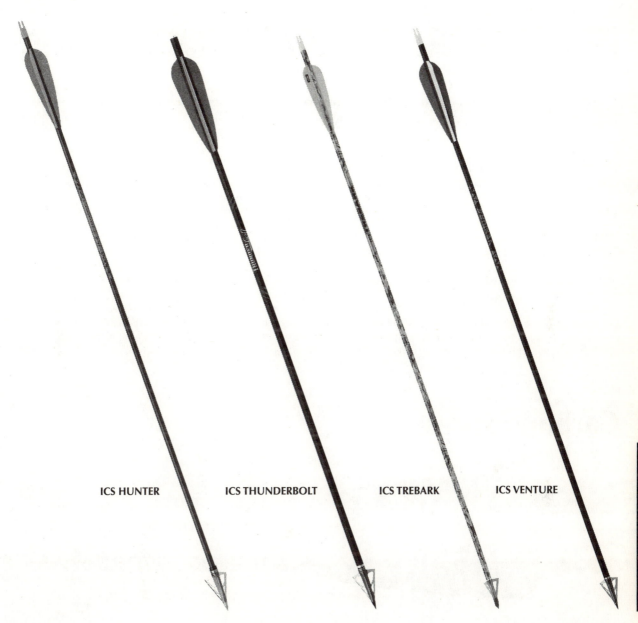

ICS HUNTER   ICS THUNDERBOLT   ICS TREBARK   ICS VENTURE

ICS HUNTER

These arrows feature a multi-layer design and plus/minus 1.5-inch straightness. The shafts have a partial graphic green camo pattern.
SRP: per dozen $73.92

ICS THUNDERBOLT

Designed for crossbow use with a ²²/₆₄ths outside diameter and offered in 20- and 22-inch lengths.
SRP: 20-inch length $48.10
22-inch length $48.50

ICS TREBARK

Beman's ICS Trebark shafts are an addition to their camouflaged hunting shaft selection. The camouflage coating on these shafts offer the ultimate in concealment with a PhotoFusion finish that's protected with Beman's Infinity Performance System (IPS). Shaft options include: 500-size shafts that weigh 7.9 grains per inch, 400-size at 9.1 gpi, 340-size at 10 gpi and 300-size at 10.1 gpi. The shafts are constructed with longitudinal unidirectional carbon fiber layers over high

strength composite fibers for better mass. The IPS coating also provides a more consistent spine and heavier weight for the shaft. Inserts and Super Nocks are included.
SRP: per dozen $76.18

ICS VENTURE

These Beman shafts represent value and multi-carbon layering. Sizes include 500, 400, 340 and 300.
SRP: $59.47

Browning Archery Arrows

BROWNING BULLETS

MICRO BROWNING BULLETS

BROWNING ARCHERY is headquartered in Tucson, Arizona, and makes bows, arrows and a full line of archery accessories.

BROWNING BULLETS

Carbon and fiberglass combination arrows are still in production and becoming available in a wider range. Browning's Bullet hunting arrows are now offered in 30/50—7.4 grains per inch—and 55/70—9.6 grains per inch models. These four-layer shafts utilize multi-directional, high-grade carbon fibers oriented at 90-degrees over a fiberglass unidirectional core. Each shaft is precision ground to a .005-inch straightness. The 30/50 shafts are fletched with three 2½-inch Duravanes and the 55/70s have three 4-inch Duravanes. For those who like to build their own arrows, 30/50 and 55/70 shafts are now available for $72.95 per 12-pack without fletching.

If you want to micro tune your arrows, Browning also offers weight tubes in 3 grains per inch and 2 grains per inch weights. These are available in a dozen per pack for approximately $15.
SRP: per six standard arrow . . $47.95

MICRO BROWNING BULLETS

Browning's Micro Bullets are designed for young archers, bows shooting lower poundages, and for shooters with shorter draw lengths. Large quantity arrow packs are offered for youth camps and situations where many arrows are needed.
SRP: per half-dozen $21.95
72 Micro Bullet arrow pack,
**   per arrow $2.69**

Carbon Express Arrows

CX CRESTED SHAFTS

CARBON EXPRESS is a Game Tracker subsidiary and makes a full line of arrows. The company is based in Flushing, Michigan. Carbon Express continues to capitalize on its BuffTuff fabric wrap technology with two shafts: the CXL Hunter 250 and 350 models. Every Carbon Express (800-241-4833) arrow will have this coating beginning in 20

CX CROSSBOLTS

These Carbon express arrows are designed for crossbows and offered in 20- and 22-inch lengths. Available with vanes or feathers.
SRP: with vanes, per dozen . . $37.50
with feathers, per dozen $44

CX DIPPED AND CRESTED SHAFTS

Each shaft is dipped in scratch resistant white and hand crested. Standard weight sizes are available and crest color options include red, green and orange.
SRP: $113.25

ARROWS

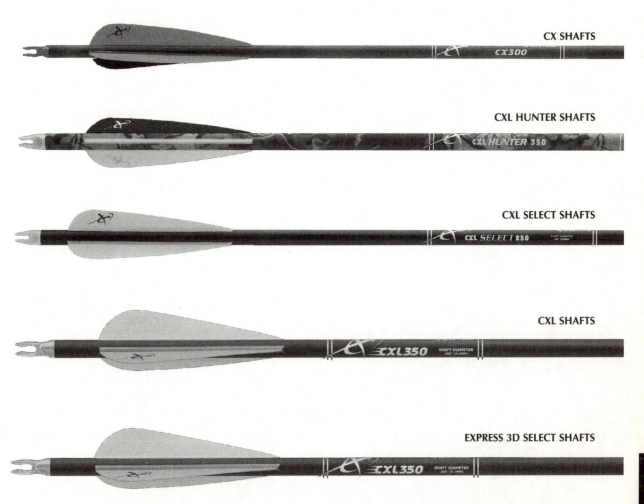

CX SHAFTS

CX300

CXL HUNTER SHAFTS

CXL HUNTER 350

CXL SELECT SHAFTS

CXL SELECT 250

CXL SHAFTS

CXL350

EXPRESS 3D SELECT SHAFTS

CXL350

CX HUNTERS

Similar to the CX shafts but camouflaged and coated with Carbon Express' durable BuffTuff. Weights include: 200, 300, and 400. All internal components are used in construction.

SRP: shafts, per dozen $188.50
 with vanes, per dozen . . . $141.54
72 bulk pack with vanes,
 per arrow $11.55

CX SHAFTS

These all-carbon shafts have internal components and are available in 100, 200, 300 and 400 weights and offer plus/minus .003-inch straightness. These are also available as fletched arrows wit feathers or vanes.

SRP: crested shafts, per doz. $133.25
 with vanes, per doz. $120.68
 with feathers, per doz. . . . $133.85
72 bulk pack, per arrow $9.90

CXL HUNTER SHAFTS

A large diameter shaft designed for speed, accuracy and maximum penetration. Coated with Buff Tuff and camouflaged. These are available as shafts only or fletched with vanes. *Weights:* 250 and 350. The 250 series features a $^{23}/_{64}$-inch diameter and weighs 11 grains per inch. The 350 series weighs 11.5 grains per inch. Both shafts are now available in Advantage. BuffTuff coating seals the arrow shaft's pores, increases its strength and makes the arrow quieter in flight. Weight tubes can also be easily installed in the CXL Hunters and are $10.50 per six for archers who want to fine-tune their arrows.

SRP: shafts. $126.60
 with vanes. $144.71

CXL SELECT SHAFTS

A group of hand selected shafts that meet the NAA equipment rules and have a maximum shaft diameter of 9.3mm.

SRP: per dozen $139.99

CXL SHAFTS

These Carbon Express shafts are available in 150, 250 and 350 weights and have plus/minus .006-inch straightness.

SRP: $104.94

EXPRESS 3D SELECT SHAFTS

The 3-D Select series—weights include 100, 200, 300 and 400— are handmatched per package for weight and straightness to ensure consistency. Each shaft is plus/minus 1 grain per package.

SRP: per dozen $116.50

ARROWS

Carbon Express Arrows

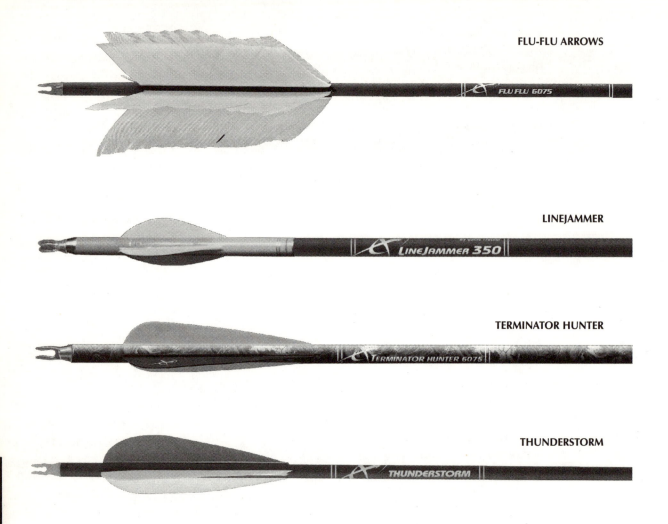

FLU-FLU ARROWS

LINEJAMMER

TERMINATOR HUNTER

THUNDERSTORM

FLU-FLU ARROWS
Great for hunting small game, these arrows feature six 4¼-inch full feathers for the ultimate arrows delivering great speed for short distances. A must have item for any serious archer. Available in 45-60 and 60-75 sizes.
SRP: 18 bulk pack, per arrow. . $9.37

LINEJAMMER
These Carbon Express arrows and shafts are created with archery competitors in mind. They are offered in 350 size and have a large exterior diameter. Available in Black BuffTuff only.
SRP: per dozen $139.99

TERMINATOR HUNTER SERIES
The Hunter series is similar to Terminator shafts and camouflaged with River Bottom camouflage.
**SRP: shafts, per dozen $80.28
with vanes installed,
per dozen $101.09
72 bulk pack, per arrow $8.26**

TERMINATOR SHAFTS
Economical priced shafts constructed of wrapped carbon composites. Available in a wide assortment of weights and shafts with plus/minus .006-inch straightness. The Hunter series is camouflaged with River Bottom camouflage.
**SRP: shafts, per dozen $61.76
with vanes, per dozen $79.76
72 bulk pack, per arrow $6.46**
Select shafts and arrows are also available at a slightly higher price.

THUNDERSTORM AND THUNDER EXPRESS
Youth arrows and products designed by Carbon Express for intermediate shooters. Thes feature carbon construction and a tunable press-fit nock. Spined for draw weights from 30 to 50 pounds.
**SRP: Thunderstorm
shafts, per dozen $55
with vanes, per dozen $70
six arrow pack $37**

**SRP: Thunder Express
shafts, per dozen $71
72 bulk pack – great for camps –
per arrow $2.15**

Carbon Tech Arrows

HIPPO

RHINO

WHITETAIL

CARBON TECH is based in Sacramento, California, and carries a full line of carbon arrows

HIPPO
Similar to Rhino with a large exterior diameter and five or six wraps of carbon for strength and durability. Sizes 23/525 and 23/400.
SRP: per dozen $126.99

RHINO
The Rhino series has plus/minus .0015 tolerances and weigh 9.5 gpi in the 35/60 size, 10 gpi in 45/70 and 11.5 gpi in 55/80 diameter shafts. Sizes 23/525 and 23/400.
SRP: per dozen $126.99

WHITETAIL
The Whitetail XP provides extreme performance with a plus/minus .0015 straightness tolerance and 7.9 grains per inch (gpi) for the 40/65 shafts and 9.5 gpi for the 65/80 diameter sizes. The Whitetail Hunter series has the same weights and diameters but .005 straightness. The Whitetail shafts have up to six wraps of carbon that incorporate a precision multi-directional carbon layer design
SRP: per dozen $94.99

ARROWS

Easton Arrows

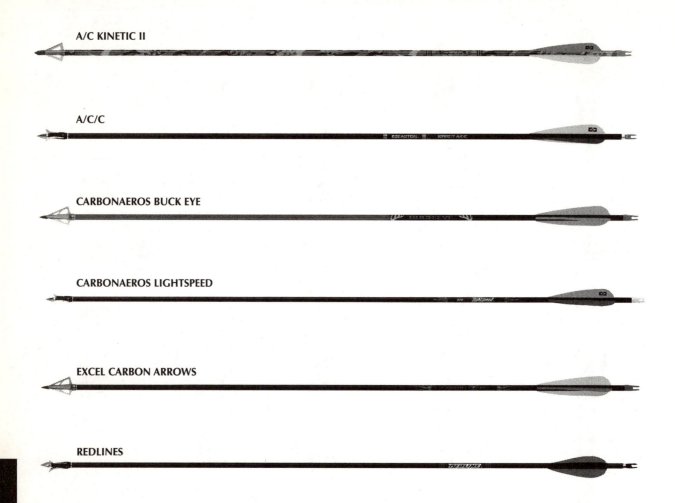

A/C KINETIC II

A/C/C

CARBONAEROS BUCK EYE

CARBONAEROS LIGHTSPEED

EXCEL CARBON ARROWS

REDLINES

EASTON If you've ever released an arrow, there's a good chance it was an Easton shaft. This company is the pioneer in aluminum arrows many moons ago. Easton still offers numerous aluminum shafts—more than a dozen styles—along with several carbon shafts. The company provides a series of dealer universities each year to keep dealers everywhere informed and up to date on arrow and bow technology. Easton is based in Salt Lake City, Utah.

A/C KINETIC II AND A/C/C- ALUMINUM CARBON

A rolling process ensures a proper carbon and aluminum bond with these shafts. Each has a plus/minus .003-inch straightness and the Kinetic has a heavier aluminum wall, plus Photofusion camouflage. Prices reflect per dozen with vanes.
SRP: A/C Kinetic $172.10

A/C/C **$163.44**

CARBONAEROS BUCK EYE

These shafts are Easton's newest offerings and they utilize the company's Infinity Performance System (IPS) coating which adds weight where it's needed—at the point-end of the shaft. This results in more kinetic energy and improved balance. The tree green colored IPS coating also protects the shaft against wear and makes it quieter to draw and release. The Buck Eye shafts include RPS inserts and factory installed Super Nocks and are offered in four popular sizes: 300, 340, 400 and 500.
SRP: per dozen $156.75

CARBONAEROS LIGHTSPEED

For bowhunters who shoot 3-D as a sideline or as warm-up practice in preparation for the hunting season,

Easton's CarbonAeros Lightspeed are new this year and have a polished matte finish and utilize multi-layered wrapped construction. Easton (801-539-1400) will provide a free brochure with all the details.
SRP: per dozen $70.25

EXCEL CARBON ARROWS

These all carbon arrows are offered in 340, 400 and 500 sizes. They feature multi-layered wrapped construction.
SRP: $64.52

REDLINES

This all carbon shaft uses Easton's C2 manufacturing process and meets strict weight and straightness standards. Redlines have a plus/minus 1.5-inch straightness and use the UNI nock system. These arrows are available in 9 sizes.
SRP: with vanes, per doz . . . $102.48

Easton Arrows

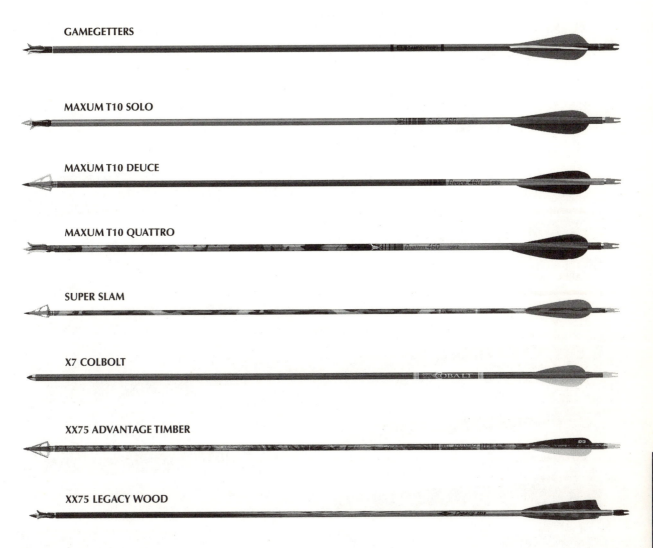

GAMEGETTERS

MAXUM T10 SOLO

MAXUM T10 DEUCE

MAXUM T10 QUATTRO

SUPER SLAM

X7 COLBOLT

XX75 ADVANTAGE TIMBER

XX75 LEGACY WOOD

ARROWS

ALUMINUM SERIES BY EASTON

GAMEGETTERS
Similar to the XX75s and available in eight sizes. A very popular economical arrow. RPS inserts are included. Gamegetter Camo Hunters and Gamegetter IIs are similar and comparable in price. These aluminum shafts must be cut to length and have inserts installed.
SRP: 3-color camo $57.79
   olive green $48.72

MAXUM T10-ALUMINUM
A new aluminum shaft that's offered in three styles: Solo bronze, deuce two tone crested look and Quattro with PermaGraphic camo. These arrows are economically priced and designed with bowhunters in mind. Inserts are included and Super UNI bushing and Super Nocks are installed.
SRP: Solo $59.80
   Quattro. $66.69

SUPER SLAM
An aluminum arrow constructed with 7178-T9 aluminum alloy with a plus/minus .0015-inch straightness tolerance. Super UNI bushings and nocks are installed. RPS inserts are included for installation after the shafts are cut to length. Available in 15 sizes! Super slam Select shafts are hand picked and cost slightly more.
SRP: $83.33

X7 COBALT
You'll recognize this target arrow by its flashy blue Cobalt color. Swage technology is used in the construction of this 7178-T9 aluminum arrow. Available in 11 sizes from 191114 to 2512. Great for 3-D shooting also.
SRP: $91.89

XX75
A very popular Easton aluminum shaft known for performance and value. These provide a plus/minus .002-inch straightness and have factory installed UNI Bushings and Super Nocks. Available in bronze and Advantage and Mossy Oak camouflage. A XX75 Legacy with wood grain pattern and feather fletching is offered for slightly less cost.
SRP: per dozen $81.32
slightly cheaper in solid color

Gold Tip Arrows

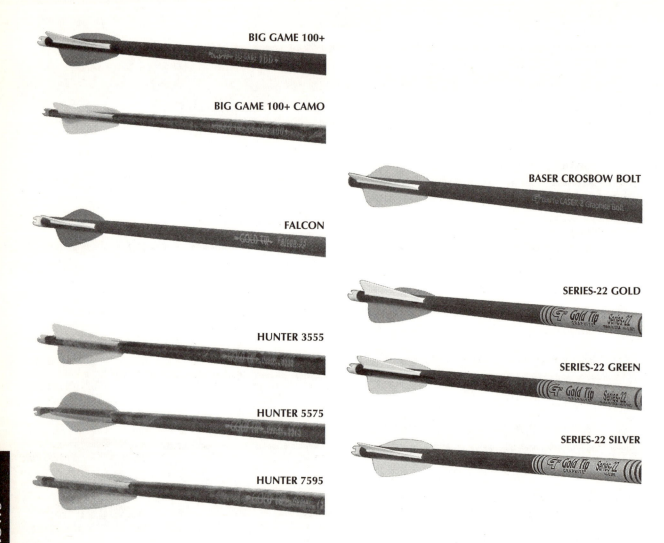

BIG GAME 100+

BIG GAME 100+ CAMO

FALCON

HUNTER 3555

HUNTER 5575

HUNTER 7595

BASER CROSSBOW BOLT

SERIES-22 GOLD

SERIES-22 GREEN

SERIES-22 SILVER

GOLD TIP arrows are distributed by Orem, Utah based Gold Tip.

BIG GAME 100+

Big Game 100+ shafts combine a +/-0.003-inch straightness tolerance with unmatched strength and an ultra-smooth finish. These shafts are spined for approximately 75 to 100 pounds of draw weight. Additional layers of graphite provide added weight and strength to meet the minimum arrow weights imposed by some states and countries. Shafts are available with vanes or feathers and with Realtree Hardwoods camouflage.
SRP: . . . . **$76.93 to $93.73**
Add $14 for camouflaged arrows and shafts

FALCON

Gold Tip's youth series provides the ultimate in durability and strength. These shafts were tested at Boy Scouts of America archery ranges.
SRP: shafts, per dozen **$36.33**
   shafts with vanes,
   per dozen **$37.33**

HUNTER

For hunters who avoid switching to graphite and carbon shafts because of the expense, Gold Tip introduces the economical Hunter shafts. Available in 3555, 5575 and 7595 as bare shafts or with feathers or vanes. Also available in Realtree Hardwoods camouflage finish.
SRP: Standard shafts, per dozen,
   . . . . **$51.35 to $68.33**
Add approximately $18 per dozen more for camouflaged models.

LASER CROSSBOW BOLTS

These bolts are designed to provide unsurpassed durability and kinetic energy for maximum penetration. These bolts are available in 20- and 22-inch lengths and with or without vanes.
SRP: per dozen . . . **$51.73 to $62.93**

SERIES-22

These competition shafts offer one of the largest diameters allowed in IBO competition. Shafts are available in one spine size (.325) and three grades: +/-0.006-inch Silver Label, +/-0.003-inch Green Label and +/-0.001-inch Gold Label.
SRP: . . . . **$69.93 to $121.73**
Silver series is least expensive and Gold series is most expensive.

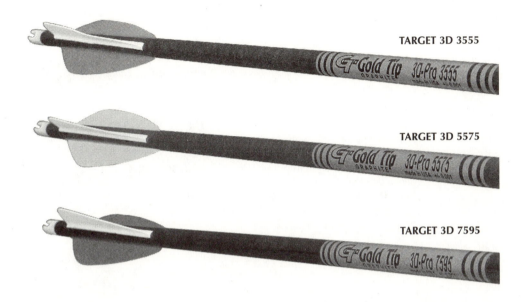

TARGET 3D 3555

TARGET 3D 5575

TARGET 3D 7595

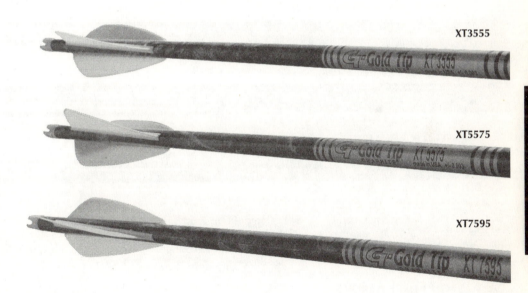

XT3555

XT5575

XT7595

TARGET 3-D

These shafts are Gold Tip's premier competition shafts. Each shaft is straight to within +/-0.001 inch nad has a wide .390-inch diameter. Available in Gold or Green grades with Gold shafts in sizes 3555, 5575 and 7595.
SRP: per dozen . . $95.13 to $111.93
Add up to $14/dozen for X-Cutter series.

XT SERIES

This series is Gold Tip's best all-around hunting arrows. The shafts are precision crafted with five layers of strategically placed graphite to create a durable and consistent arrow shaft. These shafts have a straightness tolerance of +/-0.003 inch. Lock Nocks and inserts are standard. The Camo XT series is coated with Realtree Hardwoods and is available with 3555, 5575 and 7595 shafts and as unfletched shafts or with vanes or feathers.
SRP: per dozen . . $83.93 to $100.73

The standard XT series is available minus the camouflage finish. Same specifications as camo series and as raw shafts or with vanes or feathers. Feathers are more expensive than vanes.
SRP: per dozen . . . $65.73 to $82.53

North American Archery Group Arrows

BRAVE

BRAVE WARRIOR

NORTH AMERICAN ARCHERY GROUP arrows are distributed by the North American Archery Group of Gainesville, Florida.

BRAVE 24-INCH
Designed to be used with the Brave youth bow. Fiberglass shaft, plastic vanes and chromed field points. Three per pack.
Item 3800-003 . . . . SRP varies

BRAVE WARRIOR 28-INCH
Same as Brave arrows but 28 inches long.
Item 3600-003 . . . . SRP varies

PSE Arrows

CARBON FORCE COMPETITION PRO

PSE CARBON FORCE Competition Pro 400

CARBON FORCE DOMINATOR

PSE CARBON FORCE Dominator 200

CARBON FORCE EXTREME

PSE CARBON FORCE Extreme 300

PSE (Precision Shooting Equipment) is based in Tucson, Arizona and makes one to the archery industry's widest selection of bows.

PSE CARBON FORCE ARROWS
PSE Carbon Force arrows are available in three models: Competition Pro, Extreme and Dominator. The high-performance Competition Pro shafts have a guaranteed .001 straightness—one of the best in the industry—and will be offered as shafts only. The Dominator series will offer a .006-inch guaranteed straightness. This series is now coated in PSE's Fall Brush camouflage and the exterior coating is so durable that it's nearly impossible to scratch with a knife blade.

SRP: Competition Pro, shafts only $99
Dominators with fletching, per dozen $79.99

RADIAL CROSS WEAVE
Target shooters and 3-D enthusiasts will welcome PSE's new Radial Cross Weave ultra-high performance shafts. This woven—not rolled and ground—shaft technology could be the future standard in carbon shaft construction. The technology comes from the aerospace and fishing rod industries. Since there is also less waste during construction and no grinding will be performed on the finished product, this will translate into a great value and premium product for shooters because there's less manual labor involved and much improved straightness and strength per shaft produced. This shaft could debut as a hunting shaft as early as 2004. You'll notice its unusual construction process by a unique jagged, on-the-shaft pattern when viewed under bright lights. When the shaft is damaged—such as when you shoot a Robin Hood, which could occur more often—the shaft unwinds instead of breaking off and splintering. This could result in superior penetration through mass retention and less break offs in hunting applications.
SRP: *Unavailable until the shafts are in mass production.*

ARROWS

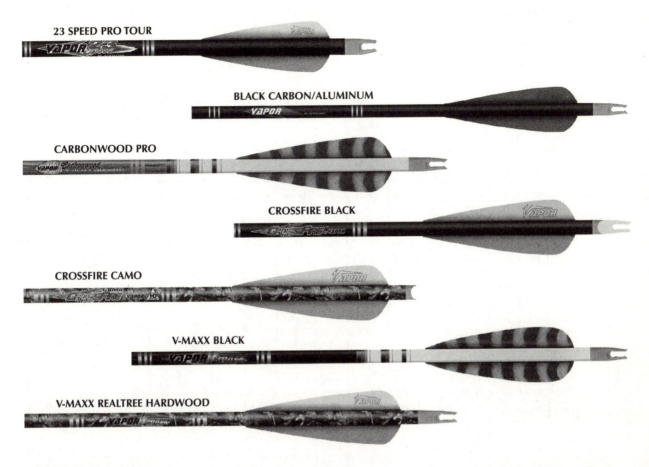

23 SPEED PRO TOUR

BLACK CARBON/ALUMINUM

CARBONWOOD PRO

CROSSFIRE BLACK

CROSSFIRE CAMO

V-MAXX BLACK

V-MAXX REALTREE HARDWOOD

BLACKHAWK VAPOR ACA all carbon arrows utilize carbon or carbon over aluminum construction. All Blackhawk Vapor arrows are now coated with Radiant Armor Carbon Coating and are unaffected by chemicals or extended use. The company is based in Austintown, Ohio.

23 SPEED PRO TOUR ARROWS
These top quality sahfts are selected for tournament archers who demand precision arrows with exact tolerances and weights.
**SRP: shafts only, per dozen . $119.95
with vanes, per dozen $124.95
with shafts per half-dozen . . . $62.95**

BLACK CARBON/ ALUMINUM SHAFTS
These Blackhawk arrows have carbon layers wrapped over an aluminum core.
**SRP: shafts, per dozen $99.95
with vanes, per dozen $104.95
six pack with vanes $64.95**

CAMO PRO SERIES
Blackhawk's more economical carbon arrows with less exact tolerances. These arrows shoot and fly with precision. Offered in Timber HD, Hardwoods Green and X-Tra gray.
**SRP: shafts, per dozen $79.95
with vanes, per dozen $84.95
with vanes, half-dozen $59.95**

CARBONWOOD PRO SERIES
V-Maxx Carbonwood series shafts with a wood-grain finish and flashy crest are offered for those who want arrows with a traditional look.
**SRP: Carbonwoods six-pack
    with vanes. $59.95
Carbonwood Pro shafts or arrows,
    per dozen $84.95**

CROSSFIRE CROSSBOW ARROWS
These shafts are designed for high performance crossbows and utilize 120-gram unidirectional carbon material along with the EXP 120 manufacturing process for parallel seams. The shafts are offered in one spine—the 30.06

series—and are rated for use with 95- to 200-pound crossbows. Crossfire shafts yield a plus/minus .004 straightness and a larger outside diameter of $^{22}/_{64}$ or .344-inch.
**SRP: standard black, per doz.. $64.95
Hardwoods HD green camo,
    per dozen $69.95**

V-MAXX 22/64 SERIES
Blackhawk's V-Maxx arrows are specially designed for the hunter who uses fixed-blade broadheads. The V-Maxx series of shafts offers a larger $^{22}/_{64}$ outside diameter that makes them easier to remove from most foam targets. The shafts have 10 grains-per-inch weight and permit maximum helical fletching and rest clearance while providing forgiving tuning capabilities.
**SRP: Realtree's Hardwood HD green
    or Standard black shafts,
    per dozen . . . $99.95 and $104.95
six-pack $58.95**

SHAFT & COMPONENT SPECIFICATIONS

ARROWS

Shaft Size	Shaft Weight — XX75[8] (Grains per Inch)	XX78[7]	X7[15]	Shaft Weight @ 29" (Grains)	Spine @ 28" Span (Deflection in inches)	Stock Shaft Length[5] — 75[6]/78[7] (Inches)	X7[15] (Inches)	Conventional Nock Size[2] (Inches)	UNI System[1] Bushing (Grains)	"G" Nock[2] (Grains)	Super UNI System[1] Bushing (Grains[5])	Super Nock (Grains[5])	3D Super Nock (Grains[5])	NIBB Point (Grains[5])	One-piece Bullet Point	RPS[4] Insert Alum. (Grains)	RPS[4] Insert Carbon (Grains)	Broad-head Adapter Ring[6] (Grains)
1214	5.93	—	—	172	2.501	26	—	—	—[13]	—	—	—	—	—	45	—	—	—
1413	5.94	—	—	172	2.036	26	—	7/32	—	—	—	—	—	—	35	—	—	—
1416	7.15	—	—	207	1.684	27	—	7/32	—	—	—	—	—	46	52	—	—	—
1512	—	—	5.84	169	1.553	—	27	—	5	7	—	—	—	49[3]	—	—	—	—
1514	—	—	6.83	198	1.379	—	26	—	5	7	—	—	—	61[3]	—	—	—	—
1516	7.34	—	—	213	1.403	27 1/2	—	1/4	6	7	—	—	—	48	54	—	—	3[14]
1612	—	—	6.27	182	1.298	—	28	—	6	7	—	—	—	55[3]	—	—	—	3[14]
1614	—	—	7.73	224	1.153	—	28	—	5	7	—	—	—	51	—	—	—	3[14]
1616	8.36	—	—	242	1.079	28 1/2	—	1/4	7	7	—	—	—	56	63	—	—	3[14]
1712	—	—	6.70	194	1.099	—	28 1/2	—	7	7	—	—	—	62[3]	—	—	—	3[14]
1713	7.42	—	—	215	1.044	29	—	1/4	7	7	—	—	—	54	—	—	—	—
1714	—	—	8.07	234	0.963	—	29	1/4	7	7	—	—	—	56	—	—	—	—
1716	9.03	—	—	262	0.880	29	—	1/4[9]	9	7	—	—	—	60	68	10	—	—
1812	—	—	7.30	212	0.879	—	29 1/2	1/4[9]	9	7	—	—	—	67[3]	—	—	—	—
1813	7.86	—	—	228	0.874	30	—	—	—	—	—	—	—	56	—	14	8	—
1814	—	—	8.57	249	0.799	—	29 1/2	1/4[9]	8	7	—	—	—	60	—	—	—	—
1816	9.27	—	—	269	0.756	30	—	1/4[9]	9	7	—	—	—	63	—	12	7	—
1912	—	—	7.60	220	0.778	—	30	—	9	7	—	—	—	70[3]	74	—	—	—
1913	8.34	—	—	242	0.733	31	—	9/32[9]	9	7	—	—	—	64	—	17	10	—
1914	—	—	9.28	269	0.658	—	30 1/2	9/32[9]	9	7	—	—	—	64	—	—	—	—
1916	10.05	—	—	291	0.623	31	—	—	9	7	—	—	—	72	82	16	9	—
2012	—	—	8.00	232	0.680	—	31 1/2	—	(10)[10]	7	5	13	12	83[3]	—	22	12	—
2013	9.01	—	—	261	0.610	32 1/2	—	9/32[9]	(10)[10]	7	5	13	12	68	—	21	12	—
2014	—	—	9.56	277	0.579	—	31 1/2	—	(10)[10]	7	5	13	12	71	—	—	—	—
2016	10.56	—	—	306	0.531	32	—	9/32[9]	—	—	4	13	12	80	90	20	11	—
2018	12.28	—	—	356	0.464	32 1/2	—	5/16[9]	—	—	4	13	12	89	—	19	10	—
2020	13.49	—	—	391	0.426	33	—	5/16	—	—	—	13	12	64	—	18	10	—
2112	—	—	8.42	244	0.590	—	31 1/2	—	(10)[10]	7	7	13	12	88[3]	100	25	14	—
2113	9.30	—	—	270	0.540	32 1/2	—	5/16	—	—	7	13	12	78[11]	100	25	14	—
2114	9.86	9.94	9.94	286	0.510	32 1/2	32 1/2	5/16[9]	(11)[10]	7	7	13	12	78	100	25	14	—
2115	10.75	—	—	312	0.461	33	—	5/16[9]	(11)[10]	7	7	13	12	83	100	25	14	—
2117	12.02	12.13	—	349	0.407	33	—	5/16[9]	—	7	7	13	12	97	100	25	14	—
2212	—	8.84	8.84	256	0.505	32 1/2	32 1/2	—	13[10]	7	9	13	12	102[3]	100	31	16	—
2213	9.83	9.92	9.92	285	0.460	33 1/2	33 1/2	5/16[9]	13[10]	7	9	13	12	88	100	30	16	—
2214	—	—	10.41	302	0.425	—	33	—	13[10]	7	9	13	12	103[3]	100	—	—	—
2215	10.67	10.77	—	309	0.420	33	—	5/16[9]	—	7	9	13	12	95	100	30	16	—
2216	12.02	12.13	—	349	0.376	33	—	5/16[9]	—	—	9	13	12	98	100	29	15	—
2219	13.77	13.89	—	399	0.337	34	—	11/32	—	—	8	13	12	107	—	26	14	—
2312	—	9.48	9.48	275	0.423	33	33	—	(15)[10]	7	11	13	12	99[3]	100	37	19	—
2314	10.67	10.76	10.76	309	0.390	33 1/2	33 1/2	11/32	(14)[10]	7	10	13	12	—	100	34	18	—
2315	11.67	11.77	—	338	0.342	34	—	11/32	—	—	11	13	12	—	100	37	19	—
2317	13.26	13.38	—	385	0.297	34	—	11/32	—	—	11	13	12	—	100	37	19	—
2412	—	9.65	9.65	280	0.400	34	34	11/32	(17)[10]	7	12	13	12	110	100	40	20	—
2413	10.40	10.50	10.50	302	0.365	34	34	11/32	(17)[10]	7	12	13	12	110	100	40	20	—
2419	14.55	—	—	422	0.268	34 1/2	—	11/32	—	—	12	13	12	—	100	37	19	—
2512	—	10.28	10.28	298	0.321	34 1/2	34 1/2	—	(20)[10]	7	15	13	12	108[3]	100	52	25	—
2514	11.33	11.43	—	329	0.305	34 1/2	34 1/2	11/32	(18)[10]	7	14	13	12	—	100	48	23	—
2613	—	11.49	11.49	333	0.265	—	34 1/2	—	(22)[10]	7	17	13	12	150	100	58	27	—

— Indicates not available
1 UNI—Universal Nock Installation System
2 Nock size for standard swaged nock taper.
3 This NIBB point will provide approximately an 8% F.O.C. All other NIBB points are approximately 7% F.O.C. F.O.C. is Front-of-Center balance position on the arrow shaft.
4 RPS = Replaceable Point System with 8-32 AMO-Standard thread
5 Length is approximate stock shaft length for each size.
6 XX75 Mossy Oak Break-Up, Advantage Timber, Yukon, Camo Hunter, GameGetter, GameGetter II, Jazz, Platinum, Legacy.
7 XX78 Super Slam Select, Super Slam.
8 Jazz, Legacy, GameGetter and GameGetter II, are produced without reduced diameter taper and can also use the next largest conventional nock size.
9 Super UNI Bushing is factory-installed on these shafts. Parenthesis indicates smaller (A/C/E Nock) UNI Bushing size is available as an accessory. Except Super Slam Select.
10 2113 shafts use 2114 X7/XX75 NIBB points and 2114-2117 components.
11 NIBB point grain weights are ±0.5 grain. All other components are ±1 grain.
12 3D Super Nock also available; 12 grains.
13 Weight calculated for 29" length.
14 Shaft sizes 1716, 1813 and 1816 use A/C/E 3-60; sizes 1913 and 1916 use A/C/C 3-71 broadhead adapter rings.
15 X7 Eclipse and Cobalt.
16 1214 accepts "G" Nock directly: 7 grains.
Note: sizes 1416, 1516, 1616 and 1713 are not suitable for bowhunting.

EASTON SHAFT SELECTION

1. Determining Correct Hunting Arrow Length

Bows with cut-out window

The Correct Hunting Arrow Length for bows with a broadhead cut-out sight window (including bows with overdraws) is determined by drawing back an extra-long arrow and having someone mark the arrow one inch in front of where the arrow contacts the most forward portion of the arrow rest.

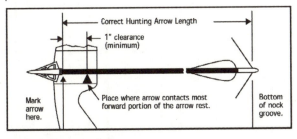

Bows without cut-out window

The Correct Hunting Arrow Length for bows without a cut-out sight window (which will not allow a fixed blade broadhead to be drawn past the front of the bow handle), mark an extra-long arrow one inch in front of the riser as shown below.

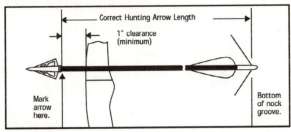

Bow Draw Length

Draw length is measured at full draw from the front of the bow to the bottom of the nock groove. Actual arrow length and draw length are only the same if the end of the arrow shaft is even with the front of the bow at full draw.

USING THE EASTON HUNTING SHAFT SIZE SELECTION CHARTS

1. Once you have determined your Correct Hunting Arrow Length and Calculated Peak Bow Weight, you are ready to select your correct shaft size:
   - 1.1 Compound bows. In the "Bow Weight" column (left-hand side of the CHART) select the column with the type cam on your bow. Then locate your Calculated Peak Bow Weight in that column.
   - 1.2 Recurve bows. In the "Bow Weight" column (right-hand side of the CHART) locate your Actual Peak Bow Weight at your draw length.
   - 1.3 Long bows. See Legacy chart below.

TUNING THE ARROW SHAFT

Our Hunting Shaft Size Selection Chart indicates that more than one shaft size may shoot well from your bow. You may decide to shoot a lighter shaft for speed, or a heavier shaft for greater durability and penetration. Also, large variations in shooting style, bow efficiency, type of wheels or cams, and type of release may require special bow tuning or a shaft size change. Easton's "Arrow Tuning and Maintenance Guide" provides additional information on tuning.

Easton's "Arrow Tuning and Maintenance Guide" available online at www.eastonarchery.com or call Easton at 801-539-1400.

2. Determining Actual Peak Bow Weight for Compound Bows

Compound bows must be measured at the peak bow weight as the bow is being drawn and not while letting the bow down.

The suggested shaft sizes in the charts on pages 26-27 were determined using a "Standard" Setup which includes:
- Use of a release aid.
- 75-100 grain arrow point weight.
- Compound bow with brace height greater than $6\frac{1}{2}$".

If your setup differs from the "Standard" Setup, use the Variables (following) to make adjustments to determine the Calculated Peak Bow Weight so the correct arrow size can be selected on the Chart on pages 26-27.

Variables to the "Standard" Setup for Compound Bows:
- Finger release - Add 5 lbs.
- Point weight over 100 grains – Add 3 lbs.
- Bows with brace heights less than $6\frac{1}{2}$" – Add 5 lbs.

Overdraw Compound Bows

If you are using an overdraw, make the calculations (if any) in the Variables section, and then modify the Calculated Peak Bow Weight of your bow using the chart below.

Bow Weight	Overdraw Amount				
	1"	2"	3"	4"	5"
For 60#-70# Actual/Calculated Peak Bow Weight, add to bow weight—	1#	3#	6#	9#	12#

3. Determining Actual Peak Bow Weight for Recurve Bows

Your local archery pro shop is the best place to determine the actual draw weight of your bow. Actual Peak Bow Weight for recurve bows should be measured at your draw length.

2. Move across that row horizontally to the column indicating your Correct Arrow Length. Note the letter in the box where your Calculated Peak Bow Weight row and Correct Hunting Arrow Length column intersect. The "Shaft Size" box below the CHART with the same letter contains your recommended shaft sizes. Select a shaft from the Chart depending on the shaft material and type of shooting you are doing.

EASTON HUNTING SHAFT SIZE SELECTION CHART

COMPOUND BOW Calculated Peak Bow Weight - Lbs.		Correct Hunting Arrow Length											RECURVE BOW Bow Weight - Lbs. Finger Release 75-100 grain points
Medium Cam	**Single or Hard Cam**	22.5 **23"** 23.5	23.5 **24"** 24.5	24.5 **25"** 25.5	25.5 **26"** 26.5	26.5 **27"** 27.5	27.5 **28"** 28.5	28.5 **29"** 29.5	29.5 **30"** 30.5	30.5 **31"** 31.5	31.5 **32"** 32.5	32.5 **33"** 33.5	
37 to 41	32 to 36		A	B	B	C	C	D	E	F			32 to 36
42 to 46	37 to 41	A	B	B	C	C	D	E	F	G	H		37 to 41
47 to 51	42 to 46	B	B	C	C	D	E	F	G	H	I	J	42 to 46
52 to 56	47 to 51	B	C	C	D	E	F	G	H	I	J	J	47 to 51
57 to 61	52 to 56	C	C	D	E	F	G	H	I	J	J	K	52 to 56
62 to 66	57 to 61	C	D	E	F	G	H	I	J	J	K	L	57 to 61
67 to 72	62 to 66	D	E	F	G	H	I	J	J	K	L	L	62 to 66
73 to 78	67 to 72	E	F	G	H	I	J	J	K	L	L	L	67 to 72
79 to 84	73 to 78	F	G	H	I	J	J	K	L	L	L		73 to 78
85 to 90	79 to 84	G	H	I	J	J	K	L	L	L			79 to 84
91 to 96	85 to 90	H	I	J	J	K	L	L	L				85 to 90

Group A

Shaft Size/Spine	Shaft Model	Shaft Wt. Grs/Inch	Wt@29"
1813/875	75	7.86	228
1716/880	75	9.03	262
780	Rdln	6.30	183

Group B

Shaft Size/Spine	Shaft Model	Shaft Wt. Grs/Inch	Wt@29"
1913/730	75	8.34	242
1816/755	75	9.27	269
690	Rdln	6.27	182

Group C

Shaft Size/Spine	Shaft Model	Shaft Wt. Grs/Inch	Wt@29"
2013/610	75	9.01	261
1916/625	75	10.05	291
3L-18/620	A/C/C	7.47	217
600	Rdln	6.92	201

Group D

Shaft Size/Spine	Shaft Model	Shaft Wt. Grs/Inch	Wt@29"
2113/540	75	9.30	270
2016/530	75	10.56	306
3-18/560	A/C/C	7.82	227
500	CAeros, KII	CAWT	CAWT
520	Rdln	7.09	206

Group E

Shaft Size/Spine	Shaft Model	Shaft Wt. Grs/Inch	Wt@29"
2212/510	SS	8.84	256
2114/510	SS, 75, Max	9.86	286
2115/460	75	10.75	312
2018/465	75	12.28	356
3-28/500	A/C/C	8.11	235
500, 460	CAeros, KII	CAWT	CAWT
520	Rdln	7.09	206

Group F

Shaft Size/Spine	Shaft Model	Shaft Wt. Grs/Inch	Wt@29"
2212/510	SS	8.84	256
2213/460	SS, 75, Max	9.83	285
2115/460	75	10.75	312
2018/465	75	12.28	356
3-28/500	A/C/C	8.11	235
500, 460	CAeros, KII	CAWT	CAWT
520	Rdln	7.09	206

Group G

Shaft Size/Spine	Shaft Model	Shaft Wt. Grs/Inch	Wt@29"
2312/425	SS	9.48	275
2215/420	SS, 75, Max	10.67	309
2117/400	SS, 75, Max	12.02	349
2020/425	75	13.49	391
3-39/440	A/C/C	8.58	249
400	CAeros	CAWT	CAWT
460	Rdln	7.32	212

Group H

Shaft Size/Spine	Shaft Model	Shaft Wt. Grs/Inch	Wt@29"
2215/420	SS, 75, Max	10.67	309
2314/390	SS, 75, Max	10.67	309
2117/400	SS, 75, Max	12.02	349
2216/375	SS, 75, Max	12.02	349
3-49/390	A/C/C	8.83	256
400	CAeros, KII	CAWT	CAWT
410	Rdln	7.60	220

Group I

Shaft Size/Spine	Shaft Model	Shaft Wt. Grs/Inch	Wt@29"
2413/365	SS, 75, Max	10.40	302
2314/390	SS, 75, Max	10.67	309
2315/340	SS, 75, Max	11.67	338
2216/375	SS, 75, Max	12.02	349
3-49/390	A/C/C	8.83	256
400	CAeros, KII	CAWT	CAWT
410	Rdln	7.60	220

Group J

Shaft Size/Spine	Shaft Model	Shaft Wt. Grs/Inch	Wt@29"
2512/320	SS	10.28	298
2413/365	SS, 75, Max	10.40	302
2315/340	SS, 75, Max	11.67	338
2219/335	SS, 75	13.77	399
3-60/340	A/C/C	9.45	274
340	CAeros, KII	CAWT	CAWT
360	Rdln	8.31	241

Group K

Shaft Size/Spine	Shaft Model	Shaft Wt. Grs/Inch	Wt@29"
2512/320	SS	10.28	298
2514/305	SS, 75	11.33	329
2317/295	SS, 75	13.26	385
3-71/300	A/C/C	9.92	288
300	CAeros, KII	CAWT	CAWT

Group L

Shaft Size/Spine	Shaft Model	Shaft Wt. Grs/Inch	Wt@29"
2514/305	SS, 75	11.33	329
2613/265	SS	11.49	333
2317/295	SS, 75	13.26	385
2419/265	75	14.55	422
3-71/300	A/C/C	9.92	288
300	CAeros, KII	CAWT	CAWT

CarbonAeros & Kinetic II (CAWT)

Shaft Size	Evolution Weight Grs/In	Evolution Weight Wt@29"	Buck Eye Weight Grs/In	Buck Eye Weight Wt@29"	Epic Weight Grs/In	Epic Weight Wt@29"	Excel Weight Grs/In	Excel Weight Wt@29"	Kinetic II Weight Grs/In	Kinetic II Weight Wt@29"
500	8.02	233	7.86	228	7.28	211	7.10	206		
460									9.40	273
400	9.12	264	9.00	261	8.41	244	8.12	235	10.20	296
340	10.01	290	9.90	287	9.31	270	8.80	255	11.00	319
300	10.14	294	10.03	291	9.45	274			11.60	336

Shaft Size/Spine – indicates suggested shaft size and spine. Shaft size and spine for carbon shafts are identical.

CAWT – Refer to CarbonAeros & Kinetic II box (left) for specific model and weight.

Color Designation for Aluminum Shafts – Within each box the aluminum arrow shafts are color-coded. Red shafts are the lightest and fastest. Green shafts are medium weight offering good speed and durability. Blue represents heavier weights for excellent durability and penetration. Black represents aluminum/carbon and carbon.

SS	XX78 Super Slam Select and Super Slam Shafts (7178-T9 alloy)
75	XX75: Yukon, Platinum, Legacy, Camo Hunter, GameGetter, GameGetter II (7075-T9 alloy)
Max	Maxum T10: Solo, Deuce, and Quattro
A/C/C	Aluminum/Carbon/Composite shafts
Rdln	Redline Carbon Composite Shafts
CAeros	Buck Eye, Evolution, Epic, Excel
KII	Kinetic II

ARROWS

Shaft Model	UltraLite A/C/C UltraLite A/C/E	UltraLite Aluminum SuperLite A/C/C	SuperLite Aluminum	Lite Aluminum	Standard Aluminum
SHAFT WEIGHT CATEGORY (spanning)					
Models Used for Competition and Recreational Archery					
X10®	1000 750 600 450 900 700 550 410 830 650 500 *380				
A/C/E®	*1400 920 670 470 *1250 850 620 430 *1100 780 570 400 1000 720 520 370				
A/C Navigator	1000 810 610 480 880 710 540 430				
Vector	1050 770 580 920 700 530 840 640 480				
Carbon Redline®	100 690 460 900 600 410 780 520 360				
X7 Eclipse		1512 1812 2112 2412 1612 1912 2212 2512 1712 2012 2312	1514 1914 2214 1614 2014 2314 1714 2114 2413 1814 2213 2613		
X7® Cobalt™		2112 2412 2212 2312 2512	1914 2114 2314 2014 2213 2413		
XX75 Platinum™ Plus			1713 2013 2413 1813 2114 1913 2213	1416 1716 2016 1516 1816 2115 1616 1916 2315	
Jazz			1214 1813 2013 1413 1913	1416 1616 1816 1516 1716 1916	
Models Used for Competition, Recreational Archery and Bowhunting					
Carbon Epic™		500 400 340 300			
Carbon Excel™		500 400 340			
LightSpeed™		500 400 340			
HyperSpeed	2L-18 2-28 2-49 2-71 2-18 2-39 2-60				
A/C/C®		2-00 2L-04 3-04 3-39 3L-00 2-04 3L-18 3-49 3-00 3X-04 3-18 3-60 3L-04 3-28 3-71			
XX75 Legacy™				(1916) 45-50 (2216) 65-70 (2016) 50-55 (2315) 70-75	(2018) 55-60 (2219) 70-75 (2020) 60-65 (2117) 60-65
Models Used for Bowhunting					
Carbon Evolution™		500 400 340 300			
A/C Kinetic™ II		460 400 340 300			
Buck Eye™		500 400 340 300			
Maxum	510 (2114) 400 (2117)	460 (2213)	420 (2215) 375 (2216)	390 (2314) 340 (2315)	365 (2413)
XX78 Super Slam®		2212 2312 2512	2114 2314 2514 2213 2413 2613	2215 2315 2216	2117 2317 2219
XX78® Super Slam® Select		2212 2312 2512	2114 2213 2314 2413	2216 2315	2117
XX75 Mossy Oak® Break-Up™			2013 2213 2413 2114 2314 2514	2216 2315	2117
XX75® Advantage® Timber™			2013 2213 2413 2114 2314 2514	2216 2315	2117
XX75® Yukon™			2114 2213 2314 2413	2016 2216 2315	2117
XX75 Camo Hunter®			1913 2112 2213 2413 2013 2114 2314 2514	1816 2016 2215 2315 1916 2115 2216	2018 2117 2317 2219 2419
XX75 GameGetter® II				1716 1916 2115 2216 1816 2016 2215 2315	2018 2117 2219
XX75 GameGetter®				2016 2216	2018 2117 2219

* Special Order

ARROWS

Ace Broadheads and Arrow Points

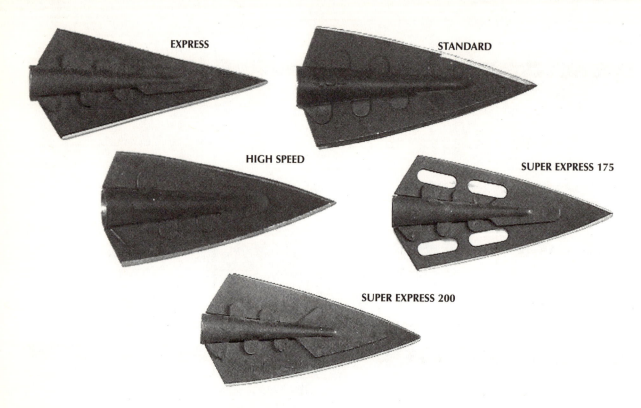

EXPRESS

STANDARD

HIGH SPEED

SUPER EXPRESS 175

SUPER EXPRESS 200

GET TO THE POINT

In archery, everything with the release can go right and the arrow can fly true, but the action of your broadhead or target point—or inaction— can be critical. A broadhead that fails to cut deep and wide enough can cause a disaster. A field point that pulls an arrow can result in the shaft being on the wrong side of the line on a bulls-eye. Whether hunting or target shooting, choose your point wisely and you'll get great results. — MDF

ACE ARCHERY TACKLE is based in Forrest, Illinois, and can be reached at 877-549-3444. The company's traditional broadheads are rugged and backed by years of use and tradition— the first one was built in the 1930s! Ace founder John Schwenk started making broadheads in 1927. The company has made more than 70 different broadhead models and has sold more than million broadheads during the past years.

ACE EXPRESS

Similar to the Super Express in design and construction but slightly smaller to create a 165-grain weight broadhead.
SRP: per six-pack $19.95

ACE HEX BLUNTS

These small game and blunt practice points are made of carbon steel and have a hollow point. Both glue-on and Screw in points are available. The glue-on point weights are: 125, 145, 160, 175 and 200-grains. The screw in points are 100, 125, 145 and 160 grains.
SRP: per six-pack $8.95

ACE HIGH SPEED

Lightweight—100 grains weight—and designed for high speed bows and set ups. This head is 1 1/16-inch wide and 2 7/16-inch long. It is a one-piece solid construction. And designed to fit on wooden shafts but can be adapted to modern arrow use.
SRP: per six-pack $18.95

ACE STANDARD

This one-piece double-edged broad-head included high carbon steel that

is spot welded and copper brazed, then heat-treated with a triple laminated tip. It uses the ACE Interlocking Ferrule. The company tests the broadheads by shooting them into concrete with no damage to the heads! These can be used on modern arrows with a ferrule adapter.
SPECIFICATIONS
Weights: 125-, 145- and 160-grain
Blades: Two
SRP: per six pack . . . . $18.95.

ACE SUPER EXPRESS

This one-piece broadheads first debuted in the 1950s and has returned today to the delight of traditional archer everywhere. This broadhead has a similar design and construction of the others in the ACE line-up and included 4 bleeder holes. The 200-grain head is solid construction without the holes. These blades are 2 13/13-inch long and 1 7/16-inch wide.
SPECIFICATIONS
Weights: 175- and 200-grain
Blades: Two
SRP: per six pack $20.95

Barrie Archery Broadheads and Arrow Points

IRONHEAD

ROCKY'S AVANTAGE

PREMIER

ASSASSIN

TI125

TI100

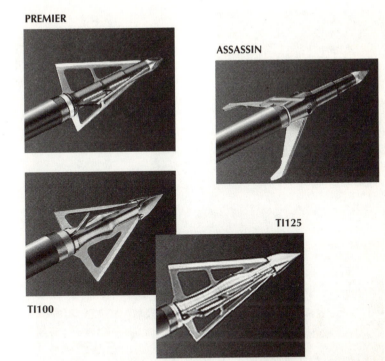

BARRIE ARCHERY/ ROCKY MOUNTAIN BROADHEADS

This southern Minnesota broadhead manufacturer was founded in 1978 and produced the first titanium broadhead in the industry. The company takes pride in producing tough, quality broadheads. Barrie Archery produces both fixed broadheads and its popular mechanical broadhead lines—the Revolution, Warhead, Xtreme, Assassin and Gator series.

IRONHEAD 125 BY ROCKY MOUNTAIN

This broadhead has a one-piece steel ferrule, Barrie Knife-Point tip that cuts on impact, UNICUT body to align blades, self-centering stainless steel Blade Lock collar and 1⅛-inch cutting diameter.

SPECIFICATIONS
Weights: 125 grain
Blades: three with 1⅛-inch cutting diameter
Available: Three or six-pack
SRP: per three $17.66
per six-pack. $32.90
Blades. $6.79

ROCKY'S ADVANTAGE

These hard-hitting, bone crushing broadheads arrive per-assembled

with surgically sharp blades and are pre-aligned. Features a Tri-Cut tip, .030 blades and Blade-Lock collars. Provides a 1 1/8-inch cutting diameter.

SPECIFICATIONS
Weights: 100 grains
Blades: three
Available: three or six-pack.
SRP: per three $17.82
per six. $33.95

ROCKY MOUNTAIN PREMIER SERIES

These broadheads are designed for today's high speed bows and provide great flight and penetration. Features cut-on impact tips, strong .030 stainless steel blades, and Blade-Lock collars. The 75-grain cuts 1⅛-inch, the 100-grain cuts 1³/₁₆-inch diameter and the 125-grain cuts 1¼-inch diameters.

SPECIFICATIONS
Weights: 75-, 100- and 125-grain.
Blades: Three.
Available: Packs of three and six.
SRP: per three $15.85
per six. $28.95
Blades. $6.79

ROCKY MOUNTAIN TI 85, TI 100 AND TI 125

These three-blade broadheads are

crafted from solidtitanium and are ten time stringer than aluminum and weigh less than half the weight of steel broadheads. Features include a space-age one piece ferrule design, cut-on impact tip, UNICUT body and patented self-centering stainless steel Blade-Lock collar. The 85- and 100-grain heads cut 1⅛-inch holes, and the 125-grain cuts 1³/₁₆-inch diameter.

THIS TROPHY SERIES FEATURES A THREE-BLADE DESIGN

ASSASSIN

This Rocky Mountain expandable broadhead has three replaceable .030-inch thick razor sharp blades behind a cut-on-impact Power Point tip. Blades open to 1½-inch cutting diameter and rest on a stainless steel collar. Blades are retained with an O-ring during flight.

SPECIFICATIONS
Weights: 85- and 100-grains.
Blades: Three.
Available: Package of three.
SRP: 85 grain. $22.20
100-grain $22.20
extra blades. $8.44
O-rings . . . . $2.68.

Barrie Archery Broadheads and Arrow Points

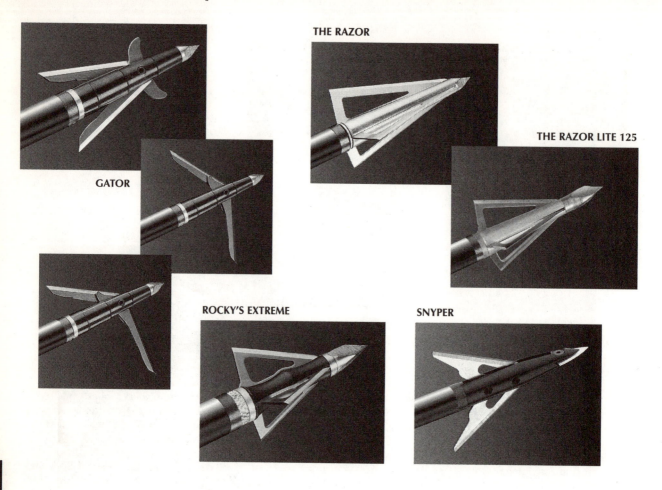

THE RAZOR

THE RAZOR LITE 125

GATOR

ROCKY'S EXTREME

SNYPER

GATOR

This unique Rocky Mountain two-blade expandable broadhead has two .030-inch thick free-floating blades. On impact the blades expand to cut 2 inches point-to-point. No O-rings required and they use a cut-on-impact high carbon steel Power Point.

SPECIFICATIONS
Weights: 80- and 100-grain.
Blades: Two
Available: Package of three.
SRP: 100-grain. $19.20
   80-grain $19.42
six extra blades $6.39

ROCKY'S EXTREME

This three-blade expandable head uses a cut-on-impact Tri-Cut tip and flies like a field point. Blades are .030-inch thick and open to cut 1⅜-inch diameter. Comes pre-assembled with a rubber band retention system.

SPECIFICATIONS
Weights: 100-grain.
Blades: Three
Available: Three pack.
SRP: $22.54
extra washers, per dozen $1.28
nine blades $8.70

SNYPER

This new Rocky Mountain broadhead has a cam-action blade system and a traditional cut-on-impact tip. The two .035-inch thick blades expand to 1⅜-inch. The blades slide rearward upon impact and begin cutting.

SPECIFICATIONS
Weights: 100-grain.
Blades: Two, plus cutting tip.
Available: Three pack.
SRP: $24.50
extra blades. $8.99

THE RAZOR
BY ROCKY MOUNTAIN

A broadhead with .020-inch thick stainless steel fixed blades that provide 1¼-inch cutting diameter.

SPECIFICATIONS
Weights: 125-grain
Blades: Three
Available: Three pack and six pack.
SRP: per three $15.85
per six. $28.95

THE RAZOR LITE

The Razor Lite is similar to the Razor with Tri-Cut tip and surgically sharpened blades.

SPECIFICATIONS
Weights: 100- and 125-grain.
Blades: Three
Available: Three and six packs.
SRP: per three $13.90
per half-dozen. $25.15
extra blades. $7.42

THE REVOLUTION - CLOSED

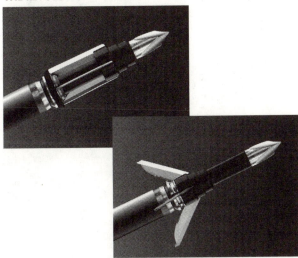

THE REVOLUTION - OPENED

WARHEAD 100 FIXED

THE WARHEAD - CLOSED

THE ULTRA

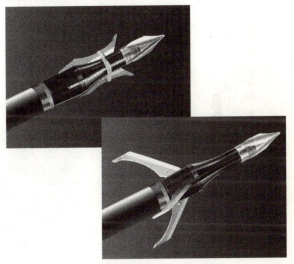

THE WARHEAD - OPENED

THE REVOLUTION BY ROCKY MOUNTAIN

The Revolution is an expandable broadhead with blades that fold back into the cutting position on impact. The broadhead comes assembled with a slide-on replacement blade cartridge and 100-grain weight. The blades expand to 1⅜-inch cutting diameter, begin cutting on impact, and are .030 thick. Titanium and aluminum bodies are available.

SPECIFICATIONS
Weights: 100-grain
Blades: Three
Available: Three pack.
SRP: standard ferrule **$23.18**
titanium ferrule **$34.95**

THE ULTRA

Utilizes double-vented reinforced blades and Rocky Mountain's heat-treated Power Point. This broadhead

has .020-inch thick stainless steel blades and self-centering stainless steel collar. The Ultra's blades expand to cut 1½-inch diameter.

SPECIFICATIONS
Weights: 125
Blades: Three
Available: Three and six packs.
SRP: per three **$14.32**
per six **$26.47**
extra blades **$6.63**

THE WARHEAD

This broadhead by Rocky Mountain also uses the slide on cartridge design and a pre-aligned Tri-Cut tip for increased penetration. Blades are .303-inch thick and expand to 1⅜ths cutting diameter.

SPECIFICATIONS
Weights: 100-grains.
Blades: Three
Available: Three pack.

SRP: **$22.04**
extra cartridges with enough blades for three broadheads **$8.75**
extra rubber bands, per dozen **$2.00**

WARHEAD 100 FIXED

This broadhead by Rocky Mountain is a replaceable blade fixed version of their expandables, and uses a unique slide-on blade cartridge to change the blades. This head has a Tri-Cut tip and cuts 1⅜-inch diameter. It can be converted to an expandable broadhead by installing the expandable blade cartidge.

SPECIFICATIONS
Weights: 100-grain
Blades: Three blades.
Available: Three and six pack.
SRP: per three **$18.99**
per half dozen **$35.95**
extra blade cartridges **$10.65**

ARROWS

Crimson Talon Broadheads and Arrow Points

CRIMSON TALON

2XJ Enterprises of North East, Maryland, has unleashed a new broadhead with curved blades that spin the broadhead and arrow in flight. The V-Lock ferrule and locking system grips the blades to provide rock solid anchoring. The blade's tips sport patent-pending mini gut hooks that also help keep the wound from closing.

SPECIFICATIONS
Weights: 100 grain
Blades: Three.
Available: Three pack.
SRP: $23.50

CRIMSON TALON

G5 Broadheads and Arrow Points

B52

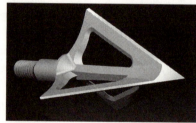

MONTEC

WARHEAD 100 FIXED

G5 is new to the archery industry and in addition to an arrow tip truing device, they also manufacture broadheads. G5 is based in Memphis, Michigan.

B52

This dark two-blade broadhead is sleek, powerful and provides excellent penetration. It has multi-tapered maul blades that are easy to sharpen and a reinforced tip. This head delivers a 1⅛-inch cutting diameter.

SPECIFICATIONS
Weights: 100 and 125 grain
Blades: Three.
Available: Three pack.
SRP: per three $24.99

B52 Sharpening Stone (Has preset angles to maintain the optimum angle while sharpening the B52 broadhead.)
SRP: $24.99

MONTEC

This new broadhead is one-piece from head to thread. It's crafted from solid stainless steel with three strong multi-tapered blades and a cut-on-impact nose. The blades angles permit easy sharpening. This head uses Monoflow air technology and cuts 1⅛-inch diameter (1 1/16-inch diameter with the 100-grain Montec).

SPECIFICATIONS
Weights: 100, 125 and 140 grain
Blades: Three.
Available: Three pack.
SRP: per three $32.99

Montec Diamond Sharpening Stone (Help you quickly and easily resharpen the Montec broadheads.)
    4-inch w/carrying case . . . $27.99
    6-inch w/leather
      carrying case. $35.99

PRESEASON MONTEC

Same as the standard Montec above, but with rounded edges. It is designed for practice and designed to create minimum wear on targets. A Lubricious coating resists rust and provides durability. These practice heads cut the same diameter as the standard Montec based on grain weight and are recommended instead of field points when hunting with Montec broadheads.

SPECIFICATIONS
Weights: 100 and 125 grain
Blades: Three.
Available: Three pack.
SRP: per three $28.99

ARROWS

Gold Tip Broadheads and Arrow Points

EZ PULL 85

EZ PULL 125

GLUE IN X-CUTTER 80

GLUE IN X-CUTTER 140

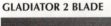

GLADIATOR 2 BLADE

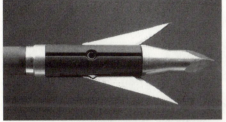

GLADIATOR 4 BLADE

GRIM REAPER - RAZORTIP

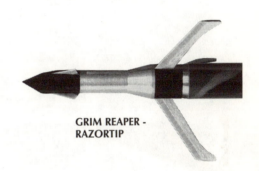

GOLD TIP broadheads and field points are available from Utah-based Gold Tip. The company makes three models of broadheads.

EZ PULL TARGET POINTS

A unique double taper makes retrieval from tight bales and foam targets effortless.

SPECIFICATIONS

Weights: Available grains include 85, 100 and 125.

SRP: per dozen $6.93
per 100 poiints $41.93

GLADIATOR

This expandable broadhead uses a patented friction bump system (no rubber bands) to ensure precision flight and dynamic opening. The expandable blade diameter is 1½ inches. Features include two rotating and opening blades and a ground aluminum chisel point.

SPECIFICATIONS

Weights: Available in 85-, 100- and 125-weights.
Blades: Two rotating.

SRP: 85- and 100-grain heads. $15.33
125-grain broadhead $16.73
replacement blades $8.33
points $1.33

GLUE IN POINTS

These field and target points can be glued onto a shaft tip and used for archery practice and plinking situations.

SPECIFICATIONS

Weights: Available in 50-, 100-, 125- and 140-grain weights in .246, Series 22 and X-Cutter models.

SRP: per dozen $11.13

GRIM REAPER

Grim Reaper Broadheads has improved its Razortip. The new design uses Trocrazor tips with mini razor blades and the Locknotch blade retention sysem that holds the blades in flight without O-rings and rubber bands. The 440C stainless steel blades open smoothly and a high strength steel cup holds the blade ring in place. You can also shoot this head as a broadhead by locking the blades open before shooting. Deliver 1⅜ths cutting diameter.

SPECIFICATIONS

Weights: 85, 100 and 125 grain
Blades: Three.
Available: Three pack.

SRP: $29.99

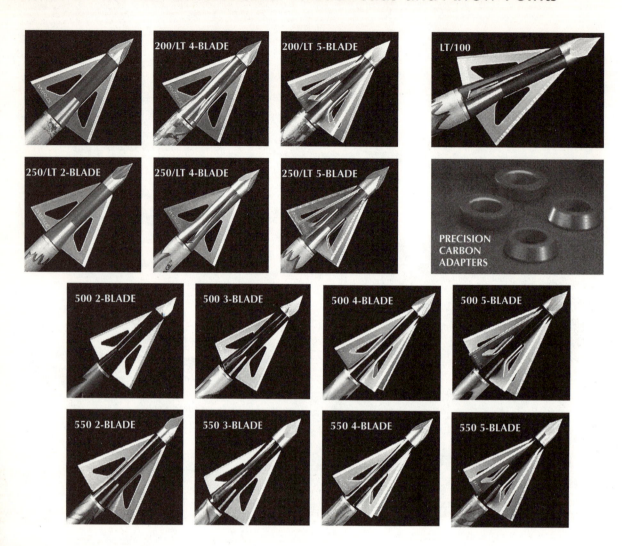

INNERLOC BROADHEADS

Each InnerLoc blade features a curved locking flange from tip to base that is inserted into the broadhead ferrule and the blades are secured into place under the tip when it is inserted into the ferrule and screwed into place. Every blade will be held securely into place—period. The stainless steel chisel point cuts on contact, and the .020-inch high-carbon, stainless steel blades are vented and reinforced by design. No O-ring or washers are required for assembly and the ferrule is made from aircraft grade aluminum. This company manufacturers a five-blade broadhead for hunters wanting more cutting edge.

InnerLoc, a Sullivan Industries company, is located in Lakemont, Georgia.

200/LT SERIES

This InnerLoc broadhead - more text to come for 200 LT Series.

SPECIFICATIONS

Weights: 85 grain 2-blade; 105 grain 4-blade and 115 grain 5-blade
Blades: 2, 4 and 5
SRP: per six $32.00

250/LT SERIES

These broadheads weigh 250 grains and are offered in 2, 4 and 5 blade designs.

SPECIFICATIONS

Weights: 95 grain 2-blade; 105 grain 4-blade and 115 grain 5-blade
Blades: 2, 4 and 5
SRP: per six $35.00

500 AND 550 SERIES

These heavyweight broadheads deliver cutting power and increase kinetic energy on target.

SPECIFICATIONS

Weights: 105 grain 2-blade and 115 grain 3-blade, 124 grain 4-blade and 135 grain 5 blade in the 500 series. In the 550 series 115 grain 2-blade, 125 grain 3-blade, 135 grain 4-blade and 145 grain 5 blade.
Blades: 2, 3, 4 and 5
SRP: per six . . . . . . $35.00 to $40.00

LT/100 GRAIN

Similar to the 200 LT but a three blade head weighing 100 grains.
SRP: per six $32.00

PRECISION CARBON ADAPTERS

These rings fit between larger broad-head bases and the smaller diameter carbon arrow shafts to assist with arrow flight and removal from targets.
SRP: per six-pack $5.00

Muzzy Broadheads and Arrow Points

MUZZY'S award winning broadheads have been available to bowhunters since the 1980s. This broadhead is designed with a weight-forward tip that can break bones and other hard surfaces. Muzzy broadheads feature stainless steel Trocar tips that's hollow ground to create three concave surfaces. The Georgia-based company produces more than 20 models of broadheads, plus other archery accessories such as the Zero Effect fall away arrow rest. The company promotes its products as: *Bad To The Bone*.

#205 AND #206

This four-blade broadhead has an 1-inch cutting diameter and screws into an insert inside of the arrow shaft. The #206 model is offered in with a Realtree camouflage finish. Optional filler inserts can turn this broadhead into a two-blade for $4.71.

SPECIFICATIONS:
Weights: 90 grain/205;
125 grain/206
Blades: 4
Available: six pack for #205 and three per pack for #206.
SRP: $33.57
replacement blades $15.14
replacement tips $9.07

#207

A lightweight 75-grain three-blade broadhead with an 1-inch cutting diameter. It screws into an insert.

SPECIFICATIONS:
Weights: 75 grain.
Blades: 3
Available: six-card pack
SRP: $33.57
replacement blades $15.14
replacement tips $9.07

#209

This 100-grain four-blade broadhead is offered in Realtree camouflage and has a threaded ferrule.

SPECIFICATIONS:
Weights: 100 grain.
Blades: 4
Available: Six-pack card standard, three pack in camo
SRP: $33.57
per three in camo $25.00
replacement blades $15.14
replacement tips $9.07

#205
#206
#207
#209
#215
#225
#235
#245
#255
#265
#285

#215

A 115-grain broadhead by Muzzy with four blades. It has a $1\frac{1}{8}$th cutting diameter.

SPECIFICATIONS:
Weights: 115 grain.
Blades: 4
Available: six-pack card.
SRP: $33.57
replacement blades $15.14
replacement tips $9.07

#225

This 100-grain broadhead screws in and has a $1\frac{3}{16}$ths cutting diameter.

SPECIFICATIONS:
Weights: 100 grain.
Blades: 4
Available: Six-pack card standard and

three pack card in Realtree camo.
SRP: $33.57
per three in camo $25.00
replacement blades $15.14
replacement tips $9.07

#235

A 125-grain three-blade Muzzy broadhead with a threaded ferrule.

SPECIFICATIONS:
Weights: 100 grain.
Blades: 4
Available: Six-pack card standard, three pack in camouflage.
SRP: $33.57
per three in camo $25.00
replacement blades $15.14
replacement tips $9.07

Muzzy Broadheads and Arrow Points

#245

This 130-grain screw-in broadhead has four blades and is green.

SPECIFICATIONS:
Weights: 130 grain.
Blades: 4
Available: six-pack card.
SRP: $33.57
per three in camo $25.00
replacement blades $15.14

#255

This 145-grain broadhead is recommended for big and dangerous game.

SPECIFICATIONS:
Weights: 145 grain.
Blades: 4
Available: six-pack card.
SRP: $33.57
per three in camo $25.00
replacement blades $15.14

#265

This Muzzy specialty broadhead weighs 120 grains and has two blades. It screws into an insert.

SPECIFICATIONS:
Weights: 120 grain.
Blades: 2
Available: six-pack card.
SRP: $33.57
per three in camo $25.00
replacement blades $15.14

#285

This Muzzy four-blade broadhead has a five-degree taper for wood or swedged aluminum shafts. It must be glued on and filler inserts are optional.

SPECIFICATIONS
Weights: 125 grain.
Blades: 4
Available: in a six-pack card
SRP: $33.57
per three in camo $25.00
replacement blades $15.14

GRASSHOPPER TIPS

These Muzzy spring-loaded blunt tips can be shot solo at stumps or added behind a Muzzy broadhead to create a low penetration turkey hunting broadhead.

SPECIFICATIONS
Weights: NA
Blades: three prongs
Available: Three pack standard blunt or as a combo 75-grain to fit behind a broadhead.

200 SERIES

300 SERIES - GLUE ON

300 SERIES - GLUE IN

GRASSHOPPER TIPS

SRP: standard blunt $45.64
 combo Grasshopper $6.57

MUZZY 200 SERIES

All 200 Series broadheads must be glued onto the carbon shaft and are sold fully assembled. Available sizes include200-2200, 20-2300, 200-22400, 200-1564 and 200-1664. They will fit AFC 2200, AFC 2300, and AFC 2400 shafts respectively. The 1564 and 1664 models fit the corresponding Beman shafts with the same size numbers. These heads have a 1-inch cutting diameter.

SPECIFICATIONS:
Weights: 100 grain.
Blades: Four
Available: six per card pack
SRP: $33.57
replacement blades $15.14
replacement tips $9.07

MUZZY 300 SERIES

This broadhead fits AFC's 2100, 2200, 2300, and 2400 shafts, plus CAE and Carbon Tech 210, 220, 230 and 240 shafts. The 1564 and 1664 models fit Beman's $^{15}/_{64}$ and $^{16}/_{64}$ shafts. The 3390 models fit ACC 3.39 shafts and the 3490 models fit ACC 3.49 shafts. The 300-3600 broadhead will fit ACC 3.60 shafts and Beman ICS and GoldTip

arrows. These heads have a $1^{3}/_{8}$ ths cutting diameter.

SPECIFICATIONS:
Weights: 100 grain.
Blades: Three
Available: six per pack
SRP: $33.57
replacement blades $15.14
replacement tips $9.07

MUZZY FIELD POINTS

These points are available in assorted weights and styles. The 100 grain glue-on field points can fit Beman, AFC and Carbon Tech shafts. Screw in points in 75-, 90-, 100-, 115-, 125-, 130- and 145-grain weights are available to help you practice in preparation for hunting with Muzzy broadheads that weigh the same.

SRP: All field points $00.20

MUZZY PERSONALIZED BROADHEADS

You can now have your name engraved on your favorite style of Muzzy broadheads. Personalized braodheads must be paid for in advance and there's a 15 character maximum. Call Muzzy at 770-387-9300 for more details or to place an order.

ARROWS

New Archery Products Broadheads and Arrow Points

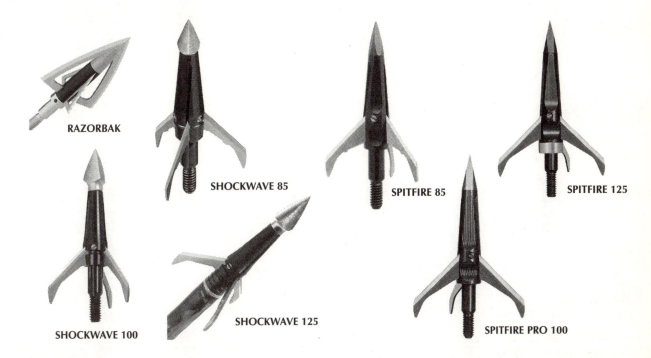

RAZORBAK

SHOCKWAVE 85

SPITFIRE 85

SPITFIRE 125

SHOCKWAVE 100

SHOCKWAVE 125

SPITFIRE PRO 100

NEW ARCHERY PRODUCTS broadhead and archery accessory manufacturer has been in business more than 31 years and prides itself in customer satisfaction. They manufacture fixed and mechanical broadheads in various weights. NAP is based in Forest Park, Illinois. The company notes that its products are: Designed to ensure the pleasure and success of archery.

RAZORBAK
The return of the popular Razorbak broadheads by NAP also means the unveiling of a new design. This new-era Razorbak has stainless steel blades set in a composite core. The main blades is .039-inch thick and the bleeder blades are .020-inch thick. The tip is designed to cut on impact.
SPECIFICATIONS
Weights: Available in 100- and 125-grains.
Blades: Four blades.
Available: Three broadheads per pack.
SRP: **$32.99**

SHOCKWAVE
These mechanical opening broadheads from New Archery Products have O-rings to hold the blades closed during flight and offer a more economical broadhead. Other features include a bone-crushing Tri-Vex point with super-sharp replaceable blades, and a strong

durable ferrule. These broadheads are sold three per package and replacement blades and replacement retention rings are available separately.
SPECIFICATIONS
Weights: Available in 85-, 100- and 125-grains.
Blades: Three blade design.
Available: Three pack of broadheads and replacement blades
SRP: **$24.99**
replacement blade. **$11.99**
retention rings, per 50. . . . . . **$3.99**

SPITFIRE
The Spitfire mechanical broadheads by New Archery Products feature a 3-blade design with a patented snap-lock blade retention system. No O-rings or rubber bands are required to hold the .030-inch thick blades in place. These broadheads cut a 1½-inch diameter circle after opening.
SPECIFICATIONS
Weights: Available in 85-, 100- and 125-grains.
Blades: Three blade design per unit.
Available: Three pack of broadheads and replacement blades
SRP: **$31.99**
replacement blade. **$16.99**
Practice blades insert into the ferrules but that do not open and cut can be obtained for $8.99

SPITFIRE GOBBLER GETTER
These mechanical opening broadheads from NAP have the same Spitfire design and use a cone-shaped silver bullet point to provide knock-down power to the turkey.
SPECIFICATIONS
Weights: Available in 100- and 125-grains.
Blades: Three blade design per unit.
Available: Three pack of broadheads and replacement blades
SRP: **$32.99**
replacement blade. **$16.99**
Practice blades that do not open and cut can be obtained for $8.99

SPITFIRE PROSERIES
The Spitfire Pro Series is similar in design and cutting dimension to the standard Spitfire and incorporates a microgroove ferrule. Practice blades can also be used with this model.
SPECIFICATIONS
Weights: Available in 85-, 100- and 125-grains.
Blades: Three blade design per unit.
Available: Three pack of broadheads and replacement blades
SRP: **$34.99**
replacement blade. **$16.99**
Practice blades that do not open and cut can be obtained for $8.99

ARROWS

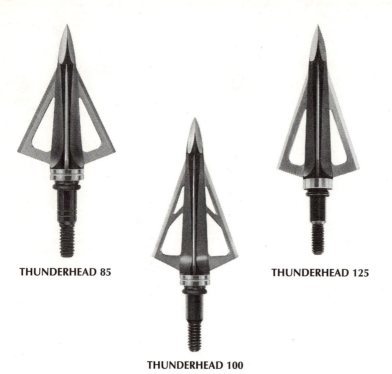

THUNDERHEAD 85

THUNDERHEAD 125

THUNDERHEAD 100

THUNDERHEAD PRO 100

THUNDERHEAD

Thunderheads feature a patented Slimline Ferrule and Trophy Tip. The .027-inch thick blades are constructed of Diamize stainless steel. This broadhead is a three-blade fixed design and the blades fit into slots and are held in place with a metal ring at the base that is backed with a rubber O-ring that helps in alignment and balancing. Replacement blades are offered separately and must be acquired to fit a specific broadhead weight model. The cutting dimensions for each style are: 1⅛-inch for the 85 grain, and 1³/₁₆-inch for the 100- and 125-grain models.

SPECIFICATIONS
Weights: Available in 85-, 100- and 125-grains.
Blades: Three blade.
Available: Six pack of broadheads and replacement blades
SRP: $33.99
replacement blade $16.99

THUNDERHEAD FOR CARBON ARROWS

Bowhunters who shoot carbon arrows can now obtain the same Thunderheads for standard arrows with an adapter to help obtain proper shaft-to-head fit. Thunderheads UBARS—Universal Broadhead Adapter Rings—make it possible. The adapter is placed behind the O-ring on the broadhead.

SPECIFICATIONS
Weights: Available in 85-, 100- and 125-grains.
Blades: Three blade.
Available: Six pack of broadheads and replacement blades
SRP: $35.99
replacement blade $16.99
Note: The UBARS are also sold separately. A package of 6 rings has an SRP of $4.99.

THUNDERHEAD PRO SERIES

Thunderhead Pro Series broadheads feature the same blades as the standard series but have micro-grooved ferrules to increase penetration. This broadhead uses a nickel plated point that's 50% harder than stainless steel. The blades have an exclusive Diamize edge. Available UBAR adapters will make these broadheads compatible with trimmer carbon shafts.

SPECIFICATIONS
Weights: Available in 85-, 100- and 125-grains.
Blades: Three blade.
Available: Six pack of broadheads and replacement blades
SRP: $38.99
Note: The UBARS are also sold separately. A package of 6 rings has an SRP of $4.99. Visit www.newarchery.com to order.

Note: The UBARS are also sold separately. These rings can be used with most popular sizes of carbon/aluminum arrows and with small aluminum shafts and with all popular broadheads. A package of 6 rings (Item 60-269) has an SRP of $4.99. Visit www.newarchery.com to order.

THUNDERHEAD REPLACEMENT PARTS

Owners of Thunderhead broadheads will want to acquire replacement O-rings and lock rings. These items are used to realign broadheads and to hold the blades in place at the base. The standard O-rings fit all models and the lock rings must be purchased to fit specific broadhead weights.

SPECIFICATIONS
Available: In a package of a dozen for the O-rings and six for the lock rings.
SRP: O-rings $1.99
lock rings $1.99

ARROWS

5-DEGREE BROADHEAD ADAPTERS

EASY PULL POINTS

5-DEGREE DART POINT

CONVERTA BLUNTS

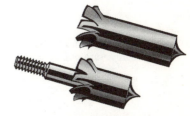

ADJUSTABLE SPEED POINTS

CONVERTA BULLET POINTS

GAME NABBER ARROWHEADS

CONVERTA 3-D/ FIELD POINTS

CONVERTA TARGET POINT

GLUE-IN TARGET POINTS

PRECISION DESIGNED PRODUCTS manufactures arrow points, broadhead adapters, field points and other accessories that attach to the business end of an arrow. The company's products have been used by many IBO and ASA shooters during their competitions. PDP is based in Independence, Kansas.

5-DEGREE BROADHEAD ADAPTERS

These adaptors are used when installing traditional broadheads into shafts with inserts. Various sizes will fit numerous styles of broadheads. Call PDP at 620-331-0333 for more details.
SRP: Starting, per dozen $3.85

5-DEGREE DART POINT

This blunt pike point is used while shooting the interactive DART video archery screen. Weighs 125 grains.
SRP: per five $9.59

ADJUSTABLE STEEL SPEED POINTS

These points come in numerous weights, including 10, 30, 50 , 60, 70, and 100 grains, and will fit popular arrows such as Express/Vapor, Gold

Tip, X-Cutter, LineJammer, CXL, and shafts sizes ranging from 2012, 2112, 2412, to 2613.
SRP: per dozen $2.34 $11.55
Note: A 5-grain set screw can help increase weight and has an SRP of $2.34. A special Speed point tool can be used to install grain weights through the Uni-Bushing. The tool has and SRP of $13.34.

CONVERTA 3-D/ FIELD POINTS

Smoother contour incerases target life, yet maintains a durable tip. Each point is stamped with size and weight for identification and accurate practice.
SRP: per dozen $2.20

CONVERTA BLUNTS

These blunts are designed for small game hunting and roving. Available in 100 and 125 grain weights.
SRP: per dozen $2.55

CONVERTA BULLET POINTS

A point with a sharp tip and precise body blend. More rounded than the 3-D points above.
SRP: per dozen $2.20

CONVERTA TARGET POINTS

Light weight and designed for flat trajectory, these target points are available in weights including 55, 65 and 75 grains.
SRP: per dozen $2.20

EASY PULL POINTS

An oversized and chamfered point to drastically enhance removal from foam targets.
SRP: per dozen $3.60

GAME NABBER ARROWHEADS

These semi-blunt points perform like a mini-broadhead and resist sticking to trees or sliding under grass while shooting small game, large birds and stumps.
SRP: per half-dozen $5.45

GLUE-IN TARGET POINTS

These target points are designed for field target and arrows without inserts.
SRP: per dozen $2.35

ARROWS

Razor Caps Broadheads and Arrow Points

RAZOR CAPS is based in Mercerville, New Jersey. This company manufacturers a heavy 200-grain broadhead that some archers seek for special hunting conditions.

RAZOR CAPS

The world's only three-blade, cut-on-contact broadhead with replaceable blades that unscrew from the ferrule. The three-blade blade unit is solid, one-piece construction of stainless steel. The blades can be resharpened. The long, lean design assists with perfect flight. The ferrules and blades are sold separately as replacement units and combined pieces can make broadheads of your desired weight. Visit www.razorcaps.com to order.

RAZOR CAPS

SPECIFICATIONS
Weights: Available in 100-, 125-, 150-, 175- and 200-grain weights.
Blades: Three blade, one piece unit.
Available: Three pack of blades or ferrules.
SRP: blades **$16.95**
ferrules **$7.95**

Satellite Archery Broadheads and Arrow Points

BEAR RAZORHEAD

BEAR RAZORHEAD LITE

BUCK MASTER VECTOR

SPEARPOINT 100

SPEARPOINT 125

SATELLITE ARCHERY broadheads and accessories are manufactured and distributed by the North American Archery Group in Gainesville, Florida. This company also makes Bear bows.

BEAR RAZORHEAD

This broadhead has been on the market since 1952 and produces 4-blade performance and results. Features a re-sharpenable two-edged .040-inch main stainless steel blade and positive-locking auxiliary blade. Able to withstand 300 pounds tensile load. Both models cut 1 1/16 th diameter on impact and feature a chisel tip point.
SPECIFICATIONS

Weights: (Lite) 110- and (Super) 145-grain.
Blades: Three stainless replaceable
Available: Three or six per pack.
SRP: Supers 3/pack **$12.99**
      6/pack **$19.99**
Lites 3/pack. **$14.99**
      6/pack **$23.99**

BUCKMASTER VECTOR

A three-blade broadhead with a hardened steel chisel point tip and .027-inch stainless replaceable blades. Produces a 1 1/8-inch diameter cutting radius.
SPECIFICATIONS
Weights: Vector 75- or 100-grain.
Blades: Three stainless replaceable

Available: Three per pack.
SRP: **$14.99**

CHUCK ADAMS SPEAR POINT

Chuck Adams designed this 3-blade broadhead for superior performance based on low friction penetration. Has cutting edges from the tip to the blades. Cuts a 1 1/8-inch diameter radius. The 125 grain Spear Point has .15-grain replaceable stainless blades and a 20-grain point. The 100-grain model has .10-grain blades and a .15-grain tip.
SPECIFICATIONS
Weights: 100- or 125-grain.
Blades: Three stainless replaceable
Available: Three per pack.
SRP: **$24.99**

Satellite Archery Broadheads and Arrow Points

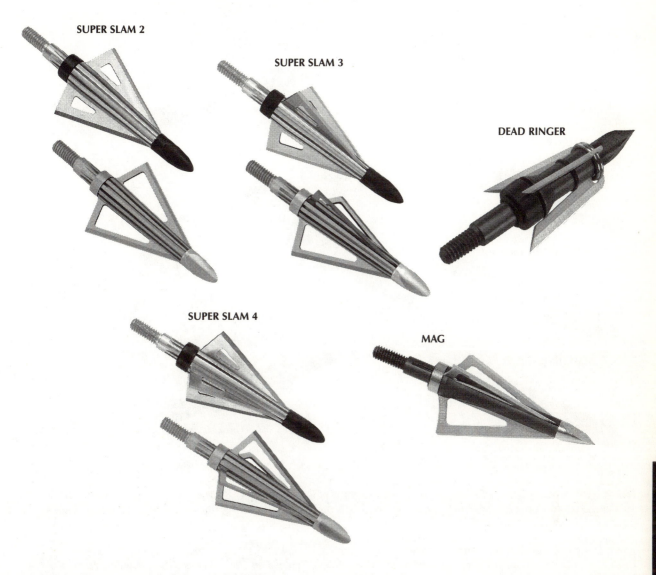

SUPER SLAM 2

SUPER SLAM 3

DEAD RINGER

SUPER SLAM 4

MAG

CHUCK ADAMS SUPER SLAM BROADHEAD SYSTEM

A revolutionary 12-slot aircraft aluminum ferrule lets the user assemble two-, three-, or four-blade configurations. Blades can be installed to align with any fletching configuration, including four fletch.

The 90- to 110-grain system utilizes .027-inch stainless replaceable blades and and the 110- to140-grain system uses dark, larger tips and dark security rings. Both systems cut 1⅛ diameter holes and have case hardened spear points.

SPECIFICATIONS
Weights: 90 to 110-grain; or 110- to 140-grain.
Blades: Three stainless replaceable

Available: Three per pack.
SRP: $27.99

DEAD RINGER

This expandable 3-blade broadhead cuts 1⁵/₁₆-inch diameter upon impact. Blades are non-vented and positioned backward for flight. Hardened steel Trocar point assists with penetration. High-tech design assures low flight pattern. Dead Ringer 75-grain model cuts 1³/₁₆ inch hole and uses .027-inch replaceable stainless blades.

SPECIFICATIONS
Weight: 75- and 100-grain.
Blades: Three stainless replaceable
Available: Three per pack.
SRP: $23.99

MAG

This broadhead series features a hardened steel chisel point with a Quick-Silver Tip, three-blade design and light weight for maximum speed. The 100- and 12 grain heads use .027-inch stainless replaceable blades and the 75-grain head uses .020-inch stainless replaceable blades. The Mag 125 cuts 1³/₁₆ diameter and the other versions cut 1⅛ diameter holes.

SPECIFICATIONS
Weights: 75-, 100- and 125-grain.
Blades: Three stainless replaceable
Available: Three or six per pack.
SRP: 3/pack. $14.99
     6/pack $24.99

ARROWS

Satellite Archery Broadheads and Arrow Points

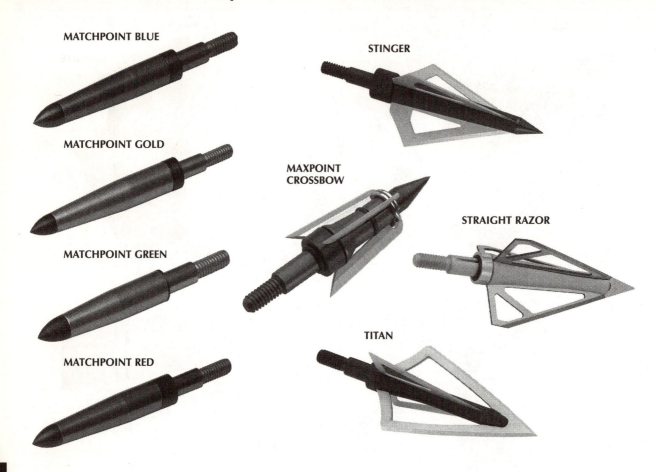

MATCHPOINT BLUE

MATCHPOINT GOLD

MATCHPOINT GREEN

MATCHPOINT RED

STINGER

MAXPOINT CROSSBOW

STRAIGHT RAZOR

TITAN

ARROWS

MATCHPOINTS

This unique point duplicates any combination of blades and any range of weights to provide a precision practice point. Design by Chuck Adams, the head is adjustable to duplicate length, balance and weight distribution of any broadhead. This kit is used for tuning a bow for hunting. The assorted colors indicate various weights.

SPECIFICATIONS
Weights: Available in 75-, 90, 100- and 125-grain.
Blades: None
Available: One per pack.
SRP: kit **$8.49**

MAXPOINT CROSSBOW BROADHEAD SYSTEM

This expandable 3-blade broadhead has a conical tip and cuts 1⁵/₁₆-inch diameter hole upon impact and opening. Blade assembly slides back instead of opening outward and low profile assures consistent flight pattern and blade penetration. Comes with matched WeightPoint for arrow flight tuning. Uses .036 stainless resharpenable blades.

SPECIFICATIONS
Weight: 100-grain.
Blades: Three stainless replaceable
Available: Three per pack.
SRP: **$25.99**

STINGER

This 3-blade broadhead uses .016 replaceable stainless blades to deliver 1³/₁₆-inch cutting diameter. Features a conical point and black body.

SPECIFICATIONS
Weights: 100- or 125-grain.
Blades: Three stainless replaceable
Available: Three per pack.
SRP: **$9.99**

STRAIGHT RAZOR

The case-hardened steel pyramid tip on this broadhead aligns with the three blades and begins cutting upon impact. The Straight Razor uses three .027-inch replaceable stainless blades.

The 100-grain broadhead cuts 1⅛ inches diameter and the 125-grain head cuts 1³/₈ diameter.

SPECIFICATIONS
Weights: 100- and 125-grain.
Blades: Three stainless replaceable
Available: Three per pack.
SRP: **$23.99**

TITAN

This broadhead is sharp to the point and begins cutting on contact. Produces high penetration with eight inches of cutting surface. Utilizes replaceable blades and a resharpenable .036-inch main blade. The replaceable blade on the Titan 125-grain head is .027 inch and .015 inch on the 100 grain head. Both broadheads cut a 1⅛ diameter hole.

SPECIFICATIONS
Weights: 100- and 125-grain.
Blades: Two stainless replaceable and one two-edge fixed blade.
Available: Three per pack.
SRP: **$23.99**

Saunders Archery Broadheads and Arrow Points

BLUDGEON

COMBO

BULLET

FIELD

TARGET

GRIP TITE

PRO GRIP

POINT PULLER

ARROWS

SAUNDERS ARCHERY is based in Columbus, Nebraska and makes field points and blunts. Visit www.sausa.com to learn more or to order these products

BLUDGEONS
Used for small game hunting, these can also stop arrows from sticking into logs or sliding under grass.
SRP: 4 pack **$7.95**
   Slip on models **$5.95**

COMBO POINTS
Great to 3-D shooting and leaves a smaller entry hole and creates less wear on targets. These are available in many sizes.
SRP: per dozen **$4.95**

FIELD, BULLET AND TARGET POINTS
The tried-and-true points that all archers have and use while practicing. These are available in numerous weights. Field points are long and pointed, bullet points are rounder and more blunt and target points are smaller.
SRP: per dozen **$3.95**

GRIP TITE ARROW PULLING PAD
A flexible super grip pad to make arrow removal easier.

SRP: **$3.95**

PRO GRIP
This soft-n-tough cylinder is big enough to easily grip when an arrow is placed in it's slot.
SRP: per two **$6.95**

POINT PULLER
Machined from carbon alloy steel and plated and then finished with foam handles, this puller will fit in your pocket but can help you remove broadheads and practice points with ease.
SRP: **$5.95**

Simmons System Archery Broadheads and Arrow Points

SIMMONS SYSTEM ARCHERY LAND SHARK BROADHEADS in Alabama produces several unique arcfhery items, like the second chance single arrow holder. Among their most unique products, however, is the Land Shark Broadheads. The flared-base, .042-inch thick blades in the 125 model are solid, and the 160-grain model .050-inch thick blades have small bleeder holes. Insert bleeder blades can be added to both models. The 160-grain broadhead cuts 1¹⁹/₁₆-inch and the 125-grain model cuts 1³/₁₆-inch wide.

SPECIFICATIONS
Weights: 125 and 160 grain
Blades: Two or four with bleeder
Available: Six pack
SRP: $25.00

LANDSHARK 125

LANDSHARK 160

Steel Force Broadheads and Arrow Points

41023

41423

41713 GLUE ON

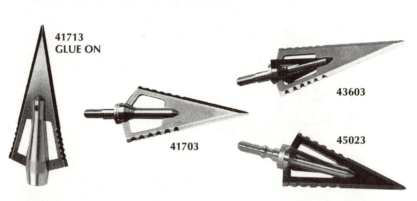

41703

43603

45023

STEEL FORCE This unique line of broadheads has serrated Sabertooth blades that cause massive tissue damage. The blades are made from .039 or .048 steel and have specially designed venting. The 49-51 Rockwell main blades can be changed and are secured into place with a quick-change blade locking system. Aluminum and titanium ferrules are available. The blade tips have a Diamond shape and free lifetime resharpening is included. Steel Force (Ballistic Archery) is based in Rosemont, New Jersey

STEEL FORCE STAINLESS STEEL SERIES: 41023/75 GRAIN
SPECIFICATIONS
Weights: 75 grain.
Blades: Two-edge single blade.
Available: Three pack.
SRP: $18.99

41413/125 GRAIN AND 41713/140 GRAIN
SPECIFICATIONS
Weights: 125- and 140-grain.
Blades: Two-edge single blade.
Available: Three pack
SRP: $21.99
Note: These blades are for gluing onto the arrow shaft and are not threaded

41423/100 GRAIN
SPECIFICATIONS
Weights: 100 grain.
Blades: Two-edge single blade cutting 1³/₁₆-inch
Available: Three pack
SRP: $18.99

41703/125 GRAIN
SPECIFICATIONS
Weights: 125 grain.
Blades: Two-edge single blade.
Available: Three pack
SRP: $18.99

43603 LD/125 GRAIN
SPECIFICATIONS
Weights: 125 grain.
Blades: Four blade lock down design.
Available: Three pack
SRP: $19.99
Note: Requires special blade pliers to change the bleeder blade

45003/100 GRAIN
SPECIFICATIONS
Weights: 100 Grains
Blades: Four
Available: Three pack.
SRP: $21.99

45023/85 GRAIN
SPECIFICATIONS
Weights: 85 grain.
Blades: Four blade.
Available: Three pack
SRP: $21.99
Note: These are designed for fast shooting compound bows

ARROWS

Steel Force Broadheads and Arrow Points

45723/125 GRAIN
SPECIFICATIONS
Weights: 125 grain.
Blades: Four blade.
Available: Three pack
SRP. $21.99

55723/150 GRAIN HELLFIRE
SPECIFICATIONS
Weights: 150 grain
Blades: Four blade, all are serrated
and cryogenically treated.
Available: Three pack
SRP: $23.50

STEEL FORCE PREMIUM SERIES
The blades do not have serrated edges

25003/100 GRAIN
AND 21003/100 GRAIN
SPECIFICATIONS
Weights: 100 grain
Blades: Four, and two in the 21003
model
Available: Three pack.
SRP: 25003 . . . . $19.99
21003 . . . . $17.99
*Note: The blades do not have serrated
edges on these broadheads.*

21533/210 GRAIN
SPECIFICATIONS
Weights: 210 grain
Blades: Two fixed, solid one-piece
construction, designed for dangerous
game.

Available: Three pack.
SRP: $32.25
Note: Moly coating is standard.

21703/100 GRAIN
SPECIFICATIONS
Weights: 125 grains
Blades: Two blade design
Available: Three pack
SRP: $17.99

25723/125 GRAIN
SPECIFICATIONS
Weights: 125
Blades: Four blade design
Available: Three pack
SRP: $19.99
*Note: This broadhead is the same
as the Sabertooth 125 but without
serrations.*

71023/65 GRAIN
SPECIFICATIONS
Weights: 65 grains
Blades: Two blade with 1-inch
cutting span
Available: Three pack
SRP: $31.75

75003/75 GRAIN
SPECIFICATIONS
Weights: 75 grain
Blades: Four
Available: Three pack.
SRP: $33.50

75503/85 GRAIN
SPECIFICATIONS
Weights: 85 grain
Blades: Four
Available: Three pack
SRP: $33.50

75703/100 GRAIN
SPECIFICATIONS
Weights: 100 grain
Blades: Four blade design
Available: Three pack
SRP: $33.50

75723/125 GRAIN HELLFIRE
SPECIFICATIONS
Weights: 125 grain
Blades: Four
Available: Three pack
SRP: $34.50
*Note: This unique Steel Force blade
is purple and gold*

STEEL FORCE TITANIUM
SABERTOOTH
Steel Force's Titanium Sabertooth
broadheads feature serrated blades,
titanium ferrules and cut-on-contact
points. The large main blades are
constructed of laser cut, grade 5
aerospace titanium.
SPECIFICATIONS
Weights: 65-125 grains
Blades: Four blade design
Available: Three pack
SRP: $33.50

Wasp Broadheads and Arrow Points

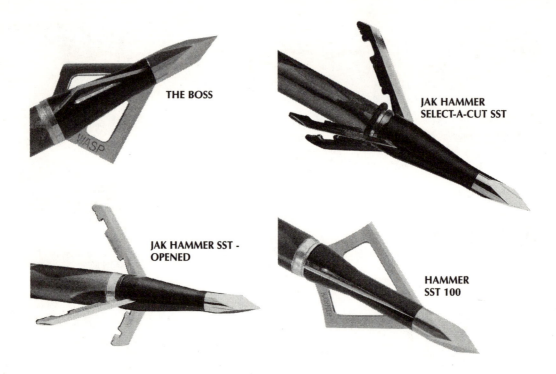

THE BOSS

JAK HAMMER
SELECT-A-CUT SST

JAK HAMMER SST -
OPENED

HAMMER
SST 100

WASP BROADHEADS uses and exclusive stainless SMART tip on many of its broadheads. The company regularly tests penetration by shooting through steel plates. WASP began business in 1971 and created the first replaceable blade broadhead.

THE BOSS BY WASP

A broadhead designed for traveling more than 300 fps with .027-inch thick blades and a sharp SST tip delivers a large wound channel on the largest game animals. Cutting diameter for the BOSS is 1⅛-inches.

SPECIFICATIONS
Weights: 100 grain
Blades: Three
Available: Six pack
SRP: $29.99

JAK HAMMER SELECT-A-CUT SST

WASP's latest innovation adds versatility to mechanical broadheads. You decide upon a 1½- or 1¼-inch cutting diameter by rotating the Select-A-Cut washer that's located between the blades and the arrow shaft. The washer has been machined at two different beveled edges to stop the blades at the preferred cutting diameter.

SPECIFICATIONS
Weights: 100 grain
Blades: Three
Available: Three pack
SRP: per three $25.99

JAK HAMMER SST AND SST 1¼ CUT

This mechanical broadhead opens up to 1¾-inch with three cutting blades. An O-ring secures the blades while in flight. A Trocar tip aids with penetration. NOTE: A newer model, the JAK-Hammer SST 1¼-inch Cut is similar in design and cuts 1¼-inch diameter. A unique feature is that you can tie the blades in place for standard per-contact flight with Spider Wire fishing line or a lightweight wire and shoot the broadhead into foam targets without the blades opening. This is a great way to check your arrow flight prior to hunting.

SPECIFICATIONS
Weights: 100 and 125 grain
Blades: Three
Available: Three pack
SRP: both models $24.99

HAMMER SST

These WASP fixed blade broadheads have a Trocar heat-treated SMART tip that provides superior penetration. An extra long front foot on each blade helps lock the blades into the ferrules so that they stay put under the toughest conditions. Cutting diameters are 1⅛-inch for the 75 grain head and 1³⁄₁₆-inch for the other weights.

SPECIFICATIONS
Weights: 75, 85, 90, 100 and 125 grain
Blades: Three
Available: Six pack
SRP: $29.99

HI-TECH CAM LOK SST

This WASP broadhead is sleek, streamlined and devastatingly simple. The SMART tip aids with the three-point positive locking blade security system. One solid, double-wound high tensile steel ring exerts continuous even pressure to lock the blades into place. Cutting diameter is 1³⁄₁₆-inch.

SPECIFICATIONS
Weights: 100 and 125 grain
Blades: Three
Available: Six pack
SRP: $29.99

Zwickery Broadheads and Arrow Points

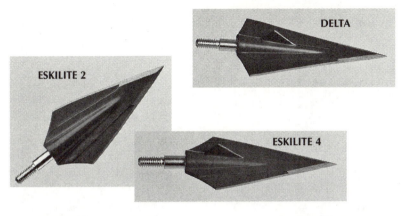

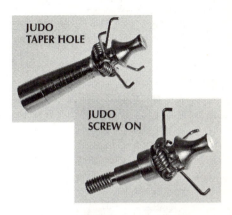

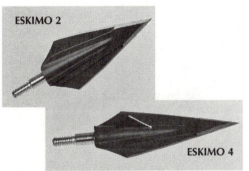

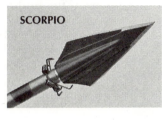

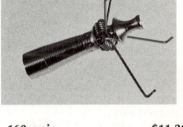

ZWICKEY ARCHERY has been manufacturing their strong, solid one-piece steel broadheads since 1938. Zwickey broadheads have grizzlies and Cape buffalo to their credit. One Alabama hunter took 50 deer with the same Zwickey Eskimo 4-edge broadhead. The company also produces the popular prong Judo point that's useful for in-the-field practice, stump shooting and small game hunting. In recent years it has created the Scropio, for behind-the-broadhead prongs, that are popular with turkey hunters. Zwickey is based in Minnesota.

ZWICKEY BLACK DIAMOND

The Zwickey broadheads are available in numerous sizes. The heads use heat treated and tempered steel. All models—Eskimo, Eskilite, and Delta—have a rugged two-blade cut on impact points and two bleeder blades. These broadheads are very popular with traditional bowhunters and can be used with modern archery gear. Four and two edge versions are available.

ZWICKEY DELTA 2½-INCH BROADHEADS
SPECIFICATIONS

Weights: 135- and 170-grains.
Blades: 2 and 4-blade configurations
Available: 6- and 3-packs.
SRP: 2-edge 135-grain $19.50
4-edge 135-grain $21.50
170-grain 2-edge screw-on. . . $13.40
4-edge screw-on 4-edge
   broadheads $14.80

ZWICKEY ESKILITE 2½-INCH BROADHEADS
SPECIFICATIONS

Weights: 110- and 135-grains.
Blades: 2 and 4 configurations
Available: 6 per pack in 110 grain, and 3 per pack in 135 grains.
SRP: 110-grain 2-blade $16.50
110-grain 4-blade $18.50
135-grain 2-blade screw-on . . $11.20
135-grain 4-blade screw-on . . $12.80

ZWICKEY ESKIMO 2½-INCH BROADHEADS
SPECIFICATIONS

Weights: 125- and 160-grain
Blades: 2 and 4 configuration
Available: Standard glue on and screw-on styles
SRP: per 6 standard 2- and 4-blade
   125 grain $16.50
per 3-pack 2 edge

160-grain $11.20
per 4-edge 160-grain
   screw-on. $12.80

ZWICKEY JUDOS
SPECIFICATIONS

Weights: 100-,125-, 135- and 120-grains
Blades: 4 prongs each
Available: 100- and 125-grain screw on for standard arrow inserts, 135- and 120-grain glue on with 5-degree taper hole
SRP: per two $6.00

ZWICKEY KONDOR
SPECIFICATIONS

Weights: 105- and 145-grains
Blades: 4 prongs
Available: screw on or 5-degere taper hole glue-on
SRP: each $4.00

ZWICKEY SCORPIO
SPECIFICATIONS

Weights: 20 grains each
Blades: 4 prongs
Available: five sizes to fit various arrow shafts: $20/64$, $21/64$, $22/64$, $23/64$, and $24/64$
SRP: per 2-pack. $3.00

Bohning Arrow Building Components

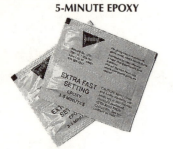

5-MINUTE EPOXY

ARROW HOLDER

UNIVERSAL ARROW PAD

STANDARD ARROW PAD

ARROW SHAFT SURFACE CLEANER (SSR)

ALCOHOL BURNER

ARROW CRESTING KIT

ARROW FLETCHING KIT

ARROW BUILDING COMPONENTS

Arrows are the objects of great interest, and prolonged despair, for some archersand bowhunters. Building your own arrows from components can bring a better understanding of arrow flight, energy and dynamics. From cutting the shafts to gluing on vanes and nocks, and from installing inserts to cresting with your special "brand," this is the equivalent of reloading for archers. Sometimes having your own arrow building components can also help you make quick repairs and put you back on the range or in your treestand in short order. Whatever level you decide to participate at, these products will help you meet your archery and arrow goals in style and with confidence. — MDF

BOHNING manufacturers numerous items to upgrade your arrows and to build them. This company also offers a wide assortment of dips and paints to crest arrows and create true flying works of art. This makes a great winter project. The Bohning Company is based in Lake City, Michigan, and can be reached at 800-253-0136 or visit www.bohning.com.

5-MINUTE EPOXY

Bonds points and inserts to all types of shafts. Available in easy-to-mix packets.
SRP: $4.45

ALCOHOL BURNER

This glass burner with a wick is excellent for hot melt adhesive applications. It uses denatured alcohol.
SRP: $11.61
extra wicks $1.00

ARROW CRESTING KIT

Use this complete package to crest aluminum, fiberglass or wooden arrows. A video takes you through the process step-by-step. Kit includes a standard crester, dip tube, Fletch-Lac thinner, six cresting colors, paint caddy, white lacquer, set of arrow hiolders, two camel hair brushes, shaft cleaner and the video.
SRP: $135.22

ARROW FLETCHING KIT

Bohning has done the shopping and assembling for you and created this kit that has everything you need to install nocks and inserts, plus attach fletchings. This kit includes an instructional video along with Fletch-Tite, Bond-Tite, Ferr-L-Tite, signature nocks, T nocks, 4- and 5-inch Fletch tite vanes, a Pro-Class fletching jig and shaft cleaner. Must specify right, left or straight clamps.
SRP: $72.58

ARROW HOLDERS

Used to dip multiple shafts at once, these racks fit all types of arrow shafts.
SRP: per dozen $30.61
per two dozen. $42.51

ARROW PADS

Use with the box to keep arrows organized and uniformly separated. The universal fits large and small diameter shafts, the standard size fits mid-range diameter shafts. Available in 100 packs.
SRP: $13.55

ARROW SHAFT SURFACE CLEANER (SSR)

This high-strength cleaner is designed for today's anodized process. It degreases and prepares aluminum and carbon shafts. Simple to use: add hot water to the powder and safely clean the shafts. Not intended for use on wood products.
SRP: pint $3.84
up to gallon. $16.21

Bohning Arrow Building Components

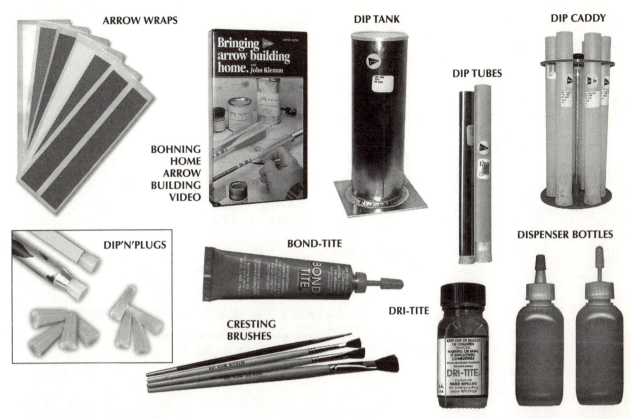

ARROW WRAPS

BOHNING HOME ARROW BUILDING VIDEO

DIP TANK

DIP CADDY

DIP TUBES

DIP'N'PLUGS

BOND-TITE

DISPENSER BOTTLES

CRESTING BRUSHES

DRI-TITE

BOHNING ARROW WARPS
Bohning's arrow wraps are available in traditional wraps, specialty wraps that include a screaming eagle, and wild wraps that include several tiger stripe patterns. These graphics are easy to install with the use of a mouse pad. Arrow wrap colors include white, yellow, orange, red green and pink. Must specify carbon or aluminum shafts.
SRP: per dozen $16.15

BOND-TITE
Bonds feathers, vanes and nocks to CARBON shafts. A waterproof, solvent-based formula. Offered in tubes, ½ pint, pint, quart, and gallon quantities.
SRP: ¾-ounce tube $2.67
to gallon $62.23

BOHNING HOME ARROW BUILDING
A step by step video guide on how to prepare, dip and fletch arrows. A must for anyone wanting to learn the process.
SRP: $18.19

CLAMP RELEASE TAPE
This special tape can be applied to the edge of the clamp to prevent adhesion build up and provide a quick clean-up.
SRP: $1.19

CRESTING BRUSHES
These quality camel hair brushes can be sued to paint lines on arrow shafts. Available in thin, ⅛-, ¼-, and ½-inch widths.
SRP: fine brush . . . . . $3.55 to $6.77

DIP CADDY
This rack by Bohning is great for Crown Dips and holds six 1-inch tubes.
SRP: $9.10

DIP'N PLUGS
Plugs to seal the ends of carbon and Uni-Bushing style shafts to prevent cresting paint from entering the end of the shaft. Available per dozen or 100 pack.
SRP: per dozen $3.60
per 100 . . . . $19.78

DIP TANKS
A convenient way and system to dip arrow shafts for cresting. The aluminum tube has a welded flat base to ensure solid performance. Specify 4- or 6-inch diameter.
SRP: 36-inch tank. . $46.18 to $61.59

DIP TUBES
Single tubes for dipping an arrow shaft. Length options include 12-, 24-, 32- and 34-inches.
SRP: 32-inch tube . . $7.93 to $14.82

DISPENSER BOTTLES
A great way to store and apply solvents and adhesives. The nearly clear bottles reveal how much mixture remains inside.
SRP: thinner $1.10
adhesiv $2.43

DRI-TITE
A waterproof dressing formulated for arrow feathers—and dry flies for fishing. It eliminates flattening and loss of body and it will not stiffen or add weight. The solution dries instantly and will not harm finishes. Available in a 1-ounce bottle and must be brushed onto the shaft
SRP: $4.58

ARROWS

Bohning Arrow Building Components

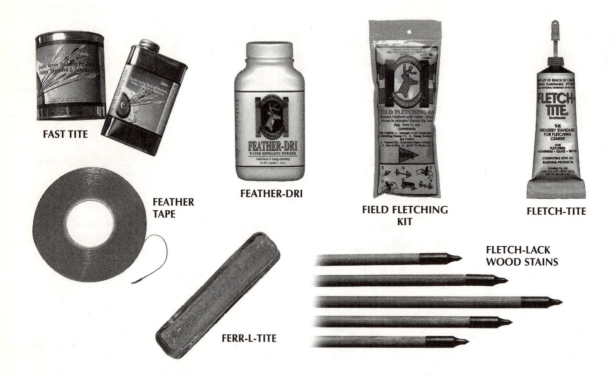

FAST TITE

FEATHER TAPE

FEATHER-DRI

FIELD FLETCHING KIT

FLETCH-TITE

FLETCH-LACK WOOD STAINS

FERR-L-TITE

FAST TITE

This water-repellent adhesion is used to quickly build arrows. Available in ½ pint, pint, quart and gallon sizes. Thinner is offered in pint, quart and gallon quantities.
SRP: ½ pint $7.13
gallon $62.23

FEATHER-DRI

A water repellant powder for feathers that is colorless and odorless and will not affect the fletch adhesion.
SRP: $6.42

FEATHER FLETCHING TAPE

This tape is easy to apply and creates a strong, reliable bond on contact. Can be used to fletch more than three dozen arrows.
SRP: roll $6.06

FERR-L-TITE

A stick of hot melt cement that's tough, elastic and waterproof. Can be used to adhere points and inserts to aluminum or wood shafts. Heat reversible. Specify stick or brick.
SRP: stick $2.22
pound brick $19.44

FIELD FLETCHING KIT

Make arrow vane and feather repairs in the field with this simple and easy to use kit. Includes everything you need to field repair 12 arrows including, fletching tool, 36 five-inch vanes, instant gel, 1 stick of Ferr-L-Tite and a dozen nocks.
SRP: $3.85

FINISH AND SOLUTION CONTAINERS

Use these containers to store and separate various cresting solutions. Sizes range from ½ pint to gallon plastic. 1-ounce and quart size glass containers are also available.
SRP: ½ pint $1.56
up to gallon container $2.97

FLAT WHITE

A dull base-coat finish to begin the cresting process. Available in ½ pint, pint, quart, gallon and 5-gallon quantities.
SRP: pint $12.78
to gallon $68.22

FLETCH-LAC BLUE AND CLEAR

This solution produces sharper, brighter colors. Can be sued to

seal wooden shafts or as a dip for aluminum shafts. Do not thin.
SRP: ½ pint $6.54
to gallon $52.14

FLETCH-LACK WOOD STAINS

Use these stains to tint raw wood shafts and bring out the natural grain as you customize the appearance of your arrows. Stain colors include shadow gray, rich mahogany, autumn glow, olive haze and walnut hue. Available in ½ pint, pint, quart and gallon quantities.
SRP: pint $7.18
up to gallon $57.37

FLETCH-TITE

A tube of glue that bonds feathers, vanes and nocks to aluminum, wood and fiberglass shafts. It's available in tubes or cans and in half-pint, pint, quart and gallon quantities.
SRP: ½ pint $6.06
to gallon $50.38

FLETCH TITE

A 2-ounce tube provides the same easy-application tip but a larger, economical size.
SRP: per 2-oz $5.31

ARROWS

Bohning Arrow Building Components

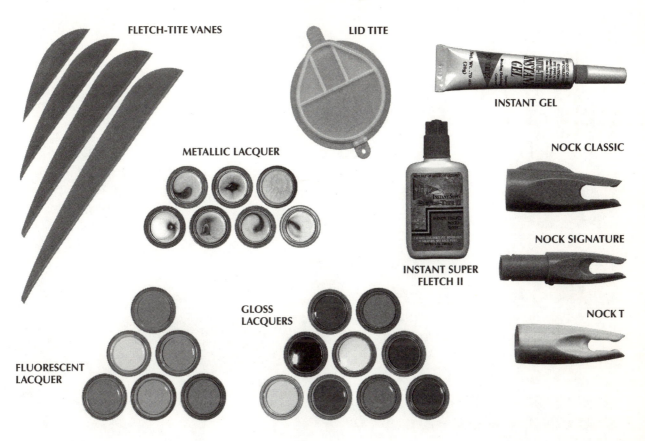

FLETCH-TITE VANES

LID TITE

INSTANT GEL

METALLIC LACQUER

NOCK CLASSIC

NOCK SIGNATURE

INSTANT SUPER
FLETCH II

NOCK T

GLOSS
LACQUERS

FLUORESCENT
LACQUER

FLETCH-TITE VANES
The base of these vanes are chemically treated to promote excellent adhesion. Must specify color and size. These vanes are offered in 36 packs, 100 packs and 1,000 packs for the archer with lots of arrows and friends. Sizes include 2-, 3-, 4- and 5-inch lengths. Colors include red, green, yellow, white, black, hot pink, teal blue, purple, orange, olive drab, bark brown, gray, dark green and several fluorescent colors.
SRP: 36 (4 and 5-inch only) . . . $2.77
per dozen $6.77

FLUORESCENT LACQUER
Add brilliant colors to your crests with these Bohning lacquers. Stabilized for long wear and life. Note: Must use a white base-coat under these colors. Options include; signal green, blaze orange, saturn yellow, rocket red, chartreuse, and aurora pink. Available in quantities from 1-ounce to one gallon.
SRP: ½-pint $10.80
to gallon $98.46

GLOSS LACQUERS
Bright true colors for cresting shafts and creating custom arrows. Easy to apply. Colors include: green, orange, purple, white, red, blue, burgundy, black and yellow.
SRP: ½-pint $7.91
to gallon $68.22

INSTANT GEL
This quick-setting gel can be used to install and repair fletching.
SRP: three gram tube $2.48
20-gram tube $9.17

INSTANT SUPER FLETCH II
An instant bond for nocks and vanes to aluminum, carbon or wood shafts. An anti-blush additive minimizes frosting.
SRP: per ounce $11.32

LID TITE
These self-sealing lids make pouring and storage of paints, adhesions and solvents a snap.
Specify quart or gallon container size

METALLIC LACQUER
Great for pin stripes and dips. Easy to apply and dries to a brilliant sheen. Make your arrows stand out in the crowd. Available in multiple quantities and colors: gold, plum, silver, jade, blue, pearl and copper.
SRP: ½-pint $9.08
to gallon $88.27

NOCKS
Bohning offers Signature, T and Classic nocks with the built-on mini vane in many sizes to fit a wide selection of shafts. Color options include: fluorescent lime, fluorescent apricot, fluorescent rose, fluorescent ruby, black, white, kiwi, mandarin, plum, yellow, green, gray, orange and red. Color selection varies by type of nock selected and not all colors are offered in all nock styles. For more details, call Bohning at 800-253-0136 or visit www.bohning.com.
SRP: Signature nocks, per doz.. $4.48
per 100 . . . . $18.18
T nocks, per 50 pack $4.30
Classic nocks, per 50 pack $4.30

ARROWS

Bohning Arrow Building Components

PAINT CADDY

STANDARD CRESTER

PRO CRESTER

NOCK OUT

POWER BOND

PRO-CLASS FLETCHING JIG

QUICK CURE EPOXY

UNIVERSAL ARROW BOX

NOCK OUT
A handy tool to assist with the removal or alignment of Signature nocks. This device will not damage the nocks.
SRP: **$1.68**

PAINT CADDY
A convenient and stable way to hold paints and brushes during the arrow cresting process.
SRP: **$7.28**

POWER BOND
The ultimate insert and point adhesion that works on all types of arrow shafts. This easy to use one-step adhesion works well on wrapped carbon applications and does not get brittle under any condition or temperature. Heat reversible. No mixing required and no mess to clean. Two drops cures in approximately 8 hours. One tube completes 300 to 400 hours.
SRP: per 2 oz. **$11.39**

PRO AND STANDARD CRESTER
This motor driven unit turns arrows up to 300 rpms and makes cresting easy and professional. A replacement chuck is available.
SRP: Standard **$102.01**
Pro **$140.73**

PRO-CLASS FLETCHING JIG
You can create a perfect fletch every time with this jig that uses a quick-set magnetic clamp adjustment. Vane and feather style options include straight, right or left helical. A crossbow bolt adapter costs $6.44.
SRP: **$54. 23**

QUICK CURE EPOXY
A double syringe with epoxy and cure that permanently bonds points or inserts to all types of shafts.
SRP: **$9.92**

SUPER COAT
A clear lacquer that cures to super hard finish. Use this as a one-coat sealer on wood shafts.
SRP: pint **$7.18**
up to gallon **$57.37**

THINNERS
These solutions (Fletch-Tite and Fletch-Lac) can be used to thin paints and various cresting solutions. Offered in quantities ranging from pint to a quart.
SRP: pint **$7.81**
to gallon **$34.36**

UNIVERSAL ARROW BOX
The industry standard arrow box that fits 34- or 336-inch shafts. This box is great for storing a dozen arrows.
SRP: 50 pack **$73.10**

Carbon Express Arrow Building Components

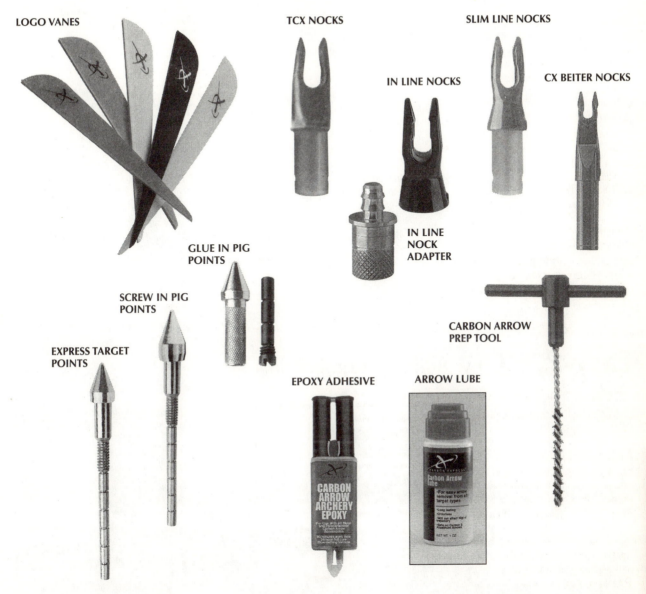

LOGO VANES

TCX NOCKS

SLIM LINE NOCKS

IN LINE NOCKS

CX BEITER NOCKS

IN LINE NOCK ADAPTER

GLUE IN PIG POINTS

SCREW IN PIG POINTS

CARBON ARROW PREP TOOL

EXPRESS TARGET POINTS

EPOXY ADHESIVE

ARROW LUBE

CARBON EXPRESS This Flushing, Michigan, based company offers components and full assembled ready to fletch shafts and ready for the range or hunt arrows with vanes. Call 800-241-4833 for more details and to order components.

CARBON EXPRESS LOGO VANES

These colorful—yellow, orange, green, white and black—vanes are available in 4-inch lengths and 100 per pack. They have the distinct Carbon Epxress logo and can be used on all carbon shafts.
SRP: 100 pack $18.92

COMPONENTS
per 6 units unless stated otherwise:
TCX NOCKS
  SRP: $5.40
IN LINE NOCKS
  SRP: $6.50
SLIM LINE NOCKS
  SRP: $4.50
  100 nocks $35.00
CX BEITER NOCKS
  SRP: per dozen $18.95
IN LINE NOCK ADAPTERS (TYPE 1)
  SRP: per dozen $6.50
IN LINE NOCK ADAPTERS (TYPE 2)
  SRP: per dozen $6.50
SCREW IN PIG POINTS
  SRP: per 12 pack $9.00

GLUE IN PIG POINTS
  SRP: per dozen $18.10
EXPRESS TARGET POINTS
  SRP: $21.70
INSERTS
  SRP: per 12 pack $5.34
SHAFT WEIGHTS (2- OR 3-GRAINS PER IN.)
  SRP: $10.50

MISCELLANEOUS ARROW CONSTRUCTION SUPPLIES
EPOXY ADHESIVE
  SRP: $12.58
ARROW LUBE
  SRP: $7.15
CARBON ARROW PREP TOOL
  SRP: $6.30

ARROWS

Easton Arrow Building Components

EASTON is based in Salt Lake City and is recognized as the leader in aluminum arrows. The company also offers components. Contact 801-539-1400 for more details and to obtain a free booklet.

ADHESIVES

HOT MELT FOR INSERT INSTALLATION
SRP: 3.30

EPOXY (AAE)
SRP: 12.40

FAST SET FLETCHING ADHESIVE GEL
SRP: (3grams) $6.23

NOCKS

Offered in black, white, green, red and yellow and in multiple styles and sizes. You must select a style to fit your arrow shaft.
SRP: per dozen $4.60
  specialty target per dozen . $12.93

SHAFTS

More than 19 models are offered, including carbon, carbon with aluminum cores and aluminum. Finishes range from black to camouflage and simulated wood grain.
SRP: aluminum target $32.76
  carbon $142.48

TOOLS

SUPER NOCK TOOL
SRP: $15.62

G NOCK TOOL
SRP: $15.62

ASSORTED NOCKS

Easy-Eye Arrow Building Components

EASY-EYE is headquartered in Allen, Michigan. (888-908-7446)

EZE-WRAPS

EZE-Eye offers more than 60 styles of arrow wraps to help you make your mark in style. The company's #401 Buck skull is a winner. Other arrow wrap options from Eze-Eye include: crests, fades, crest/fade combos, Elite wraps and X-treme graphics. Eze-Eye can also print custom wraps with your name on the wrap. The company makes a solid wrap that's highly visible in chartreuse, red, hunter orange, yellow and white.
SRP: per dozen . . . $10.00 to $12.00

SKULL GRAPHIC (DETAIL)

CREST

CREST/FADE COMBO

ELITE

FADE

XTREME TEAM USA

Flex-Fletch Arrow Building Components

FLEX-FLETCH PRODUCTS
This St. Paul, Minnesota, company makes more than a dozen target and hunting vanes. Colors and style vary widely and prices reflect current production and styles and lengths. Contact 651-426-4882 for pricing details.

G-5 Arrow Building Components

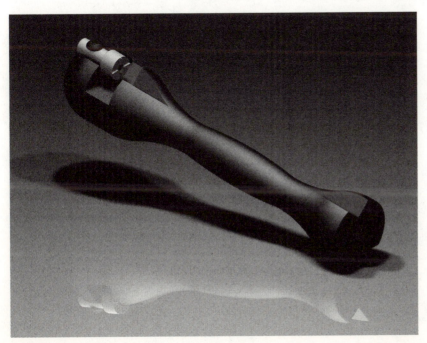

G5 This Memphis, Michigan, based manufacturer also makes broadheads and broadhead sharpeners.

ASD
The Arrow Squaring Device (ASD) by G5 is a tool that permits arrow builders and archers the ability to machine, clean and deburr the face of an insert or square the tip of the shaft for more accurate tip and broadhead alignment. This tool eliminates removing and re-gluing inserts and other steps to create an arrow that flies true. The ASD is offered in two models: one for aluminum shafts and one for carbon shafts. To operate, place the shaft in the groove and push the end of the shaft and face of the insert against the cutter and rotate the arrow shaft.
Replacement cutters are available.
SRP: aluminum **$34.99**
carbon **$36.99**

Gateway Feathers Arrow Building Components

GATEWAY FEATHERS This Douglas, Arizona company controls the quality and quantity of it feathers. Feathers are offered in 50 and 10 packs and 4 shapes, 9 sizes and 27 colors so every archer will find something to suit their taste. Sizes range from $1\frac{7}{8}$-inch to 12-inch full-length feathers. Visit www.gatewayfeathers.com for additional details.

Shapes include parabolic, shield cut, cut section, magnum and full length. Colors include white, red, chartreuse, desert brown, blue, gray, yellow, orange, pink, fluorescent yellow, black and green. Camouflaged feathers include tre brown, tre green, tre yellow, tre red, tre bark, tre purple, and tre orange. Barred feathers include white, red, green, brown, blue, yellow and orange. Must specify left or right feathers when ordering.

SRP: 4-inch parabolic, average
per 50 . . . . $16.50 - $18.99
4- or 5-inch feathers,
per 100 . . . . . . $30.00 to $35.00
Shield cut feathers, per 50 . . . $19.25
Full cut flu-flu-feathers,
per 50 . . . . $27.25

GREEN CAMO MAGNUM

GREEN CAMO PARABOLIC

GREEN CAMO SHIELD

WHITE BARRED MAGNUM

WHITE BARRED PARABOLIC

WHITE BARRED SHIELD

Fletching Size
A faster arrow can use a smaller fletch and remain stable. A slower arrow requires a larger fletch(which will make it even slower). Choose an optimum size that stabilizes the arrow over the longest distance you will have to shoot. Use the fletch size that maintains arrow speed long enough to reach the target but is as large as you can get away with for the most forgiving shot.

ARROWS

Gold Tip Arrow Building Components

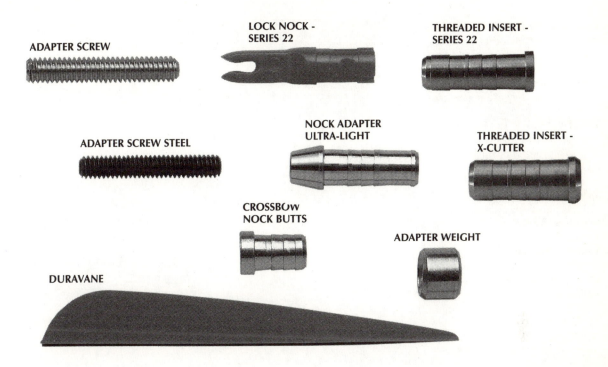

ADAPTER SCREW

LOCK NOCK - SERIES 22

THREADED INSERT - SERIES 22

ADAPTER SCREW STEEL

NOCK ADAPTER ULTRA-LIGHT

THREADED INSERT - X-CUTTER

CROSSBOW NOCK BUTTS

ADAPTER WEIGHT

DURAVANE

GOLD TIP These arrow-building components are available from Orem, Utah, based Gold Tip. The company is well known for its full line of carbon arrows.

ADAPTER SCREWS
These adapter screws help secure weights and nocks to the nock end of shafts. These adapters are available in aluminum (10-grain) and steel (30-grain) models.
SRP: per dozen $2.09
    per 120 . . . . $20.58

CROSSBOW NOCK BUTTS
These bolt inserts are available in three styles, including a 70-grain brass insert.
SRP: per dozen $2.73
brass, per dozen $4.13

DURAVANES
These durable field and range proven vanes are available in four lengths— 3-, 4-, 5- and 1.8 inch—to suit target archers and hunters. Available colors include: black, blue, brown, florescent green, florescent orange, florescent red, florescent yellow, gray, green, olive, orange, purple, red, white and yellow.

SRP: per 100 . . . . $6.93
1.8-inch vanes, per 100 . . . . . $9.73
3-D models, per 50 . . . . $9.73

GATEWAY FEATHERS
For archers who want forgiving feathers and performance. Available in: white, red, chartreuse, desert brown, blue, yellow, orange, pink, florescent yellow, black, green, and dimensional patterned bark, green, brown, yellow, orange, red and purple.Only available in 4-inch right wing parabolic format.
SRP: per 100 . . . . . $23.23 - $25.13

GOAT TUFF GLUE
Designed to help arrow vanes and feathers stick to shafts like a mountain goat does to a cliff. Available in assorted quantities.
SRP: 1oz, beginning at $5.25

LOCK NOCKS
These patented lockable nocks securely positions the nock without glues, epoxies or adhesives. Adjustments can be made quickly by loosening a small allen screw in the notch of the nock. Nocks are available in .246 (15 grain) and 22 Series (23

grain) Lock Nocks. Color choices include black, green, orange, pink, blue, white and yellow.
SRP: per dozen $5.53
    per 100 . . . . $34.95

NOCK ADAPTERS
Available models include Ultra-Light, .246, .22 series and X-Cutter nock adapters. All are designed to match the performance of Gold Tip shafts.
SRP: per dozen . . . . . $2.73 to $4.13

THREADED INSERTS
Gold Tip's threaded inserts are designed to complete the company's carbon/graphite shafts. Models include .246, 22 Series and X-Cutter. *Weight:* 47 grains each.
SRP: per dozen $2.73
    per 120 . . . . $26.53
X-Cutters . . . . per dozen $4.13

WEIGHTS
Six sizes and styles of adapter weights help archers fine tune arrow flight. Available weight in grains includes: 10, 20 and 40.
SRP: per dozen $2.09
    per 120 . . . . $20.58

Golden Key-Futura Arrow Building Components

GOLDEN KEY-FUTURA is located in Montrose, Colorado and makes rests, sights and a wide assortment of archery accessories. To order these items, or for more details, visit: www.goldenkeyarchery.com

BITZENBURGER FLETCHER

You can fletch your own arrows with this time proven fletching jig. You have a choice of straight, right wing or left wing clamps, plus standard or TM style nock receivers.

SRP: **$102**
Nock receivers **$27**

GRAYLING FLETCHER

A lighweight unit that puts on one fletch at a time with a special clamp.

SRP: **$44**

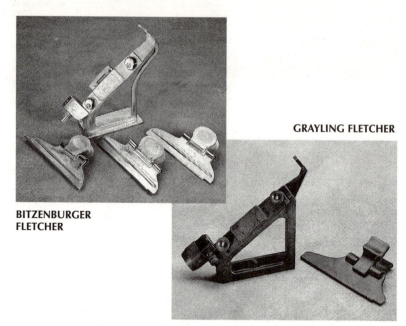

GRAYLING FLETCHER

BITZENBURGER FLETCHER

Muzzy Arrow Building Components

MUZZY The folks in Georgia who bring you Muzzy broadheads and the Zero-Effect arrow rest also offer arrow items and components for arrow building and repair.

MUZZY 10-MINUTE EPOXY

A two-part epoxy that's great for emergency field repairs and is suitable for permanent repairs of inserts and adapter, plus for gluing on broadheads and fishpoints. The epoxy sets in 10 minutes.

SRP: **$6.87**

MUZZY BUTANE TORCH

This 5½-inch tall torch is great for building arrows and shafts repairs. It can be filled with standard drug store butane and will burn for 2 to 3 hours on one refill.

SRP: **$29.27**

MUZZY BUTANE TORCH

MUZZY 10-MINUTE EPOXY

NAAG Arrow Building Components

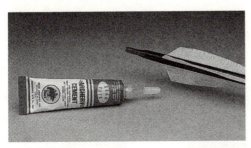

FLETCHING GLUE

NORTH AMERICAN ARCHERY GROUP (NAAG) in Gainesville, Florida, is also known for producing Bear, Golden Eagle, and Jennings bows.

ARROW NOCKS
High visible nock colors include red and orange. Available in sizes $5/16$ or $11/32$.
SRP: 12/pack. $3.49

ARROW NOCKS

FLETCHING GLUE
A tube or archery cement with applicator tip used to secure fletching to arrow shafts.
SRP: $3.49

QUICK DIP FOR ARROWS
Customize your arrows and also increase their visibility to increase recovery rate. Available in White, Fire, Fluorescent Yellow and Reflective White colors.
SRP: $11.99

PDP Arrow Building Components

5-DEGREE BROADHEAD ADAPTERS

GROOVY TOOL

CONVERTA INSERTS

PRECISION DESIGNED PRODUCTS (PDP) is based in Independence, Kansas, and in addition to its Converta field and target points used by archers everywhere, PDP also manufactures arrow shaft inserts and some tools for working on arrows.

5-DEGREE BROADHEAD ADAPTERS
A new lightweight design makes this adapter by PDP the same weight as an insert. Simply remove the insert and glue in the adapter to maintain the identical weight. A broadhead is easily attached to tapered and threaded shaft.
SRP: per dozen $6.75

CONVERTA INSERTS
All PDP inserts are stamped for permanent identification. Many sizes exist to fit all popular aluminum and carbon shafts.
SRP: per dozen . . . . $2.16 to $12.55

GROOVY TOOL
This innovative tool from PDP forms microscopic grooves inside many sizes of arrow shafts to help secure the insert in place and helps the glue grip the shaft. Never have points pull out again.
SRP: $27.90

Saunders Archery Arrow Building Components

SAUNDERS ARCHERY is located in Nebraska.

ADHESIVES
Saunders Archery has several types of adhesives:

NPV Cement $4.95
Five-Minute Epoxy $7.95
Carbon Mate Epoxy $8.95
Hunt-Bond Hot Melt $2.95

KWIK NOCK SYSTEM
These nocks have patented stepped alignment rings and can be purchased as a Uni-to Kwik nock adapter.

SRP: receivers $6.95
nocks per dozen $4.95

ROI INSERTS
Light-Speed inserts are 33% lighter than standard models. Heavy weigh versions provide more kinetic energy. Available in three styles with alignment rings.

SRP: per dozen $3.95

THE STRIPPER
A tool to remove fletching and glue from an arrow shaft in one easy stroke.

SRP: $11.95

FIVE-MINUTE EPOXY

CARBON MATE EPOXY

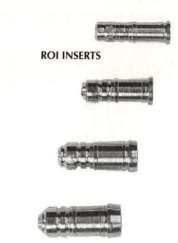

ROI INSERTS

NPV CEMENT

KWIK NOCK SYSTEM

Kwik Nock Receiver

Kwik Nock

THE STRIPPER

Sportsman Graphics Arrow Building Components

SPORTSMAN GRAPHICS BY DECALS-N-MORE is based in New Athens, Illinois and can be reached at 618-475-2300.

WRAP/CREST/TRAIL MARKER SERIES
The wraps offered by Sportsman Graphics include standard crests, reflecto-wraps, and a series that depicts white-tailed bucks, bull elk, wild boar, deer tracks, wild turkeys and monster bucks.

SRP: Standard crests, per 6 . . . $6.50
Reflecto-wraps, per 6 . . . . $6.85
Game animal series, per 6 . . . . $5.65

Steel Force Arrow Building Components

BEYOND BOND
ACCELERATOR

BEYOND BOND GLUE

BEYOND BOND COMBO

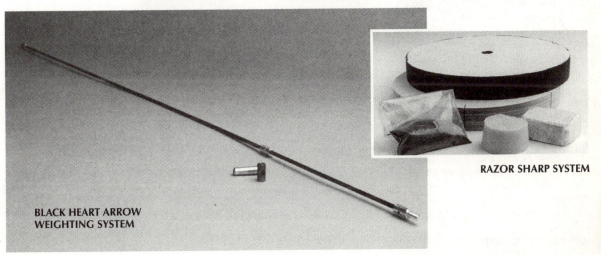

BLACK HEART ARROW
WEIGHTING SYSTEM

RAZOR SHARP SYSTEM

STEEL FORCE'S BEYOND BOND Steel Force is widely known for its serrated broadheads, and it also distributes fletching glues and accelerators, sharpening materials and arrow shaft weights. Steel Force is based in Rosemont, New Jersey.

BEYOND BOND ACCELERATOR
This accelerator speeds up the required drying time when building arrows. Spray onto the shaft before placing vane or feather into position.
SRP: 2 oz. $6.50

BEYOND BOND COMBO
This package has a bottle of Steel Forces Beyond Bond Glue and a bottle of Beyond Bond Accelerator for applying vanes and feathers to arrow shafts.
SRP: $10.50

BEYOND BOND HI-TECH GLUE
This incredibly strong high-tech glue signifantly erduces arrow building time and dries in minutes. To work best, you put glue on the feather or vane edge and spray accelerator on the arrow shaft. This glue is available in $\frac{1}{2}$ ounce and 2-ounce sizes with a resealable applicator tip bottle.
SRP: $\frac{1}{2}$-oz.. . . . . $4.95
2 oz. $12.95

BLACK HEART ARROW WEIGHTING SYSTEM
These carbon rods insert inside .245-inch inside diameter carbon arrows to add weight as needed and recommended when hunting dangerous game with bow and arrows. The weight does not affect arrow spine and center weights can be moved to change front of center percentage. The Steel Force special kit includes: three 32-inch carbon rods (can be cut to desired length), four adapters and a specially threaded insert rod.
SRP: per kit $28.50

RAZOR SHARP SYSTEM
This Steel Force broadhead sharpening kit features a special silicone carbide abrasive grit 8-inch wheel and a slotted wheel with a white rouge for create a perfect polisher/stropper like a barber shop. The kit includes additional sharpening grit, white rouge, conditioning grease and two 1x8-inch wheels that can be attached to a home arbor bench grinder.
SRP: per kit 24.95

Trueflight Arrow Building Components

TRUEFLIGHT MANUFACTURING COMPANY This Manitowish Waters, Wisconsin based company makes a wide array of feathers. Contact them at 715-543-8451 for additional details.

BARRED FEATHERS

These feathers have the distinct natural barrs in the feathers. Must specify left or right. Feathers. Color options include white, green barred, red barred, autumn brown barred, yellow-green barred, leaf green barred, orange barred, royal purple barred, chartreuse barred.

SRP: per 100 feathers

4-inch barred w/ rounded
  or shield back $46.45
5-inch barred w/rounded
  or shield back $49.20
Maxi-Fletch w/larger
  round back $52.05
Full length section so you
  can cut your own $48.10

FEATHERS

These solid colored pre-cut feathers are offered in: fluorescent white, pink, chartreuse, and scarlet red, sunshine yellow, blaze orange, kelly green, sky blue, shadow black, bronzed brown, autumn brown, leaf green, goose grey and royal purple. Must specify left or right feathers.

SRP: per 100 feathers

2½-inch round back. $16.70
3-inch round back $18.95
4-inch round back $25.10
5-inch round back $30.25
Maxi-Fletch larger feather . . . $35.05

Wet weather hunting
Plastic vanes on arrows are more forgiving on rainy days. Feather fletchings work well if treated with an odorless water repellant.

BARRED ROUND BACK

BARED SHIELD BACK

FULL BARRED FEATHER

FULL FEATHER

ROUND BACK

SHIELD BACK

ARROWS

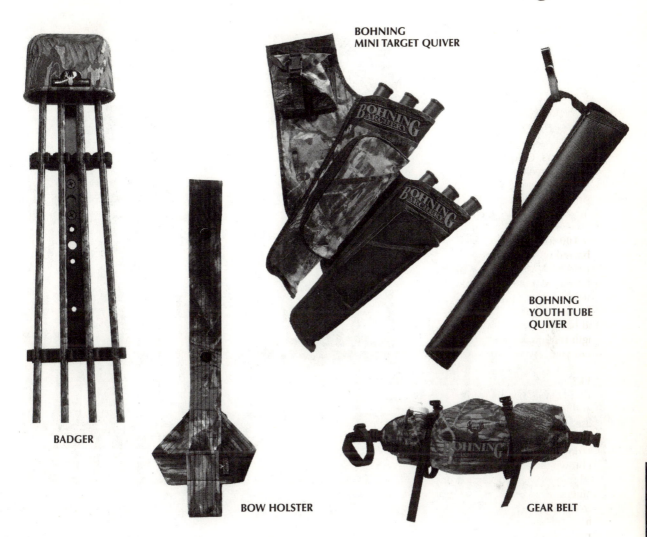

BOHNING
MINI TARGET QUIVER

BOHNING
YOUTH TUBE
QUIVER

BADGER

BOW HOLSTER

GEAR BELT

CONTROL YOUR ARROWS

Quivers are the ultimate in control for your errant arrows. It's difficult and sometimes dangerous to hold a group of arrows in your hand, thus quivers help you gain control of the situation. Whether you choose a hip, back or model that attaches to your bow, choose a quiver that meets your needs under a wide assortment of conditions. You have hundreds of models to choose from. Good luck in narrowing the field and may all your arrows soon be under control.—MDF

BOHNING
Badger
Similar to the Guardian but only designed to hold 4 arrows.
SRP: black. **$28.85**
camouflaged **$34.91**

Bow Holster
An easy snap adjustment helps you position this bow holder at the right height for quick access. The larger pocket holds single-cam bows with ease. Your bow is always in place in any hunting or shooting situation. Camouflaged in Mossy Oak Break Up.
SRP: **$6.35**

Target Quivers
These hip mounted quivers are made of durable and lightweight Cordura. These items are available in Mossy Oak and black and in LH and RH models. These quivers have three tubes and an external accessory pocket.
SRP: **$30.80**

Bowhunter's Gear Belt
This system will accept the Bohning target quiver. The belt has zippered

pockets to hold essentials, quick disconnect shoulder straps to make carrying a load more comfortable and extra straps to lash gear on the outside. A fully adjustable padded belt has a quick-disconnect system. The quiver is sold separately.
SRP: **$28.30**

Mini Target Quiver
A miniature adult version of the popular Bohning hip quiver. The quiver is 14-inches long with two arrow tubes. It's available in LH and RH and camouflaged.
SRP: **$17.92**

Youth Tube Quiver
Designed to hold smaller youth arrows for beginning target shooters.
SRP: **$9.38**

ARROWS

Guardian Quivers

GUARDIAN

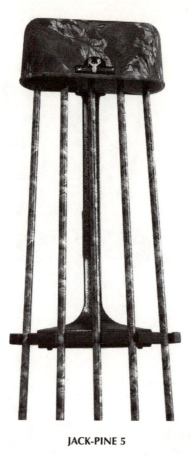

JACK-PINE 5

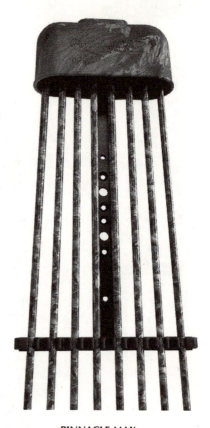

PINNACLE MAX

GUARDIAN

You can carry up to a half dozen aluminum or carbon arrows with this quiver. Mechanical broadheads can fit into the sound dampening hood liner. An aluminum stem secures the quiver sections together.

SRP: black. $29.54
camouflaged $36.20

Jack-Pine 5: 5-arrow quiver
  SRP: black. $12.56
  camouflaged $18.88
The Lynx: 4-arrow quiver
  Hood liner $3.75
  SRP: black. $16.96
  camouflaged $22.62
Pinnacle Lite: 5-arrow quiver
  SRP: black standard. $23.62

  camouflaged $28.32
Pinnacle Max: 8 arrow quiver
  SRP: black. $25.54
  camouflaged $30.14
Sentry: 3-arrow
  SRP: black. $11.87
  camouflaged $17.93

Overcoming Carbon Shaft Cling

Removing a carbon arrow, and the sometimes larger field point, can be a real chore. There are two solutions that work: Use a target made specifically for carbon shafts or try some of the new tips with the collars that make field point removal easier. —MDF

KWIKEE KOMPOUND KWIVER

KWIKEE COMBO QUIVER

KWIKEE 3

KWIKEE KWIVER

4-Arrow Kwikee Quiver for Recurves With hood to cover broadheads and an arrow gripping system that stays pliable in extreme temperatures. Ultra-Lock locking system for the attachment base and back-up knob to eliminate rattle and bracket noise. This set of gator-like jaws will grip the limbs of recurve and longbows. The grips fasten into place securely with permanently installed spring steel clips. Broadhead shield is included.

SRP: $18.99

Kwikee Combo Quiver
SRP: $24.99

Kwikee Kompound
SRP: $21.99
camouflage and colors. . . . $18.99

Kwikee 3
SRP: $19.99

Neet Quivers

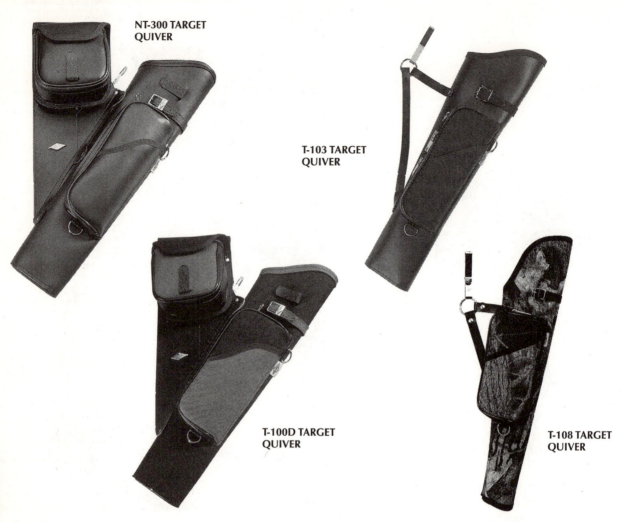

NT-300 TARGET QUIVER

T-103 TARGET QUIVER

T-100D TARGET QUIVER

T-108 TARGET QUIVER

NEET PRODUCTS

Neet has been crafting archery gear since LeRoy Young founded the company in 1956. The company produces quivers, cases, tabs, bow slings, traditional shooting gloves and other items. Many of the items are available in assorted colors. You have the option in most products of a quiver that is secured by a belt to your waist or an identical or similar product that clips to the belt.

Lined Leather Belt

Can be worn to held many of the Neet waist quivers. Sizes from 32 through 46 in even sizes and two-layer construction. Colors include black and burgundy.
SRP: $44.15

NT-300 Target Quiver

A stylish hip quiver with four arrow tubes, a large flap pocket and two zipped pockets. Includes two accessory clips. Cordura panels are available on some models and 9 colors are offered, including Advantage Timber and Mossy Oak Break Up.
SRP: camouflaged $49.35
NT-2100 Target Quiver
SRP: $51.85
NT-2300 Target Quiver
SRP: $70.52

T-100 Target Quiver

A waist quiver with a 19-inch body, three tubes and accessory clip and pencil tube.
Available in white and black vinyl and camouflaged Cordura models.
SRP: colors $24.65
camouflaged $30.25
T-100D Target Quiver
SRP: $44.95
   higher for camouflaged

T-103 Target Quiver

This hip quiver attaches to your waist with a loop and harness. This quiver has a 19-inch body, three 1½-inch diameter arrow separator tubes, a large accessory pocket and single belt clip attachment. Available in black, white and camouflage.
SRP: $19.95
camouflaged $24.40
T-104 Target Quiver
SRP: $12.85
   higher for camouflaged

T-108 Target Quiver

This hunting oriented hip quiver has an 18-inch body, a zippered pocket, arrow divider strap and is offered in right- and left-hand models. It's available in Advantage, Mossy Oak and black.
SRP: $15.85
camouflaged $17.45

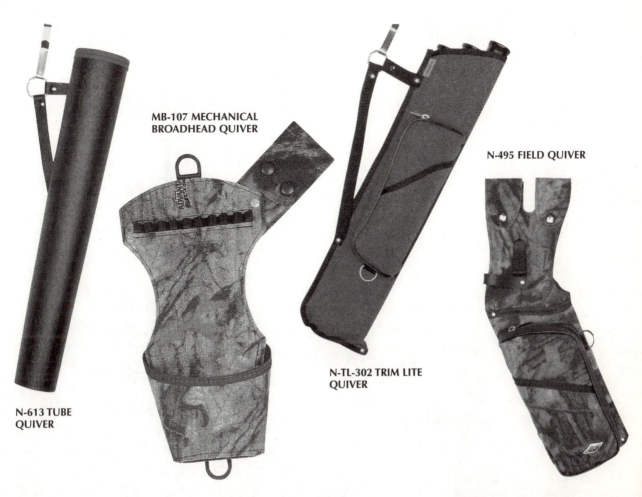

MB-107 MECHANICAL BROADHEAD QUIVER

N-495 FIELD QUIVER

N-TL-302 TRIM LITE QUIVER

N-613 TUBE QUIVER

N-613 Tube Quiver
This hip quiver has a17-inch vinyl body, 3-inch opening and single belt attachment. It is black with optional trims in red, blue and gray smoke.
SRP: $6.75
N-615 Tube Quiver
SRP: $5.75

MB-107 Mechanical Broadhead Quiver
This Neet Quiver has two molded arrow holders that will suspend four arrows. The swivel belt loop makes left to right-hand conversion simple. A firm center stave aids with arrow support. This quiver is camouflaged and comes with a web belt and adjustable web strap.
SRP: $34.95

N-495 Field Quiver
A quiver with a trim body design, snap over belt loops and arrow divider strp. It has a large storage pocket.
SRP: $21.95

N-500 Field Quiver
This Neet quiver is designed for filed use and keeps the arrows higher on your body and closer to reach. The quiver includes an accessory clip, large 8-inch zippered pocket and arrow divider. It's available in RH and LH, and in black, Advantage and Mossy Oak.
SRP: $21.95
    higher for camouflaged
N-491 Field Quiver
SRP: $18.45

Trim Lite Quivers
N-TL-301 Trim Lite Quiver
This hip quiver has two exterior pockets, is 19-inches deep and has three arrow separator tubes. It's available in RH and LH and in black, red, blue, Advantage and Mossy Oak Break Up.
SRP: $21.95
    higher for camouflaged
N-TL-302 Trim Lite Quiver
SRP: $16.75
camouflaged $18.45

N-TL-304 Trim Lite Quiver
SRP: $11.55
N-TL-400 Trim Lite Quiver
SRP: standard $46.85
camouflaged $48.50
N-TL-401 Trim Lite Quiver
SRP: $42.65
camouflaged $45.25
N-TL-404 Trim Lite Quiver
SRP: $16.25

NY-109 Target or Field Quiver
A quiver that's designed for young shooters with a 15-inch quiver body and snap over belt attachment system. It's available in RH and LH and black, camouflage and black with red, blue or gray smoke trim.
SRP: $22.65
    higher for camouflaged models

ARROWS

Arrow Accessories Quivers

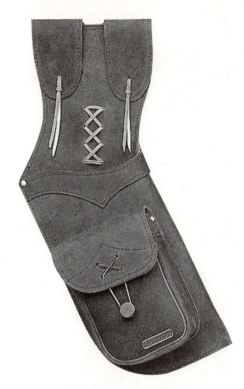

T-2595 FIELD QUIVER

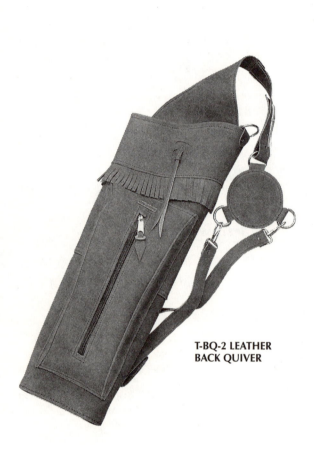

T-BQ-2 LEATHER
BACK QUIVER

T-108 Target Quiver

This model is made for young archers and clips to your belt and has an exterior storage pocket. Available in assorted colors and camo patterns.

SRP: **$15.65**
    higher for camouflaged models

T-BQ-2 Leather Back Quiver

A traditional quiver constructed of leather. This quiver is 22-inches long has a zippered accessory pocket and an arrow tube to separate arrows. It features and adjustable shoulder strap and brass plated buckles.

SRP: **$92.60**
T-BQ-3 Medium Back Quiver
    SRP: **$73.55**
T-BQ-20 Economy Back Quiver
    SRP: **$61.55**
T-BQ-30 Med Economy Back Quiver
    SRP: **$38.45**

T-2595 Field Quiver

A waist-worn hip quiver that is short in design to keep arrows close to your body. It features brass rivets, hand lacing and straps to look authentic. It's offered in LH and RH models and in burgundy leather or honey brown suede leather.

SRP: **$44.75**

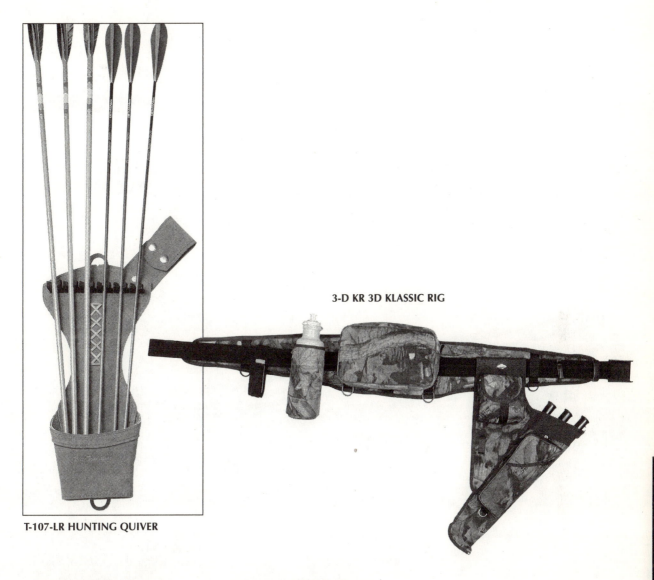

3-D KR 3D KLASSIC RIG

T-107-LR HUNTING QUIVER

T-107-LR Hunting Quiver
This Neet traditional style quiver has a swiveling belt loop to permit right- or left-hand use and a molded arrow holder securely holds six carbon or aluminum arrows. It has leather D-rings on the top and bottom to permit hanging it in a treestand.
SRP: $49.25

3-D KR 3D Klassic Rig
A system based on a foam padded support belt and the rig includes the quiver, a 2-inch wide accessory belt, fanny pack, water bottle and bow rest. Its available in LH and RH models and black, Navajo, and camouflage.
SRP: $106.25
3-D SR Standard Rig
SRP: $78.85

ARROWS

Arrow Accessories Quivers

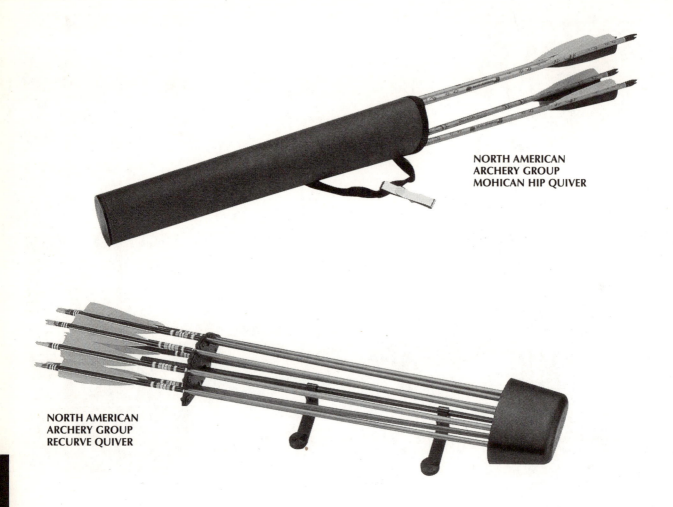

NORTH AMERICAN
ARCHERY GROUP
MOHICAN HIP QUIVER

NORTH AMERICAN
ARCHERY GROUP
RECURVE QUIVER

ARROWS

NORTH AMERICAN ARCHERY GROUP

Mohican Hip Quiver
Clips to your belt and brown simulated leather padded tube holds many full-length arrows.
SRP: **$6.49**

Recurve Quiver
A quiver designed to securely hold up to 6 arrows, and it attaches to a recurve bow. Offered in black only.
SRP: **$44.99**

Never Dry Fire
Never dry fire a bow—period. Without an arrow nocked and absorbing the energy, a bow's energy is transferred to its limbs, cables and cams. This can cause the bow to explode and seriously injure the shooter and anyone nearby.--MDF

RELEASE AIDS

RELEASE AIDS

Release Aids

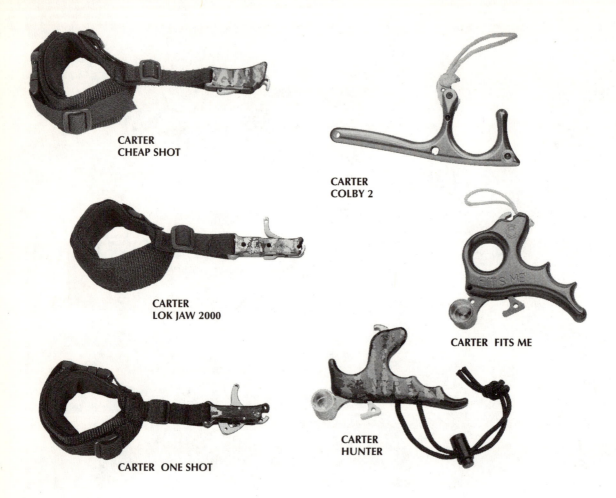

CARTER
CHEAP SHOT

CARTER
COLBY 2

CARTER
LOK JAW 2000

CARTER FITS ME

CARTER ONE SHOT

CARTER
HUNTER

RELEASE AIDS

Release aids have far out-paced the use of fingers in the archery world. They provide several key benefits and yield much smoother releases when used properly. The styles and price ranges are nearly limitless today and more models are released, excuse the pun, each year.

A good bowhunting tip that hits home with many hunters: If you use a release aid, pack an extra one in your fanny pack or daypack, or at least have one in your vehicle. When you loose this item, it's nearly impossible to make a smooth release with fingers after relying on a release aid unless you have practiced extensively. Good bowhunting and shooting. –MDF

CARTER

The housing of Carter's release aids are CNC machined from 6061 T6 aluminum and the internal pieces are CNC machined from cold roll steel and then case hardened. Each release is hand assembled and tested be fore leaving the factory. The company manufacturers a wide assortment of hunting and target releases.

Cheap Shot

This Carter hunting release aid has a wrist strap and an open (metal) jaw or closed (rope) jaw design. The closed jaw can shoot with the string, with a D-loop or with the attached rope. The wrist strap has multiple adjustments for a secure and comfortable fit.

SRP: black. **$58.99**
camouflaged **$63.99**

Lok Jaw 2000:
(Index finger release – 3/8-inch jaw. Adjustable trigger, fall-away release, open or closed jaws, and either Velcro or a super buckle wrist strap)

SRP: narrow jaw **$68.99**
Standard **$73.99**

One Shot:
(Index finger release. Jaw lock and thumb safety)

SRP: black. **$93.99**
camouflaged **$98.99**

Colby 2

This chrome release aid has a straight handle, and is offered in a hinged or spike version. Use it with the D-loop or rope.

SRP: **$104.99**

FitsMe

A Carter release that's designed to fit small to medium sized hands. It has a center hole and rope string catch.

SRP: **$153.99**

Hunter

This Carter release aid has a double sear, open jaw design and a d-loop hook. A lanyard secures the release to your wrist to prevent loss in the field.

SRP: **$153.99**

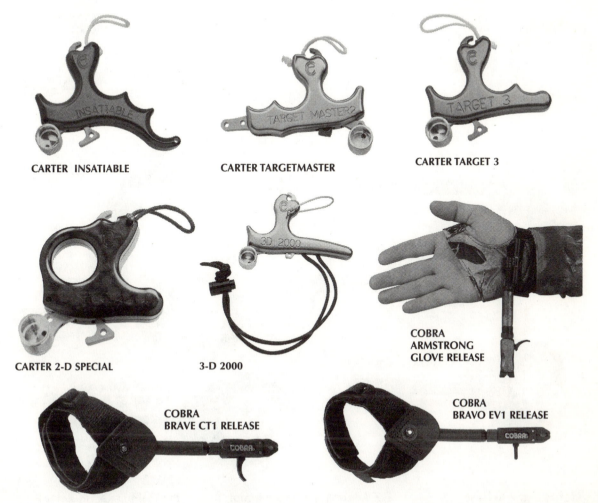

CARTER INSATIABLE

CARTER TARGETMASTER

CARTER TARGET 3

CARTER 2-D SPECIAL

3-D 2000

COBRA
ARMSTRONG
GLOVE RELEASE

COBRA
BRAVE CT1 RELEASE

COBRA
BRAVO EV1 RELEASE

Insatiable
This T-style hand-held release has finger grooves and smooth round edges. The arched handle helps place the elbow at a more natural position for better control while shooting.
SRP: **$153.99**

Target Master
This T-style release is hand held and has smooth handle, plus it can be shot with either the thumb or little finger with the simple adjustment of a set screw.
SRP: **$158.99**

Target 3
This Carter three-finger release allows you to drop your little finger off the release. A loop attaches to an enclosed jaw to hold the bow's string.
SRP: **$153.99**

3-D 2000
This release aid has a closed jaw to hold the loop and an open style, smooth handle to fit any hand. The wide separation between the index finger and middle finger creates a solid anchor. The release is supplied with a lanyard and is drilled and tapped for accessories.
SRP: **$153.99**

2-D Special
You'll remember this release aid when you see its odd design, but it is one of the most torque free aids on the market. It is available in ½- or ⅝-inch thickness and has a two-finger design.
SRP: **$153.99**

COBRA
This Bixby, Oklahoma, based manufacturer produces release aids, sights and stabilizers that are enjoyed by many archers. All Cobra release heads rotate 360-degrees and come with a lifetime warranty.

Armstrong Glove Release
The swing-away module swivels 360 degrees and the over-the-thumb glove is leather lined and covered with a Saddle Cloth camouflaged exterior. The extension and head are camouflaged also. This release is available in right-hand only and in two sizes.
SRP: **$38.56**

Brave CT1 Release
(Curved gun-style trigger)
SRP: **$17.50**

Bravo EV1 Release
Has a padded loop lock strap and peg trigger on the side of the black anodized release head. This release has distinctive COBRA gold letters.
SRP: **$17.50**

RELEASE AIDS

Release Aids

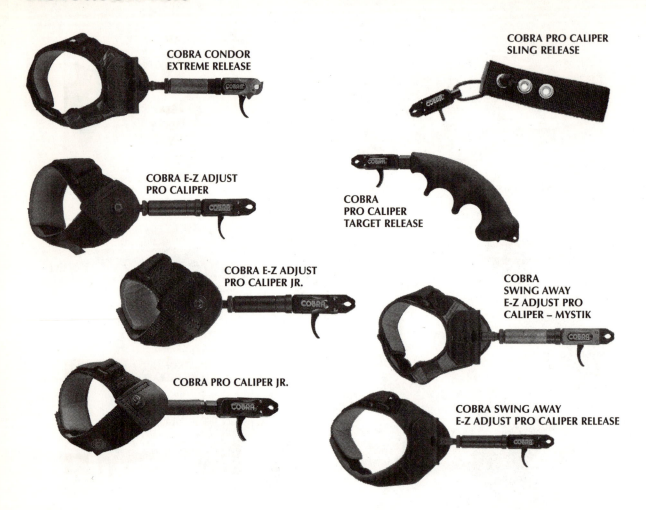

COBRA CONDOR
EXTREME RELEASE

COBRA PRO CALIPER
SLING RELEASE

COBRA E-Z ADJUST
PRO CALIPER

COBRA
PRO CALIPER
TARGET RELEASE

COBRA E-Z ADJUST
PRO CALIPER JR.

COBRA
SWING AWAY
E-Z ADJUST PRO
CALIPER – MYSTIK

COBRA PRO CALIPER JR.

COBRA SWING AWAY
E-Z ADJUST PRO CALIPER RELEASE

Condor Extreme Release
A release designed for loop bowstring shooters with an Extreme Wing on the release jaws that's easy to open with one finger. Self-loading internal springs allow you to close the release with one finger. A swing away module on the wrist strap rotates 360 degrees. The head is the E-Z adjust module that requires no tools and features a gun-style trigger. This release is available in black and Mystik.
SRP: black. **$30.99**
   Camouflage. **$34.99**

E-Z Adjust Pro Caliper
This release by Cobra requires no tools to adjust and has a padded loop wrist strap. The black anodized head has a gun-style trigger. A replacement wrist strap is available
SRP: **$23.50**

E-Z Adjust Pro Caliper Junior
  (Reduced length designed to fit women and youth)
  SRP: **$21.99**
Pro Caliper Jr.
  SRP: **$18.78**

New Generation Release
The New Generation is a swing-away model by Cobra with a release head that swivels 360 degrees. The module needs no tools for adjustment, and the black anodized release head has a gun-style trigger. The wrist collar is padded.
SRP: **$28.99**

Pro Caliper Sling Release
This is a basic release by Cobra with an adjustable sling strap that fits around the wrist. A string attaches the black anodized release head to the strap. A peg activates the precision machined center release jaws on the release head.
SRP: **$14.20**

Pro Caliper Target Release
This Cobra target release features an ergonomic grip with grooved finger slots while it rests inside a closed hand. It has a black anodized head and curved gun-style trigger.
SRP: **$21.82**

Swing Away E-Z adjust Pro Caliper–Mystik
A release that features an extension and release head in Mystik camouflage. Swing away base on the wrist strap that permits the extension and release to move out of the way while your are performing chores such as climbing to a treestand. The head rotates 360 degrees and has gun-style trigger.
SRP: **$30.99**

Swing Away E-Z Adjust Pro Caliper Release (Black only)
SRP: **$28.93**

**COPPER JOHN
EAGLE SERIES
HUNTING RELEASE**

STAN

GOLDEN KEY CASCADE #8

**GOLDEN KEY
ANSWER ANTI-PUNCH RELEASE**

GOLDEN KEY CASCADE #10

GOLDEN KEY ER-300

GOLDEN KEY AUTO-X

COPPER JOHN
Copper John is based in Auburn, New York and makes release aids, the Dead Nuts sights and arrow rests.

Eagle Series Hunting Release
This Copper John release has a wrist strap and trigger, plus an unique trigger clamp that settles around your index finger. It's offered with two, three and four-finger versions.
SRP: standard **$59.95**
   swept handle **$69.95**

STAN
These release aids are held between the fingers with a comfortable handle. Two, three and four finger models are available. Some models can be micro-adjusted. The original version has brass tip set screws and 440 stainless steel components. The newer models have thumb activation.

SRP: Original **$64.95**
   Micro adjust model **$135.00**

GOLDEN KEY-FUTURA
This manufacturer is located in Montrose, Colorado, and makes rests, sights and many archery accessories.

Answer Anti-Punch Release
The Answer can be adjusted into three shooting modes. Mode one prevents a quick punch release, mode 2 lets you deactivate the quick punch block and Mode 3 lets you shorten the trigger travel and by-pass the anti-punch option. This release has two jaws that are activated by a trigger and a lined leather wrist strap.
SRP: **$172.50**

Auto-X
An adjustable, precision made release by Golden Key-Futura that releases

through back tension to prevent punching or the unit can be adapted to a thumb release. The release has a leather wrist strap.
SRP: **$90**

Cascade #8
A T-shaped release that is CNC machined with tight tolerances. The release occurs when the trigger is relaxed, instead of when pushed. The black handle is secured to the wrist by a comfortable strap.
SRP: **$186.30**

Cascade #10
SRP: **$201.25**

ER-300
An all metal release with a loop cord to capture the bowstring. The T-handle is attached to a wide, leather wrist strap.
SRP: **$40**

Release Aids

GOLDEN KEY HIDE AWAY CALIPER RELEASE

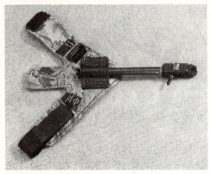

GOLDEN KEY SHARPSHOOTER

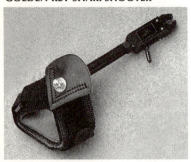

FLETCHER 3-D

FLETCHMATIC

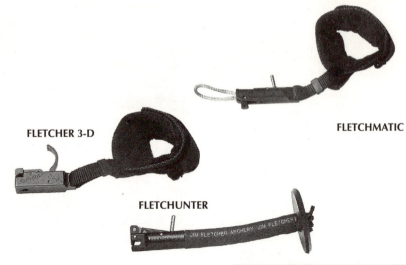

FLETCHUNTER

GOLDEN KEY TOP GUN CALIPER RELEASE

FLETCHMATIC TR

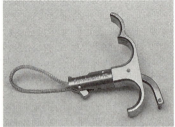

Hide Away Caliper Release

A quality, smooth shooting release with a precision adjustable head designed to retract into the strap and free up your hands when the release is not needed. This double jawed release has a camouflaged wrist strap and black anodized head with GKF logo on it. A Hide Away release wrist strap kit can be used to turn any GKF Answer or Top Gun release into a Hide Away style release.
SRP:. $75

Sharpshooter

Metal double jawed head and trigger-like prong release activator. It is offered in numerous styles with a buckle or web strap, and with an advanced strap, camouflaged strap and smaller strap for youth and ladies.
SRP: standard. $28
    camouflaged $30
    youth style. $35

Top Gun Caliper Release

This release aid is constructed with CNC machined components and can be adjusted for trigger activation speed. A comfortable black nylon wrist strap fits all sizes. The REL-2600 Model has a hide-away strap and adjustable length from wrist to fingers.
SRP: $109.25

JIM FLETCHER ARCHERY AIDS

The Fletchunter and Fletchmatic are some of the industries best known releases.

Fletcher 3-D

This release has a wide jaw with a smooth radius to eliminate string serving wear. The design is extremely accurate and forgiving in nature. The trigger is fully adjustable and the wrist strap keeps the unit in pale and ready to use. The self-locking head is anodized hunter green.
SRP:. $75

Fletchunter

This clip-on style release fastens directly to the bowstring and does not damage the serving thanks to smooth and rounded jaw edges. The over-center linkage system is fully adjustable from hair to heavy and comes in three models: The concho, the wrist strap and the swivel grip concho. The Fletchunter has a black anodized finish.
SRP: concho. $55
    wrist strap $60
    deluxe wrist strap. $70

Fletchmatic (Release uses a rope ring to wrap around the string)

SRP: concho. $55
    wrist strap $60
    deluxe wrist strap. $70

Fletchmatic T-Models

The Fletcher T-Models secure the bow-string with a rope loop and are used primarily by indoor and target archery enthusiasts. The TR unit has a three-finger handle with a thumb activated trigger. The FF unit is three finger held with a fourth finger activation. Both units feature over center hardened steel rollers, comfortable machined handles and fully adjustable triggers. These units have a gold anodized finish.
SRP:. $70

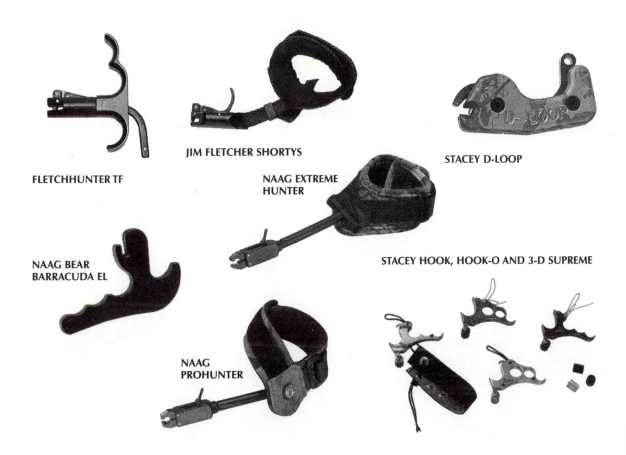

FLETCHHUNTER TF

JIM FLETCHER SHORTYS

NAAG EXTREME HUNTER

STACEY D-LOOP

NAAG BEAR BARRACUDA EL

STACEY HOOK, HOOK-O AND 3-D SUPREME

NAAG PROHUNTER

Fletchhunter T-Models

Similar to the Fletchmatic models, these releases use a steel jaw to secure the string. A third style in this series is the two-finger handle that can be used a thumb or third finger release. These units are anodized in hunter black.
SRP:. $70

Shortys

These Fletcher releases feature the Fletchunter (jaw) and the Fletchmatic (rope loop) attachment systems. The shorty is designed to fit a wide array of hand sizes and is comfortably secured to the wrist with a wide strap. The release head is similar to the other Jim Fletcher Archery Aid models.
SRP:. $70

North American Archery Group
Bear Barracuda EL

This economical hand-held, molded release has an adjustable trigger. This is an entry- level item.
SRP: $6.49

ProHunter Release

A wrist-strap release featuring a camouflaged Velcro strap, a 360-degree swivel head and adjustable trigger and dual jaws.
SRP: $19.99

Xtreme Hunter Release

This release features a 360-degree swivel head (like the Prohunter), adjustable trigger and enlarged wrist strap with comfort ribs. It has a camouflaged strap.
SRP: $24.99

Stacey Archery Sales

This Idaho-based manufacturer builds many styles of hand-held release aids, plus six styles of wrist straps with a buckle or double Velcro locking system to keep it on your wrist. The company is also known for its innovative youth bows that have all the shapes and designs like adult models.

D-Loop

Similar to Stacey's Two- and Four-Play models in style and appearance but it's designed to clip directly the bow string or rolled shut on and shot with a string loop. This model is shot only with the index finger pressure.
SRP: $79.95

Hook, Hook-O and 3-D Supreme

These Stacey creations deliver tight tolerances through CNC machining of an aluminum shell while the inner parts are machined from steel which is then case hardened and nickel plated. Each release has a travel adjustment and can be adjusted to hair-trigger lightness. All releases operate quietly and are available in: blue, silver, red, gold, purple and camouflage finishes. These releases fit over the fingers with rings. Adjustable barrel triggers give more flexibility in feel and angle of the trigger for the shooter. These will fit most popular brands of releases and provide up and down adjustment along with 360-degree rotation adjustment.
SRP: releases only $109.95

Release Aids

STACEY TWO- AND FOUR-PLAY

T.R.U. TENSION

T.R.U. CHAPPY BOSS

T.R.U. T-HANDLE PRO DIAMOND

T.R.U. SWEET SPOT

T.R.U. THE XTREME

Two- and Four-Play

These hand-held release aids can be used as a forefinger or thumb release system and rope or clip-on The Four-Play will shoot by: index pressure clip on, thumb relaxation clip-on, index finger pressure as a rope and thumb relaxation as a rope. Shooter can change system to determine best option. Other features include case-hardened inner parts, durable aluminum outer case, thumb safety and an angles string slot which lines up for a perfect release at full draw.
SRP: **$79.95**

T.R.U. BALL (TOMORROW'S RESOURCES UNLIMITED)

T.R.U. Ball is located in Madison Heights, Virginia, and produces more than 150 models of releases. Their products are very popular on the archery tournament circuits, and some models have string releases and other models have jaws. Hand grip and wrist strap versions are available in a wide variety of styles, sizes and colors.

The company also sells repair and replacement parts, plus release wrist straps and firing pins. Hats with the company's distinctive flame logo are also available.

T-HANDLE RELEASES BY T.R.U. BALL

Chappy Boss

Features no load up, firm triggers even after the release and a travel adjust-ment screw. The Chappy Boss also features a sensitivity adjustment screw and three-piece adjustable trigger. This release has been proven in tourna-ment victories everywhere and by hunters. The King George and Little Boss have thumb release options and are similar to the Chappy Boss. The Pinky Boss has pinky finger release capabilities only. All are available with standard caliper jaw, single- and double-ball jaws and talon rope head options. Available colors include black, blue and red.
SRP: . . . . **$151.99 to $164.99**

Hunting T-Handles

These releases are the hunting version of T.R.U. Ball's tournament proven hand-held releases. The Pro Diamond is ultra-quiet, has an adjustable trigger and can fasten to your bowstring while you wait in your treestand. It holds three patents for innovation and design features. The Thumb Pull model is has a loop for your thumb, the T-Handle Thumb Push utilizes a push lever to activate the release and the Pinky Pull has a lever that is operated by applied pressure by the shooter's pinky finger. All releases are available with the four common jaw options and in the three standard colors.
SRP: . . . . **$64.99 to $98.99**

Sweet Spot

This release has a string that wraps around your bow's string and locks into a small finger on the release's head. Four models are available: Ultra 4, 4 Spot, Ultra 3 and Ultra 2. The free-floating head permits you to shoot up and down hills without compromising string travel. The grips can be held with 4 to 2 fingers to ensure complete shooter comfort and control. Available colors for the Sweet Spots are black, red and blue.
SRP: **$164.99**

T.R.U. Tension

This is a T-type, in-the-fingers release that uses a wrap around double string to secure your bow's string. The release's head rotates on the same plane as the handle. Different configurations—four models avail-able—provide secure feel and control for any shooter's demand. Available colors include black, blue and red.
SRP: **$49.99**

The XTreme

This hand-held release is available with a standard caliper jaw, single or double ball, and talon rope head release system. The Extreme provides $7/16$ more draw length and features open, comfortable finger grooves. Available colors include black, blue and red. The Little XTreme, Pinky XTreme and King George XTreme are in the XTreme family line and offer smaller grips, thumb or pinky release options and caliper jaws, rope or ball jaws to grip the string.
SRP:. . . . . **$151.99 to $164.99**

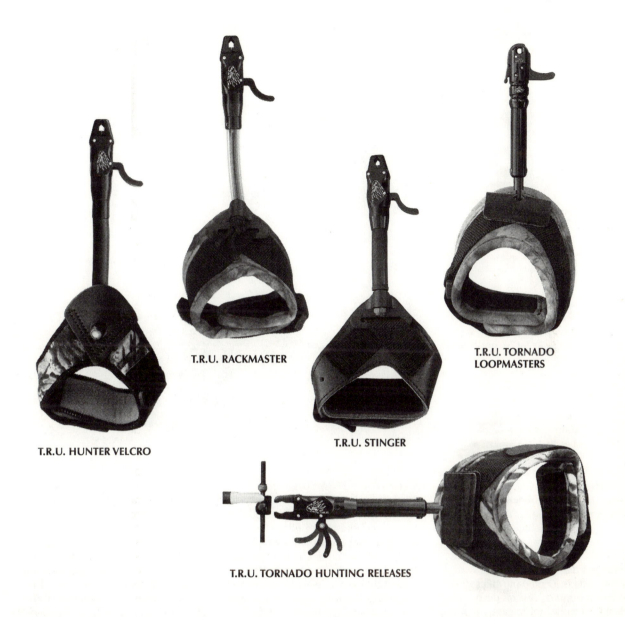

T.R.U. HUNTER VELCRO

T.R.U. RACKMASTER

T.R.U. STINGER

T.R.U. TORNADO LOOPMASTERS

T.R.U. TORNADO HUNTING RELEASES

WRIST STRAP RELEASE AIDS

Hunter Velcro

The standard caliper jaws or single- and double-ball jaw options with this release provide selection options to fit the tastes of any archer with T.R.U. Ball's Hunter series. The head rotates 360 degrees and attaches to the wrist strap with a rod. These releases are available with Velcro closures only and in several styles.

SRP: . . . . **$50 to $65**

Rackmaster

Torque-free rope connection from the wrist strap to the jaws. Versions include standard caliper jaws, single- and double-ball jaws and LoopMaster head. Black leather or camouflage cloth wrist straps are available.

SRP: . . . . **$39.99 to $52.99**

Stinger

Solid rod attaches jaws to the wrist strap, 360-degree swivel movement. Stinger Velcro has camouflaged wrist strap. Stinger Buckle incorporates buckle closure with black leather wrist strap. Both releases use standard T.R.U. Ball caliper jaws.

SRP: **$32.99**

Tornado Hunting Releases

Rotating and swiveling heads, closed-cell wrist strap has a 4-way adjustable trigger (Deluxe) or no-travel trigger (Accu-Touch) Independently operated funnel shaped jaws

SRP: . . . . **$69.99 to $164.99**

Tornado LoopMasters

360-degree rotating head. Wrist straps available in Velcro or buckle closures. Works with all jaw releases.

SRP: . . . . **$64.99 to $81.99**

RELEASE AIDS

Release Aids

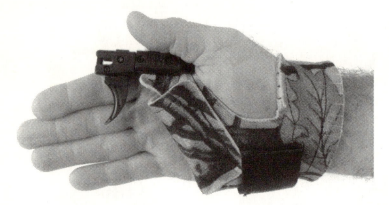

WINN C-10

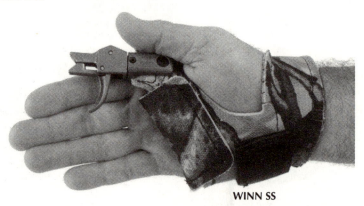

WINN SS

WINN ARCHERY

Winn Archery has been making releases for more than 20 years at its South Haven, Michigan, facility. The company's releases are made to fit securely within your hand and are attached to a glove-like base with a wrist cuff. The company takes great pride in building releases that are designed to last through years of use.

C-10

The release head and the trigger are crafted from solid hardened steel. The trigger has adjustable pull and travel features. The glove is built with 8 ounces of leather and reinforced with a Cordura overlay to prevent stretching. This release is available in X-small youth sizes through X-large adult sizes with right- and left-hand models.
SRP: **$55.50**

C-12 (Relaxed trigger release. Uses the standard Winn replacement glove)
SRP: **$55.50**

SS

This release by Winn Archery uses the company's glove base and has a solid stainless steel "Free Flight" caliper mechanism with large, easy-loading jaws that are easy on the string's serving. The trigger is adjustable and does not use springs, the trigger must be held forward at the beginning of the draw. This release will use the standard Winn replacement glove.
SRP: **$59.50**

Arrow release
Using a mechanical release will tighten your grouping of arrows to 2 to 3-inches in diameter. A mechanical release provides a more perfect and even release. When you use three fingers to hold back the string, your release will not be as crisp as with a mechanical release.

RELEASE AIDS

Arrow Rests

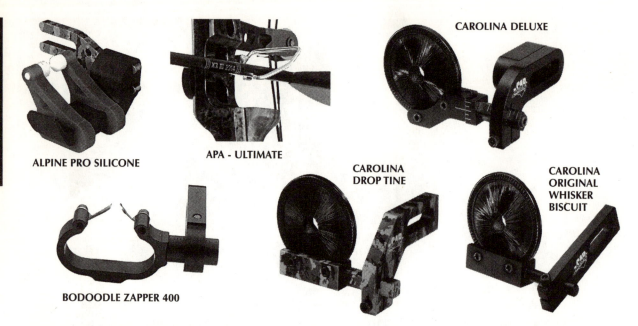

ALPINE PRO SILICONE

APA - ULTIMATE

CAROLINA DELUXE

CAROLINA DROP TINE

CAROLINA ORIGINAL WHISKER BISCUIT

BODOODLE ZAPPER 400

THE LAUNCH IS EVERYTHING

Arrow rests have drawn much attention in recent years and months. The old school of thought by archers was that a solid rest was best—the more solid, the better. Then came spring-loaded prongs and tongues that held the rest in a flexible manner. In the recent year and months, fall-away or drop-away rests have become the rage. These are designed for super fast bows and spry carbon arrows in most cases, the shooter's standard currently. From rock to solid to demand for rests that get out of the way, this is a good example of how innovative and technical archery can sometimes become.

These reviews should help you find a rest that's right for you and your shooting situations. –MDF

ALPINE ARCHERY
Pro Silicone Rest

The popular WhipserFlite arrow rest by Alpine Archery has been upgraded into their Pro Silicone fixed-position rest. The rest base and launcher support shelf are constructed of rugged extruded aluminum. The arrow rests on two white Teflon glides that are held in place by two flexible silicone triangular launchers. This rest is very simple to install and adjust. The Pro Silicone rest is also unlike any other in construction and design and can be adjusted without tools.

SRP:. $32

APA ULTIMATE

APA is based in Biggar, Saskatchewan, Canada and can be reached at 866-353-REST.

Ultimate Rest

In the solid rest category, APA Innovation's Ultimate rest is offered in a new lighter and more affordable model this year—the Ultra-Lite. The arrow rides on two stainless steel lazer-engraved cradle arms as it passes under an overhead bracket. Left and right-hand versions are offered. These rests use machined 6061-T6 aircraft aluminum brackets and stainless steel screws.

SRP: $49.99
Junior. $25.99
Release rest. $65.99

BODOODLE RESTS

Bodoodle is headquartered in Coleman, Texas and has been making rests since the mid- 70s.

Zapper 400

This unusual rest permits you to shoot arrows weighing more than 400 grains without stressing the three prongs and causing erratic arrow flight. The rest is constructed of machined aluminum and has a top-loading feature. It can

be easily converted from left to right-hand. It's available in black and camouflage.

SRP: black. $42.55
camouflaged $49.55

CAROLINA ARCHERY PRODUCTS

This company produces the famous whisker biscuit rest and is located in Hillsborough, North Carolina. For more details on their products, visit: www.carolinaarcheryprod.com.

Deluxe

This rest has the biscuit and vertical adjustments, a lockdown screw and match marks outlined on the mounting arm and brackets.

SRP: $58.00

Drop Tine

The Drop Tine rest has the famous Whisker Biscuit but the mounting arm has is curved to position the rest lower. It's available in camouflage.

SRP: $46.00

Original Whisker Biscuit

The Original is similar to the new model but with a full circle. All models will hold carbon arrows, aluminum arrows and bowfishing arrows when the donut is changed. Left and right hand models are available. Color: Black.

SRP: $36.00

CAROLINA WHISKER
BISCUIT DELUXE QS

CAVALIER AVALANCHE
EXTREME

COBRA
FRONTIERSMAN

CAROLINA WHISKER
BISCUIT DROP TINE QS

CAROLINA
REPLACEMENT
BISCUITS

CAVALIER
STINGER

CAVALIER BADGER

CAVALIER PRONGHORNS

Whisker Biscuit

A small section removed at about the 2 o'clock position permits the quick insertion of an arrow without having to start the loading process from the tip of the shaft. Rests are only available to right-hand shooters.

Whisker Biscuit Drop-Tine QS (camouflage)
　SRP: $51.00
Whisker Biscuit Deluxe QS (Black)
　SRP: $64.50

Replacement Biscuits

When your biscuit goes and starts to show a widened oval, it's time to change. Four styles are available. Fits all models on Whisker Biscuit rests.
SRP: $12.00

CAVALIER EQUIPMENT

Cavalier Equipment is from Gilbert, Arizona, and makes rests, plungers and slings.

Avalanche Extreme

The Avalanche Extreme cord activated fall-away arrow rest by Cavalier Equipment provides micro vertical and horizontal adjustments. The Avalanche Extreme's cord can be placed at variable activation positions to ensure trouble-free operation. The enhanced arrow launcher is wider and an arrow holder is optional. Several mounting brackets are offered to accommodate various risers from several major bow manufacturers.
SRP: beginning at $29.95

Badger

Designed for easy set up and a drop-designed bracket provides superior arrow and fletching clearance. The prongs are covered with Teflon sleeves. An adjustment knob on the side of the bracket is easy to use.
SRP: $15.99

Stinger

Economically priced and a simple design with sturdy construction describes this rest. It has two metal prongs to hold the arrow and slotted mounting bracket provides a wide range of adjustment to fit any bow.
SRP: $11.99

COBRA

Cobra manufactures a line of rests to compliment its sights and release aids. The company is based in Bixly, Oklahoma.

Frontiersman

A rest with a stainless steel shaft and prongs, plus independent windage, spring tension and elevation adjustments. The shaft rotates on a single bearing and Pronghorns—Cobra's exclusive sturdy prong coating—are included.
SRP: BLK $13.99
　MY camo: $15.99

Pronghorns

Slick, self-lubricating low friction material to cover arrow rest prongs and silence the release and draw process. Fit most $\frac{1}{8}$-inch diameter prongs and outperforms heat shrink tubing.
SRP: per pair $2.64

Arrow Rests

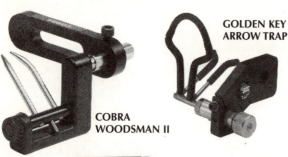

COBRA
WOODSMAN II

GOLDEN KEY
ARROW TRAP

GOLDEN KEY MIRAGE

GOLDEN KEY
HUNTER ELITE

COPPER
JOHN ALLEYCAT

GOLDEN KEY
FREE FALL

COPPER JOHN BOBCAT

GOLDEN KEY
FUNNEL

Woodsman II

This arrow rest has durable Rylon construction, independent adjustments and dual bearings to support the shaft. Pronghorn rigid covers are included to cover the two stainless steel prongs.
SRP: $9.99

COPPER JOHN

While Copper John is well known for its bow sights, the company also makes rests and release aids. Brothers Eric and Doug Springer, owners of Copper John, design many of their products while sitting in a treestand and bowhunting. A TomCAT rest will soon be offered and it will feature an arrow security system. Copper John is located in Auburn, New York.

AlleyCAT

The more advanced AlleyCAT delivers independent adjustment options. This rest has a larger mounting bracket and is more adjustable than the BobCAT.
SRP: $59.95

BobCAT

The entry-level BobCAT rest features rotary horizontal adjustment and horizontal slide adjustment. It's a drop-away string-activated rest with launchers that are shrink wrapped

with a teflon coated polymer to reduce friction at the release and increase quietness.
SRP: $39.95

GOLDEN KEY-FUTURA

Golden Key-Futura has one of the archery industry's widest assortment of arrow rests. Most models feature numerous knob-activated adjustments and two steel prongs protruding from the axle. The company released seven new rest models this year.

Arrow Trap

A new-style arrow rest with overhead tubing to hold the arrow on the rest at any angle. The prongs are spring loaded and this rest can be tuned with the Internal Tension Spring. The Speed Tune is similar in design with a camouflaged mounting bracket and gold axle sleeve but without the overhead channel found on the Arrow Trap.
SRP:. $60

Free Fall and Mirage Drop Away Rests

These Golden Key-Futura rests are designed to drop or fall when the arrow is released. The Drop Away model is mounted inside a large U-shaped bracket. The Fall Away models are two

prongs mounted to a metal axle. All are cord activated when the bow is drawn and operate when the tension is released at the release of the arrow.

Mirage Drop Away
SRP:. $105

Speed Drop
SRP:. $45

Free Fall
SRP:. $65

Premier Free Fall
SRP:. $155

Funnel Rest

A rest where your arrow and fletching pass through a multi-tabbed flexible tunnel that's mounted on an axle at the side. The Launcher Cone holds your arrow when your bow is in any position.
SRP:. $45

Hunter Elite

This premium drop-away rest has two silent launchers that are controlled by an arm that activates when the bow is drawn and a cable is pulled tight. Upon release the tension is relaxed and the prongs fall free. This rest is rugged and fully adjustable for vertical and horizontal positioning. It is available in left and right-hand models.
SRP:. $160

GOLDEN KEY POWER DROP

GOLDEN KEY SHOOT OUT

GOLDEN KEY TM SILENT HUNTER

GOLDEN KEY ROYAL HUNTER

GOLDEN KEY SPEED SET HUNTER

Power Drop

Golden Key-Futura's Power Drop rest has a drop-away action that's triggered when the cables make contact with a plunger that protrudes from the back of the rest. Innovative! The cables make contact with a large, soft rubber, tip. The Power Drop can also be set as a solid convention style rest.
SRP:. $175

Royal Hunter

The Royal Hunter rest by Golden Key-Futura has a honest-to-goodness horseshoe shaped arrow launcher that drops away at the launch. It's operated by a 12-position adjustable tension spring. Other features are a quiet, click-free adjustment and a dropped mounting bracket to permit full arrow fletching clearance.
SRP: $126.50

Shoot Out Arrow Rest

Unlike any other rest, your arrow passes through a triangle and passes over three protruding coated posts. The triangle can be converted from top or side loaded positions and mounts between two plates on the rest's lower arm. Can be easily installed as a left or right-hand model.
SRP:. $65

Speed Set Hunter

A rest with a dropped mounting bracket to ensure arrow and fletching clearance. The metal prongs of the rest are attached to a steel axle. Easy to grip adjustment knobs assist with set up and fine tuning. The Hunter model has Teflon Hush tubes on the two prongs and the standard model has steel prongs only.
SRP: coated prongs. $36
steel prongs $28

TM Hunter Series

These rests are simple and affordable. Styles include the Hunter with Teflon Hush tubes on the prongs, A Basic with bare steel prongs and Silent Hunter with sturdy and adjustable curved prongs to cradle the arrow. The Hunter Ultimate model has adjustable controls and marked calibrations to assist with adjustments.
SRP: TM Hunter. $24.59
Basic. $19.00
Silent Hunter. $32.00
Ultimate Hunter $65.00

Broadhead alignment
Make sure that your broadhead blades are in line with the fletching of your arrow. This reduces wind drag and provides truer rifling of your arrow through the air.

Arrow Rests

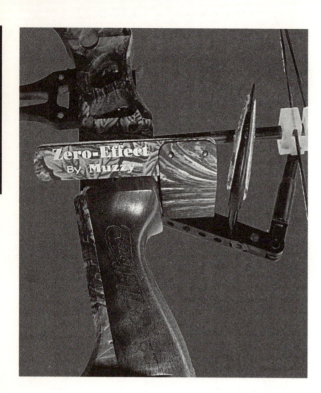

MUZZY
ZERO EFFECT

MUZZY ZERO
EFFECT LEGACY

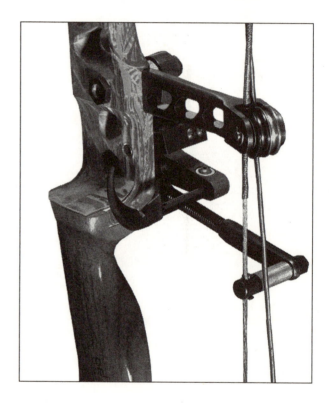

MUZZY ZERO-EFFECT RESTS

Muzzy is best known for their Bad to the Bone broadheads but also makes strings, bowfishing equipment, the Zero Effect rest and a wide assortment of archery wearables with the Muzzy Logo.

Zero Effect Arrow Rest

This odd looking rest opened the door for fall-away rests. One arm attaches to the cable and another arm cradles the arrow, until the release and then the arm drops down and the arrow floats free for the launch. Muzzy also heard from "Leftys" who howled that the earlier versions of the Zero Effect rest were offered only in right-hand versions and has introduced three left hand models. Available in left and right hand models.

SRP: **$116.65**

Zero Effect for Hoyt and Legacy Bows

Muzzy also heard from Mathews Legacy and Icon owners, and quickly discovered that those bow owners also wanted to try a Zero Effect Arrowrest. After listening, Muzzy is introducing two new Zero Effect rests—one for the Mathews bows and another model to fit the protruding spine on the newer Hoyt risers.

SRP: **$92.99**

NAAG - BEAR HAIR

NAAG - BRAVE YOUTH BOW NO-FALL

NAAG - CENTER SHOT

NAAG - MARINER BOWFISHING REST

NAAG - BEAR SHOOT AROUND

NAP - CENTEREST FLIPPER

NAAG - BEAR WEATHER

NAP - CENTEREST

NORTH AMERICAN ARCHERY GROUP

North American Archery Group makes a large assortment of bows and accessories. The following rests are available from North American Archery Group in Gainesville, Florida.

Bear Hair Rest

Designed for use on recurve and longbows. It can be cut to fit any surface.
SRP: $3.49

Bear Shoot Around Rest

Same design as Weather Rest with an additional prong to position your arrow shafts away from the bow.
SRP: $2.49

Bear Weather Rest

Pliable rubber rest with flip out arm to hold arrow.
SRP: $1.99

Brave Youth Bow No-Fall Rest

This rest is designed to prevent arrows from falling off rest as young archers develop shooting skills. The rest fits the Brave bow.
SRP: $1.99

Center Shot Rest

Simple bracket attaches to your bow and two prongs hold arrow. Available for right-hand bows only.
SRP: $12.99

Mariner Bowfishing Rest

Round design permits use of heavier fiberglass fishing arrows while protecting bow. Item 3041.
SRP: $15.65

NEW ARCHERY PRODUCTS

This Forest Park, Illinois, manufacturer has been in business for more than 30 years and strives to satisfy customers. Their arrow rest lines include Quiktune and Centerest. This company also makes the FastFlip arrow holder. All components of these products are made and assembled in the USA. Take note that the QuikTune series screws are Nylok coated and won't back out or vibrate loose, a feature that bowhunters who demand silence will appreciate. Call 708-488-2500 or visit www.newarchery for more details.

Centerest Arrowrests

This NAP arrow rest has been around for years and enjoyed by many. They are known for durability, easy installation and adjustability. The standard arrowrest has a composite arrow rest and the flipper version incorporates a flipper arm to hold the arrow. Both models are available in left- and right-hand styles. Replacement centers permit exchange of the erst without affecting the alignment.
SRP standard arrowrest $13.99
    replacement center $6.99
Centerrest Flipper $22.99
    replacement center $13.99

Arrow Rests

NAP - FASTFLIP ARROW HOLDER

NAP - QUIKTUNE 750

NAP - QUIKTUNE 800

NAP - QUIK TUNE LAUNCHERS

NAP - QUIKTUNE 1000

NAP - QUIKTUNE 3000

SAVAGE DERRINGER HUNTER

SAVAGE DERRINGER MICRO

FastFlip Arrow Holder

This unique arrow holder works with any QuikTune arrow rest and adjusts to any arrow diameter and for center-shot use. It fits left- and right-hand bows and quickly flips back out of the way upon drawing.
SRP: $15.99

QuikTune 750

This arrow rest is designed for use with al carbon and aluminum arrows and by release and finger shooters. It can be easily installed and adjusted with one wrench and it's vibration resistant. The QuikTune 750 fits both left- and right-hand bows. It has spring steel arms and Teflon silencers.
SRP: $22.99

QuikTune 800

This New Aprchery Products arrow rest features two steel prongs for the arrow to rest on. This rest can be set in high, medium and low fixed positions. It can be set with a wrench and is offered in left- and right-hand models.
SRP: $24.99

QuikTune 1000

This NAP rest features a patented triple bearing design, all-weather reliability and has Fork Tamer silencers installed. The rest is designed for hunting and archery competition applications and has a fully-independent micro-adjustable tension adjustment feature. This rest is offered in LH and RH models.
SRP: $41.99

QuikTune 3000 Micro-Adjustable

Precision adjustment without guess-work are the norm for this arrow rest that features micro-adjustment calibrations marked on the indicator knob Other features include a micro-adjust centershot, two prong fork tamers silencers and a 3-D launcher. The prongs can be changed to a single rail system that is included with the arrow rest and RH and LH models are available.
SRP: $74.99

Quik Tune Launchers

These 3-D Lizard Tongues target launchers are designed for the tournament trail and built with stainless steel. Three sizes are included with each package: light (.008), medium (.010) and heavy (.012). These will fit on most QuikTune rests.
SRP: $19.99

SAVAGE SYSTEMS

What should you focus on when considering a fall away rest? "You'll want something that moves out of the way fast enough," said Patrick Dobbs with Savage Systems." You can also avoid strings and cables that get caught in brush if you use the new inertia activated rests." Savage Systems is from Oak Grove, Louisiana and can be reached at 318-428-7733.

Derringer Hunter

Similar to the Deringer Micro with a 3/8-inch thick mounting bar. The axle will lock for fast set ups. Other features include a silent urethane return stop, stainless steel spring, and non-strip collar. Available in left and right hand models.
SRP: $29.95
    steel and Teflon launchers . $34.99

Derringer Micro Rest

This Savage Systems rest is inertia activated and has a precision micro-drive for fast adjustments that you can make with your fingers. A setscrew can then be tightened to lock the rest's axle in place while you make any other necessary adjustments. Other features on this rest include a laser engraved reference scale, lifetime play-free bushings and steel launchers with tubing or Teflon coating. Other options include left- or right-hand models.
SRP: black $52.95
    Camouflaged $57.95

SAVAGE EASY
REST HUNTER

SAVAGE JEWEL RESTS

SAVAGE READY HUNTER

SCHAFFER
TEC-1

TRAP DOOR LR
(LOW RECOIL) RESTS

Easy Rest Hunter Rest

This rest is micro adjustable and has Teflon launchers that act as an arrow holder when rotated to the up position. This rest is offered with coated or uncoated stainless steel prongs.
SRP: **$52.95**

Jewel Rests

These Savage System rests are adjustable in every possible direction and have a solid mounting bar and precision-machined aluminum body engraved with a Vernier scale. Arrows rest on two sturdy and adjustable prongs. Available finishes include: gold, platinum or black.
SRP: black.............. **$62.96**
platinum and gold **$67.95**

Ready Hunter Rests

Simple, strong and dependable describes these rests that feature a mounting bracket and U-axle for superior fletching clearance. It's available from Savage Systems with Teflon or stainless steel launchers.
SRP: **$15.95**

SCHAFFER PERFORMANCE ARCHERY

This company makes its rests in the USA and one style features the unique lizard tongue, a rest with two prongs shaped from a single base and protruding up to two sharp tips. Schaffer

is located in Burnsville, Minnesota. (952-808-2259)

TEC-1

The TEC-1 is Schaffer Performance Archery's answer to demand for an arrow rest that will fit the riser on newer Hoyt bows. This rest is offered in Realtree Hardwoods HD Green, weighs 3 ounces and can be set up as a fall-away or conventional steady rest. Dual prongs or the interesting lizard tongue rest can be installed to hold or lick the arrow. Note: The company's MAT-1, E-2 and CRS rests are similar in design with the shelf platform and two protruding steel prongs. These can be set as a conventional or fall-away rest and are similar in price to the TEC-1.
SRP: **$99.99**

SPECIALTY ARCHERY PRODUCTS

This company is based in Clear Lake, Iowa, and can be reached at 641-423-2022.

Back Drop Arrow Rest

The activation string attaches to a bow cable with a specially designed clamp. Upon activation, the rest action moves backward, not forward. A spring and brass timing adjustment knob make timing and height adjustments simple. This rest also goes through the standard arrow rest-mounting hole found on

most bow risers so installation is basic and solid. During use, the arrow rests in a durable Delrin roller that ensures silent operation. The rest can easily be converted from right- to left-hand use.
SRP:. **$77**

TRAP DOOR

Trap Door has opened a new door in drop- or fall-away arrow rests. Instead of strings and cables, the company's new drop away rests work on inertia. Trap Door is based in Bozeman, Montana, and can be reached at 406-586-1117. You can discover more details at: www.trapdoorrest.com.

Trap Door LR (Low Recoil) Rests

The standard LR (Low Recoil) model is designed to work on bows with low recoil vibration and will accommodate bows with 30- to 100-pound draw weights. The mounting and internal detection system for the inertia triggered activation are housed in a light 6061-T6 machined aluminum unit that's pre-drilled to fit all standard bows. A cover plate protects the internal controls from weather, abuse and dirt. Dampening bumpers inside the housing and a Delrin launcher assures quiet performance. The launcher attaches to a stainless steel rod that's pre-marked for adjustments.
SRP: **$86.95**

Arrow Rests

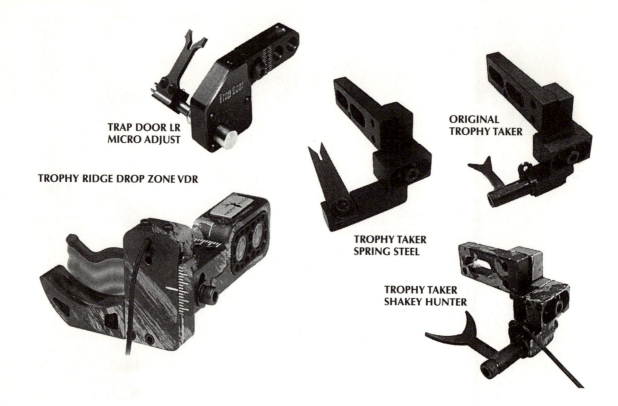

TRAP DOOR LR
MICRO ADJUST

TROPHY RIDGE DROP ZONE VDR

ORIGINAL
TROPHY TAKER

TROPHY TAKER
SPRING STEEL

TROPHY TAKER
SHAKEY HUNTER

Trap Door LR Micro Adjust
keyed and calibrated horizontal shaft for left and right adjustments independent of vertical adjustments.
SRP: **$102.50**

TROPHY RIDGE
Trophy Ridge's rests are easily spotted because they harbor the small round Harmonic Dampeners in the mounting brackets. Trophy Ridge is based in Belgrade, Montana, and can be reached at 406-388-7781.

Drop Zone VDR
(Vertical Drop Rest)
The Drop Zone VDR (Vertical Drop Rest) has a vertical arm launcher that raises the arrow as you draw with a NO-Stretch cable that tugs to activate the arm. Until you are ready to use the rest and release, the arrow is securely held in a pre-launch position on the bow's shelf with a closed-cell foam VDR rack system. The rest's V-Notched launcher arm permits you to hold the bow at extreme angles without the arrow falling off. Upon release the arm falls into a lower housing shell that also acts as a broadhead guard.

This rest is available in anodized Match-Tek black, green and brown.
SRP: **$125**

TROPHY TAKER
When the number of available rest models is important to you, Trophy Taker (406-826-0600) is a leader. This manufacturer has 32 new rest models, including left-hand, silver, black and camouflaged versions. Most models are also offered in short and long mount bars so every bowhunter and shooter will find a model that works on their bow. This Plains, Montana, based company produces numerous innovative versions of its Trophy Taker arrow rest.

Original Trophy Taker
This rest is available for left and right hand bows and with a long and short mounting bar made from durable machined aluminum. Machined hash marks help ensure precision windage and elevation adjustments and a $^{10}/_{32}$-inch hex bolt helps anchor the selection in place. Two threaded windage and elevation holes maximize adjustment options and a set

screw on the mounting bar prevents any rotation. The strong stainless steel launcher is cushioned by a completely enclosed spring. These rests—12 models are available—are available in black, silver and camouflage.
SRP: **$74.99**

Shakey Hunter
Similar to the Original Trophy Taker with a durable non-stretch and stretchable cord that can be attached to cables or the bow's cable slide. Also features a one-piece stainless steel launcher with $1\frac{1}{8}$-inch wide tip. Available in left- and right-hand models.
SRP: **$74.99**
    camouflaged **$79.99**

Spring Steel
Similar to the Shakey Hunter and Original models, the Spring Steel model comes with two widths of launchers for large or small arrows. Three spring steel launchers of various stiffness are included with each rest. These provide perfect arrow tuning capabilities and are easily changed.
SRP: **$64.99**

HUNTING & SHOOTING ACCESSORIES

Cutlery and Saws

BUCK MINI STRIDER KNIVES

BUCK STRIDER SOLUTION

LOVELESS CLASSIC KNIVES

TIGHE PAN FOLDING KNIFE

LEATHERMAN PULSE

LEATHERMAN CRUNCH

BUCK KNIVES
Buck Mini Strider Knives
Bucks Mini Strider knives are lock blades with your choice of a tanto or spear point. The ATS-34 high carbon blades are 3-inches long. These knives fold to 4-inches and weigh just 3.92 ounces. Each knife has a stainless steel belt clip.
SRP:. $180

Buck Strider Solution
This fixed blade knife has a 4½-inch long ATS-34 blade that's hardened. The handles are made of G-10 resin laminate and are resistant to heat, cold and chemicals. The knife comes with a rugged Cordua sheath.
SRP: . . . . $220.

LEATHERMAN MULTI-TOOLS
Leatherman Crunch
A multi-tool with locking pliers, wire cutters, screwdrivers, file, and serrated knife blade. The blades lock in place and released with the push of a button. This tool folds to 4-inches long.
SRP:. $98

Leatherman Pulse
This multi-tool has a pliers head, knife blade, file, screwdrivers, scissors, wire cutters, ruler and lanyard attachment.
SRP:. $72

LONE WOLF KNIVES
Lone Wolf Knives is based in Portland, Oregon, and can be reached at 503-431-6777 or visit www.lonewolfknives.com. The company produces serious cutlery that you can depend on.

Loveless Classic knives
These fixed blade knives by Lone Wolf have handles made of green canvas Micarta and attached with stainless steel rivets. The blade and handle are made form a single piece of high carbon LV-04 stainless steel. The Utility knife has a 4½-inch blade and the Semi-Skinner knife has a 3½-inch blade. A custom leather sheath is included.
SRP:. $300

Tighe Pan Folding Knife
A folding knife with a blade crafted from CPM-S30V stainless steel that's heat-treated and then sub-zero quenched. All screws and fasteners are crafted from stainless steel. The blade is 3.56-inches long and the total folded length is 4.32-inches. This knife is light and tough.
SRP:. $280

Cutlery and Saws

FOLDING SAW

KODI-PAK

PACK SAW

FRED BEAR CUSTOM KNIFE

PACK AXE

SPORTSMAN MULTI-TOOL

GRIZ PAK

NORTH AMERICAN ARCHERY GROUP
Folding Saw
This saw features a rubber sure-grip insert in the handle and sturdy blade with deep teeth for cutting wood and developing shooting lanes or firewood. Folds to compact unit for packing and to protect blade.
SRP: $14.99

Fred Bear Custom Knife
A collector quality fixed-blade knife with decorative white bone handle attached by brass rivets. Includes a soft, brown leather sheath with belt loop.
SRP: $275

OUTDOOR EDGE
Game Pack
A complete 12-piece skinning and butchering kit with knives for caping, skinning, boning and butchering. The kit also has a bone saw, carving fork, shears, steel brisket spreader, surgical game gloves and a blade sharpener. The set also works for outdoor cooking. All items are stored in a sturdy and convenient hard-side carrying case.
SRP: $88.99

Griz Pak
This skinning knife with gut hook and T-handled bone saw fit into a scent-free Zytel sheath that can be worn on a belt. The kit is also available with a Advantage camouflaged sheath.
SRP: $79.90

Kodi-Pak
A very popular knife set with a caping knife for surgical precision cuts. The kit also has a skinning knife with gut hook and a bone saw with T-handle. All items are stored in a handy sheath that can be worn on a belt.
SRP: $119.70

Pack Axe
A small packable axe with one-piece full tang construction from end to end. A rubberized Kraton handle prevents slipping. This axe is covered with a lifetime guarantee.
SRP: $49.99

Pack Saw
A folding saw that packs to 1 12-inch length and fits in a nylon storage case. Three blades are included: wood, metal and bone.
SRP: $26.99

Sportsman Multi-Tool
A multi-tool with a heavy duty pliers head, wire cutters, knife blade, broadhead wrench, chisel, bottle and can opener, and drive bit adapter with a dozen assorted screwdriver and hex heads. It all stores in a compact nylon belt sheath.
SRP: $21.60

Cutlery and Saws

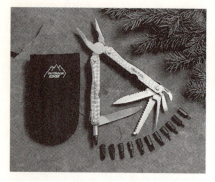

TREK TOOL

TROPHY-PAK

WHITETAIL PAK

WHITETAIL SKINNER AND
GAME SKINNER

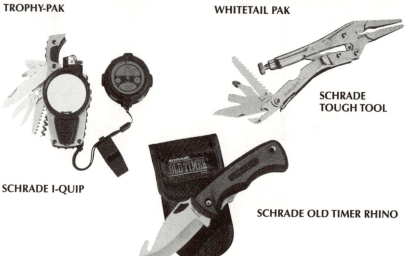

SCHRADE I-QUIP

SCHRADE
TOUGH TOOL

SCHRADE OLD TIMER RHINO

OUTDOOR EDGE CONTINUED
Trek Tool
A multi-tool with knife blade, pliers head, saw, hole punch and drive adapter with a dozen screwdriver heads and hex heads. This tool has swirl brush handles and contoured no-pinch grips.
SRP: **$21.60**

Trophy-Pak
A saw and skinning knife that are stored in a handy leather belt sheath. The blade has a gut hook for easy field dressing and triple-ground saw blade will cut brush, bone and cartilage.
SRP: **$86.99**

Whitetail Pak
An Outdoor Edge kit with the unique but effective Whitetail skinner knife and a bone saw. Both have sure grip rubberized Kraton T-handles. The complete pack weighs 14 ounces.
SRP: **$79.90**

Whitetail Skinner and Game Skinner
These knives have T-handles and an axe-like blade crafted from Chrome-Moly AUS-80 stainless steel. Each model has a gut hook and a full grain leather belt sheath. Knives with serrated blades can be obtained for slightly more.
SRP: Whitetail **$49.90**
Big Game Skinner **$59.90**

SCHRADE CUTLERY
Schrade I-Quip
A unit that's the SUV of knifes and gear enthusiasts. The I-Quip has a computer module that houses an altimeter, barometer, digital compass and digital clock. The implement pod has screwdrivers, a cutting blade, scissors, saw, caplifter, can opener and cork screw. Other features include a Led flashlight, signal mirror, survival whistle, lighter compartment and belt clip. This item is best described as a weather station and hardware store in one survival tool that's ready to roll.
SRP: **$250**

Schrade Old Timer Rhino
A folding lock knife with a gut hook on the stainless steel blade. This knife folds to 4^{7}/$_{8}$-inches and packs in a nylon sheath.
SRP: **$39.95**

Schrade Tough Tool
A multi-tool built in partnership with American Tool to produce Vice-Grip locking tools with a blade, screwdrivers, cap lifter, locking saw wire stripper and more. These tools are corrosion resistant and offered in two models.
SRP: . . . . **$33.95 to $36.95**

ALPEN APEX BINOCULARS

ALPEN MINI SPOTTING SCOPE

ALPEN PRO SERIES COMPACT
BINOCULARS

ALPEN SE BINOCULARS

BRUNTON EPOCH BINOCULARS

ETERNA COMPACT BINOCULARS

ALPEN

Alpen manufactures more than 50 styles and models of binoculars. The company is based in California and can be reached at 877-987-8370.

Alpen Apex Binoculars

A lightweight binocular with a composite body and fully multi-coated Bak-4 glass. Other features are phase coating, and high-resolution metallic prism coating. These binoculars are nitrogen filled, shock-resistant, waterproof, dustproof and guaranteed not to fog. The Apex binoculars have a lifetime guarantee.

SRP: . . . . Starting at $400

Alpen Mini Spotting Scope

Here's a mini-scope that offers huge benefits and takes up a small amount of space in your pack. It's 20X50mm and weighs only 10 ounces. The Mini-Scope features Bak-7 fully coated optics and are nitrogen filled and waterproof, dustproof, shock-resistant, and very compact. It comes with a durable, padded field case and a portable 6-inch swivel head tripod. Field of view is 147 feet at 1,000 yards.

SRP: $85

Alpen Pro Series Compact Binoculars

A small, go-anywhere pocket-sized binocular that has long eye relief and Bak-4 multi-coated optics. The porro prism designed 8X45mm and 10X45mm give wide-angle viewing. Each binocular comes with a case and carrying strap. Available models include: 8X25mm, 10X2225mm, 12X25mm and waterproof 8X45mm and 10X45mm models.

SRP: compact models. $100
Waterproof models. . starting at $125

Alpen SE Binoculars

A binocular with roof prism design, Bak-4 optics and fully multi-coated lenses. The SE series are nitrogen filled to prevent fogging and are also shock- and waterproof. Ten models are available: 8X42mm, 10X42mm, 10X50 and 12X50mm.

SRPS: . . . . Starting at $250

BRUNTON
Epoch Binoculars

A binocular with a sturdy and lightweight Magnesium-Alloy frame, variable speed focusing, hybrid aspherical ocular lenses with Flat-Light coating and SF prism material. Two versions are available: 7.5X43mm and 10.5X43mm. The 10.5 model delivers a 290-feet field of view at 1,000 yards. These binoculars are tripod compatible.

SRP: 7.5 model $1,449
10.5 model 1,499

Eterna Compact Binoculars

These compact 8X25mm binoculars have phase coating, Emerald Fire full multi-coating, Bak-4 prisms and are eyeglass compatible. Other features are wat3erprof, fog proof and nitrogen purged. The units are covered by a lifetime warranty.

SRP: $229
**Eterna Compact 10X25mm
Binoculars**
SRP: $229

SHOOTING ACCESSORIES

Optics

INSTANT REPLAY BINOCULARS

IMAGE VIEW DIGITAL BINOCULARS

LEGEND BINOCULARS

**YARDAGE PRO
ALL PURPOSE 500 MODEL**

BRUNTON CONTINUED
Eterna Monocular
When you're trying to shave ounces and cut weight, this 6X monocular from Brunton is eyeglass compatible and is waterproof and nitrogen purged. It has a 19mm long eye relief.
SRP:.....................**$149**

BUSHNELL
Bushnell is one of the most recognized names in optics and the rangefinder industry. The company's products often set the pace for others to follow. More and more archers and bowhunters are finding the useful applications—and more affordable models—of rangefinders. Distance does matter—MDF

Image View Digital Binoculars
This model combines a roof prism binocular with an 8x camera. The camera provides .35 megapixel still photographs and you can photograph what you see. This camera and binoc-

ular has 64 MB of internal memory and the images can be downloaded and sent via e-mail. The prism glass is BK-7 coated and the 10X25mm binocular provides 300 feet filed of view at 1000 yards. This unit is lightweight and very compact.
SRP:.....................**$109**

Instant Replay Binoculars
A binocular that can record up to 30 seconds of continuous video loop to capture your hunting action. The unit has 16 Megs of internal memory, and the software is provided to store, remove, view, download or edit movie clips. The Instant Replay has 8X magnification, 32mm objective lens, and Bak-4 prisms and is a mid-size binocular.
SRP:.....................**$499**

Bushnell Legend Binoculars
A binocular with Bak-4 coated roof prisms and a rubber armored design. This binocular is O-ring sealed and nitrogen purged. Available models

include 8X42, 10X42, compact 9X25 and 8X32. The Rainguard water-repellent coating prevents fog and moves water off the glass to give a better view in adverse hunting environments. Other features are twist in eyecups, knurled diopter adjustment and 100% waterproof and fog-proof construction.
SRP: 8X42...............**$339.9**

Yardage Pro All Purpose Models
These rangefinders will fit into a pack and can provide distance estimation from 20 to 500, 930 or 1,500 yards. The Yardage Pro 500 provides 6X magnification and measures out to 500 yards, can be mounted on a tripod and has a form-fitting neoprene case. The Yardage Pro Compact 800 will range out to 930 yards and provides 8X magnification. The Yardage Pro 1000 will range to 1,500 yards and has 6X magnification.
SRP: 500 model..........**$259.99**
800 Compact.............**$339.99**
1000....................**$399.99**

YARDAGE PRO LEGEND

YARDAGE PRO QUEST

YARDAGE PRO SCOUT

YARDAGE PRO SPORT

KAHLES BIINOCULARS

SHOOTING ACCESSORIES

Yardage Pro Legend

One of hunting's smallest rangefinders, the Yardage Pro Legend is about the size of a pack of cigarettes and weighs 7.2 ounces. It will easily fit in a shirt pocket and provides 6X magnification when viewing targets. Other features are plus/minus one-yard accuracy measurements, zip and rain built in modes and 100% waterproof and floatable construction. It will range distances up to 913 yards and comes with a carrying case and wrist strap. The Yardage Pro Quest is available in black and mossy Oak camouflage.
SRP: **$429.99**

Yardage Pro Quest

A new standard in rangefinders, this 8x36 porro prism binocular is 100% waterproof and can also range from 15 to 1300 yards with plus/minus one-yard accuracy. No reason to carry a binocular and a rangefinder—this unit does both. Other features are Bak-4 prisms, a center focus knob, and it can scan and provide distances in meters and yards. The Yardage Pro Quest runs on a 9-volt battery and weighs 34 ounces.
SRP: **$868**

Yardage Pro Scout

A compact range finder that uses 6X power to give you a better view as it ranges distances from 10 to 700 yards. This unit is accurate to within a yard and has scan, rain and zip modes and built-in reflect. It's powered by a 3-volt lithium battery and available in green or Realtree Hardwoods HD.
SRP: **$329.99**
Camouflage . . . . **add $20**

Yardage Pro Sport

This ultra compact and water resistant rangefinder is small and delivers 4X or 6X magnification and a 5 to 800 (or 10-700 yard for 6X) yard measuring range. It's available in gray or Advantage Classic camo. The Yardage Pro Scout weighs 6.8 ounces and comes with a carrying case. The 6X model uses a 3-volt battery and the 4X model uses a 9-volt battery.
SRP: **$219.99**

KAHLES

Kahles is based in Cranston Rhode Island, and brings Austrian optics to American hunters at an affordable price. For more details, call 866-606-8780 or visit www.kahlesoptik.com.

Kahles Binoculars

Kahles' binoculars offer close focusing and high-quality fully multi-coated lenses with an ergonomic design. The metal alloy housing has shock-absorbing rubber armoring. The binoculars are fully waterproof, nitrogen purged, fog proof and shockproof and will withstand all climatic changes during field use. Three models are available: 8x32mm, 8X42mm and 10X42mm. The binoculars are shipped with a floating case, neck strap and lens cover. The 8X32s weigh 21.5 ounces and the 10X42mms weigh 26 ounces. These premium optics are offered in gray and Advantage Timber camouflage.

SRP: 8X32mm gray **$579**
camouflaged **$609**
8X42mmgray **$679**
camouflaged **$709**
10X42mmgray **$729**
camouflaged **$769**

Optics

NIKON IMAGE STABILIZING BINOCLUAR

NIKON TEAM REALTREE CAMO HUNTING BINOCULARS

NIKON TEAM REALTREE CAMO COMPACT HUNTING BINOCULARS

NIKON TEAM REALTREE LASER 800 RANGEFINDER

NIKON TEAM REALTREE 15-45X60MM ZOOM SPOTTING SCOPE

NIKON

Nikon is located in Melville, New York, and more information about their optics line can be obtained at 800-248-6848 or visit www.nikonusa.com. The company makes a full line of binoculars and scopes.

Nikon Image Stabilizing Binocular

The 10X40mm StabilEyes uses a professional grade roof prism system the reduce vibration while being water- and fog proof. The unit has a Land and Onboard mode to switch to the condition demands. Other features include a central focus design, 13mm eye relief and phase correction coated mirrors. The unit measures 7.3x5.8x3.4-inches and weighs 45.8 ounces. It is powered by four AA batteries.

SRP: $1700

Nikon Team Realtree Camo Hunting Binoculars

Here's a binocular that blends in while providing adjustable eyecups and extra-long eye relief to be friendly for eyewear users. The Hunting Binocular will close focus to 10 feet, has multi-layer antireflective coatings on the inner glass and are lightweight. The 8X model weighs 25.3 ounces and the 10X version weighs 24.6 ounces.

SRP: 8X $199
10X $219

Nikon Team Realtree Compact Hunting Binocular

SRP: 8X $70
10X $80

Nikon Team Realtree Compact Laser Rangefinder

A small lightweight rangefinder for hunters who demand maximum concealment. This is possibly the smallest unit on the market today. It will measure from 10.5 to 437 yards with ½-yard precision and is water resistant. The rangefinder uses an 8X monocular with a 20mm objective lens to provide a 2.5mm exit pupil. The field of view is 330 feet ant 1,000 yards.

SRP: $319.99

Nikon Team Realtree Laser800 Rangefinder

SRP: $379.99

Nikon Team Realtree 15-45X60mm Zoom Spotting Scope

When you need a close-up look at a long distance, this zoom spotting scope will provide a clear, crisp look. It features multi-coated lenses and adjustable magnification. It is coated in Realtree Hardwoods and you can obtain a matching tripod and window mount.

SRP: $459.99

Optics

PENTAX DCF HR II
BINOCULARS

PENTAX DCF SP
BINOCULARS

PENTAX WATERPROOF
ANGLE COMPENSATING
LASER RANGEFINDER

SWAROVSKI ATS 80MM
SPOTTING SCOPE

PENTAX

Pentax is based in Englewood, Colorado, and makes binoculars, scopes and rangefinders. Visit www.pentaxusa.com for more details.

Pentax DCF HR II Binoculars

Affordable and lightweight describes these binoculars. They have a reinforced fiber and polycarbonate shell and are nitrogen purged waterproof. The roof prisms are phase coated and the binoculars' inner focus optical design adds to their durability. The click-stop adjustment locks in the right eyepiece diopeter. The rubber-covered exterior provides a sure grip.

SRP: 8X42 . . . . $279
10X42 . . . . $299

Pentax DCF SP Binoculars

SRP: 8X32 . . . . $499
8X43 599
10X43 . . . . $649
10X50 . . . . $749
12.5X50. . . . . $799

Pentax Waterproof Angle Compensating Laser Rangefinder

Here's a rangefinder that takes the guess out of the old question of where to aim when a target is above or below you on a steep slope. A state-of-the-art microprocessor automatically filters data and can give readings in rain and snow. The rubber armor coated unit uses a single laser beam to measure distances in feet, yards and meters. It can also provide a temperature readout, and is accurate to 12 feet and out to 500, 800, or 1,000 yards. Operates on a 9-volt battery.

SRP: 500 range model, black. . . $349
camouflage $369
800 yard model black. $369
camouflage $389
1,000 yard model black $389
camouflage $399

SWAROVSKI OPTIC

Swarovski Optic North America is based in Cranston, Rhode Island and imports scopes and binoculars from Austria or builds the units—in some cases—here in the USA

SWAROVSKI ATS 80MM SPOTTING SCOPE

This lightweight and compact scope delivers an outstanding view in every light condition and environment. The features include a wide 80mm objective lens, changeable eyepiece, coatings to reduce lens and mirror reflections. This scope is available as a straight-through design or with a 45-degree angled eyepiece. It weighs 51.9 ounces and is approximately 15½-inches long. Several eyepieces—20-60X, 20X, 30X and 45X—are available and must be purchased separately.

SRP: scope body $1,254
eyepieces start at $287

Swarovksi EL Binoculars

This series of binoculars are lightweight and provide a quality view with crisp edge-to-edge views. It has a dioptric correction system built into the pull out focus wheel and a unique body with thumb depressions. The prism is coated with Swarobright and the body is ergonomically designed from lightweight magnesium. Available in 8.5X42mm and 10X42mm.

SRP: 8.5X $1,632
10X. $1,698

Optics

SWAROVKSI SLC 8X30MM BINOCULARS

SWIFT TRILYTE 10X25MM

SWIFT TRILYTE 8X25MM

SWAROVSKI POCKET BINOCULARS

SWAROVSKI OPTIC CONTINUED

Swarovski Pocket Binoculars

Binoculars that are compact enough to fit into any pocket, yet will provide crisp views and high-contrast image quality describes these pocket models. These binoculars feature precise alignment to reduce eyestrain, central focusing, twist-in eyecups, and multi-coated glass surfaces. Available in black or forest green.
SRP: 8X20mm $554.44
10X25mm $598.89

Swarovksi SLC 8X30mm Binoculars

The features of this premium unit include a slender and compact ergonomic designed shell made of polyurethane. All lenses are coated with multi-layer coatings and the roof prism technology incorporates Swarobright interference technology to provide maximum light transmission. Swarotop coating is on all air-to-glass-lens. The other features include an easy to use diopter wheel, twist in eyecups, and special armor coatings. These binoculars weigh 19 ounces.
SRP: $954

SWIFT

Swift Trilyte 8X25mm

This binocular is waterproof, armored, and has Bak-4 phase-coated glass. The roof prism design makes them compact and they feature twist-out eyecups. These 8X25mm compact binoculars will close focus to 8 feet and have a carrying case. Rubber coated.
SRP: $349.95
Swift Trilyte 10X25mm
SRP: $359.95

WIND RIVER OLYMPIC COMPACTS

WIND RIVER PINNACLES

WIND RIVER RB800 SERIES RANGEFINDER BINOCULARS

WIND RIVER

Wind River Olympic Compacts

A compact binocular with Bak-4 and BK7 prisms, plus fully multi-coated glass and phase coating. Other features are twist-up eyecups, lens covers and neck strap. These optics are waterproof, armored and have rain shed on the exterior glass. Available in 8X25mm and 10X25mm. They are covered with a limited lifetime warranty.

SRP: 8X $274.99
10X $289.99

Wind River Pinnacles

Premium performance binoculars with fully multi-coated lenses and silver enhanced Bak-4 prisms. Contoured eyecups help block out light and can be retracted when used with eyewear. These binoculars are armor coated, are nitrogen purged and sealed waterproof, and have an ergonomic body. The exterior glass is coated with Rain shed water displacement. These are available in 8X42mm and 10X42mm.

SRP: 8X $489.99
10X $539.99

Wind River RB800 Series Rangefinder Binoculars

These 8X binoculars have a built-in range finding system. The features include roof prism design with individual focus and pull-up eyecups. The range finding system will range distances from 12 to 800 yards. These range finding binoculars weigh 23 ounces and are approximately 5 inches long. The RB800C has a built-in compass for 360-degree directional location of objects.

SRP: RB800 . . . . $874.99
RB800C $999.99

SHOOTING ACCESSORIES

Calls, Scents and Game Attractors

ACTIVE SCRAPE

BUCK FIRE

BUCK NIP

BULL RAGE

**BOOT SCENT
PADS**

COON URINE

COYOTE URINE

DOE IN ESTRUS

EXCITE

**BREEZE
DETECTOR**

CARBO WASH

ELK FIRE

WILDLIFE RESEARCH

Scents & Lures
Active Scrape (Mock scrape lure)
SRP: 1 oz. $5.99
4 oz. $14.99

Buck Fire (Doe-in-heat urine)
SRP: per 1 oz. $6.99

Buck Nip (Curiosity scent)
SRP: 1 oz. $5.99

Bull Rage (Elk lure)
SRP: 1 oz. $7.99

Boot Scent Pads
SRP: per pair $3.99

Coon Urine
SRP: 4 oz. $7.99

Coyote Urine (Cover up scent)
SRP: $7.99

Doe in Estrus (Buck lure)
SRP: 1 oz $5.99

Excite (white-tailed doe in heat estrus scent)
SRP: 1 oz. $9.99
4 oz. $24.99

Breeze Detector Powder
A bottle of odorless powder that floats in the air to reveal wind currents.
SRP: $4.99

Carbo Wash
Recommended for washing carbon-activated clothing.
SRP: 16 oz. $11.99
32 oz. $19.99

Elk-Fire
Imitates a cow elk in heat and brings bulls in looking for the cow.
SRP:1 oz $7.99
4 oz $17.99

Calls, Scents and Game Attractors

4X4 MULE DEER LURE

GRUNT'N LURE

HOT MUSK

HOT SCRAPE

KEY WICK

MASKING SCENTS

PRO DRAG

PRO WICK

RED FOX URINE

SCENT KILLER ANTI-PERSPIRANT DEODORANT

4X4 Mule Deer Lure
A full strength doe in heat urine with natural pheromones from mule deer.
SRP: $7.99

Grunt-N-Lure
Use this scent when calling bucks. It is loaded with doe in estrus, buck in rut and tarsal gland smells.
SRP: 1 oz $7.99

Hot-Musk
A unique blend of musks to create a lure effective on bucks and does.
SRP: 1 oz. $7.99

Hot Scrape
Use this doe in heat secretion at mock and natural scrapes to attract deer.
SRP: 1 oz. $4.99

Key Wick
A long think felt wick pad that's used to create a scent station near your stand.
SRP: $3.49

Masking Scents
These scents help hide the human odor and can be used in specific hunting terrains. Available in vanilla, pine, sage, cedar, earth, acorn, apple, persimmon and corn.
SRP: $5.99

Pro-Drag
A 7-inch synthetic felt pad with two tails to disperse scent and lay out a scent trail.
SRP: $4.99

Pro Wick
A small scent pad that can be tied to a limb and then have scent applied.
SRP: $3.49

Red Fox Urine
A masking scent that will not alarm deer. Arrives in a spray bottle.
SRP: 4 oz. $6.99

Scent Killer
Anti-Perspirant Deodorant
A stick deodorant that's odorless and helps keep you dry and odor free all day.
SRP: $5.99

Calls, Scents and Game Attractors

SCENT KILLER BAR SOAP

SCENT KILLER CLOTHING WASH

SCENT KILLER LIQUID SOAP

SCENT KILLER SPRAY

SELECT BUCK URINE

SELECT DOE URINE

SUPER WICK

TRAILS END 307

ULTIMATE BEAR LURE

ULTIMATE SCRAPE-DRIPPER

Scent Killer Bar Soap

A 5-ounce bar that's nonscented and kills human odor.
SRP: 5 oz. **$4.99**

Scent Killer Clothing Wash

A laundry detergent that removes odors from clothes in the wash and leaves them odorless. This product contains no UV brighteners.
SRP: Starting at 16 oz. **$6.99**

Scent Killer Liquid Soap

This soap is gentle on the skin and has an antibacterial formula that attacks human odor.
SRP: 8 oz. **$5.99**
12 oz. **$6.99**
32 oz. **$14.99**

Scent Killer Spray

This product kills odors upon contact and is available in 4-, 8- and 24 ounce sizes.
SRP: 4 oz. **$4.99**
8 oz. **$6.99**
24 oz. **$12.99**

Select Buck Urine

This is a great territorial intrusion scent and brings bucks close when they smell it.
SRP: 1oz. **$7.99**

Select Doe Urine

A natural odor of deer scent that has territorial non-threatening appeal.
SRP: **$5.99**

Super Wick

A scent station that you create. The container has a screw on cap for storage and a wick that drops down when the container is hung up on a limb.
SRP: **$5.99**

Trails End 307

A lure that's a proven top performer. When deer smell it they'll come to investigate.
SRP: 1oz. **$7.99**
4oz. **$17.99**

Ultimate Bear Lure

An intense smell with a sweet aroma that attracts bears.
SRP: 4 oz. **$12.99**
16 oz. **$29.99**

Ultimate Scrape-Dripper

This soft container can be hung over a real or mock scrape to drip scents. The dripper shuts down at night and can last up to 7 days when full.
SRP: **$12.99**

Calls, Scents and Game Attractors

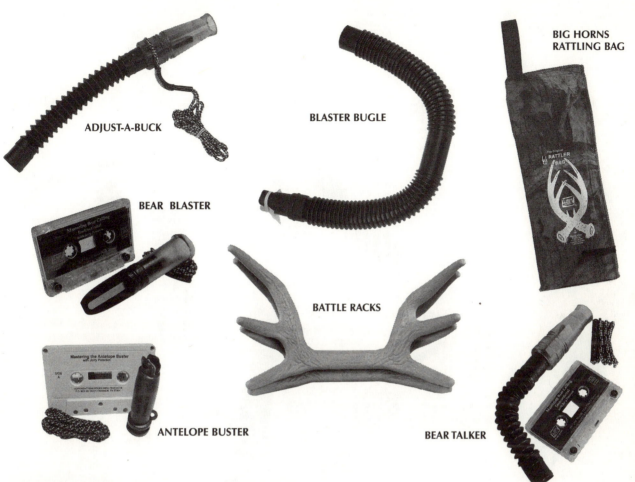

ADJUST-A-BUCK

BLASTER BUGLE

BIG HORNS RATTLING BAG

BEAR BLASTER

BATTLE RACKS

ANTELOPE BUSTER

BEAR TALKER

WOODS WISE
Woods Wise creates calls for nearly every critter found afield and in the forests and has an assortment of instructional tapes and videos

Adjust-A-Buck
This adjustable reed based call makes grunts and bleats—it's six calls in one. The expansion tube helps vary the tones. Simple O-ring slides to make adjustments.
SRP: $11.99

Antelope Buster
Use this call to imitate buck snort chuckles and to stop running pronghorns with a bark. Works well with decoys and will capture and hold any pronghorn's attention.
SRP: $12.99

Baby Squirrel Distress
This is a great locator call that makes young squirrel distress sounds.
SRP: $9.99

Bark'n Bushytail
This small call is big with response and makes excited barks to create more excitement in the squirrel community. It has air activated bellows and can be taped against your knee for hunting while sitting.
SRP: $9.99

Battle Racks
A set of full-contact antlers that are held in the middle for better balance and to avoid finger pinch while rattling. The bone Core hollow air cells help create realistic sounds.
SRP: $19.99

Bear Blaster
A call that produces variable pitches for loud distress cries to bring hungry and curious bears to your location. Take cover and be prepared when using it.
SRP: $15.99

Bear Talker
A dual-reed inhale/exhale call that imitates female and male bears. The call comes with an instructional tape and lanyard.
SRP: $17.99

Big Horns Rattling Bag
This larger rattling bag can be used to imitate large bucks and trophy bulls. It can be hung from the belt and an elastic band wraps around it to keep it quiet when necessary.
SRP: $15.99

Blaster Bugle
An elk call that makes shrill notes and deep tones when used. It comes with an audio instructional tape, camo cover and lanyard.
SRP: $26.99

Calls, Scents and Game Attractors

ABREEDING
BELLOW

BUC-N-DOE

BULLSEYE BUCK

EZY HYPERCOW

BUCK-SNORT

4-IN-1 HANDS FREE

SHOOTING ACCESSORIES

Bullseye Buck
A deer call that makes all vocalizations and snorts. You inhale to make bleats and exhale to make grunts with this call. Instructional audio and lanyard are included.
SRP: **$14.99**

Blue Doe
The lost contact call is made with this innovative call. It has a sanded reed and won't freeze and plays while wet. The expansion tube changes it from a buck to doe voice.
SRP: **$11.99**

Breeding Bellow
This call mimics a ready to breed doe and is simple to use. A how to audiotape and lanyard are included.
SRP: **$14.99**

Buc-N-Doe
This original call has removable hands-free grunt and doe bleat calls. It can be hands free, pushbutton or a tube call. It makes an assortment of calls including plain buck grunts, Contac calls, aggressive grunts, hot doe bleats and tending grunts. If a deer is near, this call will bring it closer. Includes an instructional tape.
SRP: **$14.99**

Buck-Snort
This call is realistic and easy to use, and should create action when used with rattling and calling.
SRP: **$9.99**

Callmasters Buck-n-Doe
Make buck hyper grunts and doe bleats with this call. It has 12 adjustments and a 2-reed system that's operated by inhaling and exhaling.
SRP: **$12.99**

EZY Cow
A call that's great for herd talk and it calls cows, calves and lovesick bulls.
SRP: **$9.99**

EZY Hypercow
A mouth blown call that imitates a cow in heat breeding call to drive bulls wild. It's easy to use and versatile and can be muted for softer tones.
SRP: **$9.99**

4-In-1 Hands Free
This adjustable call fits in your mouth and makes grunts of bucks and does, plus doe and fawn bleats. An elastic lanyard is included.
SRP: **$6.99**

Calls, Scents and Game Attractors

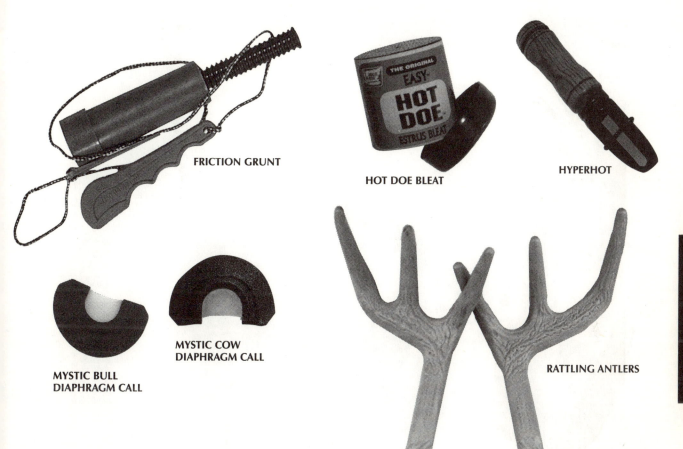

FRICTION GRUNT

HOT DOE BLEAT

HYPERHOT

MYSTIC BULL
DIAPHRAGM CALL

MYSTIC COW
DIAPHRAGM CALL

RATTLING ANTLERS

Friction Grunt
An adjustable twist tone tip and striker paddle helps make the buck's clicking courtship grunts and doe social grunts, plus rutting buck grunts and aggressive grunts.
SRP: $14.99

Hands Free Real Cow
A call designed for bowhunters and it is held in the mouth and blown. It calls cows, bulls and calves. This call will easily fit into a shirt pocket.
SRP: $8.99

Hot Doe Bleat
It's like have a deer in a container when you turn this cylinder over to imitate a hot estrus doe bleat.
SRP: $9.99

Hyperhot
The cow-in-heat elk call that makes five calls including mews and spike squeals. The call comes with a lanyard and audio instructional tape.
SRP: $14.99

Kodiak Western Doe & Fawn Bleat
Call trophy mule deer, blacktails and Coues deer with these mews and bleats. The call operates with hands free bite and blow design.
SRP: $8.99

Moose Blaster
A call that has an expansion megaphone and a red-hot XL-15 reed inside. This call makes estrus cow moans and cow protest whine and grunts. It's very compact and easy to use. For more details and to experience the thrill of a moose hunt watch the Moose Talk video with Jerry Peterson—a 70-minute VHS tape with live moose calling for $14.99.
SRP: $14.99

Mystic Bull Diaphragm Call
An in-the-mouth call with two reeds and a small frame designed to make aggressive bugles and growling chuckles.
SRP: $4.99

Mystic Cow Diaphragm Call
A call that's easy to master and it makes cow and calf calls and bugles.
SRP: $4.99

Rattling Antlers
Premium antlers made with polymer for strength and uses the Bone Core technology to create air core cells like real antlers to produce a more realistic sound and bring bucks close. This set is perfect for sparing or all-out fights.
SRP: $13.99

Calls, Scents and Game Attractors

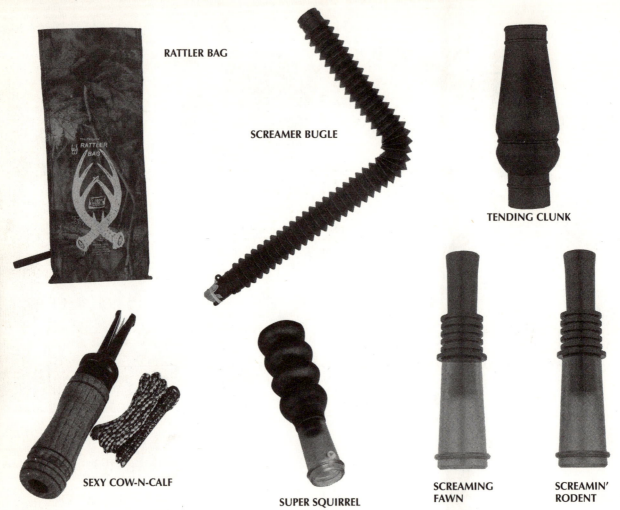

RATTLER BAG

SCREAMER BUGLE

TENDING CLUNK

SEXY COW-N-CALF

SUPER SQUIRREL

SCREAMING FAWN

SCREAMIN' RODENT

Rattler Bag
This bag can be worn on your belt and tingled with one hand to imitate sparring bucks. It will bring aggressive and curious bucks to your location. An elastic strap helps keep it quiet when not in use and the camouflaged exterior bag helps prevent movement detection while in use.
SRP: $14.99

Screamer Bugle
This elk call has an expansion tube and exclusive triple reed that permits call adjustment. Includes an instructional tape, camo cover and additional latex for over the reed controlled tuning. This call uses the EZY# triple reed system that includes a pre-tuned diaphragm with Peel-n-Stick tape mounting.
SRP: $29.99

Screaming Fawn
This call brings whitetails, mule deer and blacktails to you with loud distress calls. It will also lure in coyotes, foxes, bears and other predators.
SRP: $19.99

Screamin' Rodent
Makes a rodent in distress shrill squeal and brings all predators running for the action.
SRP: $9.99

Sexy Cow-N-Calf
A call that makes all herd talk and it's easy to use and has automatic reed alignment pins. It has a wooden barrel.
SRP: $12.99

Super Howler
A freeze-proof reed in this loud long-range call can make locator howls and female invitation howls to bring coyotes close. The call includes two reeds to make various calls.
SRP: $14.99

Super Squirrel
This call makes the alarm bark, young squirrel distress, chatters and squeals of the gray and fox squirrels. An instructional audiotape is included.
SRP: $12.99

Tending Clunk
A call that reproduces the hollow plunks and clunks of a rutting bull. To operate slap your hand over the call's opening.
SRP: $9.99

Targets & Range Equipment

BLUERIDGE SON OF A BUCK

HIGH DENSITY PRO TARGETS

BLUERIDGE

Carbon Stopper Pro
This target uses layers of 4-pound density foam to stop carbon arrows. The stand features five bull's eyes and a metal stand for secure placement.
SRP: **$41.99**

Full Body Whitetail
This buck replica is a scaled down version of the monster Buck and resembles a 125- pound buck. It has the replaceable vital area with score rings.
SRP: **$91.99**

High Density Pro Targets
This flat target by Blueridge uses 6-pound density foam to stop arrows from today's fast bows. The core bullseye is replaceable. A metal stand is included. The target is available in three sizes: 2x24x22-inches, 2x27x24-inches and 2x19x21-inches.
SRP: . . . . **$25.99 to $31.99**

Monster Whitetail
This realistic 3-D deer mimics a 175 pound buck in size and body mass. It is constructed of urethane foam and has a replaceable vital area made of self-healing Natural Tone foam. IBO score lines are marked on both sides. The Monster Buck disassembles into three pieces with removable antlers.
SRP: **$149.99**

Recycled Box Target
This box is made of recycled cardboard and is filled with compressed foam. Multiple targets are offered on the front, back and sides to provide a different level challenge for any shooter. A handle provides easy transporting.
SRP: **$16.99**

Strutting Turkey
This 3-D archery target is a life-size replica of a strutting tom. It's crafted from flexible urethane foam with a polyethylene foam interior section to enhance the stopping power and durability. Two steel stakes are included to secure the target to the ground.
SRP: **$121.99**

Son Of A Buck
This 3-D target includes two replaceable vitals—one for field points and one designed to work well with broadheads. The rear of the buck target has a pocket to secure the vital that is not in use. This target disassembles into three sections and has removable antlers. Stakes are included.
SRP: **$129.99**

3-D Target with Vital Core
When you're cramped for storage space, this rectangular foam target has a deer's chest protruding from the wall and gives a realistic section without the bulk. The features include a 2-foot square, and a 7-inch thick replaceable core. A metal stand is provided to assist with placement.
SRP: **$44.99**

Targets & Range Equipment

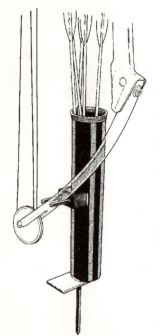

**ERICKSON'S
ARROW STAND WITH BOW REST**

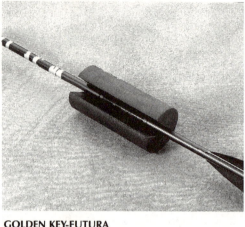

**GOLDEN KEY-FUTURA
SUPER ARROW GRIP**

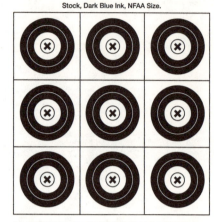

Stock, Dark Blue Ink, NFAA Size.

**MANNEY'S ARCHERY TIC TAC TOE TAR-
GET**

C.W. ERICKSON'S MFG.

This Buffalo, Minnesota, company produces bow vises, multiple brackets for
assorted uses and other archery accessories.

Arrow Stand With Bow Rest

This tube-type stand spikes into the
ground. Great for backyard use. The
foam-lined cylinder protects arrows.
The spike base has a foot ledge for
easy installation.
SRP: $30.49

GLOBAL RESOURCE INCORPORATED

This company is based in Stoughton,
Massachusetts and makes the Shockfin
vibration dampeners.

Ground Spike Bow Rest

This bow holder is secured to the
ground with a spike and can be easily
moved to any location. Holds all types
of bows and can be used in a backyard range or while turkey hunting.
Weighs 16 ounces and is 15 inches
long.
SRP: $15.69
Handy Stand Deluxe Bow and

Arrow Stand

This stand spikes into the ground and
will hold two bows and lots of arrows
in two separate tubes. The vinyl-cov-
ered rest protects a bow's finish.
Cylinders have foam-lined bottoms
and rims to protect arrows.
SRP: $71.49

GOLDEN KEY-FUTURA

This Colorado-based company makes
a wide assortment of archery gear.

Super Arrow Grip

The soft rubber cylinder has a deep
groove that securely and firmly grips
arrows when you're ready to pull them
from a target. It fits comfortably in
your hand and can pull all types and
sizes of arrow shafts, including smaller
diameter carbon shafts.
SRP: $9

MANNEY'S ARCHERY TARGETS

Manney's is based in Hibbing,
Minnesota and produces more than
two dozen types of paper targets for
use by archers. The company has been
making the bull's eyes used at ranges,
critter targets and range score cards for
more than 40 years.

**1-Spot CM 40Tic Tac Toe
(per 100 targets, small quantities
available) SRP:** $23
**3-Spot 4-Color Vegas Round
(per 100 targets) SRP:** $33
**4-Color Super 10 Ring
(per 100 targets) SRP:** $33
**5-Spot 300 Round (per 100 targets,
small quantities
available) SRP:** $23

Indoor 600 Animal Size

This assortment of animal targets printed on heavy paper. The animals
include marked kill zones. Critters
depicted include: prairie dog, rabbit,
turkey, ruffed grouse, fox, pheasant,
bobcat, skunk, raccoon and javelina.
The scoring rings are not visible past
20 yards which adds to the challenge.
SRP: . . . . $20 per 100

Targets & Range Equipment

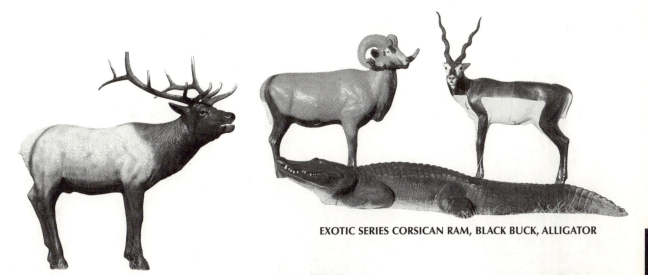

EXOTIC SERIES CORSICAN RAM, BLACK BUCK, ALLIGATOR

HD SERIES ELK

HD SERIES BIGHORN SHEEP

HD SERIES BISON

EXOTIC SERIES FALLOW DEER

McKENZIE TARGETS

McKenzie has been producing their popular and innovative 3-D targets since 1989 when the company unveiled its white-tailed deer target. These targets can be found in backyards and professional ranges worldwide and are offered in numerous styles with numerous options. You can also see these targets in use at many tournaments.

McKenzie HD Series

This series of life-like, full size 3-D targets feature high density foam and most targets can be easily and quickly disassembled for easy transporting and storage.

Bear SRP:
Bighorn Sheep SRP: $328.95
Bison SRP: $849.95
Bedded Deer SRP: $250.95
Large Deer SRP: $261.95
Medium Deer SRP: $228.95
Caribou SRP: $632.95
Elk SRP: $684.9
Mountain Goat SRP: $328.95
Wolf SRP: $222.95

McKenzie Exotic Series

These full-size lifelike 3-D foam targets cover many of the species you'd encounter in Africa and at other hunting grounds around the globe.
Alligator SRP: $240.95
Black Buck SRP: $213.95
Corsican Ram SRP: $248.95
Fallow Deer SRP: $228.95

Targets & Range Equipment

NATURAL LOOK
STANDING BEAR

NATURAL LOOK
STRUTTING TURKEY

NATURAL LOOK
MEDIUM ALERT AND GRAZING DEER

McKenzie Natural Look Targets
These tournament series targets have Super Flex foam centers for extra durability and easy arrow removal. The body is completely painted to protect the foam from harmful ultra-violet sunlight.

Medium Bear SRP:	$217.95
Standing Black Bear SRP:	$302.95
Coyote SRP:	$154.95
Mountain Lion SRP:	$229.95
Pronghorn Antelope SRP:	$217.95
Large Alert Deer SRP:	$198.95
Large Sneak Deer SRP:	$198.95
Medium Alert Deer SRP:	152.95
Medium Grazing Deer SRP:	$152.95
Mule Deer SRP:	$254.95
Quartering Deer SRP:	$180.95
Javelina SRP:	$132.95
Turkey SRP:	$116.95
Strutting Turkey SRP:	$217.95
Wild Boar SRP:	$228.95

Targets & Range Equipment

ROCK RASCALS
WOOD CHUCK, FOX, RACCOON AND BOBCAT

ROCK RASCALS BEAVER

SAFARI SERIES LION

SAFARI WARTHOG

McKenzie Rock Rascals
This small game series by McKenzie includes seven species that are painted with great detail and posed in life-like positions. All targets have IBO approved scoring rings and use a tournament proven re-bar stand system.

Beaver SRP: $115.95
Bobcat SRP: $99.95
Fox SRP: $108.00
Raccoon SRP: $99.95
Wolverine SRP:. $114.95
Woodchuck SRP: $99.95

McKenzie Safari Series
These 3-D targets will make you think that you're hunting in Africa when you spot them on a range near you or in your backyard.

African Blesbok SRP: $276.95
Chamois SRP:. $223.95
African Hyena SRP: $221.95
African Impala SRP: $244.95
African Leopard SRP: $274.95
African Lion SRP: $443.95
Warthog SRP: $242.95

Targets & Range Equipment

HUNTER EDUCATION SERIES BEAR

McKenzie Hunter Education Series

These McKenzie targets provide insight to the game species' vital zones thanks to a joint project with the National Bowhunter Education Foundation.

Bear SRP: $129.95
Deer SRP: $129.95
Turkey SRP: $85.95

Take A Closer Look

One of the best ways to discover game animals is to use a binocular and take a closer look. Look back into the shadows of brush or take a look at distant rocks and logs. You will often spot the glint of an antler tip or the white inside a deer's ear. Never look for an entire animal, always look for small parts.
A binocular can help you see better. Be certain to tuck it into your shirt or place it and any neck strap out of the travel route of your bow's string before releasing an arrow. The same holds true for any string lanyards that are holding calls around your neck.—MDF

HUNTER EDUCATION SERIES DEER

Targets & Range Equipment

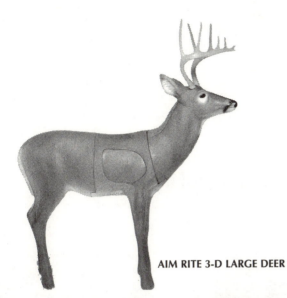

AIM RITE 3-D LARGE DEER

AIM RITE 3-D BEAR

HANDIBLOCK CROSSBOW TARGET

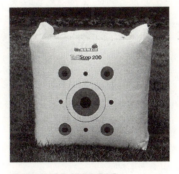

TUFF SHOT STOP BAG

CARBON BLOCK

McKenzie Aim Rite 3-D Targets

This series of targets provide bowhunters with realistic and durable targets at an affordable price.

Medium Aim Rite Deer SRP: .	**$99.95**
Medium Bear SRP:	**$124.95**
Carbon Buck SRP:	**$149.95**
Large Deer SRP:	**$124.95**
Tuff Buck SRP:	**$72.99**

McKenzie Tuff Shot Series

These block targets by McKenzie meet the needs of archers everywhere and will hold countless arrows. They are lightweight, portable and accept shooting with flied points or broadheads.

Carbon Blocks
(small) SRP:	$89.95
(large) SRP:	$99.95

HandiBlock Crossbow
Target SRP:	$79.95
Practice Target SRP:	$34.95

Tuff Stop Bag Target
SRP:	**Starting at $63.95**

Targets & Range Equipment

CARBON SIX SHOOTER

CARBON SIX SHOOTER

50,000 PLUS

3-D SERIES

OUTDOOR RANGE

MORRELL MANUFACTURING

Morrell is located in Alma, Arkansas, and produces target bags for all archers and a series of 3-D buck targets for bowhunters. Call 800-582-7438 for more details.

Carbon Six Shooter

This six-sided Morrell cube has targets on all sides and can be shot on all sides. The target is freestanding and four sides will stop broadheads. A handle permits easy carrying of this 22x22x22-inch target.
SRP: $49.99

Econo

This target has a durable polypropylene cover with NFAA style 5-spot target dots on one side and five spots on the other side. The target is stuffed with high-compressed quality fiber and will last for thousands of shots. The Econo measures 23x23x10-inches.
SRP: $29.99

50,000 Plus

It is 28x28x16 and has a patented floating center and overstuffed to grade quality fibers. This target is 100 % waterproof and will stop both carbon and aluminum arrows with ease. The 50,000 Plus is covered with a two-year warranty.
SRP: $59.99

Humongo Broadhead Targets

The Humongo is designed for broadhead use and permits easy arrow removal. This target measures 30x30x10-inches and has several inner layers of dense foam.
SRP: $34.99

Indoor Range Cube

Similar to the Outdoor Range Target but designed for indoor use. This target will stop all arrows and has flat surfaces to pin paper targets onto.
SRP: $70.00

Outdoor Range Target

This cube-type target is covered with a polymer sack with grommets to permit easy hanging. The exterior has 16 dots to aid with precision practice.
SRP: $89.99

Super Super

This 24x24x12-inch target is stuffed with high-grade fiber then wrapped with space age netting. One side depicts a deer's chest and vitals and the other side of the target has five dots for practice. It is suspended on a metal frame.
SRP: $49.99

3-D Series

These Morrell targets include an alert white-tailed buck, a black bear and a rutting buck. These targets feature easy one-finger arrow removal and the midsection can be recovered for $10. The chest cavities are wrapped with a unique fiber and burlap cover that stops arrows.
SRP: . . . . $139 to $169.

Targets & Range Equipment

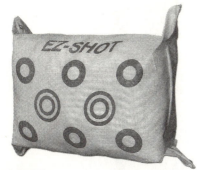

EZ-SHOT

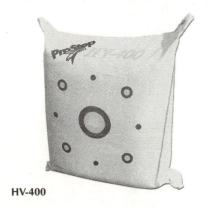

HV-400

RANGE TARGET KIT

PAPER TUNER

P&P OUTDOORS

ProStop Targets and Pittman Game Calls have combined forces and are based in Louisville, Mississippi. The companies can be reached at 800-526-4868. The company manufactures a wide assortment of deer and turkey calls, plus numerous targets and bow tuning aids.

The Blob

This cube target is made for broadheads and will also work with field tips and all types of arrows. The unique, colorfully printed sides represent turkey and deer vital regions in a life-sized scale. All arrows can be easily removed. Size is 18x18x18-inches.
SRP: **$69.95**

EZ-Shot

This economical target is hand-packed with recycled polyester bonded fiber and will stop arrows traveling at up to 260 fps. Arrows can be easily removed and two faces of the target can be shot. Size is 23x28x13-inches.
SRP: **$32.95**

HV-400

This target is designed for today's high velocity carbon arrows and has 160 layers of synthetic fibers. The target can be shot from two sides and measures 24x24x15-inches.
SRP: **$69.95**

Mini-Mag

This small target is portable and durable and can take up to 4000 shots on each side. It measures 22x22x10 inches and will stop arrows traveling up to 250 fps
SRP: **$26.95**

Paper Tuner

Accurate arrow flight depends upon proper tuning and this stand will securely hold a roll of paper for the process. The stand is lightweight, portable and easily transported and stored.
SRP: **$39.95**

Paper Roll

This roll of paper fits the Paper Tuner stand and is 450 yards long and 20 inches wide.
SRP: **$54.95**

ProStop Magnum

This target was designed in 1986 and has withstood the test of time. It is hand-packed and can stop arrows zipping along at 300 fps. The ProStop Magnum can be shot from two sides and will last thousands of arrows. Size is 24x26x13-inches.
SRP: **$46.00**

Range Target Kit

This versatile and sturdy target is sent as a ready-to-assemble kit and can be used in backyards or at professional ranges. Sturdy legs keep the target in place and above ground to prevent water damage.
SRP: **$190.00**

Super Range

This 33x34x15-inch bag is filled with high-density synthetic fiber and has a thick power pad in the rear to stop arrows with absolutely no pass through.
SRP: **$116.95**

Targets & Range Equipment

PAPER TUNER

WOODEN STAND

SAUNDERS ARCHERY

Saunders Archery has been in business many years and is based in Columbus, Nebraska. The company makes numerous innovative archery products ranging from stabilizers to targets and arrow components.

Indian Cord Mats

These machine wound targets have a durable prairie grass Indian-Cord inner layer that's covered with resilient natural burlap. The unit is economical and has a traditional appeal.
Several sizes are available and numerous stand options are available to hold the mats.
SRP: 25-inch $74.95
30-inch $84.95
36-inch $98.95
48-inch $126.95

100# Stock Faces

These heavy weight paper targets have four rings in four colors, or blue and white circles with five spots or huge 40cm circle.
26x26-inch target SRP: . . from $2.45
50x50-inch target SRP: . . . to $11.95

Mat Stands

These stands will hold the Indian Cord mats and targets securely. Numerous sizes are available and you can select from a wheeled stand to an on-the-ground easel.
Wooden stand that holds
  36- and 48-inch mats above waist
  level SRP: $51.95
Metal stand that holds
  36- to 48-inch targets at ground
  level SRP: $98.95
Metal easel stand SRP: $35.95
Dual support
  target stand SRP: $19.95

Paper Tuner

This sturdy and wide stand by Saunders Archery helps you paper tune arrows. The compact 11x114-inch finished oak frame can be clamped or mounted onto a tripod in seconds. A 17x17-inch four-color target is included along with instructions.
SRP: $24.95

Toughenized Faces

These faces have hundreds of nylon threads criss-crossing between two layers of heavy stock. They are available as squared or skirted and will cover the Indian Cord Mats.
48-inch face
  SRP: . . . . . From $10.95 to $24.95

BABY GRAND

BOWHUNTER EXTREME

LEGACY

MAGNUM EXTREME

API OUTDOORS

API makes tree stands and gear for ATVs. For additional information call 800-228-4846.

Baby Grand

This fixed position stand has a large 24x30-inch platform and will hold up to 350 pounds. The seat folds up out of the way when you need more room. The stand attaches to the tree with webbing. The Baby Grand weighs a light 16 pounds.
SRP: **$149.99**

Extreme Bowhunter

A climbing stand made with bowhunters in mind. The stand adjusts easily, has lots of padding and is light-weight to backpack. It includes shoulder straps and a body harness. The stand weighs 20 pounds and will hold 300 pounds.
SRP: **$219.99**

Legacy

This climbing stand has a wire mesh 20x29-inch platform, weighs 29 pounds and is made with rugged steel.

A cable secures the stand to the tree.
SRP: **$179.99**

Magnum Extreme

A climbing tree stand that will hold up to 350 pounds and has triple padding cushions. The stand uses a sure-grip chain to grip the tree. Comes with a full body safety harness.
SRP: **$329.99**

Tree Stands

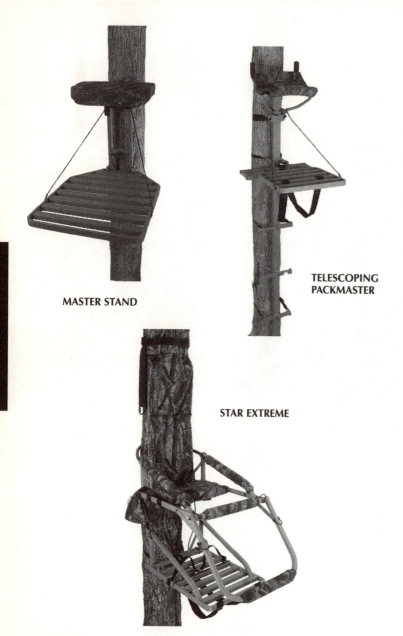

MASTER STAND

TELESCOPING PACKMASTER

STAR EXTREME

V-LOCK LADDER STAND

Master Stand
A fixed position stand with a detachable seat and 23x30-inch platform. The stand weighs 13 pounds and will support up to 300 pounds.
SRP: **$129.99**

Star Extreme
This climbing stand weighs 23 pounds, will hold 300pounds and has a roomy 20x29-inch platform. The climbing seat opens and swings out of the way for bowhunters.
SRP: **$269.99**

Telescoping Packmaster
This unique tree stand is a mobile ladder stand, fixed position stand or a telescoping ladder all in one. The package weighs 24 pounds and the ladder extends to 17-feet. It can be set up in 5 minutes and will hold up to 300 pounds.
SRP: **$279.99**

V-lock Ladder Stand
This ladder stand has a 17-feet high seat and an 18x18-inch platform. It weighs 64 pounds, will hold 300 pounds and can be disassembled into three sections for transporting.
SRP: **$199.99**

EZY CLIMB DELUXE TREE STEP **EZY CLIMB ROD TREE STEP** **EZY CLIMB ROPE TREE STEP** **EZY MIDGET T-SCREW**

EZY CLIMB FOLDING TREE STEP

SUMMIT BROADHEAD BACKPACKER CLIMBING TREE STAND

SUMMIT BUCKSTEPS

EZY T TREE STEP

CRANFORD MANUFACTURING COMPANY

Cranford makes tree steps that screw into the tree or that can be hung on the tree with a rope. Visit www.ezy-climb.com for more details. Cranford is located in Mocksville, North Carolina. All steps feature the EZY Climb screw that taps its way in the tree as you turn it.

EZY Climb Original Tree Step

This step is small, sturdy and easy to transport and place into the tree.
SRP: $3.75
EZY Climb Deluxe Tree Step
SRP: $3.25
EZY Climb Folding Step
SRP: . . . . $3.95 each
EZY Climb Rod Tree Step
SRP: $3.68

EZY T Step
SRP: $3.68

EZY Climb Folding Rope Tree Step

This step ties to a tree and can be used in areas where screw-in steps are illegal. The step folds conveniently and has a one-piece solid steel stainless steel hook.
SRP: $6.49

Midget T-Screw

This screw is used to place your stand on a tree.
SRP: $5.49

SUMMIT

Summit Tree stands are headquartered in Decatur, Georgia, and make a large selection of climbing and hang-on tree stands. Visit www.summitstands.com for more details. Body harnesses are

included with most stand models from Summit.

Broadhead Backpacker Climbing Tree stand

Here's a stand that won't weight you down and was built with bowhunters in mind. It has a 20X28-inch platform, weighs 20 pounds and holds 300 pounds.
SRP: $239

Bucksteps

A set of individual steps that attach to the tree with cam buckles and webbing. The sections are 20 inches long, weigh 10 pounds for 4 steps and will hold up to 260 pounds.
SRP: $89

Tree Stands

GOLIATH TREE STAND

HEADHUNTER MAX

HEADHUNTER MINI

**REVOLUTION
CLIMBING TREE STAND**

SWIFTREE CLIMBING POLE

Goliath Tree stand
A Summit climbing stand that will support up to 350 pounds. The stand has a 20X28-inch platform and a wide top frame.
SRP:. $279

Headhunter Max
A large version of the Headhunter hang-on stand with a 21x24-inch platform. This stand will hold 260 pounds and weighs 17 pounds. Backpacking straps are included.
SRP:. $89

Headhunter Mini
SRP:. $79

Revolution Climbing Tree Stand
A stand with an open front and the climbing bar doubles as a two-position footrest. This stand has a large cushy seat and it weighs 24 pounds. It has a weight limit of 300 pounds.
SRP:. $299

Seat-O-the-Pants 4-Point Body Harness
This harness is camouflaged and fits into a small pouch for transporting. It goes over the shoulders, between the legs and around the waist to hold you from all directions. It has a shock - absorbing tether to act as a brake if you fall. The webbing is rated to hold 6,000 pounds. Adult and youth models are available.
SRP:. . . . . Starting at $59.99

VIPER ULTRA CLIMBING STAND FOOTREST AND SUPER SOFT SEAT

SEAT-O-THE-PANTS 4-POINT BODY HARNESS

VIPER XLS CLIMBING TREE STAND

Swiftree Climbing Pole
These pole sections strap to a tree's trunk and will place you more than 17 feet above ground. The system weighs 18 pounds and will hold up to 260 pounds.
SRP:. $50

Viper XLS Climbing Tree stand
The Viper XLS has cushioned bars to rest your bow on and a super sized platform to give lots of room to maneuver. The unique cable system requires no fumbling with pins or knobs. This stand weighs 20 pounds and will climb trees from 8 to 20 inches in diameter. The weight limit is 300 pounds.
SRP:. $229

Viper Ultra Climbing Stand Footrest and super soft seat
SRP:. $259

Treestand Practice Routine
A good way to make the most of your treestand practice is to work with a partner who moves the target around while you are turned and facing the tree.
You'll have to consider a new angle and shot location when you turn around. The new situation imitates the erratic movement of game animals in the wild and can be more realistic practice. Be certain to wear a safety belt when using a treestand and that your partner is in a safe area before you release an arrow.—MDF

Other Accessories

BOHNING CAMO KIT

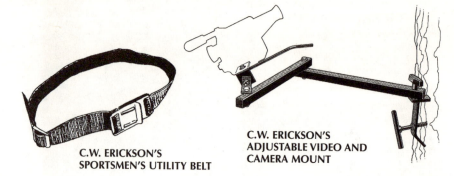

C.W. ERICKSON'S SPORTSMEN'S UTILITY BELT

C.W. ERICKSON'S ADJUSTABLE VIDEO AND CAMERA MOUNT

C.W. ERICKSON'S BOWSLING

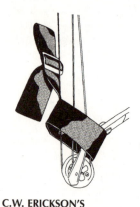

C.W. ERICKSON'S CWIK DRAW BOW HOLSTER

C.W. ERICKSON'S HIGH RISER BOW REST

BOHNING WIND CHECK

BOHNING

This company manufacturers numerous items to upgrade your arrows and to build them.

The Bohning Company is based in Lake City, Michigan, and can be reached at 800-253-0136 or visit www.bohning.com.

Camo Kit

This easy to use kit is in a camouflaged case with a mirror included. Colors inlcude: shadow gray, flat black, bark brown and forest green.
SRP: $5.76
Skin Camo Crème
SRP: $5.37

Wind Check

This small bottle of odorless powder will help you determine the most fickle wind at your stand.
SRP: $4.14

C.W. ERICKSON'S MFG.

This Buffalo, Minnesota company produces bow vises, multiple brackets for assorted uses and other archery accessories. Call 612-682-3665 for more product details.

Adjustable Video and Camera Mount

This adjustable swing arm is what the pros use to mount their cameras and video recorder to the tree to capture frame-by-frame and second by second details and action. Weighs 3 pounds and ins constructed of flat black tubing.
SRP: $63.99

Bowsling

An over-the-shoulder strap that keeps your bow securely at your side. The webbing is 2-inches wide and permits easy-on and easy-off.
SRP: $7.79

Cwik Draw Bow Holster

This holster attaches to your belt and keeps your bow at your side while relieving arm strain. Can be sued while walking and standing. Accepts long, recurve and compound bows and the item is adjustable.
SRP: $7.79

High Riser Bow Rest

Similar to the standard tree stand bow rest but an extension raises the bow 6 to 7 inches above the stand. It's fully adjustable to accommodate all tree-stand situations. Allows hands to be free but keeps the bow close and ready.
SRP: $17.10

Sportsman's Utility Belt

Use this belt to secure loads to your pack, items to your treestand or around your waist to hold a bow holder, packs, knives etc. The belt is 1½-inch wide webbing and fits waists up to 50-inches. Has a quick release buckle.
SRP: $8.39

Other Accessories

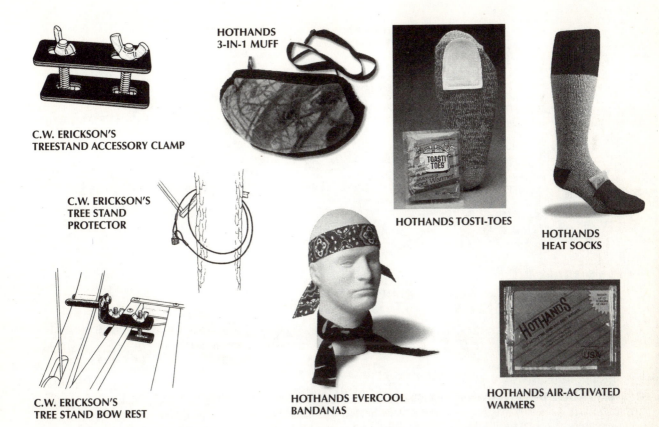

C.W. ERICKSON'S TREESTAND ACCESSORY CLAMP

C.W. ERICKSON'S TREE STAND PROTECTOR

C.W. ERICKSON'S TREE STAND BOW REST

HOTHANDS 3-IN-1 MUFF

HOTHANDS TOSTI-TOES

HOTHANDS HEAT SOCKS

HOTHANDS EVERCOOL BANDANAS

HOTHANDS AIR-ACTIVATED WARMERS

C.W. ERICKSON'S MFG.

Tree stand Accessory Clamp
This useful clamp can be used to secure many items to your treestand, plus to attach brush for concealment.
SRP: $5.59

Tree Stand Bow Rest
This handy prong can be used to securely and quietly hold your bow at the edge of your tree stand. Fits on almost all stands without drilling and vinyl cover holders secure your bow.
SRP: $9.79

Tree Stand Protector
The Protector is a 6½-foot long flexible cable to prevent theft. This item can double as a game drag.
SRP: $7.70

HOTHANDS

When the temperatures drop, these odorless air-activated heat pads might be the ticket to hunting longer and being succesful. HotHands is based in Dalton, Georgia and can be reached at 800-432-8629.

Air-Activated Warmers
These pads can be placed in pockets or gloves to keep skin and extremities warm and comfortable. Once removed from the plastic packet the air activates the pads and starts the warm up. Sizes include 4x5-inch and a compact 2½x4-inch pad.
SRP: each . . . . $.99 to $1.99

Evercool Bandanas
For hunting in hot areas where temperatures soar and the sun bakes you, these bandanas have special polymer beads that expand up to 100 times their size when soaked in water. The evaporation causes a cooling effect when the bandana is worn around the neck. Available colors include hunter green and black.
SRP: $4.99

Feet Heat Socks
These heavyweight socks have a pocket on top of the toe area to hold a heat pad. Two air-activated HotHands pads are shipped with the socks and additional pads can be purchased. The socks stay warm up to 6 hours.
SRP: . . . . $10.99 to $12.99

3-in-1 Muff
 Use the heat pads to heat this hand-warming muff. The muff is wind- and water-resistant fleece and is camouflaged with Realtree Hardwoods. A zippered pocket turns this item into a fanny pack or you can sit on an empty muff for a comfortable seat cushion. It attaches to the waist with a belt that is included.
SRP: $19.99

Tosti-Toes
These air-activated pads are designed to fit into boots and produce and average temperature of 100-degree F. An adhesive strip will help the warmer stay in place in your socks. Each package has two warmers.
SRP: per pack $1.49

Other Accessories

HUNTER'S SPECIALTIES
SCENT ELIMINATION KIT

HUNTER'S SPECIALTIES
LIMB LIGHTS

HUNTER'S SPECIALTIES
MAG LIMB LIGHTS

HUNTER'S SPECIALTIES
TRAIL MARKER TAPE

HUNTER'S SPECIALTIES
UTILITY ROPE

HUNTER'S SPECIALTIES
HOT MELT STICK

HUGHES PRODUCTS COMPANY

Hughes Products Company makes scent dispensers, very realistic rattling antlers, hunting gear and a wide assortment of archery items. A must see item that this company produces is their line of antler lamps, chandeliers and magazine racks. These will make any home or cabin more enjoyable for bowhunters. For more details, contact 336-475-0091 or visit www.hughes-productsco.com.

EZ-Fold Gambrel

When space is at a premium, such as a remote camp that you backpack in to, this folding gambrel is the ticket to properly and safely handling game. It has a 350-pound weight capacity and will hang medium size game like deer and pronghorns. The extended arms reach out 22 inches and it's only 11½-inches long when folded. A pull rope is included.
SRP: $15.95

HPX5 Broadhead Sharpener and Wrench

A neat tool that is both a broadhead wrench and blade sharpener. This unit will sharpen all styles of broadheads and knife blades with either a tungsten carbide or ceramic sharpening system,

plus it has slots to accommodate 3-, 4- and 5-blade broadheads. Yhis item is blaze orange so you will not loose it and it will fit in a shirt pocket!
SRP: $5.95

One-Man Hoist

Use this pulley system to hoist your deer or game animal up for skining and processing. This item can also be used for camp chores.
SRP: $29.95

HUNTER'S SPECIALTIES

Hunter's Specialties manufactures calls, scents and a very large assortment of archery and bowhunting oriented gear. The company is based in Cedar Rapids, Iowa.

Limb Lights

The twist type strips are reflective and wrap easily around small limbs and treesteps. They can be seen for approximately 100 yards.
SRP: $4.45

Mag Limb Lights

SRP: $4.67

Mag Hot Melt Stick

This glue stick is used to glue points and inserts to arrow shafts. It can also repair fishing rods and camp gear.
SRP: $2.58

Scent Elimination Kit

This kit includes Scent-Away soap, laundry detergent, dryer sheets and bar soap. Other items includes anti-perspirant and a scent safe storage bag.
SRP: $29.70

Scent Away Dryer Sheets

SRP: $4.90

Scent Safe Deluxe Travel Bag

SRP: $52.00

Scent Away Spray Combo

SRP: $18.31

Trail Marker Tape

This non-adhesive safety orange tape is photodegradable and perfect for marking trails and while tracking. It breaks down in sunlight and is waterproof and easy to tear. The roll is 150 feet long.
SRP: $2.52

Utility Rope

A strong 20-foot long rope that is safe, quiet and washable. Use it to haul gear up to your treestand.
SRP: $3.20

JIM FLETCHER'S FIELD TOOL

LANSKY CROCKSTICK
MULTI-SHARPENER

LANSKY
MINI-CROCKSTICK
MULTI-SHARPENER

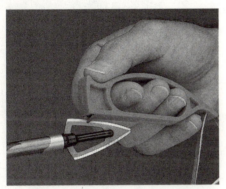

NORTH AMERICAN ARCHERY GROUP
ARCHER'S EDGE BROADHEAD SHARPENER

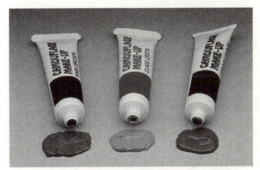

NORTH AMERICAN ARCHERY GROUP
CAMO MAKE-UP CREAM

SHOOTING ACCESSORIES

JIM FLETCHER ARCHERY AIDS

This company is based in Bodfish, California, and can be reached at 760-379-2589.

Bow Wax

This specially formulated bow wax keeps strings moist while keeping water out. It extends the life of your bowstring.
SRP: $3.20

Bow Wrist Strap

This strap keeps your bow attached to your wrist and is adjustable. It connects to the bow behind your stabilizer. It's machine washable.
SRP: $4.25

Fleece Bow Wrist Strap

A soft and quite wrist strap that keeps your bow secure to your hand. These wrist straps help you relax your hand and be a better shot.
SRP: $8.35

Fletcher's Field Tool

This compact and foldable tool has the following Allen wrenches: 3/16, 5/32, 9/64, 1/8, 7/64, 3/32, 5/64, and 1/16-inch. It also has a slot and a #1 Phillips head screwdriver head. In addition the unit has an open-end adjustable wrench and a three-blade broadhead wrench. It is truly a toolbox in your hand.
SRP: $25

LANSKY SHARPENERS

Crock Stick Multi-Sharpener

This small ceramic stick will fit in a shirt pocket and can be used to sharpen knives and broadheads. It has a triangular design and easy to grip safety end caps.
SRP: $8.00

Mini Crock Stick Sharpener

A small knife and fishhook sharpener with two removable ceramic sharpening stones. It can be used as a key ring.
SRP: $5.00

NORTH AMERICAN ARCHERY GROUP

The following items are available from the North American Archery Group in Gainesville, Florida. These items will work with their Bear and Jennings bows and for any hunter.

Archer's Edge Broadhead Sharpener

This compact hand-held unit can be used to sharpen broadheads for hunting. Compact enough to fit in shirt pocket. A must have item for hunters on the go!
SRP: $4.49

Camo Make-Up Cream

These items are sold as a kit or in bulk. Apply to face and hands to camouflage areas and increase concealment while hunting. Easily removed. Colors: green, black and brown.
SRP: . . . . $3.49.

Other Accessories

NORTH AMERICAN ARCHERY GROUP SILENT BOW HANGER

NORTH AMERICAN ARCHERY GROUP HOOK AND LINE KIT

NORTH AMERICAN ARCHERY GROUP RATTLE BAG

SIMMONS SYSTEM ARCHERY 2ND CHANCE ARROW HOLDERS

NORTH AMERICAN ARCHERY GROUP CONTINUED
Hook and Line Kit
Perfect set-up for hoisting bow and hunting gear up to your treestand after you're safely secured into position. Rope is 20-foot long and has a sturdy clip on each end. Can also be used to secure unwanted brush out of shooting lanes. Two screw-in hooks are included in the kit for securing your gear and bow in the tree.
SRP: **$3.49**

Rattle Bag
Camouflaged cloth bag with solid components to simulate battling bucks. Has clip to secure unit to your belt or pack.
SRP: **$11.99**

Silent Bow Hanger
This sturdy, rubber-coated hook can be easily screwed into a tree to hang your bow while hunting.
SRP: 3-pack **$3.49**
6-pack **$3.99**

SIMMONS SYSTEM ARCHERY
Known for its Simmons Sharks broadheads, this Jasper, Alabama, company also makes a unique arrow holder. (205-387-7174)

2nd Chance Arrow Holders
When you need a second chance without making unnecessary game spooking movement, these rubber coated screw-in arrow clips by Simmons System Archery will help hold a second arrow in a convenient and within reach location. Simply screw the holder into the tree trunk and pop an arrow between the prongs. Arrows can be removed quickly and quietly.
SRP: . . . . **$12.95 per three pack**

Invite Others
One of the best things you can do to protect your bowhunting privileges is to invite another hunter to join the ranks. If you must, spend time explaining your gear and take them to a range or proshop to try out a bow.
Don't overlook your wife as a great hunting partner.
The number of women who successfully bowhunts is growing each year. Many archery instructors will also tell you that women make better students. Almost every bow manufacturer makes models that are suitable for women and young archers.--MDF

BOWHUNTING CLOTHING

Bowhunting Clothing

HYRDO-FLEECE CLASSIC INSULATED BIB

HYRDO-FLEECE CLASSIC 4-IN-1 PARKA

HYRDO-FLEECE CLASSIC INSULATED PANT

HYRDO-FLEECE CLASSIC JACKET

BROWNING

This Utah based manufacture produces a full line of hunting apparel for men, women and young hunters. Many Browning garments utilize Gore-Tex fabric technology, such as Supprescent. The Supprescent fabric provides 100 percent waterproof protection and breathable comfort, along with an added benefit of permanent odor barrier with carbon that is permanently embedded into the fabric. There are no adhesions or stiffeners that will change the comfort of the fabric to the wearer. In addition to clothing, this technology can be found in footwear. It requires no reactivation with heat and does not require sprays or re-applications. Gore-Tex garments are tested and guaranteed waterproof. For more details, call Gore at 800-431-GORE or visit www.gore-tex.com

Hydro-Fleece Classic 4-in-1 Parka with Supprescent

This Browning parka permits layering with an inner jacket that zips in and out. Other features include two zippered pockets, and inside security pocket and hood. The shell is quiet and soft Hydro Fleece and offered in Mossy Oak camo.

SRP: S-XL $300
XXL and larger . . . . $337.

Hydro-Fleece Classic Insulated Bib with Supprescent

The perfect companion garment for the Classic parka. The bibs have front zipper, leg zippers and pockets. They are insulated and available in Mossy Oak camouflage.

SRP: S-XL $200,
XXL and larger $233

Hydro-Fleece Classic Jacket with Supprescent

This lightweight hunting jacket has Gore's Supprescent technology to eliminate human odors. The jacket has a soft fleece exterior and is available in Mossy Oak Break Up camouflage.

SRP: S-XL $225
XXL and larger $250

Hydro Fleece Classic Pant with Supprescent

These pants are the companion to the jacket above and feature a draw cord with belt loops, a rear pocket and zippered legs for easy on and off.

SRP: S-XL $155
XXL and larger $171

Hydro-Fleece Pro Series 4-in-1 Parka with Supprescent

This garment has a coat within a coat that can be zipped in or out to meet changing temperatures and weather conditions. The outer shell is made of Cordura and is quiet and rugged. It has an archer sleeve that can be adjusted for sung fit to stay out of the way of the bowstring. The parka features a detachable hood, two-zippered bellows pockets, and inside security pocket and rear storage pocket. This coat is water- and windproof. It is made scent proof with Supprescent technology and waterproof with a Gore-Tex laminate. It's offered in Mossy Oak Break-Up.

SRP: S-XL $400,
2XL and Larger. $440

CLOTHING

Bowhunting Clothing

HYRDO-FLEECE
INSULATED JACKET

HYRDO-FLEECE PANT

BUG-OUT COVER-UP PACKS

BROWNING *continued*
Hydro-Fleece Pro Series Insulated Bib with Supprescent
These bibs match the 4-in-1 parka above and are similar in design and construction. The bibs are insulated with Dupont Themolite and have an inner lining, two front pockets, a heavy duty full length front zipper and the leg zippers are full-length to permit easy on and off. It's available in Mossy Oak camouflage.
SRP: S-L $268
XXL or larger $298

Hydro-Fleece Pro Series Jacket with Supprescent
This feature packed jacket is not insulated and has similar construction and features as the parka. The jacket is lined with Gore-Tex Supprescent to eliminate odors reaching wary game species while hunting. The jacket is wind and waterproof, and has a soft and quiet Micro Fleece exterior. This jacket is designed to provide years of dependable service. The jacket is X-Change system compatible and available in Mossy Oak camo.

SRP: S-XL $260
XXL and larger $299
Hydro-Fleece Pro Series Pants with Supprescent
These pants are the companion to the above jacket and are great for bowhunting wear during normal hunting conditions. This garment has Supprescent technology. The pants have zippered legs, belt loops and a drawstring. They are available in Mossy Oak Break-Up.
SRP: S-XL $212
XXL and larger $233

BUG-OUT OUTDOORWEAR
Bug-Out manufacturers innovative bug suits to keep biting bugs away from your skin. Many spring bear hunters and early-season deer bowhunters use these products. The coat and pants are sold in a package—a bug pack! Call 877-928-4688 or visit www.bug-out-outdoorwear.com.

Bug Out Bug Packs
These handy bags contain a jacket, pants and headnet. The jacket has a full-length zipper and the pants have an elastic waistband. These garments are made of no-see-um mesh with micro fibers. The fiber will stop biting bugs and ticks and is colored olive drab.
SRP: olive . . . . . . $35.99 to $54.99

Bug Out Cover-Up Packs
These inexpensive suits come in a handy pack bag and include a jacket, pant and face mask. The jacket has a high collar, extra long sleeves and relaxed fit to permit movement. It has a full-length front zipper. The pants are cut oversized and have an elastic waistband. You can pull these on over standard clothing or other hunting garments to provide quick concealment or to better blend in under any cover. Available colors include Realtree Hardwoods, Advantage Timber, Realtree Hardwoods Blaze, Realtree Hardwoods Snow, Blaze solid and white. Sizes S-4XL large.
SRP: . . . . $39.95 to 54.99

CLOTHING

Bowhunting Clothing

CONTAIN MAXIMUM

ROBINSON OUTDOORS
DISCOVERY JACKET

ROBINSON OUTDOORS
DISCOVERY PANTS

CONTAIN SOLID

CONTAIN

Contain is based in Minnesota and makes under garments designed to control human odor. Call 800-804-8588 for more details.

Contain Maximum

The fibers of these Coolmax blend garments have built in deodorant. Contain helps prevent the formation of body odor. These items are designed to be worn next to the skin. All garments except the socks are available in Mossy Oak camouflage.

Long Sleeve T-Shirt
SPR:. $46
Long John Bottoms
SRP:. $46
Boxer Shorts
SRP:. $34
Camouflaged Head Cover
SRP:. $28
Gloves
SRP: $11.99
Hiking Socks
SRP: $16.99
Tube Socks
SRP: $12.99

Contain Solid

These undergarments actually prevent the formation of body odor thanks to deodorant fibers. The gray garments are made from an acrylic/polyester blend and can be machine-washed.
Contain Solid Long Sleeve T-Shirt
SRP: $32.99
Contain Solid Long John Bottoms
SRP: $32.99

RAIN SHIELD

Rain Shield uses 3M's ProPore to manufacture lightweight rain suits. Rain Shield is based in Minnesota and can be reached at 888-543-1984.

O2 Rainwear

A packable rain suit that comes in a small bag describes the 02 suit. The suit uses the new 3M membrane and is covered in Mossy Oak camouflage. The rain suit is breathable yet waterproof and includes a pant and jacket with hood.
SRP: $79.95

ROBINSON OUTDOORS

Based in Minnesota, Robinson Outdoors produces the Scent Blocker series of products.

Discovery Jacket

A scent control jacket by Robinson Outdoors with a zip-out removable liner and two-piece hood. The jacket has 10 pockets, a chill-out ventilation system and non-slip shoulder pad. The specially designed arm permits movement. Available in Mossy Oak Break Up and Hardwoods camouflage.
SRP: . . . . **Starting at $269**

Discovery Pants

The companion garment to the Discovery jacket. The pant has a reinforced seat, 2 large cargo pockets, two front pockets, and 20-inch water repellent leg zippers.
SRP: . . . . **Starting at 229**

SAVANNA MOCK-TURTLENECK

DAKOTA BOMBER JACKET

DAKOTA 6-POCKET PANT

SAVANNAH COVERALLS

SAVANNA BOMBER JACKET

DAKOTA HEADCOVER

SAVANNAH LONG SLEEVE MOCK-T

SAVANNAH STALKER JACKET

SAVANNAH 6-POCKET PANT

SCENT-LOK

Scent-Lok is the original creator of carbon fabric odor elimination technology and continues to improve, develop and expand the technology. These carbon fabrics actually trap gas particles released by the body during normal perspiration. Their garment line includes inner layer, outerwear and head covers and gloves. Scent-Lok has been in business for a decade. The company is based in Michigan and can be reached at 800-315-5799 or visit www.scentlok.com.

SCENT-LOK DAKOTA SERIES

This single-layer Microsuede fabric is light, burr-proof, and repels moisture. It is colorfast so camouflage patterns will not fade. The Dakota series uses Climaflex fabric that is also extremely breathable and helps keep hunters dry inside and out. Available camouflage patterns are Advantage Timber and Mossy Oak.

Dakota Six-Pocket Pants
SRP: $129.95

Dakota Single Layer Microsuede Bib Overalls
SRP: $169.95

Dakota Single layer Microsuede Mock Turtleneck
SRP: $99.95

Dakota Single Layer Microsuede Premium Bomber Jacket
SRP: $129.95

Dakota Headcover
SRP: $34.95

Scent-Lok Savanna Series

Savanna Bomber Jacket
SRP: $99.95

Savanna BDU Pants
SRP: $99.95

Savanna Lightweight Shirts
SRP: $89.95

Savanna Stalker Jacket
SRP: $114.95

Savanna Packable Coveralls
SRP: $169.95

CLOTHING

Bowhunting Clothing

SCENT-LOK SUPREME 3-IN-1 SIX-POCKET PANT

SCENT-LOK SUPREME 3-IN-1 PARKA

SCENT-LOK CLASSIC GREEN JACKET LINER

SCENT-LOK CLASSIC GREEN HEADCOVER

SCENT-LOK INSULATED GLOVES

CLASSIC GREEN SCENT-LOK PULL ON PANT LINER

SCENT-LOK SAVANNA HEADCOVER

SCENT-LOK SAVANNA T-SHIRT

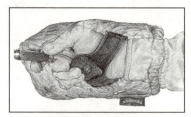

SHERWOOD ARCHERY BOW HUNTER'S RELEASE MITT

SCENT-LOK *continued*

Savanna Ultra-Light T-Shirt
SRP:.................... $59
Savanna Long Sleeve Mock T-Shirt
SRP: $79.95, $87.94
Scent-Lok Savanna Headcover
SRP: $21.95
Scent-Lok Facemask
SRP: $21.95
Scent-Lok Hunting Caps
SRP: $34.95

Scent-Lok Supreme Series
These bomber and pants offer two-layer protection with an inner light-weight garment and a touch—but quiet—outer layer that repels water and the elements.
Scent-Lok Supreme 3-in-1 Parka Length Jacket
SRP: $189.95
2XL and larger $208.95
Scent-Lok Supreme 3-in-1 Six-Pocket Pant
SRP: up to XL......... $189.95
2XL and larger........ $208.95

Scent Lok Gloves
Wear these to eliminate odors as you travel to your stand or while hunting.
SRP: $34.95
insulated............... $39.95

Classic Green Scent-Lok Liner Wear
These are the garments that got the entire human scent industry up and running. The original liners can be effectively worn under standard hunting clothing as a layering system. The Classic series are olive green in color.
Classic Jacket Liner
SRP: $75.95
Classic Headcover
SRP: $19.95
Classic Pull On Pant Liner
SRP: up to XL $75.95
XXL and larger $83.55

SHERWOOD ARCHERY
Founded in 1997 by Brian Smith and Jerry Eidenmiller, Sherwood Archery is a small, family owned business dedicat-

ed to the design and engineering of hunting equipment and apparel. Recognizing a need for functional gear designed exclusively for the bowhunter, lifelong hunter and avid archer Brian Smith researched and developed the company's signature product – the Bowhunter's Release Mitt. From this unique idea, Sherwood Archery was born. www.sherwoodarchery.com 402-680-9693

Bowhunter's Release Mitt
Protects release hand with quiet, warm fleece and 150-gram Thinsulate insulation. Innovative design allows for a smooth draw and release without fumbling with gloves, mittens or muffs. Slide hand inside and position release through the slot. Elastic cuff keeps cold out. Ambidextrous design. Mossy Oak Break-Up.
SRP: $29.95

Bowhunting Clothing

WOOLRICH
V-SYSTEM
BARRIER
PARKA

WOOLRICH CAMWOOLFLAGE JACKET

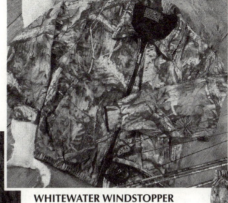

WHITEWATER WINDSTOPPER
SUPPRESCENT
JACKET

WHITEWATER
WINDSTOPPER
SUPPRESCENT PANT

WHITEWATERS OUTDOORS

This clothing manufacturer is based in Hingham, Wisconsin and can be reached at 800-666-2764 or visit www.whitewateroutdoors.com.

Whitewater Windstopper Supprescent Jacket

A jacket made of ultra-soft and quiet 100% polyester Micro Fleece to eliminate fabric scratch. The jacket is lined with Gore's Windstopper membrane with active carbon permanently embedded in. Other features include two hand warmer pockets, stretch cuffs and a stand-up collar. This jacket is available in Realtree Hardwoods and Advantage Timber. It's offered in sizes Medium through 3XL.

SRP: . . . . $140 to $160

Whitewater Windstopper Supprescent Pant

A pant similar to the Whitewater jacket in construction and fabric, and this garment has a full elastic waistband and cuffs. It is also offered in the two Jordan Enterprises camouflaged patterns.

SRP: . . . . $130 to $150

WOOLRICH

Pennsylvania is the home for Woolrich in a city with the same name. The company was established in 1830 and makes wool based clothing in many styles for outdoor wear and hunting. These garments are affordable, durable and will last for years. Visit www.woolrich.com for more details.

Camwoolflage Fleece-lined Vest

Available in sizes M-3XL, this Hardwoods camo vest has a liner, hand warmer pockets and kidney warmer. It is 80% wool and zips up the front.

SRP: $72

Camwoolflage Jacket

A hooded jacket with two lower dual entry pockets with button closures. The sleeves have adjustable cuffs.

SRP: $105

Camwoolflage Pants

The pants to match the shirt above and with side waist adjustments and two large side pockets for gear. The pants have a 36-inch inseam and are unfinished.

SRP: $76

Camwoolflage Shirt

A camouflaged wool shirt that buttons up the front. It has a high collar and two front pockets. Offered in sizes M-3XL and in Hardwoods camouflage.

SRP: $75

V-System Barrier Pant

The pants to match the above parka with similar construction and reinforced seat and gussetted crotch. Also has zipper secured pockets and side leg zippers with storm flaps. These pants are waterproof and breathable.

SRP: $170

V-System Barrier Parka

A Woolrich waterproof and breathable parka with waterproof seam sealing. This garment features a two-way zippered front, detachable hood, adjustable cuffs and 100% polyester Whisper Dry Cloth exterior with Hydromax. Available in Realtree and Advantage camouflage. You can zip an inner jacket into this parka for great layering options.

SRP: $199

Archery Sportswear

GOLD TIP HAT

GOLD TIP
SHORT SLEEVE T-SHIRT

GOLD TIP DENIM SHIRT

GOLD TIP
LONG SLEEVE T-SHIRT

GOLD KEY
BRASS
BUCKLE

GOLD KEY
DECALS

GOLDEN KEY T-SHIRTS AND PINS

GOLDEN KEY CAPS

GOLD TIP

Show your pride and enthusiasm for Gold Tip archery products as you tell others that you are a demanding archer. All have Gold Tip logos and GT insignia. Gold Tip is headquartered in Utah.

Gold Tip Hats
Assorted ball caps including camouflaged models.
SRP. . . . . starting at $13.93

Gold Tip Logo T-Shirts
Assorted colors and styles with the Gold Tip logo.
Long Sleeve T-Shirt
SRP. . . . . starting at $16.73
Short Sleeve T-Shirt
SRP. . . . . starting at $11.13

Gold Tip Polo Shirts
These upscale short sleeve polo shirts are great for on the range or around town wear.
SRP: $34.93

Gold Tip Shirts
These shirts are available in assorted colors and sizes. With these you can dress to impress.
Long Sleeve Denim Dress Shirt
SRP: $36.33
Long Sleeve Green Dress Shirt
SRP: $41.93
Long Sleeve Natural Dress Shirt
SRP: $34.93

GOLDEN KEY-FUTURA

This Colorado-based company makes a large assortment of archery gear. Wear these items to show your strong interest in archery.

Decals
Turn your truck or car into a Golden Key-Futura billborad with these decals.
SRP:. $4

Golden Key Brass Buckle
This brass buckle with the raised GKF logo will look distinctive on the range and anywhere that you go.
SRP:. $18

GKF and Dead Head Ball Caps
Numerous styles and colors are available. Camouflage hats have camo bills, other caps are single color or have a distinctive colored bill.
SRP:. $24

GKF Dead Head Logo Shirts
Quality poly/cotton blend T-shirts that will look god for years. Avalalble with GKF logo or Dead Head broadhead logo.
SRP:. $18

FRED BEAR HAT

G2 HAT

FRED BEAR POLO

FRED BEAR LONG SLEEVE SHIRT

JENNINGS DENIM SHIRT

JENNINGS LONG SLEEVE SHIRT

JENNINGS POLO

NEW ARCHERY PRODUCTS

Hats
Show your dedication to NAP's broadheads, arrow rests and stabilizers with these stylish ball caps. Each model is offered in Mossy Oak, Realtree, black, or tan with a navy bill.
Logos include: Thunderhead Broadhead, Spitfire Broadhead, and Shockwave Stabilizers. Nap is based in Illinois.
SRP: . . . . $12 each.

NORTH AMERICAN ARCHERY GROUP
The following items are distributed by the North American Archery Group of Gainesville, Florida. Here's the place to find Jennings, Bear and Golden Eagle wearables.

Archery Ball Caps
Assortment of colors (blue, camo, white, green, tan, white w/green bill and camo w/tan suede bill) with Jennings, Fred Bear and Buckmaster G2 logos.
SRP: $11.99

Fred Bear Long-Sleeve Shirt
Green short with button down collar and front. Has distinctive Fred Bear Archery logo on chest. Sizes L, XL, and XXL.
SRP: $44.99

Fred Bear Polo Shirt
Available in oatmeal color with three button front and Bear Archery logo. Sizes L, XL and XXL.
SRP: $39.99

Golden Eagle L/S Shirt
Show your pride in hunting camp with this soft, stylish shirt with a Golden Eagle logo on the chest, button front and button down collar. Sizes: L, XL and XXL. (Item 3960)
SRP: $44.99

Golden Eagle White Polo Shirt
Three button front, short sleeves and Golden Eagle logo on chest. Sizes: L, XL and XXL.
SRP: $39.99

Jennings Denim Shirt
Constructed of thick, soft denim with two buttoned front pockets and button down collar and front. Available sizes: L, XL and XXL w/ Jennings logo on chest. Color: blue.
SRP: $39.99

Jennings Long-Sleeve Shirt
Has a button-down collar and buttons down the front. Available in L, XL and XXL w/ Jennings logo. Color: Dark gray.
SRP: $44.99

Jennings Polo Shirt
A dark-blue polo shirt with a white Jennings logo on the chest. Three button front and available in L, XL and XXL.
SRP: $39.99

Archery Sportswear

MUZZY CANVAS SHIRTS

SURE-LOC POLO

MUZZY HATS

SURE-LOC T-SHIRT

MUZZY APPAREL
These items are distributed by Muzzy, the Georgia-based broadhead manufacturer.

Muzzy Canvas Shirts
Embroidered shirts with company logo on front and back. Assorted colors and sizes.
SRP: . . . . **$70.53 to $77.95**

Muzzy Hats
Thes base ball type caps have a distinctive green or gold Muzzy logo and the word MUZZY boldly printed or embroidered on the front of the cap above the bill. Color options include: Black, brown and green colors on oilskin; Realtree Hardwoods; Advantage Timber; Mossy Oak Forest Floor and Break-Up.
SRP: basic colors **$15.33**
Camouflaged **$8.67**

Muzzy Polo Shirts
Assorted colors and styles with deer and Muzzy logos.
SRP: . . . . **$20.59 to $30.53.**

Muzzy T-Shirts
These Thsirts are offered in sizes from small to XXX large and assorted colors and with multiple logos and images, including: Deer, TEAM MUZZY, Bad TO The Bone, Can't Eat, Can't Work, Fall Rut, Spring Strut.
SRPS: . . . . . . **Range from $16 to $20.**

SURE-LOC

Sure-Loc Wearables
If you're the a fan of the Sure-Loc target sights and up-scale hunting sights, then these hat and shirts will help you show your pride. Sure-Loc is headquartered in Versailles, Indiana. If you want to get a custom shooting shirt, you can have your name embroidered on any Sure-Loc shirt for $10.
SureLoc Ball Caps
SRP: **$12.99**
Sure-Loc Sweat Shirts
SRP: S, M, L, XL **$23.99**
XXL **$36.99**
Sure-Loc Polo Shirts
SRP: S, M, L, XL **$28.50**
XXL . . . . **$31.50.**
Sure-Loc T-Shirts
SRP: . . . . XXL short sleeve **$12**
long sleeve **$21.99**

BOW FISHING GEAR

MUZZY   **384**

Bow Fishing Gear

AMS SAFETY SLIDE

REEL SEAT

EVER CLEAN

BOW FISHING STARTER KIT

CLASSIC ARROW WITH GAR POINT

ECONOMY RIVER POINT

MUZZY BOW FISHING LINES

BLUE FIBERGLASS SHAFT

MUZZY

AMS Safety Slide
This innovative slide helps keep the line safely away from your arrow rest when at full draw and slides down the shaft when reeling in. End those frustrating arrow verses line launch problems with this AMS slide. Two diameters are available: $5/16$ and $22/64$.
SRP: . . . . **$3.25 each.**

Anchor Reel Seat and Rod
The anchor reel seat screws into your bow's stabilizer hole for quick mounting of the Zebco bowfishing reel. The Rod mounts in the reel seat to keep your line clear of the bow and arrow rest.
SRP: . . . . **$18 reel seat**
rod **$9.93**

Bowfishing Lines
Muzzy is your source for sturdy lines to reel in the big ones. Our inventory includes: Brownell Fast Flite, Muzzy Extreme, Brownell Gator Cord, Muzzy Tournament line, BCY 175# and 300# test lines. Lengths range from 75- to 300-feet and weight ranges span from 175-pound to the 600-pound Gator Cord.
SRP: Ranges from . . . . . **$9.65 to$40**

Bowfishing Arrow Rests
Here are two rests designed to handle bowfishing arrows and the strain caused upon release.
Wheel of Fortune II: Incorporates a brass wheel on a stainless steel shaft for smooth corrosion free operation.
SRP: **$11.65**
Tri-Loop Rest: a shoot-through metal triangle designed to accommodate unfletched arrows.
SRP: . . . . **$11.65 each**

Bowfishing Starter Kit
This package includes everything you need to grab your bow and start hunting fish! Includes a Zbeco reel filled with 150-pound test Spectra line, a reel seat, Muzzy's Tri-Loop arrow rest, an a Muzzy Classic arrow with a carp point installed. All you need is water and fish for hot bow action.
SRP: **$69.95**

Classic Arrow With Gar Point
A solid fiberglass arrow with a quick-release gar point installed. The arrow includes a nock and a hole for a cable or string attachment.
SRP: **$11.00**
Classic Arrow With Carp Point
SRP: **$11.00**

Economy River Point
This Muzzy bowfishing arrow has a solid blue fiberglass shaft with a nock, predrilled hole and is unfletched.
SRP: **$7.17**

Ever Kleen Bow Holder
This leather loop-style bow holder keeps your bow at waist level and permits faster access and quicker shots. A sturdy belt loop ensures years of dependable service.
SRP: **$9.08**

Fiberglass Shaft
Solid premium fiberglass shafts for custom finishing with any Muzzy point. 32-inches long, tapered for nocks with predrilled holes.
Blue Fiberglass Shaft
SRP: **$2.67**
White Fiberglass Shaft
SRP: **$2.67**

GATOR GETTER KIT

GLOVE FREE FINGER GUARD

FINGER SAVER

FISH BOPPER

GATOR GETTER CROSSBOW BOLTS

FLOATS

LIL' STINGER ARROW

H30 PRO SERIES SUNGLASSES

Finger Saver
This handy post screws into your bow's stabilizer hole and gives you something to wrap line around other than your fingers. The Finger Saver assists with fighting fish and while removing arrows stuck on the bottom.
SRP: $8.50

Fish Bopper
Stop those annoying flopping fish in their scales with this black mini-club. The Bopper has a string attached to prevent loosing it in water. Great for gar.
SRP: $6.00

Floats
Larger fish and gators often need to be released when you reach the end of the line. You can track their movements with these floats that are designed to work with Muzzy's slotted retriever reel.
Small Game Float, blue and white
SRP: . . . . $17.77 each
Big Game Float, yellow and white
SRP: . . . . $25.38 each
Deep Sea Float - orange
SRP: . . . . $31.92 each

Gator Crossbow Bolts and Gator Getter Kit
You can hunt gators with your crossbow and these crossbow arrows are rigged for the hunt. The same kit as above with crossbow applications is also available and includes similar components.
SRP: Gator Crossbow Kit . . . $225.33
Crossbow bolts. $23

Gator Getter Kit
Gators can provide thrills and problems. You can overcome the problems with this kit that includes: a slotted retriever reel, 2 big game floats, 600-pound Gator cord, three gator getter arrows with gator points, one extra spool of gator cord. Note that Gator arrows and gator points are sold separately.
SRP: Gator kit standard $225.33
Gator arrows $23
Gator points $7.62

Glove Free Finger Guard
These rollers permit accurate shooting even when you have wet fingers. One roller accommodates two fingers and the other roller is designed for use with one finger.
SRP: three pack $4.17

H30 Pro Series Sunglasses
These sunglasses will help you see into the water to locate fish. Interchangeable lenses can be easily and quickly installed to help you meet changing water clarity and light conditions. The sunglasses are ultra light for all-day wear.
SRP: includes three lenses . . . $59.98

Lil' Stinger Arrow
A solid premium grade fiberglass arrow with a Lil' Stinger point attached. Includes a layafletch, nock, and hole for cable or string attachments.
SRP: $9.17

BOW FISHING GEAR

Bow Fishing Gear

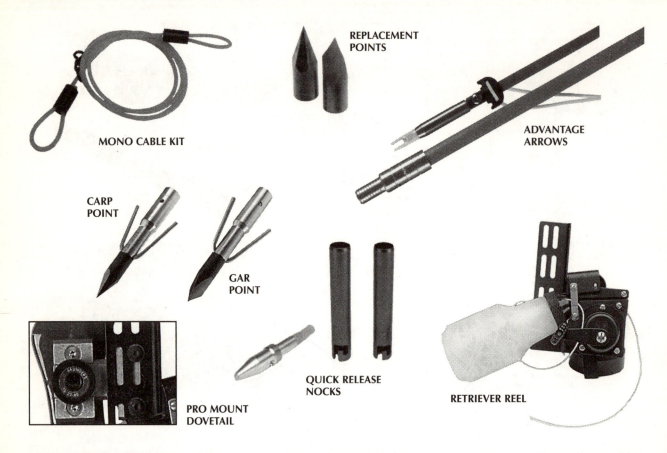

MONO CABLE KIT

REPLACEMENT POINTS

ADVANTAGE ARROWS

CARP POINT

GAR POINT

PRO MOUNT DOVETAIL

QUICK RELEASE NOCKS

RETRIEVER REEL

Mono Cable Kit
This bowfishing arrow kit includes a heavy 250-pound mono cable with swedges and swivels for complete installation.
SRP: **$3.75**

Premium Bowfishing Arrows
The Penetrator Arrow features a unique carbon/Glass and Aluminum composite with a Uni-nock system. This bowfishing arrow is fully cabled and collared. Various styles are available including: Penetrator with safety slide, Predator arrow for crossbows, and Predator arrows and Predator arrows with the newest safety slide feature and a unique Midnight camo finish. SRPs range from $17.69 to $22.69. The Advantage series of premium bowfishing arrows are fiberglass and have a full-length cable, and collar. Must install a point. The Advantage with safety slide has a Uni-nock and is Hi-Vis.
SRP: **$12.69**

Pro-Mount Dovetail
This bracket is per-drilled to fit preexisting riser holes and permits quick change over of components, such as the arrow rests listed above, to meet varying conditions.
SRP: **$17.25**

Quick Release Carp Point
Same as the Gar Point with longer tip and slightly longer barbs. Operates the same to release fish.
SRP: **$7.50**

Quick Release Gar Points
These points feature full stainless steel ferrules with the famous Muzzy Trocor point. A simple two turns of the point allows the barb to fold in the opposite direction and release fish. The short design aids in penetration.
SRP: **$7.50**

Quick Release Nock
This nock system permits removal of the nock for quick changes or fish removal on the water when quick removal counts, such as during bowfishing tournaments.
SRP: . . . . **$7.50 each**

Replacement Points
These points are designed to penetrate tough skinned fish and can be used to repleace the tips on any Muzzy fishing point. Screw on easily and quickly.
SRP: 2 to a card **$3.33**

Retriever Reels
These reels feature canisters to feed out heavy lines with no drag. The line cranks back into the canister with no tangles. The system comes loaded with Muzzy's 200-pound test Extreme line. Note; Slotted retriever reel is same as above but is designed to release a large float or ball at the end of the line. The floats can help you track large moving fish.
SRPS: standard **$57.32**
Slotted **$71.99**

Bow Fishing Gear

RIVER POINT ARROW

STINGRAY POINT

SHURE SHOT REPLACEMENT POINT

STINGRAY ARROW

SHAKESPEARE SUNGLASSES

SHAKESPEARE REEL

River Point Arrow
A fully assembled solid premium fiber-glass arrow with river point attached. Includes hole, nock and layafletch.
SRP: $7.58

Shakespeare Reel
This new reel has full brass and stain-less steel construction with special bearings and a high retrieve ratios resulting in faster landings. The reel can easily be converted from right or left-hand use and fits any anchor reel seat. Designed for seasons of depend-able performance.
SRP: $29.93

Shakespeare Sunglasses
These new wrap a rounds are designed with polarized lenses for visual acuity below the surface. They are lightweight and durable. A string can be attached to the arms to prevent loss.
SRP: $12.23

Shure Shot Point
This bowfishing point has a permanent tip and quick release barb. A twist of the tips permits the barbs to fold for-ward and release a fish.
SRP: $7.08

Shure Shot Replacement Tip
Replace worn or damaged tips on most bowfishing arrows.
SRP: $4.82

Stingray Arrow
A solid premium grade blue fiberglass arrow with a Stingray Point installed. The arrow includes a nock, layafletch (soft rubber vanes), and hole for a cable or string attachment.
SRP: $13.33

Stingray Point
This bowfishing point features a replaceable carp tip and extra-wide bite for a superior hold on large fish. Two twists release a fish. This is a rec-ommended tournament fishing point.
SRP: $8.83

Tuning
When using a launcher rest on a compound bow with a release, make certain that the arm supporting the arrow does not "give" under the weight of the shaft. To get the best arrow flight make sure that the arrow is aligned with the center of the cam-wheel when it is in its power stroke.

BOW FISHING GEAR

Bow Fishing Gear

UNI-NOCKS

UNI-NOCK ADAPTERS

3-D CARP TARGET

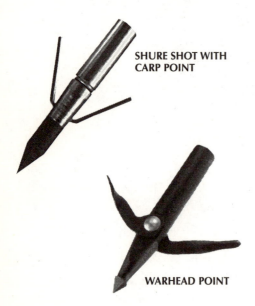

SHURE SHOT WITH CARP POINT

WARHEAD POINT

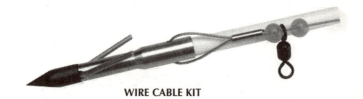

WIRE CABLE KIT

ZEBCO 808 BOWFISHING REEL

Shure Shot with Carp Point
This new muzzy point has a screw on replaceable carp tip for added convenience.
SRP: **$8.83**

3-D Carp Target
This 2-foot long carp target provides a fish when the real ones won't cooperate and is useful for practicing. It can swim underwater when rigged properly and provides realistic practice and hours of fun.
SRP: **$53.77**

Uni-Nocks And Adapters
These nocks allow easy replacement when using the Uni-Nock adapter system. These can replace the nocks on numerous bowfishing arrows listed above.
SRP: nocks **$2.67**
Adapters. **$3.95**

Warhead Point
This bowfishing point has twisted barbs that spin to improve in the water accuracy. The pyramid head positions the barbs close to the tip permitting holding power with only 2?-inch penetration.
SRP: **$4.67**

Wire Cable Kit
Includes all the items needed to cable any predrilled arrow, including a section of 300-pound test cable, swedges, swivel and orange beads.
SRP: . . . . **$2.92 each**

Zebco 808 Bowfishing Reel
Made for bowfishing, this reel has modified brass and stainless steel parts, plus a larger crank handle and lock-down drag. It arrives with 70-pound Dacron line.
SRP: **$29.93**

21 Century Longbows
Post Office Box 8461
Jacksonville, TN 75766
903-586-0715

Accu Rest
Post Office Box 566
Wauconda, IL 60084
847-487-0636

Advantage Camouflage
Post Office Box 9638
Columbus, GA 31908
800-992-9968

Allegheny Mountain
Arrowood
Post Office Box 582
Coudersport, PA 16915
814-274-2282

Alpen Outdoor
Corporation
10722 Arrow Route,
Suite #404
Rancho Cucamonga, CA
91730
909-987-8370

Alpine Archery
Post Office Box 319
3101 N&S Highway
Lewiston, ID 83501
208-746-4717

Americase
1610 East Main
Waxahachie, TX 75165
800-972-2737

Ameristep
Post Office Box 189
901 Tacoma Court
Clio, MI 48420
810-686-4035

Ames Industries
Post Office Box 44860
Tacoma, WA 98444-
0860
800-444-5869

API Outdoors/ Outland
Sports
4500 Doniphan Drive
Neosho MO 64805
800-922-9034

Apple Archery Products
245 Beshore School
Road
Manchester, PA 17345
800-745-8190

Archer's Choice
Post Office Box 279
310 Industrial Drive
Dunlap, TN 37327
423-949-4812

Archers' Edge
Post Office Box 935
Thompson Falls, MT
59873
406-827-4694

Archery Horizons
159 Elkin Avenue
Indiana, PA 15701
724-349-9313

Archery Shooters
Association
Post Office Box 399
1301 Shiloh Road
Kennesaw, GA 30144
770-795-0232

Arizona Archery
Enterprises
Post Office Box 25387
Prescott Valley, AZ
86312
928-772-9887

Arizona Rim
6401 West Chandler
Boulevard, #A
Chandler, AZ 85226
800-635-6899

Arrow Incased Systems
Post Office Box 5429
Plymouth, MI 48170-
5429
248-553-8340

Aspen Longbow
Company
W2890 Loraine Drive
Missoula, MT 59803
406-251-3300

Bad Lands
1414 South 700 West
Salt Lake City, UT 84104
801-978-2207

Barnett International
13447 Byrd Drive
Odessa, FL 33556
800-237-4507

Barrie Archery/Rocky
Mountain Broadheads
Post Office Box 482
Waseca, MN 56093
507-835-3859

Battle Lake Outdoors
Box 548
203 Main Street
Clarrisa, MN 56440
800-243-0465

Becoming an
Outdoors-Woman
1900 Franklin Street
CNR, WWSP
Stevens Point, WI 54481
877-BOWOMAN

Beman U. S. A.
5040 West Harold Gatty
Dr
Salt Lake City, UT 84116
801-539-1433

Ben Pearson Archery
Post Office Box 327
734 Brewton Industrial
Park
Brewton, AL 36427
251-867-8475

Bender's No-Glove
2803 South 22nd Street
LaCrosse, WI 54601
608-788-1339

Bighorn Bowhunting
Company
2881 31st Avenue
Greeley, CO 80631
970-356-4779

Black Scorpion
Broadheads
1585 Bird Farm Road
Jasper, AL 35503
877-431-9525

Black Widow Custom
Bows
Post Office Box 2100
1201 Eaglecrest
Nixa, MO 65714
417-725-3133

Blackwater Creek
Treestands
Post Office Box 580
Meridian, MS 39342
601-484-2987

Bloodtrailer Broadheads
RR1, Box 260A
Thornton, WV 26440
304-265-1500

Bodkin Broadheads

923 South 16th
Milwaukee, WI 53204
800-628-6604

Bodoodle
3301 US Highway 84
North
Coleman, TX 76834
800-467-8781

Bohning
7361 North Seven Mile
Road
Lake City, MI 49651
800-253-0136

Bomar Archery
1095 Goodrick Drive
Tehachapi, CA 93561
661-822-4671

Bonebuster Outdoor Inc.
P.O. Box 244
Kieler, WI 53812
608-748-4493

Boone and Crockett Club
250 Station Drive
Missoula, MT 59801-
2753
406-542-1888

Bow Maniac Stabilizers
PMB123 10152 W.
Indiantown Road
Jupiter, FL 33478
561-747-1378

Bow Tech
600 Dale Kuni Road,
Suite 220
Creswell, OR 97426
888-689-1289

Bowhunting Traditions
385 Hendrickson School
Road
Shell Knob, MO 65747
417-858-0522

Bow-Kick
6697 Victoria Shores
Laingsburg, MI 48848
517-651-6651

Bow-Pro Archery
Equipment
1605 Treanor Road
Saginaw, MI 48601
800-962-4388

BPE
890 County Road 160
Emporia, KS 66801
620-343-3783

Bracklyn Archery
Products
4400 Stillman Boulevard,
Suite C
Tuscaloosa, AL 35401
800-247-2955

Brauer Brothers
Manufacturing
1520 Washington
Avenue, 4th Floor
St. Louis, MO 63103
800-5-BRAUER

Brown Recluse Bows
153 Parkwood Drive
Royal Palm Beach, FL
33411
561-798-8858

Brownell & Co.
Post Office Box 362
Moodus, CT 06469
860-873-8625

Browning
One Browning Place
Morgan, UT 84050
800-333-3288

Browning Bows
C/o PSE
Post Office Box 5487
Tucson, AZ 85703
800-644-0283

Bruin Custom Recurves
W9664 Highway D
Antigo, WI 54409
715-623-6537

Brunton
620 East Monroe Avenue
Riverton, WY 82501
800-443-4871

BSA Optics
3911 W. 47th Avenue,
Suite 914
Fort Lauderdale, FL
33314
954-581-3165

Buck Knives
1900 Weld Boulevard
El Cajon, CA 92020
800-326-2925

Buck Stop Lures
Post Office Box 636
3600 Grow Road
Stanton, MI 48888-0636
800-477-2368

Buckmasters
C/o North American
Archery Group
4600 Southwest 41st
Boulevard
Gainesville, FL 32608-
4999
352-376-2327

Buckshot Treestands
Post Office Box 7127
Wilmington, NC 28406
910-341-7900

BuckWing Products
2650 Lehigh Street
Whitehall, PA 18052
800-555-9908

Bullet Archery Points
Post Office Box 965
Duncansville, PA 16635
814-693-6992

Bull's Eye Sights
3383 Duncan Bridge
Trail
Buford, GA 30519
800-497-3755

Bushnell Performance
Optics
9200 Cody
Overland Park, KS
66214
913-752-3400

C.R. Archery Products
Inc.
Post Office Box 10561
Lancaster, PA 17605-
0561
717-394-5769

C.W. Erickson's
Manufacturing
Post Office Box 522
Buffalo, MN 55313
763-682-3665

Cabela's
One Cabela Drive
Sidney, NE 69160
800-237-4444

Cajun Archery
2408 Darnell Road
New Iberia, LA 70560
800-551-3076

Cannon Country Game
Calls

2378 Southern Hills
Mexico, MO 65265
873-582-0121

Carbon Express by Game
Tracker
Post Office Box 380
3476 Eastman Drive
Flushing, MI 48433
800-241-4833

Carbon Impact
2628 Garfield Road
North, Suite 38
Traverse City, MI 49686
231-929-8152

Carbon Tech
4571 Pell Drive
Suite 3
Sacramento, CA 95838
800-951-8736

Carolina Archery
Products, Inc.
620 Valley Forge Road
Hillsboro, NC 27278
919-245-1400

Cartel
AIM/ARCHERY
International Marketing
95 Milk Street
Willimantic, CT 06226
888-246-8044

Carter Enterprises
Post Office Box 19
St. Anthony, ID 83445
208-624-3467

Cavalier Equipment
Company
700 N. Nelly, Suite #2
Gilbert, AZ 85233
480-497-2977

Cedar Hill Game Calls
238 Vic Allen Road
Downsville, LA 71234
318-982-5632

Championship Archery
Products
19 Morley Drive
Norwalk, OH 44857
419-668-8521

Chippewa
Post Office Box 548
Ft. Worth, TX 76101
800-362-3049

Christian Bowhunters of
America
2205 State
Route 571 West
Greenville, OH 45331
937-548-0623

Chuck Adams
Accessories
C/O North American
Archery Group
4600 Southwest 41st
Boulevard
Gainesville, FL 32608-
4999
352-376-2327

Clear Creek Company
15 South Locust
New Hampton, IA
50659
800-894-0483

Coast Cutlery
2045 Southeast Ankeny
Street
Portland, OR 97214
800-426-5858

Cobra Manufacturing
Post Office Box 667

Bixby, OK 74008
800-352-6272

Code Blue /Pradco
Post Office Box 1587
3601 Lind Road
Fort Smith, AR 72901
800-531-1201

Coffey Marketing
1678 Gillead Church Rd
Glendale, KY 42740
270-369-7323

Cold Steel
3036-A Seaborg Avenue
Ventura, CA 93003
800-255-4716

Competition Electronics,
3469 Precision Drive
Rockford, IL 61109
815-874-8001

Contico Cases
305 Rock Industrial Park Dr
St. Louis, MO 63044
800-331-7077

Copper John Corporation
173 State Street
Auburn, NY 13021
315-258-9269

Cornhuskers Archery
Post Office Box 467
201 Augusta Street
Bassett, NE 68714
888-684-2290

Cover-Up Hunting
Products
1205 State Highway JJ
Hollister, MO 65672
800-386-5503

C-Peep
Post Office Box 248
2121 East Hickory Road
Battle Creek, MI 49017
616-721-4131

Cranford Manufacturing
1927 Junction Road
Mocksville, NC 27028
336-284-2253

Custom Archery
Equipment
1826 West 213th Street
Torrance, CA 90501
310-212-5500

Custom Chronograph
5305 Reese Hill Road
Sumas, WA 98295
360-988-7801

Custom Shooting Systems
5343 State Route 10
Salt Rock, WV 25701
304-736-3639

Custom Tapered Arrows
& Shafts
15563 Co. 27 Blvd.
Pine Island, MN 55963
507-356-8857

Dakota Archery Products
916 Northeast Sixth St
Madison, SD 57042
602-256-2373

Darton Bows & Proline
Post Office Box 68
3540 Darton Road
Hale, MI 48739
517-728-4231

Dave's "Pop-Up"
Canisters
Post Office Box 182
1215 Mosley Road
Fair Port, NY 14450

585-425-7526

Deer Quest
Post Office Box 296
Belmont, MI 49306
800-795-7581

Delta Industries
117 East Kenwood Street
Reinbeck, IA 50669
319-345-6476

Dennis Kirk Game Calls
3801 Woodland Heights
Road, Suite 100
Little Rock, AR 72212
501-227-9050

Diamond Machining
Technology
85 Hayes Memorial Dr
Marlborough, MA
01752
800-530-0644

Diamondback
Camouflage
Post office Box 1419
Marble Falls, TX 78654
800-909-9972

Dodge Enterprises
E 7917 450th Avenue
Menomonie, WI 54751
715-879-5323

Doinker/Leven Industries
9025 Eton Avenue, Unit D
Canoga Park, CA 91304
818-700-2899

DoskoSport
Post Office Box 1246
4300 Barnett Boulevard
Arlington, TX 76004
888-367-5624

Double Bull
Post Office Box 923
Monticello, MN 55362
763-295-3664

Dwyer Longbow
Company
Post Office Box 221
Holmen, WI 54636
608-526-4297

E.W. Bateman & Co.
Post Office Box 109
Fischer, TX 78623
800-233-1208

Easton Technical Products
5040 West Harold Gatty
Salt Lake City, UT 84116
801-539-1400

Easy-Eye Archery
Products
7196 Arkansaw Road
Allen, MI 49227
888-908-7446

EBSA Corporation
1345 East Pleasant Valley Rd.
Shepherd, MI 48883
800-750-7910

Eclipse Broadheads
10342 Ardyce Street
Boise, ID 83704
208-322-7796

Edgemaker Company
5222 Tractor Road
Toledo, OH 43612
800-531-EDGE

EJ Sceery Outdoors
Post Office Box 6520
Santa Fe, NM 87502
800-327-4322

Ellett Brothers Inc.
Post Office Box 128

DIRECTORY OF MANUFACTURERS

267 Columbia Avenue
Chapin, SC 29036
800-845-3711

Eradicator Bow Sights
1345 East Pleasant Valley Rd
Shepherd, MI 48883
800-750-7910

Extreme Archery Products
7129 US Highway 60
Ashland, KY 41102
606-928-9447

Extreme Dimension
Wildlife Calls
94 Main Road South
Hampden, ME 04444
866-862-2825

EZE-LAP Diamond
Products
3572 Arrowhead Drive
Carson City, NV 89706
800-843-4815

Fall Woods
Post Office Box 6683
104 Dominion Circle
Huntsville, AL 35811
256-858-0430

Feather Flex Decoys
8575 West 100th Street
Overland Park, KS 66210
913-317-9600

Fedora's Custom Bows
115 Wintersville Road
Richland, PA 17087
717-933-8862

Fieldline
1919 Vineburn Avenue
Los Angeles, CA 90032
800-438-3353

Fine-Line
11304 Steele Street
Tacoma, WA 98499
800-445-0801

Finnwood Products
Post Office Box 15113
Cincinnati, OH 45215
513-761-0198

Flambeau Products
Post Office Box 97
15981 Valplast Road
Middlefield, OH 44062
800-232-3474

Flex-Fletch Products
1840 Chandler Avenue
Saint Paul, MN 55113
800-626-3844

Flight-Rite Spine Tester
7707 Gun Lake Road
Delton, MI 49046
616-795-3832

Forge Bow Company
2860 South 171st Street
New Berlin, WI 53151
414-732-7400

Foster Manufacturing
Post Office Box 458
Batavia, OH 45103
800-972-9156

Fox Archery
701 West Highway 82
Wallowa, OR 97885
541-886-9110

Foxzy Products
3240 South Central Ave
Cicero, IL 60804
708-780-3927

Fred Bear Archery
Company

C/o North American
Archery Group
4600 Southwest 41st Blvd.
Gainesville, FL 32608-4999
352-376-2327

G&S Hunting Equipment
9177 Cambridge Road
Chardon, OH 44024
800-974-8777

G5 Outdoor Equipment
Post Office Box 59
Memphis, TN 48041
810-392-8431

Game Tracker/ Eastman
Post Office Box 380
3476 Eastman Drive
Flushing, MI 48433
800-241-4833

Gamehide
1503 Easy Highway 13
Burnsville, MN 55337
888-267-3591

Games Target
Box 1515
Melville, NY 11747
516-643-5466

Gameslayers No
Non-Scents
6604 W. Slope Lane
Oconto, WI 54153
920-826-7650

Gateway Feathers
1015 West Lorenza
Parkway
Douglas, AZ 85607
520-805-0863

Genesis
3412 Oak Street
Longview, WA 98632
360-425-3908

Gibbs Archery Gear
7781 Highway 167
South
Sheridan, AR 72150
870-942-4181

Gladiator Broadheads
352 South Industrial Dr
Orem, UT 84058
800-551-0541

Global Resources
89 Lucas Drive
Stoughton, MA 02072
781-341-2441

Gold Tip
352 South Industrial Dr
Orem, UT 84058
800-551-0541

Golden Eagle
C/o North American
Archery Group
4600 Southwest 41st
Gainesville, FL 32608-4999
352-376-2327

Golden Key-Futura
Post Office Box 1446
14090 6100 Road
Montrose, CO 81402-1446
920-249-6700

Gorilla Grip
2541 South 5th Avenue
Oroville, CA 95965
530-533-8692

Gorilla Tree Stands
Post Office Box 380
3476 Eastman Drive
Flushing, MI 48433
800-241-4833

Great Northern
Bowhunting Co.
Box 777
201 North Main Street
Nashville, MI 49073
517-852-0820

Grim Reaper Broadheads
1250 North 1750 West
Provo, UT 84604-2955
801-377-6199

H&M Archery
1685 Victor Avenue
Ypsilanti, MI 48198
734-485-3044

H.S.Scents (Hunter's
Specialties)
6000 Huntington Court NE
Cedar Rapids, IA 52402
319-395-0321

Habu Bows Ltd.
4748 Traditional Trail
Coeur d'Alene, ID 83814
208-664-0667

Happy Hunter
N 5764 CTH OT
Onalaska, WI 54650
608-783-3408

Haydel's Game Calls
5018 Hazel Jones Road
Bossier City, LA 71111
800-429-3357

Heat Factory
6054 Corte Del Cedro
Carlsbad, CA 92009
800-993-HEAT (4328)

HeatMax Scent Heater
505 Hill Road
Dalton, GA 30721
800-432-8629

HHA Sports, Inc.
7222 Townline Road
Wisconsin Rapids, WI 54494
800-548-7812

High Country Archery
Post Office Box 1269
312 Industrial Park Road
Dunlap, TN 37327
423-949-5000

Highlander Archery
Products
Post Office Box 19004
3004 11th Avenue
Huntsville, AL 35804
800-758-2346

Hind Sights
Post Office Box 482
Pinckney, MI 48169
734-878-2842

Horne's Archery
Post Office Box 318
Boyd, TX 76023
940-433-3044

Horn's Products
3422 Valley Road
Marysville, PA 17053
717-957-4636

HorseBows
3314 Ridgeway Avenue
Madison, WI 53704
608-244-2845

Horton Manufacturing
484 Tacoma Avenue
Tallmadge, OH 44278
800-291-3649

Hot Shot
763 South Orem
Boulevard

Orem, UT 84058
801-221-0694

Hoyt
543 N. Neil Armstrong Rd
Salt Lake City, UT 84116
800-522-HOYT

HTM Precision
Machining
Post Office Box 28
Route 220
New Albany, PA 18833
570-363-2515

Hughes Products
Company
Post Office Box 1066
112 Todd Court
Thomasville, NC 27360
336-475-0091

Hummingbird Bows
9631 Vineyard Road,
Dept. TB
Mt. Pleasant, NC 28124
704-436-2509

Hunter Specialties
6600 Huntington Court
Northeast
Cedar Rapids, IA 52402
800-728-0321

Hunter's Choice Products
Post Office Box 326
Romeo, MI 48065
800-Archer-5

Hunter's Edge, Inc.
195 Kelly Road
Bainbridge, GA 31717
888-445-0970

Hunting Solutions
2486 Commercial Drive
Pearl, MS 39208
601-932-5832

Hunt-N-Buddy
Bowholder
Box 90 HC 4
Blanco, TX 78606
800-370-8452

Ideal Products, Inc.
Post Office Box 1006
227 East Main Street
DeBois, PA 15865
800-544-3325

Illusion
Post Office Box 6915
Rochester, MN 55903
507-281-0300

Impact Archery
1360 Union Hill Road
Alpharetta, GA 30004
770-521-9173

In-Heat Scents
Post Office Box 515
Kosciusko, MS 39090
662-289-4073

interNature
AIM/ARCHERY
International Marketing
95 Milk Street
Willimantic, CT 06226
888-246-8044

Inventive Technology
Post Office Box 266
554 S. 100 West
America Fork, UT 84003
801-756-6017

J.B. Harrison Longbows
3450 Palmdale Drive
Wasillaq, AK 99654
907-376-4969

J.K. Chastain Archery

490 South Queen Street
Lakewood, CO 80226
303-989-1120

James Greene Archery
Products
2321 Yellow Banks Road N.
North Wilkesboro, NC 28659
336-670-2186

James Valley Scents
38853 SD Highway 20
Mellette, SD 57461
800-337-5873

Jennings Archery
C/o North American
Archery Group LLC
4600 Southwest 41st
Boulevard Gainesville, FL 32608-4999
352-376-2327

Jeri-Dan Quiver
Post Office Box 8863
Erie, PA 16505
814-739-9221

Jim Fletcher Archery
(Fletchhunter)
Post Office Box 218
Bodfish, CA 93205
760-379-2589

Johnny Stewart
Wildlife Calls
6000 Huntington Court NE
Cedar Rapids, IA 52402
800-728-0321

Jo-Jan Sports Equipment
West Pointe Drive, Bldg. 3
Washington, PA 15301
724-225-5582

Juniper Mountain.
Longbows
2135 Deer Park Road
Vale, OR 97918
541-473-3812

Kadooty Manufacturing
Post Office Box 4682
Lake Charles, LA 70606
337-477-7502

Kahles
2 Slater Road
Cranston, RI 02920
800-426-3089

Keller Manufacturing
5640 Wrightsboro Road
Grovestown, GA 30813
706-556-3736

Key Industries
Post Office Box 389
400 Marble Road
Fort Scott, KS 66701
800-835-0365

King Of The Mountain
2709 W. Eisenhower
Boulevard
Loveland, CO 80537
970-962-9306

Kinsey's Archery
Products, Inc.
Post Office Box 100
1660 Steel Way Drive
Mount Joy, PA 17552-4126
800-366-4269

Kisscents
101 Main Street
Superior WI 54880
715-395-9955

KK Air International/ ICC
Cases
Post Office Box 9912

Spokane, WA 99209
800-262-3322

Knight & Hale Calls
Post Office Box 1587
3601 Jenny Lind Road
Fort Smith, AR 72901
800-531-1201

Kolpin Manufacturing
Post Office Box 107
205 DePot Street
Fox Lake, WI 53933
800-5KOLPIN

Kool-Dri Rainwear
Post Office Box 120
550 Route 897
Reinholds, PA 17569
800-523-8025

Kudlacek's Archery
3412 Oak Street
Longview, WA 98632
360-425-3908

Kwikee Kwiver Company
Post Office Box 130
7972 Peaceful Valley Rd
Acme, MI 49610
800-346-7001

Lansky Sharpeners
Post Office Box 50830
Las Vegas, NV 89016
702-361-7511

Leica
156 Ludlow Avenue
Northvale, NJ 07647
800-222-0118

Leupold & Stevens /Wind
River
14400 NW Greenbrier Pwy
Beaverton, OR 97006
503-646-9171

Liberty Bows
Post Office Box 362
Gold Beach, OR 97444
541-247-6382

Limbsaver Products
Post Office Box A
Shelton, WA 98584
877-257-2761

Little Big Horn Outdoors
1 Princeton Avenue
Fort Mitchell, KY 41017
859-331-4120

LLD Artistic Targets
4627 W. Good Hope Rd
Milwaukee, WI 53223
414-352-3238

Loggy Bayou
Post Office Box 804
Magnolia, AR 71753
870-234-2260

Lohman
4500 Doniphan Drive
Neosho, MO 64850
800-922-9034

Lone Wolf Custom Bows
3893 Grey Street
Glennie, MI 48737
517-735-3358

Lone Wolf Treestands
3314 East Grange
Avenue
Cudahy, WI 53110
414-744-4984

Longhorn Archery
Post Office Box 1285
Medical Lake, WA 99022
509-299-5574

Ludwig Manufacturing
4716 Perry Avenue North
Minneapolis, MN 55429
763-533-7176

Lynch Worldwide
500 W. Jefferson
Thomasville, GA 31792
229-228-0529

M.A.D. Calls
4500 Doniphan Drive
Neosho, MO 64850
800-922-9034

Magic Stop Targets
Post Office Box 75
Greenville, KY 42345
800-590-0796*04

Magnus Snuffers
Post Office Box 1877
Great Bend, KS 67530
620-793-9222

Mahaska Custom Bows
Post Office Box 452
Oskaloosa, IA 52577
641-673-5501

Manneys Archery Targets
Post Office Box 246
Hibbing, MN 55746
218-263-8357

Marco Nocks
9928 Road 171
Oakwood, OH 45873
800-258-6625

Mar-Den Vortex
Post Office Box 1037
124 West Maley
Wilcox, AZ 85644
888-620-9888

Martin Archery
3134 West Highway 12
Walla Walla, WA 99362-9483
800-541-8902

Master Archer Targets
Post Office Box 22
22 Railroad Street
Schenley, PA 15682
724-295-6500

Mathews
Post Office Box 367
919 River Road
Sparta, WI 54656
608-269-2728

Matlock Bows
Post Office Box 275
Chadwick, MO 65629
417-796-2733

McKenzie Targets
Post Office Box 480
Granite Quarry, NC 28072
704-279-8363

McPherson Archery
Company
Post Office Box 327
Brewton, AL 36427
251-867-8475

Mel Dutton Decoys
Post Office Box 113
Faith, SD 57626
605-967-2031

Micro Technology
932 36th Court
Southwest
Vero Beach, FL 32968
561-569-3058

Modoc Broadheads
33 South Pit Lane

Nampa, ID 83687
208-466-1827

Monarch Bows
Post Office Box 433
Darby, MT 59829
406-821-1948

Montana Black Gold
34370 East Frontage Rd
Bozeman, MT 59715
800-336-0853

Montana Camo
Post Office Box 1327
461 Knapweed Lane
Victor, MT 59875
877-226-6462

Montana Decoys
Post Office Box 2377
Colstrip, MT 59323
406-748-3092

Moosejaw Bows
Post Office Box 790
Cave junction, OR 97523
541-592-6954

Mossy Oak Apparel
Company
Post Office Box 327
201 E. Main Street
West Point, MS 39773
800-331-5624

Mountain Country
Archery
Post Office Box 445
525 Burbank Street
Broomfield, CO 80038
800-876-8600

MPI Outdoors
10 Industrial Drive
Windham, NH 03087
800-343-5827

Mrs. Doe Pee
603 Redbud Ridge
Mt. Pleasant, IA 52641
319-385-3875

MTM Molded Products/
Case-Gard
3370 Obco Court
Dayton, OH 45414
937-890-7461

Muzzy Products
Corporation
110 Beasley Road
Cartersville, GA 30120
800-222-7769

Myerco
4481 Exchange Service Dr
Dallas, TX 75236
214-467-8949

Mystik Longbows
21485 N. Cameron Road
Cuba, IL 61427
309-785-5109

Naturalgear
5310 South Shackleford,
Suite D
Little Rock, AR 72204
800-590-5590

Nature Vision
521 Dogwood Drive
Baxter, MN 56425
218-825-0733

Navajo Longbows
1824 Highway 79 South
Henderson, TX 75652
903-657-8780

Neet
5875 Easy Highway 50
Sedalia, MO 65301
800-821-7196

Nelson's Arrows
1811 Swede Hill Road
Greensburg, PA 15601
724-837-6210

Neverwear Archery
29076 Highway 190 W.
lacombe, LA 70445
504-882-5511

New Archery Products
(NAP)
7500 Industrial Drive
Forest Park, IL 60130
800-323-1279

Nic-Nock
Post Office Box 7
Shady Cove, OR 97539
800-252-1299

Nikon
1300 Walt Whitman Rd
Melville, NY 11747
631-547-4200

Norman Archery, Inc.
Post Office Drawer
95029
8317 Gateway Terrace
Oklahoma City, OK
73149
800-234-1811

North Starr Treestands
235 East Bear Lake Road
Hillsdale, MI 49242
517-439-1313

Northwind Traditional
Archery
3351 Tonawanda Creek Rd
Amherst, NY 14228
716-689-3701

Norway Industries
Post Office Box 516
Myrtle Point, OR 97458
800-778-4755

Ol'man Tree Stands
32 Raspberry Lane
Hattiesburg, MS 39402
800-682-7268

Oneida Eagle Bow
20669 30th Avenue
Marion, MI 49665
231-743-2427

Original Brite-Site
34 Kentwood Road
Succasunna, NJ 07876
973-584-0637

Outlaw Decoys
624 North Fancher Road
Spokane, WA 99212
800-653-3269

P. S. Olt Call Company
Post Office Box 550
12662 Fifth Street
Pekin, IL 61554
309-348-3633

P.A.M.S. Arrow Making
Supplies
Post Office Box 52
Lyons, MI 48851-0052
989-855-3035

Pacific Bow Butts Target
System
Post Office Box 108
Ilwaco, WA 98624
877-642-4989

Palmer Bow Company
408 North Center Street
Sabinal, TX 78881
830-988-2019

Papeep Site
Post Office Box 89
Wheatridge, CO 80033

303-424-4733

Parker Compound Bows
Route 11 South
Mint Spring, VA 24463
800-707-8149

Pee Willie Wicks
14423 Old Hammond Hwy
Baton Rouge, LA 70816-
1148
877-347-6768

Pella Products
Post Office Box 324
835 Broadway
Pella, IA 50219
641-628-3092

Penn's Woods Game
Calls
Post Office Box 306
Delmont, PA 15626
724-468-8311

Pentax
35 Inverness Drive East
Englewood, CO 80112
800-877-0155

Perfect Shot Wildlife
Attractors
2930 Empire Avenue
Brentwood, CA 94513
925-757-4383

Pete Rickard
Post Office Box 292
115 Walsh Road
Cobleskill, NY 12043
800-282-5663

Phillips Industries
2601 Davison Road
Flint, MI 48506
800-416-3100

Pine Ridge Archery
Post Office Box 310
480 Bonner Road
Wauconda, IL 60084
877-746-7434

Pittman's Game Calls
Post Office Box 204
Louisville MS 39339
800-526-4868

Plano Molding Company
431 East South Street
Plano, IL 60545
800-874-6905

Port-a-Press
1678 Gilead Church Rd
Glendale, KY 42740
270-369-7323

Precision Design
Products (PDP)
3999 CR 5200 Archery Le
Independence, KS 67301
620-331-0333

Precision Shooting
Equipment (PSE)
Post Office Box 5487
2727 North Fairview
Tucson, AZ 85703
520-594-5169

Pro Hunter
Post Office Box 226
Plymouth, WI 53073
800-236-2657

Pro Releases
33551 Giftos Street
Clinton Township, MI
48054
800-845-8515

Professional Archery
Products
Post Office Box 89
Wheatridge, CO 80033

303-424-4733

Professional Hunting
Products
Post Office Box 849
Marshall, MI 49068
616-789-1507

Pro-Hunter
Post Office Box 226
Plymouth, WI 53073
800-236-2657

Proline Bows
Post Office Box 68
Hale, MI 48739
517-728-4231

Promat Targets
333 Plumer Street
Wausau, WI 54403
800-342-1244

Prototech Industries, Inc.
5155 Portage Lane
Gurnee, IL 60031
800-523-3109

PSE Precision Shooting
Equipment
2727 North Fairview
Tucson, AZ 85705
520-884-9065

Quaker Boy Calls
5455 Webster Road
Orchard Park, NY 14127
800-544-1600

Quality Archery Designs
Post Office Box 940
117 Martins Lane
Madison Heights, VA
24572
434-846-5839

R&M Targets
227 Hathaway Street E
Girard, PA 16417
800-657-0431

R.S. Archery Products
335 West John Street
Hicksville, NY 11801
800-444-9619

Raven Arrows
993 Grays Creek Road
Indian Valley, ID 83632
208-256-4341

Razor Caps
#6 Terrapin Lane
Mercerville, NJ 08619
609-890-2010

Realtree Camouflage
Post Office Box 9638
Columbus, GA 31908
800-992-9968

Red Feather Arrows
Post Office Box 560
101 South Main
Cibolo, TX 78108
210-945-8552

Red Hawk
3424 Marquette Street
High Ridge, MO 63049
800-689-7996

RedHead/Bass Pro Shops
2500 East Kearney
Springfield, MO 65898-
0123
800-227-7776

Reflex by Hoyt
543 North Neil
Armstrong Rd
Salt Lake City, UT 84116
800-522-HOYT

Renegade Archery
Company

18706 County Highway Q
Bloomer, WI 54724
715-568-2730

Resco Arrows
Post Office Box 167
313 North Main
Everly, IA 51338
712-834-2333

Rhinehart 3-D Targets
1029 South Jackson Street
Janesville, WI 53546
608-757-8153

Rivers Edge Hunting
Products
Post Office Box 666
1360 1st Avenue
Cumberland, WI 54829
800-450-3343

Robertson Stykbows
Box 7, HCR 88
Forest Grove, MT 59441
406-538-2818

Robinson Laboratories
Post Office Box 18
110 North Park Drive
Cannon Falls, MN
55009-0018
800-397-1927

Rocket Aerohead
Corporation
Box 6749
3417 Longfellow Drive
Minneapolis, MN 55406
800-762-0281

Rocky Mountain Pack
Systems
1505 Eastridge Drive, #11
Pocatello, ID 83201
208-234-4584

Rogue River Archery
4244 Leonard Road
Grants Pass, OR 97527
541-474-4441

Ron LaClair's Traditional
Archery
Box 145
Potterville, MI 48876
517-645-7729

Rose City Archery
Post Office Box 5
Myrtle Point, OR 97458
541-572-6408

Rutherford Outdoors
5205 S. Walnut
Muncie, IN 47302
765-281-9654

Safari Club International
4800 West Gates Pass Rd
Tucson, AZ 85745
520-620-1220

Samick Sports Company
AIM/Archery International
Marketing
95 Milk Street
Willimantic, CT 06226
888-246-8044

Satellite Archery
C/o North American
Archery Group
4600 Southwest 41st
Boulevard Gainesville, FL
32608-4999
352-376-2327

Saunders Archery
Company
Post Office Box 476
1874 14th Avenue
Columbus, NE 68602
800-228-1408

Savage Systems

110 North Front Street
Oak Grove, LA 71263
800-545-4868

Savora Broadheads
1546 Bolach Avenue
Northwest
North Bend, WA 98045
800-424-6737

Scent Patch
Post Office Box 201
Staples, MN 56479
218-894-5477

Scent-Lok
1731 Wierengo Drive
Muskegon, MI 49442
800-315-5799

Schwarz Archery
Post Office Box 113
115 North Saint Paul
Avenue
Fulda, MN 56131
507-425-3327

Scott Archery
Manufacturing
101 Tug Branch Road
Clay City, KY 40312
606-663-2734

Scout Mountain
Equipment
Post Office Box 4013
1553 E. Center Street,
Suite D
Pocatello, ID 83201
888-565-7546

Scrape Juice Hunting
Products
208 Lake Lillian Road
Perry GA 30169
478-988-4594

Selway Archery
802 South 2nd
Hamilton, MT 59840
800-764-4770

Shooting Chrony Inc.
3840 East Robinson Rd.,
PMB # 298
Amherst, NY 14228
U.S.A.
Tel: 1-905-276-6292

Shrewd Precision Archery
Products
Post Office Box 235
Catawba, VA 24070
540-864-7041

Silent Pond Arrow Shafts
7 Maple Street
Whitefield, NH 03598
603-837-2323

Simms Arrows
106 Fordway
Derry, NH 03038
603-434-0569

Sims Cable
Slide/Limbsavers
301 West Busniess Park
Loop
Shelton, WA 98584
877-257-2761

SKB Cases
1607 N. O'Donnell Way
Orange, CA 92867
800-654-5992

Sonoran Bowhunting
Products
Post Office Box 17977
8195 E. Nicaragua
Tucson, AZ 85730
520-885-9314

Southern Archery
Post Office Box 204

522 Stringer Industrial
Park
Louisville, MS 39339
800-526-4868

Southern Game Calls
545 Oakhurst Avenue
Clarksdale, MS 38614
800-881-1964

Specialty Archery
Products
Post Office Box 889
10510 265th Street
Clear Lake, IA 50428
641-424-5762

Spider Legs
7056 Danville Road
Hartselle, AL 35640
256-773-5691

Sportline Manufacturing
Post Office Box 247
311 Superior Street
Antigo, WI 54409
800-842-8870

Sportsman's Outdoor
Products
9352 South 670
West Sandy, UT 84070
888-528-1775

Spot-Hogg Archery
Products
Post Office Box 226
125 Smith Street
Harrisburg, OR 97446
888-302-7768

Squires High-Tech
433 Meadows Street
Fairfield, CT 06430
203-579-5166

St. Joe River Bows
3140 Homer Road
Jonesville, MI 49250
517-849-2939

Stacey Archery Sales
6866 Jennifer Lane
Idaho Falls, ID 83401
208-523-7278

Stalker Custom Recurves
6046 Holeton Road
Carmichael, CA 95608
916-483-1241

Stanley Hips
/LonghornTargets
1211 W. Blanco Road
San Antonio, TX 78232
800-979-0915

Stearns / Mad Dog
1100 Stearns Drive
Sauk Rapids, MN 56379
800-333-1179

Steel Force Broadheads
Post Office Box 9
Rosemont, NJ
08556-0009
609-397-1990

Steiner
97 Foster Road, Suite 5
Moorestown, NJ 08057
800-257-7742

Sterling Custom Bows
62 South 200 East
Brigham City, UT 84302
801-734-2219

Sullivan Industries
(Innerloc)
1472 Camp Creek Road
Lakemont, GA 30552
706-782-5863

Summit Specialties
715 Summit Drive

DIRECTORY OF MANUFACTURERS

Southeast
Decatur, AL 35601
256-353-0634

Sure Shot Archery
Releases
476 Table Rock Road
Beaver, WV 25813
304-763-4228

Sure Shot Game Calls
Post Office Box 816
4970 Wilson Street
Groves, Texas 77619
800-643-7430

Sure Stop
20 Vernon Street
Somerville, MA 02145
617-623-3010

Sure-Loc Archery
Products
C.S. Gibbs Corperation
100 Quality Lane
Versailles, IN 47042
812-689-9926

Swarovski Optic North
America
2 Slater Road
Cranston, RI 02920
800-426-3089

Swift Instruments
952 Dorchester Avenue
Boston, MA 02125
800-446-1116

T&J Treestand Systems
2211 Brookwood Court
Joliet, IL 60435
815-725-7268

T.R.U. Ball Release
Post Office Box 1180
131 Crennel Drive
Madison Heights, VA
24572
800-724-4878

TailorMaid Bowstrings
12731 Huron River
Drive, Suite 100
Romulus, MI 48174
734-941-6611

Tarantula Outdoor
Products
9352 South 670 West
Sandy, UT 84070
801-562-8712

Tasco
9200 Cody
Overland Park, KS
66214
913-752-3400

Ten Point Crossbow
Technologies
1325 Waterloo Road
Suffield, OH

44260-9608
330-628-9245

The Block/Field Logic
101 Main Street
Superior WI 54880
715-395-9955

The Crow's Nest Stands.
190102 Balsam Drive
Wausau, WI 54401
715-675-2743

The Reaper
Post Office Box 793
7953 Webster Road
Freeland, MI 48623
877-723-7446

The Slick Tubes Company
Post Office Box 6135
Jackson, MI 49204
517-789-8941

The Wright Stand
Post Office Box 1622
Ferriday, LA 71334
318-757-1111

Third Hand Archery
Accessories
10137 Timber Creek Dr
Union, KY 41091
800-339-0232

Thunderhorn
Manufacturing
696 Highway 93 North
Hamilton, MT 59840
406-961-2449

Tiger Tuff
3 Custom Mill Court
Greenville, SC 29609
864-370-1500

Timberline Archery
Products
Post Office Box 333
201 A Rosenkranz Road
Lewiston, ID 83501
800-434-2708

Tim's Archery
1201 Eagle Way
Rock Springs, WY 82901
307-382-9196

TNT Sporting
Manufacturing
4 Willow Street
Mt. Pleasant, PA 15666
724-547-9730

Toxonics Manufacturing
1324 Wilmer Road
Wentzville, MO 63385
314-639-8500

Trailhawk Treestands
2605 Coulee Avenue
LaCrosse, WI 54601
608-787-0500

Trax America
Post Office Box 898
1150 Eldridge Road
Forrest City, AR 72335
800-232-2328

Trebark
c/o Mossy Oak
201 East Main Street
West Point, MS 39773
800-331-5624

Tree-Post
Post Office Box 7548
St. Cloud, MN 56302
320-240-2362

Tri-Triska Archery
Route 1, Box 14
West Hamlin, WV
25571
304-824-5640

Trophy Line
1904 Philadelphia Road
Jasper, GA 30143
706-692-0214

Trophy Ridge
732 Cruiser Lane, suite
200
Belgrade, MT 59714
406-388-7781

Trophy Taker
Post Office Box 1137
Plains, MT 59859
406-826-0600

Tru Hone Corporation
1721 Northeast 19th
Avenue
Ocala, FL 34470
800-237-4663

TruAngle Broadhead
Hones
6658 South State Road
13
Wabash, IN 46992
800-854-8942

Trueflight Manufacturing
Company
Post Office Box 1000
Hwy 51, South
Manitowish Waters, WI
54545
715-543-8410

Tru-Fire
N7355 State Street
North Fond du Lac, WI
54937
902-823-6866

TRUGLO
Post Office Box 1612
13475 Neutron Road
McKinney, TX 75070
972-774-0300

TS Lock
9114 E. Bennington Road
Durand, MI 48429
517-288-5854

Tuff Shot Series
Post Office Box 480
Granite Quarry, NC
28072
888-279-7985

Turbo Nocks
3424 Marquette Street
High Ridge,, MO 63049
800-689-7996

Twig Archery Company
45194 TR 432
Conesville, OH 43811
740-829-2847

Underbrush
Post Office Box 337
State Highway 1651
Stearns, KY 42647
888-376-2004

U-nique Archery
Products
7056 Danville Road
Hartselle, AL 35640
256-773-5691

United Foundation for
Disabled Archers
Post Office Box 251
20 NE 9th Avenue
Glenwood, MN 63334
320-634-3660

US Sportsmen's Alliance
801 Kingsmill Parkway
Columbus, OH 43229-
1137
614-888-4868

Vanguard USA
9157 East M-36
Whitmore Lake, MI
48189
800-875-3322

Vaper Arrows
(Blackhawk)
Post Office Box 4240
Autsintown, OH 44515
330-793-3314

Vaper Points (Blackhawk)
Post Office Box 4240
Austintown, OH 44515
330-793-3314

Vibracheck Stablilizers
10003 Raymar Street
Pensacola, FL 32534
850-857-0092

Vista/Western Recreation
Post Office Box 70
150 Pahlone Parkway
Poncha Springs, CO
81242

800-525-1181

W.A. Fisher Company
Post Office Box 1107
Virginia, MN 55792
800-874-2232 (MN only)

W.L. Gore & Associates,
Inc.
105 Vieve's Way
Elkton, MD 21921
800-431-GORE

Walker's Game Ear
Post Office Box 1069
Media, PA 19063
800-424-1069

Walls Industries
1905 North Main
Cleburne, TX 76031
817-645-4366

Warren & Sweat
Manufacturing
Post Office Box 350440
Grand Island, FL 32735
352-663-3166

Wasp Archery Products
707 Main Street
Plymouth, CT 06782
860-283-0246

Waterloo Archery, Inc.
Post Office Box 171
Waterloo, IA 50704
319-232-1842

Wayne Carlton Calls
(Hunter's Specialties)
6000 Huntington Court
NE
Cedar Rapids, IA 52402
319-395-0321

Weaver's Scent Company
3112 Heinzelman Road
West Harrison, IN 47060
812-637-6145

Wellington/Tink's
Post Office Box 244
1140 Monticello Road
Madison, GA 30650-
0244
800-624-5988

Wensel Broadheads
Post Office Box 4
Bloomfield IA 52537
641-664-2215

Western Filament
630 Hollingsworth Drive
Grand Junction, CO
81505
970-241-8780

Wheelin' Sportsmen
National Wild Turkey
Federation
770 Augusta Road

Edgefield, SC 29824
803-637-3106

Whispering Wind Arrows
77 Point Way
Hamilton, MT 59840
406-375-2300

Whitetail Plus
Box 1082
Deer Park, WA 99006
800-727-9117

Whitewater Creek
Products
3086 PCR 724
Perryville, MO 63775
573-547-8530

Whitewater Outdoors
W4228 Church Street
Hingham, WI 53031
800-666-2674

Wilderness Packs
4243 Winter Avenue
Klamath Falls, OR 97603
888-884-1577

Wildfork Archery
250 Berkley Court
Mobile, AL 36606
888-870-4253

Wildlife Research Center
1050 McKinley Street
Anoka, MN 55303
800-873-5873

Wildwood Innovations
Route 4, Box 286
Ashland, WI 54806
715-685-0020

Will-Stop Target
Company
24808 Amah Parkway
Claremore, OK 74017
800-543-8718

Wing Archery Company
227 Center Grove Road
Randolph, NJ 07869
973-989-8957

Winn Archery Equip. Co.
13757 64th Street
South Haven, MI 49090
616-637-2658

Winners Choice Custom
Bowstrings
141 East Main
John Day, OR 97845
541-575-0818

Wolverine Boots & Shoes
9341 Courtland Drive,
NE
Rockford, MI 49351
888-927-9675

Women in the Outdoors
National Wild Turkey
Federation
770 Augusta Road
Edgefield, SC 29824
800-THE-NWTF

Wood Wise Products
Post Office Box 681552
Franklin, TN 37068
800-735-8182

WoodenArrows.com
Post Office Box 70
Hazelhurst, WI 54531

Woodland Traditional
Archery
RR2, Box 83C
Rockville, IN 47872
765-569-7638

Woods & Water
1136 Bo-Di-Lac Drive
Lac du Flambeau, WI
54538
715-588-7500

Woolrich
1 Mill Street
Woolrich, PA 17779
717-769-6464

Wrangler Rugged Wear
400 North Elm Street
Greensboro, NC 27401
336-332-5397

Wyandotte Leathers
1811 Sixth Street
Wyandotte, MI 48192
734-282-3403

X-Ring Archery Products
700-B South Keeneland
Drive
Richmond, KY 40475
859-625-0935

Yellow Hammer
Outdoors
Post Office Box 20023
Tuscaloosa, AL 35402-
5900
205-759-5900

Zebra Twist / Mathews
Post Box 367
919 River Road
Sparta, WI 54656
608-269-2728

Zero-Effect (Muzzy)
110 Beasley Road
Cartersville, GA 30120
800-222-7769

Zwickey Archery
2571 East 12th Avenue
North St. Paul, MN
55109
651-777-1965

ARCHER'S BIBLE INDEX

REFERENCE

ARCHER'S BIBLE INDEX

REFERENCE

ARCHER'S BIBLE INDEX

ARCHER'S BIBLE INDEX

PHOTOGRAPHY CREDITS

Judd Cooney/Windigo Images: 2-3; Alex Bowers:
61, 189, 255, 315; Jay T. Langston: 97; George
Ryals IV: 169; Mitch Kezar/Windigo Images: 383